Criminal Justice

CRIMINAL JUSTICE

Volume 3

Racial profiling—Youth gangs
Appendices
Indexes

Edited by
Phyllis B. Gerstenfeld
California State University, Stanislaus
Department of Criminal Justice

Salem Press, Inc.
Pasadena, California   Hackensack, New Jersey

Editor in Chief: Dawn P. Dawson

Editorial Director: Christina J. Moose *Editorial Assistant:* Dana Garey
Project Editor: R. Kent Rasmussen *Photo Editor:* Cynthia Beres
Production Editor: Joyce I. Buchea *Acquisitions Editor:* Mark Rehn
Manuscript Editor: Elizabeth Ferry Slocum *Graphics and Design:* James Hutson
Assistant Editor: Andrea Miller *Layout:* William Zimmerman

Cover photo: Brand-X Pictures/Bill Fritsch

Library of Congress Cataloging-in-Publication Data

Criminal justice / edited by Phyllis B. Gerstenfeld.
    p. cm.
Includes bibliographical references and index.
ISBN-10: 1-58765-218-8 (set : alk. paper)
ISBN-13: 978-1-58765-218-9 (13-digit set : alk. paper)
ISBN-10: 1-58765-221-8 (vol. 3 : alk. paper)
ISBN-13: 978-1-58765-221-9 (vol. 3 : alk. paper)
1. Criminal law—United States—Encyclopedias. 2. Criminal justice, Administration of—United States—Encyclopedias. 3. Crime—United States—Encyclopedias. 4. Criminal procedure—United States—Encyclopedias. I. Gerstenfeld, Phyllis B.

KF9214.5.C75 2006
345.75′05—dc22

2005017803

First Printing

Contents

Complete List of Contents

Volume I

Volume II

Complete List of Contents

Volume III

Racial profiling

Definition: Police practice of using race or ethnicity as a primary reason for stopping, questioning, searching, or arresting potential suspects

Criminal justice issue: Civil rights and liberties; government misconduct; police powers; search and seizure

Significance: Increasingly recognized as a major problem in the United States, racial profiling is damaging to everyone it touches—from its victims to the police officers who employ it and society as a whole.

Criminal profiling is a recognized technique of law enforcement that is used to help identify and apprehend criminal suspects. Police investigators establish "profiles" of typical offenders of specific crimes and then try to find suspects who match those profiles. The more variables the police consider in building a profile, the greater the probability that the profile is accurate. A central problem with racial profiling is that it is based on race, or ethnicity, and only a small number of other variables, such as sex and age.

Racial profiling is based on the assumption that members of certain racial and ethnic groups are more likely than other people to commit certain types of crime. An example of a particularly common assumption is that because many young African American men commit drug crimes, young African American men in general are more likely to commit such crimes. Acting on that assumption, law-enforcement officers who see young African American men in neighborhoods known to be centers of drug crime might feel justified in stopping and questioning them, simply because they appear to fit a drug-dealer "profile." Such stops may sometimes actually help police apprehend drug dealers who might otherwise escape arrest. However, officers practicing racial profiling also stop many entirely innocent young black men whose only offense is being black.

The central problem with racial profiling is that it tends to stigmatize whole groups of people, even though most members of the stigmatized groups are law-abiding citizens. As a consequence, members of the stigmatized groups may go through their lives feeling that they are something less than full members of society and that they are always in danger of being scrutinized and distrusted.

During the 1990's, the practice of racial profiling gained so much national attention that it became an issue of public debate. Public opinion turned against the practice, which seemed unfair, undemocratic, and perhaps even un-American. Finally, in the first state of the union address of the twenty-first century, a U.S. president publicly spoke out against the practice. On February 27, 2001, President George W. Bush declared before a joint session of Congress that racial profiling was wrong and that it should be abolished in the United States. His message moved members of both parties to take action on the problem. The following June, a bipartisan bill, the End Racial Profiling Act of 2001, was presented to Congress.

However, in September, before Congress completed action on the bill, something happened that turned public opinion on racial profiling upside down. On September 11, Middle Eastern terrorists hijacked four American airliners and killed thousands of people in attacks on New York City and Washington, D.C. Because the terrorists involved in the attacks were Muslim Arabs, a cloud of suspicion of all Middle Easterners and Muslims—as well as many other immigrants and Americans of foreign descent—descended over the United States. In the new, post-September 11 atmosphere of fear, national sentiment swung back in favor of allowing law-enforcement officers to detain and arrest suspicious-looking people on the basis of evidence as limited as their physical appearance. As a result, the End Racial Profiling Act of 2001 was never passed.

The Problem

Numerous studies have shown that police in many jurisdictions stop and question or initiate investigations of members of racial minorities at rates fare greater than the minorities' representation in the general population would suggest is appropriate. Statistical evidence from across the country points to the conclusion that racial profiling, or racially biased policing, is a measurable and real phenomenon.

The Mathematics of Racial Profiling

The seductive appeal of a racial profile lies in the belief that if members of group X are disproportionately more likely to commit a particular crime than other people, it makes sense to focus attention on group X. However, if only a tiny percentage of group X members commit the crime, then such a focus may be ethically questionable, as it would burden the overwhelming majority of law-abiding members of group X. It is instructive to consider the mathematics of profiling.

If a particular crime that is committed by only 0.1 percent of the general population is committed by 1.0 percent of the members of group X, then any individual member of group X is ten times more likely to commit the crime than a member of the general population. However, 99 percent of the members of group X are law-abiding with respect to this crime. Moreover, if all the members of group X constitute less than 10 percent of the total population, then fewer than half of the people who commit the crime in question are actually members of group X.

An example of racial profiling on a large scale occurred in the California in 1999, when the state's Highway Patrol conducted a drug interdiction program called Operation Pipeline. The program utilized a profile provided by the federal Drug Enforcement Administration to make more than 34,000 traffic stops, only 2 percent of which resulted in drug seizures. Meanwhile, well over 33,000 motorists—most of whom were members of racial minorities—were detained and temporarily deprived of their rights.

In 2000, a federal General Accounting Office (GAO) study of the practices of the U.S. Customs Service revealed evidence of racial profiling by federal agents. The GAO study found that during 1998, individual white women entering the United States carried with them contraband goods at a rate that was twice that of black women. Nevertheless, the black women were X-rayed for contraband at a rate nine times greater than the rate for white women. A general finding of the study was that the rates at which women and members of minorities were selected by customs officials for intrusive searches was inconsistent with the rates at which members of the same groups were found to be carrying contraband.

U.S. Department of Justice studies of law-enforcement treatment of suspects have found similar patterns and inconsistencies. For example, one study found that African American drivers were 20 percent more likely than white drivers to be stopped by police and that individual African American drivers were 50 percent more likely than white drivers to have been stopped more than once. Moreover, among all drivers who were stopped by police, African Americans and Hispanics more than twice as likely as whites to be searched.

Effects of Racial Profiling

Individual citizens, communities, police forces, and society in general all suffer when racial profiling occurs. Individuals subjected to racial profiling can be injured in a variety of ways. They may experience anxiety, anger, humiliation, cynicism, fear, resentment, or combinations of these responses. Racially biased policing can cause psychological trauma and racial profiling can violate an individual's constitutional rights.

Racial profiling affects communities in several ways. The faith of communities in their local police tends to decline when the police engage in racial profiling because it humiliates and degrades all minorities. Profiling also degrades the legitimacy of the criminal justice system by breeding distrust between minority communities and the police.

The police tend to lose their effectiveness when the communities they are entrusted to protect lose confidence in them. Even when racial profiling is practiced only by a minority of police officers, the public is apt to lose confidence in the entire force.

One reason that racial profiling exists is that it reflects deeper societal attitudes about race. In fact, it tends to reflect the attitudes of members of *all* races about race. Support for this observation can be found in studies undertaken in the general population. In one such study, for example, subjects were shown two similar pictures. The first picture was of two young African American men, both in unkempt clothing, standing on street corner in a run-down neighborhood. One man was pointing a pistol at the other man. The second picture was exactly the same, except for the fact that both men were white.

When asked what was happening in the first pictures, must subjects—both white and black—thought that the man with the gun was either holding up the other man or was about to kill him. By contrast, when asked about the second picture, most subjects—both white and black—thought that the man with the gun was an undercover police officer. Tests such as that one show that the assumptions about race underlying racial profiling go well beyond police departments.

Progress

By mid-2004, nine states had passed legislation prohibiting racial profiling. Meanwhile, in February, 2004, Senator Russ Feingold of Wisconsin and Representative John Conyers of Michigan introduced the End Racial Profiling Act of 2004 in both houses of the U.S. Congress. The new bill was designed to do five things:

✓ prohibit racial profiling by all federal agencies
✓ require state and local police agencies applying for federal assistance to have policies that discourage racial profiling
✓ offer grants to local and state law-enforcement agencies to create programs that ensure racially neutral administration of justice
✓ require all government law-enforcement agencies to submit data to the U.S. attorney general data on the racial composition of the persons whom the agencies stop, investigate, or arrest
✓ require the U.S. attorney general to process the data collected and submit to Congress annual summaries on the use of racial profiling throughout the United States

Vic Sims

Further Reading

Cole, David. *No Equal Justice: Race and Class in the American Criminal Justice System*. New York: New Press, 1999. Introduction to the problems of racism in the American criminal justice system.

Davis, Kelvin R. *Driving While Black: Coverup*. Cincinnati: Interstate International Publishing, 2001. First-person account of a man who was unfairly arrested and eventually incarcerated because of racial profiling.

Harris, David. *Profiles in Injustice: Why Police Profiling Cannot Work*. New York: New Press, 2002. Powerful critique of racial profiling that may be the best general overview of the subject yet published.

Meeks, Kenneth. *Driving While Black: What to Do If You Are a Victim of Racial Profiling*. New York: Random House, 2000. Critique of racial profiling that offers practical advice to victims and potential victims.

Mutual Respect in Policing: Lesson Plan. Washington, D.C.: U.S. Department of Justice, Office of Community Oriented Policing Services, 2001. Federal government report on the progress made in ending racial profiling.

See also Equal protection under the law; *Illinois v. Wardlow*; Police civil liability; Police ethics; Police powers; Probable cause; Psychological profiling; Search and seizure; Stop and frisk; *Whren v. United States*.

Racketeer Influenced and Corrupt Organizations Act

The Law: Federal statute that provides both criminal and civil remedies against persons who commit a variety of common-law and statutory crimes

Date: Became law October 15, 1970

Criminal justice issues: Federal law; fraud; organized crime

Significance: The Racketeer Influenced and Corrupt Organizations Act, better known as RICO, is the primary statutory weapon used by federal prosecutors against organized crime.

After twenty years of study and debate, Congress enacted the Racketeer Influenced and Corrupt Organizations Act (RICO) as part of the Organized Crime Control Act of 1970. The statute's primary purpose is to provide an effective means for government prosecutors to act against organized crime. RICO lay dormant for a decade, however, until its architect, G. Robert Blakey of Notre Dame Law School, persuaded federal prosecutors to use it against the Mafia.

The Statutory Scheme

The general scheme of RICO is relatively simple. It applies to a defendant who, through a pattern of racketeering activity, has indirectly or directly participated in an enterprise whose activities affect interstate commerce. The critical phrases "person," "enterprise," and "pattern of racketeering activity" are broadly defined in RICO, reflecting a congressional intent to provide for the widest application of the statute in combating organized crime.

The Supreme Court recognized that RICO was to be liberally construed. The term "enterprise" thereby includes "legitimate enterprises" which have committed the requisite illegal acts. RICO prohibits four specific activities: using income derived from a pattern of racketeering activity to acquire an interest in an enterprise, acquiring or maintaining an interest in an enterprise through a pattern of racketeering activity, conducting the affairs of an enterprise through a pattern of racketeering activity, and conspiring to commit any of these offenses.

A "person," defined to include any individual or entity capable of holding a legal or beneficial interest in property, must conduct or participate in the conduct of a RICO enterprise through a pattern of racketeering activity, which requires at least two predicate acts within a ten-year period. The statute is thereby directed at conduct (the predicate acts) rather than status (organized crime). RICO therefore applies to anyone who engages in the proscribed conduct, regardless of who the perpetrator is. Federal prosecutors have generally exercised discretion in limiting RICO prosecutions to cases involving organized crime and securities violations.

The critical phrase "racketeering activity" is defined to include specific state and federal felonies. A veritable laundry list of predicate offenses includes murder, kidnapping, gambling, arson, robbery, bribery, extortion, and dealing in narcotics or other dangerous drugs. Also included as predicate acts are a number of federal crimes, including mail fraud, wire fraud, obstruction of

justice, and securities fraud. In 1984 Congress added the distribution of obscene materials to the list of predicate offenses. Several other predicate acts reflect common perceptions of organized crime, such as bribery and sports bribery, unlawful transactions with pension or welfare funds, loan-sharking, interstate transportation of wagering paraphernalia, federal bankruptcy fraud, and violation of any law of the United States concerning drug transactions.

RICO is partially intended to strike at illegal activity that operates through formal, legitimate enterprises. An enterprise is defined to include any individual, partnership, corporation, association, or other legal entity, and any union or group of individuals associated in fact even though they do not constitute a legal entity. One of the most significant features of RICO is that members of an unlawful enterprise can be prosecuted for being part of an enterprise that commits a series of predicate offenses. It is no longer necessary to prosecute individual defendants for a specific crime, such as homicide, which may be difficult to prove.

RICO is distinguished from other criminal statutes because it includes in its penalties the forfeiture of illegally acquired gains and the economic bases of misused power. RICO forfeiture can be of any property that is traceable, directly or indirectly, to the RICO violation. Forfeiture is in addition to any other fine or imprisonment imposed. Criminal forfeiture was common in England, but it is not generally incorporated into the criminal laws of the United States. A freeze on a defendant's assets can also be imposed upon the filing of a RICO complaint by the federal prosecutor.

Civil RICO

Without much thought on the floor of Congress, an amendment to the proposed RICO statute was adopted, adding a civil remedy to the statute. RICO's civil remedy provision is the most commonly utilized provision of the statute. Its popularity rests on the fact that a victim may recover treble (triple) damages and costs of litigation, including attorneys' fees. In addition, the statute can be applied against any defendant who has committed the requisite two predicate acts within a ten-year period. It is widely used in cases of securities fraud, consumer fraud, and real estate development fraud. RICO has also become a standard pleading in business disputes. In January, 1994, the Supreme Court held in *National Organization for Women v. Scheidler* that RICO can be applied against antiabortion protesters. The Court held that RICO is not limited to crimes with an economic motive. Courts frequently use the civil and criminal RICO case-law interpretations interchangeably.

RICO's Effects

RICO has been effective in the government's steady war of attrition against traditional organized crime; its record in prosecuting white-collar criminals has been mixed. Both the civil suit provision and the allowability of freezing assets have proved controversial. Plaintiffs seeking relief under RICO pursue its remedies and application to the fullest. They do not exercise the discretion and self-restraint characteristic of governmental prosecutors. Postconviction forfeitures are also receiving detailed scrutiny, although usually in state cases because of abuses in the use of the forfeited property. One final note is that roughly half the states have enacted "little RICO" laws modeled after the federal statute.

Denis Binder

Further Reading

Abrams, Douglas R. *The Law of Civil RICO*. Boston: Little, Brown, 1991. Study of the impact of RICO on American civil law.

Joseph, Gregory P. *Civil RICO: A Definitive Guide*. Chicago: American Bar Association, 1992. Handbook on RICO for legal professionals published by the leading professional attorney organization in the United States.

Organized Crime and Racketeering Section, U.S. Department of Justice. *Racketeer Influenced and Corrupt Organizations (RICO): A Manual for Federal Prosecutors*. 2d ed. Washington, D.C.: U.S. Government Printing Office, 1988. Official Justice Department report on the impact of RICO.

Philcox, Norman W. *An Introduction to Organized Crime*. Springfield, Ill.: C. C. Thomas, 1978. General study of organized crime in the United States that includes an overview of RICO and its application.

Wallance, Gregory J. "Criminal Justice: Outgunning the Mob." *American Bar Association Journal* 80 (March 1, 1994). Assessment of the impact of RICO nearly a quarter of a century after its passage.

See also Antiracketeering Act of 1934; Corporate scandals; Drugs and law enforcement; Hobbs Act; Mafia; Organized crime; Organized Crime Control Act; Political corruption; Witness protection programs.

Radio broadcasting

Definition: Coverage of crime and criminal justice issues on radio broadcasts

Criminal justice issue: Media

Significance: Since the advent of commercial radio broadcasting during the 1920's, Americans have relied upon radio reporting and commentaries for significant portions of the information they receive on crime and criminal justice.

The advent of radio broadcasting during the early twentieth century produced a revolution in American life by bringing into Americans' homes local, national, and international news, along with such features as live reports from crime scenes and the voices of judges in courtrooms.

The first American radio station began broadcasting in 1920. Within only two years, more than five hundred stations were broadcasting across the United States. Networks that linked different stations through telephone lines, so that all the stations could broadcast the same programs at the same time, began in 1926 with the creation of the National Broadcasting Corporation (NBC) in 1926. The Columbia Broadcasting System (CBS) started one year later.

Early in 1927, the Federal Radio Commission, the predecessor of the Federal Communications Commission, set the broadcast band for commercial radio and assigned frequencies to stations. News coverage began with presidential election returns of 1920 but remained only a minor segment of early programming, which was dominated by talk, music, and variety shows. Local stations reported on crimes, but there were relatively few broadcasts or summaries.

In 1925, WGN in Chicago broadcast the first major crime story on radio with intermittent coverage of the so-called Scopes monkey trial in Dayton, Tennessee. Listeners were brought to the scene and allowed to participate vicariously in the trial, which helped make on-the-spot stories irresistible to the public. Soon, radio stations were experimenting with the use of ambient sounds from scenes of news stories as well as contrived sound effects created in studios to convey a sense of immediacy and urgency—a most effective combination in reporting on crimes.

The 1930's saw several major developments in the evolution of broadcast news. In 1930, regularly scheduled news broadcasts began on the networks with celebrity announcers offering commentaries on the news. Occasionally, they included criminal justice stories that they picked up from newspapers and wire services. In 1932, on-the-spot radio reporting was established technically and journalistically when both CBS and NBC connected special lines to reporters in Hopewell, New Jersey, who were reporting on the kidnapping of Charles Lindbergh's baby. Both networks kept up vigils for seventy-two days, until the baby's body was found. The Lindbergh kidnapping trial in 1935 became the first nationally broadcast murder trial when the networks provided daily accounts and commentary on the proceedings.

Radio was ideally suited to breaking news about crimes because of its instantaneous coverage of events that gave listeners a feeling of personal involvement that no other medium could

The trial of high school teacher John T. Scopes (sitting behind radio microphone, in white shirt, with arms folded) for teaching evolution to his biology class in Tennessee was the news sensation of 1925 and was also the first major criminal justice story covered live by radio. The fact that Scopes was defended by Clarence Darrow (leaning on table), the most famous trial attorney of his time, added to the interest of the public, which followed the trial avidly on radio across the United States. *(Library of Congress)*

match. During the 1930's the networks began to broadcast realistic radio dramas about crime and detectives that drew large audiences.

The Modern Era of Radio News

The modern era of radio newscasting began in 1938 with coverage of the Munich crisis that helped precipitate World War II and continued through the war. Live broadcasts from the European and Pacific war zones drove the development of radio journalism. Improved news broadcasting was reflected in an increased immediacy in reporting on domestic crime and criminal justice. By the war's end, more than 60 percent of Americans listed radio as their primary source of news.

New technologies developed during the war years brought more advances to radio journalism. For example, lighter-weight radio transmitters allowed journalist to report live from more remote locations, and the development of high-fidelity recording tape made it easier to bring the voices of newsmakers to newscasts. Meanwhile, broadcasters increasingly depended on shorter, on-the-spot reporting of breaking news, coupled with recorded "sound bites" that added the voices of actual newsmakers to the immediate coverage. The networks provided news content "feeds" that allowed affiliate stations to tape and re-use the voices of newsmakers and the stories done by network correspondents.

Despite these advances, news programming slowly was being reduced in stature as commercial television expanded to become the major medium in the postwar years. Television news differed from that of radio in its greater emphasis on stories that lent themselves to visual elements. At that time, news broadcasting accounted for only a small part of commercial- and entertainment-driven radio, and crime subjects accounted for only about 5 percent of typical news broadcasting in the 1950's.

The period from 1946 to 1960 saw the introduction of format radio—broadcasting designed to reach specifically defined segments of the listening population. based on such criteria as age and ethnicity. This development brought new changes to radio journalism. Some stations built broadcasting formats around news, talk, and sports programs that featured heavy concentra-

tions of local, regional, and global news. However, such stations were vastly outnumbered by stations with other formats.

From 1960 to 1980, radio broadcasting expanded from the AM band by adding the FM band, and stations began replacing network-oriented programming with highly localized programming. As radio diversified to serve more fragmented audiences, radio news was redefined. Short newsbreaks, headline news, and rapidly paced stories became the norm for FM stations, but with one major exception: the nonprofit National Public Radio (NPR). Through a network of affiliated stations, NPR brought back high standards of broadcast journalism by specializing in reporting on location and using background noise, sound effects, and music to enrich news stories. NPR also offered deeper coverage and analyses of news—including criminal justice topics—than was available on commercial stations.

After 1980, radio journalism experienced a rebirth, but on a smaller scale than in earlier decades. By the mid-1980's, talk radio programs that offered discussions of issues in the news and often invited listeners to participate gained large audiences. By the mid-1990's talk radio was one of the most popular formats on the air. Talk show hosts saw themselves as playing a significant role in shaping public opinion and as having an impact on politics and public policy. Meanwhile, many broadcasters sought to achieve economies of scale by relying on satellite-delivered national news summaries and reduced their local news staffs. As a result, many stations cut back or even eliminated their local news operations, with a resultant reduction in radio reporting of crime and criminal justice.

Theodore M. Vestal

Further Reading

Douglas, Susan J. *Listening In: Radio and American Imagination*. New York: Crown, 1999. Well-documented look at how radio shaped the American psyche socially, politically, and economically.

Hilliard, Robert L., and Michael C. Keith. *The Broadcast Century and Beyond: A Biography of American Broadcasting*. 3d ed. Burlington, Mass.: Focal Press, 2001. Popular history of the most influential and innovative industry of the twentieth century.

Larson, Gary W. "Radio Journalism." In *American Journalism: History, Principles, Practices*, edited by W. David Sloan and Lisa M. Parcell. Jefferson, N.C.: McFarland, 2002. Thorough and often fascinating history of radio news from its beginnings up to the twenty-first century.

Sacco, Vincent F. "Media Constructions of Crime." *Annals of the American Academy of Political and Social Science* 539 (May 1995): 141-154. Analysis of how the news media facilitate the marginalization of competing views on crime issues.

See also News source protection; Print media; Television courtroom programs; Television crime dramas; Television news; Television police reality shows; Trial publicity.

Rape and sex offenses

Definition: Forced sexual intercourse and other forms of uninvited sexual contact

Criminal justice issues: Domestic violence; sex offenses; women's issues

Significance: Sexual assault, including rape, is a major criminal justice issue in the United States, which has the highest rape rates in the world. The legacy of English common law long placed a heavy burden on victims of sexual assault seeking redress in the courts, but since the 1970's, virtually all U.S. states have amended their statutes to ease that burden and make prosecutions easier.

According to both common law and statutory codes, rape is carnal knowledge of another human achieved forcibly and against the other person's will. Federal codes define aggravated sexual abuse by force or threat of force as knowingly causing another person to engage in a sexual act by using force against that person or by threatening or placing that person in fear of being subjected to death, serious bodily injury or kidnapping.

Definitions of rape vary by state and reflect local attitudes. For example, in Tennessee rape is defined as unlawful penetration accompanied by any of the following: force or coercion; without the consent of the victim; victim is mentally defective, mentally incapacitated, or physically helpless; fraud. The crime of rape is governed by state rather than federal laws.

Acquaintance rape is a specific form that involves two persons who already know each other. Rapes that occur during social date functions constitute a form of acquaintance rape sometimes called date rape. When victims of rape are spouses of their assailants, the assaults may be called marital or spousal rape. Rape of persons under the age of consent is called statutory rape.

Most states distinguish between acts of physical penetration, such as penal intercourse, fellatio, and sodomy, and other forms of sexual activity that do not involve penetration, such as fondling, grabbing, and pinching. Crimes involving sexual penetration are generally considered forms of sexual assault, while those involving other forms of sexual activity are generally considered sexual abuse. In some states, sexual assault offenses are further differentiated according to degree, such as first- and second-degree assault.

The federal Bureau of Justice Statistics defines twelve forms of sexual victimization, which fall under three broad types: rape, sexual coercion, and sexual contact. Each type is further differentiated according to whether it is completed or attempted or undertaken with or without force or threats of force. Sexual coercion is nonconsensual penetration under the condition of pressure, physical punishment, or reward. No penetration occurs in acts of sexual contact, such as unwanted kissing.

History

The Puritans in colonial North America tended to give equal credence to the stories of both women and men involved in sex cases and took their definition of rape from English common law: sexual congress with girls under the age of ten, or nonconsensual sexual congress with female victims above that age. Not until the seventeenth century did the idea of false accusers become predominant in rape trials. It was during this time that Sir Matthew Hale, lord chief justice of England, wrote a statement that became known as the Lord Hale Instruction, which required judges to tell juries to treat cautiously uncorroborated testimony of alleged victims because their charges were easily made and difficult to disprove. During the eighteenth century, defendants in rape cases claiming they were falsely accused generally chose from among three possible reasons on the part of their accusers: blackmail, revenge, or saying "no" when they really meant "yes." The last reason arose from a culture that expected female virginity yet encouraged sexual freedom.

After the American Revolution, most U.S. states added the concept of "incapacity to consent" to their definitions of rape. However, in the nineteenth century "incapacity," whether from drugs, alcohol, mental disorder, or even unconsciousness, no longer meant lack of consent. In addition, there was no firm understanding of what constituted consent. During the nineteenth century, defendants in rape cases were not allowed to take the stand, and the testimony of victims provided the foundations of rape trials.

English common law did not allow evidence of victims' past sexual histories to be admitted in trials unless it was pertinent to the cases. American courts upheld this principle until the nineteenth century, when courts began admitting evidence of women's prior sexual histories into trials to show that victims of rape failed to show sufficient reluctance or resistance to indicate their lack of consent. Moreover, evidence about the character of the victims was allowed to invalidate their testimony and to substantiate consent.

During the late nineteenth and early twentieth centuries, Sigmund Freud's theories about female sexual assault fantasies supported ideas about false accusers and women who say "no" when they really mean "yes." Until the 1970's, the focus of most rape trials was on the victims' characters and past sexual histories and behavior. Defenses raised questions about how quickly victims reported the crimes, how hard they physically resisted, and how their testimony could be corroborated. During the mid-1970's, changing social attitudes toward rape were reflected in new legislation. Between 1974 and 1980, every state in the Union passed some form of rape re-

form legislation that reduced the burden of proof for rape victims. For example, most states eliminated the Lord Hale Instruction. Defense attorneys found it more difficult to raise questions about victims' sexual histories as new rape shield laws restricted the use of evidence concerning the victims' past sexual behavior. Inquiries into victims' past sexual histories was allowed only when clearly pertinent to cases.

The Crime of Rape

In a stereotypical rape, a victim physically resists, incurs physical injuries, and then immediately reports the rape to the police. However, in many aspects, rape and consensual sex can often be very similar. For example, in 70 percent of rape cases, victims report no physical injuries. Most rapes go unreported for a number of reasons, including victims' denial that the rapes have occurred, their failure to understand that what has happened to them constitutes criminal rape, and their fear of being blamed or disbelieved.

Among reported rapes, 25 percent of victims make their reports within twenty-four hours of their assaults. State laws now accept victims' reports up to several years after their assaults. Most states no longer require prompt reporting and corroboration of the victim's testimony and have also eliminated or modified the physical resistance requirement. For example, in New Jersey the question of physical resistance is determined by whether the accused uses force against another person without what a reasonable person would believe to be consent to the sex act.

Consent can be indicated through physical actions, instead of words, that demonstrate what a reasonable person would believe as evidence of consent to the act. An Illinois statute states that neither a lack of verbal or physical resistance nor the victim's manner of dress constitutes consent. Some states, such as Washington, require clearly active forms of consent, such as a verbal "yes," on the part of a victim as an acceptable defense against a charge of rape. Reforms in state laws have taken into account the phenomenon of frozen fright—a condition in which a victim becomes incapable of physically or verbally resisting. The importance of this matter is shown in the fact that 49 percent of rape victims in a 1992 National Women's Survey stated that they were afraid of serious injury or death during their attacks.

Definitions of rape have continued to evolve. In some states, it has been relabeled as sexual assault. Definitions of sexual assault refer to penetration rather than sexual intercourse. For example, in 1992, New Jersey's supreme court ruled that any act of sexual penetration engaged in without the consent of the victim is sexual assault.

Rape has also been redefined in terms of gradations of sex offenses, using terms such as rape in the first degree and second-degree sexual assault. Additionally, rape definitions have been rewritten in gender-neutral terms in order to include male victims. Finally, spousal, or marital, rape is now recognized as a crime in all states. Traditionally, marital rape was exempted by law for any of three possible reasons. First, in the past it was believed that husbands "owned" their wives and could not, therefore, rape them. Also, a husband and wife were considered legally "one" and therefore, could not rape themselves. Finally, spousal rape was not considered a crime because doing so would discourage marital reconciliation.

Prevalence of Rape

Even though the United States has the highest rape rates in the world, the Federal Bureau of Investigation (FBI) has estimated that only one of every ten rapes is reported to law enforcement. Embarrassment, fear of retaliation, and fear of going to court contribute to underreporting. Rape is falsely reported 2 percent to 4 percent of the time. In 1994, the FBI reported that 53 percent of reported forcible rapes led to the arrest of the alleged assailant.

Rates are highest on the West Coast, in large metropolitan areas, and during the summer months. African American women are more likely than other women to be victims of rape. Women living in cities face up to a 20 percent chance of being raped in their lifetimes. In 2000, the U.S. Department of Justice found that 17.6 percent of all women surveyed had been victims of completed or attempted rapes. Of those women, 54 percent were under the age of eighteen when they experienced their first completed or attempted

rape, and 29 percent were under the age of eleven.

The Federal Bureau of Investigation's Uniform Crime Reports (UCR) are compiled from data submitted by 16,000 law-enforcement agencies representing 96 percent of the nation's population. According to the UCR, 1.5 million forcible rapes were reported in the United States between 1972 and 1992. The 1992 National Women's Study found that an average of 683,000 adult women were being forcibly raped annually. The same study also found that 39 percent of the victims of forcible rape had been raped more than once.

In 1999, 9 of every 10 rape victims were female. Thus, about 10 percent of all adult rape victims are male. According to the 1994 Criminal Victimization in the United States report to Bureau of Justice, there were 30,000 sexual assaults on male victims of the age of twelve and above in 1993.

The U.S. Department of Justice reported that in 1991 out of 1.8 million severe assaults against women, 45,000 were spousal rapes. Up to 14 percent of all married women have been raped by their husbands. In 78 percent of rapes, the victims know their assailants. Nine percent of these assailants are husbands or former husbands, 11 percent are fathers or stepfathers, 10 percent are boyfriends or former boyfriends, 16 percent are other relatives, and 29 percent are friends or neighbors.

In 1982, the National Institute of Mental Health estimated that 25 percent of women in college have been victims of rape or attempted rape. In another study of campus rape, 13 percent of the men accused of rape admitted to using violence, and 27 percent admitted using some degree of physical or emotional force.

In 93 percent of rapes, the victims and assailants are of the same race. Of all men arrested for rape, 52 percent are white, 47 percent African American. Forty-five percent of male assailants are under the age of twenty-five; 33 percent are between between eighteen and twenty-four. Almost 50 percent of all rapes occur in the homes of either the victims or the assailants; 20 percent occur outdoors, and 18 percent occur in cars. Most rapes do not involve weapons; however, the Bureau of Justice Statistics reports that weapons are used in about 30 percent of stranger rapes and 15 percent of acquaintance rapes.

Why They Offend

Rapists are motivated to assault their victims for various reasons. It is generally believed that rapes are not motivated by a need for sexual gratification. Rapists are often motivated by a need to dominate, control, or humiliate their victims. In many cases, especially in acquaintance rapes, the perpetrators fail to recognize their acts as rape. Many rapists share similar attitudes. For example, men who rape generally believe that sexual aggression is normal. Some men believe that women secretly want to be raped. Another attitude shared by rapists is that sexual relationships involve playing games. That attitude makes it possible for rapists to believe that when their victims say "no," they really mean "yes." This attitude is the product of a pervasive rape myth that developed from the dual sex roles assigned to women: Women are expected to be both virginal and sexual. To resolve this conflict, women must pose as virgins by saying "no," while simultaneously desiring sex and really wanting to say "yes."

Another attitude held by men who rape is that men need to dominate women, an attitude supported in pornography. This attitude holds that men should be the sexual aggressors. Men holding this attitude expect passivity from women and misinterpret passive behavior as consent to sex. Such men also equate masculinity, or the male sex role, with strong sexual performance. This attitude is reflected in all-male groups, such as fraternities and athletic teams, whose members compete to achieve the highest numbers of sexual acts. To men holding these attitudes, rape is normal sexual behavior. Such attitudes are fostered by a society that increasingly accepts interpersonal violence and perpetuates sex role stereotyping and myths about rape.

Connecticut's chief state's attorney, Christopher L. Morano, addressing a press conference in October, 2004. Morano used the conference to announce the issuance of a new kit for collecting evidence in sexual assault investigations. The new kit (in his left hand) contained equipment for collecting evidence on drug-assisted sexual assaults. *(AP/Wide World Photos)*

Investigation

Rape investigations face special challenges. For example, rape differs from other personal crimes, such as burglary, in the fact that its victims are typically the only witnesses. Rape investigations involve identifying assailants, confirming recent sexual contact, establishing the use of force or threats, and corroborating victims' testimonies. Because the victims are often the only witnesses, their bodies become the focus of crime scene investigations.

When sexual assaults occur, forensic sexual examinations should be conducted within seventy-two hours. Medical professionals, such as sexual assault nurse examiners (SANE), in hospitals and rape crisis centers examine the victims. They treat injuries, prevent possible disease, test for pregnancy, initiate counseling, and collect evidence. The examiners uses rape kits designed to protect the chain of evidence in criminal investigations. Although these kits vary from state to state, most require photographs or other illustrations of physical injuries, clothing samples from the victims, swabs or smears of fluid secretions, hair from heads and pubic areas, saliva from the victims' mouths, whole blood specimens, and reports from toxicology studies. DNA evidence collected from blood, saliva, and semen often aids in identifying assailants, as does such associative evidence as hair and clothing fibers.

Proof of sexual contact includes observations of redness and soreness at sexual penetration sites and seminal fluids and saliva at the same sites. Examiner often use a device called a colposcope to photograph internal genital injuries that may indicate recent sexual contact as well as force. Forensic examiners also use ultraviolet light to examine clothing for stains. Dried semen usually fluoresces bright green or yellow. Blood samples can determine the victims' levels of intoxication, which may be used as evidence of nonconsent. Urine specimens are collected for complete drug analyses. Lubricants, contraceptives, fibers, soil, and other debris are forms of nonbiological evidence that may corroborate victims' accounts.

Physical injuries are photographed and described on drawings. However, an absence of injuries does not necessarily mean that force has not been used or that a victim has consented. In most sexual assaults, the victims have no visible physical injuries. When victims do sustain injuries, they are most commonly bruises on the upper legs and thighs, choking bruises on the neck, upper arm bruises from punching, injuries to outer arms used to deflect blows, whip injuries to the back, bite marks on breasts, punch injuries to the abdomen and thighs, and cuts, bruises, scrapes to the face.

Examiners also interview the victims to get their accounts of the assaults. They look for symptoms of rape trauma syndrome, which is similar to posttraumatic stress syndrome. This syndrome unfolds in two phases. During the acute phase, which develops immediately after an attack, the victim experiences feelings of fear, guilt, embarrassment, disbelief, and fatigue. In cases involving delays between assaults and medical

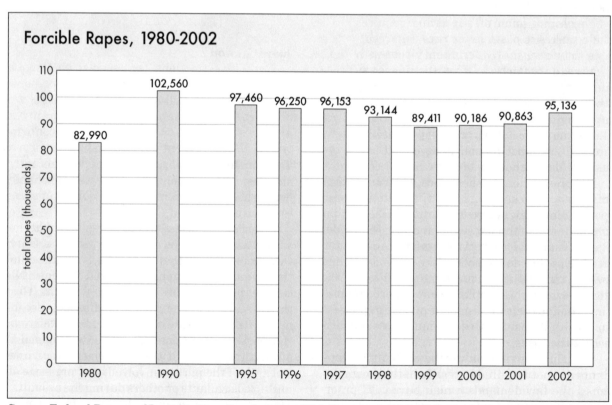

Source: Federal Bureau of Investigation, *Population-at-Risk Rates and Selected Crime Indicators.* Figures are for total completed and attempted rapes.

care, victims show loss of appetite, difficulty sleeping, tension, and headaches. In the second phase of the syndrome, the reorganization phase, victims are depressed; they withdraw from social situations, attempt to repress memories of their assaults, and sometimes engage in indiscriminate sexual behavior.

Examinations of sexual assault suspects should be made as soon as possible after they are arrested and before they bathe. Examiners collect the suspects' medical histories, examine their genitals, and collect physical evidence such as clothing and foreign debris. Investigators look especially for evidence that is transferred between victims and their assailants, such as trace evidence under fingernails. Examiners also document injuries to the suspects that may have been inflicted by the victims and photograph such identifying marks as tattoos, scars, and birthmarks.

Prosecution

The commission of any crime requires the occurrence of an *actus reus* (unacceptable act) and *mens rea* (criminal intent with respect to that act). In rape, the unacceptable act is sexual contact made without consent, and the *mens rea* is the suspect's intent of engaging in the sexual activity without the victim's consent. To prove those criteria, prosecutors must establish beyond a reasonable doubt that the victims did not consent.

For prosecutions to succeed, victims must identify their attackers and be willing to support prosecution. Law enforcement must classify rape complaints as founded (valid and prosecutable). Rape complaints are declared unfounded in cases in which police do not believe the alleged victims' stories, the assaults do not occur within the jurisdiction where the complaints are made, and victims change their minds about pressing charges. In all situations, prosecutors must be willing to accept the cases.

Securing convictions can be difficult. Defendants are not required to testify in their own defense, the law demands a high burden of proof, and convictions require unanimous decisions by juries. To prosecute sex crime, the state must

Basketball star Kobe Bryant passing through security in Colorado's Eagle County courthouse in May, 2004, during one of his many appearances there for pretrial motions as the local district attorney worked to build a criminal rape case against him. *(AP/Wide World Photos)*

first establish that sexual assaults have actually occurred. When defenses can create reasonable doubts about the occurrences, the defendants are likely to be acquitted.

Prosecutors must also establish either that the sexual assaults were committed using force or threats of force, or that no force was required for the sexual activity to be considered criminal. No consent by the victim is assumed when force or threat is present. Use of force or threats is determined from the context of the incidents, such as the presence of physical violence or weapons, use of physical or verbal threats, relative size and strength of the parties involved, and presence of multiple assailants or others during the assaults. The victims' perceptions of threats or force can be used to draw conclusions about the use of threats or force. However, the mere absence of force or threats cannot be used as evidence of consent in most states.

A defense may argue that a defendant has been misidentified. Such defenses are most frequent in stranger rape cases. A second type of defense hinges on the question of consent and is most common in acquaintance rape cases. When this defense is employed, defendants concede the occurrence of the sexual activity but deny using force or threats. Evidence establishing absence of consent may include physical or verbal resistance, physical injuries, and rape trauma syndrome.

In cases in which victims are legally viewed as unable to consent, sexual activity is deemed criminal in the absence of force or threat. When a sexual activity meets the state definition of statutory rape, no evidence of force is required. In nonstatutory cases, victims who are unconscious at the moment of assault are also considered legally unable to consent to sexual activity. The prosecution does not need to show evidence of force when victims are assaulted while incapacitated due to alcohol or drug use. Victims who are considered mentally or physically incapacitated, such as those with disabilities affecting their cognition or communication, also cannot give consent and, therefore, no force must be proven. In these cases, defendants may dispute the victims' inability to give consent or claim that they did not know the victims were unable to give consent.

Punishment

Punishments for sex crimes differ among the states. Degrees of sexual assault are usually measured by such matters as whether penetration occurred and the nature of injuries to the victims. For example, Michigan law defines sexual penetration with aggravation (accompanied by threats of injury with a dangerous weapon or serious injury to victim) as first-degree assault, punishable by a maximum of twenty years in prison. Other offenses include sexual contact with aggravation (second-degree assault), penetration without aggravation (third-degree assault), and contact without aggravation (fourth-degree assault), which is punishable by not more than one year in prison or fines of not more than five hundred dollars.

Victim of sexual assault may also pursue civil cases. In contrast to criminal trials, civil courts can require defendants to testify. Moreover, the burden-of-proof standard in civil cases requires prosecution to present only a preponderance of evidence, rather than proof "beyond a reasonable doubt," and jury decisions do not have to be unanimous. Victims pursuing civil cases must show that they have suffered harm by the defendants' actions.

A high-profile example of a civil rape case originated in Colorado in 2003, when a resort hotel employee accused basketball star Kobe Bryant of rape. Almost immediately, the local district attorney began building a criminal case against Bryant, but preparations were complicated by the fact that Bryant's financial resources were greater than those of the district attorney's office and by the massive publicity that the case attracted. Eventually, Bryant's accuser decided not to testify, and the district had to drop the case. Afterward, Bryant's accuser initiated a civil case against him. However, Bryant settled with his accuser in early 2005, and that case never reached court, either.

Evidence presented in civil rape cases is similar to that presented criminal cases; however, the victims' testimony takes on even greater importance. Civil cases normally take longer to come to trial than criminal cases. Victims may also sue third parties who share some responsibility for the circumstances that allow the rapes to occur. For example, business establishments, universities, and other institutions with large financial resources are often found liable because of their neglect in anticipating possible rapes and taking steps to prevent them. Victims may also wish to sue third parties for the purpose of prevent similar situations from occurring again.

Elizabeth M. McGhee Nelson

Further Reading

Carter, Christine. *The Other Side of Silence*. Gilsum, N.H.: Avocus Publishing, 1995. Collection of first-person accounts of date rape.

Cocca, Carolyn. *Jailbait: The Politics of Statutory Rape Laws in the United States*. Albany: State University of New York Press, 2004. Examination of the various state laws concerning statutory rape.

Dobbert, Duane L. *Halting the Sexual Predators Among Us: Preventing Attack, Rape, and Lust Homicide.* Westport, Conn.: Praeger, 2004. Up-to-date study of strategies that can be employed to prevent sexual assaults.

Hazelwood, Robert R., and Ann Wolbert Burgess, eds. *Practical Aspects of Rape Investigation: A Multidisciplinary Approach.* 3d ed. Boca Raton, Fla.: CRC Press, 2001. Study of rape that incorporates information on sex crimes from the fields of victimology, criminology, behavioral science, forensic science, and criminal justice.

Holmes, Stephen T., and Ronald M. Holmes. *Sex Crimes: Patterns and Behavior.* 2d ed. Thousand Oaks, Calif.: Sage Publications, 2002. Sociological study of the characteristics of sex offenders.

Leone, Bruno, ed. *Rape on Campus.* San Diego: Greenhaven Press, 1995. Collection of diverse views on the issue of rape on campus.

Meili, Trisha. *I Am the Central Park Jogger: A Story of Hope and Possibility.* New York: Scribner, 2004. First-person account from a woman who was raped in New York City's notorious Central Park.

Rosen, Marvin. *Dealing with the Effects of Rape and Incest.* Philadelphia: Chelsea House, 2002. Explanation of physical and sexual abuse with information to victims of abuse on surviving the aftermath.

Russell, Diana E. H. *Sexual Exploitation: Rape, Child Sexual Abuse, and Workplace Harassment.* Beverly Hills, Calif.: Sage, 1989. Broad sociological study of different forms of sex offenses, including sexual abuse of children.

Sanday, Peggy Reeves. *A Woman Scorned: Acquaintance Rape on Trial.* Berkeley: University of California Press, 1997. Scholarly study of date rape.

Smith, Merril D., ed. *Sex Without Consent: Rape and Sexual Coercion in America.* New York: New York University Press, 2001. Historical study exploring what rape meant to its victims and to society at times and places in the American past.

Warshaw, Robin. *I Never Called it Rape:*

The MS Report on Recognizing, Fighting and Surviving Date and Acquaintance Rape. New York: HarperPerennial, 1994. Survey results and first-person perspectives to explain date rape, how it happens, and what can be done.

Williams, Mary E., ed. *Abortion: Opposing Viewpoints.* San Diego: Greenhaven Press, 2002. Collection of views on abortion issues, including the quest for abortions by rape victims.

See also Abortion; AIDS; *Coker v. Georgia*; Common law; Date rape; Domestic violence; *Mens rea*; Pornography and obscenity; Prison violence; Psychopathy; Sex offender registries; Sexual harassment; Statutory rape; Victim assistance programs; Victimology.

Reasonable doubt

Definition: Absence of moral certainty of a defendant's guilt

Criminal justice issues: Constitutional protections; defendants; legal terms and principles; verdicts

Former television star Robert Blake reacts to the jury's not guilty verdict in his trial for the murder of his wife, Bonny Lee Bakley, on March 16, 2005. Blake's acquittal in the closely watched Los Angeles trial shocked many observers, but it was evident that while many of the jurors in the case privately believed Blake guilty, they concluded that the evidence presented by prosecution did not establish his guilt beyond a reasonable doubt. *(AP/Wide World Photos)*

Significance: Proof "beyond a reasonable doubt" gives jurors the amount of assurance they must have, by law, to find a defendant guilty; this proof precludes all reasonable hypotheses except the one it is intended to support.

Reasonable doubt denies jurors the amount of assurance they must attain in determining the guilt of a defendant and is vital to guaranteeing defendants' rights to verdicts that are as accurate as possible. The Fourteenth Amendment to the U.S. Constitution states that defendants may be convicted based only on proof that is beyond a reasonable doubt.

Reasonable doubt differs from determining the preponderance of the evidence, which refers to there being more evidence favoring one side than the other. Establishing reasonable doubt involves jurors' weighing of evidence in a practical and unbiased decision as to the likelihood of a defendant's guilt or innocence. Juries may convict defendants only if the prosecution proves guilt beyond a reasonable doubt. This means that jurors must decide that the evidence is convincing enough for them to declare the defendant guilty.

Twelve Angry Men

The most famous film about juries is almost certainly director Sidney Lumet's 1957 film *Twelve Angry Men* (remade for television in 1997). An intense psychological drama, it is set almost entirely within a jury room, in which twelve jurors deliberate after hearing evidence in the trial of a young Puerto Rican man accused of murdering his father. Initially, only one juror (Glen Ford) believes that the defendant should be acquitted of the crime, but he ultimately persuades the entire jury to return a verdict of not guilty by emphasizing the weaknesses in the prosecution's case. These weaknesses do not, however, mean that the jurors are convinced that the defendant is innocent. The film demonstrates that jurors may have reasonable doubts about whether the prosecution has proved its case and return a verdict of not guilty, even when they are not certain that the defendant is innocent.

Timothy L. Hall

Jurors do not, however, have to establish absolute certainty.

The reasonable doubt standard was established in the 1970 U.S. Supreme Court case *In re Winship*. In this case, the Court determined that due process demands that prosecutors prove every element of a crime beyond a reasonable doubt. However, establishing a definition of reasonable doubt in convicting defendants has been a difficult process. The 1994 case *Victor v. Nebraska* addressed the issue of whether defining reasonable doubt violates due process. As a result of this case, judges now have a standard definition to use when instructing juries during the deliberation phases of trials.

Kimberley M. Holloway

Further Reading

Garner, Bryan A., ed. *Black's Law Dictionary*. 8th ed. St. Paul, Minn.: Thomson/West, 2004.

Glannon, Joseph W. *Civil Procedure: Examples and Explanations*. 4th ed. New York: Aspen Law and Business, 2001.

Samaha, Joel. *Criminal Procedure*. 5th ed. Belmont, Calif.: Wadsworth, 2002.

See also Burden of proof; Circumstantial evidence; Convictions; Due process of law; Jury system; Pleas; Presumption of innocence; Probable cause; Simpson trials; Standards of proof; Trials; Verdicts.

Reasonable force

Definition: Amount of physical force that police officers may use while making arrests

Criminal justice issues: Arrest and arraignment; legal terms and principles; police powers

Significance: It is understood that police must sometimes use force to arrest suspects; however, excessive force is sometimes applied, and legal remedies exist for such cases.

Police officers are legally allowed to use the amount of force that is reasonably necessary to make an arrest. Courts should not substitute their own judgment for the judgment of the police officer in the field when the latter's discretion is exercised reasonably and in good faith. Nevertheless, the courts examine allegations of excessive force as potential violations of the "due process of law" that is guaranteed under the U.S. and state constitutions. Moreover, excessive force can generate civil liability under tort law and the civil rights laws, and it can itself be a crime.

The standard used for evaluating the use of force is whether an "ordinary, prudent man under the circumstances" would condone the use of force. This is a question of fact for the jury's deliberations. Factors to be considered include the need for force, the relationship between the need and amount of force applied, the extent of injuries caused by the use of force, and whether the force was used in a good faith effort to effect the arrest. In addition, courts consider whether the application of force violates accepted standards of decency. Deadly force may generally be used only against felons, and force used by a police officer to punish (rather than restrain) is strictly prohibited.

Gwendolyn Griffith

Further Reading

Alpert, Geoffrey, and Lorie A. Fridell. *Police Vehicle and Firearms: Instruments of Deadly Force.* Prospect Heights, Ill.: Waveland Press, 1992.

Geller, William, and Hans Toch, eds. *Police Violence: Understanding and Controlling Police Abuse of Force.* New Haven, Conn.: Yale University Press, 1996.

See also Arrest; Deadly force; International Brotherhood of Police Officers; King beating case; Miami riots; Police brutality; Police civil liability; Police dogs; Self-defense; Special weapons and tactics teams (SWAT); *Tennessee v. Garner.*

Reasonable suspicion

Definition: Amount of certainty that illegal actions are taking place that law-enforcement officers must have to stop suspects in public— the standard amounts to something greater than mere hunches but less than probable cause

Criminal justice issues: Investigation; police powers; search and seizure

Significance: Reasonable suspicion is an important legal concept that sets a standard that permits criminal justice professionals, such as police and correctional officials, to stop and detain suspects for further investigation.

When law-enforcement officers stop and detain suspects, they must have tangible reasons for suspecting that the suspects they stop are involved in criminal activities. What constitutes reasonable suspicion is based on such factors such as the suspects' appearances and behavior; information about the suspects gathered from previous encounters or provided by reliable sources, such as police files and databases; the locations and circumstances of the encounters with the suspects; and the officers' own training, experience, and relevant general knowledge. After stopping suspects on reasonable suspicion, the officers may detain them until their suspicions are either confirmed or proven to be unfounded.

A typical example might be a police officer who has reasonable suspicion that a suspect is carrying a concealed handgun because there is an obvious bulge around the suspect's waistband, where handguns are often hidden. The investigating officer may also know from previous encounters with the same suspect that the latter has a past arrest and conviction for weapons violations. An example of an unreasonable suspicion would be suspecting that a person seen for the first time is carrying illegal drugs because that person looks like a hippie.

Jay Zumbrun

Further Reading

Biskupic, Joan, and Elder Witt. *The Supreme Court and Individual Rights.* Washington, D.C.: Congressional Quarterly, 1997.

LaFave, Wayne R. *Search and Seizure: A Treatise on the Fourth Amendment.* St. Paul, Minn.: West Publishing, 1996.

See also Consent searches; *Illinois v. Wardlow; Maryland v. Buie;* Miranda rights; Police; Police powers; Probable cause; Stop and frisk; Suspects; *Terry v. Ohio; Whren v. United States.*

Recidivism

Definition: Tendency of parolees to return to criminal behavior

Criminal justice issues: Crime prevention; prisons; rehabilitation

Significance: While the modern criminal justice system has been placing increased emphasis on incapacitating greater numbers of offenders and for longer periods of time, recidivist rates have also been increasing, giving rise to the perception that most offenders are being caught in an ever-revolving door from which release is almost impossible.

During the 1998 U.S. presidential election campaign, recidivism became a national issue when Republican candidate George Bush accused his Democratic opponent, Massachusetts governor Michael Dukakis, of being "soft" on crime by calling media attention to the murderous behavior of a convict named Willie Horton whom Dukakis had released from prison. The Horton case be-

Polly Klaas, a twelve-year-old Northern California girl, was kidnapped from her home and murdered in 1993 by a man who had been recently paroled after serving one half of his sentence on an earlier kidnapping conviction. The public outrage at Polly's murder was compounded by the revelation that she had been killed by a parolee with a long criminal record, and it contributed directly to California's adoption of its three-strikes law. *(AP/Wide World Photos)*

came a national *cause célèbre* and the notion of incurably violent recidivists was imprinted in the minds of Americans. That notion was reinforced by another highly publicized case in 1993, when former convict Richard Allen Davis kidnapped, sexually assaulted, and murdered a young California girl named Polly Klaas. The Polly Klaas case then gave rise to the three-strikes law movement in California.

The concept of recidivism has produced a variety of definitions and special applications. However, the meaning that is most widely used defines recidivists as offenders who serve time in prisons, reenter society, and violate their parole or commit new crimes that return them to custody.

Scope of the Problem

Figures from the U.S. Bureau of Justice Statistics show that 774,588 person were on parole in the United States in 2003. In other words, more than three-quarters of a million offenders had been released from prison and were residing in and roaming freely throughout the United States. Of these parolees, approximately 50 percent had originally been convicted of felonies and 25 percent had been imprisoned for drug offenses. The majority of these offenders were under the regular supervision of parole officers, but large caseloads, geographical distances, and dwindling funds have been reducing the levels and effectiveness of post-release supervision.

Research has shown that roughly 50 percent of the 470,500 parolees newly released in 2003 were successfully discharged from their parole responsibilities. A 50-percent success rate may seem alarmingly low, but may alternatively be viewed as an extraordinary success when compared to the findings of other studies of recidivism.

In 1989, the federal government released its first comprehensive study of recidivism of prison inmates who had been released on parole in 1983. The most startling finding of that study was that within three years of their parole discharge, 62.5 percent of the former inmates had been returned to custody as the result of new crimes or parole violations. In 1994, a new version of the same study showed that the three-year recidivism rate had increased to 67.5 percent. Of particular importance is the fact that approximately one-half of those who returned to custody did so within the first six months of their release, and a full two-thirds returned within one year. The most promising finding from the study's data is the fact that the longer former inmates succeed on parole, the greater the probability they will never recidivate.

National recidivism rates are consistent with the rate of parolee failure in California, which has the largest number of parolees in the United States. the recidivism rate is a frighteningly similar 66 percent. It would appear that California is representative of the rest of the country although the fact that the majority of its recidivists are returned for such technical violations of their parole as failing "dirty" drug tests, may indicate that particular political or social pressures are at work.

Reasons for Parole Failure

In 1974, a study on the effectiveness of correctional programs published by Robert Martinson was reduced to a public perception that "nothing works." This indictment was seized by the political proponents of the "get tough on crime" movement and used as an academically produced and research-oriented justification for the dismantling and abandonment of most rehabilitative efforts in corrections over the next three decades.

Since the 1970's, the United States has been fighting a continuous war on crime, drugs, and recidivism. New sentencing strategies, such as three-strikes laws, have lengthened average prison sentences. The result has been an escalating correctional population that by 2004 had placed more than 2 million offenders in prisons and nearly another 5 million offenders in communities under probation or parole. Increased emphasis on incarcerating offenders has had both fiscal and philosophical consequences. Costs have skyrocketed as increasing numbers of offenders are incarcerated and for longer periods of time. Also, increasing numbers of prisoners are incarcerated in what are called supermax prisons, which isolate inmates as many as twenty-

three hours per day. The tendency toward more severe incapacitation policies has led to reduced remedial services for inmates and further depersonalized them and alienated them from society.

Noted criminologists, such as Joan Petersilia (2003) and Jeremy Travis, have written extensively on the problems of parolees. Typical parolees are young male members of minority groups who have limited literacy and education, meager job skills, and negligible employment histories. They are often substance abusers or addicts, and many have physical, mental, and medical complications problems. These people tend to go through the criminal justice system without getting any help for their basic problems because of shortages of resources for treatment and rehabilitation programs and the reluctance of prison administrators to acknowledge the need to try something new. The result is that many of these people become repeat offenders, and recidivism rates continue to climb.

Solutions

Criminologists, such as Petersilia and Travis, generally agree that the only way to combat recidivism is to return to corrections programs that provide rehabilitative services before offenders ar released from incarceration. They recommend that when offenders first arrive in prison, they should be properly assessed and diagnosed—both for levels of security they require and special needs, such as professionally run literacy and education programs. Criminologists also recommend that all undereducated and illiterate inmates should be required to participate in these programs with the goal of attaining high school certificates or the equivalent. Moreover, access to college education should not be denied to prisoners who wish to improve themselves. Similarly, substance abuse programs should be made available to all interested inmates and mandated for those identified as in need of such services. To encourage inmate participation in these programs, credits for sentence reduction should be offered.

Simultaneously, prisons must finance and support effective prerelease programs. The traditional bus ticket and two hundred dollars in "gate" money given to released prisoners is merely evidence of the system's disinterest in the offenders' successful reentry into society. Inmates should also be trained in ways that help them find housing and jobs upon their release. Indeed, job-training programs should be integral elements of the prison curriculum. Moreover, pre-release training should begin shortly after offenders are incarcerated and not be put off until shortly before they are released, as is generally done.

Upon their release, inmates should be provided with transitional housing—so-called "halfway houses"—to assist them in their transitions from total institutionalization to the free world. This is particularly important during the critical first six months after inmates are released. Halfway house programs provide structure, supervision, and services, while allowing former inmates an adjustment period before they are asked to face the demands and temptations of the free world.

While former inmates are in the community and under parole supervision, they should have immediate access to affordable and available aftercare services. Twelve-step programs are available worldwide and serve as the backbone for many substance abuse treatment programs, but other problems that involve personal, family, and social crises also require help. Providing all these services to former inmates is more cost-effective than dealing with the problems that arise when they return to criminal behavior that creates new victims and requires processing the same offenders through the criminal justice system and prisons again.

Reducing recidivism rates ultimately requires a fundamental philosophical shift in criminal justice and correctional policies. The current practice of warehousing offenders simply to incapacitate them must be modified. While it will always be necessary to protect society from truly violent and serious predators, rehabilitative services must be reinvigorated for the many nonviolent and petty criminals whose crimes are mostly related to substance abuse.

Kevin Meehan

Further Reading

Glaze, Lauren, and Seri Pella. *Probation and Parole in the United States, 2003*. Washington, D.C.: Bureau of Justice Statistics, 2004. The most up-to-date federal government survey of probation and parole programs throughout the United States.

Langan, Patrick A., and David J. Levin. *Recidivism of Prisoners Released in 1994*. Washington, D.C.: Bureau of Justice Statistics, 2002. Summary of the findings of the federal government study of recidivism.

Martinson, Robert. "What Works? Questions and Answers About Prison Reform." *Public Interest* 35 (1974): 2-35. Influential study of prisons that contributed to the belief that "nothing works."

Petersilia, Joan. *When Prisoners Come Home*. New York: Oxford University Press, 2003. Study by a noted criminologist of the wide variety of problems that former inmates face after they are released from custody.

Travis, Jeremy. "Invisible Punishment: An Instrument of Social Exclusion." In *Invisible Punishment: The Collateral Consequences of Mass Imprisonment*, edited by Marc Mauer and Meda Chesney-Lind. Washington, D.C.: New Press, 2002. Examination of the poor preparation for reentry into society provided to inmates by modern prison programs.

Travis, Jeremy, and Sarah Lawrence. *Beyond the Prison Gates: The State of Parole in America*. Washington, D.C.: Urban Institute, 2002. Important study of recidivism and parole by one of the leading criminologists in the field.

See also Boot camps; Community-based corrections; Halfway houses; Incapacitation; Mandatory sentencing; Prison overcrowding; Punishment; Rehabilitation; Sex offender registries; Supermax prisons; Three-strikes laws; Work-release programs.

Reckless endangerment

Definition: Willful engaging in conduct that shows a conscious disregard for safety and welfare of others

Criminal justice issues: Crime prevention; morality and public order; traffic law

Significance: Throughout the United States, laws governing reckless endangerment have been growing more popular and have been expanded to include forms of reckless behavior relating to driving vehicles, raising children, and robbery and other criminal acts. The concept of reckless endangerment is focused on the consequences of offenders' actions rather than the offenders' intent.

Although many people associate reckless endangerment primarily with irresponsible driving, the concept is a broad one and can encompass the consequences of neglectful parenting, felonious behavior, and a number of other behaviors that are regarded as socially undesirable. Laws that punish reckless endangerment are strongly influenced by the deterrence doctrine, in that they attempt to deter people from engaging in potentially harmful behavior.

What may be an extreme example of reckless endangerment laws is found in the felony-murder rule. Under this rule, offenders who participate in a felony offense can be charged with first-degree murder if their behavior results directly or indirectly in the death of another human being. This rule has even been extended to include the death of one of an offender's own partners during the felony. However, the felony-murder rule has encountered much controversy because defendants do not have to intend to kill others to be charged with first-degree murder, a fact that contradicts one of the fundamental criteria of first-degree murder.

Brion Sever

Further Reading

Fluke, John, Myles Edwards, Marian Bussey, et al. "Reducing Recurrence in Child Protective Services: Impact of a Targeted Safety Protocol." *Child Maltreatment* 6 (2001): 207-218.

Gambrill, Eileen, and Aron Shlonsky. "Assessing and Managing Risk in Child Protective Services." *Child and Youth Services Review* 23 (2001): 1-110.

Myers, Melanie. "Felony Killings and Prosecutions for Murder: Exploring the Tension Between Culpability and Consequences in the Criminal Law." *Social and Legal Studies* 3 (1994): 149-179.

See also AIDS; Child abuse and molestation; Environmental crimes; Traffic law.

Regulatory crime

Definition: Business practices banned under regulatory law instead of criminal or civil law

Criminal justice issues: Business and financial crime; white-collar crime

Significance: Laws governing regulatory crimes may be the most effective means of forcing compliance from companies because their nonpunitive nature tends to promote future corporate cooperation through persuasion.

The most common of crimes are violations of rules set by various government regulatory agencies. Among the most important federal regulatory agencies are the Federal Trade Commission, the Securities and Exchange Commission, the Occupational Safety and Health Administration, the Equal Employment Opportunity Commission, the Environmental Protection Agency, and the Federal Communications Commission. Some examples of regulatory crimes that they oversee are bid rigging, price-fixing, and failures to uphold inspection standards.

The processing of regulatory cases requires lesser standards for prosecution than in criminal and civil cases. For example, prosecutors do not need to prove guilt beyond a reasonable doubt and the matter of intent (*mens rea*) is generally irrelevant. Regulatory law is generally much flexible and proactive and involves agencies that have closer and more continuous contacts with offenders than is the case with most criminal agencies.

Regulatory law consists mainly of injunctions, consent decrees, and cease-and-desist orders. While there is no criminal aspect to punishments for offenses, regulatory sanctions may nevertheless place some degree of shame on offenders. However, the main problem with regulatory cases is that formal sanctions consist merely of fines. No such thing as a "smoking gun" that might put a grossly offending corporation out of business or send a company to prison is possible. However, gross violations can be referred to criminal authorities when regulatory agencies conclude that further investigations are warranted.

Kathryn Vincent

Further Reading

Rosoff, Stephen, Henry Pontell, and Robert Tillman. *Profit Without Honor: White-Collar Crime and the Looting of America.* Upper Saddle River, N.J.: Prentice Hall, 2002.

Simpson, Sally S. *Corporate Crime, Law, and Social Control.* New York: Cambridge University Press, 2002.

Sutherland, Edwin H. *White Collar Crime: The Uncut Version.* New Haven, Conn.: Yale University Press, 1983.

Wells, Joseph. *Corporate Fraud Handbook: Prevention and Detection.* Hoboken, N.J.: John Wiley & Sons, 2004.

See also Antitrust law; Corporate scandals; Environmental crimes; Fines; White-collar crime.

Rehabilitation

Definition: Punishment designed to reform offenders so they can lead productive lives free from crime

Criminal justice issues: Punishment; rehabilitation

Significance: While rehabilitation may be the most humane and progressive form of punishment, it is also the most difficult to achieve and has waned in popularity in the American justice system since the 1970's.

Although rehabilitation is often considered a type of punishment for criminal offenders, its objectives are therapeutic rather than punitive. While some theories of punishment claim that criminals deserve to suffer for their crimes, the rehabilitative ideal views criminal behavior more as a disease that should be treated with scientific methods to cure offenders.

Many convicts suffer from mental and physical illnesses, drug addictions, and limited opportunities for economic success, and these problems increase their likelihood of engaging in criminal activity. If the justice system simply incarcerates offenders to make them "pay their debt to society," they are likely to reenter it with all the problems that drive them to crime still in place. Moreover, they will also need to contend with the additional handicap of having a criminal record. They will also be older and still without marketable skills or education, their social relationships are likely to have deteriorated, and incarceration itself may have acclimated them to criminal culture. Thus incarcerating offenders can actually make them more likely than before to commit offenses after they are released. High recidivism rates attest to this. A rehabilitative approach to punishment attempts to treat the underlying causes of criminals' transgressions so they can return to society to become full and productive citizens. Instead of exacting revenge against criminals and making their lives even worse, rehabilitation tries to help them.

Early American prisons, such as those established at Auburn and Ossining, New York, and Pittsburgh, Pennsylvania, during the 1820's, implemented rehabilitative principles. These early programs isolated convicts from one another in order to remove them from the temptations that had driven them to crime and to provide individual inmates with time to listen to their own consciences and reflect on their deeds. Those early systems were predicated on the belief that all convicts would return to their inherently good natures when removed from the corrupting influences of society. However, those beliefs eventually gave way to more aggressive forms of treatment informed by the rise of social scientific studies into criminal behavior.

Rehabilitative Theories

Research in psychology, criminology, and sociology provided reformers with deeper understandings of deviance and sharper tools with which to treat it. Rehabilitation then became a science of reeducating criminals with the values, attitudes, and skills necessary to live lawfully. Rehabilitation has taken many forms in practice, including psychological analysis, drug and alcohol treatment, high school equivalency and other educational programs, vocational training, relationship counseling, anger-management therapy, religious study, and other services believed to meet the needs of particular offenders.

Because rehabilitation is based on the premise that every offender has different problems to overcome, programs for reform should be fashioned for individual offenders, just as doctors prescribe treatments for individual patients. Thus every sentence is individualized, and even two convicts who have committed the same crime may receive entirely different sentences. For example, an offender driven to steal because of drug addiction will require treatment different than that given to an unemployed immigrant who steals to pay for food for a family. Rehabilitative punishment is thus tailored to the offenders, rather than to the crimes.

According to rehabilitative theories, prison may not be the best venue for achieving its rehabilitative objectives because it isolates offenders from the very realities of life with which they must learn how to cope. Moreover, incarceration conditions offenders to become dependent on institutional care. Noncustodial sentences, such as parole, probation, community service, and deferred sentences serve to keep offenders functioning within their ordinary lives to some degree, while helping them learn how to manage the responsibilities they will face when their sentences expire. Such strategies are thought to be particularly important in the treatment of young offenders.

Rehabilitation seeks to reform not only individual convicts, but also the social conditions contributing to criminal culture. For example, correlations between crime, drug addiction, and poverty are well known. To some degree, these social ills cause crime. Treating individuals afflicted with these symptoms does not, by itself, stop the spread of the disease infecting so many others. Such problems transcend individual offenders. A complete criminal justice system, therefore, would seek to root out the structural conditions that create criminals. Under this theory, criminal behavior reflects the sickness of society, rather than simply deviant individuals.

Opposition to Rehabilitation

Rehabilitative justifications for punishment have lost popular support since the 1970's in the light of attacks coming from two fronts. While some argue that rehabilitation is fundamentally

The difficulty of rehabilitating people with serious drug problems is dramatically illustrated by the experience of the successful actor Robert Downey, Jr., seen here leaving a Southern California courthouse, where he was sentenced on drug and weapons charges in November, 1996. Over the next five years, Downey was in and out of drug rehabilitation programs and prison but continued his successful acting career. Despite his being under almost constant court supervision, being in rehabilitation programs, and having wealth and success, his drug problem appeared so intractable that his experience raised questions about whether drug rehabilitation programs could work for anyone. *(AP/Wide World Photos)*

immoral, others claim it is impractical. Retributivists, who cite the ancient "eye for an eye" maxim and believe that offenders should be punished merely because they deserve to suffer as payment for their transgressions, spearhead moral critiques of rehabilitation. By pampering criminals with therapy and education, retributivists argue, society fails to exact the revenge that justice demands. They further argue that this injustice is most evident in the practice of individualized sentencing, which can lead to disparate punishments for the same crimes and spare offenders from serving hard time. Such inequalities are patently unjust to retributivists.

In response to this perceived unfairness, reformers successfully lobbied for punishments to be meted out in determinate and standardized sentences corresponding to the moral desert of offenders. This movement culminated in the federal Sentencing Reform Act of 1984 and the U.S. Sentencing Guidelines, which removed most discretion from sentencing and led to skyrocketing incarceration rates.

Retributivists also find rehabilitation morally unjustifiable because it denies the offenders' responsibility for their actions by attributing their behavior to forces beyond their control, such as their sickness or circumstances. They object to the way that rehabilitation treats offenders as if they are not ultimately accountable for the choices they make. This practice, according to retributivists, reduces offenders to the level of animals or children and leads to techniques that strip offenders of their dignity.

As Anthony Burgess dramatically demonstrated in his 1962 novel *A Clockwork Orange*, it is unclear how far rehabilitative methods will go to reprogram individuals into obedient citizens. As it is now possible to inject drugs into sex offenders that will decrease their libido and to perform psychosurgery to reduce violent tendencies in convicts, it is now possible to create human beings who are effectively unable to choose whether to do good or evil. Because choice is so fundamental to any understanding of what it means to be fully human, such punishment is perceived as inhumane.

In *Discipline and Punish* (1979), the French philosopher Michel Foucault described the historical shift from spectacular corporal punishments, such drawing and quartering, to more subtle rehabilitative techniques as an increasingly efficient form of social control that blurs boundaries between incarceration and freedom. When punishment and education are conflated, penological methods seep into all of civilian life. Foucault claims that as a result human beings have become a "carceral" society.

Beyond these moral concerns, some doubt the practicality of rehabilitation. First, despite the boom in criminological research, little is still known about what causes crime and even less about how to reform criminal behavior. It is difficult to measure the success of rehabilitative methods, and recidivism rates have done little to change the thinking of those who doubt the effectiveness of rehabilitative techniques. Judging the progress of offenders is subject to interpretation, and offenders who are undergoing treatment have strong incentives to feign reform in order to expedite their own release. For the most

serious offenders, most remain skeptical that any amount of therapy can change their ways. However, it may be that the most determinative practical concern has been economic in nature: It is expensive to administer an effective rehabilitative system, and few politicians are willing to devote funds to such a disenfranchised group as unpopular as convicted felons.

Advocates of rehabilitation respond to these criticisms by claiming that their methods have not been fairly tested because they have never been supported by adequate resources. Within the political climate of the early twenty-first century, the decline of rehabilitation provides the political Right with an occasion to extend its anthem of "personal responsibility" in matters of distributive justice to justifications for punishment. Just as the poor deserve their fates and can rise from destitution by working harder, conservatives argue, criminals deserve to be held accountable for their actions. For the Left, such arguments for individual autonomy hide behind the deep social and economic injustices that segregate members of racial and economic underclasses behind prison walls.

Nick Smith

Further Reading

Allen, Francis. *The Decline of the Rehabilitative Ideal*. New Haven, Conn.: Yale University Press, 1981. Charts the rise and fall of rehabilitative punishment.

Braithwaite, John. *Crime, Shame and Reintegration*. Cambridge, England: Cambridge University Press, 1989. Argues that shame can be central to rehabilitation when done with respect for the offender.

Foucault, Michel. *Discipline and Punish: The Birth of the Prison*. Translated by Alan Sheridan. New York: Vintage Books, 1979. Philosophical work describing historical changes that led society to move away from castigating the body by means of torture to imprisoning both the body and the spirit. Capitalist society, concluded Foucault, is a carceral society of control and domination.

Garland, David. *The Culture of Control*. New York: Oxford University Press, 2001. Explains theoretical, political, and cultural trends since the 1960's that have caused a shift from rehabilitative to punitive justifications for punishment in the United States and Great Britain.

Morris, Norval, and David Rothman. *The Oxford History of Punishment: The Practice of Punishment in Western Society*. Oxford, England: Oxford University Press, 1997. Provides an overview of the transformation of the prison and the role of rehabilitation over the course of its history.

Murphy, Jeffrie. *Punishment and Rehabilitation*. New York: Wadsworth Publishing, 1994. Collection of essays on rehabilitative and other justifications for punishment.

Rothman, David. *The Discovery of the Asylum: Social Order and Disorder in the New Republic*. Boston: Little, Brown, 1971. Considers the simultaneous rise of the prison and asylum as means of treating deviants.

See also Auburn system; Boot camps; Community-based corrections; Deterrence; Forestry camps; Halfway houses; Incapacitation; Just deserts; Punishment; Recidivism; Restorative justice; Sentencing; Victim-offender mediation; Work camps; Work-release programs.

Religious sects and cults

Definition: Religious groups that are considered nonmainstream

Criminal justice issue: Civil rights and liberties

Significance: Religious and lifestyle practices of groups such as the Amish, Mennonites, Jehovah's Witnesses, Seventh-Day Adventists, and others are often subjected to challenges by secular legal authorities and civilian critics. The U.S. Supreme Court is the final arbiter of the extent to which the practices of these religious groups are protected.

Basic religious freedoms guaranteed to all Americans by the U.S. Constitution include the forbidding of religious tests for holding government offices and First Amendment guarantees that Congress may neither establish a state religion nor prohibit the free exercise of religion. All these guarantees have been extended to the actions of state and local governments by the Fourteenth Amendment. However, court interpretations of these guarantees have varied over the years.

In its 1970 *Lemon v. Kurtzman* ruling, the Supreme Court constructed a wall of separation between church and state and required a total neutrality of government toward religion when it established the so-called "Lemon test" to judge the constitutionality of laws and government actions. Under that ruling, no law may prefer one religion over another, prefer religion to nonreligion, have a primary effect that promotes religion, or cause undue entanglement between government and religious organizations. Some religions welcomed this wall of separation, but others believed the United States is a nation founded on religion and that the wall actually favors nonreligion over religion.

At the practical level, this separation means that Amish Mennonites do not have to obey school attendance laws, the Bible's Ten Commandments cannot be posted in schools, and religious groups must be given access to equal facilities on public university campuses. In 1990, however, the Supreme Court backed away from the *Lemon* doctrine in *Employment Division v. Smith* and ruled that government could require religious actors to obey general laws so long as the laws are not aimed specifically at religion or any particular religious institution. The case involved a Native American's right to smoke illegal hallucinogenic substances as part of religious ritual. Since the Court's ruling in *Boerne v. Flores* (1997), government has been able to require religious groups and actors to obey general law, so long as the laws themselves are based on compelling reason, are neutral with respect to religion, and are applied to all persons equally.

The roots of American religious freedom go back to the nation's settlement by European religious dissidents in the seventeenth century, but even then, religious bigotry was seen in the Salem witchcraft trials and religious intolerance in Massachusetts Colony. In the late twentieth century, religious rights came under attack by nongovernment civilian actors in the negative reactions of established religious bodies to the New Religion movement of the 1970's and 1980's. Anticult groups formed and members of cults and sects, such as the Society for Krishna Consciousness (Hare Krishna) and the Unification Church, were kidnapped, forced to endure deprogramming, and had their mental competency challenged in court. That period also saw a rise in anti-Semitism and attacks on Fundamentalist and predominantly African American churches.

Gordon Neal Diem

Further Reading

Cookson, Catharine, ed. *Encyclopedia of Religious Freedom*. New York: Routledge, 2003.

Davis, Derek, and Barry Hankins, ed. *New Religious Movements and Religious Liberty in America*. Waco, Tex.: Baylor University Press, 2002.

Fisher, Louis. *Congressional Protection of Religious Liberty*. New York: Novinka Publications, 2003.

See also Bigamy and polygamy; Bill of Rights, U.S.; Blue laws; Branch Davidian raid; Freedom of assembly and association; Hate crime; Ruby Ridge raid; Salem witchcraft trials.

Resisting arrest

Definition: Crime arising out of the preventing of law-enforcement officers from detaining or arresting suspects

Criminal justice issue: Arrest and arraignment

Significance: The statutory crime of resisting arrest is unusual in that it can occur only during confrontations between suspects and police officers attempting to make arrests on other charges.

Resisting arrest is a statutory crime of seeking to prevent an officer from taking a person into custody. A person may be taken into custody for the purpose of an arrest or a brief questioning. A police officer need not obtain a warrant to arrest or detain a defendant in a public place. Police officers may arrest a person for misdemeanors committed in their presence or if such misdemeanors qualify as a breach of the peace. Probable cause is the legal standard for arresting a defendant. Resisting arrest is a separate crime from the underlying offense.

Even if the underlying offense proves to be without cause or the arrest is illegal, a defendant may be liable for the separate offense of resisting arrest. A police officer has the authority to conduct a warrantless search of vehicles provided there is probable cause that a crime was committed. A person preventing a police officer from detaining the defendant or seized property may be charged with the crime of resisting arrest. A person who injures a police officer in the course of resisting arrest may be charged with more serious offenses such as aggravated assault or attempted murder. A police officer is permitted to use reasonable force in detaining a criminal suspect.

Michael L. Rustad

Further Reading

Loewy, Arnold H., and Arthur B. LaFrance. *Criminal Procedure: Arrest and Investigation.* Cincinnati: Anderson Publishing, 1996.

Quick, Bruce D. *Law of Arrest, Search, and Seizure: An Examination of the Fourth, Fifth, and Sixth Amendments to the United States Constitution.* Rev. ed. Bismarck, N.Dak.: Attorney General's Office, Criminal Justice Training and Statistics Division, 1987.

See also Arraignment; Disorderly conduct; King beating case; Nonviolent resistance; Police; *Tennessee v. Garner.*

Restitution

Definition: Punishment requiring convicted offenders to pay their victims or society for the costs incurred as a result of their crimes

Criminal justice issues: Convictions; punishment; sentencing

Significance: The use of restitution is increasing and in many states is now a mandatory sanction that courts are required, by law, to impose on offenders.

Until the late decades of the twentieth century, few formal restitution programs existed in the United States. Now, all U.S. states have restitution programs and every state gives its courts the right to order restitution to be paid by offenders. Within the United States, restitution is used as a form of punishment both in the adult and juvenile justice systems. In both cases, restitution is often part of offenders' terms of probation. Restitution is also sometimes used as an alternative form of punishment, in place of incarceration.

One type of restitution program requires offenders to pay monetary damages directly to victims. Monetary restitution may be ordered to cover such things as medical expenses, lost wages, counseling costs, loss of property, and funeral expenses resulting from the offenders' crimes. Instead of repaying the victims themselves with money, victim service restitution requires offenders to perform services for the victims of their crimes. Another type of restitution, community-service restitution, usually requires offenders to pay society back by engaging in community-service projects. Instead of being sentenced to prison or jail, offenders may be required to perform services in nursing homes, parks, hospitals, libraries, schools, animal shelters, or other public institutions. Judges may impose whatever number of service hours they regard as commensurate with the crimes committed. All these forms of restitution may be ordered for crimes against property, such as vandalism, or violent crimes against persons, such as assault.

As both a sole punishment and a condition of one's probation, restitution provides several advantages over other forms of punishment. Restitution programs save the taxpayers millions of dollars, as offenders are not placed in secure facilities, such as prisons, jails, or halfway houses. Secondly, these programs provide offenders with fresh chances to become productive citizens without suffering the negative effects of incarceration. Most important, restitution programs provide victims and communities with both tangible benefits and feelings of vindication for the harm they suffer.

Research has found that restitution programs for both juveniles and adults have higher success rates than other alternative forms of punishment. However, those who have completed restitution programs may not necessarily stay away from future contact with law-enforcement officials. Thus, while the majority of offenders complete their court-ordered restitution programs, the recidivism effects of these programs remain in doubt.

Karen F. Lahm

Further Reading

Allen, Harry E., Clifford E. Simonsen, and Edward J. Latessa. *Corrections in America: An Introduction.* 10th ed. Upper Saddle River, N.J.: Pearson Education, 2004.

Senna, Joseph, and Larry J. Siegel. *Essentials of Criminal Justice.* 3d ed. Belmont, Calif.: Wadsworth, 2001.

Siegel, Larry J. *Juvenile Delinquency: The Core.* Belmont, Calif.: Wadsworth, 2002.

See also Blended sentences; Community service; Execution of judgment; Fines; Juvenile courts; Juvenile justice system; Probation, adult; Probation, juvenile; Rehabilitation; Restorative justice; Sentencing; Victim-offender mediation; Victimology.

Restorative justice

Definition: Philosophy of justice that focuses on repairing harm caused by offenses

Criminal justice issues: Crime prevention; restorative justice; victims

Significance: Restorative justice is a modern holistic approach to justice that aims to treat both offenders and their victims, while involving the community in restitution and punishment.

A philosophical approach that is currently being used in both the adult and juvenile justice systems in the United States, restorative justice focuses on repairing the harm caused by offenses. It involves the victims of the crimes, the communities that are affected, and the offenders in the justice process. The U.S. Department of Justice has identified six components of restorative justice that must be considered in its application to any given case: the nature of the crime, the victims, the offenders, the local community, the overriding goal of justice, and the role of the criminal or juvenile justice system.

The nature of the crime, the impact on the victim and the attitude of the offender, are key factors in the success of restorative justice, and not all crimes are suitable for its application. For example, particularly violent crimes that traumatize their victims and crimes involving uncooperative offenders are generally unsuitable for restorative justice techniques.

The primary goal of restorative justice—and the one that gives it its name—is to repair damage and relationships that are harmed by crimes. This goal contrasts with the goal of retributive justice, which is to assign blame and administer punishments. Also unlike traditional retributive justice, in which victims have little involvement in the corrections process, restorative justice offers victims active roles in offender rehabilitation. For example, the victims may play a part in recommending restitution and participate in offender-victim mediation and conflict resolution, victim-offender circles, offender mentor programs, and in the supervising of community service.

Techniques

One of the most widely used techniques in restorative justice is victim-offender mediation, which brings victims and offenders together, along with trained mediators, to seek resolutions to the crimes. VOM is typically implemented after the offenders are charged, but it can also be used after the offenders complete their sentencing. During VOM, victim may share with the offenders the impact of the latters' crimes, including personal, social, and community elements. VOM is often used with burglary and other property crimes, in juvenile justice matters, and in other family court matters.

Offenders play a critical role in the success of restorative justice techniques. They must be willing to admit that they have caused harm to their victims and their communities and must be committed to repairing that harm. In addition to working with their victims, offenders must be able to identify their own needs in successful rehabilitation.

Community leaders and other community members are also involved in the restorative justice process. Their role is to work with both offenders and victims in restitution agreements. They offer resources for successful completion of the restorative programs, involve themselves in implementing restitution agreements, identify needs, and work toward crime prevention.

One example of community-led restorative justice initiatives is sentencing circles, which have been used by Native Americans for many years. The focus of circles is on the victims, their concerns, and the concerns of the community. Sentencing circles traditionally incorporate elements of both shaming and healing. The shaming works when the offenders are among their neighbors, friends, and community leaders.

A final key to the success of restorative justice is the role played by the formal criminal justice or juvenile justice system. In addition to ensuring that the restorative justice process is embraced by all the various parts of the justice system, there must be some kind of accountability within the process. As a whole, the justice system and its administrators need to know whether restorative justice measures are an effective response to criminal behavior. Research on the effectiveness of restorative justice has not yet been widely established in the United States. However, in countries in which it began earlier, such as Canada, four outcomes of restorative justice have been studied: victim satisfaction, offender satisfaction, restitution compliance, and lower recidivism rates.

Research conducted in Canada on more than thirty restorative justice programs has found that the programs have higher victim and offender satisfaction than traditional retributive justice responses, that they are better at achieving restitution compliance from offenders, and that they appear to reduce recidivism rates. It should be noted, however, that restorative justice programs are, by their very nature, likely to be more successful because they involve only positively motivated offenders and victims.

A restorative justice program that has received national attention and served as a model for other programs is the offender-victim circles held at the maximum security facility in Green Bay, Wisconsin. The circle lasts for three days and offenders convicted of serious offenses, such as murder, rape, and aggravated assault, meet with their victims in a secure environment under the supervision of psychologists and counselors.

Offenders report that meeting their victims face to face and confronting the horror of their own crimes leaves a lasting impression on them.

Obstacles

There are some barriers to overcome in implementing restorative justice programs. Some critics argue that restorative justice approaches do not address the issue of deterrence, particularly deterrence of serious crime. Others maintain that victims' rights may not be addressed equally or appropriately. Overcoming cultural barriers is also important when establishing restorative justice programs. Failure to account for cultural differences can lead to miscommunication and misunderstanding. In a brief on cross-cultural issues in restorative justice, the Department of Justice advises that differences in communication styles, such as physical proximity, body movements, paralanguage (vocal cues such as hesitations and changing timbre of voice), and density of language, should be understood by all parties involved in the restorative justice process.

Gaining the support of community members and ensuring the program meets state and federal guidelines will help ensure the success of restorative justice programs.

Monica L. P. Robbers

Further Reading

Johnstone, Gerry. *Restorative Justice: Ideas, Values, Debates*. Portland, Oreg.: Willan, 2002. Broad discussion of arguments for and against restorative justice programs.

Karp, David R., and Todd R. Clear. *What Is Community Justice? Case Studies of Restorative Justice and Community Supervision*. Thousand Oaks, Calif.: Sage Publications, 2002. Sociological study of actual restorative justice programs in action with detailed descriptions.

Rawls, John. *Justice as Fairness: A Restatement*. Edited by Erin Kelly. Cambridge, Mass.: Belknap Press, 2001. Collection of essays assembled by the distinguished American ethicist John Rawls that consider a wide variety of questions about the nature of justice.

Zehr, Howard, and Barb Toews, eds. *Critical Issues in Restorative Justice*. Chicago: Criminal Justice Press, 2004. This book provides an introduction to restorative justice and explores programs that have been implemented around the world. Both successes and failures are discussed.

See also Community service; Community-based corrections; Juvenile Justice and Delinquency Prevention, Office of; Juvenile justice system; Prison and jail systems; Punishment; Rehabilitation; Restitution; Victim assistance programs; Victim-offender mediation.

Restraining orders

Definition: Court orders in the nature of injunctions, usually temporary, that forbid parties from doing specified acts

Criminal justice issues: Crime prevention; domestic violence; victims

Significance: This remedy preserves a plaintiff's rights to avoid irreparable injury, pending final determination of the parties' rights; a variant of the restraining order helps protect victims of domestic violence.

In the usual course of a civil legal proceeding, the court makes no order affecting either party's substantive rights until the final judgment. In some situations, however, a plaintiff's rights may be irreparably damaged if the defendant continues taking some action. In such a case, the plaintiff may apply to the court for a temporary restraining order (also known as a "temporary injunction").

In order to be granted this extraordinary relief, the party seeking the order must show that immediate and irreparable harm is likely to result from a continuation of the status quo, or that the defendant is acting in a manner that will make any final judgment on the merits ineffectual. The burden is on the plaintiff to show entitlement to the order, and the court is likely to balance the relative inconveniences to the plaintiff and the defendant in determining whether the order should be issued. The temporary restraining order is effective only until a final judgment is issued. If the plaintiff is ultimately successful in the adjudication, the court may replace the temporary restraining order with a permanent injunction.

One special type of restraining order is the domestic violence restraining order. All fifty states have statutes authorizing a court to issue a restraining order against the alleged perpetrator of domestic violence, upon application by the intimate partner or former partner of the alleged perpetrator. Although the law varies among jurisdictions, this type of restraining order typically orders the respondent to refrain from further violence, harassment, or intimidation of the petitioner. It typically orders the respondent to vacate the home and to avoid contact with the petitioner at work, church, and school. The order also usually establishes custody and visitation for minor children, if necessary, and may order child or spousal support.

The typical procedure for obtaining a domestic violence restraining order is for the petitioner to make application for the court in an *ex parte* hearing—a hearing before the court in which only the petitioner is present, not the respondent. If the court finds that the statutory requirements are met, it issues a restraining order, which is then served upon the respondent. The respondent has a period of time (usually twenty-one days) in which to contest the order at a hearing. The restraining order typically is in effect for one year, unless vacated earlier by the court. Violation of the restraining order is punishable by civil or criminal penalties, and the violation itself (such as an assault) is also a separately punishable crime.

Gwendolyn Griffith

Further Reading

Haugaard, J. J., and L. G. Seri. "Stalking and Other Forms of Intrusive Contact Among Adolescents and Young Adults from the Perspective of the Person Initiating the Intrusive Contact." *Criminal Justice and Behavior* 31, no. 1 (2004): 37-54.

Meyer, J. F., and D. R. Grant. *The Courts in Our Criminal Justice System.* Upper Saddle River, N.J.: Prentice-Hall, 2003.

Neubauer, D. W. *America's Courts and the Criminal Justice System.* 7th ed. Belmont, Calif.: Wadsworth, 2002.

See also Cease-and-desist orders; Domestic violence; Stalking; Trespass; Victim assistance programs.

Reversible error

Definition: Error made during a trial that warrants a reversal of a guilty verdict

Criminal justice issues: Appeals; convictions; trial procedures; verdicts

Significance: Trial court verdicts can be reversed when appellate courts determine that defendants' cases have been seriously harmed by mistakes made during their trials.

One of the primary functions of federal and state appellate courts is to review and correct errors committed during trials. Errors can occur at any stage of the trial. Appellate courts may also review the competence and impartiality of the actors involved in the trials, including defense attorneys, judges, witnesses, and jury members.

Under English common law almost all findings of trial errors resulted in reversals, Now, however, American courts classify errors into two principal types: harmless and reversible. A harmless error is one considered to be a simple mistake made during the course of a trial that does not affect the decision of the judge or jury. By contrast, a reversible error is a mistake committed during a trial that is considered so serious that it warrants a reversal of the verdict, either because it negatively affects the outcome of the trial or because it abridges the defendant's fundamental constitutional rights.

Errors of a constitutional nature are regarded

Examples of Reversible Errors

✓ incompetent counsel
✓ judicial bias
✓ jury bias
✓ trial testimony based on coerced confessions
✓ failure of judge to recognize statutory requirements
✓ incomplete jury instructions

as more serious than nonconstitutional errors. Appellate courts have held that constitutional errors warrant reversals when there is a possibility they have contributed to decisions of the judges or juries. Nonconstitutional errors can be grounds for reversal only when appellate courts determine that they have significantly influenced verdicts.

Margaret E. Leigey

Further Reading

Traynor, Roger J. *The Riddle of Harmless Error*. Columbus: Ohio State University Press, 1970.

Whitebread, Charles H., and Christopher Slobogin. *Criminal Procedure: An Analysis of Cases and Concepts*. New York: Foundation Press, 2000.

See also Appellate process; Court types; *Habeas corpus*; Harmless error; Trials.

Right to bear arms

Definition: Right of citizens to own and carry guns

Criminal justice issues: Civil rights and liberties; constitutional protections; violent crime

Significance: The right to bear arms is a controversial subject that raises questions about exactly what kind of constitutional protection is guaranteed to citizens by the Second Amendment to the U.S. Constitution.

The right to bear arms is generally understood as the right of citizens to possess guns for their personal and community defense, for hunting and recreational target shooting, and for other lawful purposes. Many supporters of this right consider it to be a fundamental human right that is recognized by good governments. Critics consider recognition of such a right to be outdated.

Historical Roots

Connections between the right to bear arms and basic human rights have deep roots in Western philosophical tradition. In *Politics*, the fourth century B.C.E. Greek philosopher Aristotle argued that possession of arms by citizens was necessary for the preservation of their political rights. The laws of the later Roman Republic and Roman Empire did not explicitly recognize the right of citizens to bear arms, but they did acknowledge the right of citizens to defend themselves against common criminals and abusive soldiers. Likewise, the canon law, or church law, of medieval Europe affirmed a natural right of self-defense. The seminal work of canon law was the *Decretum* of the eleventh century Italian monk Gratian of Bologna, which argued that natural law is common to all nations because it exists everywhere through natural instinct. Gratian's examples of natural law included repelling violence by force, which he said could never be regarded as unjust because it is "held to be natural and equitable."

During the eleventh and twelfth centuries, many European towns began to assert their independence from monarchs and bishops who exercised temporal power. The towns bore responsibility for their own defense, which meant that their denizens had the right to bear arms and the duty to serve in their militias. The city-states of Italy became especially strong believers in militia ideology: that a civic virtue people would join a militia to defend themselves, rather than relying on foreign mercenaries for protection.

In medieval England bearing arms was considered both a right and a civic duty. Many English political philosophers attributed England's liberty to the fact that the nation was defended by militias, instead of standing armies. During the seventeenth century, England's Stuart kings made repeated attempts to assert royal control over the militias of local governments so they could build up standing armies. King James II and King Charles II both persuaded Parliament to enact gun laws that prohibited gun ownership by everyone except the wealthy and required gunsmiths to provide the government with lists of people who bought guns. The Stuart Dynasty was overthrown in 1688. The following year, Parliament enacted the English Bill of Rights, which declared "That the Subjects which are Protestants may have Arms for their Defence suitable to the Conditions, and as allowed by Law." English laws retained many strict prohibitions against hunting by commoners. Common people were allowed to have guns for other uses but not to possess items suitable only for hunting, such as nets and snares.

American Constitutional Law

All but a handful of American states have written the right to bear arms in their state constitutions. In twenty states, that right has been strengthened by voters. Apart from Massachusetts, the constitutional provisions in every state are currently interpreted as guaranteeing individuals the right to arms. Although many gun

In 1998 actor Charlton Heston became the president of the National Rifle Association, the strongest pro-gun lobbying organization in the United States. During the 2000 presidential election campaign, Heston charged that Democratic candidate Al Gore posed a threat to gun owners and raised the rhetoric of gun advocacy to a new level by holding a Revolutionary War era musket over his head during a speech and saying to Gore, "I have only five words for you: 'From my cold, dead hands,'" to a cheering audience. (AP/Wide World Photos)

control laws have been declared unconstitutional in the states, others have been upheld by courts ruling that they do not infringe constitutional rights.

A particularly controversial aspect of the right to bear arms is the meaning intended in the Second Amendment to the U.S. Constitution, which was adopted in 1791, along with the other nine amendments in the Bill of Rights. The wording of the amendment is brief and deceptively simple:

> A well regulated Militia, being necessary to the security of a free State, the right of the people to keep and bear Arms, shall not be infringed.

A much-debated question is exactly what the framers of the amendment meant by "the people." Were they thinking of collective communities, which should be allowed to arm their own militias? or, were they thinking of individual citizens? Through the nineteenth century, the Second Amendment was almost universally interpreted as guaranteeing an individual right. During the twentieth century, however, many courts and commentators argued that the amendment's allusion to "Militia" meant that the amendment guaranteed only the collective right of states to have militias, not an individual right.

In 1968, the U.S. Congress enacted the Gun Control Act, the first federal law placing any limits on the possession of ordinary guns by members of the public. Many Second Amendment challenges to the Gun Control Act were raised, but none of them has succeeded on Second Amendment grounds.

In 2001, the Fifth U.S. Circuit Court of Appeals ruled in, *United States v. Emerson*, that the Second Amendment guaranteed an individual right, and that the amendment was not infringed by a law that prohibited gun possession by persons subject to domestic violence restraining orders. Two years later, however, the Ninth U.S. Circuit Court of Appeals ruled, in *Silveira v. Lockyer* (2003), that there is no individual right to possess a gun. Other federal courts have made rulings similar to that in *Silveira v. Lockyer*.

Advocates on each side of the gun control debate assert that the U.S. Supreme Court supports their side's particular position. However, the Supreme Court has avoided addressing gun control. Three dozen different Supreme Court cases cite the Second Amendment, but the Court's last major decision on gun control was made in 1939, in *United States v. Miller*. Moreover, the Court's language in that case was sufficiently elliptical to allow both sides in the debate to claim support from the ruling.

David B. Kopel

Further Reading

Cottrol, Robert J., ed. *Gun Control and the Constitution: Sources and Explanations on the Second Amendment*. New York: Garland Publishing, 1994. One-volume edition of a longer three-volume work collecting major court cases and scholarly articles on both sides of the gun control debate.

Halbrook, Stephen P. *That Every Man Be Armed: The Evolution of a Constitutional Right*. 2d ed. Oakland, Calif.: Independent Institute, 1994. Leading argument for interpreting the Second Amendment as conferring an individual right.

Kopel, David B. "Comprehensive Bibliography of the Second Amendment in Law Reviews." *Journal on Firearms & Public Policy* 11 (1999): 5-45. Updates to this bibliography are available on the Web site of the Second Amendment Foundation (saf.org).

Kopel, David B., Alan Korwin, and Stephen P. Halbrook. *Supreme Court Gun Cases*. Phoenix, Ariz.: Bloomfield Press, 2003. Collection of the relevant text of every U.S. Supreme Court case involving the Second Amendment, gun control laws, and self-defense.

Malcolm, Joyce Lee. *To Keep and Bear Arms: The Origins of an Anglo-American Right*. Cambridge, Mass.: Harvard University Press, 1994. History of the right to arms in England, with particular attention to the seventeenth century.

Uviller, H. Richard, and William G. Merkel. *The Militia and the Right to Arms, Or, How the Second Amendment Fell Silent*. Durham, N.C.: Duke University Press, 2003. The most compelling argument for concluding that the right to bear arms should be considered obsolete in modern society.

Young, David E., ed. *The Origin of the Second Amendment: A Documentary History of the Bill of Rights in Commentaries on Liberty, Free Government and an Armed Populace, 1787-1792*. 2d ed. Ontanagon, Mich.: Golden Oak Books, 1995. Collection of all known original documents pertaining to the Second Amendment from the Founding era.

See also Bill of Rights, U.S.; Bureau of Alcohol, Tobacco, Firearms and Explosives; Constitution, U.S.; Firearms; Gun laws; National Guard; Self-defense.

Robbery

Definition: Unlawful taking of property from the immediate possession of others through the use of threat of force

Criminal justice issues: Robbery, theft, and burglary; violent crime

Significance: Essentially a combination of assault and the wrongful taking of property, robbery is considered one of the most serious crimes, and its associated punishments are among the harshest. The willingness of robbers to subject others to potential violence for pecuniary gain is a justification for its punishments being significantly greater than punishments for either underlying crime.

Robbery has been historically seen as an aggravated form of larceny, with its use or threat of force being the aggravating factor. At common law, the crime consisted of eight elements: trespass or wrongful act that damages a person or property; taking or gaining control of property; carrying away of property; taking of personal, as opposed to real, property; taking property belonging to others; intent to deprive rightful owners of their property permanently; taking of property directly from, or in the presence, of its owners; and using force or intimidation. Defenses against robbery charges often claim that the takers of

The key element of a robbery is the taking of property from the immediate possession of a victim. The use of a weapon elevates the crime to armed robbery. *(Brand-X Pictures)*

property believed it to be their own or that that they did not intend permanently to deprive the owners of their property.

As the criminal law regarding robbery has developed, the emphasis on the potential for violence posed by the crime has remained the primary focus. In fact, some states have defined robbery to include taking of property that the offenders believe to be their own. This modification of the definition is consistent with modern legislative trends to discourage self-help remedies that create the potential for physical harm. Additionally, in some jurisdictions, robbery does not include the element requiring offenders to intend to deprive owners of their property permanently. In such jurisdictions, it is unnecessary for the prosecution to prove that defendants had the specific intent of committing a larceny.

The heavy punishments associated with robbery have resulted in robbery cases frequently being litigated by defendants seeking to avoid harsh penalties. Such litigation addresses the question of whether the defendant's acts constitute a use of force. Technically, every taking of property requires the use of at least a token amount of force to seize it physically. For this reason, the amount of force actually applied by a defendant is frequently at issue. For example, the question might arise of whether the force used

was actually necessary to accomplish the taking of a purse from the arm of a women walking along a sidewalk. Although jurisdictions may vary in their general perception of whether a purse snatching should be treated as a robbery or simple theft, most jurisdictions focus on robbery's dominant characteristic—the potential for injury to victims. Consequently, if the force necessary to accomplish a purse snatching results in physical injury to the victim or a struggle over possession of the purse, or in some jurisdictions if the victim was aware of the force applied in taking the purse, then the purse snatching constitutes a robbery.

Jurisdictions, which rely upon victims' awareness of the force being applied, argue that a potential for physical injury arises when victims are aware of the applied force because the victim may resist the taking of the property and a struggle ensues. While such an analysis is consistent with the essence of the crime of robbery, it also has the effect of more severely punishing inept purse snatchers and pickpockets who inadvertently apply force that they do not intend and thereby alert their victims.

Another avenue by which defendants have challenged robbery charges is with regard to the requirement that the taking being accomplished through the use of force. At common law, robbery requires that the force be applied either immediately preceding or concurrent with the taking. Under such requirements, the use of force to retain possession of property already taken does not constitute a robbery. Moreover, it would not constitute a robbery if an offender, after taking and unsuccessfully carrying away property, were to use force to flee from apprehension. Many modern robbery statutes avoid this issue by explicitly qualifying the use of force as force used in the attempt or commission, or flight from the attempt or commission of the taking of property.

When a threat of force is the alleged instrument by which an offender obtains property, the threat must be of imminent harm. Threats of future harm generally fall under extortion statutes instead of robbery. Threats of harm do not have to be directed at the victim, but can be directed at other persons such as a relative of the victim.

Prevalence

Robbery is classified in the Federal Bureau of Investigation's (FBI) Uniform Crime Reports as a violent crime. In 2002, robberies constituted approximately 30 percent of all reported violent crimes in the United States, but only 3.5 percent of all index crimes compiled by the FBI. Only assaults constituted a larger component of violent crimes in 2002.

During the 1990's, robbery, like many other crimes, experienced a decline in the rate of criminal activity. From 1993 to 2002 the robbery crime rate declined approximately 36 percent. By 2002, the robbery rate, while still showing a slight decline from 2001, can be characterized as having stabilized.

Robbery has several distinct subcategories. Bank robbery has often been the focus of the news media and journalism, possibly because of instances in which exceptionally large sums of money have been taken. However, bank robbery constituted only 2.3 percent of robberies in the United States in 2002. A unique feature of bank robbery is the high rate of crimes in which the identities of the perpetrators are determined. Security systems at financial institutions greatly facilitate the identification and apprehension of bank robbers; consequently, in 2001 the identification, or clearance, rate for bank robbery was approximately 48 percent, a rate second only to the murder clearance rate.

In contrast, robberies of individuals on streets and public highways constitute the largest percentage of robberies and have a relatively low clearance rate. In 2002, such crimes constituted almost 43 percent of all

robberies. Most such robberies are perpetrated by offenders who are strangers to their victims—a fact that makes their identification difficult.

While overall robberies have been declining, the subcategory of residential robberies showed more than a 4 percent increase in 2002. That increase, along with a small increase in the burglary rate for 2002, apparently represents a greater willingness of criminals to invade residences, a fact that is a grave concern in many communities.

Robberies, by definition, include the use or threat of force. As might be expected, the instruments of force most often used are firearms. Brute force, using hands, fists, or feet, generally runs a close second in frequency. Thus, the vast majority of robbers either use firearms or rely solely upon their own physical strength. Although the potential for injuring victims during robberies might appear to be great, a study of bank robbery found that injuries occurred in only about 2 percent to 4 percent of the crimes.

Other Characteristics of Robbery

Robbery might be characterized as a young man's occupation, as the predominant age bracket

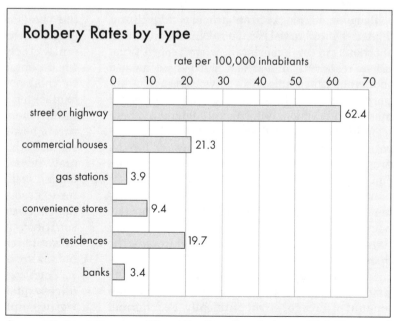

Robbery Rates by Type

rate per 100,000 inhabitants

Type	Rate
street or highway	62.4
commercial houses	21.3
gas stations	3.9
convenience stores	9.4
residences	19.7
banks	3.4

Source: Federal Bureau of Investigation, *Population-at-Risk Rates and Selected Crime Indicators.* Figures are for all robberies in the United States in 2002.

of robbers is men eighteen to twenty-five years old. However, juvenile robberies have declined at a rate even greater than that of the decline of adult robberies since the 1990's. In 2002, only 23 percent of all robberies were committed by juveniles.

Robbery is primarily an urban crime. In 2002, the robbery rate for urban areas was more than twice that of suburban counties, and more than four times that of rural counties. The prevalence of certain types of robbery also appear to be associated with population densities of communities. For example, street and highway robbery is most common in urban centers, while bank robberies constitute a much greater percentage of all robberies in rural communities than they do in urban communities.

A study of the relationship of socioeconomic factors with the crimes of homicide, robbery, and larceny in Japan has indicated that unemployment (but not poverty), and uneven distribution of wealth show positive relationships with the incidence of robbery. If the same relationship is valid in the United States, then the higher urban rate of robbery may be attributed to higher unemployment rates associated with inner cities.

Investigation

Because robbery requires the use of force or a threat of imminent force to take property from another's possession, witnesses are always present at robberies, unless the crimes also involve homicides that eliminate the witnesses. Consequently, investigations of robberies primarily are concerned with locating suspects who match descriptions provided by robbery victims. After suspects are apprehended, they must next be proven to be the actual perpetrators of the crimes. The modern proliferation of surveillance cameras in commercial enterprises and financial institutions has greatly facilitated identification of criminals who rob such establishments.

Prosecution

In criminal prosecutions of robbery cases, the force or threat element is often challenged by defendants. Pickpocketing and purse-snatching cases, for example, raise questions about the sufficiency of the force employed in the crimes. State jurisdictions vary considerably with regard to when such incidents constitute robbery. In a few jurisdictions, the rapid snatching of a purse has been characterized as a use of violence, so purse snatching thus automatically constitutes robbery. In some jurisdictions when items attached to the bodies or clothing of victims are taken by sufficient force to break the attachments, the takings are classified as robberies. For example, in one case, an offender who plucked a diamond pin from the shirt of a victim was convicted of robbery because the victim testified he had felt a jerk on his shirt.

A second issue involving the use of force concerns whether the force is actually instrumental in attempting to steal property. For example, if offenders abandon their attempts to take property and then get into physical altercations with the owners of the property, the force they exercised in such altercations does not satisfy the robbery element. Thus, in alleged attempted robberies in which offenders are unsuccessful in obtaining the property, prosecutors must prove that any physical altercations in which the offenders entered are related to their attempts to obtain or retain their victims' property.

Robbery charges often involve alleged threats of force conveyed through the offenders' actions, rather than through their words. In such cases, the prosecution must demonstrate that the offenders intended their actions to have been deliberately threatening to place their victims in fear. The intent of offenders is generally inferred from conclusions that their conduct was actually likely to place a reasonable person in fear. The fact that a victim feels threatened is not by itself determinative because the victim may be unusually susceptible to being frightened. For example, in one case, a clerk was frightened by an offender's act of quickly reaching across a convenience store counter to grab cash from an open register; however, the court concluded the clerk's reaction was insufficient proof that the offender intended that action to frighten the clerk in order to facilitate his taking of the cash.

Traditionally, robberies involving threats of force required the prosecution to prove that the victims did indeed feel threatened and were placed in fear. However, modern statutes frequently focus upon the offenders' intent rather than the question of whether the offenders are successful in achieving that intent. This focus upon an offender's intent and not the degree of success may be carried further in modern statutes with regard to the success of the robber in obtaining possession of the targeted property. Some modern statutes regard crimes of robbery to have been committed when mere attempts to obtain property involve force or threats. Under such statutes, "attempted robbery" convictions are reserved for instances in which robberies are stopped before the offenders employ force or threats.

Punishment

Robbery is a serious offense that is classified as a felony. It is generally divided into at least two degrees for punishment purposes. Forms of robbery receiving the severest punishment generally involve significant injuries to their victims, or the use or threats of use of deadly weapons, such as firearms. Even when offenders merely imply that they possess firearms when they do not, or when they display realistic toy guns, they can be convicted of the more serious degree of robbery.

David Blurton

Further Reading

Baumer, Eric, Julie Horney, Richard Felson, and Janet L. Lauritsen. "Neighborhood Disadvantage and the Nature of Violence." *Criminology: An Interdisciplinary Journal* (February, 2003). Examination of the socio-economic effects upon the quality of violence associated with assaults and robberies. Investigates whether the use of guns or physical violence is associated with the socio-demographics of the offense and whether the fact an offense occurs in a disadvantaged neighborhood rather than a middle income neighborhood has an effect on the violence.

Dix, George E., and M. Michael Sharlot. *Criminal Law.* 4th ed. Belmont, Calif.: Wadsworth, 1999. General text on substantive criminal law that includes an excellent discussion of robbery.

Kleck, Gary, and Ted Chiricos. *Unemployment and Property Crime: A Target-Specific Assessment of Opportunity and Motivation as Mediating Factors.* Columbus, Ohio: American Society of Criminology, Criminology: An Interdisciplinary Journal, August 2002. Examines the motivational and opportunity effects of unemployment upon crime with the incidence of robbery serving as one of the measures.

Lee, Matthew. *Community Cohesion and Violent Predatory Victimization: A Theoretical Extension and Cross-National Test of Opportunity Theory.* Chapel Hill: University of North Carolina Press, 2000. Study of community cohesion as a preventive element with regard to assaults and robberies.

Samaha, Joel. *Criminal Law.* 7th ed. Belmont, Calif.: Wadsworth, 2002. General substantive criminal law text discussing robbery among other topics.

See also Bank robbery; Blackmail and extortion; Burglary; Carjacking; Common law; Crime Index; Criminal law; Felonies; Pickpocketing; Shoplifting; Surveillance cameras.

Robinson v. California

The Case: U.S. Supreme Court ruling on cruel and unusual punishment
Date: Decided on June 25, 1962
Criminal justice issues: Punishment; substance abuse
Significance: This case, which held that it was cruel and unusual punishment to incarcerate drug addicts simply because of their addictions, was for some critics emblematic of the Warren court's "softness" on crime.

Robinson, the plaintiff in this case, was originally convicted under a California statute making it a crime to be a drug addict and was sentenced to ninety days in jail. The statute did not require the state to prove that the accused had either bought or purchased drugs or that he possessed them—the mere status of being a drug addict was enough to convict a defendant. Robinson appealed, and the Supreme Court overturned the conviction on grounds that incarceration for ninety days for what amounts to an illness constitutes cruel and unusual punishment.

Because of such rulings as *Mapp v. Ohio*

(1961), which extended guarantees against unreasonable search and seizure to state defendants, the Court overseen by Chief Justice Earl Warren was criticized for "coddling" criminals. *Robinson* was doubly controversial because it is based on the assumption that drug addiction is an illness over which the addict has no control. Indeed, six years later the Court declined to follow its own precedent in *Powell v. Texas* (1968), in which it upheld the criminal conviction of a chronic alcoholic, declaring that the state of knowledge regarding alcoholism was inadequate to permit the enunciation of a new constitutional principle.

The *Robinson* decision is important for making the cruel and unusual punishment clause of the Eighth Amendment applicable at the state as well as the federal level. The case was a continuation of the "due process revolution," championed initially by Justice Hugo Black, that reached its high-water mark during Earl Warren's tenure as chief justice. By means of the due process clause of the Fourteenth Amendment, the guarantees of the Bill of Rights limiting federal action were "incorporated" into the Fourteenth Amendment, thus becoming applicable to state governments. The Fourteenth Amendment, passed in the wake of the Civil War, makes all persons born in the United States citizens whose privileges and immunities cannot be restricted and whose rights of due process and equal protection cannot be denied.

Some framers of the Fourteenth Amendment indicated that the privileges and immunities extended therein included the guarantees of the Bill of Rights, but this point was left ambiguous. In *Palko v. Connecticut* (1937), the Court explicitly addressed the issue for the first time, stating that some of the rights embodied in the first ten amendments to the Constitution were so fundamental that the Fourteenth Amendment obligated states to observe them. Then, writing in dissent in *Adamson v. California* (1947), Justice Black argued that the Fourteenth Amendment obligated states to honor all aspects of the Bill of Rights. The Court has never quite adopted this view, but by the time Earl Warren's leadership ended in 1969, most of the Bill of Rights had been applied to the states.

Lisa Paddock

Further Reading

Berkson, Larry. *The Concept of Cruel and Unusual Punishment*. Lexington, Mass.: Lexington Books, 1975.

Gaines, Larry K., and Peter B. Kraska, eds. *Drugs, Crime, and Justice*. Prospect Heights, Ill.: Waveland Press, 2003.

Liska, Ken. *Drugs and the Human Body, with Implications for Society*. 7th ed. Saddle River, N.J.: Prentice-Hall, 2004.

Orcutt, James D., and David R. Rudy, eds. *Drugs, Alcohol, and Social Problems*. Lanham, Md.: Rowman & Littlefield, 2003.

See also Cruel and unusual punishment; Drugs and law enforcement; Due process of law; *Rummel v. Estelle*; Supreme Court, U.S.

Roman Catholic priests scandal

The Event: Widespread accusations, many confirmed, that large numbers of Roman Catholic priests had been sexually abusing the children and adolescents entrusted to their care

Date: 1990's-2002

Place: Boston, Massachusetts, and elsewhere around the world

Criminal justice issues: Deviancy; morality and public order; sex offenses

Significance: The gradually expanding revelations of priestly abuse of young people rocked the Roman Catholic Church both because of the nature and the extent of the abuse and because of the additional revelation that church leaders had long been aware of the problem and had responded to it only by transferring offending priests to different parishes and spending millions of dollars to silence their victims.

The molestation of children entrusted to the care of Roman Catholic priests became a worldwide news story during the 1990's and into the twenty-first century, as increasing numbers of victims came forward to describe their sexual abuse.

The first stories originated in Boston, but it was later revealed that similar abuses had occurred throughout the world. The most disturbing element of the emerging evidence was that the abuse had occurred over a long period of time.

After a police investigation began, detectives found that church records documented many incidents of such offenses as priests trading drugs for sex with minors and telling their young victims that if they were to reveal their abuse to anyone, their parents would burn in hell. One of the primary reasons that the priests had been able to abuse children for so long without suffering any punitive consequence was the Catholic Church's penchant for secrecy.

Church authorities were apparently long aware of which priests were guilty of abusing children but did nothing to have them prosecuted. Instead, the church usually sent offending priests to other parishes, where they repeated their crimes. The only other action taken by church officials was to place offenders in counseling programs. In some cases, the church paid victims and their families large sums of money in return for their silence. According to one unconfirmed estimate, the church may have paid out a total of nearly seven hundred million dollars.

The church's outpouring of money to hush accusers caused it serious structural damage. One archdiocese had to file for bankruptcy shortly before trials of two of its offending priests were about to begin. That action signaled that any further civil lawsuits brought against the Roman Catholic Church would be settled in federal courts. In December, 2002, Cardinal Bernard Law, the powerful Roman Catholic archbishop of Boston who had once been regarded as the face of American Catholicism, resigned in disgrace over revelations that he had long known about the abuse.

Eventually, it was revealed that at least 1,200 priests had been charged with sexually abusing children; some estimates went much higher. In response to the furor over the Boston incidents, other American bishops created the National Review Board (NRB), a body made up of lay members of the church. The board commissioned John Jay College of Criminal Justice in New York to investigate the scandal fully and determine the total numbers of molestations and offenders and any other behavior construed as abusive.

The college's comprehensive report received the endorsement of 98 percent of the church's American dioceses. According to the study, ap-

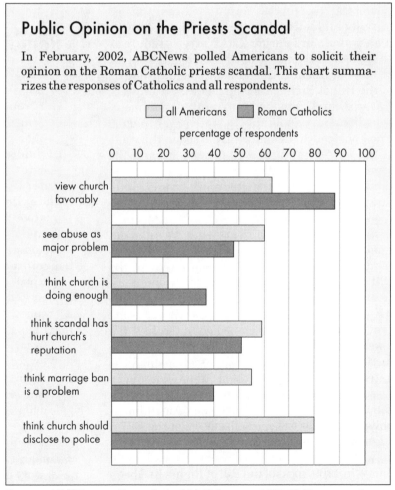

Public Opinion on the Priests Scandal

In February, 2002, ABCNews polled Americans to solicit their opinion on the Roman Catholic priests scandal. This chart summarizes the responses of Catholics and all respondents.

Source: ABCNews poll conducted in February, 2002. Poll surveyed random national sample of 1,008 adults.

Demonstration organized by the Coalition of Catholics and Survivors outside the meeting of the U.S. Conference of Catholic Bishops in Dallas, Texas, in June, 2002. The demonstrators hold pictures of alleged sexual abuse victims of Catholic priests. *(AP/Wide World Photos)*

proximately 4 percent of all American priests who served between 1950 and 2002, had been accused of sexually abusing minors. During that period, there were 10,667 victims, with boys between the ages of eleven and seventeen being the primary victims.

The frequency of molestations increased greatly during the 1960's and peaked during the 1970's before declining for two decades. More than 4,000 priests were accused of sexual abuse, but 56 percent of those accused had only one allegation against them. The bulk of the charges centered on 149 priests, each of whom had at least 10 allegations against him. Estimates of the numbers of molestation incidents and victims by outside groups placed higher numbers on all the figures.

The NRB recommended that in the future "zero tolerance" be accorded to priests guilty of sexual abuse. This meant that all priests charged

with molestation were to be expelled from the ministry, regardless of when their offenses occurred. Even if charges were unsubstantiated or pertained to incidents occurring many years earlier, accused priests could lose their positions. The NRB plan gained the acquiescence of the American bishops, but the Vatican rejected it, saying it was grossly unfair to priests who might have engaged in single sinful acts many years earlier and afterward acted with complete probity. Meanwhile, hundreds of lawsuits against the church were filed in the United States, and criminal convictions were obtained against some of the offenders.

Cary Stacy Smith

Further Reading
Boston Globe. *Betrayal: The Crisis in the Catholic Church*. Boston: Back Bay Books, 2003. Compilation of news stories on the priest scandal.

Bruni, F., and E. Burkett. *A Gospel of Shame: Children, Sexual Abuse, and the Catholic Church.* Australia: HarperPerennial, 2002. Broad and critical survey of the problem of priestly abuse throughout the world.

Jenkins, P. *Pedophiles and Priests: Anatomy of a Contemporary Crisis.* London: Oxford University Press, 2001. Scholarly examination of the scandal.

Steinfels, P. *A People Adrift: The Crisis of the Roman Catholic Church in America.* New York: Simon & Schuster, 2003. Study of the devastating impact of the scandal on the relationship between the church and its outraged lay members.

See also Child abuse and molestation; Pedophilia; Pornography, child.

The Rosenberg Case Four Decades Later

Many books have been written to protest what was perceived as the failure of justice and the misrepresentation of evidence in the Rosenberg case. Most important among them were Walter Schneir and Miriam Schneir's 1965 *Invitation to an Inquest* (new edition 1983) and Michael Meeropol and Robert Meeropol's 1986 *We Are Your Sons*, by the Rosenbergs' sons. Documents released through the Freedom of Information Act have revealed that Greenglass devised false evidence that was used against Ethel Rosenberg in the trial and that the government attempted to use its prosecution of Ethel as a tool to force Julius to confess.

In 1995 the decades-old case took another turn when the government released formerly classified documents consisting of decoded transmissions, some of them fragmentary, between Soviet operatives. These messages show that Julius Rosenberg was indeed a Soviet spy and that Ethel was at least aware of his activities, although they do not confirm her active involvement. Although the coded messages portray Julius as the leader of a spy ring, they do not specifically contain corroboration of the charges that he transmitted high-level atomic secrets. Finally, in spite of the confirmation of Julius Rosenberg's espionage activities, it is clear that false evidence was given by government witnesses at the trial.

Rosenberg espionage case

The Event: Arrest, conviction, and execution of Julius and Ethel Rosenberg for passing U.S. military secrets to the Soviet Union
Date: 1951-1953
Place: New York State
Criminal justice issues: Capital punishment; espionage and sedition; political issues
Significance: The Rosenberg espionage case prompted an international debate, pitting national security issues against First Amendment rights, and raised questions about the American justice system's vulnerability to the anticommunist political climate of the Cold War era.

Sometimes referred to as the Rosenberg-Sobell or "Atom Spy" case, the trial and execution of Julius Rosenberg and his wife, Ethel Rosenberg, is perhaps the best-known espionage case in American history. The Rosenbergs had a history of involve-ment in radical politics. In June, 1950, Julius was questioned by agents of the Federal Bureau of Investigation (FBI) after being named as a spy by his brother-in-law David Greenglass. He was arrested in July and charged with conspiracy to commit espionage under the Espionage Act of 1917. The following month saw both the arrest of Ethel and Julius's college friend Morton Sobell.

In late January, 1951, a grand jury indicted the Rosenbergs and Sobell, along with several others for espionage activities dating as far back as 1943. Among the most serious allegations were that the Rosenbergs provided the Soviets with information about the government's Manhattan Project, which was developing the atomic bomb, and delivered to them a proximity fuse that accelerated Soviet atomic bomb development.

The trial of the Rosenbergs and Sobell began in New York City on March 6, 1951. The prosecutors include Irving Saypol, who was well known for his successful prosecution of communist Alger Hiss, and Roy M. Cohn (who later gained notoriety as an aide to Senator Joseph McCarthy). The Rosenbergs' defense was handled by the father-son team of Alexander Bloch and Emanuel Bloch, who were known for their legal work on behalf of labor activists and other progressive causes. The case was presided over by Judge Irving R. Kaufman.

The prosecution's main witness, David Greenglass, told the court of how, at Julius's urgings, he had prepared diagrams of the atomic projects on which he had worked and passed them to Soviet agents in the United States. Several other witnesses told of how the Rosenbergs and Sobell tried to recruit them as spies. Sobell himself asserted his Fifth Amendment right and did not take the stand. The Rosenbergs denied all the spying charges but refused to discuss their political affiliations. The jury returned a verdict of guilty against Sobell and the Rosenbergs on March 29, 1951. Judge Kaufman sentenced Sobell to thirty years in Alcatraz Prison and the Rosenbergs to death.

After the convictions, the National Committee to Secure Justice in the Rosenberg Case began to question the proceedings openly. They pointed out that the prosecution's case rested completely on unsubstantiated circumstantial evidence and perjured testimony, that there was no documented evidence, and that references had been made throughout the trial to the Rosenbergs' leftist political beliefs. Upon public discussion of the trial proceedings, many clergy and some leading scientists, including Albert Einstein, joined the movement asking that clemency be granted to the Rosenbergs. The movement continued to gain momentum and became international in scope.

The Rosenbergs sat on death row in New York's Sing Sing Prison while several appeals were denied. During this time they were offered clemency in return for confessions but they refused the offer. In June, 1953, only days before their scheduled execution, Supreme Court justice William O. Douglas granted a stay of execution. However, in a special session two days later, the U.S. Supreme Court vacated the stay and President Dwight D. Eisenhower denied a final clemency plea. On the evening of June 19, 1953, the Rosenbergs were put to death in the electric chair.

Stephen L. Muzzatti

Further Reading

Meeropol, Robert. *An Execution in the Family.* New York: St. Martin's Press, 2003

Meeropol, Robert, and Michael Meeropol. *We Are Your Sons: The Legacy of Ethel and Julius Rosenberg.* Foreword by Eric Foner. 2d ed. Urbana: University of Illinois Press, 1986.

Schneir, Walter, and Miriam Schneir. 1965. *Invitation to an Inquest.* New York: Pantheon, 1983.

See also Auburn system; Espionage; Federal Bureau of Investigation; Hoover, J. Edgar; Palmer raids; Smith Act.

Royal Canadian Mounted Police

Identification: Canadian national police force
Date: Founded in 1873
Criminal justice issues: Law-enforcement organization; police powers
Significance: The Canadian equivalent of the U.S. Federal Bureau of Investigation, the Royal Canadian Mounted Police is a powerful police institution with a presence at the national, provincial, and civic levels.

The Canadian government created the North West Mounted Police, as the Royal Canadian Mounted Police was originally called, in 1873 to bring European law and order to both the existing aboriginal population in the newly acquired Canadian West and the settlers about to arrive. Deployed the following year, the Mounted Police was not an ordinary police force. Modeled after the Royal Irish Constabulary, it was a paramilitary law-enforcement agency.

A success in ensuring order, particularly during the Yukon gold rush at the end of the nineteenth century, the Mounted Police quickly gained international fame thanks to romanticized accounts of its exploits in works both of nonfiction and fiction. Hollywood would later make the Mounties, as the organization's officers are known, even more famous through a series of

Performing a task far removed from the stereotypes of traditional Mounties' duties, an officer of the Royal Canadian Mounted Police boards an American sailboat docked in Halifax, Nova Scotia, in July, 2004. The boat had been seized off the province's coast with more than five hundred kilograms of cocaine on board. *(AP/Wide World Photos)*

films, such as Cecil B. DeMille's *North West Mounted Police* (1940).

Despite its fame, by the end of World War I the future of the Mounted Police was anything but secure. Under the Canadian constitution, policing was a provincial responsibility, and, accordingly, individual provinces had established their own police forces. The Mounted Police, officially known as of 1920 as the Royal Canadian Mounted Police (RCMP), spent that decade spying on communists and enforcing federal rules and regulations instead of fighting crime.

The turning point for the force arrived with the Great Depression. Because of financial difficulties, five provinces in 1932 joined the province of Saskatchewan and replaced their provincial police forces with the more cost-effective RCMP. In the long run, only the provinces of Quebec, Ontario, and Newfoundland would keep their own provincial police forces. The RCMP was now in a particularly powerful position, as it worked at the national level, at the provincial level, and in some provinces even at the civic level. It was also in charge of Canada's domestic security as it continued to monitor communist espionage and subversion.

Eventually, as with the Federal Bureau of Investigation's COINTELPRO program in the United States, it was this security role and not the regular crime fighting that would fundamentally affect the RCMP. During the 1970's, RCMP illegal activities directed against Quebec separatists became public, and afterward a special inquiry by the Canadian government removed most aspects of the RCMP's security role from it. However, its regular policing role continued untainted, with a renewed emphasis on curtailing international crime, including the smuggling of drugs and of people. As a sign of the respect the RCMP has enjoyed, some of its members traveled abroad to train officers in the developing democracies of Haiti and Bosnia.

Steve Hewitt

Further Reading

Baker, William, ed. *The Mounted Police and Prairie Society, 1873-1919*. Regina, Sask.: Canadian Plains Research Center, 1998.

Kelly, William, and Nora Kelly. *The Royal Canadian Mounted Police: A Century of History, 1873-1973*. Edmonton, Alta.: Hurtig, 1973.

See also Canadian justice system; COINTELPRO; Drugs and law enforcement; Federal Bureau of Investigation; Justice; Vigilantism.

Ruby Ridge raid

The Event: Siege of private citizen Randy Weaver's Idaho home by federal law-enforcement officers
Date: August 21-31, 1992
Place: Ruby Ridge, Idaho
Criminal justice issues: Federal law; government misconduct; police powers
Significance: The Ruby Ridge incident generated new guidelines for the future conduct of federal law-enforcement agents in the execution of criminal justice.

Proclaiming himself a "white separatist" and hoping to avoid contact with the outside world, Randy Weaver moved his family to Ruby Ridge, in northern Idaho, during the early 1980's. Through a series of events that transpired between 1986 and 1989, Weaver was indicted in 1990 on a charge of violating federal weapons laws. When he failed to appear in court, six U.S. marshals dressed in camouflage clothing were sent to the Weaver property on August 21, 1992, to arrest Weaver. An ensuing gun battle left Sammy Weaver, Randy's fourteen-year old son,

and U.S. Marshal William Degan dead. The following day, four hundred Federal Bureau of Investigation (FBI) agents arrived at the Weaver premises. Randy Weaver was wounded while outside his cabin, and shortly thereafter, his wife, Vicki, was killed by FBI sharpshooter Lon Horiuchi.

Through negotiations conducted by Colonel Bo Gritz, Randy Weaver surrendered to FBI agents on August 31. In July, 1993, Randy Weaver was acquitted of weapons and murder charges. In 1995, the Weaver family was awarded $3.1 million in damages by the U.S. Department of Justice for the wrongful death of Vicki Weaver. The Justice Department found twelve FBI agents guilty of violating FBI guidelines and protections afforded U.S. citizens by the Fourth Amendment of the U.S. Constitution. Recommendations for reforming and standardizing procedures to be followed when future incidents like Ruby Ridge might occur were subsequently formulated by the justice department.

Alvin K. Benson

Further Reading

Skogan, Wesley G., and Kathleen Frydl, eds. *Fairness and Effectiveness in Policing: The Evidence*. Washington, D.C.: National Academies Press, 2003.

Walter, Jess. *Ruby Ridge: The Truth and Tragedy of the Randy Weaver Family*. New York: Regan Books, 2002.

See also Attorney general of the United States; Bureau of Alcohol, Tobacco, Firearms and Explosives; Conspiracy; Deadly force; Equal protection under the law; Federal Bureau of Investigation; Marshals Service, U.S.; Religious sects and cults.

Rummel v. Estelle

The Case: U.S. Supreme Court ruling on mandatory sentences
Date: Decided on March 18, 1980
Criminal justice issues: Fraud; punishment; sentencing
Significance: In this case, the Supreme Court found no cruel and unusual punishment in a

state's mandatory life-imprisonment statute as applied to a man convicted of three fraudulent offenses involving only $229.11.

In 1973, William Rummel was convicted under the Texas recidivist statute, which required a mandatory life sentence after three felony convictions, even for nonviolent offenses. In 1964 Rummel had been convicted of his first felony, the fraudulent use of a credit card to obtain goods worth $80.00. Four years later he had been found guilty of passing a forged check for $28.36. Finally, in 1973 he was charged with a third felony of receiving $120.75 by false pretenses. Rummel might have avoided the life sentence if he had yielded to the state's pressure to accept a plea bargain without a jury trial, but he insisted on a trial. Rummel sought relief in federal court, with the argument that his life sentence was "cruel and unusual" because it was grossly excessive and disproportionate to the penalties for more serious crimes. The district court and court of appeals rejected the argument, and Rummel appealed to the U.S. Supreme Court.

The Court voted 5 to 4 to affirm the constitutionality of Rummel's punishment. Writing for the majority, Justice William H. Rehnquist maintained that the doctrine that the Eighth Amendment prohibited sentences disproportionate to the severity of the crime was relevant only in death-penalty cases, because this penalty was unique in its total irrevocability. Rehnquist found that the Texas statute had two legitimate goals: to deter repeat offenders and to isolate recidivists from society as long as necessary after they had demonstrated their incapacity to obey the law. The states generally had the authority to determine the length of isolation deemed necessary for such recidivists. Rehnquist also made much of the fact that the Texas statute allowed the possibility of parole.

In an important dissent, Justice Lewis F. Powell, Jr., argued that the doctrine of disproportionality also applied to penalties in noncapital cases. He pointed to precedents that could be interpreted as prohibiting grossly excessive penalties, especially *Weems v. United States* (1910) and *Robinson v. California* (1962). Powell observed that in Texas, even those convicted of murder or aggravated kidnapping were not subject to mandatory life sentences. In addition, he maintained that the possibility of parole should not be considered in assessing whether the penalty was grossly disproportionate.

The *Rummel* decision would prove to be limited and uncertain in its application as a precedent. In 1983, when the Court encountered a life sentence without any chance of parole based on a recidivist statute in *Solem v. Helm*, Justice Powell would write the majority opinion while Rehnquist would write a dissent. While *Solem* did not directly overturn *Rummel*, the *Solem* majority did endorse the idea that a prison sentence might be unconstitutional if it was disproportionate to punishments for other crimes. Yet in upholding a life sentence for the possession of 650 grams of cocaine in *Harmelin v. Michigan* (1991), the Court would indicate its continued reluctance to apply the doctrine of disproportionality in noncapital cases.

Thomas Tandy Lewis

Further Reading

Demleitner, Nora V., Douglas A. Berman, Marc L. Miller, and Ronald F. Wright. *Sentencing Law and Policy: Cases, Statutes, and Guidelines*. New York: Aspen Publishers, 2003.

Tonry, Michael. *Sentencing and Sanctions in Western Countries*. New York: Oxford University Press, 2001.

_____. *Sentencing Matters*. New York: Oxford University Press, 1996.

United States Sentencing Commission. *Federal Sentencing Guidelines Manual 2003*. St. Paul, Minn.: West Publishing, 2004.

See also *Brady v. United States*; Cruel and unusual punishment; Mandatory sentencing; Plea bargaining; Supreme Court, U.S.

Saint Valentine's Day Massacre

The Event: Seven men from the Northside gang of George "Bugs" Moran were lined up and shot in a garage in Chicago

Date: February 14, 1929

Place: Chicago, Illinois

Criminal justice issues: Homicide; organized crime; violent crime

Significance: Public reaction to the largest mass slaying associated with gangland wars in American history prompted the federal government to crack down on organized crime.

On February 14, 1929, approximately twelve men dressed in police uniforms and driving stolen police cars, but actually associated with Al Capone, entered a garage at 2122 Clark Street in Chicago, where they found seven members of George

Bodies of six of the seven victims of the St. Valentine's Day Massacre. *(AP/Wide World Photos)*

"Bugs" Moran's gang. The seven were then shot to death. The dead included Pete and Frank Gusenberg, two of Moran's top gunmen, and Adam Heyer, Moran's "business manager." Moran himself was not present.

The organizer of the crime was "Machine Gun" Jack McGurn, Capone's top gunman and bodyguard and survivor of an assassination attempt carried out by the Gusenbergs. McGurn had hired Fred Burke, golfing partner of Capone and member of the "Egan's Rats" gang from St. Louis, in the belief that it would be better to use "imported" killers. Also hired were members of the Detroit Purple gang.

The crime was eventually solved, in part with the use of the new science of forensics. Calvin Goddard, a ballistics expert, observed the presence of so-called fingerprints on bullets, markings that could identify the weapon. When Burke was arrested the following year for the murder of a Michigan police officer, Goddard showed that the same weapon had been used in the Chicago massacre. Though never convicted for the gangland slayings, Burke was sentenced to life in prison for the murder of the officer.

As a result of the uproar resulting from the slayings, the federal government stepped in to remove the most notable gangsters from the scene, using any available means. Capone spent most of his declining years in federal prison for tax evasion.

Richard Adler

Further Reading

Bergreen, Laurence. *Capone: The Man and the Era*. New York: Touchstone, 1994.

Helmer, William, and Arthur Bilek. *The St. Valentine's Day Massacre*. Nashville: Cumberland House, 2004.

See also Capone, Al; Gangsters of the Prohibition era; Organized crime; Prohibition.

Salem witchcraft trials

The Event: Trial and execution of English settlers accused of practicing witchcraft
Date: 1692
Place: Salem Village, Massachusetts
Criminal justice issues: Capital punishment; hate crime; women's issues
Significance: The injustice of the Salem witch trials has come to symbolize the terrible results that can come of intolerance and hysteria.

Salem, Massachusetts, was settled by English Puritans; the church at Salem was established in 1629 as an independent Protestant church. A belief in witchcraft and the idea that humans could be direct agents of the devil was widespread in Europe at the time, and the Puritans brought the belief with them to New England. The colonial charter had laws against sorcery and witchcraft, and punishment was the death penalty.

The problems in Salem began in February, 1692, when young girls in the home of the church pastor, including the pastor's daughter, began suffering spectacular seizures and speaking incantations. The girls were soon considered bewitched, and they began to implicate people in

The Witchcraft Trials on Stage and Screen

The Salem witchcraft trials are most familiar to the public through Arthur Miller's 1953 play, *The Crucible*, which was made into a popular film of the same title in 1996. In the film adaptation, after John Proctor (Daniel Day Lewis) has an affair with his household maid (Winona Ryder), the maid accuses his wife (Joan Allen) and others of witchcraft. In the trials that follow, the judges rely on "spectral evidence"—testimony of young girls who claim to have seen visions in which the devil appears with the defendants.

In the actual historical trials, Puritan ministers Increase Mather and his son Cotton Mather famously disagreed as to the appropriateness of using such evidence to prove witchcraft charges. Miller's play is a sober testimony to the mischief that may be done when criminal defendants do not have legal representation and when judges play favorites with witnesses.

Timothy L. Hall

the community as witches; most of them were middle-aged women. It came to be believed that a servant girl named Tituba, who was said to be familiar with witchcraft practices from her home in the West Indies, and two older women named Sarah Good and Sarah Osborn had influenced the girls. A complaint was filed against them, and warrants were issued for their arrest. Sarah Good was eventually convicted and executed on July 19 of that year. Sarah Osborn died in jail in Boston. In all, over the course of the summer of 1692, twenty people were executed, mostly by hanging, ten more were condemned, and hundreds were accused.

No formal court system existed to handle these trials; they were presided over by governor-appointed commissioners. Concern over the chaotic nature of the Salem antiwitch frenzy spread throughout Massachusetts in the spring and summer of 1692. In October, the new governor of Massachusetts, William Phips, ordered a halt to the trials. He formed a new court in January of 1693 that eventually acquitted all people still accused of witchcraft. It was the questionable reliability of witnesses and evidence (adolescents made the charges and served as the primary witnesses) that led to the discontinuing of the trials. Accusations against the wife of a pastor and other people of seemingly impeccable repute raised considerable doubt as to the validity of the accusations.

Aftermath

Only a few years later, the Salem witchcraft trials were seen as a great tragedy. Most prominent people repented of their part in them, and the jurors issued a public statement of regret, saying that they had acted out of ignorance and delusion. The term "witch-hunt" eventually entered the American lexicon as a description of any paranoic, unreasoning attempt to ferret out and punish conspirators; the most famous example was the anticommunist witch-hunts of the late 1940's and 1950's.

Diane C. Van Noord

Further Reading

Boyer, Paul S. *Salem Possessed: The Social Origins of Witchcraft*. Cambridge, Mass.: Harvard University Press, 1976. Scholarly study of the colonial setting in which witchcraft fears developed in the late seventeenth century.

Norton, Mary Beth. *In the Devil's Snare: The Salem Witchcraft Crisis of 1692*. New York: Alfred A. Knopf, 2002. Reconstruction of the events of 1692 that attempts to put the witchcraft hysteria in the broadest possible context of the time and place in which it arose.

See also Due process of law; Punishment; Religious sects and cults.

Santobello v. New York

The Case: U.S. Supreme Court ruling on plea bargaining
Date: Decided on December 20, 1971
Criminal justice issues: Defendants; pleas
Significance: In this case, which granted the petitioner the right to either a resentencing or a new trial, the Supreme Court confirmed the binding nature of plea-bargaining agreements made by prosecutors with defendants in criminal proceedings.

In 1969, in New York, Rudolph Santobello was arraigned on two criminal counts of violating state antigambling statutes. At first, Santobello entered a plea of not guilty, but later, after negotiations with his prosecutors, he changed his plea to guilty to a lesser-included charge, which carried a maximum penalty of one year in prison. Between the entering of the new guilty plea and the sentencing, there was a delay of several months, and in the interim Santobello obtained a new defense attorney, who immediately attempted to have the guilty plea removed and certain evidence suppressed. Both motions were denied.

At Santobello's sentencing, a new prosecutor recommended the maximum penalty of one year in prison. The defense quickly objected, using the argument that the petitioner's plea-bargaining agreement had stipulated that the prosecution would make no recommendation regarding sentencing. The judge, rejecting the relevancy of what prosecutors claimed they would do, sentenced Santobello to the full one-year term on the grounds that he was a seasoned and habitual offender. Subsequently, the Appellate Division of the Supreme Court of the State of New York unanimously upheld the conviction.

The U.S. Supreme Court found that the prosecution had breached the plea-bargaining agreement and remanded the case to the state court to determine whether the circumstances required only resentencing before a different judge or whether the petitioner should be allowed to withdraw his guilty plea and be granted a new trial on the two counts as originally charged. The fact that the breach in the plea-bargaining agreement was inadvertent was deemed irrelevant, as was the sentencing judge's claim that he was not influenced by the prosecutor's recommendation. Chief Justice Warren E. Burger, in the Court ruling, argued that the plea-bargaining procedure in criminal justice "must be attended by safeguards to ensure the defendant what is reasonably due in the circumstances." Therefore, any agreement made in the plea-bargaining process, because it is part of the inducement used to encourage a plea of guilty, constitutes "a promise that must be fulfilled."

In its decision in *Santobello*, the Supreme Court both confirmed its formal recognition of plea bargaining, first granted in *Brady v. United States* (1970), and established its binding nature. Although in later decisions it would review and somewhat modify its position, as, for example, in *Mabry v. Johnson* (1984), it established an extremely important principle: that prosecutors and courts could not unilaterally renege on promises made in plea-bargaining agreements. The *Santobello* decision had the effect of encouraging wider use of the plea-bargaining process, an important aid in expediting justice.

John W. Fiero

Further Reading

Fisher, George. *Plea Bargaining's Triumph: A History of Plea Bargaining in America.* Stanford, Calif.: Stanford University Press, 2003.

Rosett, Arthur I. *Justice by Consent: Plea Bargains in the American Courthouse.* Philadelphia: Lippincott, 1976.

Vogel, Mary E. *Coercion to Compromise: Social Conflict and the Emergence of Plea Bargaining, 1830-1920.* Rev. ed. New York: Oxford University Press, 2005.

See also *Brady v. United States*; Criminal justice system; Criminal procedure; District attorneys; Plea bargaining; Supreme Court, U.S.

Schall v. Martin

The Case: U.S. Supreme Court ruling on preventive detention

Date: Decided on June 4, 1984

Criminal justice issues: Juvenile justice; probation and pretrial release; punishment

Significance: In agreeing with a New York State family court in this preventive detention case, the Supreme Court limited the application of the Fourteenth Amendment's due process clause.

Schall v. Martin was a preventive detention case involving juveniles. New York State had enacted a Family Court Act pertaining to juvenile delinquents and to juveniles arrested and remanded to the family court prior to trial. If the family court determined that pretrial release of juveniles might result in their disappearance or place them or the general public at risk, it was authorized to detain them. Detention occurred only after notice was given to parents and other authorities, a hearing was held, a statement of facts and reasons was presented, and "probable cause" that release might be harmful was established.

Juvenile detainees Gregory Martin, Luis Rosario, and Kenneth Morgan (along with thirty-three other juveniles introduced into the case) faced serious charges. Martin had been arrested in 1977, charged with first-degree robbery, second-degree assault, and criminal possession of a gun after he and two others struck another youth on the head with a loaded gun and beat him in order to steal his jacket and sneakers. He was found guilty of these crimes by a family court judge and placed on two years' probation. Martin was fourteen. Rosario, also fourteen, was charged with robbery and second-degree assault for trying to rob two men by putting a gun to their heads and beating them. He previously had been detained for knifing a student. Morgan, fourteen, had four previous arrests and had been charged with attempted robbery, assault, and grand larceny for robbing and threatening to shoot a fourteen-year-old girl and her brother.

Martin and the others brought suit claiming that their detention deprived them of a writ of *habeas corpus* and violated the due process clause of the Fourteenth Amendment. The federal district appeals court agreed that their detention "served as punishment without proof of guilt according to requisite constitutional standards." Gregory Schall, commissioner of the New York City Department of Juvenile Justice, appealed to the Supreme Court. The case reached the Supreme Court at a time when polls showed that crime was a major fear of the American public and when a relatively conservative Court was exercising judicial restraint and limiting the expansion of civil liberties.

Reading the majority 7-2 decision, Justice William Rehnquist acknowledged that the due process clause of the Fourteenth Amendment indeed applied to the pretrial detention of juveniles. He agreed with Schall, however, that when, as in these cases, there was "serious risk" involved to both the juveniles and the public by their release, the New York law was compatible with the "fundamental fairness" demanded by the due process clause.

Clifton K. Yearley

Further Reading

Champion, Dean John. *The Juvenile Justice System: Delinquency, Processing, and the Law.* 4th ed. Upper Saddle River, N.J.: Prentice-Hall, 2003.

Cox, Steven M., John J. Conrad, and Jennifer M. Allen. *Juvenile Justice: A Guide to Theory and Practice.* 5th ed. New York: McGraw Hill, 2003.

Shaughnessy, Edward J. *Bail and Preventive Detention in New York.* Washington, D.C.: University Press of America, 1982.

Singer, Richard G. *Criminal Procedure II: From Bail to Jail.* New York: Aspen, 2005.

See also Comprehensive Crime Control Act; Due process of law; Juvenile justice system; Preventive detention; Supreme Court, U.S.

School violence

Definition: Use of physical, psychological, or verbal force to threaten or harm students in the school, or prohibited juvenile social behavior that includes property damage, vandalism, excessive truancy, or prohibited gang affiliation

Criminal justice issues: Crime prevention; juvenile justice; vandalism; violent crime

Significance: The outbreak of school shootings such as those occurring in Littleton, Colorado, and at other high schools in the 1990's frightened students, parents, school board members, teachers, and administrators, causing them to examine what has turned out to be a growing but overlooked problem of violence in the schools, ranging from bullying to school homicides.

Administrators and teachers have always faced delinquent and troubled children in the schools. The wave of school shootings at the end of the twentieth century, especially the shooting at

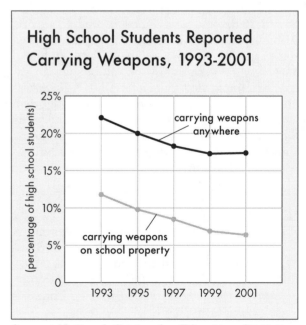

Source: National Center for Education Statistics, 2003. Figures reflect total numbers of students in grades 9-12 who reported carrying weapons at least once in the previous thirty days.

Red Lake High School on the Red Lake Indian Reservation in Minnesota, where a student went on a shooting spree and killed a security guard, a teacher, five other students, and himself on March 22, 2005. Although such instances of school violence were becoming sufficiently common to generate less public shock than they would have in earlier years, this incident was particularly shocking because of the rarity of school violence in Native American communities. *(AP/Wide World Photos)*

Columbine High School in Littleton, Colorado, brought the fear of school violence onto the national agenda for education and produced an outcry for safe schools.

Police, who already were in and out of schools working off-duty security or presenting substance abuse programs, were recruited to become full-time school police; they took on the name of school resource officers (SRO). School boards enacted "zero-tolerance" weapons policies and purchased metal detectors. Campuses were closed. Dress codes, backpack and locker searches, and name badges were mandated.

Between 1983 and 1992, vandalism by juveniles in American schools increased by 49.2 percent. More than half (56 percent) of all juvenile victimization in 1991 occurred in three campus locations: classrooms, lunchrooms, and playgrounds. School bathrooms, which historically had been associated with illegal smoking by students, proved less of a problem.

School violence has ranged from verbal threats that result in minor scuffles to an occasional beating leading to criminal charges of assault and battery. Knives and clubs are often used. Pushed by school board policies (especially in the wake of school shootings), teachers, who had often overlooked bullying incidents in the past, began to crack down on any signs of violence—thus expanding the definition of school violence. Teachers were encouraged to send home students who drew violent depictions of killings in any context (such as in war), wrote essays or produced videos involving killing, or who brought toy guns or anything else resembling a weapon to school.

First National Report of Feeling Unsafe at School

In 1978, the release of the "National Safe Schools Study" to Congress included the first statistics regarding violence in American schools. The report showed that approximately 282,000 students and 5,200 teachers were physically assaulted in high schools every month. Harris and Gallup polling data during the late 1980's revealed that half of all teens believed schools were becoming more violent. By 1995, Gallup polling reported that teenagers felt safer at home and in their neighborhoods than they did at school. Nearly half of all youths in the 1993 American Teachers National Survey by Harris Polls reported they felt unsafe. Of teachers, 77 percent reported that they felt unsafe at school.

Rates of crimes involving physical violence rose in American middle schools, which had been considered immune to school violence. By 2000, twenty-two hundred representative principals of elementary, middle, and high schools were asked by the National Center for Educational Statistics of the U.S. Department of Education about the levels of violent crime, disorder, and disciplinary actions taken in their schools. The report, titled *Crime and Safety in American Public Schools*, showed the most violent school crime was experienced by 20 percent of schools, most of which were in urban areas. Such schools had experienced at least one serious incident (including rape, sexual battery other than rape, physical at-

tacks or fights with a weapon, and threats of physical attack with a weapon and robberies).

Schools experiencing serious violence were likely to have police involvement as part of their history. The majority of these schools reported at least one of these incidents to law-enforcement personnel. Twenty-nine percent reported no violent incidents, while 71 percent reported the occurrence of at least one violent incident that school year, most often an attack involving a weapon, which they had reported to police. "Schools reporting violence experienced at least one physical attack or fight without a weapon (64 percent). Threats of physical attack without a weapon (52 percent) and vandalism (51 percent) were the second most reported crimes, followed by theft or larceny (46 percent), and possession of a knife or sharp object (43 percent). Of those crimes presented to principals, sexual battery other than rape (2 percent), rape or attempted rape (1 percent), and robbery with a weapon (0 percent) were least likely to have occurred at school."

The initial wave of school shootings in the 1990's began with a sixteen-year-old boy's attack on his schoolmates in Pearl, Mississippi, in 1997 and included a rampage by two boys at Columbine High School in Littleton, Colorado, in 1999, which left thirteen dead. In investigations, the FBI published *The School Shooter: Threat Assessment Perspective*, and the Secret Service published *Safe School Initiatives*. Both reports provide a law-enforcement behavioral profiling analysis. The FBI shooter characteristics report, published in 2000, was criticized as a rushed response, too much like the serial killer profiles that dominated early FBI profiling attempts. The Secret Service report identified thirty-seven incidents and forty-one shooters in twenty-six states by 2002 and included more mental health and personal family-school background characteristics. Other

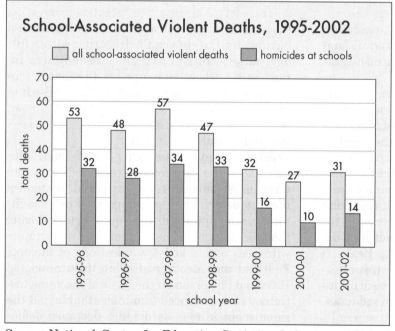

Source: National Center for Education Statistics, *Indicators of School Crime and Safety*, 2003. Figures are for all student, staff, and nonstudent school-associated violent deaths in the United States.

identification characteristics were published in *Early Warning, Timely Response: A Guide to Safe Schools*, a joint historical publication between the Department of Education, the Department of Justice, and National Institute of Mental Health in 1998. *Early Warning, Timely Response* has become a standard guide for state departments of education and local schools putting together a Safe School Plan.

William Bourns

Further Reading

Casella, Ronnie. *At Zero Tolerance: Punishment, Prevention, and School Violence*. New York: Peter Lang, 2001. Examines how the U.S. criminal justice system has responded to violence, both in communities and in schools. Based on research conducted in high schools and a prison.

Davis, Stan. *Schools Where Everyone Belongs: Practical Strategies for Reducing Bullying*. Wayne, Maine: Stop Bullying Now, 2004. A hands-on, research-based guide to intervening and preventing bullying in any school.

Devine, John. *Maximum Security: The Culture of Violence in Inner-City Schools*. Chicago: University of Chicago Press, 1997. An exposé of inner-city school violence, based on the author's experience with the School Partnership Program between New York University and New York City schools, which focused on dropout prevention strategies.

Sexton-Radek, Kathy, ed. *Violence in Schools: Issues, Consequences, and Expressions*. New York: Praeger, 2004. Collection of essays presents a comprehensive view of the various types of school violence and preventive steps.

Wessler, Stephen. *The Respectful School: How Educators and Students Can Conquer Hate and Harassment*. Alexandria, Va.: Association for Supervision and Curriculum Development, 2003. Wessler, a former state prosecutor, describes how words can hurt as well as heal and what educators can do to create a respectful school environment that promotes positive interactions among staff members and students.

See also Campus police; Drive-by shootings; Juvenile justice system; Vandalism; Violent Crime Control and Law Enforcement Act; Youth gangs.

Scottsboro cases

The Event: Celebrated cases arising from the arrest, on false charges of rape, of nine young African American men who were subsequently convicted by all-white juries and subjected to years of incarceration

Date: March 25, 1931-July, 1937

Place: Alabama

Criminal justice issues: Appeals; civil rights and liberties; juries

Significance: The Scottsboro cases showed the racist nature of justice in the American South and led to the U.S. Supreme Court's establishment of new rules concerning lawyers and juries.

On March 25, 1931, Alabama authorities arrested nine young black men, Olen Montgomery, Clarence Norris, Haywood Patterson, Ozie Powell, Willie Roberson, Charlie Weems, Eugene Williams, Andrew Wright, and Leroy Wright, and charged them with raping two white women, Ruby Bates and Victoria Price. The alleged rape took place on top of a boxcar on a freight train moving rapidly through Jackson County in northeastern Alabama. The "Scottsboro boys," as the nine African Americans were called, denied having seen the girls on the train, but within five days an all-white grand jury indicted them for rape, and a week later, April 6, the first defendants were brought to trial before an all-white jury.

The Initial Trials

After two days of testimony, largely from Price and Bates, the jury found Clarence Norris and Charlie Weems guilty of rape and sentenced them to death. The court-appointed defense attorney, who appeared to be quite drunk during the proceedings, did not bother to cross-examine witnesses and asked few questions of anyone. The next day, another all-white jury convicted Haywood Patterson on the basis of the same testimony and sentenced him to death. He had the same inept lawyer as did the first two defendants.

On April 8 and 9, four more of the accused, including fifteen-year-old Eugene Williams, sat in the Scottsboro courthouse and heard similar evidence and the same verdict: death by the electric chair. The final trial took place on the afternoon of April 9 but ended in a mistrial for the thirteen-year-old Leroy Wright. Several members of the jury rejected the prosecution's demand for a life sentence for the youngest of the accused, wanting Leroy to die instead. After the mistrial he was released and not retried. In short, in three days of legal proceedings, eight of the nine defendants were sentenced to death after quick trials before all-white juries and with inadequate legal representation.

The Appeals

The convictions made newspaper headlines across the country and caught the attention of the National Association for the Advancement of Colored People (NAACP). The group quickly sent a team of lawyers to Alabama to appeal the verdicts in state and federal courts. The American Communist Party also dispatched a prominent lawyer, Samuel Leibowitz, to Scottsboro (it hoped to use the case to build its membership in the African American community). The NAACP and the Communist Party fought for months over who would have chief responsibility for the appeals. Finally, Leibowitz took full charge of the case. The Alabama Supreme Court denied the appeals of all the convicted men except Eugene Williams. The court ordered his release because he was a juvenile at the time of his conviction. The appeal to the federal courts had much greater success, however, and in November, 1932, the U.S. Supreme Court ordered new trials for all seven of the "boys" now sitting on death row. The Court ruled in this case, *Powell v. Alabama* (1932), that none of the defendants had been provided with an adequate lawyer, so they had been denied their right to due process under the Fourteenth Amendment.

Second Series of Trials

During a second series of trials in March, 1933, in Decatur, Alabama, a safer distance from the scene of the alleged crime, but also before all-

Defendant Haywood Patterson during the 1933 trial. *(National Archives)*

white juries, Haywood Patterson and Clarence Norris were found guilty again and sentenced to death. This happened even though one of the supposed victims, Ruby Bates, reversed her earlier testimony and denied that any rape had taken place. The trial judge, however, in an unusual move, set aside the conviction of Patterson and ordered a third trial for him. At that new trial in December, the jury heard from Price one more time but not from Bates, who by this time was attending Communist Party rallies in the North calling for the immediate release of the Scottsboro boys. The third all-white jury convicted Patterson a third time and ordered his execution. A few days later, at Norris's second trial, he also was sentenced to the electric chair. Testimony from a farmer who claimed to have witnessed the event from his hayloft about a quarter of a mile away from the fast-moving train helped make the state's case.

In the new round of appeals the Alabama supreme court upheld the new convictions, and the prisoners remained on death row. They continued to be abused by vicious guards and wardens. In 1935 the U.S. Supreme Court stepped in once more and reversed the convictions of Norris and Patterson. The Court held in *Norris v. Alabama* (1935) that neither defendant had received a fair trial because of a "long-continued, unvarying and wholesale exclusion of Negroes from jury service" on the part of the state of Alabama. A short time later, the first black man in the state's history was placed on the Jackson County grand jury, and the defendants were quickly reindicted.

In January, 1936, Haywood Patterson stood trial for a fourth time. The same witnesses presented the same testimony, but this time the jury recommended a seventy-five-year sentence rather than electrocution, and Patterson was returned to the state prison. The Alabama Supreme Court upheld this conviction, and the U.S. Supreme Court this time found no reason for reversal. In July, 1937, Clarence Norris was tried for a third time, convicted, and sentenced to death. Andy Wright and Charlie Weems got ninety-nine years and seventy-five years respectively. In a major surprise, the state dropped all charges against Eugene Williams, Olen Montgomery, Willie Roberson, and Roy Wright. After six years on death row, they were released.

Aftermath

A year later, Alabama governor Bibb Graves reduced Norris's death sentence to life imprisonment but denied pardons to the remaining Scottsboro defendants despite promises he had previously made to lawyers for the NAACP. Not until 1943 did a new governor release Charlie Weems, followed the next year by Norris and Andrew Wright. Both men immediately violated their paroles by leaving the state. Norris was hunted down and returned to prison in 1944. Two years later he got a second parole; Ozie Powell was also released. Andy Wright was returned by Georgia authorities and sent back to prison. In 1948, Haywood Patterson escaped from Kilby State Prison and headed to Detroit. The FBI tracked him down as a parole violator, but Michigan governor G. Mennen Williams refused to extradite him to Alabama. Patterson died four years later after spending more than seventeen years in prison for a crime he never committed. The last surviving "Scottsboro boy," Clarence Norris, received a pardon from Alabama governor George Wallace in October, 1976. Norris died in quiet obscurity in 1989.

The Scottsboro cases demonstrated the great biases and inequalities in American law, especially for African Americans in the South. Nine defendants suffered greatly because of biased juries, inadequate lawyers, and the disregard for the basic constitutional rights of black Americans. Still, the U.S. Supreme Court made two key decisions in the cases that helped affirm these basic rights in the future. *Powell v. Alabama* and *Norris v. Alabama* established the right to effective council in death-penalty cases and the guarantee of an unbiased jury.

Leslie V. Tischauser

Further Reading

Carter, Dan T. *Scottsboro: A Tragedy of the American South*. Rev. ed. Baton Rouge: Louisiana State University Press, 1979.

Goodman, James E. *Stories of Scottsboro*. New York: Pantheon Books, 1994.

Horne, Gerald. *"Powell v. Alabama": The Scottsboro Boys and American Justice*. New York: Franklin Watts, 1997.

Miller, Loren. *The Petitioners: The Story of the Supreme Court of the United States and the*

Negro. New York: Pantheon Books, 1966.

National Association for the Advancement of Colored People. *Guide to the Papers of the NAACP, Part 6: The Scottsboro Case, 1931-1950*. Frederick, Md.: University Publications of America, 1986.

Record, Wilson. *Race and Radicalism: The NAACP and the Communist Party in Conflict*. Ithaca, N.Y.: Cornell University Press, 1964.

See also Appellate process; Counsel, right to; Equal protection under the law; *Gideon v. Wainwright*; Jim Crow laws; Miscarriage of justice; *Powell v. Alabama*.

Search and seizure

Definition: The law-enforcement practice of searching people and places in order to seize evidence or suspects

Criminal justice issues: Constitutional protections; privacy; search and seizure

Significance: The Fourth Amendment requires an appropriate balance between criminal investigations and protection of people's privacy and possessions.

Search and seizure law provides a focal point for the collision of competing objectives within the justice system. On the one hand, police must search for and seize evidence and suspects in order to enforce the criminal laws. On the other hand, the Fourth Amendment's prohibition on "unreasonable" searches and seizures aims to avoid granting too much power to police officials and to preserve people's privacy and liberty. The U.S. Supreme Court has regularly been presented with cases requiring the justices to interpret the Fourth Amendment in a way that satisfies the dual goals of protecting people's rights and simultaneously permitting police officers to conduct effective investigations.

Historical Origins

American search and seizure law can be traced to English origins. Although the roots of search and seizure in English common law are not clear, the English gradually developed the practice of using warrants to justify government intrusions into citizens' homes, usually in a search for stolen goods. Eventually, English kings began to use general warrants justifying unlimited searches. These warrants did not specify the places to be searched or the items being sought. In effect, law-enforcement officers could use the general warrants to search as they pleased. For example, warrants came to be used to discover whether people possessed any books or pamphlets that criticized the king. Because of these abusive practices, during the mid-eighteenth century Parliament passed resolutions condemning general warrants, and English courts began to limit the government's use of such warrants.

In the American colonies, people felt victimized by "writs of assistance," general warrants used by British officials to conduct exploratory searches of people's homes and businesses. These searches were frequently used to determine whether all proper taxes and duties had been paid to the king for goods produced, bought, or sold. Disputes about such British tax policies and search and seizure methods contributed to the American Revolution.

After independence from Great Britain was achieved, the authors of the Bill of Rights had keen memories of their dissatisfaction with British search and seizure practices. As a result, they wrote the Fourth Amendment in order to set explicit limits on the government's ability to conduct searches and undertake seizures. According to the Fourth Amendment, "The right of the people to be secure in their persons, houses, papers, and effects, against unreasonable searches and seizures, shall not be violated, and no warrants shall issue, but upon probable cause, supported by oath or affirmation, and particularly describing the place to be searched, and the persons or things to be seized." The drafters of the Bill of Rights thus sought to prevent unreasonable searches by requiring the use of specific warrants that were to be issued by neutral judges after the presentation of evidence justifying the need for a search.

Legal Doctrines

For most of American history, the Fourth Amendment had little impact on police searches because the Supreme Court paid little attention to such issues. Moreover, the Fourth Amendment was initially applied only against federal law-enforcement officials and not against state or local police. Some state judges interpreted their state constitutions to place limits on local enforcement activities, but police officers in many areas searched people and homes with impunity. Such searches were sometimes carried out for purposes of intimidation and harassment of the poor, members of racial minority groups, or political opponents of the local mayor or police chief.

The Supreme Court's development and enforcement of strong search and seizure rules began with the case of *Weeks v. United States* in 1914. Here the Court invalidated federal officers' warrantless search of a home by creating the "exclusionary rule." The Court declared that if any federal searches violate the Fourth Amendment, no evidence discovered during those searches can be used against a defendant in court, even if the evidence demonstrates the defendant's guilt. By making exclusion of evidence the remedy for improper searches and seizures, the Supreme Court effectively declared that it was more important to protect people's rights to privacy and liberty than to make sure that every criminal law was strictly enforced. Advocates of the exclusionary rule assumed that it would deter police from conducting improper searches.

In 1949, the Supreme Court declared that the Fourth Amendment's protections are also applicable against state and local police, although the justices declined to apply the exclusionary rule to such officers (*Wolf v. Colorado*). In 1961, however, the Court began to treat state and local police searches in the same manner as federal searches by applying the exclusionary rule to all law-enforcement officers (*Mapp v. Ohio*). The Court's decision generated an outcry from local law-enforcement officials, who claimed that the justices were preventing the police from catching guilty criminals. During the 1960's, many politicians criticized the Supreme Court's decisions on this and other cases having to do with the rights of criminal defendants.

One such critic was Richard Nixon, who, after winning the presidency in 1968, used his appointment powers to place on the Supreme Court new justices who believed that the search and seizure rules were too harsh on the police. One Nixon appointee, Chief Justice Warren E. Bur-

ger, wrote an opinion containing strident criticisms of the exclusionary rule and expressed the view that Fourth Amendment rights could be protected without excluding useful evidence found during improper searches (*Bivens v. Six Unknown Named Agents*, 1971). Eventually, the Supreme Court's composition changed to contain a majority of justices who shared Burger's view. Thus, during the 1980's in particular, the Supreme Court issued many new decisions making it easier for law-enforcement officers to conduct searches and seize evidence without obtaining proper warrants.

For example, in *United States v. Leon* (1984), the Supreme Court created a "good-faith" exception to the exclusionary rule by permitting police to use evidence seized under a defective warrant that had been based on inadequate justification. Because the error had been made by the judge who issued the warrant rather than by the police officers who conducted the search, the Court permitted the evidence to be used. In another example of relaxed standards, the justices permitted police to search an apartment based on an erroneous belief that the suspect's girlfriend possessed the authority to consent to the search (*Illinois v. Rodriguez*, 1990).

The Supreme Court has identified a variety of situations in which police officers can search and seize people or evidence without any warrant. Such situations include automobile searches, stopping and frisking suspicious persons on the street, searches incident to an arrest, and searches conducted in emergency circumstances. In each of these circumstances, society's need to enforce laws and preserve criminal evidence could be defeated if officers were always required to obtain a warrant before conducting a search. Automobiles, for example, are mobile and could disappear with important evidence if the Supreme Court did not define some circumstances in which warrantless searches are permissible. In defining these circumstances, however, the justices seek to limit the conditions that justify a search in order to withhold from police officers the power to conduct searches on a whim.

A Difficult Balance

American search and seizure laws reflect changing decisions about the most appropriate balance between the need to investigate crimes and the Fourth Amendment's mandated goal of protecting people from governmental intrusions. During the 1960's, when many Americans became keenly aware of the concept of constitutional rights and the existence of harsh and discriminatory law-enforcement practices, the Supreme Court gave great emphasis to the protection of rights, even if it meant that some guilty offenders would go free. During the 1970's and 1980's, however, fear of crime became a growing concern for many Americans. The greater attention given to issues of law and order by the public and politicians was reflected in changes in the Supreme Court's composition and, eventually, in changes in legal doctrines affecting search and seizure. By the mid-1990's, the Supreme Court had relaxed many of the restrictions placed on police officers' search and seizure methods during the 1960's.

Although the rearrangement of priorities gave police officers a freer hand in conducting searches and using improperly obtained evidence, the changes did not represent an abandonment of the Fourth Amendment's restrictions on search and seizure. Even the justices who believed that greater emphasis should be placed on crime control still identified some circumstances in which police officers' search and seizure activities went beyond constitutional boundaries. For example, in *Minnesota v. Dickerson* (1993), the Court invalidated the seizure of cocaine from a man's pocket, asserting that police engaged in a warrantless stop-and-frisk search of a suspicious person on the street had erred in extending their inquiry beyond a search for a weapon.

Another factor also helped to protect the Fourth Amendment. By the late twentieth century, police officers and judges had become better trained, more professional, and less connected to and controlled by local patronage politics. Thus these officials had greater legal knowledge and ethical sensitivity than their predecessors and sought on their own to respect citizens' Fourth Amendment rights.

Debates about search and seizure are likely to continue because of the difficulties involved in achieving a consensus among policymakers, scholars, and judges about the appropriate interpretation of the Fourth Amendment. The inevitable collisions between the social goals of vigorously investigating crimes and protecting citizens from governmental intrusions virtually guarantee that courts will continually be presented with situations in which the Fourth Amendment must be interpreted to strike an appropriate balance between these goals. The most significant conflicts about search and seizure have generally focused on the exclusionary rule. Many scholars and judges believe that the Fourth Amendment is merely an empty promise if police officers are permitted to use improperly obtained evidence, yet the Supreme Court gradually permitted greater use of such evidence during the 1980's. As society's values change and new justices are appointed to the Supreme Court, there are likely to be further developments in search and seizure doctrine. Thus it is difficult to imagine that search and seizure issues will ever disappear from the nation's justice policy agenda.

Christopher E. Smith

Further Reading

Bodenhamer, David. *Fair Trial: Rights of the Accused in American History.* New York: Oxford University Press, 1992. General historical review of criminal defendants' constitutional rights, including search and seizure.

Del Carmen, Rolando V. *Criminal Procedure: Law and Practice.* 6th ed. Belmont, Calif.: Thomson/Wadsworth, 2004. Comprehensive and readable review of criminal procedure that includes detailed discussions of search and seizure legal doctrines.

Hall, John Wesley. *Search and Seizure.* 3d ed. Charlottesville, Va.: LEXIS Law Publishing, 2000. Textbook focusing on search and seizure issues.

LaFave, W. R. *Search and Seizure: A Treatise on the Fourth Amendment.* 3d ed. St. Paul, Minn.: West Publishing, 1995. Comprehensive overview of search and seizure.

McWhirter, Darien A. *Search, Seizure, and Privacy.* Phoenix, Ariz.: Oryx Press, 1994. Written to make subjects such as search and seizure and the exclusionary rule interesting for high school and undergraduate college students.

Wetterer, Charles. *The Fourth Amendment.* New Jersey: Enslow, 1998. Discusses the various aspects of search and seizure law and how the courts have interpreted the amendment.

Search warrants

Definition: Written legal documents issued by magistrates and judges authorizing law officers to execute searches of specified locations

Criminal justice issues: Arrest and arraignment; police powers; search and seizure

Significance: Search warrants are often crucial to the lawful obtaining of evidence used in criminal proceedings, which depend on evidence that meets the requirements of the U.S. Constitution's Fourth Amendment.

In the justice system, warrants are written legal document obtained from judges, magistrates, and justices of the peace, unless otherwise specified by a legal statute, that direct law officers to execute specific actions appropriate to their positions. Several varieties of warrants are used, but the most commonly issued are warrants of arrest and search warrants.

Search warrants are written authorizations for law enforcement to inspect stated premises, usually to search for materials related to the commission of crimes. Obtaining search warrants requires law enforcement to convince judges or other magistrates that criminal activity has taken place or is about to take place and that there is an urgent need to conduct searches to acquire evidence. Law enforcement presents its requests to the judge in the form of written affidavits that must establish probable cause for conducting the searches. Probable cause is usually based on either an officer's own observations or the observations of private citizens or police undercover informants.

Any evidence gathered from a private premise without a valid search warrant is regarded as illegal and inadmissible in court under the exclusionary rule, under rules set forth by the U.S. Supreme Court's decisions in *Weeks v. United States* (1914) and *Mapp v. Ohio* (1961).

Police officers armed with warrants are authorized to search only the places specified in the warrants, and they typically can seize only the property that the warrants describe. However, when investigators conducting legal searches discover additional incriminating evidence, they may seize it as well. Investigators are permitted to seize any unlisted items, provided they are contraband or offer evidence of criminal activity. For example, if investigators using a warrant to search for a weapon believed to be in a particular apartment were to find only packages of cocaine during their lawful search for the weapon, they would be authorized to seize the cocaine and use it against the suspect in court.

The Fourth Amendment

The Fourth Amendment to the U.S. Constitution governs police search and seizure procedures. Before search warrants can be issued, it requires that probable cause for conducting searches be supported by oaths, that specific descriptions of the items or persons to be seized be listed, and that detailed descriptions of the premises in question be provided.

The amendment is intended to protect citizens against "unreasonable searches and seizures." It was written in response to abuses American colonists suffered under British rule. Prior to the American Revolution, British soldiers were given legal "writs of assistance" to rummage and ransack colonists' homes whenever they so chose. The Fourth Amendment was carefully constructed to guard against searches of that nature. However, the judiciousness with which certain modern searches are permitted has been challenged extensively both in court and elsewhere. In *California v. Acevedo* (1991), the Supreme Court ruled that searches of bags or other receptacles in car trunks are permissible and not "unreasonable" without warrants if probable cause is found to exist.

The terrorist attacks on the United States of September 11, 2001, helped to compromise the rights guaranteed by the Fourth Amendment. Following the attacks, the U.S. Congress passed the Patriot Act, which permitted searches authorized by such vague authorities as "TITLE I- Sec. 106 Presidential authority" and "TITLE II-Sec. 213 Authority for delaying notice of the execution of a warrant," as well as a whole host of others.

In actual practice, most police searches occur without warrants issued by magistrates or judges because the courts have defined a number of situations in which warrants are not necessary—either because the searches are reasonable under the circumstances or because the Fourth Amendment does not apply because of a lack of a reasonable expectation of privacy. Circumstances under which law enforcement is not required to obtain warrants include consent searches approved by persons in control of the premises to be searched; plain view searches of places in which crime-related materials or contraband in "plain view" reveals to police evidence of criminal activity; and searches made in conjunction with arrests.

Automobiles may also be searched without warrants when they are validly stopped and police have probable cause to believe they contain contraband or evidence. Other exceptions to the warrant requirement include emergency circumstances in which police are authorized to conduct searches when waiting for warrants would place the evidence or public safety in jeopardy, and searches of discarded garbage that has been taken outside premises for collection. Also, individual persons may be searched for weapons when police can establish reasonable suspicion that criminal activity is afoot.

Holly E. Ventura

Further Reading

Bloom, Robert M. *Searches, Seizures, and Warrants*. Westport, Conn.: Praeger, 2003. Up-to-date text on all aspects of search warrants and related issues.

Del Carmen, Rolando V. *Criminal Procedure: Law and Practice*. 6th ed. Belmont, Calif.: Thomson/Wadsworth, 2004. Comprehensive and unusually readable textbook on criminal procedure that pays considerable attention to issues relating to warrants and search and seizure issues.

LaFave, W. R. *Search and Seizure: A Treatise on the Fourth Amendment*. 3d ed. St. Paul, Minn.: West Publishing, 1995.

Comprehensive overview of search and seizure with special attention to the constitutional issues that it raises.

McWhirter, Darien A. *Search, Seizure, and Privacy*. Phoenix, Ariz.: Oryx Press, 1994. Excellent survey of search and seizure and the exclusionary rule that was written to make the subjects interesting for high school and undergraduate college students.

See also Bench warrants; Consent searches; Fourth Amendment; *Illinois v. Gates*; *Illinois v. McArthur*; *Kyllo v. United States*; *Mapp v. Ohio*; *Maryland v. Buie*; No-knock warrants; Plain view doctrine; Police powers; Probable cause; Search and seizure; *Wilson v. Arkansas*.

Secret Service, U.S.

Identification: Federal law-enforcement agency that performs both investigative and protective tasks

Date: Founded in 1865

Criminal justice issues: Business and financial crime; federal law; investigation

Significance: With their dual responsibilities of protecting federal government officials and investigating financial and other federal-government-related crimes, the men and women of the Secret Service are central figures in U.S. law-enforcement work.

During the U.S. Civil War, more than seven thousand varieties of paper currency circulated in the

In the Line of Fire

On November 1, 1950, Secret Service officer Leslie Coffelt was killed while defending President Harry S. Truman from an assassination attempt, when Puerto Rico nationalists attempted to storm the president's temporary residence while the White House was undergoing remodeling. Fifty-five years later, Coffelt remained the only Secret Service officer or agent to lose his life while protecting a president from an assassination attempt.

United States. Confusion over these currencies allowed counterfeiting to flourish. After the war, the federal government responded after the war by creating the Secret Service to prevent the counterfeiting and dissemination of fake treasury notes and currencies. President Abraham Lincoln signed the bill creating the agency on April 14, 1865—the same day on which he was to be shot by John Wilkes Booth. The new agency fell under the auspices of the Department of the Treasury.

Throughout the rest of the nineteenth century, government currency remained in disarray, and money markets were rife with corruption and illicit activity. At one point, every individual state had its own coin and paper currency. Meanwhile, more than one-third of all paper currency in circulation in the United States was believed to be fake.

Through its first few decades of operation, the Secret Service shut down hundreds of illegal money operations throughout the country. However, the agency was also required to investigate many cases that fell outside its narrow investigative realm. For example, presidents directed the Secret Service to investigate persons associated with the Teapot Dome scandal during the 1920's, frauds committed by members of the government, and various people who might pose threats to the government and the citizens of the United States. The most frequently targeted groups by the Secret Service were members of groups that exhibited antigovernment sentiment, such as the Ku Klux Klan.

Responsibilities

The primary investigative responsibility of the Secret Service has been and continues to be counterfeiting and other financial crimes. Along with hundreds of support personnel, special agents are assigned to carry out these investigations. During the early 1980's, Congress began expanding the investigative responsibilities of the Secret Service. The agency's responsibilities now encompass credit card fraud; crimes involving

---

People Who Receive Secret Service Protection

✓ incumbent presidents, vice presidents, and their immediate families
✓ former presidents and their spouses during the presidents' first ten years out of office
✓ presidential and vice presidential candidates and their families up to 120 days before general elections
✓ U.S. dignitaries visiting foreign countries on behalf of the U.S. government
✓ foreign ambassadors and their families who are visiting the United States on behalf of their countries
✓ all other individuals to whom the president deems it necessary to offer protection

---

specific types of forgery; fraud stemming from false identification; cybercrime; all crimes relating to U.S. financial institutions; certain crimes relating to terrorism, especially issues of school violence and domestic hate groups; certain types of money laundering; and major identity theft cases. In fact, the Secret Service is the only federal agency that has explicit federal investigative power over identity theft cases.

By a tragic irony, President Lincoln was shot the same day that he signed the bill creating the Secret Service, which would later take on the task of protecting presidents. Outraged citizens petitioned Congress to find ways to protect future presidents. However, Congress waited thirty-six years before it responded. Meanwhile, two more presidents would be assassinated: James A. Garfield in 1881 and William McKinley in 1901.

In 1906, five years after McKinley's assassination, Congress passed a law giving the Secret Service responsibility for protecting presidents. In 1917, Congress expanded on this protection by making verbal and written threat against presidents and members of their families federal offenses. This law was further broadened in 1951 to protect vice presidents and their families.

The protective responsibilities of the twenty-first century Secret Service have grown exponentially. Two divisions of Secret Service personnel are responsible for various protective assignments. The first are special nonuniformed agents who act as personal bodyguards for governmental dignitaries. Many years of guided training are required before agents are assigned to special protective duties.

The second division consists of uniformed Secret Service officers who carry out their duties much like regular police officers. Created by President Warren G. Harding in 1922, the uniformed officers provide a visible security presence in places such as the White House, the vice president's residence, buildings in which presidential offices are located, all U.S. Treasury buildings, all foreign embassies in Washington, D.C., and other federal facilities throughout the United States that the president deems necessary to protect.

The Secret Service Today

The Secret Service now employs approximately 5,000 people in field offices in both the United States and overseas. Approximately 1,200 of these people are uniformed officers assigned to protect federal facilities affiliated with the president, vice president, 170 foreign embassies, and the Treasury Department. Most facilities that these officers are assigned to protect are located in the metropolitan District of Columbia area.

An additional 2,100 employees are special agents who are assigned to investigative and protective duties in Washington D.C., throughout the continental United States, and overseas. Special agent are trained for both protective and investigative capacities and are expected to be able to perform the duties and responsibilities of both roles at any time and any place.

Paul M. Klenowski

Further Reading

Melanson, Philip H., and Peter F. Stevens. *The Secret Service: The Hidden History of an Enigmatic Agency*. New York: Carroll & Graf, 2002. This work gives the most complete and accurate look at the history of the United States Secret Service.

Motto, Carmine J. *In Crime's Way: A Generation of Secret Service Adventures*. Boca Baton, Fla.: CRC Press, 1999. Firsthand stories by a retired Secret Service agent who specialized in counterfeiting investigations.

Petro, Joseph, and Jeffrey Robinson. *Standing Next to History: An Agent's Life Inside the Secret Service*. New York: Thomas Dunne Books, 2005. Rich, anecdotal memoir of Petro's twenty-three-year career in the Secret Service, during almost half of which he protected presidents and vice presidents

Seidman, David. *Secret Service Agents: Life Protecting the President*. New York: Rosen, 2003. Part of a series of books on "extreme careers" written for young adults, this book discusses the history and duties of the Secret Service and the education and preparation required for prospective agents.

See also Counterfeiting; Cybercrime; Homeland Security Department; Identity theft; Justice Department, U.S.; Money laundering; President, U.S.; Teapot Dome scandal; Treasury Department, U.S.

Seditious libel

Definition: The criminal act of undermining government by publishing criticism of it or of public officials

Criminal justice issues: Espionage and sedition; media; political issues

Significance: Reaction against the concept of seditious libel contributed significantly to the growth of a broader concept of freedom of the press.

Part of the common-law heritage of American justice, the crime of seditious libel gave way to a more libertarian view of the press's role in American politics. The concept of seditious libel developed as part of English common law and was transplanted to the American colonies. Primarily concerned with the preservation of government, it viewed criticism that tended to lower the respect of the people for government as a criminal "assault." Under the doctrine of seditious libel, it did not matter if the offending words were true; indeed, since damaging words based on truth were likely to be more effective, the law held that "the greater the truth, the greater the libel." In seditious libel trials, the role of the jury was limited to determining the fact of publication. The judge determined whether the words were libelous.

Prosecutions for seditious libel were relatively rare in colonial America, though the concept did give rise to one of the eighteenth century's most famous trials. In 1735, John Peter Zenger, printer of the *New York Weekly Journal*, was charged with seditious libel for his criticisms of the colony's governor. Though Zenger admitted that he had published the offending material, he maintained that it was true and that truth was an adequate defense. Despite the judge's determination that his words were libelous, the jury refused to convict Zenger and found him not guilty. His resultant popularity may well have discouraged other prosecutions.

Seditious Libel and Partisan Politics

Seditious libel was still a crime when the Bill of Rights was adopted in 1791, and contemporary opinion seems to have held that the First Amendment's protection of freedom of the press did not eliminate it. Freedom of the press was held primarily to mean that there should be no censorship before publication, or "prior restraint." After publication, authors and printers could be held accountable for what was published. In the heightened tensions of the nation's first party system in the 1790's, the Federalists and Jeffersonian Republicans criticized each other in the press in terms that ranged from the vigorous to the scurrilous.

Fearing that their opponents threatened the very stability of the government, the Federalists persuaded Congress to pass the Sedition Act of 1798. This act made it a crime to bring the president or Congress into disrepute. It also modified the law of seditious libel to allow truth as a defense and to permit juries to determine whether a publication was libelous. The act was employed in a very partisan manner: All those prosecuted under it were Republicans; all the judges were Federalists. Thomas Jefferson and his followers argued that the law was unconstitutional. The act expired in 1800, and after Jefferson's election to the presidency in 1800, Congress repaid the fines of those convicted under the act. The Sedition Act created a strongly negative reaction in public opinion. While the act never came before the Supreme Court and seditious libel was never formally repudiated, the increasingly democratic nature of American politics ensured that any government initiating a seditious libel prosecution would be subject to ridicule. For the next century little was heard of the crime.

Later History of Seditious Libel

Though the common-law crime of seditious libel was seldom used as the basis of prosecutions, the attitude that the federal government needed protection from the writings of subversives surfaced periodically in the twentieth century, particularly during times of crisis. During World War I, the Espionage Act of 1917 made a variety of forms of antigovernment expression illegal, particularly after it was amended by a new sedition act in 1918. During the Cold War, the Smith Act of 1940 was used to prosecute the leaders of the American Communist Party partly on the grounds that the party's publications had seditious purposes. As late as the 1960's, efforts were made by opponents of the Civil Rights movement to use the law of libel to silence their opponents in the press. The Supreme Court's decision in *New York Times Company v. Sullivan* (1964), however, established the principal that political figures had to prove "actual malice" rather than mere inaccuracy to sustain a charge of libel.

Though seditious libel has never been declared a dead letter, the absence of its use and the relative rarity of other prosecutions utilizing the concept of sedition are a mirror of the extent to which American government has come to accept the view that vigorous public debate, including strong criticism of the government and its officials, is necessary to the existence of a free society.

William C. Lowe

Further Reading

Brill, Stephen. *Trial By Jury*. New York: Simon & Schuster, 1990. Study of jury decisions in libel cases that shows the difficulty jurors face when asked to apply the actual malice test.

Kalven, Harry. "The *New York Times* Case: A Note on 'The Central Meaning of the First Amendment'" *Supreme Court Review* (1964): Analysis of the Supreme Court's ruling in *New York Times Co. v. Sullivan* by one of the foremost First Amendment scholars of that era.

Levy, Leonard, Kenneth Karst, and Dennis Mahoney. *The First Amendment*. New York: Macmillan, 1990. Exploration of the role that the First Amendment of the Bill of Rights has played in fostering free expression in American history.

Lewis, Anthony. *Make No Law*. New York: Random House, 1991. Very readable case study of the Supreme Court's 1964 *New York Times Co. v. Sullivan* ruling.

Van Alstyne, William. *First Amendment: Cases and Materials*. 2d ed. Westbury, N.Y.: Foundation Press, 1995. Broad study of the protections provided by the First Amendment, with numerous examples of court rulings.

See also Clear and present danger test; Deportation; Palmer raids; Smith Act; Treason.

Self-defense

Definition: The lawful use of force to defend against an unprovoked, imminent attack when no feasible means of escape exists

Criminal justice issues: Defendants; homicide; violent crime

Significance: Self-defense comprises one of the principal affirmative defenses against charges of homicide, assault, and battery; an understanding of the concept is essential to both law enforcement and adjudication.

British common law is the source of the doctrine of self-defense in American jurisprudence. John Locke, in his *Second Treatise on Government* (written during the 1680's), observes that the right to defend one's life is a basic principle of natural law. Locke further argues that since property is essential to the preservation of life, natural law is also the source of the right to defend one's property.

Since self-defense is an affirmative defense, the defendant has the initial burden of proof. For defendants to claim self-defense successfully as a justification for their actions, several conditions must be met. Defendants claiming self-defense must not have provoked the attacks on them, their danger must have been immediate, the force they used in their defense must have been reasonable and proportionate, and they must

have had no safe means of escape. In addition to these conditions, certain other limitations are placed on the defense of property.

Provocation and Imminent Danger

As a general rule, a person who provokes an attack cannot successfully claim self-defense. Two important exceptions to this rule exist, however. First, persons provoking an attack and then withdrawing "in good faith" with no intention of continuing the attack may claim self-defense if they use force against a retaliatory attack. Second, if a person provokes an attack with less than deadly force and the victim responds with deadly force, then the initial aggressor may claim self-defense. A man provoking a fist fight with an evenly matched opponent, for example, may claim self-defense if he kills his opponent after the opponent introduces a gun to the fight. In this case the initial victim of the assault used unlawful deadly force against a less than deadly attack.

For a person to claim self-defense, the danger to the person must normally be immediate or imminent. A person may not retaliate for an attack by chasing or searching out an attacker, nor may a person use force to prevent an expected attack that is not imminent.

Some states permit a claim of self-defense when the danger is not immediate but the claimant believes that force is necessary to prevent an attack on the present occasion. When an attacker is leaving to get a weapon, for example, the danger is not immediate, but it is present. Most states, however, still adhere to the rule that the danger must be immediate. A problem arises concerning situations in which a person falsely believes that danger is imminent. The general test is whether a reasonable person confronted with the same set of objective circumstances would believe that danger was imminent.

Reasonable and Proportionate Force

The requirement of reasonable and proportionate force necessitates an evaluation of all the factors surrounding an incident. The relative size, physical condition, and even emotional state of the attacker may all play a role in determining what response to an attack is reasonable and proportionate. An obviously intoxicated football player, for example, might threaten a bartender

A well-publicized homicide case involving a self-defense claim began when Alpna Patel (left) stabbed her husband, Viresh Patel (right) to death in Baltimore in 1999. Her claim of self-defense was complicated by cultural factors, as she and her husband were of Indian background and their marriage had been arranged. The jury in her first trial acquitted her of first-degree murder but could not reach unanimity on second-degree murder and voluntary manslaughter charges. The credibility of her self-defense claim was challenged by jurors who doubted her ability to overpower her much stronger husband. In her second trial, Patel was convicted of manslaughter and sentenced to prison, but after she had served most of her sentence, Maryland's court of appeal overturned her conviction. *(AP/Wide World Photos)*

with death and then jump across the bar to carry out his threat. An elderly five-foot-two bartender may be justified in reaching for a weapon and using deadly force to prevent such an attack. However, if the situation were reversed, with a football player tending bar and an diminutive elderly person launching the attack, the football player might not even be justified in using his fists against his small attacker.

With one notable exception, in most states self-defense is limited to situations in which a safe retreat is not possible. If the attack occurs at one's home, however, the obligation to retreat normally does not exist. Some states have extended this "castle doctrine" to a person's place of business. In cases of domestic violence, when a married couple occupies a home together, each has the obligation to retreat, if possible, from an attack by the spouse. Although some states do not apply the "castle doctrine" to live-in partners, this seems to be changing.

Limitations on Defense of Property

In frontier America the use of deadly force to protect one's property was justifiable under the self-defense doctrine. Theft of horses, cattle, farm equipment, or other necessities could jeopardize survival in that environment, and law enforcement was generally unavailable. As society has developed, various safeguards have arisen so that the loss of property does not threaten physical survival. Consequently, protection of property is now limited to less than deadly force under the doctrine of self-defense in nearly all states. Most states ban the use of "booby traps" designed to maim and possibly kill intruders because of this restriction on resort to deadly force in defense of property.

Generally a person may claim self-defense when coming to the aid of a third party if that assisted party has a claim to self-defense under the circumstances. A person resisting lawful arrest, for example, cannot claim self-defense; therefore, someone helping that person cannot claim self-defense.

Battered Spouses and Children

Several states permit abused spouses and children to introduce psychological evidence in support of the claim to self-defense. The relative size, age, and physical condition of persons involved in a confrontation is significant in determining whether danger is imminent and what type of force is reasonable or proportionate. It seems to follow that psychological impairments might also be fairly considered in evaluating the immediacy of danger, the possibility of retreat from one's home, and the type of force that a battered child or wife would reasonably employ.

Jerry Murtagh

Further Reading

Fletcher, George P. *A Crime of Self-Defense: Bernhard Goetz and the Law on Trial*. New York: Free Press, 1988. Study of the case of Bernhard Goetz, a New York City resident who shot several young men who harassed him on a subway train.

Kuttner, Henry. *Deadly Force: The True Story of How a Badge Can Become a License to Kill*. New York: Morrow, 1983. Critical analysis of the use of deadly force by law-enforcement officers.

Samaha, Joel. *Criminal Law*. 3d ed. St. Paul, Minn.: West, 1990. Excellent overview of self-defense.

See also Aggravating circumstances; Battered child and battered wife syndromes; Defenses to crime; Excuses and justifications; Gun laws; Manslaughter; Mitigating circumstances; Murder and homicide; Reasonable force; Right to bear arms.

Self-incrimination, privilege against

Definition: Privilege found in the Fifth Amendment to the U.S. Constitution that protects persons from being compelled to be witnesses against themselves in state or federal criminal proceedings

Criminal justice issues: Confessions; defendants; immunity; interrogation

Significance: The privilege against self-incrimination is an important procedural safeguard against the awesome power of the government in the accusatorial system of criminal justice, designed to protect the individual.

The privilege against self-incrimination originated in England in the twelfth century, when English subjects were summoned to appear before the ecclesiastical courts, the courts of High Commission, and the infamous Star Chamber to take oaths *ex officio*. Without being informed whether they were being accused of any crime,

suspects were obliged to swear that they would answer truthfully any and all questions put to them.

To object, subjects invoked the ancient maxim *nemo tenetur* ("no man is bound to accuse himself"), insisting that they could not be required to accuse themselves of crimes before formal judicial proceedings, and the courts relented. Parliament prohibited administration of oaths *ex officio* and, by the eighteenth century, English courts had extended to defendants and witnesses in criminal trials the right to refuse to testify against themselves. Because the accused was disqualified from testifying at the trial, the privilege became the chief protection against forced confessions.

The Fifth Amendment

The privilege was carried over to the American colonies. The fact that twelve of the twenty-three rights in the Bill of Rights (the first ten constitutional amendments, ratified in 1791) deal with criminal procedures is some indication of the importance of balancing individual rights against the government's power to prosecute crime. The Fifth Amendment reads, in part: "No person . . . shall be compelled in any Criminal Case to be a witness against himself." The Fifth Amendment acted as a limitation only on the federal government for a time. Beginning in the 1930's, the Supreme Court relied on the Fourteenth Amendment to reverse state criminal convictions based on confessions that it determined were involuntary under a "totality of the circumstances" evaluation (*Brown v. Mississippi*, 1936). Then, in *Malloy v. Hogan* (1964), the Court decided that the right against self-incrimination itself was so fundamental that it should be applied in state criminal prosecutions, under the so-called incorporation doctrine.

The values underlying the privilege against self-incrimination form the core of the American criminal justice system, which is based on an accusatorial rather than an inquisitorial system of criminal justice. The privilege obliges the government to meet its burden of proving guilt beyond a reasonable doubt without forcing the accused to join the prosecution. The Supreme Court has recognized the premium this system places on individual dignity, even the dignity of those accused of serious crime. The privilege obliges the government to play by the rules: Police and prosecutors may not rely on physical abuse, inhumane techniques, or deceit and trickery. A criminal defendant need not testify at all. The prosecutor may not comment on the failure to testify, and the jury may not take the defendant's silence as any indication of guilt.

The privilege is not without limits. It applies in civil or administrative proceedings only if an answer might tend to be incriminating in a later criminal proceeding. It can be claimed only by individuals and not by corporations, and thus business records usually may be seized. It protects only evidence elicited from the defendant, not incriminating statements of a third party. It is limited to testimonial evidence; a defendant may be obliged to furnish real evidence such as fingerprints or a blood sample. Even a person with a valid claim of privilege may be compelled to testify if the government grants immunity and promises not to use the testimony in any later criminal prosecution.

Interrogations

The Supreme Court first took a Sixth Amendment/right to counsel approach to custodial interrogations and held that accused persons had the right to be informed by their lawyer of their privilege against self-incrimination, once an investigation had focused on them (*Escobedo v. Illinois*, 1964). Then in 1966, the Court decided the landmark case *Miranda v. Arizona*, and held that without a waiver, the assistance of counsel during interrogation is necessary to vindicate the right against self-incrimination.

The police must deliver the well-known Miranda warning to the suspect: He has a right to remain silent; anything he says may be used against him in court; he has a right to a lawyer's assistance before and during interrogation; a lawyer will be appointed if he cannot afford one. If the suspect requests a lawyer or invokes the right to remain silent, then the interrogation is supposed to stop. Unless the suspect is expressly and fully afforded this warning and knowingly and voluntarily waives these rights, any confession or statement is not admissible in evidence at trial.

This decision touched off a heated public argument over the advisability of requiring this warning, which was part of a larger debate over the appropriateness of the U.S. Supreme Court elaborating rights for those accused of crime. In numerous subsequent decisions, the Supreme Court has refined the Miranda holding and its exceptions in an apparent effort to accommodate legitimate interests in law enforcement. The central requirement of a formal warning has remained intact.

Thomas E. Baker

Further Reading

Berger, Mark. *Taking the Fifth: The Supreme Court and the Privilege Against Self-Incrimination*. Lexington, Mass.: Lexington Books, 1980. Useful summary of U.S. Supreme Court rulings on self-incrimination issues.

Garcia, Alfredo. *The Fifth Amendment: A Comprehensive Approach*. Westport, Conn.: Greenwood Press, 2002. Part of the publisher's Contributions in Legal Studies series, this book examines the interconnections among the Fifth Amendment's three clauses relating to criminal justice: the privilege against self-incrimination, the right to a grand jury indictment, and protection against double jeopardy.

Levy, Leonard W. *Origins of the Fifth Amendment*. New York: Oxford University Press, 1968. Though old, still one of the best available histories of the Fifth Amendment, which provides the constitutional basis of the protection against self-incrimination.

Meltzer, Milton. *The Right to Remain Silent*. New York: Harcourt Brace Jovanovich, 1972. Very readable book on the privilege against self-incrimination written for younger readers.

Taylor, John B. *Right to Counsel and Privilege Against Self-Incrimination: Rights and Liberties Under the Law*. Santa Barbara, Calif.: ABC-Clio, 2004. Comprehensive and up-to-date text on the privilege against self-incrimination in the post-September 11, 2001, environment.

See also Bill of Rights, U.S.; *Brady v. United States*; Constitution, U.S.; Counsel, right to; Criminal justice system; Criminal procedure; Defendants; Due process of law; Fifth Amendment; Immunity from prosecution; *Minnick v. Mississippi*; Miranda rights; *Miranda v. Arizona*; *Nolo contendere*; Supreme Court, U.S.

Sentencing

Definition: Handing down to convicted defendants of specified penalties, such as incarceration or probation

Criminal justice issues: Convictions; probation and pretrial release; punishment; sentencing

Significance: Sentences are not simply punishments; they may include nonpunitive responses such as psychological treatment.

Historically, when people committed acts of violence, the focus was on making matters whole again, often through restitution to the victims or the victims' families. With the rise in state power and the inability of the peasantry to pay monetary compensation, society increasingly resorted to corporal forms of punishment such as branding, whipping, and execution. It was not until the nineteenth century that prison was accepted as a reformed method of corporal punishment.

Types of Sentences

There are currently four basic types of sentences: fines, whereby governments collect money from convicted offenders; community sentences, whereby the convicted follow behavioral rules, such as restitution or treatment programs; incarceration in jails, prisons, and community treatment facilities; and capital punishment, whereby the convicted are executed.

The specific blend of these sentencing forms may depend on which of five sentencing goals are held most important. Those who believe in deterrence hope that punishment will prevent offenders or potential criminals from committing additional crimes. Those who seek long prison terms hope that they can select and incapacitate future criminals. Those who focus on punishment for its own sake seek retribution for past acts. Those who focus on rehabilitation hope to teach offenders not to commit future bad acts. Those who focus on restitution hope that offenders' future behavior will be altered through their efforts to compensate victims and that victims will regain some sense of wholeness. In addition to these sentencing goals, many argue that sentencing laws and decisions are highly responsive to political pressures and that organizational considerations such as courtroom efficiency and the capacity of the correctional system have a major impact on such decisions.

Prison sentences are either indeterminate or determinate. Indeterminate sentences give offenders both a minimum and a maximum sentence, say from five to fifteen years, whereby the corrections department is given the discretion to release inmates based on appropriate behavior. Determinate sentences set a single period of incarceration, although judges may be given the discretion to pass sentences from a wide range of possibilities. This discretion has increasingly been restricted by mandatory sentencing laws, such as Massachusetts's requirement of a one-year sentence for illegal firearms possession. Similarly, recent sentencing-guideline statutes allow judges to vary sentences only slightly, often by only a few months, in the case of multiple-year sentences. Studies have shown that between indeterminate and determinate sentencing systems, there is little overall difference in the time inmates actually serve.

Recent attempts at innovation involve community sentences, such as shock incarceration boot camps, high-tech solutions such as electronic monitoring, and efforts to include offenders in "restoring" victims to their previctimized state.

Sentencing Process

The three branches of government—the legislative, judicial, and administrative—have different levels of responsibility for setting criminal sentences. A legislature takes increasing responsibility if it establishes mandatory sentences or strict sentencing guidelines. Often a judge, the prosecutor, and occasionally a jury make choices within a broad range of options set by the legislature, giving them the primary power in sentencing. Correctional officials may have significant responsibility if the sentences are indeterminate, for they largely decide when an inmate will be released from prison.

The vast majority of defendants plead guilty before trial as a result of a plea bargain with the prosecutor. Such agreements usually include sentence recommendations. Most judges either accept such agreements or must give mandatory or highly restricted sentences. Thus, many argue that prosecutors are now the most powerful sentencing agents in the criminal justice system.

Actual sentences are handed down at sentencing hearings, which, for the majority of defendants, take place either the same day or the day after they are convicted. For the majority of defendants, the only information the judge has in sentencing are attorney recommendations and the prior conviction record of the defendant. Some jurisdictions require a presentence report, especially for serious crimes. A probation agent or court official gives the information to the judge for consideration after investigating the crime, its victims, and the defendant.

Legal Rights in Sentencing

Compared to the guilt phase of the criminal process, the U.S. Supreme Court has recognized very few defendants' rights during the sentencing phase of a criminal proceeding. Defendants have the right, under the Sixth Amendment to the Constitution, to have an attorney assist them at the sentencing hearing, but only if an actual jail or prison term is imposed. Defendants do not have the right of allocution—that is, the right to address the court on their own behalf. They also have no right to a presentence report nor do they have the right to see or comment on a presentence report or to call witnesses on their own behalf unless they face the death penalty. Defendants also have no right to cross-examine witnesses or to ask that judges give reasons for their decisions.

Sentencing decisions can easily be biased by unfair information, but the U.S. Supreme Court has said that the quantity of information is very important, saying that a judge may consider almost any information, including alleged prior criminal acts for which the defendant has not been convicted. Some lower courts have even said that judges may consider charges for which defendants have been found not guilty. Also, if judges believe that defendants lied when testifying, they can use this belief to punish defendants at sentencing. If defendants refuse to provide information about another person's criminal activity, they can also be additionally punished at sentencing. Evidence that may not be admitted in criminal trials because it was illegally seized may be admitted during sentencing hearings. Evidence showing the impact of the crime on victims or victims' families is allowed, as are victims' personal characteristics. Only victims' or family members' opinions about how a defendant should be sentenced are not allowed.

While the U.S. Supreme Court has recognized very limited rights for defendants, some state legislatures and courts have recognized that defendants have additional rights during sentencing, and some judges, using their discretion, may also provide defendants with such additional benefits.

Peter Gregware

Further Reading

Allen, Harry E., Clifford E. Simonsen, and Edward J. Latessa. *Corrections in America: An Introduction*. 10th ed. Upper Saddle River, N.J.: Pearson Education, 2004. Introductory discussion of the history of corrections, sentencing, incarceration, alternatives to confinement, types of offenders under correctional supervision, and reintegration.

Byrne, James, Arthur Lurigio, and Joan Petersilia, eds. *Smart Sentencing: The Emergence of Intermediate Sanctions*. Newbury Park, Calif.: Sage Publications, 1992. Collection of a broad range of views on issues and controversies surrounding such community sanctions as electronic monitoring and boot camps.

Demleitner, Nora V., Douglas A. Berman, Marc L. Miller, and Ronald F. Wright. *Sentencing Law and Policy: Cases, Statutes, and Guidelines*. New York: Aspen Publishers, 2003. Comprehensive text on all aspects of sentencing, with numerous case studies and texts of relevant laws and the actual federal guidelines.

Krantz, Sheldon, and Lynn Branham. *The Law of Sentencing, Corrections, and Prisoners' Rights*. St. Paul, Minn.: West Publishing, 1997. Excellent legal text that includes most of the important legal decisions related to sentencing and offers examples of state sentencing systems.

Stith, Kate, and Jose A. Cabranes. *Fear of Judging: Sentencing Guidelines in the Federal Courts*. Chicago: University of Chicago Press, 1998. Critical evaluation of the impact of federal sentencing guidelines on court decisions.

Tonry, Michael. *Reconsidering Indeterminate and Structured Sentencing*. Washington, D.C.: U.S. Department of Justice, Office of Justice Programs, National Institute of Justice, 1999. Federal government report on impact of sentencing guidelines on the entire U.S. justice system.

_____. *Sentencing Matters*. New York: Oxford University Press, 1996. Excellent history of sentencing with an analysis of contemporary reforms, such as sentencing guidelines, intermediate sanctions, and mandatory penalties.

United States Sentencing Commission. *Federal Sentencing Guidelines Manual 2003*. St. Paul, Minn.: West Group, 2004.

Zimring, Franklin, and Gordan Hawkins. *Incapacitation: Penal Confinement and the Restraint of Crime*. New York: Oxford University Press, 1995. Examination of the relationship between theories of incapacitation and its actual impact.

See also Bifurcated trials; Community-based corrections; Community service; Concurrent sentences; Discretion; Indeterminate sentencing; Just deserts; Mandatory sentencing; Plea bargaining; Rehabilitation; Sentencing guidelines, U.S.; Suspended sentences; Three-strikes laws; United States Sentencing Commission.

Sentencing guidelines, U.S.

Definition: Parameters established by Congress and state legislatures that courts must follow to determine the maximum and minimum sentences allowed for any criminal offense

Criminal justice issues: Punishment; sentencing

Significance: In the "get-tough-on-crime" era, many people feel that criminals should be spending more time behind bars. Sentencing guidelines seek to ensure lengthy prison sentences for offenders.

In the criminal courts of the United States, the judge decides what punishment the convicted offender will receive in the sentencing phase of a trial. The U.S. court system was set up so that judges could carefully weigh all the factors in each case and determine the most appropriate punishment for each offender. Traditionally, a judge might decide in one case that the offender would benefit from doing community service work or attending some type of treatment program. In another case, the judge might decide that the crime was so heinous that the offender needed to spend a lengthy sentence in prison. The judge had the discretionary power to decide each sentence on a case-by-case basis.

By the 1970's, many observers felt that criminals were punished too lightly for their crimes, and some said that criminals should spend more time behind bars. In addition, critics felt that judges had too much discretionary power and that sentences were being arbitrarily meted out. For example, an African American man who was convicted of a first-time burglary offense may have gotten the same sentence as a white man with three prior convictions. As for the most extreme sentence, death, African Americans were being handed this sentence much more often than whites who had committed similar crimes.

In an attempt to address both concerns, sentencing guidelines were proposed. Eventually, most states and the federal government adopted some type of sentencing guidelines. These vary by jurisdiction. Regardless of the specific content of the guidelines, they all serve the same function: to take complete discretion in sentencing away from the judge and to establish specific parameters within which a person can be sentenced. As a result, each offender within the same jurisdiction who is convicted of the same kind of crime will receive a similar sentence, regardless of age, race, sex, or any other factor.

Although these parameters have satisfied some critics, many judges are not happy with sentencing guidelines because they restrict judges' discretionary powers. These judges feel their role is to hand out a sentence after having considered the person's crime, criminal history, remorse, and other factors. Under sentencing guidelines, judges may be forced to hand down sentences they feel are either too severe or too light. In extreme cases, judges have resigned in order to avoid handing out a sentence with which they did not agree.

Neil Quisenberry

Further Reading

Tonry, Michael. *Reconsidering Indeterminate and Structured Sentencing*. Washington, D.C.: U.S. Department of Justice, Office of Justice Programs, National Institute of Justice, 1999.

Tonry, Michael, and Richard Fraser. *Sentencing and Sanctions in Western Countries*. New York: Oxford University Press, 2001.

Ulmer, Jeffery T. *Social Worlds of Sentencing: Court Communities Under Sentencing Guidelines*. Albany: State University of New York Press, 1997.

United States Sentencing Commission. *Federal Sentencing Guidelines Manual 2003*. St. Paul, Minn.: West Publishing, 2004.

See also Community service; Discretion; Indeterminate sentencing; Judges; Just deserts; Mandatory sentencing; Punishment; Sentencing; United States Sentencing Commission.

September 11, 2001, attacks

The Event: Terrorist hijackings of commercial jetliners that were used to kill several thousand people in attacks on New York City and Washington, D.C.

Date: September 11, 2001

Place: New York City; Washington, D.C.; rural Pennsylvania

Criminal justice issues: Homicide; international law; terrorism; violent crime

Significance: Often simply called "Nine-Eleven," the terrorist attacks on the United States of September 11, 2001, changed the attitudes of the American public and the policies of the federal government and all levels of law-enforcement regarding the threat of terrorism to American society.

In June, 2002, the Gallup Organization conducted a poll of Americans and found that terrorism, national security, and fear were the most serious problems facing the United States. The terrorist attacks of September 11, 2001, had changed the attitudes of many Americans, making them more fearful and concerned about the world than ever before.

Americans began demanding more from law enforcement, whose agencies are expected to protect and defend Americans against any future terrorist attacks. Crimes involving political and religious motives and international organizations became the most important policy issue for many Americans. Because terrorism is a form of crime, it draws the attention and resources of the entire criminal justice system. In the twenty-first century, criminal activity in the form of international terrorism dominates other policy issues, such as drugs, the economy, and education. Because of Nine-Eleven, terrorism and national security are thus the most fundamental issues facing Americans.

Homeland Security and the Patriot Act

In response to Nine-Eleven attacks. the U.S. Congress created the Department of Homeland Security to consolidate the administration and coordination of law-enforcement agencies. The National Strategy for Homeland Security and the Homeland Security Act of 2002 served to activate and organize the United States to stop terrorist attacks. The main purpose for the establishment of the Department of Homeland Security was to unite the large number of law-enforcement organizations and institutions involved in efforts to provide safety for citizens. Federal agencies, including the Federal Bureau of Investigation (FBI), were brought together under the unified control of the Homeland Security Department and were required to divert their resources and efforts toward investigating and preventing terrorist attacks. Federal agencies immediately began tightening security at airports and national borders.

In 2001, Congress also passed the USA Patriot Act (an acronym for "Uniting and Strengthening America by Providing Appropriate Tools Required to Intercept and Obstruct Terrorism") to provide more power and discretion for federal law-enforcement agencies to investigate, especially through the use of electronic surveillance against suspected terrorists. Under that law, law-enforcement officers can use roving wiretaps against terrorist suspects who attempt to evade law enforcement by changing locations and communication devices. They can also employ "delayed notification search warrants" to prevent suspected terrorists from being tipped off about investigations. They can also access business records and monitor computer activity on Internet servers more easily. Finally, the Patriot also made punishments more severe for terrorists or those who aid them and their activities.

One of the most important consequences of the government response to Nine-Eleven was the large-scale diversion of federal law-enforcement resources to investigating possible terrorist ac-

tivities. In fact, as early as October, 2001, so many FBI agents were focusing their attention upon preventing new terrorist attacks, that some observers feared that the bureau's traditional investigative responsibilities were being dangerously neglected. Indeed, it is possible that a long-term consequence of the Nine-Eleven attacks may be a significant reduction in the federal role in traditional law-enforcement activities. If so, criminal investigations traditionally handled by

The Events of September 11, 2001

At 8:45 A.M. on September, 11, 2001, an airliner flying out of Boston crashed into the north tower of New York City's World Trade Center, ripping a hole in several upper floors and starting a fire so intense that people on higher floors could not evacuate the building. At first, the crash was believed to be an accident. However, when a second airliner struck the Trade Center's south tower eighteen minutes later, it was clear that neither crash had been accidental. Fearing that a large-scale terrorist attack was underway, government agencies shut down local air-

The jet fuel of the airliners that terrorists crashed into New York City's World Trade Center towers turned the buildings' upper floors into infernos. Eventually the burning floors of both buildings collapsed and the weight of the falling floors above them caused the entire buildings to collapse. *(AP/Wide World Photos)*

ports, bridges, and tunnels. Less than one hour after the first crash, the Federal Aviation Administration ordered—for the first time in history—a stop to all flight operations throughout the United States. Only moments later, a third airliner crashed into the Pentagon Building outside Washington, D.C.

Meanwhile, the intense fires in the Trade Center towers—fed by the airliners' jet fuel—so weakened the buildings that they could no longer support their upper floors. At 10:05 A.M., the entire south tower collapsed; twenty-three minutes later, the north tower collapsed. Between those events, a fourth airliner crashed in a field outside Pittsburgh, Pennsylvania.

As was later determined, all four airliners had been hijacked by operatives of a shadowy Middle Eastern organization known as al-Qaeda that was determined to kill as many Americans and do as much damage to the United States as possible. By any measure, the scheme was a great success. The cost of the physical damage of the attacks could be measured in billions of dollars. Although the extent of human fatalities was not as great as was initially feared, about three thousand people lost their lives—a number greater than all the American fatalities during the Japanese attack on Pearl Harbor on December 7, 1941. In addition, the sense of security from outside threats that Americans had long enjoyed was shattered. The impact of the terrorist attacks on American criminal justice would be profound.

federal agencies may be transferred to state and local agencies.

Preventing Future Attacks

The attacks on the World Trade Center and the Pentagon demonstrated that major cities within the United States were not safe, and law-enforcement officials have realized the need for increased awareness of the activities of such international criminal organizations. Since September 11, 2001, the entire American criminal justice system and U.S. intelligence agencies have increased their efforts to gather information that may help avert future attacks. Many international terrorist organizations use criminal activities such as credit card fraud and drug trafficking to secure resources for their operations. For example, one year after the September 11 attacks, the federal government uncovered an illegal cigarette smuggling operation based in North Carolina that was suspected of raising funds for a terrorist organization.

Because organizations that employ terrorist tactics for political purposes are closely connected to international crime networks, the United States has devoted additional personnel and resources in efforts to cut off their supplies of money and weapons. Most important, law-enforcement agencies work to prevent the acquisition of nuclear materials and weapons by al-Qaeda and other terrorist groups. The law-enforcement agencies of many other countries have increased their levels of communication and cooperation with the United States in this work.

Balancing National Security and Freedoms

In the aftermath of Nine-Eleven, the U.S. criminal justice system entered a new phase in which suspects have been detained and prosecuted based upon evidence of their connections to organizations responsible for terrorism. For example, the federal government created a list of both citizens and noncitizens deemed "enemy combatants" and confined many of them to military facilities with no concrete plans for their formal prosecution. Many people, including legal scholars, charged that this practice is a denial of the basic constitutional rights that are accorded to sus-

Victims of the Nine-Eleven Terrorist Attacks

Place	Male	Female	Unknown	Total
World Trade Center	2,128	621	—	2,749
Pentagon	108	71	5	184
Somerset County, Penn.	20	20	—	40
Totals	2,256	712	5	2,973

Source: Federal Bureau of Investigation, *Crime in the United States*, 2002.

pects in civilian criminal courts. Many people also charged that Muslims have been discriminated against because of their religious and political beliefs and associations.

Since Nine-Eleven, the U.S. Supreme Court has ruled that American citizens can challenge the government's actions in federal court, but that right has not been granted to noncitizens. It is therefore clear that the Nine-Eleven attacks have significantly altered constitutional protections, government power, and attitudes toward political crimes in the criminal justice system.

Scott P. Johnson

Further Reading

Chang, Nancy, and Howard Zinn. *Silencing Political Dissent: How Post-September 11 Anti-Terrorism Measures Threaten Our Civil Liberties*. New York: Seven Stories Press, 2002. Critical examination of the effect on civil liberties of post-Nine-Eleven antiterrorism legislation, such as the Patriot Act.

Cronin, Audrey, and James M. Ludes. *Attacking Terrorism: Elements of a Grand Strategy*. Washington, D.C.: Georgetown University Press, 2004. Outline of a strategy for fighting future terrorism with a warning that the battle will be a long and arduous process.

Leone, Richard C., Greg Anriq, Jr., and Greg Anriq. *The War on Our Freedoms: Civil Liberties in an Age of Terrorism*. New York: BBS Public Affairs, 2003. Three experts on civil liberties warn of the consequences of the war on terrorism to American freedoms, while documenting how each generation of Americans has witnessed struggles between order and liberty.

Lyon, David. *Surveillance After September 11.* Cambridge, England: Polity Press, 2003. Lyon examines the changes in the security atmosphere such as the integration of databases containing personal information, biometric identifiers, such as iris scans, and how consumer data is being merged with data obtained for policing and intelligence, both nationally and internationally.

Schulhofer, Stephen J. *The Enemy Within: Intelligence Gathering, Law Enforcement, and Civil Liberties in the Wake of September 11.* New York: Century Foundation Books, 2002. Examination of the wide-ranging new surveillance and law-enforcement powers acquired by the federal government that have eroded civil liberties.

See also Border patrols; Electronic surveillance; Freedom of assembly and association; Hate crime; Homeland Security Department; Patriot Act; Skyjacking; Ten-most-wanted lists; Terrorism.

Sex discrimination

Definition: Unequal treatment of similarly situated individuals based on their sex

Criminal justice issues: Business and financial crime; civil rights and liberties; women's issues

Significance: Strong federal legislation has made it illegal for employers and institutions to treat men and women differently in such matters as employment and access to educational opportunities.

Discrimination is the treatment of individuals with similar abilities and potential in a different manner because of some distinguishing characteristic. Sex discrimination is the use of gender as the basis for such unequal treatment. Federal and state antidiscrimination laws, most of which were enacted during the 1960's and 1970's, prohibit sex discrimination, as do federal and state constitutions. Sex discrimination laws cover a wide array of issues, including employment rights and education opportunities.

Civil Rights Act of 1964

Title VII of the federal Civil Rights Act of 1964 is titled "Equal Employment Opportunity" and expressly prohibits discrimination in employment based on several criteria, including sex. The act applies to certain private employers, employment agencies, and labor organizations. Title VII also prohibits discriminatory and unlawful employment practices, including the use of gender as the basis for hiring and firing decisions. Thus, when equally qualified male and female candidates apply for the same job, gender may not be the determining factor of which of them is hired.

Likewise, Title VII forbids sex discrimination in compensation, working conditions, employment terms, and privileges afforded employees. Moreover, test scores used for selection or referral of persons for jobs may not be adjusted or altered based on sex. People with the same qualifications must therefore receive equal pay, equal opportunities for obtaining jobs and promotions, and equal benefits. However, even more than four decades after the passage of the Civil Rights Act of 1964, women are estimated to receive about 25 percent less compensation than equally qualified men holding the same kinds of jobs. Sex discrimination still exists in the twenty-first century.

Title VII also prohibits the unlawful employment practice of classifying, limiting, or segregating employees based on gender in a manner that might deprive employees of various employment opportunities, such as advancement and training opportunities. job. In addition, employment agents and labor unions may not make gender-based decisions to refer clients and members for employment, and it is unlawful for labor organizations to make membership decisions on the basis of gender.

Title VII does, however, permit good-faith employment qualification and ability test exceptions that may result in discrimination based on sex. Under these exceptions, employers may impose specific job qualifications that can be shown to be necessary for job performance. For example, an employer might set as a job qualification the ability to lift a minimum weight that would disqualify most women from the job. If, however, a woman applicant were able to lift the required weight, then gender could not be used to disqualify her. Courts have also held that arbitrary

Seeking Equal Pay for Equal Work

American women have struggled for equal pay for many years, and thousands of women have joined together to file class-action sex-discrimination suits against large corporations. The first major victory came in 1973 in a suit against American Telephone and Telegraph (AT&T); the giant communications company paid out $38 million to more than 13,000 women. In a class-action suit filed against Wal-Mart during the first years of the twenty-first century, hourly and salaried female employees of the world's largest retailer sought lost wages and punitive damages. Both sex discrimination cases were based on claims of unequal pay when compared with men in similar positions and failure of the companies to promote women to management positions.

country than in another, and the same employer could provide disparate pay for the same job in the two separate locations.

Penalties for Violating the Civil Rights Act

Intentional violations of Title VII may subject violators to a variety of punishments and sanctions, such having to pay compensatory and punitive damages, based on the size of the employer; injunctions to terminate unlawful employment practices; orders that may require reinstatement or hiring of employees; awards of back pay; and payment of attorney and expert witness fees.

Because intentional violations may subject violators to monetary damages, jury trials are also available. When employers prove they have not intentionally discriminated, then sanctions may be limited to equitable relief to stop their discrimination and the payment of attorney fees alone.

Officers and employees of the federal Equal Employment Opportunity Commission (EEOC) are also subject to penalties under Title VII for failing to maintain the confidence of parties who file discrimination claims. Moreover, any employee who makes such information public may be charged with a misdemeanor and made to pay a fine or be subject to imprisonment.

The fact that a person may be subject to penalties under the federal Civil Rights Act does not relieve such a person from compliance with anti-discrimination laws adopted by states and their political subdivisions. Furthermore, it is unlawful for employers to retaliate against employees who oppose employment practices that constitute sex discrimination or who file claims, provide testimony, or otherwise participate in investigations of sex discrimination cases under Title VII.

The Education Amendments of 1972

Title IX of the Education Amendments of 1972 prohibits gender discrimination with respect to education programs and related activities that receive federal financial assistance in the form of grants, loans, or contracts. However, several types of educational institutions are exempt from Title IX, such as single-gender schools and military training facilities. Title IX requires that both sexes have equal opportunities to seek education programs, and anything that might discriminate

weight and height requirements for employment are illegal.

The 1991 Civil Rights Act added a disparate impact category to unlawful employment practices. Under this provision, if a complaining party were to show that an employment practice would have a disparate gender impact, then the employer would have to show that the practice is job related and required by business necessity. Such a defense is not, however, available in intentional sex discrimination cases. Complaining parties may also demonstrate that alternative employment practices are available to employers that do not result in disparate impacts based on sex.

Title VII of the Civil Rights Act of 1964 does not require preferential treatment of members of any gender group in order to correct imbalances that may exist, but this fact does not prevent voluntary attempts to correct the imbalance. Reverse discrimination claims have met with some success in the courts when men have claimed to be victims of general discrimination in hiring, firing, and promotion practices designed to increase the numbers of women workers. Employers may also provide different levels of compensation, terms, conditions, and privileges of employment at different locations as long as they are not based on sex discrimination. For example, the cost of living may be higher in one area of the based on gender and interfere with this opportunity would be in violation of Title IX. Educational institutions may, however, require separate living facilities for each gender, and they are not required to provide benefits related to abortions.

The rights under Title IX also include equal access to sports opportunities. Educational institutions do have some flexibility in complying with the law, however, and are not required to offer exactly the same sports or even equal numbers of sports for both genders. However, educational institutions are required by the Title IX regulations to accommodate the athletic interests and abilities of each gender when selecting sports to support. Similar to Title VII, Title IX does not require preferential treatment of a person or group of persons on the basis of gender in order to correct any imbalance that may exist. Failure to comply with this act could result in termination of federal financial assistance.

Constitutional Protections and the ERA

The Fifth and Fourteenth amendments to the U.S. Constitution and comparable provisions under state constitutions require governments to provide equal protection for all their citizens. In interpreting the Constitution in gender-based discrimination cases, the U.S. Supreme Court has imposed a heightened standard of review, sometimes referred to as a middle-tier scrutiny, in which governmental entities imposing gender-based classification must demonstrate an "exceedingly persuasive justification" by proving that the classification meets two requirements: an important governmental purpose for the classification, and a substantial relationship between the purpose and the means used to achieve it. The Supreme Court has held that this heightened scrutiny does not apply in gender-based discrimination claims under the Civil Rights Act, as private entities are not subject to constitutional requirements.

In 1972, Congress approved the Equal Rights Amendment (ERA) to the U.S. Constitution and submitted it to the states for ratification. That amendment would have expressly prohibited government from denying or abridging equal rights based on sex, but it eventually failed because of lack of timely ratification by at least thirty-eight states.

Other Sex Discrimination Issues

Prior to passage of the Civil Rights Act of 1964, Congress enacted the Equal Pay Act of 1963. That law prohibits gender-based discrimination with respect to compensation in situations in which men and women perform substantially similar work under the same working conditions in the same locations. Since the early 1990's, the Department of Labor has found violations of antidiscrimination laws, such as the Equal Pay Act, among approximately one-half of all companies whose federal contracts have been audited. These audits have resulted in multimillion-dollar settlements because of gender-based pay disparities and lack of management opportunities for women.

In 1978, Congress passed the Pregnancy Discrimination Act as an amendment to Title VII of the Civil Rights Act. Under this act, it is illegal for employers to deny the use of sick leave to employees because of pregnancy or childbirth or to exclude such conditions from health benefit plans. Likewise, the 1991 Civil Rights Act defined the terms "discrimination on the basis of sex" and provided that this means any discrimination based on "pregnancy, childbirth, or related medical conditions." One gender-based exception under the Civil Rights Act, however, is that employers are not required to pay for health benefits for abortions, unless a pregnant woman's life is endangered or medical complications arise after an abortion. In the 1991 act, Congress also appointed a Glass Ceiling Commission to study artificial barriers to advancement in the workplace for women and minorities.

Parties continue to raise gender discrimination issues in many venues in order to change laws to meet the needs of modern society. Arguments have concerned matters such as abortion and reproductive rights; access to Medicaid; same-sex marriage, adoption, and inheritance rights; domestic abuse and the battered woman's syndrome defense; pregnancy, health care, and family care; and marriage, divorce, alimony, and child custody. If the past is any example, future changes in the law to correct discrimination are likely to remain controversial and move forward at a slow pace.

Carol A. Rolf

Further Reading

Ficks, Barbara J. *American Bar Association Guide to Workplace Law: Everything You Need to Know About Your Rights as an Employee or Employer*. New York: Random House, 1997. Easy-to-read guidebook to workplace law, including sex discrimination issues.

Gavora, Jessica. *Tilting the Playing Field: Schools, Sports, Sex, and Title IX*. San Francisco: Encounter Books, 2003. Discussion of the negative impact that Title IX has had on men's college sports programs throughout the country.

Lindgren, J. Ralph, Nadine Taub, Beth Anne Wolfson, and Carla M. Palumbo. *Law of Sex Discrimination*. 3d ed. Belmont, Calif.: Wadsworth, 2004. Useful undergraduate text that explores several ways to combat sex discrimination in the twenty-first century.

Macklem, Timothy, and Gerald Postema, eds. *Beyond Comparison: Sex and Discrimination*. Cambridge, England: Cambridge University Press, 2003. Study of sex discrimination that views its history from the standpoint of the needs of women to lead meaningful lives, rather than comparing women's lack of opportunities to those afforded to men.

Rowland, Debran. *The Boundaries of Her Body: A History of Women's Rights in America*. Naperville, Ill.: Sphinx Publishing, 2004. Discussion of Title VII and gender discrimination case law.

Simon, Rita J. *Sporting Equality: Title IX Thirty Years Later*. Emeryville, Calif.: Transaction, 2004. Frank discussion of the effects of Title IX on sports programs at educational institutions.

Stockford, Marjorie A. *Bellwomen: The Story of the Landmark AT&T Sex Discrimination Case*. Piscataway, N.J.: Rutgers University Press, 2004. Tells the story of a lawsuit brought by women against a large corporation and the multimillion-dollar settlement that changed forever the discriminatory practices of AT&T.

See also Abortion; Constitution, U.S.; Equal protection under the law; Privacy rights; Sexual harassment; Victimology.

Sex offender registries

Definition: Law-enforcement databases that contain the names, crimes, and current addresses of convicted sex offenders released from custody

Criminal justice issues: Crime prevention; deviancy; sex offenses

Significance: The practice of registering released sex offenders has been adopted in all fifty states and represents a major law-enforcement attempt to reduce recidivism.

The recidivism threat posed by sex offenders has long been a focus of concern. California established the first sex offender registry in 1947. The motivation for the subsequent spread of these systems has been a concern that most released sex offenders are not rehabilitated in any meaningful sense. Recidivism studies have shown mixed results, but prison overcrowding and budgetary pressures have increased the number of offenders released from incarceration. Registration requires that released offenders give local law-enforcement authorities their names, descriptions of their crimes, and their new addresses. There is also usually a requirement that released offenders must regularly update their address information.

Laws establishing sex offender registries frequently include provisions for various forms of public notification, based on the belief that the registration process by itself does not suffice to protect the public. Some notification systems require citizens to apply to local police departments for information on file there, while others post it on the Internet.

Megan's Law

The first major piece of legislation requiring notification was New Jersey's 1994 Megan's Law, which was enacted in response to the rape and murder of a seven-year-old child named Megan Kanka by a paroled sex offender who lived in Megan's neighborhood. The man's legal history was unknown to his neighbors. Besides registration and notification procedures, the New Jersey law included provisions for involuntary civil commitment and a DNA database. In 1994, the federal government got involved in sex offender registration when Congress passed the Jacob Wetterling Act. This federal law requires states to establish registration systems for child molesters and other sexually violent offenders. Most offenders had to register for ten years, while those in the most serious "sexually violent predator" category were registered as long as they were still so designated. The law also contained a provision allowing the release of registration information to the police and the public. A federal version of Megan's Law, passed by Congress in May, 1996, required release of this data when necessary for public safety. Finally, the Lyncher Act in October, 1996, required the Federal Bureau of Investigation (FBI) to establish a national sex offender registry and stiffened registration requirements. Aggravated offenders and recidivists as well as sexually violent predators had to register for life.

Later federal legislation and U.S. Supreme Court decisions concerning registration and notification have reinforced the earlier federal laws and expanded their scope. For example, the Protect Act of 2003 gave states three years to establish offender Web sites. Meanwhile, convicted sex offenders were naturally anxious not to have their names publicized and some undertook legal action to prevent having their names placed on Web sites. Several cases reached the Supreme Court. In the Court's *Connecticut Department of Public Safety v. Doe* (2003) decision, offenders were not required to have "dangerousness" hearings before being included on state Web sites. Decided on the same date, the Court's *Smith et al. v. Doe et al.* ruling upheld Alaska's inclusion of offenders whose convictions occurred before the state's registration law took effect. The Court held that Alaska's law was a nonpunitive civil public safety measure.

Despite solid legislative and judicial backing of sex offender registration, criminologists analyzing the laws' impact have noted several potential problems. One is possible overconfidence in the laws' contributions to public safety. It has been noted that the registries do not list first-time sex offenders. The effectiveness of the registries is also predicated on the assumption that offenders will consistently register. However, there have been numerous cases of sex offenders who move and do not reregister.

Possible Effects of Public Shaming

A more ominous concern is the possibility that the public shaming and ostracizing effects of registries and notification requirements may actually serve to strengthen the "deviant" identities of offenders, driving wedges between them and support sources in their communities. This tendency may, in fact, have reinforced the traditional "loner" stance of pedophiles, driving them toward finding companionship with children, who may become their new victims. Moreover, the stress and threat of public exposure can discourage offenders from seeking treatment during incarceration and after release, thus leading to increased recidivism.

Among recommendations made for combating sex offender recidivism are increased cross-jurisdictional sharing of registry information. This can lessen possible crime "displacement" effects but may require revision of current state statutes. There is also a need for more evaluation research, especially regarding recidivism and possible vigilantism. There have been some preliminary analyses but not enough studies with robust sample sizes and vigorous methodologies.

Eric W. Metchik

Further Reading

Edwards, William, and Christopher Hensley. "Contextualizing Sex Offender Management Legislation and Policy: Evaluating the Problem of Latent Consequences in Community Notification Laws." *International Journal of Offender Therapy and Comparative Criminology* 45, no. 1 (2001): 83-101.

Holmes, Ronald M., and Stephen T. Holmes, eds. *Current Perspectives on Sex Crimes.* Thousand Oaks, Calif.: Sage Publications, 1993.

Wright, Richard. "Sex Offender Registration and Notification: Public Attention, Political Emphasis and Fear." *Criminology and Public Policy* 3, no. 1 (2003): 97-104.

See also Bureau of Justice Statistics; Child abuse and molestation; Criminal history record information; Geographic information systems; Indecent exposure; Pedophilia; Pornography, child; Pornography and obscenity; Psychopathy; Rape and sex offenses; Statutory rape; Victimology.

Sexual harassment

Definition: Unwelcome gender-based treatment of individuals in workplaces and other arenas

Criminal justice issues: Civil rights and liberties; sex offenses; women's issues

Significance: Although sexual harassment may not involve actual physical sex acts, its victims may seek legal redress under federal civil rights legislation.

Sexually based harassment has a deep history, especially in the workplace, where men have long subjected women to subtle and not-so-subtle remarks and actions designed to degrade them and make them more submissive. However, since the passage of the Civil Rights Act of 1964, victims of sexual harassment have been provided with increasingly strong legal remedies.

Title VII of the Civil Rights Act of 1964 prohibited employment discrimination based on color, national origin, race, religion, or sex. The full implications of prohibiting sex discrimination in employment did not begin to become clear until the U.S. Supreme Court's 1986 *Meritor Savings Bank v. Vinson* ruling, in which the Court ruled that on-the-job sexual harassment is illegal. Moreover, the Court defined sexual harassment as "unwelcome sexual advances, requests for sexual favors, and other verbal or physical conduct of a sexual nature" where "such conduct has the purpose or effect of unreasonably interfering with an individual's work performance or creating an intimidating, hostile, or offensive working environment" that is "sufficiently severe or pervasive to alter the conditions of employment and create an abusive working environment."

Forms of Harassment

The Supreme Court's *Meritor* ruling identified two forms of sexual harassment: hostile environment harassment and quid pro quo harassment. The first form occurs when employees of one sex are repeatedly subjected to abusive insults, intimidation, crude jokes, ridicule, or even whistles by members of the opposite sex. For hostile environment harassment to exist, it need not be directed toward any one person, so long as members of one gender are pervasively victimized.

The key element of offensive environments is that the offensive behaviors are gender-based; the behaviors themselves do not necessarily have to involve anything overtly sexual. For example, simple pranks and petty thefts might be seen as part of a pattern of upsetting workers of a particular sex. More overtly sexual examples might include the posting of nude or sexually suggestive pictures of women on bulletin boards, repeated compliments conveying unwelcome sexual connotations, and giving openly favorable treatment to employees known to be having sexual relationships with supervisors.

Quid pro quo harassment involves more overtly sexual behavior. For example, it exists when employees are forced into implicit "understandings" that tolerating behaviors such as pinching and fondling in the workplace or that engaging in sex with bosses may be conditions for continued favorable employment conditions, even though nothing explicit may be said on these matters. Quid pro quo harassment also exists when employees who refuse sexual advances suffer less favorable work conditions.

The courts recognize that women are more sensitive than men to nuances of action and words. In *Oncale v. Sundowner Offshore Services* (1998), the Supreme Court ruled that sexual harassment can also apply to men who are "forcibly subjected to sex related, humiliating actions," whether gay or not.

Sexual harassment may be committed by bosses, coworkers, clients, or customers. To seek legal relief, victims of sexual harassment must make their situations known to their employers' chief executives. Accordingly, the Supreme Court ruled in 1998 (*Burlington v. Ellerth* and *Faragher v. Boca Raton*) that victims of sexual harassment must at least try to report unwelcome conduct to the top boss. Under the principle of vicarious liability, however, employers are liable if harassing supervisors invoke the authority of their chief executives and employees suffer from tangible adverse actions as a result. Failure to implement procedures to handle sexual harassment complaints makes employers liable.

Victims of sexual harassment often conclude that they have no alternatives but to quit their jobs—a situation known as constructive discharge. In *Pennsylvania State Police v. Suders* (2004), the Supreme Court ruled that employers are, in effect, firing employees when they allow "unendurable working conditions" to provoke reasonable persons to quit, provided that the victims make efforts to complain, at least orally, about their harassment before quitting.

Remedies

In ideal situations, victims of sexual harassment register their complaints, and their employ-

During the U.S. Senate Judiciary Committee hearings on the nomination of Clarence Thomas to the Supreme Court in October, 1991, law professor Anita Hill, who had worked with Thomas in two federal government agencies a decade earlier, caused a sensation by testifying that Thomas had frequently "embarrassed and humiliated" her with sexually explicit jokes and remarks. Despite Hill's testimony, Thomas's nomination was narrowly approved by the full Senate, but his reputation may have suffered irreversible damage. Hill herself afterward became a national symbol of female victims of sexual harassment, and she frequently spoke out on women's issues. (AP/Wide World Photos)

ers stop the harassment. When employers fail to do so, victims of sexual harassment may file written charges with the federal Equal Employment Opportunity Commission, which can investigate and mediate disputes.

In sexual harassment cases, lawsuits are the remedy of last resort. In successful suits filed between 1986 and 1991, judges could only order employers to stop the harassment and create and enforce rules against sexual harassment. Courts could also order employers to rescind adverse actions against victimized employees and award back wages. The federal Civil Rights Act of 1991 added another remedy—monetary damages, in addition to back wages. Compensatory damages are for "pain and suffering," that is, the psychological effects. Punitive damages are penalties imposed on employers who notoriously resist efforts to stop harassment. However, the law specified ceilings on amounts of damages based on the number of employees. For example, companies with fewer than fifteen employees were exempt from paying damages, while employers with more than five hundred employees were subject to a maximum of $300,000 in damages.

Sexual Harassment in Other Arenas

Sexual harassment is prohibited in many other federally financed activities and institutions, such as educational institutions, hospitals, and prisons. Since 1972, federal legislation pertaining to the financing of educational institutions and other programs has tended to include provisions banning sex discrimination. Some antidiscrimination provisions have been interpreted as banning sexual harassment as well. For example, in *Franklin v. Gwinnett County School District* (1992), the Supreme Court invoked Title IX of the Education Amendments Act of 1972 to ban sexual harassment in a case that involved a male high school coach who coerced a female student into having sex. Title IX has no cap on damages.

Some workers or students may charge sexual harassment against employers or teachers for spite, without any legitimate basis. Victims of unfounded charges can sue for libel or slander after charges are proved to be false. However the reputations of falsely charged persons may nevertheless suffer permanent damage. There are no legal remedies for random whistling at women from automobiles or consensual dating or flirting on the job.

Michael Haas

Further Reading

Crouch, Margaret A. *Thinking About Sexual Harassment: A Guide for the Perplexed.* New York: Oxford University Press, 2001. Practical handbook for victims of sexual harassment that outlines the legal remedies available to them.

Foote, William E., and Jane Goodman-Delahunty. *Evaluating Sexual Harassment: Psychological, Social, and Legal Considerations in Forensic Examinations.* Washington, D.C.: American Psychological Association, 2004. Guidebook for professionals who counsel, interview, and evaluate persons who claim to be victims of sexual harassment.

Johnson, Marjorie A. *Harassment Prevention: Everything You Need to Know to Prevent and Resolve Workplace Harassment.* Chicago: Commerce Clearing House, 2003. Guide designed to help employers identify and stop sexual harassment in their workplaces.

Lindgren, J. Ralph, Nadine Taub, Beth Anne Wolfson, and Carla M. Palumbo. *The Law of Sex Discrimination.* 3d ed. Belmont, Calif.: Wadsworth, 2004. Undergraduate textbook that explores the legal ramifications of sex discrimination and harassment in the twenty-first century.

Patai, Daphne. *Heterophobia: Sexual Harassment and the Future of Feminism.* Lanham, Md.: Rowman & Littlefield, 1998. Study of the implications of sexual harassment in broader issues of female identity.

Swisher, Karin L., ed. *What Is Sexual Harassment?* San Diego: Greenhaven Press, 1995. Exploration of all aspects of sexual harassment, with many examples.

See also Date rape; Hate crime; Indecent exposure; Pornography and obscenity; Rape and sex offenses; Sex discrimination; Sex offender registries; Stalking; Vicarious liability.

Sheriffs

Definition: Chief law-enforcement administrators of counties who are usually elected officials

Criminal justice issues: Jurisdictions; law-enforcement organization

Significance: As chief county law-enforcement administrators, sheriffs are responsible for maintaining public order within their jurisdictions.

In addition to maintaining public order, the duties of sheriffs may also include the execution of the mandates and judgments of criminal and civil courts, the delivery of writs, the summoning of juries, and the maintenance of county jails. The responsibilities of sheriffs are often so vast that sheriffs' offices are the largest employers of law-enforcement personnel in many areas of the country. Around 1990, more than one in five law-enforcement officers served in sheriffs' departments. In states that legally require sheriffs, the duties and responsibilities of the office vary widely as do the requirements for holding the office. It is not unusual in many states for individuals to be elected who possess little or no educational training in law enforcement.

Sheriffs in England

The office of sheriff originated in England prior to the Norman Conquest of 1066. Each shire, or county, was administered by a representative of the king known as a reeve. The appointed reeve was usually a baron who was an ally of the king. These officials had nearly absolute power within their jurisdictions. Eventually the title "shire reeve" evolved phonetically into "sheriff." The sheriff in the English countryside collected taxes, commanded the militia, delivered writs, and served as judge and jury in all criminal and civil cases. After the reign of William the Conqueror (r. 1066-1087), the sheriff's power and status were dramatically diminished. Under King Henry II (1154-1189) the position assumed a law-enforcement role. By the end of the Protestant Reformation in England, specifically during the reign of Queen Elizabeth I (1558-1603), most of the duties and powers once reserved exclusively for the sheriff had been assumed by the newly created offices of constable and justice of the peace.

Early American History

The English settlers of colonial America referred to their first law-enforcement officials as constables, as they had responsibilities very similar to those of their English namesakes. However, the governor of colonial New York appointed sheriffs who functioned in much the same manner as they had in England, exercising considerable power in their respective counties. The sheriff in colonial New York was also responsible for the total oversight of elections, which led to widespread claims of corruption and abuse of power. The office of sheriff was stripped of much of its power following the American Revolution (1775-1783) and sheriffs as the law-enforcement agents of frontier justice did not emerge until after the American Revolution.

Prior to the Civil War of the early 1860's, American sheriffs were typically appointed to their positions by state, territorial, or city governments, and they exercised wide-ranging powers. Their many duties included maintaining order, collecting taxes, apprehending criminals, conducting elections, and maintaining local jails. Frontier sheriffs led particularly dangerous lives. They were poorly trained and often ill-equipped to deal with the hardships required of their office.

In the Western territories of California, Oregon, Utah, New Mexico, Colorado, Nevada, and Texas they were called upon to travel great distances to apprehend criminals and perform other duties. When granted the authority, sheriffs also appointed deputy sheriffs to assist them in carrying out the duties of their office, especially the apprehension of fleeing criminals. It was not uncommon for sheriffs to "deputize" dozens of volunteers when circumstances required, especially during emergency situations. As the former Western territories achieved U.S. statehood, sheriffs increasingly became elected officeholders.

The Modern Sheriff

By 1900 population shifts in many states from the countryside to the cities required the creation of new law-enforcement agencies, such as city and state police departments. These new agencies as-

sumed much of the work and duties performed by sheriffs' offices. The complexities of organized crime and other developments, especially the automobile and the expanding highway system, necessitated the creation of highly trained and skilled state and federal police agencies capable of dealing with the challenges of modern criminal activity. Most sheriffs, generally popularly elected, did not have the training or professional qualifications to deal with the modern criminal, who could move rapidly from one jurisdiction to another.

Another often-heard complaint was that the sheriffs in many communities were nothing more than servants of the local elites. In 1940 sheriffs around the country who were concerned about the level of professionalism and expertise needed to survive in the ever-changing field of criminal justice began organizing what evolved into the National Sheriffs' Association (NSA). The NSA offers training, information, and other services to sheriffs, deputies, and other personnel throughout the United States, allowing law-enforcement professionals to network and share information about trends in law enforcement and policing. In 1972 the National Sheriff's Institute (NSI) was established by the NSA to provide sheriffs and their administrative staffs with high-quality, low-cost training and programs. Jail administration, liability issues, crime prevention, and public relations are but a few of the many concerns addressed by NSI classes. The NSA also publishes the *Sheriff* magazine, *Community Policing Exchange*, *Sheriff Times*, and several other periodicals.

There are more than 3,000 sheriffs' departments in the United States, which serve as a critical part of today's law-enforcement community. Issues of concern for modern sheriffs as they enter the twenty-first century include funding, community policing, coping with law-enforcement stress, and rising medical costs. In many sparsely populated and unincorporated areas of the United States, the locally elected sheriff is still the primary source of law-enforcement protection. Alaska and New Jersey are the only states that do not maintain sheriffs' offices. Sheriffs are elected in forty-six states, and most states require that all law-enforcement personnel, including sheriffs, undergo training before acting in their capacity as law-enforcement officers.

Donald C. Simmons, Jr.

Further Reading

Cohn, Paul, and Shari Cohn. *Careers in Law Enforcement and Security*. New York: Rosen Publishing Group, 1990. Discusses the role of the modern American sheriff.

Daniels, Bruce C., ed. *Town and Country: Essays on the Structure of Local Government in the American Colonies*. Middletown, Conn.: Wesleyan University Press, 1978. Study of municipal and county government during the colonial era that includes discussions of the role of sheriffs in law enforcement.

Duncombe, Herbert Sydney. *Modern County Government*. Washington, D.C.: National Association of Counties, 1977. Discusses sheriffs in the context of county government organization.

Keith-Lucus, Bryan. *The History of Local Government in England*. New York: Augustus M. Kelly, 1970. One of the best historical treatments of the role of the sheriff in English and early American colonial government.

Prassel, Frank R. *The Western Peace Officer: A Legacy of Law and Order*. Norman: University of Oklahoma Press, 1971. History of law enforcement on the Western frontier during the nineteenth century, with attention to the influence of that era on modern law enforcement.

Rosa, Joseph G. *The Gunfighter: Man or Myth?* Norman: University of Oklahoma Press, 1969. Addresses the question of whether gunfighting sheriffs really existed in the Old West.

See also Highway patrols; Law enforcement; Marshals Service, U.S.; Outlaws of the Old West; Police; Police chiefs; *Posse comitatus*; Vigilantism.

Sherman Antitrust Act

The Law: Federal law outlawing contracts and conspiracies in restraint of trade as well as monopolization or attempts to monopolize by firms in interstate or foreign commerce

Date: Became law on July 20, 1890

Criminal justice issues: Business and financial crime; federal law

Significance: The Sherman Act effectively put a stop to collusive actions by business firms such as price-fixing, and it restricted the power and growth of large firms.

As the economy of the United States grew and modernized following the Civil War, large and aggressive firms developed, first in railroading, then in industry. A conspicuous firm was Standard Oil Company, led by John D. Rockefeller. The firm was efficient and progressive in developing petroleum refining, but it was heavily criticized for such actions as receiving preferential rebates from railroads and engaging in discriminatory price cutting to intimidate competitors. In 1882 the firm was reorganized in the form of a trust, facilitating acquisition of competing firms. Although the trust form went out of use, the term "trust" became a common name for aggressive big-business monopolies.

Opposition to big-business abuses became widespread among farmers and in small-firm sectors such as the grocery business. Both political party platforms in the election of 1888 contained vague antimonopoly statements. Senator John Sherman of Ohio introduced antimonopoly bills beginning in 1888. In 1890 his bill was extensively revised, primarily by Senators George F. Edmunds of Vermont and George F. Hoar of Massachusetts. With little debate and only one opposing vote in Congress, the bill was signed into law by President Benjamin Harrison on July 20, 1890.

The Sherman Antitrust Act outlawed "every contract, combination in the form of trust or otherwise, or conspiracy, in restraint of trade or commerce among the several States or with foreign nations." The law also made it illegal for any person to "monopolize or attempt to monopolize any part" of that trade or commerce. The attorney general was empowered to bring criminal or civil proceedings against violators. Further, private individuals could sue offending firms for triple the value of their losses.

Early Applications

In the law's early years, relatively few cases were brought. Several targeted railroads, despite their regulated status. The law also proved potentially damaging to labor unions, giving rise to triple-damage suits against strikes, picketing, and boycotts. A prosecution directed against the sugar trust was dismissed by the Supreme Court in 1895 for lack of jurisdiction, on grounds that manufacturing was not commerce (*United States v. E. C. Knight Company*). Collusive behavior among a number of separate firms, however, was not granted such a loophole. In 1898, activities by six producers of cast-iron pipe to agree on contract bids were held illegal in *United States v. Addyston Pipe and Steel Company*. These two cases indicated that activities involving several firms were much more likely to be found illegal than the operations of a single-firm monopolist. Perhaps in response, the decade of the 1890's witnessed an unprecedented boom in formation of giant corporations through mergers and consolidations. The culmination was the formation of United States Steel Corporation in 1901, capitalized at more than $1 billion.

Busting Big Trusts

Public outcry arose over these mergers. Some large firms were successfully attacked. A giant railroad merger was thrown out in 1904 (*Northern Securities v. United States*). In 1911 two of the most notorious "trusts," Standard Oil and American Tobacco, were convicted of antitrust violations. In each case, the offending firm was ordered broken into several separate firms. Entry into petroleum refining became much easier, making possible the appearance of such new firms as Gulf Oil and Texaco. Prosecution of the ultimate corporate giant, U.S. Steel, was dismissed in 1920.

In 1914, Congress amended the Sherman Act to try to identify more specific actions to be prohibited. The Clayton Act outlawed price discrimination, tying and exclusive-dealing contracts, mergers and acquisitions, and interlocking directorships, where these tended to decrease competition or create a monopoly. The Federal Trade Commission was also established in 1914, charged with preventing "unfair methods of competition" and helping enforce the Clayton Act.

After World War II

Until 1950, Sherman Act prosecutions tended to be relatively effective and stringent against collusive actions by separate firms in interstate commerce—such as price-fixing and agreements to share markets, to boycott suppliers or customers, or to assign market territories. On the other hand, individual large firms were left relatively free, even if they held substantial monopoly power. The last condition appeared to change in 1945, when the government successfully prosecuted the Aluminum Company of America (ALCOA) on grounds that its market share was large enough to constitute a monopoly and that the firm had deliberately set out to achieve this monopoly. While few other firms met the market-share criterion, *United States v. Aluminum Company of America* established a precedent for successful actions against United Shoe Machinery Company (1954) and against American Telephone and Telegraph (AT&T). In the AT&T case, settled in 1982, the telephone industry was drastically reorganized. The various regional operating companies became independent, and entry into long-distance telephone service was opened up for new competitors. In 1950, Congress strengthened the restrictions on mergers by the Celler-Kefauver Anti-merger Act.

Evaluations

After more than a century, the Sherman Act remains an important constraint on business activity, although much of the litigation has shifted into areas involving the Clayton Act and its amendments. Some economists believe that antitrust legislation interferes with efficiency and technological innovation and may even inhibit competition. Others believe that it is important in maintaining a sense of fairness, preventing collusion, and keeping open the opportunity for new firms to enter established industries.

Paul B. Trescott

Further Reading

Blair, Roger D., and David L. Kaserman. *Antitrust Economics*. Homewood, Ill.: R. D. Irwin, 1985. Historical and economic overview of trusts and antimonopoly activities.

Cefrey, Holly. *The Sherman Antitrust Act: Getting Big Business Under Control*. New York: Rosen Publishing Group, 2004. Up-to-date examination of the history and purposes of the Sherman Antitrust Act.

Hovenkamp, Herbert. *Federal Antitrust Policy:*

The Law of Competition and Its Practice. 2d ed. St. Paul, Minn.: West Publishing, 1999. Detailed treatment of federal antitrust enforcement.

Shenefield, John H., and Irwin M. Stelzer. *The Antitrust Laws: A Primer.* 2d ed. Washington, D.C.: AEI Press, 1996. Brief and understandable summary of the principal antitrust statutes.

Sullivan, E. Thomas, and Jeffrey L. Harrison. *Understanding Antitrust and Its Economic Implications.* 3d ed. New York: Matthew Bender, 1998. Reviews the scope and economic rationale of the U.S. antitrust laws.

See also Antitrust law; Attorney general of the United States; Consumer fraud; Precedent; White-collar crime.

Shoe prints and tire-tracks

Definition: Prints and impressions left by shoes and vehicle tires at crime scenes
Criminal justice issues: Evidence and forensics; investigation; technology
Significance: Evidence left by shoe prints and vehicle tires is commonly found at crime scenes and frequently contributes to solving investigations by helping to identify the suspects and vehicles involved in the crimes.

Shoes and tires are surprisingly complex and have many identifiable characteristics. Shoes are made up of many parts, but investigators are generally concerned only with the shoes' outsoles, which are commonly known simply as soles. Many types of modern shoes—especially those manufactured for sports—have identifying logos or motifs on their soles. They may also have distinct grooves and divisions designed for specialized uses.

Vehicle tires are also complex and are commonly identified by their unique ridges and grooves. Because tire manufacturers patent the

A forensic scientist explains the patterns made by athletic shoes owned by the defendant in a North Carolina murder trial in 2003. The defendant, Michael Peterson, was charged with murdering his wife, on whose sweat pants was found a shoe mark matching that of one of Peterson's shoes. Peterson was eventually convicted and sentenced to life in prison without possibility of parole. *(AP/Wide World Photos)*

treads on their products, each unique tread pattern can appear on one manufacturer's tires.

A key concern of the first investigators to reach crime scenes is preservation of possibly transient evidence. Shoe-print evidence can be especially sensitive to disintegration or contamination. Moreover, shoe prints are easily susceptible to destruction because they are often found outside primary crime scenes. To preserve such evidence, it is important to strictly control access to crime scenes and to establish entry and exit paths from the scenes that do not interfere with print evidence.

Shoe-print and tire-track evidence should be photographed as soon as possible. Shoe prints found in dust can be lifted with a technique known as electrostatic lifting. Both shoe prints and tire-tracks made in soft surfaces, such as

Shoe and Tire Patterns on the Web

Many manufacturers of shoe outsoles and tires advertise their products on the Internet, where the products distinctive patterns can be inspected. Manufacturers are generally helpful in identifying prints made by their products. Law-enforcement organizations also keep files of shoe-print and tire-track patterns. The Federal Bureau of Investigation has a large database that may be accessed by professionals.

mud, can be cast in a variety of materials. Prints and tracks made in snow can be preserved with colored aerosols and photographed, or they can be cast with special materials.

Items of evidence found at crime scenes possess either class or individual characteristics. Evidence with individual characteristics—such as human fingerprints—can be matched to its source with a high degree of certainty. Evidence with class characteristics can be matched only to groups and not to particular sources. Both shoe-print and tire-track evidence possess class characteristics. However, as shoes and tires are used over time, they take on individual characteristics, such as nicks and scrape marks. Eventually, tires and shoes may develop distinctive wear patterns and leave impressions that indicate to investigators exactly which particular shoes or tires of the same types have made the impressions.

Ayn Embar-Seddon
Allan D. Pass

Further Reading

Adams, T., A. Caddell, and J. Krutsinger. *Crime Scene Investigation*. 2d ed. Upper Saddle River, N.J.: Prentice-Hall, 2004.

Genge, Ngaire E. *The Forensic Casebook: The Science of Crime Scene Investigation*. New York: Ballantine, 2002.

Houck, Max M., ed. *Mute Witnesses: Trace Evidence Analysis*. San Diego, Calif.: Academic Press, 2001.

_____. *Trace Evidence Analysis: More Clues in Forensic Microscopy and Mute Witnesses*. San Diego, Calif.: Academic Press, 2003.

See also Crime labs; Crime scene investigation; Fingerprint identification; Forensic psychology; Forensics; Latent evidence; Trace evidence.

Shoplifting

Definition: Usually small-scale theft of items from retail establishments by consumers

Criminal justice issues: Business and financial crime; crime prevention; juvenile justice; robbery, theft, and burglary

Significance: Although individual acts of shoplifting are typically petty, the aggregate annual costs of the crime to American retailers are measured in billions of dollars, and the survival of many retailers depends on their ability to prevent shoplifting—a crime in which retailers themselves play a role in the apprehension of suspects.

Shoplifting goes back at least as far as sixteenth century England, when shoplifters became so prevalent that retail merchants sought laws punishing those that stole their products. As Western societies became more urbanized and consumers purchased more goods from stores, shoplifting became one of the most prevalent crimes in developed countries. During the nineteenth century, the scale of shoplifting rose to new levels, as advertising of products became a growing industry in its own right. Manufacturers and retailers used advertising to increase product sales, but mass advertising also increased demand for products that many people could not afford to buy, thus encouraging ever more people to take up shoplifting when they entered stores.

Nature of the Crime

At first, the rise of shoplifting was little understood. The rising numbers of women who were caught shoplifting was initially attributed to the desire of women to acquire goods they could not afford. In 1830, a new word entered the English language—"kleptomania," the uncontrollable urge to steal for the simple pleasure of committing thefts without being caught. The mere thrill of successfully committing crimes became the accepted reason for shoplifting items of little value or interest to the shoplifters. During the twentieth century, kleptomania occurred primarily among young women and was associated with depression and anxiety. As the century progressed, however, kleptomania became a less acceptable explanation for shoplifting and merchants became more willing to prosecute even those who said they were suffering from mental illness and were compelled to steal.

It was becoming clear that shoplifting was a crime often committed by people who could not afford basic necessities, as well as by those suffering from such psychological problems as obsessive-compulsive behavior that left them unable to control their impulse to steal. Alcoholics and drug addicts also stole to raise money to support their habits. In the United States, shoplifting became a means for adolescents to impress friends and to earn acceptance within groups. Adolescent girls in particular who were seeking the approval of their peers shoplifted for the thrill of committing crimes and not getting caught.

During the 1960's and 1970's, some radical groups advocated shoplifting as a means of attacking the capitalist economic system and undermining retailers. The radical leader Abbie Hoffman exemplified his dislike of the system by titling his manual on becoming a hippie *Steal This Book* (1971). However, proponents of using shoplifting to attack the system were ignored by most people.

During the 1990's and early years of the twenty-first century, shoplifting cases involving celebrities were widely publicized. Examples include former Olympic gymnastics champion Olga Korbut, tennis star Jennifer Capriati, and actor Winona Ryder. However, celebrity shoplifters represented an insignificant part of the larger problem. Shoplifting thefts created huge losses for retail stores and led to higher prices for consumers. It was estimated that by the 1990's, stores were suffering billions in losses from "leakage"—the industry term for shoplifting. As stores utilized better methods of spotting and catching shoplifters, shoplifters themselves began using more clever means of stealing.

Throughout the history of shoplifting, those guilty of the crime have used a variety of techniques to fool retailers and escape with their stolen items. A common simple technique is switching tags of lower-priced items to more expensive items, which shoplifters try to pay for at the lower prices. Another method is hiding stolen goods inside clothes or bags. Many shoplifters steal clothes by taking them into changing rooms and putting them on, under the clothes they are wearing when they enter the stores or hiding them in bags containing items for which they have already paid.

More complex methods of shoplifting involve people acting in concert. A simple technique used by small teams has one person distract a salesperson while another steals items. A second method involves shoplifters working with store employees, who ignore their thefts. In a modifica-

Shoplifting became a focus of media attention in 2002, when actor Winona Ryder was tried and convicted on two counts of felony theft in connection with her shoplifting from a Beverly Hills department store in 2001. She is pictured here with her attorney during her December, 2002, sentencing hearing, at which she was sentenced to three years of supervised probation, payment of restitution, and 480 hours of community service. In June, 2004, before Ryder completed her probation, the felony convictions were reduced to misdemeanors. *(AP/Wide World Photos)*

tion of this technique, employees ring up their confederates' purchases at much lower prices or run items through checkstands without ringing them up.

Prevention, Apprehension, and Prosecution

As merchants have waged an escalating war against shoplifters, they have grown less willing to accept their losses and have more aggressively sought to find, arrest, and prosecute shoplifters. Many merchants now use cameras and electronic detection systems to protect their merchandise, while fighting to increase the penalties for shoplifters. Increasingly common sights in retail establishments are signs warning, "This store prosecutes all shoplifters."

In contrast to most crimes, in which police are primarily responsible for investigating and apprehending offenders, shoplifting is a crime that is often initially investigated by merchants. Detection of shoplifting combines high-tech surveillance including hidden cameras and electronic devices attached to products and old-fashioned human surveillance. Most merchants rely on their employees to watch for suspicious behavior and apprehend shoplifters in the act of stealing.

Surveillance from specially placed cameras provides security, especially in places not observed by employees. Many merchants place surveillance cameras on ceilings that monitor their entire stores. Some cameras are placed behind two-way mirrors, especially in store areas in which shoplifting is most likely to occur and in spaces that ceiling cameras cannot observe. Videotaped evidence of shoplifting is especially valuable in prosecuting shoplifters, as it is generally more persuasive at trial than eyewitness testimony.

A crude but effective method for deterring shoplifting is the use of grossly oversized packaging, especially of small high-value items, such as DVDs and music CDs, that might otherwise be easily slipped into pockets and purses. Such packages—which also cannot be opened easily—make it difficult for the items to be removed from stores unobserved.

A more high-tech line of defense is the attachment of electronic detection devices to products, particularly those most likely to be stolen. Such devices trigger alarms if they pass through store

exits without first being deactivated by clerks at the time of purchase. Another device is the use of price tags with bar codes that identify individual products. As purchases with these tags are processed through checkstands, bar code readers bring up the products' names on registers so that clerks can match the items with their price tags. At the same time, detection devices embedded in product packaging are disabled. Some merchants use price tags that release ink when they are improperly removed, rendering the stolen products unusable and visibly marking the shoplifters.

Most states have laws permitting retailers to detain shoplifters while calling for police assistance. This merchant privilege gives store employees the power effectively to arrest shoplifters caught in the act and detain them until police arrive. However, stores must take great care not to detain suspects without adequate probable cause to avoid liability for charges of unlawful imprisonment, assault, or slander that may subject them to paying damages.

Merchants who catch shoplifters have the choice of prosecuting them, releasing them without charges being filed while banning them from reentering the store, or taking no action whatever. As shoplifting has become a more costly business, merchants have become more willing to prosecute. However, many stores are still content to release shoplifters with warnings, while banning them from ever returning.

Douglas Clouatre

Further Reading

Caputo, Gail A. *What's in the Bag? A Shoplifting Treatment and Education Program.* 2 vols. Lanham, Md.: American Correctional Association, 2003. Program for professional counselors helping shoplifters to reform.

Cleary, James, Jr. *Prosecuting the Shoplifter: A Loss Prevention Strategy.* Boston: Butterworth-Heinemann, 1986. Survey of techniques that merchants can use to deter shoplifting, with advice on procedures for handling shoplifters whom they catch.

Segrave, Kerry. *Shoplifting: A Social History.* Jefferson, N.C.: McFarland Publishing, 2001. Fascinating brief study of the rise and proliferation of shoplifting in American history.

Sennewald, Charles, and John Christman. *Shop-*

lifting. Boston: Butterworth-Heinemann, 1992. Legal textbook on the crime of shoplifting.

Whitlock, Tammy C. *Crime, Gender, and Consumer Culture in Nineteenth Century England.* Burlington, Vt.: Ashgate, 2005. Broad study of the rise of retail consumerism in England during the Industrial Revolution, with some attention to shoplifting.

See also Celebrity criminal defendants; Misdemeanors; Robbery; Surveillance cameras; Theft; Three-strikes laws; Youth gangs.

Simpson trials

The Event: Two trials concerning O. J. Simpson's role in the murder of his former wife and her friend produced conflicting results

Date: January 24-October 3, 1995 (criminal trial); October 23, 1996-February 12, 1997 (civil trial)

Place: Los Angeles, California

Criminal justice issues: Media; verdicts; violent crime

Significance: The Simpson trials became major cultural events, attracting the interest of tens of millions of people, but resulted in divisive social attitudes and numerous calls for judicial reform.

On June 12, 1994, Nicole Brown Simpson and her friend Ronald Goldman were savagely stabbed to death outside Simpson's Los Angeles home. Five days later, Simpson's former husband, Hall of Fame football star and media celebrity O. J. Simpson, was arrested and charged with the murders following an ambiguous suicide note and a nationally televised car chase.

The Criminal Trial

O. J. Simpson's wealth and celebrity permitted his attorney Robert Shapiro to assemble a high-priced "dream team" for the defense that included F. Lee Bailey, Johnnie Cochran, Alan M. Dershowitz, Peter Neufeld, Barry Scheck, and Gerald Uelman. Following six months' preparation, an eight-month criminal trial was presided over by Judge Lance Ito.

Los Angeles County prosecutors, including Marcia Clark and Christopher Darden, showed that Simpson had motive and opportunity. They presented extensive physical evidence pointing to him: bloody gloves, socks, shoe prints, hair, and fiber traces. The defense focused on irregularities in the collection, documentation, and analysis of the evidence, arguing that through incompetence and racially motivated conspiracy, the police had contaminated or planted evidence to link the DNA of Simpson, his former wife, and Goldman.

Forensic scientist Henry Lee declared that there was "something wrong" with the evidence, and defense attorneys expanded on that theme. Testimony by Mark Fuhrman, the police detective who had found the bloody glove outside Simpson's home—especially his lies about not having used "the N-word"—permitted the defense to shift the focus from the murders to an alleged police conspiracy to frame Simpson, a man who had, in fact, long received special consideration. When prosecutor Darden asked Simpson to try on the gloves in court, and the gloves appeared to be too small for Simpson's hands, the defense took up the mantra, "If it doesn't fit, you must acquit."

Cochran even flirted with jury nullification, inviting the jury to send a message to society about police racism. Some critics saw this as analogous to ignoring fact and law to acquit whites who murder blacks, as in the famous Emmett Till lynching case of the 1950's. Simpson was acquitted, and national reaction to the jury verdict revealed visceral disagreement between many black and white Americans, who seemed to have different views about the likelihood of police conspiracies.

The Civil Trial

A year later, Simpson defended himself again, this time against civil suits brought by Ron Goldman's parents and estate and Nicole Brown Simpson's estate. Differences between the civil and criminal trials included the kinds of evidence that could be introduced, the standards of proof (preponderance of evidence rather than reasonable doubt), and venues and jury composition. Television was excluded, and in general the judge, Hiroshi Fujisaki, exercised tight control. The civil trial jury found Simpson "liable" for the

In one of the most notorious courtroom blunders in modern criminal history, prosecutors in O. J. Simpson's criminal murder trial asked him to put on leather gloves that they asserted he had worn on the night he allegedly committed double murder. The fact that the gloves were obviously too small for Simpson dealt a devastating blow to the prosecution's case, as the defense took up the mantra, "If it doesn't fit, you must acquit." (AP/Wide World Photos)

William Dwyer, for example, the lesson is that judges cannot passively allow lawyers to become overly contentious. To Lee, the effect of the case has been to make it clear that in forensic science "only the highest professional standards would be tolerated in the future." Prosecutor Clark went so far as to suggest that a ballot measure to eliminate affirmative action programs in California, approved by voters in November 1996, would not have passed "if white Californians had not been so infuriated by the Simpson verdict."

The Simpson trials led to conflicting results, complicating judgments about their ultimate legal or social legacy. Simpson emerged a free man, one of the most famous defendants of all time—liable but not guilty.

Edward Johnson

attacks, and he was assessed more than $33 million in compensatory and punitive damages.

Legacy of the Trials

Public attention was riveted during the two-and-a-half year media saturation of the Simpson saga. The criminal trial received, communications scholar Janice Schuetz claims, "the most extensive coverage of any event in history." Its live verdict was watched by an estimated 150 million viewers, becoming a defining moment in Americans' collective memory.

The trials prompted much soul-searching about the jury system. Some observers argued that, regardless of Simpson's guilt or innocence, the first jury's verdict was correct, given the higher standard of reasonable doubt. Many critics faulted the jury for incompetence or bias. Other candidates for reform included the defense, the prosecution, the judge, the police, the expert witnesses, the jury consultants, the media, the adversary system itself, or the influence of wealth, celebrity, or race on justice.

Critics have drawn diverse lessons and consequences from the Simpson case. To federal judge

Further Reading

Bugliosi, Vincent. *Outrage: The Five Reasons Why O. J. Simpson Got Away with Murder*. New York: W. W. Norton, 1996. The prosecutor of convicted murderer Charles Manson provides a detailed analysis of the evidence in Simpson's criminal trial and a pugnacious critique of the performance of the prosecution.

Dwyer, William L. *In the Hands of the People: The Trial Jury's Origins, Triumphs, Troubles, and Future in American Democracy*. New York: Thomas Dunne Books/St. Martin's Press, 2002. A federal judge sets the Simpson trials in the context of his defense of juries as "America's most democratic institution," faulting Judge Lance Ito's passivity and the lawyers' contentiousness.

Knappman, Edward W., ed. *Great American Trials: Two Hundred and One Compelling Courtroom Dramas from Salem Witchcraft to O. J. Simpson*. New York: Barnes and Noble, 2004. Includes a concise overview of key events in the criminal trial.

Lee, Henry C., and Frank Tirnady. *Blood Evi-*

dence: *How DNA Is Revolutionizing the Way We Solve Crimes*. Cambridge, Mass.: Perseus, 2003. Lee, an expert witness in Simpson's defense, offers an extensive discussion of the DNA evidence in that case and others.

Petrocelli, Daniel, with Peter Knobler. *Triumph of Justice: The Final Judgment on the Simpson Saga*. New York: Crown, 1998. The successful lead attorney for the plaintiffs describes the strategies involved in Simpson's civil trial.

Schuetz, Janice, and Lin S. Lilley, eds. *The O. J. Simpson Trials: Rhetoric, Media, and the Law*. Carbondale: University of Southern Illinois Press, 1999. A collection of essays by scholars discussing the interaction of legal and rhetorical strategies in the trials.

Toobin, Jeffrey. *The Run of His Life: The People v. O. J. Simpson*. New York: Random House, 1996. An account of the criminal trial by the attorney/journalist who revealed in *The New Yorker* (and thereby began the implementation of) the defense's "race card" strategy.

See also Bloodstains; Burden of proof; Celebrity criminal defendants; Celebrity trial attorneys; Chain of custody; DNA testing; Domestic violence; Double jeopardy; Jury nullification; Reasonable doubt; Standards of proof; Trial publicity.

Skyjacking

Definition: Hijacking of aircraft in flight by armed persons or groups, usually for the purpose of perpetrating other crimes

Criminal justice issues: International law; terrorism

Significance: A form of air piracy, skyjacking has been a major international concern since the late 1960's; however, the use of skyjacked aircraft as flying bombs on September 11, 2001, added a new and frightening security threat for the United States and all other countries.

Before the September 11, 2001, terrorists attacks on the United States, most skyjackings were undertaken for the purpose of using passengers as hostages to secure the release of political prison-

ers or to gain passage to certain locations, such as Cuba. More than one-half of all skyjackings between 1947 and 2004 were committed by political refugees; these included twenty-seven skyjackings of airplanes redirected to Cuba in 1968 alone. In 1969, there were eighty-two skyjacking attempts throughout the world. Several of these were undertaken by Palestinian nationalists who attempted to use them as political propaganda for their causes or as efforts to force Israel to release Palestinian prisoners from jail. A small number of skyjackings have been undertaken for monetary gain. The most famous of these occurred in 1971, when a skyjacker known only as "Dan Cooper" escaped with a large ransom. He has never been fully identified or arrested since then.

History and Prevalence

The first documented skyjacking occurred in Peru in 1931, when a pilot flying a tiny Ford Tri-Motor was confronted by a group of armed political insurgents. His refusal to fly them to their destination led to a ten-day standoff that was eventually resolved through negotiation. The first skyjacking of a commercial airliner is believed to have occurred in 1948, when a Cathay Pacific seaplane crashed in the sea after a failed takeover by an armed passenger.

The next ten years saw few recorded skyjackings of commercial airliners. After the communist takeover in Cuba in 1959, however, skyjackings of commercial airliners by persons who wanted to fly from Cuba to the United States or from the United States to Cuba began. Most skyjackers were refugees fleeing from Cuba and the rule of Fidel Castro. Between 1967 and 1972, more than 150 skyjackings occurred around the world. Most were undertaken for political reasons, and many of the skyjackers demanded to be flown to the Middle East or Cuba.

In late November, 1971, a different form of skyjacking occurred, when a man who would become known to the world as "D. B. Cooper" boarded a Northwest Orient Airline Boeing 727 in Portland, Oregon. Cooper pulled off the only major successful skyjacking for money in U.S. history and became an antigovernment cult hero in the process. His story began when he purchased an airline ticket to Seattle. Shortly after the plane took off, he gave a flight attendant a note demanding four parachutes and $200,000 in unmarked cash. After the flight attendant passed the note to the plane's pilot, she reported seeing objects in Cooper's briefcase that might be parts of a bomb, so the pilot took Cooper's threat seriously and reported Cooper's demands to the airline, which in turn notified the Federal Bureau of Investigation (FBI), which had investigative jurisdiction over skyjackings.

At that time, airline flight crews were trained to accede to skyjackers' demands and hope for peaceful resolutions to situations. As Cooper's flight circled the Seattle airport, the FBI assembled 10,000 twenty-dollar bills—which weighed more than twenty pounds—and the four parachutes that Cooper demanded. The plane then landed in Seattle, where all the other passengers and all but one of the flight attendants left the aircraft. After the plane took off, Cooper demanded to be flown to Mexico. He also ordered the pilots to fly the plane at an altitude of 10,000 feet and an airspeed of not more than 200 miles per hour. Meanwhile, he had the stairs on the aft entry of the Boeing 727 lowered. About fifteen minutes after takeoff, the pilot noticed a warning light that indicated the plane's rear door was open. Cooper was gone, along with two parachutes and the money.

The two U.S. Air Force jets following the airliner did not see Cooper exit the aircraft. Since Cooper evidently parachuted from the plane at an altitude of about 10,000 feet, in the midst of high winds and freezing rain, there was good reason to believe that he may not have survived the jump. Cooper was never found, but FBI agent Ralph Himmelsbach, who was in charge of the investigation, concluded that Cooper was killed while parachuting. Nine years later, a young boy found almost $6,000 of Cooper's ransom money near the Columbia River. No other trace of Cooper or his ransom has ever been found, and in 2005, the case remained the only unsolved domestic skyjacking in U.S. history. Meanwhile, D. B. Cooper became a popular legend and the subject of films and television programs.

Cooper's crime inspired some copycat skyjackings in the United States. For example, in August, 1972, another Boeing 727, which was flying from Miami, Florida, to New York City, was sky-jacked by a U.S. citizen and an Ethiopian national, who managed to board the plane with a shotgun and a revolver. At that time, passengers boarding airliners were not screened. These hijackers attempted to emulate each step of Cooper's plan, but their scheme was disrupted when their plane was damaged during its landing. They demanded a second airplane but eventually surrendered to FBI agents after a long standoff. Both men were convicted of air piracy and sentenced to lengthy prison terms.

During the 1980's and 1990's, politically motivated skyjackings became more frequent around the world, especially in the Middle East. However, there were few major skyjacking incidents in the United States until September 11, 2001. On that date, Muslim extremists who had established residence in the United States hijacked four American airliners simultaneously and used them as suicide missiles against targets in New York City and Washington, D.C. This new use of skyjacking introduced a more terrifying aspect to skyjacking that posed a huge security threat to the world's nations.

Investigation

Skyjacking presents unique challenges to law enforcement, especially since 2001. One of these challenges is posed by the exceptional mobility of aircraft, which makes it possible for skyjackers to perpetrate crimes that range across states, nations, and even oceans. Skyjacking of aircraft is covered under federal law, as are several other crimes involving aircraft in the special aircraft jurisdiction of the United States.

As the investigative arm of the U.S. Department of Justice, the FBI has long had jurisdiction over investigations of skyjackings under Title 28, Section 533, of the United States Code. Since 2001, the FBI has listed protecting the United States and its citizens from terrorist attacks as its top priority, and that fact in turn makes combating skyjacking a top FBI priority. To meet that priority, the FBI cooperates extensively with law-enforcement agencies of other nations.

In late 2001, the U.S. Congress passed the USA Patriot Act to toughen security against future terrorist attacks. Congress also passed the Aviation and Transportation Security Act, which created the Transportation Security Administration (TSA). Originally placed under the federal Department of Transportation, that new agency was moved to the new Department of Homeland Security in 2003. TSA was made responsible for airport security, and prevention of skyjackings became an integral part of its mission. TSA employees have replaced civilian security contractors at airports throughout the United States. TSA established new guidelines for carry-on and stowed luggage, began utilizing improved methods of conducting inspections of passengers and their luggage, and established guidelines for interception of suspected terrorists. Meanwhile, state, local, and federal law-enforcement agencies, including the FBI, have worked diligently to investigate suspected terrorist organizations and individuals to prevent future terrorist skyjackings.

Prosecution and Punishment

Several international conventions have sought to gain agreements and cooperation from various countries regarding the issue of skyjacking. For example, the 1958 Geneva Convention on the High Seas defined air piracy as "any illegal acts of violence, detention or act of depredation, committed for private ends by the crew or the passengers of a private ship or a private aircraft." In 1963, the Tokyo Convention obliged contracting states to take all appropriate measures to restore control of aircraft hijacked in flight to their lawful commanders and required the states in which hijacked aircraft land to allow their passengers and crew to continue to their intended destinations. Other international treaties pertaining to skyjacking were signed at conventions in The Hague in 1970 and Montreal in 1971.

Despite these international treaties and other attempts at international cooperation in the handling of skyjackings, there has been little real progress among nations. Skyjacking is an international problem, but not all nations are willing to cooperate in combating it. Even the United States has not always cooperated fully with other nations. On several occasions, it has refused to return skyjackers to the countries where they hijacked aircraft. In some cases, the United States has regarded the skyjackers as political refugees from countries with totalitarian regimes, such as Cuba.

The events of September 11, 2001, have changed the way skyjackers are treated in the United States and other nations. For example, in 2003, six Cuban refugees sought freedom from the rule of Fidel Castro by forcing the pilots of an aging Cuban DC-3 passenger plane to take them to Florida. All six refugees were convicted of air piracy in a U.S. district court and sentenced to twenty-year prison terms. Afterward, assistant U.S. attorney Harry C. Wallace, Jr., said the verdict sent "a clear message that while we are sympathetic to people who want to come to the United States, we will not tolerate the use of violence or the threat of violence."

Edgar J. Hartung

Further Reading

Choi, J. *Aviation Terrorism: Historical Survey, Perspectives and Responses*. Indianapolis: Palgrave Macmillan, 1994. Review of the history of aviation terrorism from its beginnings through hijackings of the 1960's and 1970's to the sabotage bombings during the 1980's. Includes detailed case studies of important incidents.

Gero, D. *Flights of Terror: Aerial Hijack and Sabotage Since 1930*. Osceola, Wis.: Motorbooks International, 1997. History of skyjacking that concentrates on the hostile actions committed against commercial aircraft from the earliest days of air travel through the 1990's. Provides detailed reference information in a factual and readable format. Each entry lists the date, airline, aircraft serial number, location, details of the action, and whatever reasons are known.

Himmelsbach, R. *Norjak: The Investigation of D. B. Cooper*. Woodburn, Oreg.: Norjak Project, 1980. The story of D. B. Cooper's skyjacking as told by the former FBI agent who headed the Cooper investigation.

Moore, K. *Airport, Aircraft, and Airline Security*. 2d ed. Woburn, Mass.: Butterworth-Heinemann, 1991. Study of airport and airline security that also covers skyjacking and terrorism against air carriers and methods used to combat terrorism.

St. John, P. *Air Piracy, Airport Security, and International Terrorism*. Westport, Conn.: Quorum Books, 1991. Now somewhat dated but highly readable work that provides a fascinating history of international aircraft terrorism and examines the difficulties of combating the problem. Current safety measures and policies of individual countries are analyzed, and a coordinated seven-stage plan is proposed to combat air piracy.

Wallis, R. *Combating Air Terrorism*. Dulles, Va.: Brassey's, 1993. Focusing on the principal air terrorist acts since the mid-1980's, explains how the international community is working to make airways safer, describing the areas that need more attention.

See also Carjacking; Federal Bureau of Investigation; Homeland Security Department; International law; Justice Department, U.S.; Kidnapping; Marshals Service, U.S.; Multiple jurisdiction offenses; Patriot Act; Terrorism.

Slave patrols

Definition: Summoned bodies of citizens charged with enforcing laws restricting the activities and movement of slaves in the antebellum South

Criminal justice issues: Civil rights and liberties; law-enforcement organization

Significance: Slave patrols provide an example of the piecemeal, militia-style law enforcement of the pre-Civil War South and served as a blueprint for the vigilante groups of the postbellum South.

The British American colonies began to establish informal slave patrols during the late seventeenth and early eighteenth centuries in reaction to public fears of slave rebellion. South Carolina, with its majority black population, was the first colony to establish formal slave patrols in 1704, followed by Virginia in 1727 and North Carolina in 1753. By the end of the eighteenth century, slave patrols existed in every state where slavery was legal. The patrols' makeup and the extent of their activities varied from state to state and often from locality to locality according to the size of the slave population and the threat of runaways and insurrection. Patrollers were typically white men between the ages of sixteen and sixty, chosen from militia and tax rolls to serve terms that varied in length.

Slave patrols usually worked at night in small groups, looking for slaves wandering from their home plantations without permission, evidence of unlawful slave assemblies, and other illegal activities. Patrollers were assigned broad authority to act as police, judge, and jury, including the right to enter plantations without a warrant, search slave quarters and other plantation property, and arrest or summarily punish slaves at will. Brutality, vindictiveness, and other abuses of power were common under this system; just as common, however, were complaints of laxity and ineffectiveness on the part of the patrols in suppressing slave assemblies and reducing the number of runaway slaves. Slave patrols operated sporadically in many locations, especially those in which slaves were relatively few in number. In some areas, they were little more than loosely organized posses activated in the event of real or perceived threats.

Evidence indicates that public attitudes toward slave patrols were mixed and that many southerners simply considered them a necessary evil. Nonslaveholders often bore most of the burden of patrolling, leading to resentment and abuses of power leveled against both slaves and their owners. Men with the means to avoid patrol duties by hiring substitutes or simply paying the fines for not serving often did so. Nevertheless, few southerners advocated doing away with the patrols, which continued to exist until slavery was abolished. Over time, slave patrols assumed other law-enforcement duties in many localities, becoming de facto police forces in some southern towns and cities.

Slave patrols intensified their activities during the Civil War, often joining forces with local militias. Although they ceased to operate after the war, slave patrols provided the inspiration for the activities of the Ku Klux Klan and other "night riders" who terrorized southern blacks during the Reconstruction era.

Michael H. Burchett

Further Reading
Hadden, Sally E. *Slave Patrols: Law and Violence in Virginia and the Carolinas*. Cam-

bridge, Mass.: Harvard University Press, 2001.

Stampp, Kenneth M. *The Peculiar Institution: Slavery in the Antebellum South*. New York: Vintage Books, 1989.

Wyatt-Brown, Bertram. *Southern Honor: Ethics and Behavior in the Old South*. New York: Oxford University Press, 1983.

See also Corporal punishment; Criminal justice in U.S. history; Lynching; Marshals Service, U.S.; Vigilantism.

Smith Act

The Law: Federal legislation, officially known as the Alien Registration Act, that required aliens to register with the U.S. government and made it a crime to advocate overthrowing the American government by force

Date: June 28, 1940

Criminal justice issues: Espionage and sedition; federal law; political issues

Significance: The Smith Act became the U.S. government's primary legal tool for attacking the American Communist Party during the early years of the Cold War.

As World War II approached, fears of foreign-inspired subversive activity grew in the United States. Concerned especially that the buildup of American defenses might be threatened by sabotage, Congress reacted by passing the Alien Registration Act, which came to be more generally known as the Smith Act for its major proponent, Congressman Howard W. Smith of Virginia.

The Smith Act had two major thrusts. The first sought greater control over aliens living in the United States. Under the act, aliens had to register with the government, be fingerprinted, carry identity cards, and report yearly. (The registration requirement was dropped in 1982.) Those involved in what were regarded as subversive activities could be deported. The other major provisions of the act were directed at disloyal activities. These made it a crime for anyone to advocate the overthrow of the federal government or other American governments by force or violence, to enter a conspiracy to advocate such a course of action, or to become a knowing member of such a group. Penalties for those convicted under the act included a ten-thousand-dollar fine, up to ten years in prison, or both.

Though a wartime measure, the Smith Act was used relatively little during World War II. As postwar tension between the United States and the Soviet Union developed into the Cold War, however, the act came to the fore as concerns about the possibility of communist subversion in the United States rose. By the late 1940's, there were increasing concerns about the activities of members of the American Communist Party and sympathetic groups, and charges of communist penetration of the government were increasingly made. The administration of President Harry S. Truman was charged with being slow to meet the communist challenge at home. Partly in response, the Truman administration used the Smith Act to attack the party's organization.

In 1948 Eugene Dennis and ten other communist leaders were arrested and charged under the act. They were convicted and sentenced to prison. They appealed, arguing that the Smith Act was an unconstitutional violation of the First Amendment's protection of free expression. Their appeal was denied by the Supreme Court in 1951.

Use of the Smith Act continued during the 1950's. Altogether, more than 140 arrests were made under the act. Later Supreme Court decisions in *Yates v. United States* (1957) and *Brandenburg v. Ohio* (1969) broadened the extent of expression protected by the First Amendment, but the Smith Act itself continued to be held as constitutional.

William C. Lowe

Further Reading

Abraham, Henry J., and Barbara A. Perry. *Freedom and the Court*. 7th ed. New York: Oxford University Press, 1998.

Ngai, Mae M. *Impossible Subjects: Illegal Aliens and the Making of Modern America*. Princeton, N.J.: Princeton University Press, 2004.

See also Clear and present danger test; Palmer raids; Rosenberg espionage case; Seditious libel.

Sobriety testing

Definition: Methods of determining whether drivers are operating vehicles while under the influence of alcohol or drugs

Criminal justice issues: Arrest and arraignment; police powers; substance abuse; traffic law

Significance: An important tool in combating drunk driving, sobriety testing can be crucial to establishing probable cause for making arrests and providing evidence to secure convictions of suspected drunk and drugged drivers.

Police officers administer sobriety tests to drivers they suspect of driving while impaired by alcohol or drug ingestion for two reasons. First, they need to establish probable-cause foundations for making arrests; second, the results of the tests are used to aid in prosecutions to establish that violations of law have occurred. Sobriety tests are of two basic kinds: field and chemical. Field sobriety tests (FSTs) are subjective in nature; that is their validity relies upon the observations of the arresting officers. Chemical sobriety tests are considered to be objective, as their results are obtained through laboratory analyses.

One objective measure of a driver's sobriety is the level of the driver's blood alcohol concentration (BAC). That level is calculated scientifically by measuring the amount of ethanol (ethyl alcohol, an odorless form of alcohol) in a person's bloodstream from blood, breath, or urine samples. All fifty U.S. states have legally defined presumptive limits of blood alcohol concentration. Under those definitions, drivers of motor vehicles are presumed to be under the influence of alcohol when their blood alcohol concentration exceeds the limits of the states in which they are driving. The limit is .08 percent in most states, and .10 percent in others.

Field Sobriety Tests

Field sobriety tests are designed to give officers in the field approximate ideas of the sobriety of suspected drunk-driving offend-

ers. Such tests do not confirm either illegal intoxication or sobriety; they serve only as guidelines. Officers carrying breath-analyzer equipment in the field can administer objective tests immediately. Otherwise, they must ask suspects to submit to subjective tests.

Every law-enforcement agency in America has a policy for administration of subjective field sobriety tests, but the National Highway Traffic Safety Administration (NHTSA) has developed a standardized set of tests since the early 1970's to assist officers in their arrest decisions.

The most commonly used standardized field test is called the horizontal gaze nystagmus (HGN) test. This test is designed to help officers observe whether any jerkiness (or bounce) appears in the eyes of suspected offenders when their eyes follow a stimulus from side to side. Eye jerkiness may indicate intoxication, but officers are trained to know that such eye movements may be

One of the oldest and most revealing field sobriety tests requires suspect drivers to walk in a straight line, heel to toe. The difficulty of performing this test successfully while under the influence of alcohol can be easily confirmed by any person who has consumed several drinks. *(Brand-X Pictures)*

present even without intoxication, as in the case of certain nerve disorders.

Officers also watch for other subjective symptoms of intoxication, such as bloodshot and watery eyes, slurred speech, and poor balance. Other field sobriety tests include balance and coordination trials, such as walking in a straight line, heel to toe; counting on fingers; and reciting the alphabet. When officers believe that suspects have been driving while intoxicated, the tests have served their purpose as pre-arrest indicators of intoxication and arrests are made. Suspects are then transported to facilities for the administration of chemical sobriety tests.

Chemical Sobriety Tests

In most states, suspects arrested for driving while under the influence of alcohol (DUI) may choose the types of chemical sobriety tests that are administered to them. Some states require offering two options; others require three. Failure to submit to a chemical test after arrest usually results in revocation of driving privileges.

Chemical sobriety tests include tests of samples of blood, breath, and urine. Blood and urine tests are usually administered when arresting officers suspect that the drivers have ingested drugs other than alcohol. Such tests are conducted in hospitals and jail facilities. Persons administering blood tests must be medically certified to draw blood. However, breath tests may be administered by anyone certified to operate a breath analyzer, and arresting officers frequently administer such tests. Urine samples may be taken by any person associated with the arrest. Both law enforcement and arrested drivers prefer breath tests, probably because their results are known immediately and do not require the time-consuming analyses of blood and urine tests.

Breath tests are conducted on the theory that alcohol escapes from the body through the breath. Most law-enforcement agencies use breath-analyzer machines produced under the trade names of Intoxilizer, Intoximeter, and Breathalizer because of the wide acceptance of their results by courts. When officers in the field carry a portable breath analyzer, the field sobriety tests they administer are considered to be objective.

Blood samples, which are usually drawn at community hospitals, are maintained under strict chain of custody standards until they are analyzed by laboratories. Afterward, they are either used in trials or are destroyed. Urine samples are usually collected at police stations, jail facilities, or hospitals. The samples are witnessed by officers who thereafter maintain the same chain of custody standards that are used with blood samples.

Regardless of the types of sample taken, officers are aware that blood alcohol concentrations in human bodies diminish at the rate of approximately .02 percent per hour. Consequently, the samples must be collected as soon as possible after arrests are made.

Charles L. Johnson

Further Reading

Dietrich, James J. *Horizontal Gaze Nystagmus: The Science and the Law—A Resource Guide for Judges, Prosecutors, and Law Enforcement.* Washington, D.C.: National Highway Traffic Safety Administration, 1999. Practical guide to administering horizontal gaze nystagmus tests to suspected drunk drivers.

Homel, Ross. *Policing and Punishing the Drunk Driver: A Study of General and Specific Deterrence.* New York: Springer-Verlag, 1988. General study of methods of combating drunk driving through law enforcement.

Jacobs, J. B. *Drunk Driving: An American Dilemma.* Chicago: University of Chicago Press, 1992. Broad synthesis by a law professor on all aspects of drunk driving in the United States, from myths about the nature of the problem to the trend toward tougher enforcement of drunk driving laws.

Jasper, Margaret, et al. *DWI, DUI and the Law.* New York: Oceana, 2004. Lay guide to drunk driving laws in the United States. Covers criminal justice procedures, drunk driving statistics, and other related subjects.

Laurence, Michael D., John R. Snortum, and Franklin E. Zimring, eds. *Social Control of the Drinking Driver.* Chicago: University of Chicago Press, 1988. Sociological study of the causes and effects of drunk driving.

Robin, Gerald D. *Waging the Battle Against Drunk Driving: Issues, Countermeasures and Effectiveness.* Westport, Conn.: Greenwood Press, 1991. Fascinating study of the modern movement against drunk driving, with special attention to such grassroots movements as Mothers Against Drunk Driving.

Taylor, Lawrence E., and Steven Oberman. *Drunk Driving Defense*. New York: Aspen, 2003. How-to guidebook written by a lawyer to help people beat drunk-driving charges. While the ethics of publishing such a book may be questionable, the book provides revealing insights into the problems of prosecuting drunk driving offenses.

Watson, Ronald R., ed. *Alcohol, Cocaine, and Accidents*. Clifton, N.J.: Humana Press, 1995. Collection of ten research papers on the roles of alcohol and cocaine in motor vehicle, aviation, and aquatic accidents that are addressed to policymakers and people in law enforcement. Particular attention is given to the behavior of young people.

Wilson, R. Jean, and Robert E. Mann, eds. *Drinking and Driving: Advances in Research and Prevention*. New York: Guilford Press, 1990. Interdisciplinary collection of articles on a wide variety of aspects of drunk driving. The first section covers efforts to understand impaired drivers, the second section examines efforts to deter drunk driving, and the third section examines other preventive measures.

See also Alcohol use and abuse; Chain of custody; Drug testing; Drunk driving; Highway patrols; Hit-and-run accidents; Mothers Against Drunk Driving; Probable cause; State police; Toxicology; Traffic law; Vehicle checkpoints.

Solem v. Helm

The Case: U.S. Supreme Court ruling on cruel and unusual punishment

Date: Decided on June 28, 1983

Criminal justice issues: Constitutional protections; punishment

Significance: In this case, the Supreme Court interpreted the Eighth Amendment's prohibition on cruel and unusual punishments to limit the ability of states to impose life sentences for multiple convictions on nonviolent felony charges.

In 1979, Jerry Helm was convicted of issuing a "no account" check for one hundred dollars. This was his seventh felony conviction in South Dakota. In 1964, 1966, and 1969, he had been convicted of third-degree burglary. He had been convicted of obtaining money under false pretenses in 1972, and in 1973 he was convicted of grand larceny. Moreover, his third drunk-driving conviction in 1975 counted as a felony offense. All the offenses were nonviolent, none involved personal, physical victimization of another person, and alcohol was a contributing factor in each case.

Although the maximum penalty for writing a "no account" check in South Dakota was normally five years in prison and a five-thousand-dollar fine, Helm was sentenced to life imprisonment without possibility of parole because defendants convicted of four felonies under South Dakota law may be given the maximum penalty for class 1 felonies—even if they have never actually committed a class 1 felony. The purpose of the state's tough sentencing law was to put habitual offenders away forever so that they could not commit additional offenses.

On appeal, the South Dakota Supreme Court rejected Helm's claim that the sentence of life without parole for a nonviolent offense constituted cruel and unusual punishment in violation of the Eighth Amendment. The U.S. Court of Appeals disagreed and invalidated Helm's sentence. When the U.S. Supreme Court reviewed the case, a narrow five-member majority agreed with Helm's argument.

In a prior decision (*Rummel v. Estelle*, 1980), the U.S. Supreme Court had permitted Texas to impose a life sentence on a man who, over the course of a decade, was convicted of three separate theft offenses in which he stole less than $250. The Supreme Court regarded the *Helm* case as different because South Dakota, unlike Texas, did not permit people with life sentences to become eligible for parole. Thus the realistic impact of Helm's sentence was much harsher than that of life sentences imposed in other states where prisoners typically earn an eventual parole release if they exhibit good behavior. The Court decided that Helm's punishment was disproportionate to his crimes because sentences of life without parole are typically reserved for people convicted of first-degree murder, kidnapping, or treason—not for people who commit nonviolent offenses involving modest amounts of money.

The importance of *Solem v. Helm* is that the Supreme Court placed limitations on the ability of the states to impose severe sentences on people convicted of multiple nonviolent felonies. The case also reinforced the Court's view that the Eighth Amendment contains an implicit requirement that sentences cannot be disproportionate to the crimes committed.

Christopher E. Smith

Further Reading

Berkson, Larry. *The Concept of Cruel and Unusual Punishment*. Lexington, Mass.: Lexington Books, 1975.

Demleitner, Nora V., Douglas A. Berman, Marc L. Miller, and Ronald F. Wright. *Sentencing Law and Policy: Cases, Statutes, and Guidelines*. New York: Aspen Publishers, 2003.

Tonry, Michael. *Sentencing and Sanctions in Western Countries*. New York: Oxford University Press, 2001.

United States Sentencing Commission. *Federal Sentencing Guidelines Manual 2003*. St. Paul, Minn.: West Publishing, 2004.

See also Bill of Rights, U.S.; Cruel and unusual punishment; *Rummel v. Estelle*; Sentencing; Supreme Court, U.S.

Solicitation to commit a crime

Definition: Enticing or inducing someone to commit a crime

Criminal justice issues: Defendants; legal terms and principles

Significance: As the typical first step toward commission of a crime, solicitation is requesting, commanding, encouraging, or advising another person to engage in criminal conduct. The act of solicitation establishes complicity in a future crime. Prosecution of solicitation is a way to prevent future criminal acts.

The term "solicitation" is attached to an intended crime, for example, solicitation to commit burglary. The crime of solicitation is of the same legal grade and degree as the most serious crime solicited, and convicted solicitors are sentenced accordingly. The act of solicitation is a crime even if the person solicited declines, the person solicited is incapable of committing the crime, or the person for whom the solicitation was intended did not hear or receive the solicitation.

Merely discussing a criminal act can be considered solicitation. Solicitation is a crime similar to conspiracy and is added to charges in a quarter of all cases, usually as a bargaining chip in pretrial negotiations. When civilians solicit, the act of solicitation in itself is considered to be a crime. When police, police informants, or undercover agents solicit, it may sometimes be considered entrapment, but it is rarely prosecuted as a crime.

Renunciation is a defense for solicitation. To renounce solicitation, defendants must have subsequently persuaded the solicited persons not to commit the crimes or have prevented the commission of the crimes, and have demonstrated a voluntary recanting of their intent to solicit, facilitate, or commit the crimes.

Gordon Neal Diem

Further Reading

Duff, R. Antony. *Criminal Attempts*. New York: Clarendon Press, 1996.

Kessler, Kimberly, and Larry Alexander. "*Mens rea* and Inchoate Crimes." *Journal of Criminal Law and Criminology* 87 (June 22, 1997): 1138-1193.

See also Accomplices and accessories; Attempt to commit a crime; Conspiracy; Criminal intent; Criminal law; Entrapment; Inchoate crimes; *Mens rea*; Privacy rights.

Solicitor general of the United States

Definition: The fourth-ranking member of the Department of Justice and the primary legal spokesperson for the executive branch of the government

Criminal justice issues: Appeals; federal law; law-enforcement organization

Significance: Solicitors general play a key role in the appellate process, as they determine which cases the government will appeal to the Supreme Court and mediate interdepartmental disputes on matters of legal policy.

The office of solicitor general was created by Congress as part of the Department of Justice in 1870. Its purpose was to provide the attorney general and by extension the executive branch with legal advice. The solicitor general is the only official required by statute to be "learned in the law." In the modern Department of Justice the solicitor general is a presidential appointee who ranks fourth in authority behind the attorney general, the deputy attorney general, and the associate attorney general. The solicitor general is primarily responsible for deciding what federal cases the government will appeal to the Supreme Court. These decisions are based on a number of factors, including the "ripeness" of the issue, the Court's crowded docket, policy considerations, and the government's legal resources.

The solicitor general determines the government's position and argues the case before the Supreme Court if the Court accepts the case. The Supreme Court accepts about 75 percent of cases in which the solicitor general is a party or an *amicus curiae* (friend of the court) as compared with fewer than 5 percent of other petitioners. This makes the solicitor general the "gatekeeper" affecting the flow of cases to the Supreme Court. The Court grants the solicitor general special privileges with regard to court procedures in recognition of this role as the government's attorney. At times, the Court will ask the solicitor general for an opinion on complicated cases. By tradition, the Court expects the solicitor general not to be narrowly partisan but to take a longer view of issues and to do so with candor. This special relationship with the Supreme Court has led the solicitor general to be informally called the "tenth justice."

Because of this dual role as representative of the executive branch and counselor to the Court, solicitors general have taken an independent stance and viewed their primary loyalty to be to the idea of law and justice. This has led to tension with the executive branch. For example, Rex Lee, solicitor general from 1981 to 1985, refused on more than one occasion to put forth arguments advanced by the Reagan administration if he thought they were weak or inappropriate. This refusal to be, as he put it, "pamphleteer general," finally led to his resignation. His successor, Charles Fried (1985-1989), was less reluctant to ask the Court to reverse matters for political reasons, which caused him to lose credibility and ef-

Notable Solicitors General

Tenure	Solicitor general	Later distinctions
1890-1892	William Howard Taft	president of United States, 1909-1913; chief justice of United States, 1921-1930
1912-1918	John W. Davis	argued more cases before the Supreme Court than any other attorney
1929-1930	Charles Evans Hughes	associate justice of Supreme Court, 1910-1916; chief justice, 1930-1941
1935-1938	Stanley Reed	associate Supreme Court justice, 1938-1957
1961-1965	Archibald Cox	Watergate special prosecutor, 1973
1965-1967	Thurgood Marshall	associate Supreme Court justice, 1967-1991
1973-1977	Robert Bork	Supreme Court nominee, 1987

fectiveness before the Court. Independence remains a vital characteristic of the office and makes it a crucial component of the American justice system.

Melvin Kulbicki

Further Reading

Clayton, Cornell C. *The Politics of Justice: The Attorney General and the Making of Legal Policy*. Armonk, N.Y.: M. E. Sharpe, 1992.

Cole, George F., and Christopher Smith. *American System of Criminal Justice*. 10th ed. Belmont, Calif.: Thomson/Wadsworth, 2004.

Johns, Margaret, and Rex R. Perschbacher. *The United States Legal System: An Introduction*. Durham, N.C.: Carolina Academic Press, 2002.

See also Attorney general of the United States; Justice Department, U.S.

Solitary confinement

Definition: Confinement of prisoners in isolation from other prison and jail inmates

Criminal justice issues: Medical and health issues; prisons; punishment

Significance: A difficult challenge to prison administrators has long been how to punish inmates for offenses committed within prison walls, when extending sentences may mean nothing to prisoners already facing long sentences or possible execution. One solution has been to place prison offenders in solitary confinement. However, some critics charge that solitary confinement may merely aggravate the prisoners' problems.

Modern prisons generally have four reasons for placing inmates in solitary confinement: administrative detention, protective custody, short-term disciplinary segregation, and long-term detention in special housing units or supermax prisons.

Inmates placed in administrative detention are put in special sections of prison segregation units when they are charged with serious rule vi-

One of the difficulties of deterring prisoners who are already serving long prison sentences from committing additional crimes while in prison is finding sanctions that mean something to them; one proven deterrent is isolating misbehaving prisoners in solitary confinement. *(Brand-X Pictures)*

olations, and investigations are in progress. They may also be placed in administrative detention when they voice concerns for their own personal safety because of their fears of sexual assaults by other prisoners, gang violence, or retaliation for having informed on other prisoners. When prison officers find that the prisoners' fears are well grounded, they may then place the inmates in long-term protective custody units or transfer them to other prisons.

Inmates found guilty of serious prison-rule violations, such as fighting with other inmates, assaulting staff members, or trying to escape, are placed in punitive or disciplinary segregation. Such isolation is usually limited to a maximum of sixty days at a time because of court restrictions.

The physical conditions of solitary confinement are typically spartan. Inmates are generally locked up alone for up to twenty-three hours a day in small cells.

Inmates in solitary confinement receive their food on trays passed through slots in their doors known as "pie flaps," and they eat all their meals within their cells. Inmates are permitted to exit their cells only after they have been handcuffed by extending their hands through the pie flaps in the doors. Inmates are generally allowed to exercise outside their cells for one hour per day, either alone or in small groups, in small, fenced-in units, which have been dubbed "recreation cages." Medical personnel visit periodically to attend to inmates' medical and psychological needs.

> ## Contents of a Typical Solitary-Confinement Cell
> ✓ four plain concrete walls
> ✓ one heavy metal door with a "pie flap"
> ✓ one narrow, barred window
> ✓ one stainless steel sink/toilet combination
> ✓ one bolt-down metal-frame bed or concrete sleeping slab
> ✓ one small storage container for personal items
> ✓ one bolted-down table
> ✓ one bolted-down chair
> ✓ one small bookshelf
> ✓ one reading light
>
> Inmates serving long terms in solitary confinement may also have shower stalls in their cells. Depending upon the conditions imposed on a prisoner, a cell may or may not contain a small television set, a radio, or limited amounts of reading material.

The prisoners may also be allowed some educational and religious programming in their cells.

Critics of solitary confinement argue that it is unduly restrictive and punitive and creates boring claustrophobic environments that can lead to, or intensify, mental illness. Proponents of solitary confinement counter that little empirical evidence has been gathered to prove that solitary confinement causes mental disorders. They also point out that when inmates complain about solitary confinement, they typically criticize the treatment they receive at the hands of the guards, not their living conditions.

Psychologists and psychiatrists testifying in court often offer conflicting testimony on the impact of solitary confinement on mental health. Consequently, when judges examine the conditions of solitary confinement, they generally focus most of their attention on the food and physical conditions of the confinement units, not on the prisoners' psychological conditions.

Robert Rogers

Further Reading
Kupers, Terry. *Prison Madness: The Mental Health Crisis Behind Bars and What We Must Do About It*. San Francisco: Jossey-Bass Publishers, 1999.
Neal, Donice, ed. *Supermax Prisons: Beyond the Rock*. Lanham, Md.: American Correctional Association, 2003.
Toch, Hans, and Kenneth Adams. *Coping: Maladaptation in Prisons*. New Brunswick, N.J.: Transaction Books, 1989.

See also Auburn system; Cruel and unusual punishment; Incapacitation; Mental illness; Prison escapes; Prison violence; Supermax prisons; Walnut Street Jail.

Spam

Definition: Unsolicited and usually unwanted electronic mail
Criminal justice issues: Business and financial crime; computer crime; fraud; privacy
Significance: Since the rise of the Internet and e-mail, computer users have been deluged with an ever-growing flood of spam, much of which contains fraudulent solicitations and offers. The irritation and disruptions to normal communications caused by the sheer volume of spam have prompted many calls for criminalizing spam itself.

What is now known as "spam" has existed since the mid-1970's. It originated as postings to newsgroups, evolved into advertisements and solicitations, and soon got out of hand, with individual members receiving numerous unwanted e-mails.

With the rapid expansion of the World Wide Web during the 1990's, the problem of unsolicited e-mail began to grow exponentially. By 2005, most Internet e-mail users were receiving dozens— sometimes even hundreds—of pieces of spam every day.

Spam messages include legal and illegal solicitations of all kinds, running from advertisements—including a large proportion of pornographic advertisements—to chain letters and jokes. Volume is not the only problem that spam presents to computer users. Many spam messages contain computer viruses and worms that can inflict serious damage on the computers receiving the unwanted messages. The annoyance that spam causes computer users is difficult to exaggerate. In addition to offending users with unwanted—and often repugnant—solicitations, spam forces users to spend time and resources filtering and removing spam, while increasing their anxieties about the safety and security of their computers.

During the 1990's, increasing numbers of lawsuits were being filed against the purveyors of spam, known as spammers, in state and federal courts—primarily under fraud statutes. The Coalition Against Unsolicited Commercial E-mail (CAUCE) is one of a number of groups that have lobbied for criminalizing spam in the United States and Europe. During the 2003-2004 session of the U.S. Congress, at least six pieces of legislation designed to regulate spam were introduced. By the year 2005, no blanket national law made spam illegal, but by then as many as twenty-one states had passed, or were then considering, laws to criminalize spam.

One problem with criminalizing spam is the fact that much of it falls under laws protecting legitimate commerce and trade. The state of California found a way around this problem by enacting a law requiring that spam messages be labeled as advertising and that they offer ways for recipients to have their names removed from mailing lists. The California law was upheld by an appeals court as constitutional.

Existing federal and state laws protect citizens from fraud and illegal pornography. The Federal Trade Commission, the Federal Bureau of Investigation, the Internet Fraud Complaint Center, and the National White Collar Crime Commission all investigate complaints concerning spam. However, spam messages are difficult to trace back to their senders. Moreover, even when the senders are identified, they are rarely prosecuted or sued unless criminal activity and criminal intent can clearly be demonstrated.

On January 1, 2004, the federal Controlling the Assault of Non-Solicited Pornography and Marketing Act (CAN-SPAM) of 2003 took effect. A so-called "opt out" law, this legislation gave e-mail users a way to remove themselves from mailing lists. In addition, the CAN-SPAM Act forbade fraudulent e-mail subject lines, made it illegal to send e-mail to addresses that are improperly "harvested," forbade sending e-mail with pornographic content without clear identifying labels, and provided both criminal and civil penalties for violators.

Some critics have warned that the CAN-SPAM Act might actually increase the volume of spam in the United States. The fear is that by signaling to the world that spam is legal in the United States, foreign spammers might send more messages than ever. Also, requiring recipients to read unwanted e-mails to opt out is considered unfair.

Most spam being sent in 2005 remained illegal. Nothing in the law will stop illegal spammers from sending spam. The general consensus toward fighting spam seems to be on the side of private sector response. Individual computer users should use devices such as firewalls and antivirus programs to protect their computers from invasive e-mail threats. Internet service providers are developing "black hole" technologies to help prevent spam from reaching subscribers. These are seen as more effective than additional layers of legislation.

Donald R. Dixon

Further Reading

Clifford, Ralph D., ed. *Cybercrime: The Investigation, Prosecution, and Defense of a Computer-Related Crime*. Durham, N.C.: Carolina Academic Press, 2001.

Feinstein, Ken. *Fight Spam, Viruses, Pop-Ups and Spyware (How to Do Everything)*. New York: McGraw-Hill, 2004.

Poteet, Jeremy. *Canning Spam: You've Got Mail (That You Don't Want)*. Indianapolis: Sam's Publishing, 2004.

Thomas, Douglas, and Brian D. Loader, eds. *Cybercrime: Law Enforcement, Security, and Surveillance in the Information Age.* New York: Routledge, 2000.

See also Computer crime; Cybercrime; Fraud; Trespass.

Special weapons and tactics teams (SWAT)

Definition: Specialized police units designed to resolve dangerous crises

Criminal justice issues: Morality and public order; police powers; violent crime

Significance: Nearly every major municipal police department in the United States now includes some type of SWAT unit, and these tactical units are gradually moving from acting as urban-emergency response teams to performing more routine police duties.

Heavily armed members of a Miami-Dade County SWAT team returning to their station after spending six hours in a futile search for burglars in a high-rise Florida bank building in early 2003. *(AP/Wide World Photos)*

Special weapons and tactics teams, or SWAT teams as they are better known, were first established by the Los Angles Police Department in response to the Watts riot of 1965. The brainchild of future Los Angeles police chief Daryl Gates, SWAT teams were designed as paramilitary units to counter urban insurgencies that regular police officers were not trained or equipped to handle. In fact, many modern SWAT teams now get much of their equipment, weapons, and training directly from the U.S. military.

The units were originally called "special weapons attack teams," but the name was changed to make the units sound more technical and less aggressive. More American cities began creating SWAT teams after an incident in Austin, Texas, in 1996, when a sniper named Charles Whitman barricaded himself in a university tower and began randomly firing upon people below. That incident brought to national attention the idea of training and equipping specialized police units to deal with exceptionally dangerous situations.

The first SWAT teams were especially designed to deal with situations involving hostages and barricaded suspects. However, they were soon used to control violent political groups such as the Black Panthers and the Symbionese Liberation Army.

SWAT teams place a high emphasis on teamwork and set high standards for their members. Candidates for SWAT team placement are carefully selected and must meet strict qualifications. They must have good service records, meet certain physical requirements, and demonstrate that they can react quickly in stressful situations. The criteria are strict because SWAT members are involved in highly volatile situations and carry weapons that can cause a great amount of damage.

In the twenty-first century, SWAT teams are being used in everyday police situations and are no longer limited to responding to hostage and barricaded suspect situations. Their current responsibilities now include serving search warrants to high-risk suspects, especially those believed to possess firearms. SWAT teams also often participate in drug raids, riot control, and in some areas are used to stabilize violent domestic disputes and vicious animals.

The use of SWAT teams in everyday policing has been controversial. Some critics argue that SWAT teams are increasing the militarism of police forces, thereby eroding the line between domestic law enforcement and martial law. SWAT operations that have resulted in the loss of innocent lives have also been cited as a reason the tactical units should not be used. Proponents of SWAT teams counter, however, that dangerous situations will always arise that police officers cannot control. Proponents also note that the increasing number of violent criminals in American society and the growing threat of terrorism will continue to make SWAT teams necessary, and that in the long run, SWAT teams will save many more lives than they cause to be lost.

Mark Anthony Cubillos

Among the primary reasons for stopping speeding drivers and issuing them citations is to deter them from repeating their dangerous behavior. In addition to the costs of speeding tickets—which can be substantial—repeated violations can raise drivers' insurance premiums and possibly cost drivers their driving licenses. (Brand-X Pictures)

Further Reading

Goranson, Christopher D. *Police SWAT Teams: Life on High Alert.* New York: Rosen, 2003.

Snow, Robert L. *SWAT Teams: Explosive Face-offs with America's Deadliest Criminals.* Cambridge, Mass.: Perseus Books, 1996.

See also Criminal justice system; Criminals; Deadly force; Drugs and law enforcement; Law Enforcement Assistance Administration; No-knock warrants; Police; Police brutality; Police ethics; Police powers; Reasonable force; Symbionese Liberation Army; Terrorism.

Speeding detection

Definition: Methods of determining when motorists exceed legal speed limits

Criminal justice issues: Crime prevention; traffic law

Significance: Driving at excessive speeds contributes to one-third of all motor-vehicle accidental fatalities in the United States and causes many injuries and considerable property damage every year. These costs give traffic-law-enforcement authorities strong incentives to detect and punish motorists who exceed posted speed limits.

Exceeding speed limits and driving at excessive speeds in unsafe conditions is both illegal and highly dangerous. Most highways and motor vehicles are built for safe motor vehicle operation at the speeds traveled by most motorists. Nevertheless, speeding on American roadways is common and contributes to as many as one-third of all accidents involving fatalities. A 2002 study by the National Highway and Traffic Safety Administration reported that speeding is such a pervasive behavior that about three-quarters of surveyed drivers admitted having driven above posted speed limits, on all types of roads, within the previous month. More than one-quarter of the drivers admitted having violated speed limits on the days they were interviewed.

An ongoing question is why so many American motorists ignore posted speed limits. One possible explanation is that drivers see so little evidence of enforcement that they expect not to be caught. However, the ratio of citations issued to mere warnings to speeding motorists has steadily climbed since 1997, reflecting a public concern with the safety hazards posed by speeding motorists. Speeding is clearly one crime in which deterrence works, and the key to effective deterrence is detecting and punishing speeding drivers.

The Basis of Speed Limits

Posted speed limits are generally designed to meet the needs of 70 percent of all drivers and are enforced with standard deviations of approximately 15 percent. That is, drivers who operate their vehicles at speeds 15 percent above or below the posted ranges are considered to be unsafe and may be cited.

When planned intelligently, speed limits are determined scientifically through the application of traffic engineering principles. Speed limits are enforced with scientific equipment, and speeding convictions are validated by testimony based on the scientific principles underlying such speed-detection devices as radar.

Traffic-enforcement officers are responsible for enforcing traffic codes and citing violations. Their primary focus is often on the most common violation, speeding. There are three primary purposes for stopping speeding motorists. The first is to stop violations of the law for public safety. The second is to deter other drivers from speeding. The third purpose is to change drivers' future driving behaviors.

The benefits of maintaining traffic safety by reducing speeding are both numerous and obvious: increased safety on the roadways for both motorists and pedestrians, lower insurance costs, lower health care and tax costs, and government revenue generation and gains from asset forfeitures.

Traffic-law enforcement can also play an important role as a crime-solving tool. Because most criminals use motor vehicles for transportation to and from crime scenes, as well as their every-day transportation, traffic officers are often involved in preventing and helping to solve crimes. Traffic stops often detect evidence of more serious offenses. Well-trained, alert, and motivated officers often intercept criminals whom they stop for simple traffic violations.

Methods of Detection

One of the most effective devices for detecting speeding vehicles is radar, which was originally developed as a military technology during World War II to detect enemy aircraft. Speed-measuring radar works on a similar principle by bouncing radio signals off approaching vehicles and calculating oncoming vehicles' speed by measuring changes in frequency in the returning signals as the vehicles move toward the radar transmitters. The mere presence of traffic radar can deter would-be speeders.

A modern enhancement to traffic radar is photo-radar, which combines cameras and radar transmitters to detect and photograph speeding vehicles. The pictures taken can be used to identify drivers' faces and the license plates of their vehicles. That information can be used to send citations to the registered owners of the speeding vehicles.

Michelle R. Hecht

Further Reading

Hand, B., A. Sherman, and M. Cavanagh. *Traffic Investigation and Control*. New York: Macmillan, 1980.

Langford, Les. *Understanding Police Traffic Radar and Lidar*. Rev. ed. Pleasant Grove, Utah: Law Enforcement Services, 1998.

Royal, Dawn. *National Survey of Speeding and Unsafe Driving Attitudes and Behavior, 2002*. Washington, D.C.: National Highway Traffic Safety Administration, 2004.

Sawicki, Donald S. *Traffic Radar Handbook: A Comprehensive Guide to Speed Measuring Systems*. Brasstown, N.C.: Grove Enterprises, 1993.

See also Highway patrols; Hit-and-run accidents; Police; State police; Traffic courts; Traffic fines; Traffic law; Vehicle checkpoints.

Speedy trial right

Definition: Constitutional right of defendants to have their cases tried without unreasonable delays

Criminal justice issues: Constitutional protections; probation and pretrial release; trial procedures

Significance: The constitutional guarantee that accused persons have the right to a speedy trial is one of the fundamental features of U.S. constitutional law.

The Sixth Amendment to the U.S. Constitution provides that in all criminal prosecutions the accused shall enjoy the right to a speedy trial. Applying the due process clause of the Fourteenth Amendment, the U.S. Supreme Court ruled in *Klopfer v. North Carolina* (1967) that this right applies to state trials as well. Chief Justice Earl Warren wrote that "the right to a speedy trial is as fundamental as any of the rights secured by the Sixth Amendment," and like the right to counsel, he reasoned, it should also be applied to the states.

Not only do trial delays create an enormous backlog of cases that clog the judicial system, but they also make it difficult for the accused to present an adequate defense. Even if the accused person is free on bail, employment may be disrupted, reputations harmed, and financial resources depleted.

Delay is a common defense tactic, because there are many instances in which delay favors the accused. Most often it puts pressure on the prosecution to make concessions. To avoid a lengthy trial a prosecutor may offer to reduce the charges against a defendant in return for a guilty plea. There is also the danger that a person on bail awaiting trial may commit other crimes or forfeit bail.

The term "speedy trial" is vague at best, and over the years the U.S. Supreme Court has attempted to clarify its meaning. In *Barker v. Wingo* (1972) the Court stated that the factors to be considered in determining whether a delay is justified are, generally, the length of the delay, the reason for the delay, the defendant's claim to the right to a speedy trial, and prejudice toward the defendant. In *Barker* a delay of five and a half years caused by sixteen state-requested continuances was allowed because of the need to convict a codefendant before proceeding against the accused and because of the illness of the chief investigating officer. When Willie Barker was eventually brought to trial, he was convicted and given a life sentence. The Court held that since the defendant did not ask for a speedy trial and did not assert that his right had been violated until three years after his arrest, he had not been deprived of his due process right to a speedy trial.

Most states have statutes that fix the period of time during which an accused must be brought to trial. In addition, to ensure that a person's trial in a federal court not be unduly delayed or that a suspect not be held in custody indefinitely, the U.S. Congress passed the Speedy Trial Act of 1974. According to this act, which was supposed to go into effect by 1979, federal cases had to be brought to trial within one hundred days of a person's arrest. If cases were not tried within this period, federal prosecutors faced the possibility that their charges against defendants would be dismissed. Despite the planned five-year delay in the implementation of the Speedy Trial Act, the federal courts were backlogged with cases to such an extent that Congress was forced to postpone its implementation indefinitely.

Raymond Frey

The Sixth Amendment

In all criminal prosecutions, the accused shall enjoy the right to a speedy and public trial, by an impartial jury of the State and district wherein the crime shall have been committed; which district shall have been previously ascertained by law, and to be informed of the nature and cause of the accusation; to be confronted with the witnesses against him; to have compulsory process for obtaining witnesses in his favor, and to have the assistance of counsel for his defence.

Further Reading

Campbell, Andrea. *Rights of the Accused*. Philadelphia: Chelsea House, 2001.

Garcia, Alfredo. *The Sixth Amendment in Mod-*

ern American Jurisprudence. Westport, Conn.: Greenwood Press, 1992.

Lewis, Thomas T., ed. *The Bill of Rights.* 2 vols. Pasadena, Calif.: Salem Press, 2002.

Smith, Christopher E. *Courts and Trials: A Reference Handbook.* Santa Barbara, Calif.: ABC-Clio, 2003.

See also Bail system; *Barker v. Wingo*; Bill of Rights, U.S.; Citations; Criminal prosecution; Defendants; Indictment; Plea bargaining; Trials.

Sports and crime

Criminal justice issues: Business and financial crime; media; victimless crime; violent crime

Significance: Once regarded as an unpleasant but normal part of sports, criminal behavior by athletes and fans now receives focused attention by the criminal justice system. Arrests of both athletes and fans for misbehavior on and off the field of play help to illustrate how many of the problems of violent behavior directly related to sport relate to violent problems in other areas of society.

The concept of "sports crime" has no one specific definition but encompasses three main areas of importance: crowd and fan violence, criminal behavior of players outside the field of play, and criminal behavior of players on the field of play. Each of these areas of sport crime presents the criminal justice system with its own specific challenges.

Crowd and Fan Violence

Compared to other countries—particularly in Europe and South America—the United States has relatively law-abiding and peaceful sports fans. However, while the frequency of violent behavior by fans and the severity of fan violence is substantially higher in many other countries, there is enough sport-related crowd and fan violence in the United States to merit considerable attention from the U.S. criminal justice system.

The most common form of crowd violence is fights among fans attending sporting events.

While many of these fights are minor in nature and do not escalate beyond verbal arguments, the modern trend appears to be toward greater frequency and higher levels of violence. For example, in 2002 a Massachusetts court convicted a man for the involuntary manslaughter of another man during an argument that arose over the amount of slashing and checking that was occurring during a youth hockey practice in which their sons were participating. Fan violence has become prevalent enough at sporting events that some stadiums, such as Philadelphia's Veterans Stadium, have set up temporary jails during football games to house fans who become overly intoxicated or engage in abusive and violent behavior.

In addition to fans assaulting other fans, there have also been growing numbers of incidents in which fans have assaulted athletes, both on and off the field. A particularly notable instance of fan violence directed toward an athlete occurred in Germany in 1993, when a German fan of tennis star Steffi Graf stabbed tennis star Monica Seles during a tennis match. Violence of that level directed at athletes is almost unknown at U.S. sporting events. Less violent incidents are not uncommon, however. For example, in November, 2004, near-riotous conditions erupted during the midst of a professional basketball game between the Detroit Pistons and the visiting Indian Pacers, when a fan threw an object at a player who responded by jumping into the stands after him. Soon, a large numbers of players and fans were fighting in the stands and on the court. Afterward, a number of arrests were made and several star players received long suspensions.

In 2002, a Chicago White Sox fan and his fifteen-year-old son jumped onto the playing field during a White Sox game with the Kansas City Royals and physically attacked the Royals' first base coach. That incident attracted national headlines. Earlier, another man had run onto the same field and tackled an umpire for what he regarded as an unfair call against his team. In response to those events, Illinois lawmakers introduced a new law that extended the offense of criminal trespass to places of public amusement, specifically targeting people who illegally enter playing fields, locker rooms, or stages.

Violence at sporting events can also occur at a group level among crowds in what often turn into riotous circumstances before, during, and after games. A form of crowd violence, which has become so common that it is now often expected, occurs during what have been labeled "celebratory riots" by fans of winning teams. Such riots may occur in spectator stands, on playing fields, or outside stadiums. To some extent, they follow old traditions of joyous fans doing such things as pouring onto football fields and tearing down goal posts after important or unexpected victories.

Crowd riots also can occur after losses by home teams. In 1999, for example, after the Michigan State men's basketball team suffered a loss in the National Collegiate Athletic Association's (NCAA) basketball championship tournament, crowds in East Lansing, Michigan, set sixty-one fires, threw frozen beer cans at police, and caused over $250,000 worth of damage. In response, law-enforcement officers made 132 arrests, of which 10 resulted in felony sentences. During the 2005 NCAA basketball tournament, Michigan State was again eliminated in the championship bracket and students in East Lansing again rioted.

Although there is some debate over the specific causes of crowd riots, most research suggests that the events occurring during games have less to do with providing incentives for rioting than the circumstances surrounding the events. In fact, police records show that many rioters ar-

One of the worst brawls in modern American sports history occurred during a professional basketball game between the Indiana Pacers and the Detroit Pistons at the latters' Auburn, Hills, Michigan, arena on November 19, 2004. After a minor scuffle between Pacer center Ron Artest and Piston center Ben Wallace, Artest lay down on a table, and a Detroit fan threw a drink on him. Artest responded by jumping into the stands to retaliate. Soon players were involved in a free-for-all that spilled onto the court. *(AP/Wide World Photos)*

rested after sporting events do not even attend the games that trigger the riots.

Athlete Crimes "Off the Field"

Some of the most celebrated criminal cases in modern U.S. history have involved athletes. The criminal proceedings against such well-known athletes as former football star O. J. Simpson, boxer Mike Tyson, and basketball star Kobe Bryant have attracted the most attention and publicity, but many more cases are disposed of quickly in the courts and receive little attention from the media. Arrests and convictions of both professional and amateur athletes for crimes such as sexual assault, aggravated battery, drug possession and sales, domestic violence, drunk driving, and even homicide no longer have the shocking impact on the public they once had. After Charles Barkley made the controversial statement in a 1993 shoe commercial that children should not view athletes as role models, Americans became more accustomed to seeing athletes charged for criminal offenses.

Although it is not known whether athletes commit crimes at a rate greater or less than that of nonathletes, it is clear that the criminal behavior of athletes has an association with the nature of sports in American society. Research conducted on athletes who engage in criminal behavior off the field of play has found many similarities between the causes of athletes' criminal behavior and the criminal behavior of nonathletes. More specifically, however, research has found that the specific cultural environment surrounding sports and athletes can contribute to criminal behavior of athletes outside the sporting arena.

For most professional athletes, socialization from an early age often encourages aggressive and violent behavior. From childhood through professional careers, athletes find themselves in a world that puts heavy emphasis on heroic values and winning. The consequent combat sport subculture rarely tolerates losing, even if it means playing "outside the lines" to win. Not only do athletes learn to be aggressive and to win at any cost, but coaches, teammates, and fans also frequently reward the overly aggressive behavior of athletes.

In addition, athletes often are involved in sport cultures in which failing to live up to the ex-

pectations of peer groups—such as being masculine and tough—is often punished by receiving less playing time or being ignored by the television media. When athletes carry these values into life outside sports, their illegal behaviors are often ignored or downplayed by many in the community because of admiration for the athletes' abilities. The resulting lack of punishment leads to a sense of entitlement on the part of athletes who may conclude that their actions, no matter how criminal, have few negative consequences.

Athlete Crimes "On the Field"

Legal concern with excessive violence in sport in the United States is far from a recent development. As far back in U.S. history as 1905, President Theodore Roosevelt threatened to outlaw, by executive order, the sport of football following a game in which a University of Pennsylvania football player assaulted an opposing player. Roosevelt stated that the player had been beaten to a "bloody pulp." After Roosevelt's time, however, threats of criminal and civil litigation against athletes was virtually nonexistent in the United States for more than a half century. The situation changed during the 1970's, when several landmark court cases began to challenge the use of excessive violence in sport and attempted to hold those engaged in such behavior criminally responsible for their violent actions.

The most famous court case occurred in 1975, when David Forbes of the National Hockey League's (NHL) Boston Bruins "checked" Henry Boucha of the Minnesota North Stars into the boards with his "elbows up." Boucha retaliated by punching Forbes. Both players were given seven minutes of penalty time, during which they continued arguing. As the players finally left the penalty box to return to their team benches, Forbes followed Boucha and hit him over the head with his hockey stick. After Boucha fell to the ice, Forbes continued his attack and slammed Boucha's head into the ice. Boucha suffered a fractured eye socket and required twenty-five stitches for facial cuts.

NHL officials concluded that an unprecedented ten-game suspension of Forbes was warranted, but a Minnesota grand jury indicted Forbes for aggravated assault with a dangerous weapon. The jury in Forbes's criminal trial voted

9 to 3 in favor of conviction, but since it could not reach a unanimous verdict, a mistrial was declared. Forbes was never retried. Interestingly the nine jurors who voted for conviction later stated that their reason for wanting to convict Forbes was that they believed his assault was technically "out of play." Had the incident occurred during play, they would have been reluctant to convict.

In 2004, the Forbes case remained the only modern American criminal prosecution of an athlete in a major professional league for activity engaged in during a game. However, there have been recent examples of semi-professional players who have been convicted of participant-on-participant violence during games. In addition, other countries such as Canada have had a history of criminally charging and convicting players for actions occurring during professional games. Hockey player Marty McSorley was tried in Vancouver for criminal assault during a game in 2002, and Todd Bertuzzi was also tried in Vancouver for assault in 2004. Both cases received worldwide attention and may eventually have an impact on the criminal justice system in the United States.

Barriers to Prosecuting Violence "On the Field"

The justice system faces many societal pressures when it attempts to charge athletes for criminal assaults during play because of the unique context of sporting events. Many prosecutors hesitate to burden courts with assaults that the public may regard as nonthreatening to public safety. Prosecutors are also concerned that they should be focusing on more "serious" criminals whose behavior better warrants their attention. Moreover, many people fear that holding athletes criminally responsible for overly aggressive actions during play may drastically change sports as they are known. Arguments that athletes should be immune to prosecution for assaults in sports competitions arise from concerns that players may become tentative and lack the intensity required to make games entertaining for spectators.

Lawyers prosecuting sports violence cases face an unusual set of legal obstacles that make logistical aspects of their task more difficult than in other kinds of cases. For example, victims of as-

saults on the field often do not see themselves as victims and—like many fans—regard their victimization as "part of the game." Moreover, many athletes view victims of violence in competition who are willing to testify against their attackers as traitors to their teams and place pressure on victims not to testify.

In cases of sports violence, the prosecution must typically prove that the defendants committed assault and battery against their victims with intent to cause harm. It is quite difficult to prove *mens rea* during sporting events that involve quick decision making and physical contact as integral parts of competition. Prosecutors thus have difficulty proving intent.

Even when intent to cause harm is established, prosecutors must deal with the defense of consent—a special problem in sports because athletes who participate in inherently violent sporting events are, in effect, consenting to the types of physical contact that commonly occur in the events. The question that arises next is the extent of implied consent that athletes give during games. While consent is limited to acts that occur in the ordinary and normal conduct of a game, what constitutes "ordinary and normal conduct" is difficult to define. For example, a professional boxer who enters the ring against an opponent gives consent to be repeatedly punched in the face, within the rules of boxing; however, the boxer does not consent to being repeatedly hit below the belt, because boxing forbids that kind of hitting. Hard body checks in hockey games and hard tackles in football games are almost always considered ordinary parts of those sports and are often not against the rules. However, problems of definition arise when a boxer's punch, a hockey player's body check, or a football player's tackle goes beyond what players consider normal. Examples might include a hockey player's check on the back of an opponent's neck using a hockey stick or a football player's blindside tackle of an opponent who has stepped out of bounds.

Legislative attempts to outlaw excessive violence in sports have generally failed. In 1980, for example, Ohio congressman Ronald Mottl wrote the Sports Violence Act and the Sports Violence Arbitration Act, which intended to "deter and punish through criminal penalties, the episodes of excessive violence that characterize professional sports." Similarly, Congressman (later Senator) Tom Daschle of South Dakota attempted to introduce a similar bill in 1983 seeking to impose civil law remedies by an arbitration board. Both attempts were unsuccessful.

Ryan K. Williams

Further Reading

Buford, Bill. *Among the Thugs*. New York: Vintage Books, 1993. Very personal look into British football (soccer) hooligans by an American journalist. Buford followed a group of violent supporters of the Manchester United team to matches throughout Europe and attempted to discover some of the underlying causes of their aggressive behavior. Buford helps readers to distinguish between traditional hooliganism and other forms of crowd violence.

Dunning, Eric. *Sport Matters: Sociological Studies of Sport, Violence, and Civilization*. New York: Routledge, 1999. Covers a wide range of issues surrounding the study of modern sport. Topics include spectator violence in both the United Kingdom and North America as well as issues surrounding the globalization of sport and gender issues in sport.

Feinstein, John, and Terry Adams. *The Punch: One Night, Two Lives, and the Fight That Changed Basketball Forever*. Boston: Little, Brown, 2002. Discusses an on-the-court incident in a 1977 National Basketball Association game in which Kermit Washington struck opposing player Rudy Tomjanovich and shattered the bones in his face.

Goldstein, Jeffrey H. *Why We Watch: The Attractions of Violent Entertainment*. London: Oxford University Press, 1998. Attempts to answer the question of why violence in popular entertainments is both appealing and difficult to regulate. Contributors look at the appeal of violence in a wide range of entertainment categories including movies and television. Also contains chapters on sports, children's toys, and games and even religion.

Messner, Michael, and Donald Sabo. *Sex, Violence, and Power in Sports: Rethinking Masculinity*. Freedom, Calif.: Crossing Press, 1994. Examines the culture of male sports and its relation to concepts of masculinity. Messner and Sabo investigate the ways racism, sexism, and homophobia on the part of athletes can result in violent consequences.

Tatum, Jack. *They Call Me Assassin*. New York: Avon Books, 1980. Controversial unrepentant memoir by a former professional defensive football star who is most remembered for a hit on receiver Darryl Stingley in 1978 that left the latter permanently paralyzed.

See also Celebrity criminal defendants; Criminal intent; Criminal liability; Gambling; Moral turpitude.

Stakeouts

Definition: Tactical deployments of law-enforcement officers to specific locations for the purpose of surreptitiously observing criminal suspects to gather information or to stop crimes from occurring

Criminal justice issues: Crime prevention; investigation; technology

Significance: Stakeouts are frequently high-profile tactical operations that can present risks to officers, offenders, and bystanders alike. As forms of police intervention, they may involve armed and violent criminal suspects. To avoid exposure and to minimize risks, stakeouts require careful tactical planning and complex team efforts.

The action-packed portrayals of police stakeouts that are often presented in novels, films, and television shows are misleading. The fictional kinds of stakeouts, in which cops sit in vehicles for an hour or so and then arrest multiple suspects, would rarely succeed in real life. Real stakeouts tend to be undramatic, tedious, and personally demanding.

Stakeouts take two basic forms: temporary and planned. Temporary stakeouts tend to be impromptu actions, undertaken as unexpected situations develop. They can also be high-risk operations. Most temporary or impromptu stakeouts result when officers are in the preliminary stages of investigations or discover pending criminal activity that requires immediate action.

To succeed, surveillance and stakeout teams

must blend into neighborhoods to avoid being detected themselves. Fictional stakeouts often show officers sitting in their cars for hours in the suspects' neighborhoods. However, occupied vehicles parked for prolonged periods rarely go unnoticed. If investigators fail to be in harmony with their surroundings, they are likely to be identified, or—in stakeout jargon—"burned" or "made." The best results in temporary stakeouts occur when they are conducted from fixed and secure positions, such as buildings.

Planned stakeouts are more complex operations, whose success results from team efforts, not lone detective improvisation. Stakeout operations may offer opportunities to interrupt serial offenses, such as robbery, drug deals, and other offenses. For example, a crime analyst studying convenience-store robberies who discovers patterns in the methods of the robberies and trademark behaviors of the robbers would have reason to suspect that the robberies are part of a series. Moreover, the analyst might even see something in the patterns to suggest that certain stores are likely to be hit next. Drawing on the analyst's conclusions, a police lieutenant would organize a surveillance team to stake out the threatened stores. A major operation might have teams working both inside and outside the stores, so that careful coordination of their efforts would have be planned in advance.

Thomas E. Baker

Further Reading

Adams, James A., and Daniel D. Blinka. *Electronic Surveillance: Commentaries and Statutes*. Notre Dame, Ind.: National Institute for Trial Advocacy, 2003.

Lyman, Michael D., and Gary W. Potter. *Organized Crime*. Upper Saddle River, N.J.: Prentice-Hall, 2004.

Monmonier, M. S. *Spying with Maps: Surveillance Technologies and the Future of Privacy*. Chicago: University of Chicago Press, 2002.

Rossmo, D. Kim. *Geographic Profiling*. Boca Raton, Fla.: CRC Press, 2000.

See also Electronic surveillance; *Katz v. United States*; *Kyllo v. United States*; *Olmstead v. United States*; Privacy rights; Private detectives; Stop and frisk; Surveillance cameras; Wiretaps.

Stalking

Definition: Willful, malicious, or repeated following of another person

Criminal justice issues: Deviancy; domestic violence; victims

Significance: Stalking is a serious crime associated with other forms of criminal behavior.

Although stalking is perceived as a public health concern in the twenty-first century, the first antistalking legislation was not passed until 1990. Within five years, antistalking laws existed in all fifty states, and there is now a model antistalking code. However, the frequency with which stalking occurs is difficult to determine because of the varying interpretations of the law in each state. Part of the difficulty in determining stalking rates also stems from the low likelihood of a victim reporting the crime (about 50 percent), which makes enforcement difficult as well. Fear of reprisals keeps reporting rates low. Rates are also affected by the age of the subjects under study, the funding agency, and the venue in which the study is conducted.

If the law is narrowly interpreted, proof of a lethal intent may be necessary to pursue legal ac-

Preventing Stalking

The best strategy to prevent being stalked is to reduce opportunities for potential stalkers. It is always best to be aware of one's surroundings, to walk with other people and in well-lit areas, and to vary one's routes. Predictable patterns make it easier for stalkers to follow their targets. Further, in the modern age of the Internet, minor identifying information can assist stalkers in obtaining more personal information; home telephone numbers should be unlisted for the same reason.

Stalking victims should take special care to secure their residences with locks and alarms. They should also inform roommates, coworkers, and authorities of their situation. Law-enforcement officers cannot offer assistance if they do not know that crimes are occurring.

It is estimated that fewer than 25 percent of victims of stalking file for restraining orders, which require complainants to provide the names of their stalkers and to show that the stalking is part of a pattern of behavior. *(Brand-X Pictures)*

tion. Less than 25 percent of stalking victims file a criminal restraining order. To do so, the victim must know the name of the offender, show that the stalking behavior was a pattern and not an isolated incident, and show that the offender was trespassing. Many stalkers, however, do not come in contact with the victim, and some victims do not know the offender.

Another problem for victims is that the criminal justice system (and society) engages in victim-blaming. If the offender is not a stranger, and there is an interpersonal nature to the relationship, the victims are viewed as being at least partially responsible for their circumstances. The crime may then be trivialized, and the victim may not be taken seriously.

Despite these problems, there is now much knowledge about the categories of stalking and the reasons stalkers commit the crime. For example, most stalking occurs between parties after a relationship ends. Some stalkers delude themselves into believing that relationships exist between themselves and their victims. However, other stalkers do not seek relationships at all with their targets. Further, statistics suggest that 200,000 persons are stalked annually, and

between 81 percent and 90 percent of women killed by their husbands or boyfriends were stalked prior to their deaths. The National Sexual Victimization of College Women Survey showed that 13 percent of college women had been stalked within a six- to nine-month period, and the National Institute of Justice determined that more than one million women and 400,000 men had been stalked.

Links to Other Crimes

Stalking is clearly linked to other types of crime, including domestic violence and sexual harassment. All of these offenses involve issues of power and control. Victims are often stalked by persons who are their current or former intimate partners; many of these stalkers are domestic violence offenders. The crime of stalking is commonly intended to scare the victim into believing that the stalker is omnipotent. These intimidation tactics are used against victims of domestic violence or sexual harassment, and they are useful in perpetuating the feelings of helplessness among victims.

Stalking on college campuses is extensive and is closely linked to dating abuse. Stalking frequently occurs after a relationship ends, and it is likely to involve actual violence as well as threats of violence. In fact, the highest risk of a stalking victimization occurs with undergraduate students or in places where alcohol is present. Victims in these settings claim unwanted phone calls are the most common form of stalking experienced.

Stalking is also associated with a history of other criminal acts, substance abuse, and psychiatric disorders. Stalkers tend to suffer from some type of personality or mental disorder. Further, many stalkers come from abusive homes. Interestingly, most offenders are white men, and most are of above-average intelligence. Women make up from 10 percent to 13 percent of stalkers, and they are likely to fit the category of an obsessional stalker (one who repeatedly follows or threatens another person in an attempt to frighten, cause harm, or control the victim). Conversely, most victims are white women, who claim they have been spied upon or followed. This behavior can affect a target physically and emotionally; victims tend to lose weight and become depressed, anxious, and irritable. Many experience difficulty sleeping and concentrating. Between 20 percent and 30 percent of victims seek psychological counseling as a result.

Gina M. Robertiello

Further Reading

Fisher, B. S., F. T. Cullen, and M. G. Turner. *The Sexual Victimization of College Women*. Washington, D.C.: National Institute of Justice, Bureau of Justice Statistics, 2000.

Haugaard, J. J., and L. G. Seri. "Stalking and Other Forms of Intrusive Contact Among Adolescents and Young Adults from the Perspective of the Person Initiating the Intrusive Contact." *Criminal Justice and Behavior* 31, no. 1 (2004): 37-54.

Meloy, J. R., and C. Boyd. "Female Stalkers and Their Victims." *Journal of the American Academy of Psychiatry and the Law* 31, no. 2 (2003): 211-219.

Pathe, M. T., P. E. Mullen, and R. Purcell. "Same-gender Stalking." *Journal of the American Academy of Psychiatry and the Law* 28, no. 2 (2000): 191-197.

Phillips, L., R. Quirk, B. Rosenfeld, and M. O'Connor. "Is it Stalking? Perceptions of Stalking Among College Undergraduates." *Criminal Justice and Behavior* 31, no. 1 (2004): 73-96.

Sfiligoj, T. M. "A Comparison of Stalkers and Domestic Violence Batterers." *Journal of Psychological Practice* 8, no. 1 (2003): 20-45.

Tjaden, P., and N. Thoennes. "Prevalence and Consequences of Male-to-Female and Female-to-Male Intimate Partner Violence as Measured by the National Violence Against Women Survey." *Violence Against Women* 6, no. 2 (2000): 142-161.

See also Arrest; Breach of the peace; Cybercrime; Date rape; Domestic violence; Restraining orders; Sexual harassment; Trespass; Victimology.

Standards of proof

Definition: Rules determining how much and what sort of evidence is enough to win cases in courts of law

Criminal justice issues: Evidence and forensics; professional standards; trial procedures

Significance: Without well-established and uniformly applied standards of proof, no one would be assured of a fair trial.

There are three separate standards of proof, two for "civil" (noncriminal) cases and another for criminal cases. In most civil cases, the standard is generally said to require proving a case "by a preponderance of the evidence." This means convincing the court that one side's position is more likely true than the other side's position. In these cases, the same standard applies to both sides.

In some civil cases, such as those involving fraud, the party bringing the lawsuit is required to prove a case by providing "clear and convincing evidence." Under this standard, the court must be persuaded that the accusation or claim is highly probable, not merely more likely true than not true.

These civil standards are basically "judge-made"; that is, they were developed as part of the English common law, and those traditions have been followed by American courts. The distinction between the two types of civil cases has its origin in ancient English law, where there were two court systems, one of law and one of "equity." Cases heard in law courts were decided under the "preponderance" standard, while those heard in courts of equity were decided under the "clear and convincing" standard.

Although most modern American court systems have only courts of law, the ancient distinction still remains. Sometimes the standard to be applied is included in the law the court is asked to enforce; where the statute does not say, however, the courts resort to the common-law tradition and to their understanding of the legislature's purposes in passing the law.

In a criminal case, the party bringing the case is the government, which is usually far more powerful and with much less to lose than the other side. A much higher standard of proof is applied to the government: Before it can win, it must prove its position "beyond a reasonable doubt." That means the accused person cannot be found guilty unless the court is convinced that the government has definitely proved every necessary part of its case. This standard has long been followed in both England and the United States, and it has been expressly required in American criminal cases since 1970, when the U.S. Supreme Court formally adopted that language in *In re Winship* (1970).

Douglas E. Baker

Further Reading

ABA Standards for Criminal Justice: The Prosecution Function. 3d. ed. Washington, D.C.: American Bar Association, 1992.

Reid, Sue Titus. *Criminal Justice.* 6th ed. Cincinnati: Atomic Dog Publishing, 2001.

Samaha, J. *Criminal Law.* 8th ed. Belmont, Calif.: Thomson/Wadsworth, 2004.

See also Burden of proof; Criminal procedure; Evidence, rules of; Presumption of innocence; Reasonable doubt; Simpson trials; Sobriety testing.

Stanford v. Kentucky

The Case: U.S. Supreme Court ruling on cruel and unusual punishment

Date: Decided on June 26, 1989

Criminal justice issues: Capital punishment; juvenile justice

Significance: In this case, the Supreme Court held that the Eighth Amendment's prohibition against cruel and unusual punishment did not prevent the execution of individuals who were juveniles at the time they committed the crimes for which they were executed.

The Supreme Court's decision addressed two cases, one involving a seventeen-year-old male convicted of first-degree murder for having robbed a gas station and then raped, sodomized, and shot to death a station attendant, and the other involving a sixteen-year-old sentenced to death for having robbed a convenience store, stabbed the attendant, and left her to die. Both criminal defendants had been tried as adults.

The Supreme Court held that the Eighth Amendment's "cruel and unusual punishment" clause did not bar states from executing individuals who were sixteen and seventeen years of age at the time they committed the applicable crimes. The Court noted that such executions were not the kinds of punishment considered cruel and unusual at the time the Bill of Rights was adopted. Furthermore, the Court concluded that the executions at issue in the case were not contrary to "evolving standards of decency that mark the progress of a maturing society." Justice Sandra Day O'Connor concurred in this holding but wrote separately to emphasize her belief that the Court had a constitutional obligation to assure in each case that a particular defendant's blameworthiness was proportional to the sentence imposed. Justice Antonin Scalia, who wrote the majority opinion and the opinion of four justices on this point, argued that the Court had never invalidated a punishment solely because of an asserted disproportion between the punishment and the defendant's blameworthiness.

Justices William J. Brennan, Thurgood Marshall, Harry A. Blackmun, and John Paul Stevens dissented. These justices stated that the "cruel and unusual punishment" clause of the Eighth Amendment bars the execution of any person for a crime committed while the person was under age eighteen. Justice Brennan, writing for the dissenters, asserted that such executions violated contemporary standards of decency. He pointed out that the laws of a majority of states would not have permitted the executions at issue in this case and that in the vast majority of cases involving juvenile offenders, juries did not impose the death penalty. The justice concluded by arguing that the imposition of the death penalty for juvenile crimes served the interests of neither retribution nor deterrence. Capital punishment in these cases did not serve the interests of retribution since, according to Justice Brennan, the penalty was disproportionate to the defendants' blameworthiness. The punishment did not advance the interests of deterrence since juveniles were not likely to make the kind of cost-benefit analysis that would dissuade them from committing a crime for fear of receiving the death penalty.

Timothy L. Hall

Further Reading

Bedau, Hugo Adam, and Paul Cassell. *Debating the Death Penalty: Should America Have Capital Punishment? The Experts on Both Sides Make Their Best Case.* Oxford, England: Oxford University Press, 2003.

Berkson, Larry. *The Concept of Cruel and Unusual Punishment.* Lexington, Mass.: Lexington Books, 1975.

Bohm, Robert M. *Deathquest: An Introduction to the Theory and Practice of Capital Punishment in the United States.* Cincinnati: Anderson Publishing, 2003.

Cox, Steven M., John J. Conrad, and Jennifer M. Allen. *Juvenile Justice: A Guide to Theory and Practice.* 5th ed. New York: McGraw Hill, 2003.

See also Bill of Rights, U.S.; Capital punishment; Constitution, U.S.; Cruel and unusual punishment; Juvenile justice system; Punishment; Supreme Court, U.S.

Stare decisis

Definition: Deciding of cases on the basis of judicial precedent in similar cases

Criminal justice issues: Appeals; law codes; legal terms and principles; trial procedures

Significance: This principle gives continuity and predictability to the entire body of common-law decisions.

Stare decisis comes from a Latin term meaning "to stand by things that have been settled." Under this principle of law, judicial decisions that have been made in cases similar to the one under consideration are accepted as authoritative. *Stare decisis* involves, in addition to how judges in the past decided similar cases, what the basic judicial principles followed were. (It is accepted that specific circumstances will vary.) Often more than one case will be cited to illustrate the stability and continuity of the principles judged to apply in the current case. The principle applies only to the actual decision and not to the arguments substantiating that decision. Thus, a later case could be decided similarly to an earlier one but for different reasons.

Many arguments on questions of the law have already been settled in earlier cases. When the same point is again in controversy in a trial court, the earlier precedent is judged to be binding on the later court decision. This principle provides a degree of certitude as to what the law actually says about similar issues. It gives a consistency to court decisions that might not be possible if earlier decisions were not consulted. Appellate courts similarly follow the principle of *stare decisis*, but they are not under the same obligation as is a trial court. If two principles of the law come into conflict, or if the court seeks to remedy a continued and obvious injustice, appellate courts can deviate from judicial precedent and break new ground.

Precedents can be overruled and, in fact, have been many times. Courts often look at the presumed results of a decision. Occasionally such a prediction will prompt the judge to alter a decision. The judicial philosophy of a particular judge or justice can also influence a court decision. Judicial activists are more likely to overturn a precedent than are judges who believe it is their duty to defer to legislative intent. In the absence of clear legislation, that philosophy tends to follow decisions of earlier courts.

In *Helvering v. Hallock* (1940), Supreme Court Justice Felix Frankfurter called *stare decisis* "a principle of policy and not a mechanical formula," especially when adhering to the principle would involve "collision with a prior doctrine more embracing in its scope, intrinsically sounder, and verified by experience." It is not unusual for the U.S. Supreme Court to overrule its own decisions. The New Deal era Court, for example, did that several times. The most celebrated Court reversal was *Brown v. Board of Education* in 1954, which overruled the "separate-but-equal" segregation doctrine of *Plessy v. Ferguson* (1896).

Overruling judicial precedent is a serious responsibility because it not only changes what has been accepted as law but also implies that the judge or judges making the earlier rules were either mistaken or philosophically wrong. A court must show respect for the knowledge and intelligence of previous judges. Even when an earlier decision can be shown to be legally or constitutionally flawed, stability is a consideration. If changing a decision would disrupt society excessively or create political chaos, judges are reluctant to break with the continuity of precedent.

Closely related to *stare decisis* is the principle of *res judicata* ("a matter settled by judgment"). This means that once a matter is judicially settled by the courts, continued suits on the same matter will not be permitted. Once decided, a decision is laid to rest.

William H. Burnside

Further Reading

Garner, Bryan A., ed. *Black's Law Dictionary*. 8th ed. St. Paul, Minn.: Thomson/West, 2004.

Holmes, Oliver Wendell, Jr. *The Common Law*. Boston: Little, Brown, 1909.

Pekelis, Alexander H. *Law and Social Action*. New York: Da Capo Press, 1970.

Schwartz, Bernard. *The Law in America: A History*. New York: McGraw-Hill, 1974.

See also Annotated codes; Appellate process; Case law; Common law; Evidence, rules of; Judicial review; Judicial system, U.S.; Opinions; *Payne v. Tennessee*.

State police

Definition: Law-enforcement organizations that operate directly under the authority of state governments, rather than under municipalities

Criminal justice issues: Law-enforcement organization; police powers; traffic law

Significance: State police carry out certain specific functions, principally highway safety and criminal investigations.

The U.S. Constitution assigned to the states the responsibility for maintaining law and order. Until 1900, however, the states entrusted policing mainly to local communities. In case of riots or other serious disorders, governors called out the militia. In Texas, the Rangers, a mounted militia, kept the peace in isolated areas in addition to fighting Native Americans and patrolling the Mexican border. Between 1865 and 1875, Massachusetts experimented with a state constabulary. During the late nineteenth century, public sentiment remained hostile toward the idea of professional state police forces.

Early State Police Forces

During the 1890's, the United States underwent rapid industrialization and grew more interdependent, its parts connected by a vast network of railroads. Crime became more mobile and complex, challenging the resources of local police. At the dawn of the twentieth century there was a pressing need for more specialized, better-trained police at the state level.

The first state to meet that need was Pennsylvania. Like many other newly industrialized areas of the Northeast and Midwest since the Civil War (1861-1865), Pennsylvania suffered chronically from severe social unrest, especially among workers in its coal mines and factories. A fierce, lengthy strike in the anthracite mines in 1902 aroused public opinion to demand that other, more civilized means be found of calming industrial disputes than the indiscriminate clubbing of mine workers by private police. This outcry set in motion a reform movement led by Governor Samuel W. Pennypacker to create a state police. The governor sent John C. Groome, a former officer in the Philippine Constabulary, to Ireland, where he studied the Royal Irish Constabulary. In 1905 Groome organized the Pennsylvania State Police, recruiting 228 men with military backgrounds, some of whom had also been officers in the Philippine Constabulary. They were given rigorous training and then deployed in four units in western Pennsylvania, where they proved to be impartial and effective at quelling disorder.

Fourteen states established police forces over the next twenty years, the eastern states generally following Pennsylvania's example. Western states, such as Nevada and Colorado, created forces that were extremely brutal and partial to the interests of wealthy absentee employers, especially in the mining industry. During the 1920's, modern highways spread out across the United States, creating a new task for state police: traffic control. This required a new approach to policing. Persons wealthy enough to own or drive automobiles were likely to be prosperous merchants and professionals rather than foreign-born coal miners. Police had to be recruited and trained who could deal civilly with middle-class taxpayers, offering traffic safety programs and mildly enforcing traffic regulations.

At the same time, the expense of installing the technology to fight crime led many states to establish bureaus of criminal identification. By 1940 highway patrols or state police were at work in more than 80 percent of the states. They had earned reputations as "elite lawmen." Since World War II, state police have continued to be concerned mainly with traffic control, while assuming a more significant role in criminal investigation. State police agencies are characterized by their narrow, specific mandates, reflecting public distrust of centralized policing in the European tradition.

Because most police work is done by municipal police forces and county sheriffs' offices, state police are involved mostly in highway safety and statewide criminal investigations. *(Brand-X Pictures)*

Organization of State Police

The term "state police" is broadly understood to refer to the various agencies of law enforcement that function directly under the authority of the governments of the states, in contrast to county and local police agencies and federal police agencies. This broad definition of state police includes highway patrols, state police forces, and a variety of state investigative agencies. In 1993 there were 87,000 state police in the widest sense of the term, which amounted to 9.7 percent of all sworn law-enforcement personnel in the United States. In contrast, there were 110,000 federal, 173,000 county, and 465,000 municipal police. All U.S. states except Hawaii have state policing agencies. Twenty-six states have highway patrols and twenty-three have state police agencies. Thirty-five states have investigative agencies that are separate from highway patrols or state police. There are, in addition, a great number of specialized investigative bodies, such as fire marshals and fish and wildlife agents. All state law-enforcement entities derive their authority to investigate wrongdoing or enforce the law from the state legislatures, from which they receive most of their funds.

State law enforcement is organized differently from state to state. In some states several agencies are centralized in one department. The Iowa Department of Public Safety, which is headed by a commissioner who reports to the governor, oversees the divisions of state patrol, criminal investigation, fire marshal, capitol security, communications, and administrative services. In other states, law-enforcement agencies are organized in various departments. The California Highway Patrol, for example, is organized in the Business, Transportation, and Housing Agency while the state's investigative agencies are grouped together in the Division of Law Enforcement under a director appointed by the state attorney general. Some state police agencies are controlled by commissions and others by state governors.

State Police Powers

State police in the narrow sense, in contrast to highway patrols, have state-wide powers to arrest persons suspected of both criminal and traffic offenses. Most state police agencies have plainclothes and uniformed agents. They provide the auxiliary services of record-keeping, training, communications, and forensics. Pennsylvania has the largest state police agency and Idaho the smallest.

State highway patrols are usually limited to enforcing traffic regulations, but they are empowered to assist any law-enforcement officer upon request. The investigation of crime is generally left to separate state investigative agencies. California has the largest highway patrol and Wyoming the smallest.

Investigative agencies with statewide authority to arrest have primary jurisdiction in certain crimes. Criminal investigative personnel are plainclothes officers who provide a variety of auxiliary services. They are distinguished from other state investigative agents, such as fish and game inspectors, whose powers are limited to a particular area of enforcement. Florida has the largest state bureau of investigation and North Dakota and South Dakota the smallest.

Role of State Police Broadly Considered

All state law-enforcement agencies require that applicants be U.S. citizens and state residents. Most state police agencies provide a basic course of instruction and training, usually at police academies, and in-service training. The minimum educational requirement is usually a high school diploma or equivalent. The investigative agencies of California and several other states require that applicants must have completed two or more years of college, concentrating on police sciences.

Regardless of how differently state police systems are organized, they share common functions within law enforcement. They investigate certain crimes as prescribed by state law and provide forensic and other technical services to local police. They also provide specialized investigators, such as narcotics squads, to assist investigations by local agencies. State police enforce, with the power of arrest, state traffic laws and laws pertaining to certain criminal offenses. Usually state constitutions assign to county and municipal police the general responsibility for enforcing state laws and keeping the peace. If rural or unincorporated areas are unwilling or unable to perform these functions, they may contract or arrange for service by state police, as is the case in Alaska, Rhode Island, and Connecticut.

On rare occasions state governments may call upon their police to temporarily assume law-enforcement duties in municipalities, as in New York City in 1935 and Trenton, New Jersey, in 1983. With a few exceptions, the state police's authority to carry arms and to arrest is limited to the areas within state borders. States may enter into mutual agreements with one another that allow their respective police to cross borders in pursuit of fugitives.

State police forces provide information to themselves, to local police within their states, and to other state and federal agencies. Every state has access to the National Crime Information Center of the Federal Bureau of Investigation (FBI). They all have computer information systems for processing criminal records. The effectiveness of communication is improved by regional cooperation, as in the New England State Police Compact, under which police forces share resources in the investigation of organized crime. In most cases state law-enforcement agencies are responsible for collecting, transmitting, and publishing states' crime statistics. State law-enforcement agencies also supply forensic services to their own personnel and to other criminal justice agencies. For the most part, the employees of states' forensic institutions are civilians.

Examples of State Police Forces

Established in May 1905, the Pennsylvania state police was the first state police force in the United States. It is also the largest. Its organization is centralized under a commissioner, who is appointed by the governor and has the rank of colonel. Reporting directly to the commissioner is the Bureau of Professional Responsibility, the Office of General Counsel, the Office of the Budget, and Public Information. A chief of staff responsible for several bureaus of technical and administrative services also reports to the commissioner. A deputy commissioner responsible for a bureau of highway patrol, a bureau of criminal investigation, and five area commands also reports to the commissioner. In addition to the main forensic laboratory in Harrisburg, there are four regional crime laboratories serving local police. The Bureau of Criminal Investigation includes divisions of general investigation, organized crime, fire marshal, and drug-law enforcement.

Recruits to the Pennsylvania state police must be U.S. citizens, state residents, and high school graduates, and they must meet certain physical requirements. Cadets undergo a twenty-week trooper course at the training academy in Hershey followed by field training and periodic inservice instruction.

Founded in 1929, the California Highway Patrol has grown to be the largest agency of its kind in the United States that focuses on traffic control. Situated in the Business, Transportation, and Housing Agency, it is led by a commissioner, who is appointed by the governor. It is one of two primary state law-enforcement agencies, the other being the California Division of Law Enforcement, which is responsible for criminal identification and investigation and forensic and other technical investigative services. The California Highway Patrol requires its recruits to be U.S. citizens, holders of valid California driver's licenses and high school graduates. Moreover, they must meet certain physical and legal requirements. Recruits undergo a basic training course of twenty-two weeks at the academy in Yolo County.

Charles H. O'Brien

Further Reading

Bechtel, Kenneth H. *State Police in the United States: A Socio-Historical Analysis*. Westport, Conn.: Greenwood Press, 1995. Thorough, well-balanced study that examines the evolution of state policing in the political, economic, and social context of the early twentieth century.

Fisher, Scott M. *Courtesy, Service, Protection: The Iowa State Patrol*. Dubuque, Iowa: Kendall-Hunt, 1993. Detailed history of one state's state police force.

Johnson, David R. *American Law Enforcement: A History*. St. Louis, Mo.: Forum Press, 1981. Includes a chapter on the history of the state police.

Smith, Bruce. *The State Police: Organization and Administration*. Montclair, N.J.: Patterson Smith, 1969. Early, but still influential, study favorable to the concept of a centralized, professional state police force.

Stark, John. *Troopers: Behind the Badge*. West Trenton: New Jersey State Police Memorial Association, 1993. Journalist's lively, anecdotal account of the men and women in the New Jersey state police, one of the larger state police agencies.

Stephens, Donna M. *Soldiers of the Law: Oklahoma Highway Patrolmen During the Early Years, 1937-1964*. Philadelphia: Xlibris Corporation, 2003. Historical study of the early development of Pennsylvania's state police.

Torres, Donald A. *Handbook of State Police, Highway Patrols, and Investigative Agencies*. Westport, Conn.: Greenwood Press, 1987. Thorough treatment of the organization and administration of state police forces. This book is enhanced by many tables illustrating state police organization, illustrations of state uniforms and badges, and a detailed catalog of state police agencies.

See also Criminal justice system; Highway patrols; International Brotherhood of Police Officers; National Guard; Police; Sheriffs; Sobriety testing; Speeding detection; Traffic fines; Traffic law.

Status offenses

Definition: Offenses such as truancy, incorrigibility, or running away from home that are considered crimes when they are committed by juveniles but are not considered crimes when committed by adults

Criminal justice issues: Juvenile justice; victimless crime

Significance: Although status offenses generally pose no immediate threats to public safety, they may create cases difficult to resolve, require significant expenditures of court and community resources, and result in the removal of children from their homes.

Juvenile courts have jurisdiction over a broad range of behaviors including some behaviors that are illegal for minors but not illegal for adults. Indeed, part of the reason that the juvenile court system was originally established arose from the fact that adult courts lacked authority to deal

Most Common Status Offenses

✓ Curfew violations
✓ Incorrigibility (disobeying parents)
✓ Possession of alcohol
✓ Running away from home
✓ Truancy from school

with youths who ran away from home, refused to obey their parents, or failed to attend school. Most modern juvenile courts continue to handle status offense cases.

There are a number of reasons for enforcing status offenses. Some people believe that juvenile court involvement is needed because status offenders place themselves at risk or because status offense behaviors will lead to more serious types of criminal activity. Also, because juvenile courts are often sensitive to community demands for assistance, they are frequently willing to support parental or school authorities in their efforts to deal with problem behaviors exhibited by children.

Although there are compelling arguments for court involvement in status offense cases, not all courts have the resources or expertise necessary to deal effectively with such cases. Status offense cases can be complex and may be the products of years of family dysfunction, neglect, abuse, or ineffective parenting. Because of these complications, some courts limit their involvement in status offense cases or avoid them even when legal intervention is possible. Effective community resources for handling these cases do not always exist.

Preston Elrod

Further Reading

Elrod, Preston, and R. Scott Ryder. *Juvenile Justice: A Social Historical and Legal Perspective*. Gaithersburg, Md.: Aspen, 1999.

Lemmon, John H. "Invisible Youth: Maltreated Children and Status Offenders in the Juvenile Justice System—Politics, Science, and Children's Issues." In *Controversies in Juvenile Justice and Delinquency*, edited by Peter J. Benekos and Alida V. Merlo. Cincinnati: Anderson Publishing, 2004.

See also Alcohol use and abuse; Juvenile courts; Juvenile delinquency; Juvenile Justice and Delinquency Prevention Act; Juvenile justice system; *Parens patriae*.

Statutes

Definition: Laws enacted by legislative bodies and interpreted by courts, administrative agencies, and practicing lawyers of the appropriate jurisdictions
Criminal justice issue: Law codes
Significance: Statutes, or laws written by legislatures, are often contrasted with common law—that is, law arising primarily from judicial decisions and only later, if ever, codified in statutory or similar form.

In the United States, Great Britain, and other English-speaking countries, most law was traditionally of the common-law variety, the decision of legal questions being based on results in prior cases (precedent) and judges' own sense of equity or fairness in the case at hand. In the twentieth century the vastly increased pace of regulatory legislation, including antitrust, securities, environmental, labor, and various antidiscrimination laws, together with tax and commercial law statutes, meant that statutory law had become as important or more important than common law, especially at the federal level.

Courts and practicing attorneys still spend much of their time dealing with the interpretation and application of federal and state statutes. In this sense, the difference between the English-speaking countries and the so-called civil law jurisdictions, such as France and Italy, which do not have a common-law tradition and have always relied primarily on statutory law, has been reduced in recent times.

Statutes create work for lawyers at all levels of the legislation and interpretation process. Many senators, congressmen, and state legislators are themselves practicing attorneys, and legislative committees employ staff attorneys to provide technical assistance in drafting various bills. At the administrative level—for example, the Internal Revenue Service (IRS) for tax laws and the

Justice Department for antitrust or antidiscrimination statutes—still more lawyers are required to write regulations and supervise enforcement efforts.

Finally, many private attorneys emphasize statutory law in their day-to-day practice, especially in specialty areas that are largely statutory in nature. This type of practice is highly challenging, because it requires familiarity with legislative and administrative sources together with more widely known judicial or court decisions. Thus, a tax lawyer must remain up-to-date about new and proposed tax legislation, IRS regulations and rulings, and judicial decisions in tax-related cases.

A major debate has focused on the interpretation of statutes. While U.S. Supreme Court Justice Antonin Scalia and others have argued that statutes should be interpreted according to their literal language, their opponents have argued that legislative history, including committee reports and floor debates, should be accorded greater and at times decisive weight. A parallel debate has focused on the degree of deference that courts should accord to administrative agency decisions that delineate the scope or breadth of particular statutes. How these debates will turn out is uncertain, but the vehemence with which they have been conducted highlights the increasing importance of statutory law throughout the American legal system.

Michael A. Livingston

Further Reading

Conklin, Curt E. *An Historical and Bibliographic Introduction to the United States Statutes at Large.* Washington, D.C.: Government Publications Press, 1992.

Demleitner, Nora V., Douglas A. Berman, Marc L. Miller, and Ronald F. Wright. *Sentencing Law and Policy: Cases, Statutes, and Guidelines.* New York: Aspen Publishers, 2003.

Dubber, Markus Dirk. *Criminal Law: Model Penal Code.* New York : Foundation Press, 2002.

Federal Criminal Code and Rules. St. Paul, Minn.: West Publishing, 2003.

See also Animal abuse; Bill of attainder; Common law; Judges; Statutes of limitations; United States Code; United States Statutes at Large.

Statutes of limitations

Definition: Laws that disallow prosecution of crimes after specified periods of time elapse

Criminal justice issues: Law codes; prosecution

Significance: Offenders may be protected forever from prosecution if the maximum time periods set by the statutes for their crimes expire without the government's initiation of legal action.

Statutes of limitations are temporal in nature, that is, they deal with time limitations for prosecutions in criminal cases or for initiation of litigation in civil matters, such as torts or contracts. In criminal cases, the clock begins to tick at the moment of the crime, while the cause of action in civil cases generally accrues when the event occurs although sometimes it is postponed until the discovery of the condition that is the subject of the lawsuit.

The philosophical justifications for statutes of limitations include fairness. With the passage of time, witnesses' memories fade, their whereabouts may be undiscoverable, and evidence may be lost—all developments that can hurt defendants' opportunities for fair trials. The existence of statutes of limitations also encourages criminal justice officials to investigate crimes and proceed in an expeditious manner. In addition, the acts also permit closure for both innocent and guilty suspects, who need not fear arrest for minor crimes that occurred years earlier. A further benefit of the statutes is that they reduce the caseloads of unresolved crimes, allowing criminal justice personnel to concentrate on current crimes.

Every U.S. state selects the crimes that are subject to statutes of limitations and sets their individual durations. Misdemeanors frequently have two-year statutes of limitations, while serious crimes typically carry longer time periods. Murder and a small number of other crimes are generally exempted, leaving offenders forever subject to trial and punishment.

Statutes of limitations may be tolled or suspended under certain circumstances. For example, the clock stops when an accused person leaves the state to avoid being prosecuted. Some states allow exceptions for repressed memories of childhood abuse, which is often sexual in nature, and delay the imposition of the statute until a victim remembers the incidents.

The running of time under a criminal statute of limitation continues from occurrence of the offense until prosecution is commenced. What constitutes commencement of prosecution varies by state and may include the moment when either a complaint is filed, a warrant of arrest is issued, an indictment is handed down by a grand jury, or an information is filed. Statutes of limitations are the equivalent of affirmative defenses; therefore, it is the defendant's responsibility to raise the issue of the prohibition, and it is the prosecution's duty to show that the event occurred within the allotted time.

Susan Coleman

Further Reading

Gardner, Thomas J., and Terry M. Anderson. *Criminal Law*. 8th ed. Belmont, Calif.: Wadsworth/Thomson Learning, 2003.

Inciardi, James A. *Criminal Justice*. 7th ed. Fort Worth, Tex.: Harcourt College Publishers, 2002.

See also Brinks bank robbery; Canadian justice system; Criminal prosecution; Double jeopardy; Murder and homicide.

Statutory rape

Definition: Sexual intercourse with a person under the age of legal consent, regardless of whether or not the underage partner consents

Criminal justice issues: Juvenile justice; sex offenses

Significance: Statutory rape laws criminalize consensual sexual relations between unmarried adults and minors, regardless of the relationships between the participants. Questions of whether such offenses are to be prosecuted as felonies or misdemeanors depend on the specific provisions of individual state statutes.

Most state rape laws prohibiting sexual intercourse between legal adults and persons considered to be legal minors specify minimum ages of

Felony vs. Misdemeanor Statutory Rape in Louisiana

Known as "carnal knowledge of a juvenile" in Louisiana, statutory rape can be prosecuted there as either a felony or a misdemeanor offense. The distinction rests primarily on the ages of the offenders and their underage sex partners.

Type of offense	Age requirements	Punishment
Felony	Offenders are at least nineteen years old and have consensual sexual intercourse with nonspousal partners between twelve and seventeen years of age, or offenders are at least seventeen years old and have consensual sex with nonspousal partners between twelve and fifteen years of age.	Convictions are punishable by incarceration for up to ten years at hard labor.
Misdemeanor	Offenders are between seventeen and nineteen years of age and have consensual sexual intercourse with nonspousal partners between fifteen and seventeen years of age, and the differences between their ages are greater than two years.	Convictions are punishable by up to six months imprisonment.

the perpetrators or age differences between the perpetrators and their underage sex partners. The consent of victims and the belief by the perpetrators that their victims are of the age of consent are usually considered irrelevant.

Often, relationships exist between the parties to the act, and the offenses are reported to authorities by the parents of the younger partners—who are typically female—even though the parents may have known about their children's relationships for a period of time. It is usually a change in the parents' views of the perpetrators that move them to initiate complaints. Extenuating circumstances such as pregnancy, sexually transmitted diseases, or the parents' own inability to control their children result in the parents' pressing charges.

The necessity of criminal statutes against statutory rape remain apparent. A 1989 survey of male college undergraduates revealed that 7 percent of all respondents expressed a willingness to have sexual relationships with underage girls if they could avoid detection or punishment. Moreover, organizations such as the Renee Guyon Society, the North American Man Boy Love Association, the Childhood Sensuality Circle, and the Howard Nichols Society have been founded to encourage sexual activity between adults and youthful participants under the age of consent. In the absence of aggressive enforcement and prosecution of violations of criminal statutes on the books, underage children appear to be moving ever closer to losing the legal protections presently guaranteed to them by state governments.

Bernadette Jones Palombo

Further Reading

Cocca, Carolyn. *Jailbait: The Politics of Statutory Rape Laws in the United States*. Albany: State University of New York Press, 2004.

Dobbert, Duane L. *Halting the Sexual Predators Among Us: Preventing Attack, Rape, and Lust Homicide*. Westport, Conn.: Praeger, 2004.

Hazelwood, Robert R., and Ann Wolbert Burgess, eds. *Practical Aspects of Rape Investigation: A Multidisciplinary Approach*. 3d ed. Boca Raton, Fla.: CRC Press, 2001.

Holmes, Stephen T., and Ronald M. Holmes. *Sex Crimes: Patterns and Behavior*. 2d ed. Thousand Oaks, Calif.: Sage Publications, 2002.

Rosen, Marvin. *Dealing with the Effects of Rape and Incest*. Philadelphia: Chelsea House, 2002.

See also Abortion; Common law; Date rape; Rape and sex offenses; Sex offender registries.

Sting operations

Definition: Undercover police operations in which officers pose as criminals in order to trap law violators

Criminal justice issues: Government misconduct; police powers

Significance: Sting operations are now a major law-enforcement tactic, especially in dealing with drug trafficking, prostitution, and property theft crimes. Undercover sting operations can be effective law-enforcement tactics in combating crime. However, even for such cases prosecutors must be careful to apply fair-play and constitutional standards in their pursuit of criminals.

In typical sting operations, police officers pose as would-be purchasers ("fences") of stolen property; when criminals attempt to sell them stolen goods, the officers arrest them. Sting operations also often involve officers posing as buyers of illegal drugs to catch pushers. Studies have shown that sting operations are also effective against career burglars and motor vehicle thieves. However, studies of the effectiveness of sting operations in combating illegal drug activities have been inconclusive.

Sting operations are often criticized as unethical or even illegal forms of entrapment. They raise a host of issues not relevant to routine catch-the-crook-red-handed police work. For example, the police are not allowed to entrap people by inducing them to commit criminal acts that they are not otherwise predisposed to commit. Presenting predisposed criminals with apparent opportunities to commit a crime is the goal of sting operations, and it in itself does not constitute entrapment. However, there is often a thin line between a successful sting operation and illegal entrapment.

Recognizing the need to separate legal sting operations from illegal entrapment, the Federal Bureau of Investigation (FBI) has issued detailed descriptions of acceptable and unacceptable operations to its agents. A document with eighteen single-spaced pages, the FBI guidelines have been criticized as so overly complex and technical that they are likely to be violated frequently in real-life sting operations.

Another controversial area in sting operations is the use of intermediaries. In the Abscam scandal that involved U.S. Congress members during the 1970's, the FBI was criticized because its operation drew on the help of known criminals. Another issue is the belief by many that the mere existence of sting operations may lead innocent citizens to live in fear that "Big Brother" is watching them all the time.

Cliff Roberson

Two Big-Time Sting Operations

One of the most successful sting operations in modern history was conducted in Washington, D.C., from 1974 to 1980. Local police joined with agents of the Federal Bureau of Investigation and the Treasury Department to pose as members of the "New York Mafia." During a five-month period, the federal officers purchased some $2.4 million worth of stolen property for only $67,000 and arrested a total of 180 sellers.

In 1988, the FBI operated a high-tech electronic store in Miami that was used by drug traffickers to purchase electronic equipment, such as beepers, cell phones, and computers. Based on leads generated by these sales, the FBI arrested 93 drug traffickers in one seventeen-month period.

Further Reading

Dempsey, John. *An Introduction to Policing*. 2d ed. Belmont, Calif.: Wadsworth, 1999.

Miller, Linda, and Karen M. Hess. *The Police in the Community: Strategies for the Twenty-first Century*. Belmont, Calif.: Wadsworth, 2002.

See also Asset forfeiture; Defenses to crime; Drugs and law enforcement; Entrapment; Gambling; Political corruption.

Stop and frisk

Definition: Power of police to stop and search suspects or their property when there is reason to believe that the suspects have committed crimes or may be carrying concealed weapons

Criminal justice issues: Investigation; police powers; search and seizure

Significance: To protect the police from potentially armed suspicious persons during initial street encounters, police officers are permitted to conduct limited detentions and conduct limited searches for weapons.

Under the Fourth Amendment to the U.S. Constitution police officers are permitted to conduct warrantless searches incidental to a lawful arrest provided that the arrest and subsequent search is reasonable and is based on probable cause. Probable cause has been defined by the courts as enough information to make a police officer believe that a crime has been, is being, or is about to be committed and that the person arrested is the suspect in the crime.

Most suspicious activities observed by the police during routine patrols, however, do not present enough elements of suspicion to reach the probable cause requirements for arrests. Therefore, the justification for a search incidental to an arrest does not exist. This situation presents a serious constitutional dilemma for police officers who are concerned for their safety while initially investigating suspicious persons in a patrol environment.

The police are sworn to respond to suspicious activities within their jurisdictions, all of which present potential dangers, yet many do not result in arrests upon initial investigation. To alleviate all doubts as to the nature of suspicious activities, however, the police must make an initial contact with the suspicious person. Such encounters may be viewed by suspicious persons as illegal invasions of their privacy and therefore an abuse of police power. To balance the police's right to investigate suspicious activities with less than probable cause while protecting the suspicious person's rights against police abuse, the U.S. Supreme Court established a legal doctrine that clarified and balanced these competing interests. This doctrine has come to be known as the "stop and frisk" doctrine.

In *Terry v. Ohio* (1968) the U.S. Supreme Court established a number of procedural rules that apply to initial police investigatory contacts on the street when the police have less than probable cause to arrest. The Court, in defining the parameters of constitutionally permitted police contacts, established that contacts based on reasonable suspicion rather than probable cause are permissible under certain limited circumstances. Reasonable suspicion is defined as information based on more than a mere hunch or intuition that criminal activity is afoot but less than the information needed to make a probable cause arrest. Reasonable suspicion contacts are commonly referred to as "stops" and are generally short-term in duration. Particularly concerned with the safety of police officers engaged in reasonable suspicion stops, the courts have allowed the police to conduct limited, non-intrusive, outer garment searches of suspicious persons for potential weapons that could be used against the police. Such limited searches are known as "frisk" or "pat down" searches. If the "frisk" reveals that the suspicious person is carrying an illegal weapon, probable cause to arrest is then established and a full search incidental to a lawful arrest is allowed.

Frank Andritzky

A primary justification for permitting police to frisk, or "pat down," suspects is to ensure their safety by allowing them to determine whether the suspects are carrying dangerous weapons. *(Brand-X Pictures)*

See also Arrest; Automobile searches; Bill of Rights, U.S.; *Illinois v. Wardlow*; Loitering; Miranda rights; Plain view doctrine; Police powers; Probable cause; Racial profiling; Reasonable suspicion; Search and seizure; Suspects.

Further Reading

Bloom, Robert M. *Searches, Seizures, and Warrants*. Westport, Conn.: Praeger, 2003.

LaFave, W. R. *Search and Seizure: A Treatise on the Fourth Amendment*. 3d ed. St Paul, Minn.: West Publishing, 1995.

McWhirter, Darien A. *Search, Seizure, and Privacy*. Phoenix, Ariz.: Oryx Press, 1994.

Wetterer, Charles M. *The Fourth Amendment: Search and Seizure*. Springfield, N.J.: Enslow, 1998.

Strategic policing

Definition: Style of police management that relies on an assessment of performance goals and allocates resources to meet those goals most efficiently

Criminal justice issues: Law-enforcement organization; police powers; professional standards

Significance: The move to strategic policing changed the view of police administration from one of cost-of-service, response-based policing to one of outcome-oriented performance. This can be thought of as a shift in

Understanding Outputs and Outcomes

To implement successful strategic policing, one must understand the differences between outputs and outcomes. One simple framework for seeing these differences involves two key questions: What is the police department trying to accomplish? How does it plan to accomplish that goal? Outcomes are used to answer the first question, while outputs are used to answer the second. Outputs are the tools used to accomplish outcomes.

Imagine a traffic unit, whose reason for existing is to reduce traffic injuries. The unit does not exist for the purpose of writing tickets; the writing of tickets is simply one way in which it hopes to reduce fatalities. The number of tickets written is an output measure, while the number of crashes is an outcome measure. Under strategic policing, the department's success is judged not by how many citations it writes but by how well it meets its goals of reducing accidents.

central focus from one of "what one does" to "what one is trying to accomplish."

A major push to "reinvent" government began in the federal bureaucracy during the early 1990's, central to which was a move toward smarter, more efficient operation of government programs. As the federal government began to administer its agencies based on this new way of thinking, state governments followed suit. Not long after, county and municipal administrations instigated similar changes. As government agents, many police chiefs and county sheriffs saw the expectations of their governments changing and so began embracing strategic policing as a way to meet the expectations of this new brand of management.

Strategic policing is a method of police administration and management that is outcome- and performance-focused, rather than output- and accounting-focused. During the Reform and Professional eras of American policing, many police departments had adopted output-related management styles, in which accounting practices were brought to bear on information about the tasks police undertake. Police departments established their annual goals and budget requirements based on output-based indicators, such as the numbers of traffic citations, arrests, motorists assisted, and the like. Departments' success

was judged based on how well they met or exceeded their output goals.

Under the move to strategic policing, police administrators shifted focus from outputs to outcomes. While a traffic-related output assessment might count the things police do, such as number of citations issued, a traffic-related outcome assessment might count the things police officers try to affect, such as number of fatal crashes. Rather than judging a department to be successful based on their output goals, departments are rewarded for having a meaningful impact on the community and for meeting their outcome goals.

The move to strategic policing has been important for fundamental reasons. While output goals were traditionally established based on accounting projections and other scientific methods, strategic policing ensures that agencies seriously evaluate their outcome expectations. Often this involves closely working with all members of the department, as well as members of the community. Working together, the department establishes service priorities and then constructs outcome measures that will assess whether or not the department is adequately addressing those priorities. If the community agrees that traffic fatalities are a serious problem, the department may establish the number of fatal crashes as an outcome-related measure. While the number of traffic citations is an informative gauge, it does not measure the thing police are interested in changing—crashes.

Timothy M. Bray

Further Reading

Brady, T. V. *Measuring What Matters, Part One: Measures of Crime, Fear, and Disorder.* Washington, D.C.: National Institute of Justice, 1996.

Bureau of Justice Statistics. *Performance Measures for the Criminal Justice System.* Washington, D.C.: Bureau of Justice Statistics, 1993.

Langworthy, R. H. *Measuring What Matters: Proceedings from the Policing Research Insti-*

tute Meetings. Washington, D.C.: National Institute of Justice, 1999.

National Institute of Justice. *Measuring What Matters, Part Two: Developing Measures of What the Police Do*. Washington, D.C.: National Institute of Justice, 1997.

See also Community-oriented policing; Law enforcement; Neighborhood watch programs; Police.

Strict liability offenses

Definition: Offenses for which people are responsible, whether they mean them to occur or not

Criminal justice issues: Defendants; law codes

Significance: Strict liability offenses do not require criminal intent on the part of offenders, who are deemed responsible even though they do not intend to break the law. The principle is a sharp contrast with the usual legal principle making intent a requirement for guilt.

An action generally must have several components to constitute a crime: The action or behavior itself must be regarded as illegal, an act must take place (*actus reus*), and a guilty mind (*mens rea*) must be behind the action. There must also be concurrence of the act and the guilty mind. That is, both need to occur at the same time. Additionally, some harm must be incurred that is a result of the act. However, strict liability offenses differ from most offenses in that they do not require criminal intent, or guilty mind. In other words, their actors are held accountable for crimes whether they actually want or intend for crimes to occur.

Statutory rape is the most commonly cited example of a strict liability offense under the criminal law. Persons who engage in sexual activity with partners who are deemed underage are guilty of statutory rape even if they do not know that their partners are minors.

Another class of strict liability offenses crimes encompasses unintended criminal actions by corporations. Officers in charge of corporations can be held criminally responsible for actions that lead to serious harm even if they do not intend for the harm to occur. Strict liability offenses are also present in the law of torts, product liability, corporate law, and criminal law. Strict liability is applied to many situations that the law views as inherently dangerous.

The purpose of strict liability offenses laws is to discourage reckless behavior and needless loss. Strict liability cases are comparatively easy for prosecutors to prosecute, as they do not need to establish intent. Another benefit of applying strict liability to particular events is that accelerating prosecution can make it easy for victims to get on with their lives.

A serious concern about prosecuting of strict liability offenses is that cases occur in which criminal intent should be considered. For example, it may be unfair to bring statutory rape charges against adults who have good reason for believing their sexual partners to be of legal age, as would be the case when they meet in bars or other venues that do not admit minors. Moreover, it has been argued that the very fact that prosecutors can make their cases without establishing criminal intent is inherently unfair.

Sheryl L. Van Horne

Further Reading

Feinman, Jay M. *Law 101: Everything You Need to Know About the American Legal System*. New York: Oxford University Press, 2000.

Simester, Andrew, ed. *Appraising Strict Liability*. New York: Oxford University Press, 2005.

See also Criminal intent; Criminal law; Criminal liability; *Mens rea*; Sexual harassment; Vicarious liability.

Subpoena power

Definition: Power of courts to require persons to appear in court to testify or to produce documents that are relevant to cases

Criminal justice issues: Courts; judges; trial procedures; witnesses

Significance: The word "subpoena" comes from a Latin word that literally means "under penalty"—which is the essence of the legal authority behinds a subpoena.

Whereas a summons merely indicates that legal action is being taken against the person receiving it, that person would not be breaking the law by not appearing in court. However, a subpoenaed witness is ordered to appear to give testimony at a specified time and place and is subject to penalty if the order is disobeyed. An individual receiving a subpoena to appear as a witness may be ordered to testify in court, before an administrative or other body, or to a court reporter. The Sixth Amendment to the U.S. Constitution guarantees that criminal defendants have the right to have witnesses subpoenaed in their favor, and it is typically wise to do so in order to guarantee that the witnesses will appear at the legal proceedings.

Subpoenas are issued for a variety of reasons by a variety of legal authorities, including a lawyer for the parties involved in a suit, a grand jury for witnesses to a crime, a prosecutor, a court clerk, a coroner, legislative committees, and administrative agencies. There are two basic types of subpoenas. The type referred to simply as a subpoena requires that an individual testify as a witness. The other type, a *subpoena duces tecum*, requires that witnesses must bring with them any documents or papers in their possession that may be relevant to the case under investigation. Before formal charges have been filed in a case, investigatory subpoenas may be issued requiring witnesses to appear at a hearing and to bring with them any pertinent documents or papers. Likewise, after formal charges are filed in a case, subpoenas can again be issued requiring witnesses to appear at a hearing or in court to give depositions or produce relevant documents or papers.

A valid subpoena must be issued by an officer authorized by the court, and it must typically be delivered personally within the proper time and to the proper place. It is very important that a person who has been subpoenaed appear at the specified time and place stated in the subpoena. An individual failing to do so can be held in contempt of court, fined, or imprisoned and may also be liable for damages sustained by the aggrieved party. For legitimate reasons, such as illness or a family death, a subpoenaed individual may postpone the appearance date.

It is wise for individuals to consult a lawyer if they object to a subpoena. A lawyer may raise objections to a subpoena prior to the appearance date by making a motion to quash the subpoena or by filing a formal objection in writing. In either case, a hearing will be held to consider the lawyer's request, and a decision will be rendered as to whether or not the subpoena will be enforced.

Alvin K. Benson

Further Reading

Meyer, J. F., and D. R. Grant. *The Courts in Our Criminal Justice System*. Upper Saddle River, N.J.: Prentice-Hall, 2003.

Neubauer, D. W. *America's Courts and the Criminal Justice System*. 7th ed. Belmont, Calif.: Wadsworth, 2002.

Rabe, Gary A., and Dean John Champion. *Criminal Courts: Structure, Process and Issues*. Upper Saddle River, N.J.: Prentice-Hall, 2002.

See also Discovery; Expert witnesses; Hearings; *Mandamus*; News source protection; Obstruction of justice; Summonses; Testimony; Watergate scandal; Witnesses.

Suicide and euthanasia

Definition: Suicide is the intentional taking of one's own life; also known as "mercy killing," euthanasia is the intentional taking of the life of another or allowing, through intentional neglect, another life to end.

Criminal justice issues: Medical and health issues; murder and homicide

Significance: Suicide ranks among the ten leading causes of death in the United States, and when it occurs, law enforcement generally investigates its circumstances. Euthanasia takes many forms, some of which are illegal and require criminal justice responses.

Suicide occurs among almost all population groups, but rates of suicide vary greatly by demographic group. For example, during the year

Arguments for and Against Physician-Assisted Suicide

Arguments for	*Arguments against*
Decisions about time and circumstances of death are personal; competent persons should have the autonomous right to choose death.	Assisted suicide is morally wrong because it contradicts strong religious and secular traditions supporting the sanctity of life.
Like cases should be treated alike. If competent, terminally ill patients may hasten death by refusing treatment, those for whom treatment refusal will not hasten death should be allowed the option of assisted death.	There is an important difference between passively letting someone die and actively killing a person. The two options are not equivalent.
Suffering may go beyond physical pain; there are other physical and psychological burdens for which physician-assisted suicide may be a compassionate response to suffering.	There is a potential for abuse; persons lacking access to care and support may be pushed into assisted death; moreover, assisted death may become a cost-containment strategy.
Although society has a strong interest in preserving life, that interest lessens when a person becomes terminally ill and has a strong desire to end life. A complete prohibition on assisted death excessively limits personal liberty.	Physicians have a long ethical tradition against taking life. Their Hippocratic oath pledges them not to "administer poison to anyone where asked" and to "be of benefit, or at least do no harm."
Assisted deaths already occur secretly, as when the administration of morphine may be a covert form of euthanasia. Legalization of physician-assisted suicide would promote open discussion of the subject.	Physicians occasionally make mistakes, and there may be uncertainties in diagnoses, and the state has an obligation to protect lives from such mistakes.

Source: Ethics in Medicine, University of Washington School of Medicine (http://eduserv.hscer.washington.edu/bioethics/topics/pas.html).

2001, American men had a suicide rate of 17.6 per 100,000 population, which was more than four times greater than that of women (4.1). Men tend to be at greater risk of suicide than women for a variety of reasons, including their higher rate of alcoholism, their greater familiarity with firearms, and their lower inclination to seek help for mental troubles.

Likewise, the rate of suicide among white Americans as a group is typically about double that of African Americans (11.9 vs. 5.3). This difference may be accounted for by the fact that whites tend to have more favorable attitudes toward suicide, and they tend to be more likely than African Americans to internalize their aggressive feelings and blame themselves for life's problems. While African Americans tend to externalize their aggression, perhaps because of

their history of facing discrimination, they also have a homicide rate four times greater than that of white Americans (22.1 vs. 4.9 per 100,000). Risk of suicide is also high among people with damaged ties to society and people living under unusual stresses, such as those who are divorced or widowed, those low in religiosity, the unemployed, and the poor.

Police Suicide

Police are generally believed to have higher than average suicide rates, but data supporting that view may be inconclusive. Job stresses that might contribute to police suicide include frequent danger of death and injury, public dislike of police, and having to work changing and often inconvenient shifts. These stress factors can, in turn, increase marital and other problems.

The findings of more than twenty-five studies of police suicide have been mixed. A common flaw in many of the studies has been a failure to compare police suicide rates to race- and gender-matched control groups. For example, a *New York Times* story published during the early 1990's reported on the "high" rate of suicide among police in New York City: about 21 per 100,000 population. The *Times* pointed out that this rate was almost twice the national average of 12, but the story neglected to take into consideration the fact that the composition of the police matched that of a demographic group—white male adults—that already had a high suicide rate. That failing diminished the report's conclusions about police suicide rates. In actuality, the suicide rate among New York City police is lower than that for all men of working age.

Well-designed studies make such controlled comparisons. For both the United States as a whole and Germany, once controls are incorporated for demographic factors such as age and gender, police are not at an elevated risk for suicide. However, no study has focused specifically on police officers on patrol. It may be that suicide risk for such officers is much higher than that for the many officers who work primarily in clerical and managerial capacities, away from dangers on the streets.

Suicide in Correctional Facilities

Correctional officers and prison guards also work in unsafe environments. Moreover, they serve clients who are criminals and receive low pay in return. Nevertheless, studies undertaken with controls for demographic factors, find that the suicide rate of prison guards is not significantly higher than that of the rest of the working-age population.

On the other hand, suicide rates among inmates of jails and other correctional facilities tend to be higher than those for demographically comparable nonprison populations. Suicide rates in state prisons range between 13 and 17 per

100,000—figures at or below the rates for all men of comparable age. However, in jails—in which overcrowding is common—suicide rates are triple those of state prisons and well above what would be expected for all men in the same age group.

Prisoners who commit suicide are most apt to do so during the first week of their confinement. The most suicides occur during the first twenty-four hours of prisoners' confinement, a period of rapid and stressful change. New prisoners experience sudden breaks with work, loss of daily contacts with families and loved ones, loss of familiar environments, and sudden subjection to rigorous institutional regimentation. Feelings of disorientation, depression, and anxiety and other psychological states associated with suicide risk are high during this time frame.

Euthanasia

Passive euthanasia involves aiding the termination of other persons' lives by withdrawing life-support assistance, such as medical treatments, medications, respirator equipment, respirators,

Wearing an artificial stock to dramatize his attitude toward what he regarded as archaic laws, Jack Kevorkian conducts a press conference before his arraignment on assisted-suicide charges in Pontiac, Michigan, in September, 1995. The best-known advocate of assisted suicide in the United States, Kevorkian is a medical doctor who repeatedly challenged laws against the practice during the 1990's, when he helped more than one hundred people commit suicide. In 1999, he was finally convicted of second-degree murder in Michigan and was sentenced—at the age of seventy-one—to ten to twenty-five years in prison. (*AP/Wide World Photos*)

nutrition, and water. Active euthanasia involves the administration of treatments or medications designed to end life. Euthanasia is considered to be voluntary when victims request it and involuntary when persons other than the victims request it. Physician-assisted suicide differs from active voluntary euthanasia in that physicians do not perform the actual killings but merely provide the means for suicide, such as a prescription for a lethal dose of drugs. In some jurisdictions all forms of euthanasia are illegal. In 1999, a Michigan court sentenced Dr. Jack Kevorkian to prison after he had assisted in the suicides of 130 persons.

The first nation to legalize assisted suicide was the Netherlands, which went through a long process of legal decisions between 1973 and 2001 before the practice was fully legal. Oregon became the first U.S. state to legalize the practice, when its voters approved the Death with Dignity Act in 1997. Over the next two years, forty-three people in the state committed suicide with the assistance of physicians. However, most persons who received permission for assisted suicide never completed it. This is an indication that mandatory waiting periods and rigorous application procedures tend to discourage the practice.

Little systematic research has been done on why people choose assisted suicide over unassisted suicide. However, in contrast to the pattern for suicide in general, about two-thirds of people who apply for permission for assisted suicides are women.

Some research has been done in the impact of physician-assisted suicide and euthanasia on society. The one consequence has been the promotion of more favorable attitudes toward suicide in general. Research in thirty-one nations has found that societies with high public approval rates of euthanasia tend to have higher acceptance of suicide in general. In the United States, the percentage of people supporting suicides of terminally ill patients rose from 39 percent in 1977 to 63 percent in 1998. An analysis of a variety of factors found that the increase in television coverage of euthanasia in this time period was a leading predictor of increased public support for suicide. A study in the Netherlands determined that legal endorsements of assisted suicide were associated with increases in suicide in general.

Steven Stack

Further Reading

Berger, Arthur S., and Joyce Berger, eds. *To Die or Not to Die? Cross-Disciplinary, Cultural, and Legal Perspectives on the Right to Choose Death*. New York: Praeger, 1990.

Brody, Baruch A., ed. *Suicide and Euthanasia: Historical and Contemporary Themes*. Dordrecht, Netherlands: Kluwer, 1989. Collection of articles on a variety of suicide issues from the nation that has pioneered in the legalization of assisted suicide.

Humphry, Derek. *Final Exit: The Practicalities of Self-Deliverance and Assisted Suicide for the Dying*. 2d ed. New York: Dell, 1996. Classic guide to methods of committing suicide with discussions of related legal issues. This book has been controversial because of public perceptions that it encourages readers to commit suicide; however, its emphasis on the practical difficulties of committing suicide may have the opposite effect.

Institute of Medicine. *Reducing Suicide: A National Imperative*. Washington: National Academies Press, 2002. Overview of the distribution and causes of suicide, together with policy recommendations for its reduction.

Larue, Gerald A. *Euthanasia and Religion: A Survey of the Attitudes of World Religions to the Right to Die*. Los Angeles: Hemlock Society, 1985. Broad survey of the place of suicide in religious beliefs, published by an organization that advocates legalizing assisted suicide.

Lester, David. *Why People Kill Themselves: A 2000 Summary of Research Findings on Suicide*. 4th ed. Springfield, Ill.: C. C. Thomas, 2000. Summary of all research on suicide published in English between 1990 and 1997, compiled by a leading authority in the field of assisted suicide.

Roleff, Tamara L., ed. *Suicide: Opposing Viewpoints*. San Diego, Calif.: Greenhaven Press, 1998. Collection of essays addressing suicide from different perspectives; designed for young adult readers.

Rosenfeld, Barry. *Assisted Suicide and the Right to Die: The Interface of Social Science, Public Policy, and Medical Ethics*. Washington, D.C.: American Psychological Association, 2004. Analyzes how social science can be used to inform the debates on end of life matters such as how untreated depression may form the basis for requests for physician-assisted suicide.

See also Coroners; Document analysis; Kevorkian, Jack; Medical examiners; Murder and homicide; Mental illness; Victimless crimes.

Summonses

Definition: Judicial instruments used to initiate legal proceedings or to call for the appearance of persons before courts or other bodies

Criminal justice issues: Courts; pleas; trial procedures

Significance: Important instruments in criminal justice, summonses expedite proceedings by using the full weight of the courts and other government bodies to order defendants, witnesses, and other persons to make appearances.

In a civil action summonses are formal notices issued by clerks of the court that notify defendants of actions against them. A summons normally gives notice of the nature of the lawsuit and demands that the defendant appear to answer the allegations. Failure to answer, either through further pleadings or by not appearing in person, generally subjects the defendant to a default judgment.

Other forms of summonses include jury summonses, which command citizens to appear before the court to serve as jurors. A jury summons carries the authority of the court, and a failure to appear in response to it may subject the person to severe civil or criminal penalties. A summons may also be used in lieu of a subpoena to order a witness to appear to give testimony.

In criminal matters summonses are also used to command the appearance of defendants before the court. Whereas a warrant generally requires the arrest of the named person, a summons simply commands the person's appearance before the court. This technique is used frequently when dealing with misdemeanors or violations. For example, the owner of a tavern may receive a summons to appear before a magistrate to answer for

violations of liquor laws or health codes. Likewise, motorists typically receive summonses when they are issued citations for moving violations. The tickets issued by police officers are forms of summonses that command the motorists to appear before courts or otherwise answer the allegations.

Summonses may also be issued by officials charged with enforcing various legal codes of municipalities, counties, and states. They might include a summons directing a food vendor to appear before health inspectors for serving food without a license or for operating a restaurant that fails to meet health code regulations. This type of summons, much like a traffic ticket, usually serves two purposes in the sense that it is both the actual complaint and the summons to appear.

Carl J. Franklin

Further Reading

Del Carmen, Rolando V. *Criminal Procedure: Law and Practice.* 6th ed. Belmont, Calif.: Thomson/Wadsworth, 2004.

Samaha, Joel. *Criminal Procedure.* 3d ed. St. Paul, Minn.: West Publishing, 1996.

See also Citations; Judges; Jury duty; Subpoena power.

Supermax prisons

Definition: Control-oriented prisons designed for inmates considered so incorrigible, disruptive, escape-prone, or violent that they pose threats to the staffs and inmates of conventional maximum-security prisons

Criminal justice issues: Deviancy; prisons; violent crime

Significance: Supermax prisons are a modern innovation in American corrections. By separating the most dangerous inmates from general prison populations and keeping those inmates in what amounts to long-term solitary confinement, supermax prisons appear to have reduced levels of prison violence. However, no studies have yet shown what effect the prisons are having on the inmates themselves and on crime problems generally.

Supermax prisons are based upon the concept of selective incapacitation—the notion that because most offenses are committed by a small minority of offenders, incapacitating that minority will reduce crime by an amount disproportionate to their numbers. The concept grew out of a now-classic study of juvenile offenders in Philadelphia published by Marvin E. Wolfgang, Robert M. Figlio, and Thorsten Sellin in 1972. Replications of the Philadelphia study elsewhere produced remarkably similar results. Consequently, policy analysts concluded that if this small group of chronic recidivists—both in society and in prison—could be identified and isolated, the total crime rate should drop considerably. Supermax prisons are thus designed to incapacitate these violent recidivists who do not respond well to treatment.

It has been estimated that up to 20 percent of inmates in prison are remorseless psychopaths who are not motivated to change. However, psychopaths and other dangerous repeat offenders generally "burn out," or moderate their behavior, with the passage of time. Meanwhile, less-serious offenders in traditional prisons feel safer and more secure when separated from the hard-core repeat offenders and tend to take fuller advantage of the vocational and therapeutic programs offered to rehabilitate them.

Handcuffed prisoners transferring to other federal prisons being led through one of Alcatraz's grim cell blocks. This photograph was taken in March, 1963, shortly before the prison was shut down. (AP/Wide World Photos)

Alcatraz: The First Supermax Prison

The first supermax prison in America was Alcatraz Island. Built by the federal government on a small island in the frigid, shark-infested waters of San Francisco Bay in 1934, Alcatraz held a comparatively small number of violent and notorious criminals, including "Machine Gun" Kelly and Al Capone, in tiny cells. Alcatraz proved to be a secure facility but was expensive to operate because of its isolation. All its supplies, including fresh water, had to be shipped to it by boat, and

all its waste materials had to be shipped off the island. Less than thirty years after it opened to prisoners, Alcatraz was closed down in 1963 and replaced by a federal penitentiary in Marion, Illinois.

Marion Penitentiary soon developed problems of its own. Designed as a traditional congregate penitentiary, it was ill equipped to deal with exceptionally violent offenders placed in it. In response to the staff's ever-tightening security, the prison's inmates carried out a work strike in 1980. Prison officials responded by shutting down the prison factory and terminating all education classes. After two correctional officers were killed by inmates in separate incidents in the prison's most secure housing unit in October, 1983, and an inmate was found murdered in his cell four days later, federal Bureau of Prisons officials decided to place the penitentiary on permanent lock-down status. From that time, Marion's inmates were confined alone within their cells for more than twenty-three hours each day, and group programs were virtually eliminated.

In 1985, Marion inmates challenged their living conditions in federal court in the case of *Bruscino v. Carlson*. The judge in that case ruled that conditions in Marion met constitutional requirements. After a federal appellate court upheld that decision in 1988, and the U.S. Supreme Court let the ruling stand in 1989, there was a rapid expansion of supermax prisons throughout the country. By the early twenty-first century, the federal government and a majority of the states were operating supermax prisons. These facilities ranged from the Bureau of Prison's Florence, Colorado, facility—which replaced the Marion Penitentiary—to California's Pelican Bay State Prison, which opened in late 1989.

Supermax Prison Design

Virtually all supermax prisons have certain things in common. They all have tight perimeter security and severely restricted inmate movement within their walls. They all have small concrete-encased solitary cells. These cells generally measure about seven by twelve feet in area and are typically furnished with metal doors; narrow, barred windows; small steel sinks and toilets; shower stalls; small steel desks with pull-out stools; small steel bookshelves anchored to the walls; and raised concrete slabs or metal-frame beds. Radio and television receivers may or may not be allowed.

Supermax inmates typically spend twenty-three hours a day alone in their cells, eating, exercising, and taking part in whatever programming is available through video, correspondence, or written materials. Individual inmates rarely, if ever, have contacts with other inmates. Their human contacts are generally restricted to counselors, clergy members, and medical personnel who see them in their cells. When inmates leave their cells, they are handcuffed, placed in leg irons, and escorted to their destinations by at least two correctional officers. When they are al-

lowed to have visits, they are separated from their visitors by concrete, steel, and thick glass and must communicate by speakerphones or, in more extreme cases, via video screens.

Critics of the Prisons

Proponents of supermax prisons argue that they deter as well as incapacitate. Inmates housed in supermax prisons must serve a minimum of two years in solitary confinement before becoming eligible for transfer back to traditional penitentiaries.

Opponents of supermax prisons note that the facilities are more expensive to build and operate than standard maximum-security institutions. Staff-to-inmate ratios are generally higher because inmates spend so much time locked down within their cells that everything they need must be carried to them. Moreover, in contrast to most prisons, in which inmates perform many of the routine cooking, cleaning, and maintenance chores that keep the institutions running smoothly, all chores in supermax prisons must be done by staff members.

Critics also charge that the criteria for selecting inmates for supermax prisons are vaguely

---

The Philadelphia Study

Marvin E. Wolfgang, Robert M. Figlio, and Thorsten Sellin studied 9,945 boys who were born in Philadelphia in 1945. In sociological terminology, that group is known as a birth cohort. Approximately 3,500 of the boys developed criminal records between the ages of ten and eighteen. The researchers examined the records of all the boys until they turned eighteen and published their findings in *Delinquency in a Birth Cohort* in 1972.

What Wolfgang and his colleagues found was that a tiny group of chronic recidivists, who constituted only about 6 percent of the group, committed more than one-half of all crimes attributed to the entire birth cohort. Moreover, that small group of hardcore recidivists was responsible for fully 69 percent of all aggravated assaults, 71 percent of all homicides, 73 percent of all rapes, and 82 percent of all robberies committed by the cohort.

worded and capriciously applied. For example, some prisoners are sent to the facilities because they have become labeled as "troublemakers" for making themselves nuisances to administrators by filing frequent grievances and lawsuits. Members of gangs are sometimes sent to supermax prisons because of their gang membership, even if they have no histories of serious assault or escape.

Supermax prisons are also criticized for fostering repressive environments in which staff abuses are more likely to occur. Courts have documented abuses at Pelican Bay. Inmates who are mentally ill or prone to mental illness may deteriorate further in solitary confinement over extended periods of time. Moreover, supermax prisons typically offer inmates no work, treatment programs, or vocational training to prepare them for successful reintegration into the community.

It has also been charged that some supermax prisons have been built at the behest of politicians wanting to appear "tough on crime," even when correctional officials themselves do not think the facilities are needed. In any case, in the modern rush to build supermax prisons, little research has been conducted to prove their actual effectiveness. The Bureau of Prisons has reported that levels of violence have gone down throughout the federal prison system since supermax prisons were introduced. States such as California and Texas have also reported curbing waves of violence in their prison systems with the widespread use of solitary confinement. However, other states have not reported reductions in inmate-on-inmate assaults since the introduction of their supermax prisons. Findings on the impact of supermax prisons on inmate-on-staff assaults have also been mixed.

Robert Rogers

Further Reading

Alarid, Leanne, and Paul Cromwell. *Correctional Perspectives: Views from Academics, Practitioners, and Prisoners*. Los Angeles: Roxbury, 2002.

Briggs, Chad S., Jody L. Sundt, and Thomas C. Castellano. "The Effect of Supermaximum Security Prisons on Aggregate Levels of Institutional Violence." *Criminology* 41, no. 4 (2003): 1341-1376.

Kurki, Leena, and Norval Morris. "The Purposes, Practices, and Problems of Supermax Prisons." In *Crime and Justice: A Review of Research*, edited by Michael Tonry. Chicago: University of Chicago Press, 2001.

Neal, Donice, ed. *Supermax Prisons: Beyond the Rock*. Lanham, Md.: American Correctional Association, 2003.

Pizarro, Jesenia, and Vanja M. K. Stenius. "Supermax Prisons: Their Rise, Current Practices, and Effect on Inmates." *Prison Journal* 84, no. 2 (2004): 248-264.

Toch, Hans. "The Future of Supermax Confinement." *Prison Journal* 81, no. 3 (2001): 376-388.

Wolfgang, Marvin E., Robert M. Figlio, and Thorsten Sellin. *Delinquency in a Birth Cohort*. Chicago: University of Chicago Press, 1972.

See also Cruel and unusual punishment; Incapacitation; Mental illness; Prison and jail systems; Prison escapes; Prison violence; Recidivism; Solitary confinement.

Supreme Court, U.S.

Identification: Highest court in the U.S. justice system

Criminal justice issues: Appeals; civil rights and liberties; constitutional protections; courts

Significance: As the highest court of appeal in the United States, the Supreme Court has played an important role in shaping the American criminal justice process, especially in regard to the interpretation of the rights of criminal suspects.

The legal basis for the creation of the U.S. Supreme Court can be found in Article III of the U.S. Constitution, which was ratified in 1789. The Constitution does not spell out the Court's specific responsibilities and powers, but the Court has come to play a central role in the American political system in interpreting the constitutional bases of laws and exercising the power of final judicial review over all appeals that reach it from state and lower federal courts.

The Court's power of judicial review empowers it to declare governmental acts unconstitutional. Judicial review is controversial because it appears undemocratic when a president signs a law approved by a majority of the people's representatives in Congress, only to have a majority of the Court's nine justices—none of whom is elected by the people—declare the law unconstitutional. The principle of judicial review was established in 1803, in the landmark case of *Marbury v. Madison*, in which the Supreme Court ruled that the power was implied within the judiciary's duty to interpret the law.

Early History

During the late eighteenth century and the nineteenth century, the Supreme Court played a significant role in defining the structure and institutions of the American political system. The Court issued rulings that defined the powers of the national government and its relationship with the states and also interpreted the powers of the executive and legislative branches of government. During that period, however, the Court performed only a minor role in matters related to civil liberties, including the rights of criminal defendants. After the U.S. Congress passed the Judiciary Act of 1925, the Court began expanding its role in the political system by interpreting the scope of the freedoms listed in the Bill of Rights and the due process clause of the Fourteenth Amendment.

Also known as the Judges' Bill, the Judiciary Act of 1925 established the Supreme Court's discretionary jurisdiction, which has given the Court more flexibility in case selection. The modern Court selects cases for review without interference from Congress, although Article III of the U.S. Constitution gives Congress the power to define the process of how cases are appealed to it. The power of Congress to define the appellate jurisdiction of the Supreme Court is one of the checks within the system of checks and balances established by the Framers of the Constitution. However, commercialization, urbanization, and industrialization made laws so complex that Congress decided that the Court was better able to select cases for itself.

The Judiciary Act also established the writ of *certiorari* petition, which has since become the most common way for cases to be accepted for review by the Supreme Court. Parties appealing decisions to the Court must file writs of *certiorari* requesting that relevant lower court records be delivered to the Supreme Court. Four of the nine justices on the Court must vote in favor of a writ of *certiorari* petition for a case to be granted review.

Throughout the twentieth century, the Supreme Court incorporated nearly all the protections of the Bill of Rights to make them apply to state governments through the due process clause of the Fourteenth Amendment. Before the Bill of Rights protections were extended to the states, their protections were guaranteed in federal courts, but not necessarily in state or local courts. However, the Fourteenth Amendment, which was ratified immediately after the Civil War to protect newly freed slaves, asserted that states could not deny due process to all their citizens. The Court used the Fourteenth Amend-

After former California governor Earl Warren was appointed chief justice of the United States in 1953, he presided over an era of sweeping liberalizations of defendants's rights and the extension of most of the provisions of the Bill of Rights to the states. *(Supreme Court Historical Society)*

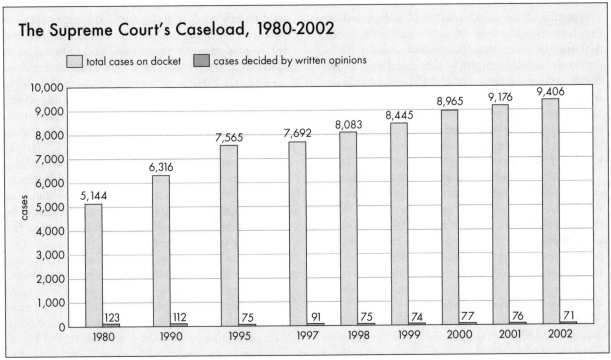

The Supreme Court's Caseload, 1980-2002

☐ total cases on docket ■ cases decided by written opinions

Source: Office of the Clerk, Supreme Court of the United States.

ment's due process clause as a vehicle to require the individual states to respect most of the freedoms and protections enumerated in the Bill of Rights.

The Court and Rights of Criminal Defendants

The incorporation of the Bill of Rights upon states was especially significant for persons accused of crimes because about 90 percent of criminal cases are tried in state and local courts. Before the Bill of Rights protections were incorporated, it was common for criminal defendants to be treated roughly by law-enforcement officials during searches and seizures and interrogations and by prosecutors and judges in trials in ways that are now no longer permitted. Criminal suspects were frequently denied due process of law in states whose constitutions and local practices ran contrary to the rights of criminals defined in the federal Bill of Rights.

The Warren Court

With the appointment of Earl Warren as chief justice of the United States by President Dwight D. Eisenhower in 1953, the Supreme

Court began an era of liberal interpretations of criminal defendants' rights. Warren expanded the meaning of criminal defendants' rights by nationalizing most of the liberties during the 1960's and by establishing a code of conduct for police officers in dealing with criminal suspects. Landmark decisions by the Warren court revolutionized the criminal justice system by providing more protection for criminal defendants. For example, the Court's decision in *Gideon v. Wainwright* in 1963 required states to provide attorneys for defendants accused of felonies who could not afford their own representation. The Court's 1966 *Miranda v. Arizona* decision required police officers to inform suspects of their right to remain silent and their right to counsel.

The Warren court did not rule directly on the constitutionality of the death penalty. However, in *Trop v. Dulles* (1958), it established that punishments had to meet evolving standards of decency or risk violating the Eighth Amendment's cruel and unusual punishment clause.

The Warren court also nationalized a controversial principle known as the exclusionary rule in its landmark *Mapp v. Ohio* decision in 1961.

The exclusionary rule bars illegally obtained evidence from being used in court against criminal defendants. The rule is controversial because guilty defendants might be set free if crucial evidence is excluded from trials. The rule applies to illegal police searches and coercive interrogations conducted by police officers without the presence of attorneys to advise suspects. Hence, the exclusionary rule relates to provisions in the Fourth, Fifth, and Sixth Amendments.

While political liberals applauded the Warren court's rulings, conservatives were offended by them and viewed the Supreme Court as "soft on crime." It was common during Warren's era to see billboards calling for Warren's impeachment, especially in conservative states such as Texas and Indiana.

Conservative Counterrevolution

In reaction to the Warren court's liberal decisions, Richard M. Nixon campaigned for the presidency in 1968 on a "law and order" platform. A Republican, Nixon promised the voters that he would appoint conservative justices to the Court who would favor law-enforcement officers, or what he called the "peace forces." After Nixon

was elected, he had the unusual fortune of appointing four justices to the Court during his first term. His appointments included Chief Justice Warren Burger, who served on the Court from 1969 until 1986.

Republican Presidents Ronald W. Reagan and George Bush followed Nixon's lead by appointing six justices to the Court during the 1980's and early 1990's, including Chief Justice William H. Rehnquist in 1986. Meanwhile, no Democratic president appointed a justice between 1968 and 1993. The increased conservatism the Republican appointments gave to the Court significantly altered the Court's rulings in a variety of areas, including criminal justice.

During the 1980's and 1990's, the Supreme Court handed down rulings that created exceptions to allow illegally obtained evidence to be used in criminal trials. For example, the Court allowed police officers to conduct searches with invalid warrants when they acted in "good faith." The Court also created a "public safety" exception to allow police to coerce suspects into providing information about locations of dangerous weapons in public places. This exception allowed police to avoid the problems associated with issuing

The Rehnquist court during the 1990's. Clockwise from upper left: Ruth Bader Ginsburg, David Souter, Clarence Thomas, Stephen Breyer, Anthony Kennedy, Sandra Day O'Connor, Chief Justice William H. Rehnquist, John Paul Stevens, and Antonin Scalia. (Richard Strauss, Courtesy the Supreme Court of the United States)

Miranda warnings during emergency situations in which speedy police action was crucial. The Supreme Court also created the "inevitable discovery" exception to admit illegally obtained evidence into court under the presumption that if such evidence had not been obtained illegally, it would have been found eventually.

Exceptions such as these are examples of how Warren court decisions have been interpreted in a more conservative manner by the Burger and Rehnquist courts. However, while legal scholars agree that a conservative counterrevolution has, in fact, occurred since Warren retired in 1969, many of his court's landmark decisions, such as *Gideon*, *Miranda*, and *Mapp*, have not been overturned. However, these decisions have been interpreted to provide more support for law-enforcement officials, prosecutors, and judges in their battle against criminal defendants.

The post-Warren court has also made conservative rulings in matters of sentencing and punishment. In *Gregg v. Georgia* (1976), for example, the Court ruled that the death penalty did not violate the Eighth Amendment's cruel and unusual punishment clause. The Rehnquist court has also made it easier to apply the death penalty by issuing decisions that limit the number of federal appeals for death row inmates, to allow states to execute defendants under the age of eighteen, and to allow relatives of murder victims to issue emotional statements to juries during the sentencing phases of death penalty trials. Although more than one-half of death row inmates are of African American and Hispanic heritage, the Court ruled in *McCleskey v. Kemp* (1987) that the death penalty was not being implemented in a racially discriminatory manner. Clearly, the rights of criminal suspects have been limited by the decisions of the Burger and Rehnquist courts, while a movement favoring a strict enforcement of the laws has been expanded.

Scott P. Johnson

Further Reading

Baum, Lawrence. *The Supreme Court*. 8th ed. Washington, D.C.: CQ Press, 2004. Comprehensive study of the Court.

Campbell, Andrea. *Rights of the Accused*. Philadelphia: Chelsea House, 2001. Overview of the constitutional protections in the Bill of Rights through detailed discussion of landmark Supreme Court cases and their histories, as well as fundamental principles. Well written and easily understood.

Cole, George F., and Christopher E. Smith. *The American System of Criminal Justice*. 10th ed. Belmont, Calif.: Wadsworth Publishing, 2004. Standard textbook that covers all aspects of criminal justice in the United States, with extensive attention to the role of the Supreme Court.

Epstein, Lee, and Thomas G. Walker. *Constitutional Law for a Changing America: Rights, Liberties, and Justice*. 5th ed. Washington, D.C.: CQ Press, 2003. Up-to-date study of constitutional law with considerable attention to the role of the Supreme Court.

Greenberg, Ellen. *The Supreme Court Explained*. New York: W. W. Norton, 1997. Clear guide to how the Supreme Court works, with examples of how specific cases go through the Court.

Hall, Kermit. *The Rights of the Accused: The Justices and Criminal Justice*. New York: Garland Publishing, 2001. Broad study of the role of the Supreme Court in the U.S. criminal justice system.

Lewis, Thomas T., ed. *The Bill of Rights*. 2 vols. Pasadena, Calif.: Salem Press, 2002. Comprehensive coverage of the Bill of Rights, with articles on each of the amendments, the Constitution, the incorporation doctrine, and many other topics, as well as 280 individual court cases.

Lewis, Thomas T., and Richard L. Wilson, eds. *Encyclopedia of the U.S. Supreme Court*. 3 vols. Pasadena, Calif.: Salem Press, 2001. Comprehensive reference to the Court, with alphabetically arranged articles on all the Court's justices, many of its rulings, and many other subjects.

O'Brien, David M. *Constitutional Law and Politics*. 6th ed. New York: W. W. Norton, 2005. General study of the role of the U.S. Constitution in U.S. government and justice.

See also Bill of Rights, U.S.; Capital punishment; Constitution, U.S.; Counsel, right to; Court types; Due process of law; Incorporation doctrine; Judicial review; Judicial system, U.S.; Jurisdiction of courts.

Surveillance cameras

Definition: Video cameras mounted on elevated locations in public areas such as highways, parking lots, and spaces within or between buildings

Criminal justice issues: Civil rights and liberties; crime prevention; privacy

Significance: Widely practiced throughout the United States, the electronic monitoring of people in public areas represents an important application of technology in the face of increasing concern about crime in such areas. Moreover, surveillance cameras can deter crime while reducing demands on personnel time. At the same time, criminal courts are finding that evidence from surveillance cameras increases guilty pleas.

The commission of crimes in public spaces has long been a focus of concern, especially to law-enforcement authorities. Much of the impetus for the development and implementation of closed-circuit television surveillance (CCTV) has come from Great Britain, which has the most extensive CCTV monitoring in the world—including thousands of surveillance cameras in London alone. The growth rate of surveillance cameras in the United States is estimated at about 15-20 percent each year, supported by an enormous influx of public funds.

CCTV monitoring is usually operated remotely from central stations that are typically police headquarters. The actual monitoring of the cameras themselves is done by police or civilian personnel, who make surveillance videotapes that are kept on file for various periods. The amounts of personnel time that different agen-

In early 2004, a surveillance camera in a University of Nebraska building in Omaha caught this image of a recent prison escapee whose whereabouts had been previously unknown. Although fortuitous discoveries of fugitives by surveillance cameras are rare, the pictures the cameras record often assist law enforcement in identifying and tracking criminal offenders. *(AP/Wide World Photos)*

cies allot to monitoring cameras and recordings vary greatly.

The impact of CCTV monitoring the commission of crimes is difficult to measure, as reported results vary greatly: Changes in crime rates range from reductions as high as 90 percent to increases of up to under 20 percent. Interpreting figures for crime increases is complicated. If one by-product of surveillance cameras is better detection of crime, then increases may actually be signs of success.

The problem of interpreting these figures reflects a duality in the basic goal of CCTV: deterring crime, while facilitating the detection and prosecution of crime. There is some evidence that surveillance cameras are more effective in deterring property crimes than violent crimes, as the latter are more likely to be impulsive and to be committed under the influence of alcohol and drugs. Under those conditions, offenders are less aware of the presence of surveillance cameras.

Another question about the impact of surveillance cameras is whether they actually deter crime or merely displace it to other locations that lack surveillance. There is some evidence that this may be the case.

Public Concerns

Studies of public opinion about surveillance cameras commonly find approval ratings exceeding 90 percent of respondents. Moreover, surveillance cameras can enhance communications among police agencies and area businesses, while helping to revive businesses located in "trouble" areas. The police can also demonstrate their acquisition of the most up-to-date technology.

Despite the apparent effectiveness of surveillance cameras in combating crime, the use of cameras has raised several concerns about violations of citizens' civil rights and liberties. For example, the unfettered discretion of CCTV operators has led some analysts to speculate that minority group members may be disproportionately represented among those being monitored. There are also concerns that the monitoring itself may be used for controversial purposes beyond the scope for which it is initially approved. The right of people to know when they are being monitored has also been emphasized.

There is also a potential for abuses arising from inaccurate or misinterpreted videotaped information. Sound tracks are often not part of the tapes, pictures may be out of focus, and people in the tapes may be difficult to identify definitively. Nevertheless, the use of CCTV is steadily rising, and its potential in terms of crime deterrence and investigation has only begun to be realized.

Eric W. Metchik

Further Reading

Gill, Martin, ed. *CCTV*. Leicester, England: Perpetuity Press, 2003.

Goold, B. J. *CCTV and Policing: Public Area Surveillance and Police Practices in Britain*. New York: Oxford University Press, 2004.

McGrath, J. E. *Loving Big Brother: Performance, Privacy and Surveillance Space*. New York: Routledge, 2004.

Newburn, Tim, and Stephanie Hayman. *Policing, Surveillance and Social Control: CCTV and Police Monitoring of Suspects*. Portland, Oreg.: Willan Publishing, 2002.

See also Electronic surveillance; Prison escapes; Privacy rights; Robbery; Shoplifting; Stakeouts; Wiretaps.

Suspects

Definition: Persons under investigation for possible criminal activity
Criminal justice issues: Arrest and arraignment; defendants; investigation
Significance: Procedures for the proper investigation, arrest, and booking of criminal suspects are well defined by statutory law and court rulings.

People can be suspected of committing crimes at three basic levels. The lowest level occurs when a law-enforcement officer has a mere "hunch," or slight suspicion, that someone has committed a criminal act or is about to commit one. For example, slight suspicion would exist if the officer were to observe a known drug dealer conversing with a known drug user. However, those two persons might well be talking about completely innocent topics, and there is probably less than a 50 percent chance that a crime is developing. At that level of suspicion, the officer can only follow the suspects, to see if a crime develops, or confront, them in a nonthreatening manner.

The second level of suspicion is reasonable suspicion. This level exists when there appears to be a greater than 50 percent chance that a crime has taken place or is about to take place, based on the "totality of the circumstances" as described in the U.S. Supreme Court's *Terry v. Ohio* (1968) ruling. Reasonable suspicion by itself is insufficient cause for making an arrest, but it is sufficient cause for a stop and frisk.

Stop and frisk is the temporary stopping of suspects long enough to conduct brief investigations and pat-downs of their exterior clothing for concealed weapons. If no evidence of criminality is found, the suspects are immediately released. Significantly, suspects who refuse to identify themselves during such stops may be arrested under a ruling made by the Supreme Court in *Hiibel v. Sixth Judicial District Court of Nevada* (2004).

The third and highest level of suspicion is probable cause which exists when law-enforcement officers have tangible evidence of criminality. Officers holding such evidence may arrest the suspects.

Booking Suspects

When suspects are juveniles who meet the standard of probable cause, they are held in sight-and-sound separation from adult suspects. Adults however, are usually taken directly to jail facilities for booking. During booking, detailed descriptions of them are made, details of the offenses are recorded, criminal background checks are conducted, fingerprints and photographs are taken, and personal property is confiscated. After suspects are booked, pretrial hearings are held to determine the legitimacy of the probable cause and whether the booked suspects need defense attorneys and possible pretrial release on bail or other special provisions.

Once in custody, suspects must be told of their Miranda rights, and the arresting officers must ascertain that the suspects understand those rights before they are questioned about their alleged offenses. Miranda rights include the sus-

pects' right to remain silent and the right to an attorney. Reading of these rights also includes the warning that anything the suspects say might be recorded and later used against them.

Suspects may also have to appear in police "show-ups" or "lineups," which are used to help witnesses and victims make identifications. In both procedures, the suspects have the right to have attorneys present if criminal proceedings against them have begun—usually by the filing of indictments.

Show-ups bring witnesses and victims into police stations to view and possibly identify suspects. They are conducted when photographs of the suspects are not available and lineups are not possible. According to the U.S. Supreme Court's ruling in *Neil v. Biggers* (1972), show-ups are permissible when conducted soon after the offenses occur, when witnesses have proper lighting and opportunities to observe the suspects for substantial periods at the time the offenses occur and are confident of their ability to identify suspects, and can provide detailed descriptions of the suspects prior to the show-ups. When formal lineups are used, the Supreme Court has ruled that they not be "impermissibly suggestive" and should place each suspect among at least four other persons who are not suspects.

Criminal suspects may also be subject to investigative techniques involving tracking and electronic eavesdropping equipment, such as computers, cell-phone taps, wiretaps, and bugs. Most of these procedures require warrants. Suspects are often cleared of suspicion by law-enforcement use of DNA evidence, polygraph tests, and the establishment of alibis.

Camille Gibson

Further Reading

Becker, Ronald F. *Criminal Investigation*. Gaithersburg, Md.: Aspen Publications, 2000.

Gilbert, James N. *Criminal Investigation*. Upper Saddle River, N.J.: Prentice-Hall, 2001.

Osterbug, James W., and Richard H. Ward. *Criminal Investigation*. 3d ed. Cincinnati: Anderson, 2000.

See also Arrest; Bail system; Booking; Defendants; Miranda rights; Police lineups; Probable cause; Reasonable suspicion; Stop and frisk.

Suspended sentences

Definition: Postponements of the execution of sentences handed down by courts

Criminal justice issues: Convictions; pardons and parole; sentencing

Significance: The power to suspend sentences allows courts discretion in awarding actual punishments while satisfying statutory requirements for justice.

Depending upon federal and state sentencing guidelines, suspended sentences may be rendered in a number of ways. Courts may suspend pronouncement of sentences on convicted defendants. They may impose sentences at the time of conviction and then suspend the actual implementation of those sentences; or, they may impose sentences, incarcerate the convicted defendants and later suspend the remainder of their sentences.

When courts impose suspended sentences by delaying their renderings of the sentences, they review the cases at designated future dates and later render sentences that are appropriate for their later judgments. For example, a court may suspend sentence on payment of court costs. If the convicted individual pays the costs as ordered, the court will render the sentence as costs of court with no incarceration. If the convicted individual fails to pay costs as ordered, the court may at a later date impose a sentence that includes incarceration. Many states allow the sentences of first-time offenders—especially for less serious crimes—to be postponed in this manner. Such suspensions help make space in overcrowded prisons for repeat offenders and those who perpetrate more serious crimes.

Courts may pronounce sentences and then suspend incarcerating the defendants, subject to additional requirements. For example, a court may hand down a suspended sentence of eighteen months, court costs, and admission of the convicted defendant to a drug-treatment facility. A court might also hand down a suspended sentence of three months, court costs, and performance of one hundred hours of community service. In both examples, the sentences rendered may be consistent with sentencing guidelines for the crimes committed, while giving the convicted defendant some choice in the matter of being incarcerated at the time of sentencing. Most states use some form of suspended sentencing whenever possible, not only to relieve overcrowding in prisons, but also to render sentences more likely to reduce recidivism, or repeat offenses.

The form of suspended sentence that is most common falls under the guidelines of parole. After convicted defendants serve some portion of the sentences, they petition to have their incarceration terminated or postponed. Granting of parole does not nullify the original sentence, as persons who violate their parole terms may be required to serve out their full sentences.

Suspended sentences are not considered final judgments. Suspended sentences render the case proceedings inactive within the courts subject to re-activation upon violation of conditions imposed with the suspension.

Taylor Shaw

Further Reading

Hoffman, Peter B. *History of the Federal Parole System*. Chevy Chase, Md.: U.S. Department of Justice, 2003.

Tonry, Michael. *Sentencing Matters*. New York: Oxford University Press, 1996.

_____, ed. *The Future of Imprisonment*. New York: Oxford University Press, 2004.

See also Appellate process; Blended sentences; Execution of judgment; Parole; Probation, adult; Sentencing.

Symbionese Liberation Army

Identification: Paramilitary antigovernment and anticapitalist organization

Date: Founded in early 1973

Place: Oakland, California

Criminal justice issues: Kidnapping; political issues; violent crime

Significance: The short-lived Symbionese Liberation Army was a violent organization that blended criminal and radical political ideologies and gained national attention through a high-profile kidnapping.

Although the Symbionese Liberation Army (SLA) did not come into existence until the spring of 1973, eight of its members had known each other earlier through the Black Cultural Association, an African American prisoner organization in the California correctional system's medical facility at Vacaville. The Black Cultural Association had as members both visiting political radicals and incarcerated criminals. Donald DeFreeze, who organized the SLA and was its leader, escaped from prison and turned to the radicals for a safe place to live.

The SLA's murder of Marcus Foster, the superintendent of the Oakland school system was an attempt to be recognized and was followed by the release of the SLA's first public political statement to justify its activities. Meanwhile, two SLA members were arrested for Foster's murder and one was convicted.

In February, 1974, the SLA became the focus of intense news-media attention when its members kidnapped Patricia Hearst, the granddaughter of newspaper tycoon William Randolph Hearst, from her Berkeley apartment. The organization then demanded a ransom in the form of a massive free-food distribution to the poor. Shortly afterward, SLA leaders announced that Hearst had voluntarily joined their organization. In May, 1974, six SLA members were killed in a shoot-out with the Los Angeles SWAT team that ended in a fiery conflagration. The following year, the remaining SLA members staged a bank robbery in which a bank customer was killed. The organization's final action was a failed attempt to kill police officers in Los Angeles.

The life of the organization ended in September, 1975, when Patricia Hearst and another SLA member were captured. For her part in the bank robbery, Hearst was convicted in 1976 (she was later pardoned). Five other former SLA members who had participated in the robbery pleaded guilty to a variety of charges when they were finally arrested in 2002.

Donald A. Watt

Further Reading

Boulton, David. *The Making of Tania Hearst.* London: New English Library, 1975.

Hearst, Patricia, and Alvin Moscow. *Patty Hearst, Her Own Story.* New York: Avalon Books, 1988.

Payne, Les, and Tim Findley, with Carolyn Craven. *The Life and Death of the SLA.* New York: Ballantine Books, 1976.

See also Bank robbery; Celebrity criminal defendants; Federal Bureau of Investigation; Special weapons and tactics teams (SWAT); Terrorism.

T

Tax evasion

Definition: Deliberate failure to pay legally due taxes or to submit required returns and other documents

Criminal justice issues: Business and financial crime; fraud; white-collar crime

Significance: Although tax evasion is a felony offense punishable by fines and imprisonment, as well as civil penalties, the scale of the crime is immense because as many as one in five Americans admits to cheating on income tax returns.

In 1913, the Sixteenth Amendment to the U.S. Constitution gave the U.S. Congress the power to lay and collect taxes on incomes, from whatever source derived, without apportionment among the states, and without regard to any census or enumeration. To implement that power, Congress passed the Internal Revenue Code (IRC) or tax code. That code provides that any person who willfully attempts, in any manner, to evade or defeat a tax imposed by the code is guilty of a felony and subject to fine, imprisonment, or both. Another section of the code also makes it a felony to fail to file required tax returns.

Responsibility to Pay Income Tax

Any person who willfully makes and submits a return, statement, or other document that contains any false information is guilty of tax evasion under the code. It is also a crime willfully to aid or assist other persons or corporations to evade a legally due tax. Among specific types of violations possible under the tax code are deliberately underreporting or omitting income, overstating deductions, keeping multiple sets of books, making false entries in books and records, claiming personal expenses as business expenses, claiming false deductions, and hiding or transferring assets or income.

The federal tax code relies on the concept of voluntary compliance by taxpayers. It is thus the responsibility of individual taxpayers to file correct returns in a timely fashion and to determine and pay the correct amounts of taxes that are due. The vast majority of Americans recognize that responsibility by properly reporting and paying their tax obligations. However, the Internal Revenue Service (IRS), which collects federal income taxes, estimates that 17 percent of all taxpayers do not comply with the tax laws in one way or another.

The IRS further estimates that individual taxpayers—mostly middle-income earners—do 75 percent of the cheating, and corporations do most of the rest. Cash-intensive businesses and service industry workers are considered as the worst offenders. For example, the IRS claims that restaurant waiters underreport their tips by an average of 84 percent. According to the IRS, most cheaters deliberately underreport income, while only 6.8 percent of deductions that are claimed are overstated or simply false. Tax cheating done by self-employed people approaches 100 percent, but much of such cheating may be trivial. For example, using a postage stamp for which a business deduction is taken to mail a personal letter is technically a form of tax cheating.

The federal tax code is complex and is amended annually. In 2004, the complete code filled more than 4,500 printed pages. The sheer size and complexity of the code naturally creates many situations in which it is not clear how a tax law should be applied. As a consequence, honest differences in interpretation lead to frequent disputes between taxpayers and the IRS.

Part of the confusion in tax laws arises from the fact that some tax rules are written for purposes other than raising revenue for the government. For example, the federal government tries to help alleviate housing problems of poor citizens by giving special tax breaks to those who invest in low-income housing. The government also attempts to stimulate manufacturing industries by allowing rapid tax write-offs to buyers of new business equipment. There are also many special interest groups, such as oil and insurance companies, that have successfully lobbied for tax laws designed to give them special treatment. Indeed, the special provisions of the federal tax code outnumber the laws of general application.

Honest Disputes

Honest disputes and misinterpretations of provisions of the complex tax code are not considered tax evasion. In federal criminal tax cases, the statutory willfulness requirement is the voluntary, intentional violation of a known legal duty. Federal courts have held that it is not the purpose of the law to penalize frank differences of opinion or innocent errors made despite the exercise of reasonable care. In one case, for example, a U.S. district court held that a taxpayer's reliance on a certified public accounting firm's assurance that it would either file the taxpayer's income tax return before the due date or file a request for an extension of time to file constituted "reasonable cause" for the taxpayer's failure to file the return.

The court in that case refused to adopt a per se rule that a taxpayer has a nondelegable duty to file a tax return when due. However, while reliance on the firm's assurance was sufficient to protect the taxpayer from criminal liability, the taxpayer was still required to pay a civil penalty for the failure to file the return on time.

Tax avoidance is the minimization of an individual's tax liability by taking advantage of legally available tax saving opportunities. The difference between tax avoidance and tax evasion is that the latter entails the reduction of tax liability by using illegal means.

Arguments that some provisions of the tax code are unconstitutional does not excuse the failure to comply with the tax code requirements for filing returns, providing required documents, or failing to pay required taxes. The courts have held that taxpayers cannot ignore the duties imposed by the IRC without risking criminal prose-

Former baseball star and manager Pete Rose being escorted by federal marshals to a federal courthouse in Cincinnati, where he was sentenced to prison on tax-evasion charges in July, 1990—one year after he was banned for life from Major League Baseball for betting on games. Throughout the ensuing decade, Rose protested his innocence of the gambling charges (a position that he later recanted), but the undeniable fact remained that he served prison time for violating the nation's tax laws. (AP/Wide World Photos)

cution. Taxpayers who refuse to comply with those duties must take the risk or being wrong. It makes no difference whether the claims of invalidity are frivolous or have substance.

Investigation

When IRS tax auditors find evidence of possible tax violations, they forward the suspect documents to the criminal investigation unit of the IRS. That unit is directed at taxpayers who willfully and intentionally violate their responsibilities to pay income, employment, and excise taxes. The criminal investigation division's general fraud program encompasses a wide variety of investigations involving tax and money laundering crimes perpetrated by individuals and organizations from small business owners and self-employed persons to large corporations. General fraud cases constitute the main component of the criminal investigation division's efforts to force taxpayer compliance with the Internal Revenue Code.

The IRS also has an Illegal Source Financial Crimes Program. This program attempts to recognize illegal source proceeds that are part of the untaxed underground economy and are considered threats to the voluntary tax compliance system. The federal government considers that failure to investigate these cases would erode public confidence in the tax system. Within the guidelines of the Illegal Source Financial Crimes Program, the criminal investigation division commits resources to investigations that involve proceeds derived from illegal sources. The program covers tax and tax-related violations set forth in the U.S. Code, as well as money laundering and currency violations. Linked to the investigation of the criminal charges within this program is an emphasis for the effective utilization of the forfeiture statutes to deprive individuals and organizations of illegally obtained assets.

Prosecution

The IRS uses informers in its efforts to find and prosecute tax evaders and pays them about 8 percent of the first $100,000 it collects and 1 percent of the balance. (Rewards received by inform-

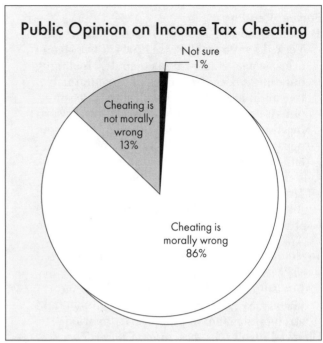

Source: Roper Center for Public Opinion Research, University of Connecticut. *Time* magazine survey, January, 1987. Figures based on interviews with 1,014 adult Americans.

ers are taxable income.) Identities of informers are kept secret, but tax cheats usually know who has reported them. In most cases, informers are former spouses and disgruntled business associates. In a recent year, the IRS paid out a total of only $1.5 million for tips, on $72 million collected. The IRS places low priority on investigating tips and has been accused of looking for ways to avoid paying rewards.

Penalties and Punishments

Tax evasion is a felony that is punishable by fine and/or prison. Careless mistakes on tax returns may add 20 percent penalties to taxpayers' tax bills. Deliberate fraud may add 75 percent civil penalties and also subject taxpayers to criminal liability. However, the line between negligence and fraud is not always clear, even to the IRS and the courts. The maximum punishments for tax evasion crimes are generally five years imprisonment and $100,000 in fines for each act of tax evasion. Civil penalties can range as high as 100 percent of the taxes legally due.

Cliff Roberson

Further Reading

Berson, Susan A. *Federal Tax Litigation*. New York: Law Journal Press, 2004. Coverage of every aspect of federal tax disputes, including handling tax controversies at the administrative audit and appeals levels of the IRS, alternative dispute resolution procedures, asserting the "innocent spouse defense," advice on negotiating with the IRS, and representing clients who are targets of investigations.

Callahan, David. *The Cheating Culture: Why More Americans Are Doing Wrong to Get Ahead*. Orlando, Fla.: Harcourt, 2004. Broad study of declining ethical standards in modern American society.

Pechman, Joseph A. *Tax Reform, the Rich and the Poor*. 2d ed. Washington, D.C.: Brookings Institution, 1989. Brief and simple overview of tax issues by a leading tax researcher and strong proponent of progressive taxation.

Slemrod, Joel, ed. *Does Atlas Shrug? The Economic Consequences of Taxing the Rich*. Cambridge, Mass.: Harvard University Press, 2000. Fifteen conference papers and commentaries examining important moral and economic aspects of taxing the wealthy.

Yancey, Richard. *Confessions of a Tax Collector: One Man's Tour of Duty Inside the IRS*. New York: HarperCollins, 2004. Revealing memoir of an Internal Revenue Service agent who looks at income tax from the inside.

See also Background checks; Capone, Al; Consumer fraud; Corporate scandals; Fraud; Insurance fraud; Internal Revenue Service; Money laundering; Organized crime; Perjury; Treasury Department, U.S.; White-collar crime.

Teapot Dome scandal

The Event: Federal government debacle involving oil field leases
Date: 1920's
Criminal justice issues: Business and financial crime; government misconduct
Significance: This shocking scandal undermined the honor of the federal government and led to closer scrutiny of the activities of government officials.

By federal law passed in 1920, the oil field reserves at Teapot Dome, Wyoming, and at Elk Hills, California, were set aside for use by the U.S. Navy. In 1921, Albert B. Fall, secretary of the interior, persuaded the secretary of the Navy, Edwin Denby, to transfer these valuable properties to the Department of the Interior. U.S. president Warren G. Harding unwisely signed the secret order. After receiving generous bribes worth more than $400,000, Fall proceeded to lease Teapot Dome reserves to oilman Harry F. Sinclair and Elk Hills reserves to oilman Edward L. Doheny in 1922, without holding any competitive bidding.

As details of the crooked dealings began to emerge in early 1923, federal hearings led to the indictment of Fall, Sinclair, and Doheny in 1924. President Calvin Coolidge appointed attorneys Owen Roberts and Atlee Pomerene to litigate the case for the federal government. Their efforts helped Coolidge to return the administration of the pertinent oil fields back to the secretary of the Navy in early 1928. Applying the finest traditions of American jurisprudence, Roberts and Pomerene meticulously amassed all of the pertinent evidence necessary to convict Fall in 1929 for conspiracy and accepting bribes. Fall was fined $100,000 and sentenced to one year in prison. He was the first cabinet officer ever jailed for crimes committed while serving in office. The wealthy and influential Sinclair and Doheny were acquitted, undermining public faith in the court system.

Alvin K. Benson

Further Reading

Stratton, David H. *Tempest Over Teapot Dome: The Story of Albert B. Fall*. Norman: University of Oklahoma Press, 1998.

Thorndike, Jonathan L. *The Teapot Dome Scandal Trial: A Headline Court Case*. Berkley Heights, N.J.: Enslow, 2001.

See also Conspiracy; Corporal scandal; Fraud; Political corruption; President, U.S.; Secret Service, U.S.; Watergate scandal.

Telephone fraud

Definition: All uses of telephones to defraud or cheat victims

Criminal justice issues: Business and financial crime; fraud; technology; white-collar crime

Significance: Because telecommunications have become integral parts of modern personal and professional life, the impact on victims of frauds and crimes that use telephones is similar to violations of trust and personal space.

Telephone fraud takes a variety of forms. One of the most common forms, telemarketing fraud, is the use of telephones to deceive people with false or misleading information to persuade them to make purchases or investments. Closely related to this is the use of telephones in the furtherance or commission of crimes. Other forms include the theft of telephone service and defrauding telephone customers.

Telemarketing Fraud

Telemarketing fraud involves lies, misrepresentations, intentional perversions of the truth, and other deliberate deceptions practiced for the purpose of gaining unfair advantages or injuring the rights or interests of others or providing unauthorized benefits to the initiators of frauds. Lying is an essential component of telephone fraud; without it, a telephone communication may constitute nothing worse than mere abuse. Moreover, the lies themselves must involve present or past facts; false claims about the future cannot constitute fraud. The lies must also be material or important to the parties making decisions, such as purchasing or investment decisions. Opinions do not constitute lies, unless those expressing them claim to have superior knowledge or state them as fact.

For an act to constitute fraud, three elements must be present. The first is the intention to make another party rely on the lie to change its position in a transaction. If the lie serves only to protect the liar's ego or reputation, an intention to defraud may not exist. Also, if the liar does not know that the statement is false, the lie may constitute only an innocent misrepresentation and not fraud.

A second requirement is that the party hearing the lie must actually and justifiably rely on it in making a decision. If decision that is made would have been the same, without the lie, the lie might not be fraud. Also, if the lie is not meant to be believed, it might not be fraud. For example, a salesman's puffery or exaggerated claims might not be fraud. If the party has reason to be suspicious of the claim, there might not be reliance. There is an obligation for the party to investigate or inquire about a suspicious claim.

A final requirement for considering a lie to be fraud is that monetary damage must result. If the lie merely causes hurt feelings or results in a decision with no monetary value—such as adopting a philosophical belief—the lie might not be fraud. The party must show a causal relationship between the lie and the damages suffered.

Other types of telemarketing fraud include promissory fraud, which involves promises that are made with no intention of keeping them, and negligent misrepresentation—assertions made as facts by persons who have no reason to believe their assertions are true. Specific telemarketing tactics and schemes include bait and switch, home improvement and repair scams, confidence tricks, false advertising, identity theft, prize offers in exchange for money or identity information, false billings, selling of products of spurious use, creating false companies or charitable organizations, and securities trading and investment schemes.

Telephone Service Frauds

Another broad form of telephone fraud is telephone service fraud, which may be practiced both by and on telephone service providers. An example of a service fraud perpetrated on telephone customers is "cramming"—charging customers for services they either do not receive or do not request, such as voice mail, paging, and Internet access.

Most service frauds are perpetrated by telephone users. For example, "phone phreaking" is the stealing of long-distance telephone services by manipulating the electronic dial tones, codes, or electronic signals used by telephone systems. Other methods of tampering with equipment or installing unauthorized equipment may also constitute service fraud, as does tapping into business private branch exchange (PBX) lines.

Some schemes affect third parties, such as the use of false identities or counterfeit credit cards over the telephone to receive services. Yet another of the many variations of service fraud is placing calls and transferring their charges to unsuspecting third parties by use of captured telephone numbers and stolen identities.

Telephone fraud can be a federal offense. The United States Code defines "wire fraud" as the use of interstate wire communications to carry out schemes to defraud. Violations of that law need involve no more than the devising, or intent to devise, schemes that involve, at least in part, some sound or voice transmission being wired in interstate commerce. Wire fraud includes telemarketing schemes but also extends to making false insurance claims over the telephone or plotting crimes.

Prevalence

Telephone fraud has existed almost as long as telephones themselves. Telephone service fraud was especially common during the 1960's and 1970's, when the high costs of long-distance services prompted the development of schemes to steal telephone service. During the early 1970's, a magazine called *Youth International Party Line* even published articles explaining how to steal service. Since that time, advances in telephone technology have made stealing service much more difficult.

The U.S. Congress has estimated that telemarketing fraud costs American consumers about forty billion dollars per year. A nonprofit consumer organization called the Alliance Against Fraud in Telemarketing, which formed in 1989, has claimed that one in every six private telephone users is cheated by telemarketers each year. *Billing World* magazine has estimated that up to 10 percent of telephone company revenue is lost to subscription fraud and other scams, some as simple as service subscribers signing up with fake names. The impact of telephone use to further other kinds of criminal schemes is inestimable.

Investigation

Telecommunication frauds are difficult to investigate and prosecute, but efforts to do so are necessary to protect telephone users, especially the most vulnerable citizens, including the elderly, less educated, and mentally challenged. However, all telephone users are vulnerable to the messages and practices of telephone fraud.

Telemarketing and telephone service fraud is investigated by the offices of state attorneys general, the Federal Communications Commission, and the Federal Trade Commission. Most investigations are undertaken in response to complaints of victims, who may also sue perpetrators of fraud for damages in civil court and conduct private investigations.

Telephone service providers use electronic equipment designed to detect ringback tones and changes in phone line power levels that may reveal illegal uses of telephone services. Telephone companies also respond to complaints from telephone users and investigate accused customers. Law enforcement uses wiretaps and electronic surveillance to pursue wire fraud.

Prosecution and Punishment

The Telephone Consumer Protection Act of 1991 and Federal Trade Commission Telemarketing Sales Rule of 1994 require telemarketers to identify themselves to the people whom they call and to disclose the purpose of their calls. Telemarketers are also required to disclose the full costs of payment agreements they offer and are prohibited from making misrepresentations. They are further required to respect consumer do-not-call lists, limit the hours during which they make calls, limit their use of automatic dialing systems and pre-recorded messages, and not send unsolicited advertising messages by fax. The National Do Not Call Registry fines businesses that initiate calls to registered telephone numbers, unless the businesses can show they have already established a business relationship with the phone owner whom they call. Registered charitable organizations, professional poll takers, and representatives of political campaigns are exempt from registry rules. Some state registries include businesses such as real estate, insurance, and newspapers in lists of exempted callers.

Penalties for telemarketing and telephone service fraud take into account the seriousness of the individual offenses. Frauds for small amounts—less than five hundred dollars—may be prosecuted as class A misdemeanors. Frauds for larger amounts may rise to class C felonies, which are punishable by fine and up to five years in prison.

In addition to being a criminal offense, fraud is also a tort in civil law, which means that its victims can recover damages from offenders. Victims may receive out-of-pocket costs, which are the differences between fair market prices for goods or services and the prices charged in fraudulent contracts. This measure is used in property and real estate fraud. Victims can receive benefit-to-bargain costs, which are the differences between the values of what has been promised and the value actually received. This is the measure used in service fraud and cases in which there are fiduciary relationships that obligate the liars to protect their victims, such as real estate agents and home buyers. Victims may also recover some of the costs of their litigation and, only occasionally, damages for emotional distress.

Wire fraud offenses are often attached to more serious criminal offenses. Such offenses may raise the penalties for the criminal acts that involve interstate wire communications.

Gordon Neal Diem

Further Reading

Ayres, Ian, and Gregory Klass. *Insincere Promises: The Law of Misrepresented Intent*. New Haven, Conn.: Yale University Press, 2005. Detailed discussion of promises, lies, and misrepresentations of fact.

Champion, Fred. *America's Guide to Fraud Prevention*. New York: Kroshka Books, 1997. Practical handbook offering advice on how to avoid becoming a victim of corrupt practices, fraud, and deceptive advertising in areas including telephone sales and telemarketing.

Corwall, Agnes S., ed. *Telecommunications: Issues in Focus*. New York: Nova Science Publishers, 2002. Discussions of issues of the future, including billing, telemarketing, and law-enforcement surveillance.

Dunn, Robert L. *Recovery of Damages for Fraud*. Westport, Conn.: Law Press Corporation, 2004. Detailed state and local information and cases on recovery for damages and defense from recovery.

Grabosky, Peter, and Russell Smith. *Crime in the Digital Age: Controlling Telecommunications and Cyber Illegalities*. New Brunswick, N.J.: Transaction Publishers, 1998. Extensive discussion of theft of services, piracy, telemarketing fraud, funds transfer crimes, the use of telecommunications in crime, terrorism, electronic vandalism, and more.

Schulte, Fred. *Fleeced! Telemarketing Rip-Offs and How to Avoid Them*. Amherst, N.Y.: Prometheus Books, 1995. Exposé on telephone schemers.

Sifakis, Carl. *Frauds, Deceptions and Swindles*. New York: Checkmark Books, 2001. Collection of brief articles on 150 of the most common American frauds and the people who have created them.

See also Cable and satellite television signal theft; Consumer fraud; Cybercrime; Electronic surveillance; Fraud; Insurance fraud; Mail fraud; Privacy rights; White-collar crime; Wiretaps.

Television courtroom programs

Definition: Fictional and so-called reality television presentations of the courthouse side of the U.S. criminal justice system

Criminal justice issues: Courts; media; trial procedures

Significance: Televised courtroom dramas reflect the changing attitudes of Americans toward their criminal justice system, even as they inform and shape those opinions.

Since the earliest days of American television programming during the late 1940's, courtroom dramas have been a staple of American entertainment, both in their own right and as a frequent element in such other genres as Westerns and science-fiction shows. Their appeal is not surprising. Perhaps because of the immense wealth of the American continent, the United States has been able to resolve through judicial hearings such seminal societal issues as corporate concentration of wealth (the Sherman Antitrust Act and the Supreme Court decisions based on it) and the exploitation of labor (through federal laws governing minimum wages and maximum hours of employment).

Likewise, from the days of the Salem witch trials, judicial proceedings have earmarked American history. Moreover, the search for the proper balance between individual liberty and the authority of the state—the issue in criminal proceedings—particularly touches that deeply ingrained part of the American political culture which reveres individualism but recognizes the state's mandate to safeguard the interests of society.

Real World Versus Television Programming

Television, like all entertainment, unfolds in and reflects the popular culture of the time. Although in any given year numerous television shows can be found with a courtroom locale and with prosecutors as well as defense attorneys as their central characters, almost every decade has witnessed the emergence of a dominant legal drama in tune with the mood of the United

States. During the 1950's, when television in general was simplifying life for a war-weary America seeking tidy solutions to complex problems, that drama was *Perry Mason*, the stories of an infallible defense attorney based on Erle Stanley Gardner's popular series of novels. Mason not only successfully defended his innocent clients but also regularly unearthed the guilty in each weekly episode.

During the turbulent 1960's, when the Vietnam War and the Civil Rights movements called authority into question, the pat formula of *Perry Mason* gave way to the more complex world of *The Defenders*, an hour-long drama aimed at educated viewers and revolving around a father-son duo committed to protecting the innocent but not always successful in doing so.

By the 1980's, character development and interrelationships had become nearly as important as plot to success on television, and the subject of the decade's premier legal drama became not a key lawyer but the McKenzie, Brackman firm of

Scene from a 1998 episode of *The People's Court* featuring a case in which the plaintiff sued a topless dancer, Tawny Peaks (standing, second from right), for injuring his neck when she struck him with her size 69HH breasts during a bachelor party. *(AP/Wide World Photos)*

L.A. Law. Indeed, weekly shows often gave as much time to the legal work that goes on inside law offices as to the attorneys' courtroom appearances—an approach which enabled their characters to focus frequently on civil as well as criminal law. Nonetheless, amid the office politics, romances, and in-office client negotiations, this drama offered its share of criminal proceedings, often revolving around the most controversial issues and events of the decade.

Defense attorneys operating in such shows as *The Practice* continued to do active business during the 1990's; however, rising crime rates and the resultant fears of urban America made an industry of the original and spinoff *Law and Order* series, which paired courtroom drama with police action. By then, the police dramas, too, had followed a similar path of evolution—from the tough-guy interrogation techniques of Joe Friday on *Dragnet* in the police-friendly 1950's to the precinct-lawyer-protecting-the-accused in the post-*Miranda* 1970's of *Hill Street Blues* to the slam-them-against-the-wall interrogations on-screen in *Homicide* and *N.Y.P.D. Blue* during the 1990's. The pairing of the *Law and Order* detectives with their soulmates in the district attorney's office tapped deeply into the American psyche, and the spinoffs and original continued to dominate the airwaves during the early twenty-first century.

Courtroom Television and the Real World

Advertisements for *Law and Order* announcing the new weekly episodes as "ripped from today's headlines" underscored the degree to which television drama had become linked to real-world events by the 1990's. That relationship, however, has by no means been one-sided. Beginning with the more controversial themes introduced in *The Defenders,* courtroom dramas have informed viewers and fleshed out their knowledge of such changing legal parameters as *Miranda v. Arizona*'s effect on police interrogations, Supreme Court guidelines governing capital punishment, mandatory sentencing, jury nullification, and the state's police authority under 2001's Patriot Act. The education process has also included civil law cases revolving around corporate liability, child

Courtrooms on the Small Screen

Television show	Ran	Type
The Defenders	1961-1965	courtroom drama
The Guardian	2001-2004	law drama
Hill Street Blues	1981-1987	police drama
JAG	1995-2005	military law drama
Judge Judy	1996-	reality courtroom
Judging Amy	1999-	court drama
L.A. Law	1986-1994	law drama
Law & Order	1990-	crime drama
The Lawyers	1969-1972	law drama
NYPD Blue	1993-2005	police drama
The People's Court	1981-1993	reality courtroom
Perry Mason	1957-1974	law drama
The Practice	1997-	law drama

custody issues, and the ability of minors to "divorce" their parents.

Fed by such shows and the media's coverage of the occasional celebrity trial, the public has steadily increased both its knowledge of and its desire for more real-life dramas far removed from the courtroom world Perry Mason once inhabited. In turn, television programmers have responded with more offerings, including shows with novel focal points, such as Fox's short-lived *The Jury* in the summer of 2004 and an entire cable television channel, Court TV, devoted to its namesake.

Joseph R. Rudolph, Jr.

Further Reading

Carlson, James M. *Prime Time Law Enforcement Crime Show Viewing and Attitudes Toward the Criminal Justice System.* New York: Praeger Special Studies, 1985. An early but still authoritative study of the impact of television viewing on the attitudes of viewers toward their legal system.

Jancovich, Mark, and James Lyons, eds. *Quality Popular Television: Cult TV, the Industry, and Fans.* London: British Film Institute, 2003. As the title suggests, the book's essays provide superb background reading on the impact of television on popular culture.

Jarvis, Robert M., and Paul R. Joseph, eds. *Prime Time Law: Fictional Television as Legal Nar-*

rative. Durham, N.C.: Carolina Academic Press, 1998. Excellent individual chapters on the most celebrated American police and courtroom television dramas, plus essays on British courtroom drama and such broad topics as "Women Lawyers."

Lenz, Timothy O. *Changing Images of Law in Film and Television Crime Stories.* New York: Peter Lang, 2003. Although films receive more attention than television dramas, the book's distinction between the liberal and the conservative slant of many of these dramas makes this volume essential reading.

Rapping, Elayne. *Law and Justice as Seen on TV.* New York: New York University Press, 2003. Read this book for the introductory chapters on fiction and entertainment genres, but do not ignore the essays grouped under the heading of news and documentary genres.

See also Criminal justice system; Due process of law; Films and criminal justice; Gag orders; Jury system; Literature about criminal justice; Radio broadcasting; Television crime dramas; Television news; Trials.

Television crime dramas

Definition: Fictional dramas made for television that revolve around issues of crime, police work, and public and private investigators

Criminal justice issues: Investigation; media

Significance: Television crime dramas have evolved to reflect real changes in society and audience expectations, but the real world of criminal justice has always been, and continues to be, more mundane than the televised depictions that have shaped public views of American criminal justice.

Broadcast television is essentially a creation of the late 1940's and early 1950's, and since its inception, televised crime dramas have been significant sources of information about crime and policing for large numbers of citizens. Many citizens have limited contacts with real criminal justice professionals and tend to get their ideas about police work and crime from television. Indeed, the types of affluent viewers sought by prime-time television advertisers are probably the segment of the population with the least direct experience with serious and violent crime, and they are thus the same segment of the population that derives its understanding of crime through media sources.

The proportion of broadcasting time that television devotes to dramas about "cops and criminals" far outweighs the prevalence of either in the population. Television audiences thus may form more concrete impressions about this side of life than they do about other professions and other social problems.

Television Versus Other Media

The ways in which police work is depicted in television dramas differ from depictions in films, books, and television news coverage. For example, American films and detective novels, from the 1930's onward, generally depicted a morally corrupt world in which police officers and private detectives operate. Police detectives, other government agents, victims, witnesses, and criminals who populated film and fictional crime stories inhabited interlocking and ambiguous worlds of multiple motives, guilt, and innocence. Often, nothing was truly as it appeared to be. Such worlds contrasted sharply with that of the first "police procedural" television series, *Dragnet* (1951-1959, 1967-1970), which originated as a radio series in 1949. Like those of many modern television police dramas, the plots of *Dragnet* were developed from real police cases that had few ambiguities. The procedural has served as the basic model for television police programs produced since the early 1950's.

Television crime drama has seen many significant changes over the years, but it has always rested on strong themes of social restoration and has contained considerably less ambiguity than either films or novel fiction. Crime drama episodes generally develop along predictable lines. First, good persons, families, or communities are disrupted, wounded, or trespassed upon—usually by acts of violence. Second, the police officers or detectives—in whom viewers have already developed confidence—aim to interrupt the activities of the perpetrators and bring them to justice. Finally, capture of the criminals restores the world to wholeness or restores the public's faith in the guarantors of justice.

The most significant changes in television's treatment of criminal justice have been shifts in the ways in which representatives of law and the moral order are shown to accomplish their larger tasks. Each new generation of crime dramas claims to represent greater "realism" than its predecessors, implying that previous programs were fraught with naive views of the subject.

Departures from Reality

Throughout television's brief history, its programs have placed increasing emphasis on violent crimes, crimes that are aberrant or atypical, and crimes that are committed by strangers to their victims. All these trends are departures from the realities of crime in the United States. For example, the proportion of all crimes in the United States that are violent is generally around 12 percent, most violent crimes involve rather obvious methods and motives, and most violence occurs among persons who are not strangers to one another.

Media researchers have also noted that television crime dramas have tended to favor stories about disproportionate numbers of criminal perpetrators who are professionals and wealthy. Perpetrators are often portrayed as powerful, intelligent, and ruthless figures who present "worthy opponents" for the investigators and law-enforcement officers who confront them. Television dramas also overemphasize the need for law-enforcement officers to use force to apprehend suspects. Finally, the most common crime in police dramas is murder—a crime that most police officers encounter rarely. Television's increasing emphasis on serious and aberrant crimes may reflect increased social concerns about such crimes, but it may also contribute to exaggerated public fears of such crimes.

Television's increasing focus on violence, aberrant events, and challenging criminals also shifts viewer attention away from what has been termed the "order maintenance" function of policing. Most police activities, in most places—even more densely populated, higher crime areas—center around traffic control and nonspecific aid

As *Dragnet's* Sergeant Joe Friday, actor Jack Webb personified honest, hard-working police detectives to two generations of American television watchers. In keeping with changing audience preferences, a new version of *Dragnet* that was launched on cable television in 2003, with Ed O'Neill as Friday, placed much greater emphasis on action than the original show, in which guns were rarely drawn and almost never fired. *(AP/Wide World Photos)*

to the public, and otherwise to constabulary duties and petty thievery. Work in these areas is most typical of the average police officer's experiences. Similarly, the activities of real-life private detectives, which generally center on suspected marital infidelity and business-related record searches, are generally much more banal than television would lead viewers to believe.

Crime Drama in a Different World

Since the 1970's, television crime dramas have tended to move away from beat and patrol policing, such as that depicted in the *Adam-12* series (1968-1975, created by Jack Webb, who had also done *Dragnet*), with its "service" orientation, and toward a focus on detective work and specialized policing. One explanation is that in the quest for more affluent audiences, networks may have favored shows with more educated, middle-class officers and quasi-officers, such as detectives and supervisors, handpicked task force officers, crime scene analysts, medical examiners, and forensic psychologists.

Crime dramas have also responded to the diversification of police forces. Beginning in the late 1960's and early 1970's with *The Mod Squad* (1968-1973) and *The Rookies* (1972-1976), African American and Latino police officers made their appearance. To some extent, this trend has followed a real-world trend. However, at the same time, it may be said that because crime dramas are still engaged in producing a healed, remoralized world for viewers, the diversification of the television squadroom reflects the desire to restore legitimacy to the police in the eyes of minority communities. The presence of nonwhite officers as regular characters, with as many dimensions as their white counterparts, has been lauded by most, but some critics see it as an attempt to neutralize criticism of the genre, in its previous depiction of African Americans and Latinos as criminals, gangsters, informants, and occasional victimization-prone "sidekicks," such as *Starsky and Hutch*'s "Huggy Bear."

The 1970's also saw the debut of women police officers and private investigators on television. The first program to focus on a woman was *Police Woman* (1974-1978); followed by *Get Christie Love!* (1974-1975); which featured a black woman officer; and then the highly rated *Charlie's Angels* (1976-1981). Although *Charlie's Angels* at times seemed to be more about hairstyling and jiggling than combatting crime, it had as its main characters women who had their police-academy hopes dashed by sexism in the roles they were assigned. It was the private detective agency that offered them real investigation and criminal pursuit opportunities. *Cagney and Lacey* (1982-1988) moved the role of the television policewoman forward by relying less upon last-minute rescues by male officers and by directly confronting the role of gender in squadroom politics. Female victims of violence were also depicted in more depth—a departure from the tendency of earlier shows to soft-pedal the details and impact of domestic abuse and sexual assault.

Modern Detectives: New Heroes

Cagney and Lacey was also a harbinger of the most significant change in crime dramas: the now-expected narrative interweaving of the characters' personal and emotional lives with the traditional procedural format. First, the individual personalities of police officers in crime drama have become more important to the progression of the story. In early shows, officers were loyal to the law in the abstract and to their colleagues in the criminal justice system. Personalities of television police officers were consistent with their assigned roles: They were competent and respectful, never excessive or emotional. There was an expected routine; the routine was there for a good reason and would inevitably lead to the capture of the criminal. For example, Sergeant Joe Friday of *Dragnet* could be interested in "just the facts" without seeming out of touch. Everyone was best served by sticking to the book and not encouraging histrionics, either by displaying emotion themselves or by encouraging it among victims and witnesses.

Since the 1950's, television police officers have been increasingly depicted as mavericks who are demonstrative about the moral transgressions that accompany serious crime, and the reserved personalities of earlier years were seen as inadequate. This trend was especially evident in the dramas of the 1970's, such as actor Robert Blake's *Baretta* (1975-1978) and *Starsky and Hutch* (1975-1979). In this new generation of dramas, reserved police officers were seen as being too much "agency" figures. Officers were now depicted as having personal lives, as having emotional attachments to crime victims, and as being somewhat contemptuous of the law-and-order establishment, whose top brass might be seen as complacent, and whose red tape and constitutional protections of suspects tied their hands. However, the new protagonists, in their own way, held true to the old ideals of justice, if not its cogs and wheels.

The new norm of multidimensional officers also spawned several series featuring private, rather than government, detectives, which further distanced them from the protocols (and apparent drudgery) of rule-bound police agencies. Of these programs, *The Rockford Files* (1974-1980) was the most successful. Rockford (James

Garner) was not an agency man either, though he was also less cynical than his counterparts in the *film noir* and novels of an earlier era. Similarly, the series *Mannix* (1967-1975) followed an iconoclastic private eye (Mike Connors), who strikes out on his own after clashing with his boss over rules, boundaries, and paperwork.

Even more lighthearted series of the era, such as *CHiPs* (1977-1983), made their officers accessible and gregarious. Often the main characters in crime series of the 1970's had trademark affectations, such as Baretta's habit of carrying a pet cockatoo on his shoulder, or Theo Kojak's (Telly Savalas) penchant for sucking on lollipops in *Kojak* (1973-1978)—a habit retained when a new *Kojak* series was launched in 2005. The best example of this tendency was the popular *Columbo* series (1971-1978) featuring a Los Angeles police detective, Lieutenant Columbo (Peter Falk), with his distinctively rumpled raincoat, omnipresent cigar, dilapidated car, and offbeat technique of getting suspects to incriminate themselves through careless errors, rather than grilling them in the old-school, harsh-light, accusatory manner. A typical Columbo episode might have the detective rambling on about his car troubles, while the suspect—who is unaware of being a suspect—looks for any excuse to get away from him. Eventually, Columbo says something that ruffles the suspect's composure.

Despite these trends, several successful series of the 1970's resisted these sorts of innovations. The second-longest-running police drama in American television history was *Hawaii Five-O* (1968-1980), whose four main detectives were decidedly cut from the reserved, persevering Joe Friday cloth. The *Streets of San Francisco* series (1972-1977) paired a seasoned, old-fashioned "street-smart" detective (Karl Malden) with a young, occasionally overeager college graduate (Michael Douglas), reflecting a real shift in the expectations of law-enforcement agencies, as well as a symbolic torch-passing.

Post-1970's Templates

Sociologist Todd Gitlin's study of decision making among network executives, *Inside Prime Time* (1983), found that most executives regarded crime dramas as obsolete by the late 1970's. Just about everything that could be done

in the form, it was thought, had been done. According to Gitlin, the first major new crime show of the 1980's, *Hill Street Blues* (1981-1987), challenged that judgment. That show's eventual success provided a new way of thinking about crime drama. Audiences would eventually change their expectations of those who represented law and order.

Hill Street Blues set a new template for television. It was unconventional in the numbers of returning characters it used and in offering several story lines in every episode. Moreover, it left many cases unresolved from week to week. *Hill Street Blues* also introduced to television drama a new tone of long-term pessimism about the ability of the police to make broad strides against serious crime. However, the bleakness of the show's narratives was punctuated by moments of satisfaction regarding just deserts for specific offenders and hope for the healing of specific victims. Other successful series that followed took on a similar tone, investing hope in the small victories of individual characters rather than peace and justice in the abstract.

By the 1990's, personality flaws, squadroom conflicts, and personal struggles in the lives of police officers were becoming even more central. *NYPD Blue* (1993-2005) and *Law & Order* (1990-   ) featured officers who were active or recovering alcoholics and were self-absorbed and who had serious illnesses, hair-trigger tempers, womanizing tendencies, and troubled relatives. Generally it was accepted that their personal-life entanglements made them vulnerable to projections of excessive zeal upon particular cases. All of these "imperfections," far from disqualifying officers as symbolic agents of justice, only enhanced their dedication and skill in this respect.

Homicide: Life on the Street (1993-1999) depicted the lives and work of detectives in Baltimore. It eschewed violent action segments and car chases altogether and reflected a more realistic view of homicide detective work—which was often plodding, frustrating, and slow. *Homicide* was not nearly as popular as *Law & Order* and *NYPD Blue*, both of which combined traditional appeals to audiences, blending casebook proceduralism with complex characters and near-existential resignation to a world of darkness.

In promotions for coming episodes, *Law & Or-*

der has claimed that its stories are "ripped from the headlines," but it would be more accurate to say that real high-profile crimes are used as touchpoints to explore contemporary legal issues. Half of each episode, usually, is devoted to post-arraignment developments—in which a district attorney makes charges stick, investigates further, negotiates a plea bargain, or takes the accused to trial.

Modern Crime Dramas and International Trends

Significant declines in crime in the United States that began during the 1990's have not tempered television's trend toward pessimism in its crime dramas. To some extent, this ongoing trend reflects police caseloads that remain historically high despite declining crime rates, due to new initiatives and changes in enforcement expectations. However, it is curious that almost no major crime drama series has backed away from the post-1970's message that almost nothing can be done about violence, or even petty crime. A small but revealing sign of this tendency is the fact that television shows set in New York City have continued to show the city's famed subway cars as covered in graffiti and grime years after those conditions had waned. It appears that it is still necessary for many shows to put each case and character into a visual context that seems to say that criminality and chaos reign supreme.

Meanwhile, as television has gone global, so have crime dramas. While the United States exports its own shows to many countries, the crime dramas made in other countries usually match or exceed the popularity of American shows. There are both differences and similarities between American and foreign crime shows.

In Great Britain, popular crime dramas have tended to maintain the "hard-boiled" detective role at their centers, despite their tendency to take on other dimensions. Such shows have included *The Bill* (1984-   ), which centers on a single police precinct in London; *The Sweeney* (1975-1978), about an elite unit assigned to armed robbery, which has been praised for its gritty realism; *Cracker* (1993-1996), about a psychologically oriented detective; and, to some extent, the miniseries *Prime Suspect* (1991-   ), which has a female chief of detectives.

Similarities to U.S. dramas are especially evident in *The Bill*. This show started as a standard police procedural but gradually became more focused on the personal troubles of officers, problems of corruption, and interpersonal relationships among officers on the job. It also diversified its characters, including the addition of an openly gay officer. Detectives in British shows are often more organizationally deviant and single-minded in their pursuit of criminals than their American counterparts. At the same time, British shows, such as *Z Cars* (1962-1978), were earlier in showing their officers drinking to excess, womanizing, and otherwise acting personally deviant against the image of the clean-cut law enforcers.

Socioeconomic class has also played a more overt role in British television, according to a study by Glen Creeber, creating conflicts for detectives ("inspectors" in Britain) who are upwardly mobile, introspective, and educated. These traits allow them to remain

A makeup artist touches up one of the innumerable actors who have played corpses in the popular *CSI* television dramas. With the emphasis that these programs place on realistic forensic details of homicide investigations, it is possible that these series have had more actors play corpses than all other television dramas combined. *(AP/Wide World Photos)*

Top-Rated Network Television Programs, January 24-30, 2005

Rank	Program	Network	Type of program
1	*American Idol* (Tues.)	FOX	Talent competition
2	*American Idol* (Wed.)	FOX	Talent competition
3	*CSI	CBS	Police procedural
4	*E.R.	NBC	Drama about medical emergencies in a hospital
5	*CBS Sunday Movie*	CBS	Feature film
6	*CSI: NY	CBS	Police procedural
7	*Cold Case	CBS	Police procedural
8	*CSI: Miami	CBS	Police procedural
9	*Medium	NBC	Drama about a woman who uses psychic powers to solve mysteries
10	*Numb3rs	CBS	Drama about application of mathematics to police investigation
11	*Without a Trace	CBS	Drama about the FBI's missing persons squad
12	*Apprentice 3*	NBC	"Reality" series about corporate business
13	*Everybody Loves Raymond*	CBS	Family sitcom
14	*Law and Order: Special Victims Unit	NBC	Police procedural
15	*60 Minutes*	CBS	News feature series
16	*Extreme Makeover: Home Edition*	ABC	Reality series about home remodeling
17	*Law and Order: Criminal Intent	NBC	Police procedural
18	*Two and a Half Men*	CBS	Family sitcom
19	*Extreme Makeover: Home Edition*	ABC	Reality series about home remodeling
20	*Desperate Housewives*	ABC	Family sitcom

Source: Nielsen Media Research. *Programs with criminal justice themes are asterisked.

fiercely independent and even defiant, although they also wish to maintain their toughness and credibility on the street and among their working-class rank-and-file subordinate officers.

South America's largest nation, Brazil, presents a different kind of contrast. There, television crime dramas do not always cast police as heroes. Sometimes they are shown as self-interested or corrupt. Even sympathetic officers are shown as battling rampant corruption among their peers while trying to serve the public good.

In post-Soviet Russia, commercial television networks have broadcast American crime dramas, such as *NYPD Blue*, and created their own domestic shows, which are highly rated. Elena Prokhorova's analysis of themes in Russian shows found similarities to the transformations that took place in U.S. dramas during the 1980's and 1990's. Characters in Russian shows have became highly personalized, and deep pessimism about crime has arisen. As in reality, organized crime plays a significant role in the new Russian

crime dramas. The hope of achieving justice amid burgeoning crime and violence is consistently reduced to small personal victories: islands of order amid chaos. As similar as this trend is to changes in the American shows, it also reflects a particular sort of cynicism as a backlash to the ideological messages of earlier Soviet crime dramas. Soviet programs were unabashedly optimistic. They tended to focus on embezzlement and presented dedicated, smart, and untroubled officers as representatives of the state.

At the beginning of the twenty-first century, there is some indication that U.S. crime dramas are becoming more preoccupied with threats from organized crime, international syndicates, and transnational terrorism, as might be expected in the wake of the September 11, 2001, terrorist attacks. However, the long-term overall popularity of crime drama around the world, and the overlapping themes that can be seen in recent decades, suggest that the appeal of crime drama goes beyond any social feature unique to the

United States. Perhaps there is something fundamental about the relationship between television, modernization, and the appeal of crime and police dramas worldwide.

Pamela Donovan

Further Reading

Creeber, Glen. "Old Sleuth or New Man? Investigations into Rape, Murder and Masculinity in *Cracker* (1993-1996)." *Continuum: Journal of Media and Cultural Studies* 16, no. 2 (2002): 169-183. Examination of the depiction of social class, gender relations, and masculinity in recent British crime dramas.

D'Acci, Julie. *Defining Women: Television and the Case of "Cagney and Lacey."* Chapel Hill: University of North Carolina Press, 1994. Examination of gender issues, feminism, and policing through the case of one television series.

Dominick, J. R. "Crime and Law Enforcement on Prime-Time Television." *Public Opinion Quarterly* 37, no. 2 (1973). Classic content analysis unearthing contrasts between reality and fiction.

Gitlin, Todd. *Inside Prime Time*. 1983. Berkeley: University of California Press, 2000. Sociological study of how decisions are made by executives in television networks.

Kamalipour, Yahya R., and Kuldup R. Rampal, eds. *Media, Sex, Violence and Drugs in the Global Village*. New York: Rowman & Littlefield, 2001. Collection of articles examining treatments of social problems in the media, particularly television, in different parts of the world.

Lane, Philip J. "The Existential Condition of Television Crime Drama." *Journal of Popular Culture* 34, no. 4 (2001): 137-151. Examination of parallels between existential philosophy and dilemmas faced by characters in modern crime dramas.

Perlmutter, David D. *Policing the Media: Street Cops and Public Perception of Law Enforcement*. Thousand Oaks, Calif.: Sage Publications, 2000. Ethnographic study of one town's police force, the officers' views of "cop shows" and the public, and the public's view of police.

Prokhorova, Elena. "Can the Meeting Place Be Changed? Crime and Identity Discourse in Russian Television Series of the 1990's." *Slavic Review* 62, no. 3 (Fall, 2003): 512-525. Descriptive account of late Soviet and post-Soviet crime drama, with themes of chaos and struggles over personal identity.

Silver, Alain, and Elizabeth Ward, eds. *Film Noir: An Encyclopedic Reference to the American Style*. 3d ed. Woodstock, N.Y.: Overlook Press, 1992. Articles on American-style detective films and their cultural origins in post-World War II social dislocations.

Terrace, Vincent. *The Complete Encyclopedia of Television Programs, 1947-1979*. New York: A. S. Barnes, 1979. Collection of synopses of regularly scheduled series on broadcast television.

See also Cold cases; Films and criminal justice; Literature about criminal justice; Police detectives; Print media; Private detectives; Radio broadcasting; Television courtroom programs; Television police reality shows.

Television news

Definition: Coverage of criminal justice on national and local television broadcasts

Criminal justice issue: Media

Significance: It is a well-documented fact that television news offers distorted coverage of crime. Although there are differing explanations for why television news is saturated with coverage of crime and violence, the fact that such coverage distorts public perceptions of crime and affects criminal justice policies is beyond contention.

As the United States becomes ever more a media nation, public perceptions of the world are increasingly influenced by media consumption. Such perceptions include public views on the nature and extent of crime and violence in the nation. Public perceptions help to shape what society expects and is willing to permit as acceptable criminal justice policies. Whether the public wishes to rehabilitate, educate, or demand vengeance upon criminal offenders is based, to a large extent, on such perceptions.

More than any other source, the news media are responsible for shaping public views on crime and criminal justice issues. Such media-driven perceptions combine with real-world experiences to make citizens feel safe or fearful when they leave their homes at night or walk to their cars after work. It is a well-researched and widely accepted truth that a vast majority of Americans receive their images of crime and their knowledge of the criminal justice system from what they see and read in the news media. One study places that majority as high as 76 percent. It is thus important to understand how the news media approach these issues.

The fact that public perceptions of crime rates do not reflect actual rates of crime is beyond contention. A vast majority of citizens are misinformed on crime in this country. For example, although crime rates have fallen since the mid-1990's, the public has continued to believe that crime rates have continued to rise—and in almost epidemic proportions. The news media are the primary source of such misperceptions, and public misperceptions drive government criminal justice policies.

Disproportionate News Media Coverage of Crime

The phrase "if it bleeds, it leads" has come for many to describe the news media's approach to crime coverage, and this is particularly true of television news. The reason is simple: Crime stories attract more viewers than less sensational stories. Larger audiences mean higher television ratings, and higher ratings mean greater advertising revenue.

Some representative statistics on homicide demonstrate the overemphasis on violent crime in television news. For example, although homicides traditionally account for only 0.1 to 0.2 percent of all arrests made in the United States, they account for more than 25 percent of all crimes reported on the evening television news programs. Moreover, although the numbers of homicide arrests in the United States dropped 32.9 percent between 1990 and 1998, television news stories on homicide increased by 473 percent over the same time period. The trend in print media coverage of homicide was similar, but the increase in homicide coverage was not as great.

Offenses committed by juveniles are also disproportionately covered in the news media. Between 1993 and 1998, the rate of homicides committed by juvenile offenders dropped by 68 percent. During that same period, polls found that 62 percent of Americans thought that the rate of juvenile homicide was rising. This public misperception was almost certainly a result of overemphasis on juvenile crime in the news media. This overemphasis is particularly evident in local television news coverage. One study of local television news stories focusing on youths during that same time period found that about 74 percent of the stories pertained to incidents of crime and violence. That figure contrasts with the 40 percent of metropolitan newspaper stories on youths that focused on crime and violence. While violence perpetrated by youths is overreported in the news media, violence against youths is underreported.

Threat to Society

People working in the news media tend to justify their overreporting of crime by calling it a service to society. In their view, crimes tear at the moral fiber of society and endanger the innocent. They see occurrences of criminal behavior as more important than events that do not threaten society or endanger the innocent. Overreporting of crime and violence is thus justified, as they are simply more important than events that do not threaten society and the innocent.

Crimes committed in what are believed to be safe areas or by persons who are expected to be innocent receive particular attention in the news media because they are unexpected, and unexpected events are more newsworthy. This same logic helps to explain why crimes committed by youths are overreported: Youths are expected to be innocent, and when they commit crimes, it is unexpected. Violent events in places such as schools and day-care centers are especially newsworthy because they are places that have long been regarded as safe havens for the innocent.

Theodore Shields

Further Reading

Chermak, Steven M. *Victims in the News: Crime and the American News Media*. Boulder, Colo.: Westview Press, 1995. Examination of the role of victims in media coverage of crime news.

Klug, Elizabeth A. "Juvenile Crimes Are Vastly Overreported by the Media." *Corrections Compendium* 26, no. 6 (June, 2001). Carefully documented study of how the news media overreports juvenile offenses.

Lipschultz, Jeremy H., and Michael L. Hilt. *Crime and Local TV News: Dramatic, Breaking, and Live from the Scene.* Mahwah, N.J.: Lawrence Erlbaum Associates, 2002. Analysis of local television news that emphasizes theories of market-driven journalism and lack of interest in public affairs coverage as factors explaining media emphasis on crime.

Potter, Gary W., and Victor E. Kappeler, eds. *Constructing Crime: Perspectives on Making News and Social Problems.* Prospect Heights, Ill.: Waveland Press, 1998. Collection of fifteen essays examining media and crime. The essays examine how popular images of crime are generated, the effects of these images, and who benefits from the images that are constructed.

Sherwin, Richard K. *When Law Goes Pop: The Vanishing Line Between Law and Popular Culture.* Chicago: University of Chicago Press, 2002. Study by a legal scholar and former prosecutor of the corrupting influence on the criminal justice system of television and film treatments of criminal justice.

Sorenson, Susan B., Julie G. Peterson Manz, and Richard A. Berk. "News Media Coverage and the Epidemiology of Homicide." *The American Journal of Public Health* 88, no. 10 (October, 1998). Study of the discrepancies between news media coverage of homicide and actual trends in homicide.

Surette, Ray. *Media, Crime, and Criminal Justice.* 2d ed. Pacific Grove, Calif.: Brooks/Cole Publishing, 1998. Perhaps the definitive work on media coverage of criminal justice, this book explores media treatments of crime and offers extensive discussions of relevant Supreme Court decisions and summaries of research on media and crime issues.

Yanich, Danilo. "Location, Location, Location: Urban and Suburban Crime on Local TV News." *Journal of Urban Affairs* (Summer/Fall, 2001). Examination of the tendency of local television news to overemphasize crime in neighborhoods that are expected to be safe.

See also Gag orders; News source protection; Print media; Radio broadcasting; Television courtroom programs; Television police reality shows; Trial publicity.

Television police reality shows

Definition: Television program featuring actual police operations

Criminal justice issue: Media

Significance: While police reality shows may help to educate the public about real-life police work, they can also contribute to fostering distorted views of law enforcement and raising viewers' own fears of becoming victims of violent crime. Reality shows also pose the threat of violating the privacy of the people caught on camera.

During the 1980's, American television networks began broadcasting programs about police that fit in what later became known as the "reality television" genre. One of the first such programs was *America's Most Wanted* (1988-   ), which invited members of the audience to phone in information about suspects profiled on the show through recitations of facts, photographs, and dramatized re-creations of events. *COPS*, which began in 1989 and ranked as one of the longest-running television shows in U.S. history in 2005, depicts real police officers at work and has become the epitome of reality-based police shows. Other television reality police shows have included *Top Cops* (1990-1993), which featured reenactments of heroic real-life police work, and *Rescue 911* (1989-1996), which featured both documentary film footage and dramatized reenactments of police and firefighters in emergency situations.

What sets the reality genre apart from fictionalized programming is that reality programs use real-life film footage shot and edited to make viewers feel that they are part of the action. Hand-held cameras are often used to increase the viewers' sense of being there. Pictures are often unclear, and the lighting is often poor. All these elements add to the reality of the program, reminding viewers that what is important is the action, not the camera work. Camera crews literally follow real police officers around as they go about their duties, and real criminals and real victims are shown to audiences. Police officers typically present background information, framing the action from a law-enforcement perspective, and conclude by supplying moral lessons to conclude each vignette.

Pros and Cons of Reality Shows

An important benefit of reality shows to television networks is that they are cheap to produced, as there are no big-name actors to be paid, no scriptwriters to hire, and no sets to build. At the same time, reality programs receive high ratings, which translate into increased advertising revenue and high profits.

Another benefit of reality police shows is that

John Walsh, host of the Fox network's long-running show *America's Most Wanted*. (AP/Wide World Photos)

members of the general public can gain insights into how real police work is done. Such programs almost invariably place police in a positive light, showing officers capturing offenders, handling dangerous and difficult situations effectively, responding to public calls for help, and explaining everything that is happening to audiences.

Despite their ostensible efforts to present police work realistically, reality programs distort reality in a variety of ways. For example, they generally emphasize violent crime and present a misleading picture of the role combatting such crime plays in everyday police work. In this regard, reality shows are similar to television crime dramas; however, they do not go as far as televised dramas to in emphasizing unusual crimes.

Reality shows also focus on the most dramatic elements of police work, such as hot pursuit of suspects, and neglect or ignore the tedious paperwork officers have to do and the slow days when police work consists mostly of uneventful patrols. In general, the shows make police work appear to be more glamorous and exciting than it typically is. The shows can also distort social realities in subtle ways. For example, the law-enforcement personnel depicted on *COPS* are mostly white people, while the show's suspects tend to be disproportionately nonwhite.

These distortions taken on greater significance than they might in dramatic shows because audiences of reality shows are inclined to assume that what they see is, in fact, reality. Moreover, the "reality" audiences see may actually be manufactured in various ways. For example, the format of *COPS* may encourage viewers to believe that the events they see are occurring at a pace similar to the way in which the actual events have occurred. Many hours often pass between citizen calls for help and successful resolutions of problems, but the quick editing used in *COPS* often gives audiences the impression that the action is fast-paced, dramatic, and sensational. People appearing on *COPS* may be real officers, criminals, and victims, but their awareness of the cameras' presence may cause them to behave differently than they would otherwise. Moreover, much of what they do and say may be edited out of the footage broadcast on the show, which uses only footage that supports the messages the show tries to impart.

Implications for Criminal Justice

Reality shows such as *COPS* may help educate the public about law enforcement and crime, but placing cameras in the midst of police may hinder the officers' ability to perform their duties or infringe upon the rights of the people with whom they are dealing. Indeed, in 1999 the U.S. Supreme Court ruled that the presence of media violated the right of a citizen to privacy when a media crew entered a home during a police search.

Although many people may watch reality shows purely for entertainment, audiences may alter their views about police because of the shows. For example, people who watch such programs are more likely than others to fear they may become victims of violent crime. Studies have shown that people who watch the shows are more likely than others to prefer harsher punishments for criminals and are more likely to hold racist attitudes.

Sheryl L. Van Horne

Further Reading

Fishman, Mark, and Grey Cavender, eds. *Entertaining Crime*. New York: Aldine de Gruyter, 1998. Scholarly research of crime shows, focusing mostly on reality crime shows in the United States, Great Britain, the Netherlands, and France.

Lesce, Tony. *Cops: Media vs. Reality*. Port Townsend, Wash.: Loompanics Unlimited, 2000. Study of the relationship between reality show footage and actual police work, with attention to the impact of the shows.

Murray, Susan, and Laurie Ouellette, eds. *Reality TV: Remaking Television Culture*. New York: New York University Press, 2004. Historical account of the changing of television and the growing popularity of the reality genre.

Perlmutter, David D. *Policing the Media: Street Cops and Public Perceptions of Law Enforcement*. Thousand Oaks, Calif.: Sage Publications, 2000. Study of how the media portray police work and how media portrayals differ from reality.

See also Films and criminal justice; Literature about criminal justice; Print media; Radio broadcasting; Television courtroom programs; Television crime dramas; Television news.

Ten-most-wanted lists

Identification: Federal Bureau of Investigation program that publicizes the names and images of the most dangerous and sought-after criminal fugitives

Date: Begun in March, 1950

Criminal justice issues: Federal law; investigation; media

Significance: Since the inception of this Federal Bureau of Investigation (FBI) program, most-wanted lists have helped to raise public awareness of law-enforcement work while serving as an effective tool in apprehending criminal fugitives.

In 1949, a journalist writing for the International News Service (INS) asked the FBI for a list of the ten "toughest guys" that the agency was then seeking and published the list in the *Washington Post*. The list attracted so much public interest that FBI director J. Edgar Hoover decided to make publication of most-wanted lists a regular FBI program. On March 14, 1950, the agency issued its first official list of the ten most-wanted fugitives. Since then, the lists have occasionally been expanded to include more than ten names as special circumstances justified exceptional additions.

Because the ten-most-wanted lists are part of a federal law-enforcement program, the fugitives listed by the FBI must be sought for violating federal laws. The primary crimes with which most of the fugitives are charged—such as murder, rape, assault, and robbery (except bank robbery, which can be a federal offense)—are violations of state laws over which the federal government has no jurisdiction; however, when the fugitives cross state lines to avoid prosecution or punishment, they become guilty of violating federal laws and thus become eligible for the ten-most-wanted lists. In 1962, the U.S. Congress passed the Unlawful Flight to Avoid Prosecution Act, which authorized the FBI to pursue fugitives from justice who cross state lines, regardless of the nature of their original offenses. Since the 1960's, it has been illegal to flee across state lines to avoid prosecution, custody, or confinement for any felony or capital crime or to flee to avoid giving testimony in felony proceedings.

Suggestions for names to put on the lists are made by agents in the FBI's fifty-six field offices. Their suggestions are reviewed by special agents in the criminal investigative division of the FBI who are familiar with the bureau's fugitives and the Office of Public and Congressional Affairs. After the suggestions are narrowed down, they receive a final review by the FBI's deputy director or director.

Criteria for Selection

The selection of only ten fugitives to list is a complicated process because at even given moment, the FBI may be seeking as many as twelve thousand different fugitives. Fugitives selected for the list are those who have lengthy records of committing serious crimes and who are considered particularly dangerous to society. No fugitive's name goes on the list unless there is some reasonable hope that publicizing the fugitive

might actually assist apprehension. Hence, a fugitive who is already widely known from other publicity might not be listed.

Names are removed from the list when the fugitives die, are captured, or no longer fit list criteria. The latter may occur when a fugitive is no longer regarded as a major threat to society, but this rarely happens. As names are dropped from the list, others are added.

Since the program's inception, the makeup of the lists has reflected the changing nature of crime in America as well as the changing criteria of the FBI. During the program's early years, bank robbers, burglars, and car thieves dominated the list. During the 1960's, political radicals charged with destruction of government property, sabotage, and kidnapping predominated. During the 1970's, as international organized crime and political terrorism increased, the makeup of the lists changed again. Since the early 1990's, organized crime figures, international drug dealers, serial murderers, and international terrorists have predominated.

Impact of the Program

Of the approximately five hundred fugitives whose names were listed between 1950 and 2005, more than 90 percent were apprehended. One of the reasons for this success rate is the FBI's use of television and radio to draw the widest possible public attention to its lists of fugitives. Among the broadcast programs that have publicized the lists are John Walsh's *America's Most Wanted* (1988-   ) and *Unsolved Mysteries* (1987-   ) on television and radio's *FBI, This Week*, an ABC network program produced in cooperation with the FBI. In 1995, the FBI began posting its lists on the Internet. Other commercial uses of the lists are prohibited, as the program exists for the sole purpose of getting the public to help track down fugitives.

Publicity has had a psychological impact on the fugitives themselves, some of whom have voluntarily turned themselves in when they have realized that they are targets of nationwide manhunts. Nevertheless, some fugitives evade capture for many years.

U.S. attorney general Janet Reno announcing the addition of Juan Garcia-Abrego to the FBI's ten-most-wanted list in March, 1995. The reputed leader of a Mexican drug cartel, Garcia-Abrego was the first international drug trafficker to make the list. *(AP/Wide World Photos)*

The ten-most-wanted list program has attracted a number of criticisms. First, some people have charged that it is merely a publicity event and a waste of taxpayers' money. The FBI rebuts this charge by pointing out that the program's main purpose is to generate publicity that will enlist public cooperation in the pursuit of dangerous criminals.

It has also been charged that the lists too often target small-time criminals, while organized crime leaders and major drug traffickers remain at large. This charge may be refuted by the fact that high-ranking crime leaders rarely become fugitives because they can afford to hire expensive lawyers for their legal defense. The FBI rarely needs help in locating such people.

A third criticism of the list is its frequent inclusion of political radicals on the list. It might be conceded that some names have found their way onto the FBI's list because of the personal political agendas of FBI leaders such as Hoover, but the FBI would counter that criminal offenders cannot be allowed to legitimize their crimes on political grounds.

Peter B. Heller

Further Reading

Matera, Dary. *FBI's Ten Most Wanted*. New York: HarperCollins, 2003. Profiles of some of the most notorious fugitives on the FBI list, including Osama bin Laden, the al-Qaeda leader who is believed to have masterminded the September 11, 2001, terrorist attacks on the United States. Also includes an appendix listing all the names that have appeared on FBI lists.

Newton, Michael, and Judy Newton. *The FBI Most Wanted: An Encyclopedia*. New York: Garland, 1989. Case-by-case descriptions of all the fugitives who made the FBI's list between 1950 and 1988, with details on their crimes.

Swierczynski, Duane. *The Encyclopedia of the FBI's Ten Most Wanted List: 1950 to Present*. New York: Checkmark Books, 2004. More up-to-date collection of profiles of fugitives listed by the FBI.

Walsh, John, and Philip Lerman. *Public Enemies: The Host of "America's Most Wanted" Targets the Nation's Most Notorious Criminals*. New York: Pocket Books, 2002. Anecdotal appraisal of publicized searches for fugitives by the host of television's *America's Most Wanted*.

See also Attorney general of the United States; Federal Bureau of Investigation; Hoover, J. Edgar; Organized crime; Prison escapes; September 11, 2001, attacks; Unabomber.

Tennessee v. Garner

The Case: U.S. Supreme Court ruling on police use of deadly force
Date: Decided on March 27, 1985
Criminal justice issues: Arrest and arraignment; police powers
Significance: This case significantly limited the power of police officers to use deadly force in effecting arrests.

Most arrests do not entail problems, but occasionally the accused will resist arrest or flee. There are also occasions when law-enforcement officers must make an instantaneous decision on the severity of any threat posed to the officers. The common law developed the rule that law-enforcement officers could use all necessary and reasonable force, including deadly force, to arrest a suspected felon, regardless of whether the suspect committed an act of violence or posed a threat to the arresting officers.

The common-law rule became increasingly controversial during the 1960's and 1970's, but courts adhered to it. There were numerous objections of constitutional, legal, and humanistic natures. The main objection was that, in essence, the rule allowed police officers to become judge, jury, and even executioner. Indeed, many jurisdictions that did not use capital punishment allowed officers to use deadly force through "fleeing felon" statutes modeled after the common law.

In *Tennessee v. Garner*, a fifteen-year-old boy, Edward Garner, broke a window and entered an unoccupied residence in suburban Memphis on the night of October 3, 1974. A neighbor called the police. Two police officers responded and intercepted the minor as he ran from the back of the house to a six-foot cyclone fence in the backyard. By shining a flashlight on the suspect, the officers could tell that the suspect was a youth and apparently unarmed. There was therefore no indication that the boy had committed a felony involving violence, nor did he pose an apparent threat to the officers' safety. The suspect ignored the officers' directive to stop. Instead, he tried to escape. One officer took aim and fatally shot the suspect in the back as he climbed over the fence. The officer had acted in accordance with his training, the Tennessee fleeing felon statute, and police department policy. The deceased had ten dollars worth of money and jewelry in his possession, stolen from the house.

The decedent's father brought suit against the officers, their superiors, and the city under the federal civil rights statute to recover damages for wrongful death caused by violation of the decedent's constitutional rights. The lawsuit was filed in federal court in a successful attempt to circumvent the common law. The Supreme Court overturned the common-law rule in a 6-3 decision. Justice Byron White delivered the majority opinion, which held that deadly force may be used to effectuate an arrest only in cases where it is necessary to prevent the escape of the suspect and the officer has probable cause to believe that the suspect poses a significant threat of death or serious physical injury to the officer or others. The Court noted that most major police departments had forbidden the use of deadly force against nonviolent suspects. The practical effect of *Tennessee v. Garner* was that lawsuits involving wrongful-death causes of action against state law-enforcement officers will be brought in federal courts and will invoke federal constitutional law.

Denis Binder

Further Reading

Alpert, Geoffrey, and Lorie A. Fridell. *Police Vehicles and Firearms: Instruments of Deadly Force*. Prospect Heights, Ill.: Waveland Press, 1992.

Del Carmen, Rolando V. *Civil Liabilities in American Policing*. Englewood Cliffs, N.J.: Prentice-Hall, 1991.

Fyfe, James J., ed. *Readings on Police Use of Deadly Force*. Washington, D.C.: Police Foundation, 1982.

Skolnick, Jerome H., and James J. Fyfe. *Above the Law: Police and the Excessive Use of Force*. New York: Free Press, 1993.

See also Arrest; Deadly force; Discretion; Police brutality; Police dogs; Police ethics; Reasonable force; Supreme Court, U.S.; Wiretaps.

Terrorism

Definition: Coercive use, or threat, of violence to terrorize a community or society to achieve political, economic, or social goals

Criminal justice issues: International law; political issues; terrorism; violent crime

Significance: Long a significant factor in other parts of the world, large-scale terrorism became a primary law-enforcement issue in the United States after the surprise terrorist attacks of September 11, 2001, and threats of terrorism have reshaped criminal justice in the United States.

Terrorism is notoriously difficult to define for several reasons. The first reason is the problem of perspective: One person's terrorist may be another person's freedom fighter. For example, many people in the Middle East regard the al-Qaeda operatives who perpetrated the September 11, 2001, attacks on the United States as heroes. By contrast, the Sons of Liberty during the American Revolution were regarded as terrorists by the British.

A second problem is the mismatch of analytical units that can lead to circular thinking. For example, if an organization or group is labeled as "terrorist," then its actions are automatically seen as "terroristic," even though it was labeled terrorist because of its earlier terroristic actions and statements. A third problem is that "terrorism" can be meaninglessly overinclusive. Some people have argued that the definition of terrorism used in the Patriot Act of 2001 is overly broad. In sum, defining terrorism has been one of the most intractable aspects of the study of crime. Because of difficulties including the inherent biases, clarity of purpose, and disagreements about which phenomena to include, no one definition can be relied upon.

Under the definition used here, terrorism almost always involves some form of coercion, through either actual or threatened violence. Not all violence need be against human targets. For example, the Weather Underground, a radical leftist organization of the late 1960's and 1970's, attacked mainly structures and attempted to limit harm to human life. Similarly, the Narodnaya Volya (People's Will) of nineteenth century Russia was adamant about the protection of the innocent and targeted only the czar and his support system.

At its core, terrorism is a technique of communication. Acts of terror are designed to communicate messages to audiences larger than those targeted by the acts themselves. When the Provisional Wing of the Irish Republican Army blows up a police station in Belfast, it does so not to deliver a message to the police officers who are attacked, but to send a message to the wider audiences of the British and Ulster Protestant authorities.

Because terrorist target selection is often symbolic, terror is sometimes called "propaganda of the deed." Allied with this point, the message communicated is often a sociopolitical one; some form of change is desired. For example, the Zapatista rebels of Mexico desire agrarian reform and got the attention of the national government by taking hostages and capturing key government facilities.

Finally, terrorism can be practiced by either insurgents or governments. Insurgent organizations often try to place their issues before wider, perhaps national, audiences to bring about changes in how things are done. In contrast, governmental terror usually strives to quiet dissent or to oppress some within governmental control. In addition to these general types of terror, there are also variations on these themes, including transnational terror, cyberterrorism, ethnonational terror, and narcoterrorism.

Historical Antecedents

Violent oppression and opposition may be endemic to the leadership of humans by other humans, but some of the earliest accounts of activities that would now be recognized as terrorism come from the ancient Holy Land of the Middle East. During the Roman occupation of what was then called Judea, in what is now Israel, Jewish Zealots known as Sicarii killed Jewish moderates, burned financial records, and staged other assaults on Roman/Jewish order. Their goal was to provoke Roman authorities to commit counteratrocities that would turn all Judeans against Roman rule. The name of the Sicarii comes from their choice of weapon: a dagger or short sword called the sica that they used to dispatch enemies in crowded public places in broad daylight. Attackers would strike their victims, then feign horror at what they were seeing and thereby escape detection. The Sicarii campaign of terror made all Judeans feel unsafe and helped to incite Jews to open rebellion against the Romans.

Another early Middle Eastern terrorist movement was that of the Hashishim, or Assassins, who operated from the eleventh through the thirteenth centuries. Their name literally means "hashish eaters," so called because they were known to ingest hashish before making their attacks. The Assassins desired to invoke the coming of the Messiah, as well as to protect their religious autonomy from Seljuk oppression, by killing government officials. Again, daggers were the weapon of choice, largely for religious reasons.

The Thuggee, or Thugs, of India were professional assassins in a cult that operated for several centuries, until British rule was firmly implanted in India. The Thugs killed mostly randomly, paying homage to their god Kali. In contrast to other organizations of terror, the Thugs used silk ties to strangle their victims, an artistic flourish rarely employed before or since.

The first use of the term "terrorism" in the modern sense of the word comes from the time of the French Revolution. The Jacobins were the first to use the term and used it with affection, but the positive connotations they invested in the term did not last very long. However, the rapid evaporation of positive connotations of "terrorism" should not be read to indicate that since the French Revolution all terrorists have been regarded as monsters.

One of the most significant and fascinating terrorist organizations of the nineteenth century was Russia's Narodnaya Volya, whose "Narodniki" members were anticzarist socialists. Possessing an egalitarian organization and a well-read membership, the Narodniki aimed at achieving a "blow at the center." Even more interesting than their organization is their commitment—uncommon in the modern world—to protecting the innocent. The Narodniki targeted specific individuals and would, at their own peril, protect nontargets from the violence they sought to visit upon the czarist regime. They wrestled philosophically with their right to resort to violence for the furtherance of their political aims and concluded that they could secure this right only by forfeiting their own lives.

Modern Trends

The twentieth century witnessed many important changes in the application and perception of terrorism. For example, the struggle against Eu-ropean imperialism in the developing world saw the birth of a number of terrorist organizations, including the Jewish Irgun, who struggled against the British rule in Palestine, and the Irish Republican Army, with its attempt to drive all British authority from Ireland.

Since the mid-twentieth century, religiously inspired terrorism has proliferated greatly, most notably in the Middle East. However, religious purposes have blended with more secular aims. Organizations such as Hezbollah, Hamas, Palestinian Islamic Jihad, al-Gama'a al Islamiyya, al-Aqsa Martyrs' Brigade, and others have mingled religious and political agendas, sometimes cooperating, sometimes clashing. Many newer groups have formed from splits from older groups. These splits often occur over religio-political disagreements.

Agents of the Bureau of Alcohol, Tobacco, Firearms and Explosives searching for evidence at the federal Bureau of Land Management's Litchfield horse facility in Northern California in October, 2001. The facility was firebombed by members of the Earth Liberation Front. In a manifestation of modern ecoterrorism, the radical environmentalist organization was protesting the federal government's roundups of wild horses. *(AP/Wide World Photos)*

The impact of Middle Eastern terrorism on American criminal justice takes several forms. First, the United States has been involved in the region for many years—most prominently in its support of the Jewish state of Israel, which has been almost constantly in conflict with its predominantly Muslim neighbors since its creation in 1948. One result of American involvement in the Middle East has been to make the United States itself a target of some of the region's organizations that practice terrorism. Al-Qaeda, the organization behind the September 11, 2001, attacks, is but one notable example.

A second point is that in the pursuit to understand criminal behavior, Middle Eastern terrorism presents an opportunity to study morally justified violence in order to bring about a lasting peace among humans. Finally, it is in the best interests of all the world's peoples to end terrorism's violence, regardless of whether Americans are targets.

Leftist Terror

Many organizations on the left side of the political spectrum have sought to launch workers' revolutions with terrorist violence. Notable examples have included Russia's Red Army Faction, Italy's Red Brigades, Mexico's Zapatistas, Peru's Tupac Amaru and Sendero Luminoso, and America's own Weather Underground. Such groups attempt to raise the consciousness of the proletariat in order to bring about revolutions against the upper classes and replace existing regimes with Marxist or socialist governments.

After the end of the Cold War and the dissolution of the Soviet Union during the early 1990's, a major funding and ideology source for Marxism-motivated terror groups dried up, and leftist organizations were weakened. The Weather Underground collapsed due to a perceived failure to bring about the desired changes in consciousness in the American underclass.

Single-Issue and Domestic Terrorism

Some organizations form around single sociopolitical issues and employ terror to further those

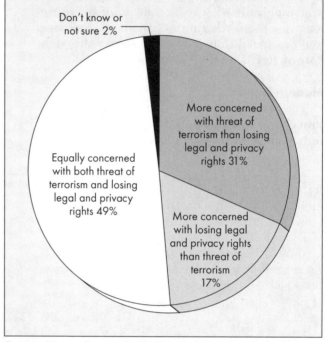

Public Concerns About Terrorism and Losing Privacy and Legal Rights

In August, 2003, a TIPP/Investor's Business Daily/ Christian Science Monitor Poll asked a cross section of Americans which of the views noted below most closely reflected their concerns about terrorism and the loss of privacy and legal rights.

Don't know or not sure 2%

More concerned with threat of terrorism than losing legal and privacy rights 31%

Equally concerned with both threat of terrorism and losing legal and privacy rights 49%

More concerned with losing legal and privacy rights than threat of terrorism 17%

Source: Roper Center for Public Opinion Research. Figures are based on responses of a national sample of 901 adults. Because of rounding off of decimals, percentages do not add up to 100.

issues. For example, radical opponents of abortion bomb abortion clinics, hoping to end abortions through violence because they believe they are protecting unborn people by doing so. Groups such as Earth First! employ coercive means to protect the environment.

Far from being less significant due to their narrower platforms, single-issue terror organizations may be more problematic for law enforcement than ideologically broader groups precisely because they are more focused. Although target selection by such groups may be more predictable, the members' fervent beliefs and commitments to their causes may make them even more vicious and tenacious than other types of terrorists.

Terrorism has played a role in American history from the inception of the nation. The Sons of Liberty and the Minutemen of the American Revolution were prototerrorists and insurgents, respectively. On the political Left are groups such as the Weather Underground and the Symbionese Liberation Army, and on the political Right are groups such as the Order; the Covenant, Sword, and the Arm of the Lord; and other organizations of the Christian Identity movement. Also on the Right are groups such as the Ku Klux Klan, Posse Comitatus, Aryan Nation, and others with neo-Nazi and hate-based ideologies.

Prevalence of Terrorism

It may not be an exaggeration to say that there is no place on Earth in which human beings live in any numbers that is not, or has not been, affected by terrorism. Terror has been the resort of groups as diverse as Earth First!, the Jewish Defense League, Hamas, and the Liberation Tigers of Tamil Eelam of Sri Lanka.

With a few notable exceptions, before 2001, Americans observed terrorism only from afar, on television and through other media. The events of September 11 gave Americans a healthy respect for the threat of terrorism. Americans need not live in fear, as strengthened law-enforcement systems and logistical difficulties make the mounting of future attacks against U.S. targets difficult. However, America's time of complacence regarding terrorism is most assuredly at an end.

Investigation

Inadequate government responses to nonstate terrorism may be the most important factor in the success and continuation of terrorism. If states respond either repressively or too meekly, they may encourage terrorists and worsen their own situations. However, finding a proper balance between strong armed response and diplomacy is inherently difficult and made even more so by the fact that every case may require a unique and unprecedented solution.

Two major issues confront the investigation of terrorism in America. First, intelligence gathering and analysis is crucial to the prevention of terrorist attacks. Second, resources including additional officers and equipment are needed to extend the blanket of coverage and enhance response capabilities of local law enforcement.

The best way to meet terrorist threats is to be forewarned and prepared. Having and understanding information regarding preparations, funding sources, travel, and ties makes interdiction of terrorism possible. Local law enforcement

---

Terrorist Incidents Involving the United States

1993 February 26 bomb attack on New York City's World Trade Center kills six people and injures more than one thousand.

1995 Bombing of a federal office building in Oklahoma City, Oklahoma, kills 168 persons.

1996 Muslim extremist Osama bin Laden, of al-Qaeda, issues a declaration of war against the United States.

1998 Simultaneous bombings of U.S. embassies by al-Qaeda in Kenya and Tanzania on August 7 kill 224 persons, mostly Africans. Two weeks later, the United States stages missile attacks on suspected terrorist bases in Afghanistan and the Sudan.

2000 October 12 suicide bombing on the USS *Cole*, while it is docked in Yemen, kills seventeen U.S. sailors. Al-Qaeda is believed to be behind the attack.

2001 On September 11, al-Qaeda agents hijack four American jetliners; they fly two of the planes into the World Trade Center towers, which collapse, killing about three thousand people. A third plane is flown into the Pentagon building, and the fourth is downed—apparently because of passenger intervention—in rural Pennsylvania. On October 7, the United States launches an invasion of Afghanistan, the apparent base of al-Qaeda operations.

plays a major role in this undertaking by being a major source of valuable information that, when combined with other intelligence, enables agencies responsible for intelligence analyses to determine levels of threat.

Logically, then, to prevent terrorism, all that would be required would be total scrutiny of all activities and sufficient personnel to analyze intelligence as it is received. In a tyrannical state, this solution may be possible, provided there are sufficient resources. However, aside from the inherent logistic difficulties, another major problem exists in this model. In a democracy, the wholesale invasion of privacy attendant to total surveillance will not be tolerated. In the United States, the Fourth Amendment to the Constitution of the United States guarantees citizens protection from search and seizure of their homes and persons except in cases in which warrants have been issued upon probable cause of wrongdoing. The goal and challenge for law enforcement in this regard is to provide the maximum amount of protection to citizens that is consonant with constitutionally guaranteed civil liberties.

Despite limitations on the intelligence gathering ability of law enforcement posed by the U.S. Constitution, and by policies, laws, and regulations that contain the spirit of the Constitution in this regard, much can be done by law enforcement to investigate potential terrorists. For example, information that can be gathered without warrants—but through subpoenas—includes bank records, flight itineraries, telephone records, and credit card transactions. Additionally, recording of conversations with third parties, vehicle tracking, and observing buildings from the air are all permissible investigative activities not requiring demonstration of probable cause.

Resources

As the first line of defense and as an important source of intelligence, local law-enforcement agencies need to have sufficient resources and training to provide the high-quality service Americans need from them. However, during the first several years after September, 2001, the needed resources were slow in arriving, despite the obvious need and acts of heroism shown by local law enforcement. Meanwhile, additional duties have been required of police, while no additional personnel have provided to assist. These increased demands have meant that already thinly stretched services are further taxed, decreasing the ability of dedicated officers to provide the levels of service they want to offer.

Only since September 11, 2001, has there been a concerted effort to bridge communication barriers among U.S. law-enforcement agencies, to provide sorely needed resources, and to enhance cooperation among different agencies. Part of the reason for this is that the American criminal justice system is a patchwork of different agencies. Organizations at the same jurisdictional levels have traditionally not had to cooperate, so coordination across jurisdictional levels likely will be that much more of a challenge.

Prosecution and Punishment

Prosecution of suspected terrorists has been undertaken primarily at the federal level, even though many of these suspects have committed crimes that are normally punishable at the state level. This is due primarily to the greater resources of the federal agencies involved with the investigation—primarily the Federal Bureau of Investigation (FBI)—and prosecution—primarily through the U.S. attorney's offices.

Punishments for terrorists, in the United States and abroad, have varied from nothing or home detention to summary execution. Leading figures of the Weather Underground were released from custody because of the illegal means used by the FBI to gather intelligence against them. In Italy, the "pentiti" (repentant) law allowed many Red Brigades members to escape significant punishment in exchange for information that was used against other members of the organization. In the United States, Timothy McVeigh was executed for his role in the terrorist bombing of the federal office building in Oklahoma City, Oklahoma, in 1995.

These wide variations in punishments are due in part to at least three issues. First, the threats offered by different terrorist organizations are not all of the same level; some are more dangerous than others. Second, when terrorist organizations enjoy some measure of popular support within their own countries, their governments may wish to avoid appearing repressive by "overpunishing" them. Finally, in cases in which security forces

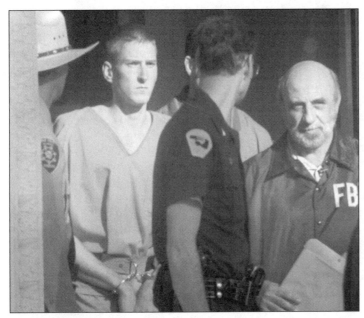

Timothy McVeigh shortly after his arrest in April, 1995, for the bombing of the Oklahoma City federal office building. *(AP/Wide World Photos)*

overstep their authority by conducting illegal searches or seizures, the evidence they collect may be deemed inadmissible—as in the case of the Weather Underground in the United States.

Responses to Terrorism by Democracies

Because of their need to preserve civil liberties, democracies face the greatest challenges in dealing with terrorism. As has been discussed, how a government responds to terror may be one of the most significant determinants of whether terrorism continues. Weak responses may encourage terrorists to continue their campaigns, while overly violent responses by a government may polarize citizens and strengthen the position of terrorists.

The "hard-line" approach to fighting terrorism outlined by Paul Wilkinson in *Terrorism Versus Democracy* (2001) makes several important points. First, security forces in democratic states must act within the scope of their own authority and abide by relevant laws and democratic principles. Second, intelligence is central to success. Third, despite the importance of intelligence, security forces must be fully accountable to democratic institutions of government. Fourth, terrorist propaganda efforts must be countered as fully

as possible. Finally, under most circumstances, governments should refrain, to the greatest extent possible, from conceding to terrorist demands.

Although there is much good in Wilkinson's model, it also has weaknesses, as it tends to paint with a broad brush. For example, acting aggressively to counter propaganda may make a government appear as if it has something to hide. Additionally, cases have arisen in which making concessions to terrorists has led to cessations of hostilities.

The use of military forces in the pursuit of terrorists can be problematic. In a domestic context, a full military response to a terrorist threat would involve martial law, which requires the suspension of civil liberties, establishment of curfews, censorship, summary punishments, and other things. The use of the military in aid of civil power can be effective, provided the troops have proper training. However, an army is not a ready tool for peacekeeping and is not well suited for use in domestic crises. Thus, using an army for domestic terror response should be undertaken with care and circumspection.

Legislation against terrorism takes several forms. It may be preventive by attempting to address the underlying issues that have given rise to terrorists' claims. It may be aimed at deterrence by making punishments so grim as to discourage would-be terrorists from risking capture. Finally, it may be enforcement-based, aiming to equip law enforcement with sufficient powers to detect, prevent, arrest, and successfully prosecute terrorists. Laws themselves cannot guarantee victory; many terrorists fight against the governments that write the laws. Also, humans interpret and enforce law, and so the law is only as effective a tool as its users make it.

Michael J. DeValve

Further Reading

Hoffman, B. *Inside Terrorism*. London: Victor Gollancz, 1998. Broad conceptual review of issues relating to world terrorism.

Kushner, H., ed. *Essential Readings on Political Terrorism: Analyses of Problems and Perspec-*

tives for the Twenty-first Century. New York: Gordian Knot Books, 2002. Collection of articles written by leading scholars on terrorism.

Laqueur, Walter. *No End to War: Terrorism in the Twenty-first Century.* New York: Continuum International Publishing, 2003. Up-to-date survey of world terrorism that attempts to project future trends.

Mack, R. L. *Equal Justice: America's Legal Response to the Emerging Terrorist Threat.* Ann Arbor: University of Michigan Press, 2004. Study of post-September 11 legislative and judicial responses to terrorism, with a discussion of the challenge of balancing of civil liberties protections and national security needs.

Rapoport, David C., and Yonah Alexander, eds. *The Morality of Terrorism: Religious and Secular Justifications.* 2d ed. New York: Columbia University Press, 1989. Collection of essays that includes several classic readings on justifications of terrorism and historical perspectives that are invaluable for understanding current terrorism issues.

Smith, B. *Terrorism in America: Pipe Bombs and Pipe Dreams.* Albany: State University of New York Press, 1994. Detailed review of domestic terrorism through the early 1990's that is perhaps the finest source on that subject.

Wilkinson, Paul. *Terrorism Versus Democracy: The Liberal State Response.* Portland, Oreg.: Frank Cass, 2001. Presents an enlightened review of issues facing democracies in responding to terrorism.

See also Antiterrorism and Effective Death Penalty Act; Bombs and explosives; Cybercrime; Espionage; Immigration and Naturalization Service; International law; Patriot Act; September 11, 2001, attacks; Skyjacking; Symbionese Liberation Army; Treason; Unabomber; Weather Underground.

Terry v. Ohio

The Case: U.S. Supreme Court ruling on search and seizure

Date: Decided on June 10, 1968

Criminal justice issue: Search and seizure

Significance: In this case, the Supreme Court ruled that arresting officers who have reasonable suspicion that they are dealing with armed suspects are permitted to conduct limited searches of the suspects' outer clothing—a procedure sometimes known as "stop and frisk."

In October, 1963, veteran Ohio detective Martin McFadden observed suspicious activity by two men in a Cleveland business district. Suspecting a daylight robbery, McFadden approached John Terry and Richard Chilton and identified himself as a police officer. When his attempts to question the men on their activities were ignored, McFadden seized the two and patted down their outer clothing. Feeling a weapon on each, McFadden removed the guns and arrested the men for carrying concealed weapons. In a pretrial motion, Terry and Chilton contended that the guns were seized during an illegal search. The Court of Common Pleas overruled the motion and sentenced the men to three years. Chilton died before the case was appealed.

In June, 1968, the Supreme Court ruled 8 to 1 to uphold Terry's conviction. Writing for the majority, Chief Justice Earl Warren concluded that the issue at hand was "whether it is always unreasonable for a policeman to seize a person and subject him to a limited search for weapons unless there is probable cause for an arrest." In deciding this issue, the Court divided the case into the "seizure" and the "search." The decision defined a seizure as occurring any time a police officer restrains an individual's freedom to walk away.

Determining the constitutionality of the search required a balance between the Fourth Amendment's protection from unreasonable searches and seizures on one hand, and the safety to the individuals involved on the other. Warren concluded that a limited search was allowable if based on "specific reasonable inferences" drawn from "the facts in the light of [the officer's] experience." In addition, the Court stipulated that "the issue is whether a reasonably prudent man in the circumstances would be warranted in the belief that his safety or that of others was in danger." Dissenting from the decision, Justice William O. Douglas looked to the legal differences between "probable cause" and "reasonable suspicion." Relying on the protection found in the Fourth Amendment, Douglas saw the search in question as an "infringement on personal liberty" because McFadden had no probable cause for arrest prior to the search.

Terry v. Ohio allowed a significant change in police procedures. It provided a police officer, once identified as such, with a legal right to perform a limited search of suspicious individuals by means of a protective pat-down. This provision helped to lower the number of injuries and deaths during initial confrontations between individuals and police officers. In addition, the police were authorized to seize any nonthreatening contraband, such as drugs or drug paraphernalia, found during a *Terry* search. Recognizing the potential for abuse in allowing "stop and frisk" actions by police, however, the Court was careful to outline the Fourth Amendment limitations that apply to stop and frisk searches. In *Sibron v. New York*, a companion case to *Terry*, the Court held that if the reason for the search is to find evidence rather than to check for weapons, then any evidence found is inadmissible.

Jennifer Davis

Further Reading

Del Carmen, Rolando V. *Criminal Procedure: Law and Practice*. 6th ed. Belmont, Calif.: Thomson/Wadsworth, 2004.

LaFave, W. R. *Search and Seizure: A Treatise on the Fourth Amendment*. 3d ed. St. Paul, Minn.: West Publishing, 1995.

McWhirter, Darien A. *Search, Seizure, and Privacy*. Phoenix, Ariz.: Oryx Press, 1994.

Wetterer, Charles M. *The Fourth Amendment: Search and Seizure*. Springfield, N.J.: Enslow, 1998.

See also *Atwater v. City of Lago Vista*; Automobile searches; Bill of Rights, U.S.; Evidence, rules of; *Illinois v. Wardlow*; *Maryland v. Buie*; Miranda rights; Police powers; Reasonable suspicion; Search and seizure; Supreme Court, U.S.

Testimony

Definition: Evidence provided by witnesses in trials that is given under oath, either orally or in the form of affidavits or depositions

Criminal justice issues: Evidence and forensics; trial procedures; witnesses

Significance: Testimony is critical in criminal trials because it provides support for arguments and positions advocated by either side in a legal proceeding.

Although testimony can loosely be defined as evidence, it is distinguishable from evidence derived from writings or other sources. For evidence to be testimony, a witness must present it under oath to a judge or tribunal, in person or through a sworn deposition.

Testimony is a component in three aspects of the legal process: grand jury hearings, preliminary hearings, and trials. A grand jury consists of a body of citizens who determine if there is probable cause to believe that a crime has been committed. In order to make that determination, they hear testimony from witnesses presented by the state, or prosecution. If they determine that probable cause exists, they return an indictment against the defendant. In a preliminary hearing, a judge hears testimony from prosecution witnesses and makes a decision as to whether or not an individual should be held for trial. In a criminal or civil trial, witnesses are questioned through direct and cross-examination, and a judge or jury listens to the testimony in order to reach a verdict. In all three instances, witnesses take oaths in which they swear or affirm to tell the truth.

Testimony in a grand jury is usually secret and is not used in later trials. However, testimony in a preliminary hearing is preserved for later use, either by a court reporter or a tape recorder. The testimony provided in a preliminary hearing might be used in a trial to refresh a witness's memory or to demonstrate inconsistencies in the testimony. The testimony in a preliminary hearing may also be used at trial if a witness dies or becomes unavailable to testify.

The prosecution in a criminal case and the plaintiff in a civil case present their testimony first because they have the burden of proof. Testimony is provided in brief question and answer format; witnesses usually do not tell their stories in a continuous narrative. In direct examination, the attorneys question the witnesses who support their side of a case. Typically, the questions are open-ended in order for the witnesses to elaborate on their testimony, thus presenting a strong case. In cross-examination, the attorneys question the witnesses on the opposing side. The attorney may attempt to obtain testimony by using closed-ended or leading questions so that the witness does not have a chance to elaborate on answers. During closing arguments, attorneys make convincing arguments and provide reasons for the jurors or judge to return a verdict in their favor. They draw on the testimony of witnesses to help support their arguments.

Ann Burnett

Further Reading

Loftus, Elizabeth F. *Eyewitness Testimony*. 2d ed. Cambridge, Mass.: Harvard University Press, 1996.

Weiss, K. "Confessions and Expert Testimony." *Journal of the American Academy of Psychiatry and Law* 31 (2003): 451-458.

Wrightsman, L. S., E. Greene, M. T. Nietzel, and W. H. Fortune. *Psychology and the Legal System*. Belmont, Calif.: Wadsworth, 2002.

See also Court reporters; Cross-examination; Discovery; Evidence, rules of; Expert witnesses; Eyewitness testimony; Grand juries; Hearsay; Perjury; Preliminary hearings; Subpoena power; Trial transcripts; Witnesses.

Texas v. Johnson

The Case: U.S. Supreme Court ruling on flag burning

Date: Decided on June 21, 1989

Criminal justice issue: Constitutional protections

Significance: The First Amendment protects symbolic forms of expression, including the right of a protester to burn an American flag as part of a political demonstration.

While the Republican National Convention was taking place in Dallas in 1984, Gregory Lee Johnson participated in a political demonstration to protest the policies of the Reagan administration and of certain Dallas-based corporations. In front of city hall, Johnson doused an American flag with kerosene and set it on fire. While the flag burned, protesters chanted, "America, the red, white, and blue, we spit on you." Several witnesses testified that they had been seriously offended, but no one was injured or threatened with physical injury.

Following the demonstration, a witness collected the flag's remains and buried them in his backyard. Johnson was charged with the desecration of a venerated object in violation of the Texas Penal Code. He was convicted, sentenced to one year in prison, and fined two thousand dollars. The Court of Appeals for the Fifth District of Texas at Dallas affirmed the conviction. The Court of Criminal Appeals of Texas, however, reversed the lower courts. By a 5-4 vote, the U.S. Supreme Court affirmed the appeals court's decision.

Justice William J. Brennan, joined by Justices Thurgood Marshall, Harry Blackmun, Antonin Scalia, and Anthony Kennedy, wrote the majority opinion. Brennan noted that the First Amendment protects "expressive conduct" as well as written and spoken words. While a state can prevent "imminent lawless action," in this case Johnson's symbolic expression of displeasure with government policies did not lead to a disturbance of the peace and did not oppose the state's interest in maintaining order. Instead, Johnson's expression was restricted because of the content of his message. "If there is a bedrock principle underlying the First Amendment," Brennan observed, "it is that the Government may not prohibit the expression of an idea simply because society finds the idea itself offensive or disagreeable."

Toleration of Johnson's criticism reaffirms the freedom that the flag represents. Brennan stated:

The way to preserve the flag's special role is not to punish those who feel differently about such matters. It is to persuade them that they are wrong. . . . We can imagine no more appropriate response to burning a flag than waving one's own, no better way to counter a flag burner's message than by saluting the flag that burns.

Chief Justice William Rehnquist, in a dissenting opinion joined by Justices Byron White and Sandra Day O'Connor, emphasized the unique role of the flag and the "profoundly offensive" nature of Johnson's conduct. In a separate dissent, Justice John Paul Stevens argued that Johnson had been prosecuted not for his criticism of government policies but for the method he chose to express his views.

This case is important for establishing that flag burning as a symbolic form of expression is protected by the First Amendment.

Joseph A. Melusky

Further Reading

Curtis, Michael, ed. *The Flag Burning Cases.* Vol. 2 in *The Constitution and the Flag.* New York: Garland, 1993.

Goldstein, Robert Justin. *Burning the Flag: The Great 1989-1990 American Flag Desecration Controversy.* Kent, Ohio: Kent State University Press, 1996.

_____, ed. *Desecrating the American Flag: Key Documents of the Controversy from the Civil War to 1995.* Syracuse, N.Y.: Syracuse University Press, 1996.

_____. *Saving "Old Glory": The History of the American Flag Desecration Controversy.* Boulder, Colo.: Westview Press, 1995.

Miller, J. Anthony. *"Texas v. Johnson": The Flag Burning Case.* Springfield, N.J.: Enslow, 1997.

See also Bill of Rights, U.S.; Civil disobedience; Supreme Court, U.S.

Theft

Definition: Illegal taking of money or property from others with the intent of depriving rightful owners of their possessions

Criminal justice issues: Fraud; robbery, theft, and burglary

Significance: The most frequently committed crime in the United States, theft takes many forms and costs Americans billions of dollars in annual losses.

Theft is an inclusive term for various forms of taking property from others, including organizations and institutions, with the intent of permanently depriving the rightful owners of possession. Criminal codes in the United States classify theft under a variety of forms, but the underlying thread throughout all definitions is the same: the illegal taking of property with the intent of depriving rightful owners of their possessions.

Definitions

English common law defined two types of theft: grand larceny and petit larceny. The line separating the two hinged upon the value of the goods stolen. Grand larceny is a felony, while petit larceny is a misdemeanor. In common law, in which "theft," "larceny," and "stealing" are used interchangeably, specific conditions must be met for a theft to occur. First, something must be taken with the express intent of stealing it. Under this principle, thieves must take the property into their possession, thereby securing control of it. Next, the stolen goods must be moved from their rightful place, and a trespassing must occur in which the goods are removed from the rightful owner's possession. Also, the stolen property must be something tangible, such as money or watches, and must belong to someone else. Finally, there must be an intent to steal.

Other variations of theft include using false pretenses, which occurs when an individual makes false representations, either spoken or written, with the intent to cheat or defraud a victim. The misrepresentation must be one of either past or present fact, and not of opinion or false promise. In addition, the offender must receive the title to the property, as possession alone does not denote a crime. Throughout legal history, gaining custody of property using false pretenses was called "larceny by trick."

Another crime, similar to theft by false pretense but generally regarded as more serious, is a confidence game—or "con game"—known as "larceny by deception." In this form of theft, falsehoods must take a more tangible form than mere spoken words. Embezzlement is often regarded as a form of theft, but slight differences exist. In embezzlement, the stolen property need only be legally possessed or accessed by the offender; in theft, the stolen property must actually be in the offender's possession. An additional distinction centers on "conversion" of the property; that is, a sale or pledge regarding the embezzled property, or the spending of embezzled funds. Embezzlement commonly occurs in businesses, as when employees borrow money from their employers and never repay it.

Robbery is a violent form of theft that is often viewed as a combination of assault and battery and larceny—hence its definition, "aggravated larceny." Each element of larceny is present in robbery, along with additional elements. Violence, or the threat of imminent violence, is the focal point of robbery, and the larceny must take place in the victim's presence. Robbery may be said to occur when a person is forced under threat of violence to give something of value that the robber wants, such as money, jewelry, a watch, or a car. Moreover, the stolen items must be either on the victim's body or nearby; otherwise, the larceny might be attempted without the threat of violence. For purposes of punishment, states distinguish between two different levels of robbery. Simple robberies occur when victims are verbally intimidated into handing over their possessions; armed robbery occurs when the offenders use deadly weapons in their crimes.

Burglary is a form of theft that involves unlawful trespass into a building with the intent to steal something of value. Force to gain entry need not be present for an offense to be classified as burglary. In most states, burglaries are classified in three categories: forcible entry, unlawful entry in which no force is used, and attempted forcible entry.

The passing of bad checks is considered a form of theft in all states, and this crime also takes a variety of forms. One form is the passing of a check from a financial institution in which one does not have an account. Another form is the passing of "short checks"—checks written on valid accounts that the check passers know to contain insufficient funds to cover their checks. Checks made out on such accounts "bounce."

Receiving and buying stolen property are crimes when the receivers know that the goods they are getting have been stolen. Accepting stolen goods is a crime only when the receivers know that the goods have been stolen; merely suspecting that the goods might be stolen is often not enough to make the receipt of the goods a crime.

During the early twentieth century, a new form of theft became commonplace: securities theft, a crime in which fraudulent corporate securities are sold to unwary investors hoping to gain wealth. Every state has statutes requiring the licensing of sellers and registration of the securities to be sold. In addition, sale of unregistered commodities, the sale of securities by unlicensed agents, and the giving of false information are criminal offenses. In 1934, the Securities and Exchange Act was passed, requiring registration, with a federal agency, of securities to be sold in interstate commerce, and providing for punishment of individuals for the sale of securities on the basis of false information.

During the late twentieth century, with the proliferation of credit cards and computers, identity fraud became a common crime. It, too, can be a form of theft. Offenders create fictitious identities or manipulate existing identities of other persons to evade detection or gain money illegally. Variations of identity fraud include identity theft, the appropriation of other persons' individual identifying information; takeovers of personal accounts by appropriating social security numbers and personal account numbers; credit card fraud; and check fraud. The latter crime includes such offenses as check kiting, counterfeiting, and forgery.

History

Modern laws pertaining to theft have their origins in the ancient laws of larceny. For instance, trespass laws were designed to protect real property (that which is permanently affixed to the ground) from damage and destruction. Larceny laws were designed to protect movable personal property from being stolen. Until the Industrial Revolution, larceny was the only kind of theft defined in statutes and was a felony offense punishable by death.

Many famous law codes throughout history have dealt with theft. During the early eighteenth century B.C.E., the Babylonian king Hammurabi wrote at length about stealing. The code of Hammurabi contained 282 clauses detailing how Babylonians were to behave on a daily basis. Theft was punished severely, often resulting in the death penalty. Forms of theft punished with death included thefts from the palace entrance or temple treasury, receiving or selling stolen goods, making false claims regarding the goods of others, kidnapping (a form of theft), and burglary. However, the manner of death was not specified in the code. In the Torah, the first five books of the Bible, Moses received four methods of dealing with theft.

Before the twelfth century, all Western law originated in Roman law, also known as civil law. Much of that law is still used in European countries. During the late twelfth century reign of England's King Henry II, court decisions were written down and cataloged for future use. When the courts heard new cases involving issues similar to those considered in earlier cases, they based their rulings on the earlier precedents.

This practice became known as *stare decisis*, a Latin term for "let the decision stand." Under this rule, once a legal issue has been resolved as it applied toward a particular set of facts, a court did not reconsider that legal issue in a later case if the circumstances were similar. Modern law is a continuation of this reasoning.

Prevalence

Although other types of theft still occur, identity fraud is the form of theft issue that is commanding the most attention in the early twenty-first century. Due to the phenomenal growth of electronic, or e-, commerce, the use of the Internet for bank transactions has grown exponentially. In 2002, the Federal Trade Commission (FTC) reported that approximately one in eight adult Americans had been a victim of identity theft during the preceding five years. The FTC warned that the thefts cost businesses $48 billion

During rioting and other civil disturbances, theft often becomes an epidemic problem as breakdowns in social order tend to make people think that it is all right to loot or that in the midst of mass confusion, their apprehension is unlikely. Here, police officers stand guard over looters captured during the 1992 rioting in Los Angeles that followed the acquittal of the police officers who were caught on videotape savagely beating motorist Rodney King. *(AP/Wide World Photos)*

and individual victims $5 billion in 2002 alone. The most common type of identity fraud is credit card theft, followed by making unauthorized purchases on existing accounts, phone and utility fraud, and bank fraud. Interestingly, about 38 percent of theft victims do not report the crimes.

MasterCard and Visa, the two primary credit cards used in America, use similar definitions of what does and does not constitute fraud by identity theft. Both organizations consider identity theft to consist of two fraud categories—account takeovers and fraudulent applications. Based on these two categories, the associations' aggregate identity theft-related losses from domestic operations rose from $79.9 million in 1996 to $114.3 million in 2000, an increase of about 43 percent.

While the credit card companies use a narrow definition of identity theft-related fraud, federal and state law-enforcement organizations consider identity theft to pertain to virtually all categories of credit card fraud. Under this broader definition, the total fraud losses suffered by MasterCard's and Visa's domestic operations rose from approximately $760 million in 1996 to more than $1.1 billion in 2000, an increase of about 45 percent. Although this figure is less than 0.1 percent of U.S. member banks' annual sales volume during 1996 through 2000, it is still a sobering figure.

Despite public concerns about security and privacy, consumer confidence in online commerce has grown. During the 2000 holiday season, consumers spent an estimated $10.8 billion online, a 50 percent increase over the previous year's amount.

Investigation and Prosecution

Theft investigations usually begin with complaints made to police. Investigators must first determine whether an offense has been committed, and, if so, under what section of the code it falls. Investigators must also determine whether there is sufficient evidence to warrant proceeding further. They then determine who the parties to the offense are. It is important to identify exactly who was involved in the offense and to what degree. This includes the perpetrator, aider, and abettor or counselor. These individuals have to identify any possible accessories after the fact, which are different from parties to the offense.

Each state has its own laws regarding the prosecution of theft, but uniform codes do exist. The criminal prosecution of thieves is contingent upon the types of theft for which they are charged.

Pickpocketing thefts include the removal of items such as wallets from victims' purses and pockets. Pickpocketing usually occurs in crowded areas, public conveyances, and other places where the thieves can disguise their activities in the confusion of crowds. Similar to pickpocketing are thefts from persons who are unconscious, such as drunks. However, when the victims are physically manhandled or force is used that goes beyond incidental jostling, the thefts are prosecuted as strong-arm robberies. Closely related to pickpocketing is purse-snatching. As with stealing from unconscious victims, when more force is used than is necessary for merely snatching of a purse from a victim's arm, then the theft is prosecuted as a strong-arm robbery.

Shoplifting is the theft of merchandise from business establishments. It differs from burglary in that offenders have legal access to the premises from which they steal, and no trespass or unlawful entry is involved. Shoplifting also includes the theft of merchandise displayed outside buildings such as department stores, hardware stores, supermarkets, fruit stands, gas stations, and other retail establishments.

In the federal Uniform Crime Reports, thefts of items from inside motor vehicles of all types are classified as larcenies; however, some state laws classify such thefts as burglaries. Items typically stolen from vehicles include cameras, clothes, and packages. Thefts of motor vehicle parts and accessories from the vehicles themselves are classified differently. Items commonly stolen include radios, tape decks, engines, hubcaps and wheel covers, manufacturers' emblems, license plates, mirrors, and wheels.

Thefts from inside buildings can be prosecuted in several different ways. For example, thefts from buildings such as churches, restaurants, schools, libraries, and other public and professional offices during the hours when they are open to the public are treated as larceny thefts. However, if the same kinds of thefts are associated with unlawful entry, they are prosecuted as burglaries. Likewise, thefts from coin-operated devices and machines are treated differently if they are associated with illegal entry into the buildings in which the machines are housed. There are also a wide variety of miscellaneous forms of theft, such as thefts from fenced enclosures, boats, and airplanes.

Punishment

The lengths and severity of punishments for persons convicted of theft depend upon several factors. The first factor is the question of whether the crime is classified as a felony or misdemeanor. Felony convictions are punished by prisons terms, fines, or both. Misdemeanor convictions are usually punished by brief sentences to county jails, fines, or both. Punishments for theft in other countries can be far more severe. For example, in countries that follow Islamic law, thieves can be punished by having their hands cut off.

Cary Stacy Smith

Further Reading

Cassell, E., and D. A. Bernstein. *Criminal Behavior*. Boston: Allyn & Bacon, 2000. Sociological study of criminal behavior that includes some discussion of how thieves work and what motivates them.

Dix, George E., and M. Michael Sharlot. *Criminal Law*. 4th ed. Belmont, Calif.: Wadsworth, 1999. A general text on substantive criminal law, including an extended discussion of the various forms of theft.

General Accounting Office. *Identity Theft: Prevalence and Cost Appear to Be Growing*. Washington, D.C.: Government Printing Office, 2002. Federal government report on identity theft based on interviews and quantitative research. Perhaps the most accurate picture of the nature of identity victimization to date.

Hage, Brian S., et al. *Identity Theft in the United States*. Morgantown, W.Va.: National White Collar Crime Center, 2001. Excellent explanation of what the crime of identity theft is, who tends to be targeted, profound statistics on the extent of the problem, and steps for dealing with the crime.

Hale, M., and C. Gray. *The History of the Common Law in England*. Chicago: University of Chicago Press, 2002. General survey of the history of English common law, from which the United States derives the principles underlying its laws pertaining to theft.

Schmalleger, Frank. *Criminal Justice Today: An Introductory Text for the Twenty-first Century*. 8th ed. Upper Saddle River, N.J.: Pearson/Prentice-Hall, 2005. Widely used college textbook on criminal justice in the United States, with extensive coverage of issues relating to theft.

Sullivan, Bob. *Your Evil Twin : Behind the Identity Theft Epidemic*. New York: John Wiley & Sons, 2004. Comprehensive examination of the scope of identity theft crimes and methods of prevention, with many examples of real cases by an identity theft expert.

Whitebread, Charles H., and Christopher Slobogin. *Criminal Procedure: Regulation of Police Investigation: Legal, Historical, Empirical, and Comparative Materials*. 4th ed. New York: West Publishing, 2000. Textbook on police investigation procedures that includes a detailed explanation of the procedures used in investigations of theft.

See also Burglary; Cable and satellite television signal theft; Common law; Consumer fraud; Criminals; Cybercrime; Embezzlement; Fraud; Identity theft; Motor vehicle theft; Pickpocketing; Victimology.

Three-strikes laws

Definition: Laws mandating lengthy prison sentences for third felony convictions

Criminal justice issues: Judges; punishment; sentencing

Significance: Three-strikes laws are largely symbolic in most of the United States, but in California they have helped to swell the prison population and have escalated the critical problems of overcrowding and fiscal crisis.

As the politically motivated get-tough-on-crime campaigns against crime and drugs escalated during the 1980's, government policymakers moved to adapt the baseball concept of "three strikes and you're out" to sentencing of repeat offenders, and multiple states and the federal government rushed to create politically popular draconian mandatory minimum sentencing laws.

The goal behind these laws was to punish serious and violent repeat offenders with prison sentences as long as from twenty-five years to life, while reducing victimization and improving community safety through the casting out and incapacitating of the worst criminals. Despite the initial popularity of the concept of three-strikes laws, they have been little used in most states. However, one state, California, has pursued the concept with such vigor that it has become an integral part of the state's corrections and fiscal landscape.

The Nation

In 1993, voters in the state of Washington responded to a particularly heinous violent sexual crime by a recidivist parolee by approving an initiative that mandated life in prison without the possibility of parole for persons convicted of committing serious offenses such as murder, rape, and robbery a third time. Within two years, more than twenty-five other states and the federal government approved their own variations of three-strikes laws. While there was some variation in the crimes covered by these new laws, the principles of "three strikes" and long mandatory sentences adopted in Washington were followed in virtually all the new laws.

Over the next decade, state legislatures and court systems showed appropriate restraint by sentencing only a few thousand criminals under three-strikes laws throughout the entire nation. For example, between 1993 and 2004, the state of Washington sentenced fewer than two hundred criminals under its three-strikes laws. Generally, the original intent of the law was upheld, as most of the criminals sentenced under these laws were violent robbers, sex offenders, murderers, and individuals convicted of serious assaults.

California

Meanwhile, by 1994, both the legislature and voters of California had adopted three-strikes laws. California's laws included a unique feature: the provision of a second-strike enhancement that doubled sentences, as well as the ability of

---

Three Strikes in California

Many people argue that three-strikes laws are inherently unethical and cite cases in California, which has an especially strict law. One of the most notorious cases is that of Leandro Andrade. In 1995, Andrade shoplifted nine videocassettes from two K-Mart stores to give as presents to his nieces for Christmas. His crime was completely nonviolent, and he did not even resist arrest. However, because he had two prior felony convictions, he was given *two* sentences of from twenty-five years to life and could not hope for release before the year 2046.

In another California case, Gary Ewing received a twenty-five-year sentence for stealing three golf clubs, worth a total of $400, from a country club. In 2003, the U.S. Supreme Court voted 5 to 4 to uphold Ewing's sentence. Justice Sandra Day O'Connor wrote, "To be sure, Ewing's sentence is a long one. . . . But it reflects a rational legislative judgment, entitled to deference, that offenders who have committed serious or violent felonies and who continue to commit felonies must be incapacitated."

---

prosecutors to file third-strike charges on nonviolent and nonserious felony offenses, many of which would ordinarily have been treated as misdemeanors. For example, shoplifting offenses could be prosecuted as petty theft if the offenders had prior convictions.

California's approach was controversial and raised important issues relating to the Eighth Amendment's cruel and unusual punishment clause and the principle of proportionality. In the 2003 landmark companion cases of *Lockyer v. Andrade* and *Ewing v. California*, the U.S. Supreme Court voted 5 to 4 in favor of allowing California to set the sentencing laws approved by its voters.

The most striking result of California's three-strikes law has been a large increase in the state's prison population. Of the 160,000 inmates incarcerated in California in early 2004, about 25 percent were second and third strikers. The large number of prisoners has placed unprecedented strains on the state's budget. The average cost of housing an inmate in California was

$31,000 per year in 2004. As prisoners age beyond fifty, their increasing health problems raise the average cost of housing to between $60,000 and $75,000 per year. Implementation of the three-strikes law in California not only has raised the numbers of inmates but also has led to forecasts of a greatly increased proportion of older inmates in the future, as three-strikes offenders grow older in its prisons. A study of California's three-strikes law estimated that during its first decade, the law cost taxpayers more than $8 billion in increased corrections costs. Moreover, more than 50 percent of that extra expenditure went to incarcerating nonviolent third strikers.

The 1990's found California, like the rest of the nation, experiencing significant crime reductions. Experts believe that reductions in crime were more likely to be due to the robust economy of that period, the increased availability of jobs, the maturation of community policing, and other criminal justice and corrections systems improvements rather than to the advent of three-strikes laws. Support for this observation can be found in the fact that the national reduction in crime occurred fairly evenly throughout the nation, including the one-half of the states that had no three-strikes laws.

In November, 2004, Californians voted on an initiative that would have eased the state's three-strikes law by allowing judges to impose milder prison sentences on nonviolent offenders. That measure failed to pass.

Kevin Meehan

Further Reading

Clark, John Austin, James Henry, and D. Alan Henry. *"Three Strikes and You're Out": A Review of State Legislation*. Washington, D.C.: National Institute of Justice, 1997. Federal report on the impact of three-strikes laws throughout the United States four years after the first such laws were enacted.

Ehlers, Scott, Vincent Schiraldi, and Jason Ziedenberg. *Still Striking Out: Ten Years of California's Three Strikes*. Washington, D.C.: Justice Policy Institute, 2004. Close study of the impact of the three-strikes law in California, with particular attention to the cost of the program to taxpayers.

LaCourse, R. David, Jr. *Three Strikes in Review*. Seattle: Washington Policy Center, 1997. Critical assessment of the effect of Washington State's three-strikes law.

Tonry, Michael. *Sentencing Matters*. New York: Oxford University Press, 1996. Comprehensive history of sentencing with an analysis of contemporary reforms, such as sentencing guidelines, intermediate sanctions, and mandatory penalties.

United States Sentencing Commission. *Federal Sentencing Guidelines Manual 2003*. St. Paul, Minn.: West Publishing, 2004. Summary of the federal guidelines for prison sentences that serve as the basis for sentencing in most states.

Zimring, Franklin E., G. Hawkins, and S. Kamin. *Punishment and Democracy: Three Strikes and You're Out in California*. New York: Oxford University Press, 2001. Scholarly study of the impact and implications of California's controversial three-strikes law.

See also Criminal records; Cruel and unusual punishment; Discretion; Incapacitation; Judges; Mandatory sentencing laws; Prison overcrowding; Recidivism; Sentencing; Supreme Court, U.S.; Violent Crime Control and Law Enforcement Act.

Tison v. Arizona

The Case: U.S. Supreme Court ruling on capital punishment

Date: Decided on April 21, 1987

Criminal justice issues: Capital punishment; sentencing

Significance: In this case, the Supreme Court created a flexible standard for applying the death penalty to felony-murder accomplices who demonstrate reckless disregard for human life even though they do not directly participate in killing a victim.

On July 30, 1978, brothers Donny, age twenty-one, Ricky, age twenty, and Raymond Tison, age nineteen, smuggled guns into the Arizona State Prison and helped in the escape of their father,

Gary, who was a convicted murderer, and another convicted murderer. The group changed cars and made their escape on a desert highway. When they had a flat tire, they flagged down a passing car containing young parents, a baby, and a teenage cousin and held the family at gunpoint. Gary Tison ordered his sons to load their possessions into the young family's car. As the brothers loaded the car and pushed their own disabled car into the desert, their father and the other prison escapee brutally murdered the entire family, including the baby, with shotgun blasts at close range.

The escaping group traveled for several more days before encountering a police roadblock. During the ensuing shoot-out, Donny was killed, Gary escaped into the desert but soon died from exposure, and Ricky, Raymond, and the other convict were captured.

As accomplices to the killing of the young family, Ricky and Raymond Tison were charged with felony murder. When they were sentenced to death, they appealed their sentences based on a Supreme Court decision (*Enmund v. Florida*, 1982) which had declared that felony-murder accomplices cannot be sentenced to death if they do not directly participate in the actual killing. After the Arizona Supreme Court upheld the sentences, the Tisons took their case to the U.S. Supreme Court.

In a 5-4 decision, the U.S. Supreme Court created a flexible standard for imposing the death penalty. The Court declared that felony-murder accomplices could receive the death penalty if they demonstrated "reckless disregard for human life," even if they did not directly participate in the killing. The justices used this new standard to uphold the capital sentences imposed on the Tisons because they viewed the brothers' active involvement in supplying weapons to convicted murderers and kidnapping the young family as a demonstration of "reckless disregard."

In *Tison v. Arizona* the Supreme Court gave state prosecutors greater flexibility to seek the death penalty against accomplices who participate in crimes that result in homicides. This new flexibility came at the price of greater inconsistency in the application of capital punishment. Under the prior rule, it was relatively clear which offenders were eligible for the death penalty,

based on their direct participation in a killing. By contrast, under the *Tison* rule, jurors and judges applying the vague "reckless indifference" standard have broad opportunities to impose capital punishment based on their negative feelings toward the accomplice or their revulsion at the crime without precise consideration of the defendant's actual participation.

Christopher E. Smith

Further Reading

Banner, Stuart. *The Death Penalty: An American History*. Cambridge, Mass.: Harvard University Press, 2002.

Bedau, Hugo Adam, and Paul Cassell. *Debating the Death Penalty: Should America Have Capital Punishment? The Experts on Both Sides Make Their Best Case*. Oxford, England: Oxford University Press, 2003.

Bohm, Robert M. *Deathquest: An Introduction to the Theory and Practice of Capital Punishment in the United States*. Cincinnati: Anderson Publishing, 2003.

Latzer, Barry, ed. *Death Penalty Cases: Leading U.S. Supreme Court Cases on Capital Punishment*. 2d ed. Boston: Butterworth-Heinemann, 2002.

See also Accomplices and accessories; Capital punishment; Cruel and unusual punishment; Felonies; Murder and homicide; Supreme Court, U.S.

Toxicology

Definition: Science concerned with the effects of harmful and toxic substances on living organisms

Criminal justice issues: Evidence and forensics; investigation; technology

Significance: Toxicology plays a prominent role in many investigations of homicides, accidental deaths, and suicides.

In its most elementary form, toxicology is the study of poisons. However, scientific advances and research have complicated definitions of toxicology. Some scientists regard toxicology as the study of chemistry and chemical composition, while others regard it as the study of biological poisoning. Here, toxicology is defined as the study of the chemical composition, symptoms, identification, and treatment of foreign substances (to include poison, alcohol, industrial chemicals, poisonous gas, and illegal drugs) on living organisms.

The study of toxicology encompasses many scientific disciplines, including chemistry, biochemistry, epidemiology, pathology, physiology, and pharmacology—all of which are concerned with substances that can be ingested or inhaled or that can make direct contact with skin and eyes. The adverse effects of these toxins—which are commonly known as poisons—may include illness, injury, and death, depending on the types and amounts of the toxins that enter the body.

History of Toxicology

The scientific field of toxicology is comparatively modern, but study and use of toxic substances has a long and well-documented history in human societies. In fact, knowledge of dangerous toxins can be traced back to prehistoric humans, who used their senses of touch and taste to recognize poisonous plants and animals. Early humans extracted the poisons they found for use in medicinal healing and the manufacture of poison-tipped weapons for hunting and warfare.

Scientific toxicology began to take shape during the Renaissance. During the early sixteenth century, the Swiss scientist Paracelsus, who is regarded as the founder of biochemistry, instituted what is now called the dose-response relationship, a significant tenet in toxicology. He posited that everything had the potential to imitate a poison and it was the dosage that dictated the body's response. Small doses yielded harmless effects, while larger doses resulted in higher degrees of toxicity.

The first important work on toxicology was published in 1813 by the Spanish physician and chemist Mathieu Orifila, who is now regarded as the founder of the field of toxicology. He was the first person to established connections between the chemical and biological properties of poisons.

Forensic Toxicology

Forensic toxicology was developed to solve the "invisible" crime of poisoning. Poisoning has been a popular method of committing murder for millennia. In the ancient world, the many illustrious figures who were victims of poisoning included the Greek philosopher Socrates, Egypt's Queen Cleopatra, and several Roman emperors. Not only were carefully selected and administered poisons impossible to identify, but the very fact that they had been administered might also go undetected.

The first murder trial to showcase toxicological testimony occurred in England in 1751, when the medical testimony of four doctors resulted in a woman being found guilty of murdering her father with arsenic. The verdict in that case was later criticized because the doctors had used sensory data rather than scientific measures to identify the presence of arsenic in the murdered man's food. The first scientific use of toxicology in the courtroom occurred in 1840, when traces of arsenic were found in the body of a man, whose wife was subsequently found guilty of poisoning him.

Throughout history, detection of poisoning crimes and identification of the poisons used have posed difficult challenges to investigators. The effects of most poisonous substances can be misdiagnosed as symptoms of common medical diseases, thereby rendering the toxins virtually untraceable. In modern crime investigation, toxicological sections have become commonplace parts of crime labs. Their task is to identify foreign substances in bodies and communicate their findings to law-enforcement investigators.

Toxicological Analyses

A standard toxicological procedure includes preliminary examinations of blood and urine samples and sometimes strands of hair. In some cases, full autopsies are needed so that tissue samples can be removed from various organs. Tests of the samples can detect the presence of chemicals and other foreign substances that have been ingested into the body.

In early times, the poison of choice for murder was arsenic, as it was readily available as a rat poison. Its effects on humans vary with the amounts ingested. Large doses are fast-acting and cause damage to the brain, liver, and spinal cord. Conversely, small doses ingested over extended periods of time show subtle effects such as nerve damage, headaches, nausea, numbness, and muscle weakness. Both methods of ingestion ultimately kill, but smaller doses are less detectable.

Lisa Landis Murphy

Further Reading

Klassen, C. D., and J. B. Watkins. *Casarett and Doull's Essentials of Toxicology.* New York: McGraw-Hill, 2003. Detailed explanations of the basic concepts and principles associated with toxicology.

Levine, B. *Principles of Forensic Toxicology.* Washington, D.C.: AACC Press, 2003. Book designed for use in one-semester undergraduate courses that explores the principles and theories associated with forensic toxicology.

Olson, K. R. *Poisoning and Drug Overdose.* New York: McGraw-Hill, 2003. Accessible reference guide to aid clinicians in the diagnosis and treatment of toxic poisoning and drug overdose.

Rudin, N., and K. Inman. *An Introduction to Forensic DNA Analysis.* 2d ed. New York: CRC Press, 2001. Comprehensive reference guide to DNA for lay readers.

Timbrell, J. A. *Introduction to Toxicology.* New York: CRC Press, 2001. User-friendly introductory text for students that serves as an outline to the basic tenets and origins of toxicology.

Trestrail, J. H. *Criminal Poisoning: An Investigational Guide for Law Enforcement, Toxicologists, Forensic Scientists, and Attorneys.* Totowa, N.J.: Humana Press, 2000. Comprehensive guide to the identification of toxic poisons used in homicides.

Williams, P., R. James, and S. Roberts, eds. *The Principles of Toxicology: Environmental and Industrial Applications.* New York: John Wiley & Sons, 2002. Guide for health professionals in the fundamentals of toxicology in both occupational and environmental settings.

See also Autopsies; Bloodstains; Coroners; Crime labs; DNA testing; Drug testing; Forensic palynology; Forensics; Latent evidence; Medical examiners; Sobriety testing; Trace evidence.

Trace evidence

Definition: Forms of physical evidence at crime scenes that are usually not visible to the naked eye

Criminal justice issues: Criminology; evidence and forensics; investigation; technology

Significance: Trace evidence is an integral part of many police investigations because it employs scientific methods to establish direct links between suspects and crime scenes. Trace evidence can provide powerful clues for reconstructing crimes for which little other evidence exits.

During the early part of the twentieth century, Edmond Locard, a French scientist who directed the world's first crime laboratory, articulated a principle of criminology that became known as Locard's Exchange Principle. It holds that when two physical objects come into contact with each other, each leaves particles on the other. Locard observed that no crime scene can ever be completely free of evidence; although no evidence may be seen by the naked eye, some evidence is always left behind. Locard's principle has served as the foundation for the forensic study of trace evidence.

Trace evidence alone may be inadequate to build cases against criminal suspects, but it can establish links between suspects and crime scenes or victims of crimes. The types of trace evidence analyzed most often at crime scenes are hair and fibers. Large amounts of hair found at a crime scene often indicate a struggle; they are commonly found on floors near weapons or points of contact between victims and their assailants. Rooted hair may provide DNA evidence. Carpet and clothing fibers are also commonly found in places where assailants and their victims come into contact with one another.

Other important types of trace evidence include paint residue, dust and dirt, and firearm residue. Chips of paint from vehicles, doors, and furniture are often found on weapons and clothes. Paint chips from vehicles can often be used to identify the vehicles' production years and makes and models. Dust and dirt residue can be used to determine places where people have been, where they reside, and what kinds of animals they have come into contact with. Residues left by ammunition can indicate whether suspects have fired firearms, but tests for such residues must be conducted within six hours of the time that weapons are fired.

Another broad category of trace evidence is used to identify the characteristics of persons involved in crime scenes. This type of evidence includes bodily fluids, bite marks and other wounds, shoe prints, and tool marks. Bodily fluids, which can provide useful evidence whether they are fresh, coagulated, or dry, include blood, semen, saliva, and sweat. The dryness of blood specimens can be used to estimate how much time has passed since crimes have been committed. Bite marks—which might be found on either victims or suspects—can be particularly useful in identifying suspects, as every person's teeth leave unique impressions. Likewise, every person has a walk that leaves shoe prints that are unique because of both the way in which people walk and the distinctive wear on their shoes.

Wounds made by weapons can often be used to determine the size, shape, and length of the weapons. Even tools leave identifying marks that can be used to link suspects with crime scenes.

Lisa Landis Murphy

Further Reading

Houck, M. *Mute Witnesses: Trace Evidence Analysis.* San Diego, Calif.: Academic Press, 2001.

_____. *Trace Evidence Analysis: More Clues in Forensic Microscopy and Mute Witnesses.* San Diego, Calif.: Academic Press, 2003.

Lee, H., H. C. Lee, and T. Timedy. *Blood Evidence: How DNA Is Revolutionizing the Way We Solve Crimes.* Cambridge, Mass.: Perseus Publishing, 2004.

See also Autopsies; Bloodstains; Crime labs; DNA testing; Fingerprint identification; Forensic palynology; Forensic psychology; Forensics; Latent evidence; Medical examiners; Shoe prints and tire-tracks; Toxicology; Trace evidence.

During a 2003 murder trial in Virginia Beach, Virginia, a Federal Bureau of Investigation DNA expert demonstrates how a person firing a rifle would deposit DNA traces on the weapon. *(AP/Wide World Photos)*

Traffic courts

Definition: Courts that deal with infractions of traffic laws that are considered less serious than misdemeanors and felonies

Criminal justice issues: Courts; traffic law

Significance: Traffic courts alleviate crowding in the justice system, for if traffic violations led to full criminal trials, the system would be overwhelmed with juries, lawyers, and convictions. Costs would be enormous, and many persons would be upset with the police and justice system for the vigorous enforcement of what are perceived to be insignificant crimes.

Traffic courts were established to handle routine traffic violations, such as speed law violations, driver and vehicle safety code infractions, parking tickets, and offenses against other rules of the road. Traffic crimes did not fit well into traditional state criminal court systems.

There are more than 150 million licensed drivers in the United States and a total of more than 25 million automobile accidents every year, more than 50,000 of which involve fatalities. The costs of these accidents reach more than $30 billion a year. The purpose of traffic law enforcement and traffic courts is to reduce the number of accidents and deaths. One result is that more than 20,000 traffic citations are filed every day in the United States.

Routine traffic violations are handled differently from more serious offenses such as driving under the influence of alcohol or drugs (DUI). For crimes such as speeding or running through a traffic sign, there is no need to prove criminal intent, as is true with other types of crimes. Simply committing the act is proof of guilt. Traffic courts were established specifically to handle proceedings involving what are legally called "traffic infractions." Most U.S. states have three types of criminal acts: misdemeanors, felonies, and infractions. Infractions are dealt with by civil rather than criminal procedures. The right to an attorney or trial by jury may not apply in cases involving infractions. Convictions do not result in prison or probation, and fines are often held to $50 or less. More serious traffic crimes, such as driving under the influence, are handled in more traditional court proceedings, in which defendants have the right to an attorney and a trial by jury.

Creating Order on the Highways

Highways can be very dangerous. Traffic laws have done a good job in creating order out of potential chaos. Drivers generally respect speed laws, traffic signs, and traffic lights, even when no police cars are visible. The success of the system is illustrated by the fact that the long-term trend has shown a decrease in traffic fatalities. The National Safety Council reports that there is only one serious traffic accident for every 60,000 miles driven, and Americans drive more than 2 trillion miles a year. The effect of traffic law enforcement by police and courts is demonstrated by the success of state laws requiring motorcyclists to wear helmets. Prior to passage of laws requiring helmets, only 50 percent of cyclists wore helmets, but after vigorous enforcement by the police and judges, that number grew to almost 100 percent, and the number of deaths in motorcycle accidents dropped dramatically. In the three states that refused to pass such laws, the number of fatalities remained at a very high level.

The strict enforcement of laws and efficient procedures in traffic courts have, according to many studies, led to fewer accidents and better driving habits. Studies of speed law enforcement have shown that it is not so much the severity of the penalty as the likelihood of being caught and convicted that reduces violations. On the other hand, studies have not indicated that there is any real benefit to sending traffic law violators to traffic school.

Leslie V. Tischauser

Further Reading

Haas, Carol. *Your Driving and the Law: A Crash Course in Traffic Tickets and Court, Auto Accidents and Insurance, and Vehicle-Related Lawsuits*. Bountiful, Utah: Horizon, 1991.

Hand, B., A. Sherman, and M. Cavanagh. *Traffic Investigation and Control*. New York: Macmillan, 1980.

U.S. Department of Transportation. *Traffic Safety and Crime: Keeping Pace*. Washington, D.C.:

National Highway Traffic Safety Administration, 1996.

See also Citations; Drunk driving; Hit-and-run accidents; Misdemeanors; Traffic fines; Traffic law; Traffic schools.

Traffic fines

Definition: Monetary penalties imposed for traffic violations

Criminal justice issues: Punishment; traffic law

Significance: Traffic fines are a serious issue because safety on the roadways is a substantial problem; however, public opinion views traffic offenses as noncriminal acts, even when serious injuries result, and traffic fines appear not to deter chronic offenders from repeating their offenses.

Traffic fines are imposed by states as sanctions to deter bad driving of motor vehicles. However, studies have shown that traffic fines are not effective in deterring chronic traffic offenders, particularly drunk drivers. Improving road safety is difficult when many in the general public do not view most traffic offenses as serious issues.

Amounts of traffic fines are usually tied directly to the types of driving violations, with more serious violations receiving higher fines. Police officers may make arrests and issue citations, summonses, tickets, and other documents for violations of traffic laws. Depending on the seriousness of violations, motorists may be required to appear in court or simply to pay fines for their violations.

Car crash caught on film by an overhead surveillance camera that was triggered when the car on the left ran the red light in the intersection. In addition to capturing a picture of the traffic violation, the camera recorded the time and place of the incident. *(AP/Wide World Photos)*

Fines are usually nominal amounts designed to be high enough to impress upon drivers the seriousness of their violations, without being so high that drivers may be unable to pay them and consequently face imprisonment. New technologies such as traffic cameras are now increasingly used to detect traffic violations, such as running stoplights; citations are simply mailed to the registered owners of the offending vehicles; and fines are paid without the need for appearances in court.

Police agencies have long recognized that enforcing traffic laws uniformly is more important than having uniformity in the traffic laws themselves. Traffic fines may vary from jurisdiction to jurisdiction, but the general public expects fairness. Drivers get upset when they perceive that they are being ticketed and fined while other drivers who are doing the same things, or worse, are not. Police officers are thus expected to be consistent in their awarding of tickets.

Police officers who take money directly from drivers instead of issuing them tickets are practicing a form of corruption. In years past, small towns in isolated regions occasionally ran "speed-trap" operations in which police and court officials worked in tandem to collect excessive fines from motorists passing through their communities.

David R. Forde

Further Reading

Boyle, John M. *National Survey of Speeding and Other Unsafe Driving Actions.* Washington, D.C.: U.S. Dept. of Transportation, National Highway Traffic Safety Administration, 1998.

Carroll, Alex. *Beat the Cops: The Guide to Fighting Your Traffic Ticket and Winning.* Santa Barbara, Calif.: Ace, 1995.

Haas, Carol. *Your Driving and the Law: A Crash Course in Traffic Tickets and Court, Auto Accidents and Insurance, and Vehicle-Related Lawsuits.* Bountiful, Utah: Horizon, 1991.

Matheson, Tim. *Traffic Tickets, Fines, and Other Annoying Things.* Secaucus, N.J.: Citadel Press, 1984.

See also Citations; Misdemeanors; Night courts; Traffic courts; Traffic law; Traffic schools.

Traffic law

Definition: Branch of law comprising rules for the orderly and safe flow of pedestrian and vehicular traffic

Criminal justice issues: Law codes; traffic law

Significance: Violations of traffic laws are usually considered minor criminal offenses, although in some jurisdictions less serious traffic offenses have been decriminalized and are called infractions.

Although there may be separate rules of procedure in traffic cases, the basic procedure, especially in serious offenses, is the same as in criminal cases. The state or municipality is the party that brings the charge. The burden of proof is beyond a reasonable doubt, and the same constitutional protections are afforded as apply in criminal cases.

The penalties meted out for most minor traffic violations are fines. In addition, most states have established point systems in which points are assessed on one's driving record for each moving traffic violation. The number of points assessed varies according to the seriousness of the violation. When persons accumulate a certain number of points within a period of time, their driver's licenses may be suspended. In some states persons can remove points or even avoid conviction for minor traffic offenses by attending traffic school. An indirect consequence of traffic conviction may be an increase in insurance premiums through loss of a safe driver discount or because a bad driving record places a driver in a higher risk category. Professional drivers must also consider the effects of traffic violations on their employment records.

As a general rule, a traffic law applies only if a violation occurs on a public street, highway, or public way. There are important exceptions, however. In many jurisdictions the offense of drunk driving can occur anywhere, even on private property. The definition section and the cited section of the traffic code should always be carefully reviewed to determine under what circumstances a violation can occur.

In almost all traffic offenses, a specific intent to violate the law is not necessary. Accordingly, persons cannot use as a defense that they did not see a stop sign or did not know that they had exceeded the speed limit. These matters, however, may be raised in mitigation.

Traffic Tickets

The usual procedure that is followed when a motorist appears to have violated a minor traffic law is for the officer to stop the vehicle and issue the driver a citation or ticket. This advises the person of the date, time, and place for the court appearance and of the particular offense for which the motorist is charged. The U.S. Supreme Court has ruled that the mere stop and issuance of a ticket is not an arrest. It is therefore not necessary for an officer to read a motorist the Miranda rights, which are warnings to suspects that they enjoy certain constitutional safeguards during questioning by law-enforcement officials. Any statements or admissions made at the time of the stop can be used in court against the driver without showing that the Miranda rights were read. It is most important at the time of a stop for the driver to give only essential information to the officer. Many persons have lost cases in court by telling police officers that they were going too fast to stop at a red light or by saying that they were driving only sixty-five miles per hour when an officer accused them of driving seventy miles per hour in a fifty-five mile per hour zone.

After the issuance of the ticket the officer usually provides information as to how to avoid a court appearance by merely paying a fine in person or by mail. It should be noted that before alleged offenders are allowed to leave, a computer check is made to determine whether they have valid driver's licenses and whether there are any warrants outstanding against them. In the past, nonresident drivers were required to post a bond with cash, a credit card, or an automobile club card. If they failed to make court appearances, which was often the case, the bond was forfeited and the case closed. Because almost all states have become signatories to the Non-Resident Violator Compact, the bond requirement may be waived for minor violations and nonresident drivers treated the same as local residents by being given the option of mailing in the fine or appearing in court at a later date.

Failure to appear in court or pay the fine has serious consequences. A local resident who ignores a citation will ultimately discover that a warrant has been issued, and the next encounter with a police officer will trigger an arrest. Out-of-state residents who ignore traffic tickets may find that the motor vehicle authority in their state has suspended their driving privileges under the Non-Resident Violator Compact.

Speeding Offenses

Speeding is the most common type of traffic violation, followed by stop sign and red light violations. Speed laws may be absolute in that the mere fact that a driver has exceeded the speed limit constitutes a violation. An example of such a law was the 55-mile-per-hour speed limit imposed by the federal government in the 1970's as an energy conservation measure but later repealed.

More commonly, speeding laws are drafted so that a violation occurs only if the speed is unreasonable and improper. To make enforcement easier, the law establishes speed limits and provides that they be posted. Drivers who exceed the posted speed limit are then considered to be in violation unless they show that the speed they were driving was reasonable and proper under the circumstances. Thus, if someone is charged with exceeding the posted 25-mile-per-hour speed limit in a business district during the early hours of the morning, a good argument could be made that a faster speed was not unreasonable or improper, because there was little or no vehicular or pedestrian traffic at that time.

The assured clear distance law regulates another type of speeding violation. Rear-end collisions are usually the result of violating this law. The basic rule of the road is that a motorist who is traveling behind another vehicle must be able to stop without colliding with the vehicle in front or any discernible object ahead in the path of travel.

With any traffic offense it is most important to carefully read the section of the traffic code under which a citation is issued. Each and every element of the offense must be present and proven by the arresting authority. It is not enough, for example, to be merely exceeding the posted speed limit in a school zone. A careful reading of the code section would probably disclose that children must actually be coming to or leaving school

Because the U.S. Supreme Court has ruled that stopping a motorist to issue a ticket for a traffic violation is not an arrest, officers are not required to issue cited motorists the Miranda rights that must be read to persons being arrested. Nevertheless, anything that cited motorists say to officers issuing citations may be used against them in court, should their cases go to trial. *(Brand-X Pictures)*

hit-and-run accidents, drag racing, and fleeing from police officers are likewise classified as serious traffic offenses in most states. In a drunk driving case, an arrest is made at the scene and the driver is transported to a lockup facility or patrol post. The Miranda rights are read to the driver as soon as practicable after the arrest so that any statements made by the driver may be used in court.

In the other serious traffic offenses, drivers may simply be given traffic citations to appear in court. In the case of nonresidents, cash or surety bonds are usually required. Court appearances in these serious cases are required, however, and cannot be avoided by the mere payment of fines. If a jail or prison sentence is to be imposed, accused persons are entitled to a court-appointed attorney if they are unable to pay for one. As to the right to a jury trial, the law varies from state to state. Under the U.S. Constitution as interpreted by court decisions, a defendant has the right to a jury trial when the offense charged carries with it a term of imprisonment of more than six months.

during opening or closing hours or at recess. This would be true even though flashers were operating warning of the school zone.

Testing devices require careful scrutiny. If a radar device is used, the traffic code, administrative rules, and case law should be researched to determine compliance. There are always very specific and definite rules as to calibration—that is, the check that has to be made to determine if the device is in good working order. The officer operating the radar device must also be trained and qualified in its use. Evidence that these requirements have been met must be introduced before any radar reading may be used as evidence against an allegedly errant drive.

Serious Traffic Offenses

Not all traffic violations are of such a minor nature that they are handled by a traffic ticket and a fine. Vehicular homicide and drunk driving are serious crimes punishable by possible jail or even prison terms. Driving under a suspended license,

Civil Liability

A violation of a traffic law may cause an accident that results in property damage or personal injury. The issue then arises as to who is liable for the damages. In states that have a no-fault insurance law, it may be that the parties can only recover their losses from their own insurance companies. In states without a no-fault law, the loss can be recovered from the other party provided the other party was at fault.

Fault in a motor vehicle accident is usually determined by a violation of a traffic law if the violation caused the accident. Accordingly, if one driver running a red light resulted in an accident, the driver in legal terms would be negligent per se and the proximate cause of the accident. The driver or the driver's insurance company would be liable for the damages to the driver and owner of the other vehicle. If both drivers violated the law, the issue of contributory negligence would apply, which would prevent or limit recovery by either driver.

Persons involved in traffic accidents should not admit fault at the scenes or enter guilty pleas in traffic court, as these acts would be admissions that can be used at trial to recover for damages. A driver cited for a violation of a traffic law under such circumstances who seeks to avoid the inconvenience and expense of contesting a traffic charge should enter a plea of no contest. Such a plea would not be admissible at a civil trial.

Gilbert T. Cave

Further Reading

Bello, Phil. *How to Win in Traffic Court: The Non-Lawyers Guide to Successfully Defending Traffic Violations*. Gibbsboro, N.J.: Major Market Books, 1989. Typical handbook offering advice on contesting traffic tickets. This book and the four titles that follow below all contain easily understood explanations of traffic laws and what elements must be present before violations can occur. Because some of the terms and procedures are keyed to particular states, care must be exercised in their use.

Carroll, Alex. *Beat the Cops: The Guide to Fighting Your Traffic Ticket and Winning*. Santa Barbara, Calif.: Ace, 1995.

Glass, James A. *Traffic Court: How to Win*. Arcadia, Calif.: Allenby Press, 1988.

Langford, Les. *Understanding Police Traffic Radar and Lidar*. Rev. ed. Pleasant Grove, Utah: Law Enforcement Services, 1998.

Matheson, Tim. *Traffic Tickets, Fines, and Other Annoying Things*. Secaucus, N.J.: Citadel Press, 1984.

Royal, Dawn. *National Survey of Speeding and Unsafe Driving Attitudes and Behavior, 2002*. Washington, D.C.: National Highway Traffic Safety Administration, 2004.

Shankey, Michael. *The MVR Book: A Motor Services Guide*. Tempe, Ariz.: BRB Publications, 1996. Excellent research tool for obtaining basic information on traffic laws and licensing, together with addresses for motor vehicle bureaus or their equivalent in each of the fifty states and the District of Columbia.

Van Kirk, Donald J. *Vehicular Accident Investigation and Reconstruction*. Boca Raton, Fla.: CRC Press, 2000. Practical manual for law-enforcement professionals involved in investigating traffic accidents that is also accessible to novices. Accurate reconstructions of accidents are often crucial to determining fault, making it possible to separate motorists who have violated the law from those who are victims of other drivers' mistakes.

See also Alcohol use and abuse; Arrest; *Atwater v. City of Lago Vista*; Citations; Drunk driving; Hit-and-run accidents; Mothers Against Drunk Driving; Night courts; Sobriety testing; State police; Traffic courts; Traffic fines; Traffic schools.

Traffic schools

Definition: Government and commercially run institutions that provide driver education classes and other types of driving-related training

Criminal justice issues: Punishment; rehabilitation; traffic law

Significance: Traffic schools, both private and public, provide rehabilitation for drivers convicted of driving offenses, instruction for new and inexperienced drivers, and specialized instruction for drivers with special needs.

In 1995, more than 41,000 people were killed in traffic accidents in the United States, and the cost of motor vehicle crashes was estimated at $4,000 per second. These statistics point to the need for safer driving, and the task of producing safer drivers falls mainly to traffic schools and driver education. It is projected that approximately one in every five Americans will be involved in an alcohol-related crash at some time during their driving lives. The court system must deal with persons driving under the influence of alcohol or drugs (DUI).

One approach to the problem of driving under the influence and to other traffic violations is the mandatory enrollment of convicted drivers in traffic school programs. Many states use the successful completion of a traffic school program to reduce or remove DUI and other traffic violations from the offender's record. To rehabilitate traffic offenders, private traffic schools offer a variety of programs. Many states employ a point system for various traffic offenses: The more serious the offense, the greater the points are assigned, until a specific total number of points is reached and a person's driver's license is suspended. In some cases the successful completion of an approved traffic school course is sufficient for removing points from one's driving record. In some instances, driver education courses in public and private schools, as recognized by the courts, also serve to provide the appropriate training so that court-imposed penalties may be reduced.

Rehabilitation is not the only purpose of traffic schools. New and inexperienced drivers enroll in traffic schools to acquire skills and experience in driving. In most states, teenage drivers who have reached the legal driving age must undergo some form of driver training in order to obtain permanent licenses. This training is often conducted in schools in which driver education is an established part of the curriculum. Teachers who give driver education classes are licensed upon completion of specially designed programs as part of their college or university training. The Driving School Association of America (DSAA), representing 350 driving schools in the United States and Canada, serves as a medium of exchange for ideas and policies relating to driver training at all levels. It is also possible to enroll in and complete traffic school courses at home through videotaped programs and on-line Internet courses.

A number of specialized traffic schools meet the specialized needs of certain programs. Commercial truck, bus, and cab drivers receive special training in the operation and handling of their vehicles. There are schools for race car drivers, airplane pilots, school-bus drivers, motorcyclists, persons with disabilities, and off-highway vehicle operators. Law-enforcement officers require specialized training. Business executives and others who may face dangers such as kidnappings and terrorist attacks can receive specialized defensive driver training.

Traffic school training involves more than just learning to handle an automobile. Traffic laws, safe driving procedures, vehicle operation, emergency repairs, emergency driving measures (such as swerving and panic stops), accident avoidance, and accident reporting are also covered.

Gordon A. Parker

Further Reading

Carroll, Alex. *Beat the Cops: The Guide to Fighting Your Traffic Ticket and Winning.* Santa Barbara, Calif.: Ace, 1995.

Glass, James A. *Traffic Court: How to Win.* Arcadia, Calif.: Allenby Press, 1988.

Matheson, Tim. *Traffic Tickets, Fines, and Other Annoying Things.* Secaucus, N.J.: Citadel Press, 1984.

See also Alcohol use and abuse; Criminal records; Drunk driving; Jaywalking; Rehabilitation; Traffic courts; Traffic fines; Traffic law.

Treason

Definition: Violation of allegiance toward one's country or sovereign, especially the betrayal of one's country by waging war against it or by consciously and purposely acting to aid its enemies

Criminal justice issues: Capital punishment; espionage and sedition; federal law; international law

Significance: Treason holds a special place in American criminal justice for two reasons—its heinousness and the fact that it is the only crime specifically defined in the U.S. Constitution. However, the Constitution's narrow definition of treason has had the effect of making treason prosecutions rare occurrences.

At the time when the U.S. Constitution was being drafted, in 1787, treason had long been considered the greatest of crimes against humanity. The Framers of the Constitution discussed the wording of the document's treason clause at length and relied upon the common law and the English Statute of Treasons for their definition of the crime. Aware of abuses of treason in England, whose laws allowed the suppression of political and religious speech, the Framers were concerned with limiting the scope of the crime while at the same time protecting national security. They also worried that treason excited hatred and fear against those charged with the crime. The Constitutional Convention chose to explicitly entrust cases in which treason was alleged to the judicial power.

Article III, section 3 of the Constitution defines treason precisely:

> Treason against the United States, shall consist only in levying War against them, or in adhering to their Enemies, giving them Aid and Comfort. No Person shall be convicted of Treason unless on the Testimony of two Witnesses to the same overt Act, or on Confession in open Court.

> The Congress shall have Power to declare the Punishment of Treason, but no Attainder of Treason shall work Corruption of Blood, or Forfeiture except during the Life of the Person attainted.

The Constitution's treason clause limits treason to making war on the United States or aiding enemies of the nation. Moreover, the clause prohibits the legislature or the judiciary from redefining treason. Finally, no one can be convicted of treason unless at least two witnesses testify to the same overt act or the accused person confesses in an open court. The two-witness rule helps to ensure that an innocent person is not convicted on the testimony of a single biased or self-interested witness. Finally, the clause gives Congress the power to establish the punishment for treason.

Treason Cases in History

Throughout American history, only about thirty-five treason cases have been pressed to trial by the federal government. No one has yet been executed upon a federal treason conviction, and presidents have frequently pardoned those convicted or mitigated their sentences. (In 1953, Ethel and Julius Rosenberg were executed after being convicted of conspiracy in connection with selling atomic secrets to the Soviet Union, but they were not charged with treason.) Cases of alleged treason have rarely had a central bearing on national security policy. Instead, the federal government has relied upon cooperation between Congress and the president to maintain national security.

Many U.S. states have their own treason laws, but they have seldom used them. Only twice have states completed treason prosecution cases. The first instance was Rhode Island's conviction of Thomas Dorr in 1844. The second case was Virginia's conviction of John Brown in 1859. Both men were charged with levying war against the states.

The treason clause of the federal Constitution was first interpreted in the Whiskey Rebellion trial of 1795. The case arose when armed settlers in eastern Pennsylvania protested a federal excise tax on distilled whiskey, but they were soundly defeated by militia under the personal command of President George Washington. Two ringleaders in the rebellion were convicted of treason but were pardoned by Washington.

Another interpretation of the treason clause occurred in the 1807 trials of Aaron Burr and his co-conspirators in federal court. A former vice president, Burr was charged with plotting to lead the southwestern United States into secession from the Union with the intention of establishing a confederacy under his leadership. He was indicted and tried for treason but was acquitted, in large part because of Chief Justice John Marshall's narrow interpretation of the constitutional meaning of treason. In a trial of two of Burr's confederates, Marshall confined the meaning of levying war to the actual waging of war. Marshall's ruling made it extremely difficult to convict anyone of levying war against the United States, short of actually participating in armed actions. Marshall's rulings in those cases ensured that treason would thereafter be a legal, rather than a political, concept, thereby limiting the number of treason indictments and trials in later history.

Most U.S. treason trials have arisen during times of national crises and wars. For example, during the War of 1812, acts such as selling provisions to the British, releasing prisoners to the enemy, and attacking troops enforcing embargoes were prosecuted as treason. However, all of the accused were acquitted. In 1851, a jury acquitted a defendant accused of treason for forcibly interfering with the recapture of escaped slaves under the Fugitive Slave Law.

A number of persons were convicted of treason during the Civil War and its aftermath. Such acts as participating as a member of a state militia company in the seizure of a federal fort or fitting out and sailing a privateer were held to be the

Noted Cases of Americans Accused of Treason

Name	The charges
Benedict Arnold	U.S. general accused of plotting to surrender West Point to British forces in 1780.
Aaron Burr	Former vice president accused of conspiring to take over western territories of the United States during Thomas Jefferson's administration.
Mildred Gillars, a.k.a. "Axis Sally"	American who broadcast propaganda for Germany during World War II.
Iva Toguri, a.k.a. "Tokyo Rose"	Japanese American accused of broadcasting propaganda to U.S. servicemen for Japan during World War II, when she became trapped in that country while visiting relatives.
Ezra Pound	Poet who broadcast propaganda for Italy during World War II.
Alger Hiss	Diplomat accused of spying on the United States for the Soviet Union during the 1930's and 1940's.
John Walker, Jr.	Former naval warrant officer who sold military secrets to the Soviet Union from 1967 to 1985.

levying of war and thus treason. Cases of confiscation of property or refusal to enforce obligations given in connection with sale of provisions to the Confederacy, likewise, were found to be giving aid and comfort to the enemy. After the war, Jefferson Davis, the former president of the Confederacy, successfully argued that rebels whose government achieved the status of a recognized belligerent could not be held for treason. Davis himself thus was not tried for treason.

During the 1899-1903 Philippine insurrection against U.S. occupation, armed efforts to overthrow the government were found to be acts of levying war. Some rebels were convicted of treason, but strict enforcement of the two-witness requirement resulted in some of the convictions being reversed.

After the nineteenth century, the president and Congress relied upon statutory criminal protections against disloyalty and no longer considered the treason charge as the principal bulwark of state security. Such federal laws as the Espionage Act of 1917, the Smith Act of 1940, the Uniform Code of Military Justice, the Patriot Act of 2001, and seditious conspiracy statutes have provided alternatives for prosecutors to deter or punish crimes that threaten national security without resorting to treason indictments. As mid-twentieth century Supreme Court justice

Robert H. Jackson observed, "We have managed to do without treason prosecutions to a degree that probably would be impossible except while a people was singularly confident of external security and internal stability."

During World War I, Congress passed legislation making it a crime to speak or publish words intended to bring the government into contempt or to interfere with the success of the military. Nearly one thousand people were convicted under these statutes. Remarkably, however, only three cases of treason arose at that time when feelings ran high against unpopular opinions or attitudes.

During World War II, in *Cramer v. United States* (1945), the Supreme Court interpreted the constitutional requirement that treason be proved by the testimony of two witnesses so expansively as to provide a remarkable degree of protection against the overuse of treason indictments. On the other hand, in *Haupt v. United States* (1947), the Court sustained a conviction based on evidence that did not satisfy the requirements of *Cramer*. That ruling facilitated seven treason prosecutions of American nationals, including Iva Toguri (known as "Tokyo Rose") and other radio-broadcast defendants, for aiding the Axis Powers during the war. The last case of treason before the Supreme Court was *Kawa-*

kita v. United States in 1952, involving a U.S. citizen who brutalized U.S. prisoners in a Japanese war-materials plant during World War II.

Investigation

The Federal Bureau of Investigation (FBI) has primary responsibility for investigating treason allegations under its mandate to protect the United States against terrorist and foreign intelligence threats. The mission of the bureau's Intelligence Program is to position the FBI optimally to meet current and emerging national security and criminal threats by aiming core investigative work proactively against threats to U.S. interests.

United States attorneys in the Department of Justice have the power to prosecute those accused of treason. Under the federal criminal justice system, federal prosecutors have wide latitude in determining when, whom, how, and even whether to prosecute possible violations of federal criminal law. The prosecutors' broad discretion in such areas as initiating or forgoing prosecutions, selecting or recommending specific charges, and terminating prosecutions by accepting guilty pleas has been recognized on numerous occasions by the courts.

Punishment

The punishment for a person found guilty of treason is death or imprisonment for not less than five years and a fine of not less than ten thousand dollars. Persons convicted of treason are also barred from holding any office under the United States.

Any U.S. citizen who has knowledge of an act of treason against the nation and fails to report the act to government authorities promptly may be found guilty of misprision of treason—an early common-law concept under which a person was required to report or prosecute one known to have committed a felony. The punishment for misprision of treason is a fine or imprisonment of not more than seven years, or both.

Theodore M. Vestal

Further Reading

Chapin, Bradley. *The American Law of Treason: Revolutionary and Early National Origins.* Seattle: University of Washington Press, 1964. History of treason during colonial times and the American Revolution through the trial of Aaron Burr in 1807.

Hurst, James Willard. *The Law of Treason in the United States: Collected Essays.* Westport, Conn.: Greenwood Publishing, 1971. Definitive analysis of the doctrinal development of the law of treason in the United States from its English origins to the late twentieth century. An appendix lists all cases in which construction of the treason clause was involved.

Lucas, Eileen. *The Aaron Burr Treason Trial: A Headline Court Case.* Berkeley Heights, N.J.: Enslow Publishers, 2003. Brief study of Burr's trial, for young readers.

Melton, Buckner F., Jr. *Aaron Burr: Conspiracy to Treason.* New York: John Wiley & Sons, 2001. Well-written and accessible account of Burr's treason trial by a constitutional law authority who examines the ethical and legal issues underlying the case.

West, Rebecca. *The New Meaning of Treason.* New York: Viking Penguin, 1964. Eloquently written analysis of British traitors such as the fascist dubbed "Lord Haw-Haw" during World War II and spies in the communist cause during the 1950's and 1960's.

See also Attorneys, U.S.; Capital punishment; Constitution, U.S.; Criminal prosecution; Espionage; Federal Bureau of Investigation; Federal Crimes Act; Justice Department, U.S.; Patriot Act; Punishment; Seditious libel; Terrorism; War crimes.

Treasury Department, U.S.

Identification: Primary federal agency tasked to promote the prosperity and stability of the U.S. economy by assisting in regulating financial institutions and markets and enforcing laws dealing with money, taxes, and related matters

Date: Established in 1789

Criminal justice issues: Business and financial crime; federal law; fraud

Significance: The Department of Treasury works to create a prosperous capitalist economy by regulating federal laws dealing with economic matters throughout the United States. This objective is also linked to the world economy, as the Treasury also works to assist and promote a healthy and vibrant economy for the many nations of the world.

In 1789, the U.S. Congress created the Treasury Department of the United States and outlined and prescribed all the new department's duties and responsibilities for maintaining, protecting, and assisting in the growth of the nation's economy. The modern Treasury Department is the main federal agency tasked with maintaining and securing the economic safety of the United States.

The Treasury Department's duties include a wide range of activities—from advising the president on any and all economic issues, to enhancing and creating corporate governance in financial institutions, assisting other nations to build a stable world economy, predicting and preventing global economic crises, and regulating and protecting the economy of the United States by enforcing the economic and tax laws needed to regulate appropriate growth and stability of the national economy.

Organization of the Department

The Treasury Department is organized in two major components: the departmental offices and the operating bureaus. The departmental offices are responsible for the formulation of policy and management for the entire department. The operating bureaus carry out the specific tasks assigned by the department and employ 98 percent of the department's personnel. Twelve different bureaus are tasked with numerous different responsibilities; however, they share a central mission: protecting and maintaining the United States economy.

The basic functions of the Treasury Department as a whole include producing postage stamps, currency, and coinage; managing all federal finances, collecting federal taxes, duties, and all other moneys owed to the government; paying all bills that the United States owes to other nations; supervising national banks and credit institutions; advising other branches of the government, including the president, on financial and

tax-related policies and issues; enforcing federal finance and tax laws; and investigating and prosecuting persons who counterfeit U.S. currency and persons who evade paying taxes on regulated goods and services.

Of the twelve bureaus of the Treasury Department, only four have enforcement and investigative duties. Before 2003, however, four other bureaus operated under the auspices of the Treasury Department. However, under the Homeland Security Act, in 2003 those bureaus were transferred to other departments and given revised investigative and protective missions. The four bureaus are the Bureau of Alcohol, Tobacco, Firearms and Explosives (ATF), the Federal Law Enforcement Training Center, the U.S. Customs Service, and the U.S. Secret Service.

The four remaining Treasury Department bureaus with enforcement and investigative responsibilities are the Alcohol and Tobacco Tax and Trade Bureau, the Internal Revenue Service, the Financial Crimes Enforcement Network (FinCEN), and the Office of Inspector General.

Alcohol and Tobacco Tax and Trade Bureau

The Homeland Security Act of 2002 divided the Treasury Department's Bureau of Alcohol, Tobacco, Firearms and Tobacco into two bodies with separate missions. The core of ATF was moved to the new Homeland Security Department, and the remainder of it was reconstituted within the Treasury Department as the Alcohol and Tobacco Tax Bureau (ATTB). The Homeland Security Act called for the tax collection functions to remain with the ATTB under the Department of the Treasury. The ATTB now collects alcohol and tobacco taxes owed to the federal government and works to ensure that alcoholic beverages are produced, labeled, advertised, and marketed in accordance with federal law. These duties date back to 1789, when Alexander Hamilton, the first Treasury secretary, suggested that under the new U.S. Constitution, Congress should impose a tax on imported spirits to help pay the Revolutionary War debt.

Internal Revenue Service

The largest of the twelve Treasury bureaus, the Internal Revenue Service (IRS) is responsible for determining, assessing, and gathering inter-

The Fall of Al Capone

After years of being investigated by agents of the Federal Bureau of Investigation and other law-enforcement agencies, Al Capone—perhaps the most notorious mobster of all time—was finally brought down by U.S. Treasury Department special agents. On June 16, 1931, Capone pleaded guilty to tax evasion and Prohibition violation charges; four months later, he was convicted at trial. He was sentenced to eleven years in federal prison, fined $50,000, charged $7,692 for court costs, and ordered to pay all back taxes that he owed, including interest charges, that totaled $215,000. After serving time in California's Alcatraz Penitentiary, Capone was released in 1939. By then, his health was broken by syphilis, and he quietly lived out the remaining years of his life in Florida.

nal revenue in the United States. The IRS deals directly with more Americans than any other institution, public or private, in the United States. It also is one of the world's most efficient tax administrators and collects more than two trillion dollars in taxes every year.

A major goal of the IRS is to ensure that all Americans understand and carry out their tax obligations to the government. This is not an easy task to accomplish. To ensure that all federal tax laws are carried out and administered fairly and justly, the IRS maintains a criminal investigation unit that employs about twenty-nine hundred special agents. They investigate violations of tax, money laundering, and Bank Secrecy Act laws. Although the IRS shares the jurisdictions of money laundering and Bank Secrecy Act violations with other federal agencies, it is the only agency that has sole investigative jurisdiction over criminal violations of the Internal Revenue Code.

The special agents who make up the law-enforcement arm of the IRS are some of the most elite financial investigators in the world. Individual financial investigations may take hundreds of hours and require the scrutiny of many thousands of financial records and tax statements. The agents focus their investigative efforts on legal-source tax crimes, illegal-source financial crimes, and narcotics and terrorist-related financial crimes. Agents also investigate public and governmental corruption, tax evasion, health care fraud, telemarketing fraud, money laundering, and other forms of financial fraud. IRS agents have one of the highest conviction rates among federal law-enforcement agencies, and many of the people whom they help to convict pay severe fines; some are awarded lengthy prison sentences.

Financial Crimes Enforcement Network (FinCEN)

The Financial Crimes Enforcement Network (FinCEN) is tasked with bringing people and information together to fight the complex crime of money laundering, which is now considered to be the third-largest business in the world. FinCEN was established by the Treasury Department in 1990, and since its inception it has worked to maximize information sharing and gathering among all branches of law enforcement and its other partners in the regulatory and financial sectors.

FinCEN's network system approach encourages cost-effective methods to combat money laundering both domestically and globally. FinCEN has been designated by the Department of the Treasury as one of the principal agencies to establish, oversee, and implement policies to detect and prevent money laundering, terrorist financing, and international organized crime financial activities. FinCEN's primary goals are to support law-enforcement investigative efforts, foster interagency and global cooperation against domestic and international financial crimes, and provide U.S. policymakers with strategic analyses of domestic and worldwide money laundering developments, trends, and patterns. FinCEN officials try to accomplish these goals through information collection, analysis, and sharing, as well as technological assistance and innovative, cost-effective implementation of the Bank Secrecy Act and other Treasury authorities. FinCEN offers online access to both national and international law-enforcement agencies who are deeply involved in the fight against money laundering.

FinCEN's staff includes approximately two hundred employees, many of whom are intelligence research specialists from both law-enforcement and financial communities; law-enforcement support staff; and law-enforcement and legal analysts. In addition, at any given moment about forty long-term detailees from twenty different law-enforcement and regulatory agencies around the United States work in the bureau. As members of a collective bureau, these individuals are tasked with connecting the links among the individuals and financial institutions who engage in the illegal act of money laundering. This task is quite arduous; however, FinCEN maintains and operates one of the largest repositories of information on money laundering activities available to law enforcement nationally and internationally.

Office of Inspector General

The Department of the Treasury's Office of Inspector General (OIG) was established in 1989 by the secretary of the treasury. The OIG is led by an inspector general who is appointed by the president of the United States with the consent of the U.S. Senate. The inspector general reports indirectly to the secretary of the treasury through the deputy secretary and provides the secretary with independent and unbiased reviews of all department operations.

The inspector general is also required to keep both the secretary and the entire Congress up to date on all problems and concerns relating to the administration of Treasury Department programs and operations. Serving with the inspector general is a deputy inspector general, who is responsible for assimilating all current bureau reports and investigations. In addition to the inspector and deputy, the office keeps a staff of one hundred full-time civil servants who are responsible for record keeping, external auditing, report writing, and internal investigations.

In regard to investigations, it is vital that all erroneous or criminal behavior be dealt with at once. Audits and investigations that indicate any form of specious or suspected criminal activity are usually passed on to the Department of Justice for further investigation and appropriate action. It is the main goal of the office of the inspector general to act as an internal investigation mechanism for the Department of the Treasury so that a fiduciary environment in which the U.S.

economy can grow and prosper can be maintained.

One of the main tasks of the civil servant staff is to create and submit semiannual reports on the activities and investigations of the inspector's office. Disclosures of problems, abuses, and deficiencies in the Treasury Department are highlighted and brought to the attention of the Congress and the secretary of the treasury. The reports also offer recommendations of what the department should do with regard to corrective action plans when particular abuses and deviancies are reported. Overall, the office of the inspector general plays an integral role for the Department of Treasury by making sure that all operations of the twelve bureaus are carried out efficiently and without corruption or deceit.

Paul M. Klenowski

Further Reading

Berson, Susan A. *Federal Tax Litigation*. New York: Law Journal Press, 2004. Coverage of every aspect of federal tax disputes, including handling tax controversies at the administrative audit and appeals levels of the IRS.

International Business Publications USA. *U.S. Department of Treasury Handbook*. 2d ed. Washington, D.C.: International Business Publications USA, 2001. Handbook explaining the organization and functions of the Treasury Department, published for international businesspersons and government leaders.

Johnson, David. *Illegal Tender*. Washington, D.C.: Smithsonian Institution Press, 1995. Fascinating history of the early years of counterfeiting and the rise of the U.S. Secret Service under the Treasury Department.

Melanson, Philip H., and Peter F. Stevens. *The Secret Service: The Hidden History of an Enigmatic Agency*. New York: Carroll & Graf, 2002. This work gives the most complete and accurate look at the history of the United States Secret Service, which was formerly under the Treasury Department.

The Use and Counterfeiting of U.S. Currency Abroad. Washington, D.C.: U.S. Department of the Treasury, 2003. One of a series of annual Treasury Department reports to Congress on the department's ongoing fight against counterfeiting.

Yancey, Richard. *Confessions of a Tax Collector: One Man's Tour of Duty Inside the IRS*. New York: HarperCollins, 2004. Personal memoir of a veteran agent of the IRS.

See also Bureau of Alcohol, Tobacco, Firearms and Explosives; Counterfeiting; Forgery; Fraud; Internal Revenue Service; Money laundering; Secret Service, U.S.; Tax evasion; Telephone fraud.

Trespass

Definition: Unlawful intrusion onto property, persons, or rights of others

Criminal justice issues: Privacy; vandalism

Significance: Trespass is a complex area of both civil and criminal law that takes many forms and has close ties to other criminal offenses; because trespass touches on so many aspects of daily life, it is the basis for frequent legal disputes and concerns.

When someone enters the property of another without permission, there is a possibility of a civil or criminal offense if harm or injury occurs. There are several types of trespass, remedies for the offense, and grounds for defenses against charges of trespass.

Trespass Involving Property

Real property consists of immovable areas on the ground and their vegetation and structures, as well as the right of the property's owners to possess, enjoy, dispose of, and control the property's use. Part of that right is the right to exclude others from the property. Trespass to land is the unlawful interference with the ownership of real property involving intentional, negligent, or reckless behavior that results in damage.

Trespass to land usually involves traveling on the surface of other persons' real property. Such trespass may entail treading down a lawn, destroying vegetation, entering a structure, or obstructing entry to the property. Such acts constitute trespass whether they are performed by a person or a person's employees, servants, or animals.

Trespass may also involve going above or below someone's property. Branches and roots of trees on one property may be regarded as illegally encroaching on the real property of a neighbor. Timber trespass occurs when intruders remove trees or harvests from trees without the owners' permission. Unauthorized drilling for oil under another person's land is also a form of trespass. Aircraft and balloons may be regarded as trespassing on the airspace of a property if they damage the property below. On the other hand, boating or swimming past someone's property in a lake or stream is not considered trespassing.

Environmental trespass may involve air or soil pollution, whether from public (such as smelly sewers) or private (such as factory waste dumping) sources. Continuing trespass occurs when the intrusion is not temporary, as when someone dumps trash on another person's land and does not remove it.

Recreational trespass involves damage to parklands, lakes, and rivers, as well as plants and forests, whether publicly or privately owned. Camping, picnicking, or playing football is trespass when it takes place on land owned by others. Bottomlands trespass occurs when a property owner adjacent to a lake or stream tries to place anchors or docks on the bottomlands of another person's property without permission. Refuge trespass applies to any unlicensed person who hunts, traps, injures, molests, or destroys wildlife on government land or waters.

Vehicle prowling is a form of trespass that occurs when someone unlawfully enters a motor home or a sailboat or vessel equipped for mechanical propulsion that has a cabin with permanently installed sleeping quarters or cooking facilities.

A charge of trespass can apply to a public facility or a place of public accommodation, such as a cinema, hotel, shopping mall, or public street, if individuals are disruptive. Examples may include overly aggressive panhandlers, unruly drunks, loud or obnoxious persons, or gang members who claim space as part of their turf and try to exclude others. In a business establishment, protesters and strikers can be charged with trespass.

Aggravated trespass involves activity that disrupts, obstructs, or intimidates individuals from engaging in lawful activity. The most common offense occurs near facilities for abortions, where protesters may behave in a threatening manner so that those seeking abortions are fearful of entering.

Trespass on the case occurs when the resulting damage is a remote consequence of the act of entering another's property. A possible example is a duck that has been shot down by a hunter that lands on valuable property not owned by the hunter.

Trespass also applies to personal property. Conversion is taking someone's personal property, such as finding a hat in someone's basement and leaving the premises with the hat but without asking permission. Trespass to chattels occurs when someone substantially interferes with an individual's personal property; for example, one who steals authorization codes to make unauthorized long-distance telephone calls is trespassing on the telephone company's telephone lines and switching systems. The same applies to repeated, unwelcome faxes or telephone calls. In the time of slavery, damage to a slave by someone other than the slaveowner was a form of trespass to chattels.

Some attorneys have argued that unwelcome e-mail ("spam"), computer viruses and worms, and Web site intrusions by hackers constitute computer trespass because the intrusion is on the electrons involved in cyberspace.

The offense of breaking and entering is a form of criminal trespass. Entry is trespass; breaking (subsequent damage or theft of property) constitutes criminal trespass. However, the charge of criminal trespass becomes incidental if more violent crimes are committed when the trespass takes places.

Trespass Involving Persons

Stalking, which occurs when one individual persistently tracks down and follows another person, involves trespass when the stalker gains entry into the property or house of an individual, even though no harm may be intended, because of the psychological effect on the person stalked. Aggravated stalking occurs when stalking continues even after a court has issued a restraining order again the stalker.

Audio trespass is concerned with noise pollution. From high-decibel boomcars to drag racing,

loud noise can cause hearing loss, disturb sleep, increase stress, and even interfere with the ability to hear such emergency signals as police sirens.

Chemical trespass or toxic trespass exists when toxic chemicals are present in the human body at medically unacceptable levels. The sources include polluted tap water used for drinking and such toxic chemicals as pesticide sprays that enter the airspace of real property and find their way into the lungs or onto the skin of those at home.

Establishing Criminality

Criminal trespass occurs when trespassers intentionally enter properties belonging to others, using force, and injuries directly result. For example, a pet owner who deliberately sends a dog to attack a person or dog on another's property is liable for criminal trespass. However, pet owners are not criminally liable when their pets merely stray onto other properties, even though the other property owners have the right to use reasonable force to remove the animals. Police officers are empowered to arrest those suspected of criminal trespass, but they usually leave other forms of trespass to civil suits.

Charges of criminal trespass may be incidental to other offenses. Courts judge first-degree from second-degree criminal trespass on a case-by-case basis. Criminal trespass can be either a felony or a misdemeanor, depending on the extent of damage caused by the trespass. Computer trespass, for example, is commonly a felony.

Stalking can be established as criminal if a reasonable person's response to the actions of the stalker would be to feel fearful, intimidated, terrorized, frightened, threatened, harassed, or molested. The stalker must also cause the victim to experience any of these feelings to an intense degree.

In the case of trespass to chattels, criminality can be determined from four tests:

✓ Is the chattel dispossessed?
✓ Is use of the chattel made unavailable for a long period?
✓ Is the condition, quality, or usefulness of the chattel impaired?
✓ Is there is actual harm to the chattel?

Remedies and Penalties for Trespass

Property owners who post "No Trespassing" signs on their property may mistakenly believe that there is an absolute right to use force to resist a trespasser. Instead, there is a legal procedure to follow to stop intruders from entering properties, such as shopping malls. Owners or lawful tenants must first issue proper trespass warnings. The latter are verbal or written warnings phrased precisely in the manner prescribed by law, which usually requires that the warnings indicate the names of the owners and how long entry is barred. Moreover, landowners who fail to post notices of dangerous conditions on their land may be liable for injuries incurred by trespassers.

In cases of recreational trespass, the posting of signs large enough to be read, even without protective fences, are sufficient notice. Persons who merely picnic on someone else's land and knowingly disregard no-trespassing signs are engaging in civil trespass.

Persons who do not heed proper trespass warnings may be taken into custody by licensed security officers and later arrested by government police. However, second and third warnings are often issued for nonviolent trespassing before arrests are made. Such lawbreakers as shoplifters are subject to immediate detention pending police arrest.

Property owners can ask courts for injunctions to stop civil trespass. The courts may issue cease-and-desist orders to chronic trespassers. They may also order mandatory injunctions to remove structures encroaching on property if the trespasser has acted intentionally and in bad faith. If a tree is involved, the owner of the property on which the tree overhangs may trim branches of the tree so long as the integrity of the tree is not compromised. In cases of stalking and repeated trespass, courts may issue restraining orders.

If someone strikes oil under another property owner's land, the owner of the land is entitled to royalties, provided that the deed of ownership includes mineral rights.

Laws prescribe a variety of penalties for criminal trespass that may include imprisonment and fines, depending upon the circumstances and the specific laws. Deliberate destruction of or damage to property can be treated as criminal trespass and involve liability for double or triple compensatory damages. There are two ways to determine compensatory damages—the replacement costs of the damages or the differences in property values before and after the trespass. In addition, punitive damages can be awarded when a wrongful act is deliberately committed without just cause or excuse.

Trespass causing emotional distress—notably stalking offenses—may result in awards of punitive damages if the offenses are deemed beyond the bounds of decency, recklessly ignoring the victim's emotions. Victims of trespass may also recover attorney's fees.

Defense Against Criminal Trespass

The most common defense against a charge of civil trespass is that the act of crossing into someone else's property was unintentional or harmless. Judges often dismiss trespass charges when no damage results. The law recognizes a nuisance instead of a trespass when the intrusive activity is minor or the intrusion results in intangible distress, such as interference with someone's enjoyment of peace and quiet when a dog barks excessively.

Criminal trespass does not apply in certain cases:

✓ When the buildings or vehicles entered have been abandoned.
✓ When the premises are open to members of the public and the trespassers comply with all lawful conditions imposed on access.
✓ When alleged trespassers may reasonably believe that the property owners or their agents would permit entry.
✓ When the alleged trespassers enter to prevent harm emanating from one property to visit another.
✓ When there are legal reasons to enter, such as serving subpoenas or legal documents.

Exceptions

An easement is a right of a nonowner to enter another person's property for legitimate purposes. For example, if one residence is behind another, and both are accessed by the same driveway, the landlocked resident in the rear has an easement to use the driveway, even if it is owned solely by the resident in front. Census workers, firefighters, letter carriers, police, regulatory inspectors, tax assessors, and utility personnel also have easements to enter properties to engage in their necessary business.

When owners fail to keep up their property, the owners of adjacent properties may want to use and own the land. Such lands can be acquired in court by the neighbors through the principle of adverse possession after the neighbors demonstrate continuous, exclusive, and open use of the land in question for their benefit for five or more years. In some states, the nonowners must also pay all property taxes on the disputed land.

If there are weeds on a steep slope that can be removed only by entering an upslope property, the owner of which refuses access, a court may award the downslope property owner an easement by prescription if the latter fulfills all the conditions of adverse possession except for payment of property taxes. A property owner can avoid loss of ownership through either method by granting written permission to use the land for a specific purpose, sometimes known as the principle of neighborly accommodation.

The principle of implied dedication can establish a right to use private property without a charge of trespassing. For example, owners of beachfront properties might allow a government agency to pave an access road to a beach on privately owned land, thereby enabling the public to gain access to the road and the beach. However, if users of the road prove to be disruptive, they may be found to be engaging in civil or criminal trespass.

Michael Haas

Further Reading

Jordan, Cora. *Neighbor Law: Fences, Trees, Boundaries and Noise.* 4th ed. Berkeley, Calif.: Nolo Press, 1994. Nontechnical explanations by an attorney of laws governing trespass of real property.

Katsh, M. Ethan. *Law in a Digital World.* New York: Oxford University Press, 1995. Broad discussion of the legal implications of computer trespass issues.

Kennedy, Caroline, and Ellen Alderman. *The Right to Privacy.* New York: Vintage, 1997. Layperson's guide to privacy rights protected by the U.S. Bill of Rights.

Martz, Clyde O. *Rights Incident to Possession of Land.* Boston: Little, Brown, 1954. Comprehensive analysis of the legal principles of trespass.

See also Burglary; Cease-and-desist orders; Computer crime; Cybercrime; Defenses to crime; Felonies; Misdemeanors; Privacy rights; Punitive damages; Restraining orders; Spam; Stalking.

Trial publicity

Definition: Information about trial disseminated through print or broadcast media
Criminal justice issues: Media; trial procedures

The criminal trial of Michael Jackson on child molestation charges in Southern California gave new meaning to the term "media circus" in early 2005. Virtually every day the pop music star made an appearance at the Santa Barbara County courthouse, crowds of zealous fans greeted his arrival as if he were arriving at an awards show. Jackson himself contributed to the festive atmosphere by dressing flamboyantly and walking to the courthouse surrounded by hefty bodyguards, one of whom always held an umbrella over him in the fashion of the entourages of traditional West African kings. *(AP/ Wide World Photos)*

A Musical Lampoon of the News Media

The Academy-Award winning film *Chicago* (2002), based on a musical by Bob Fosse and Fred Ebb, depicts the legal travails of a nightclub singer (Catherine Zeta-Jones) and a chorus girl (Renée Zellweger) during the 1920's. Both women are arrested for murder and are represented by the same media-hound lawyer (Richard Gere). The lawyer's efforts for each client wax and wane as the publicity their cases generate goes up and down. By this measure, his efforts for the chorus girl increase as public interest in the nightclub singer wanes. Eventually, both women—though acquitted of their crimes—are relegated to the dustbin of media attention, and the lawyer moves on with new clients.

Chicago may be an accurate reflection of the public's fickle interest in headline cases in the past, but its theme is not equally relevant in modern American society. In the early twenty-first century, media coverage of sensational legal cases typically morphs into book deals and made-for-television films. In the current media environment, sensational criminal cases—such as those involving O. J. Simpson, Robert Blake, Kobe Bryant, and Michael Jackson—can occupy the public's attention for long periods of time.

Timothy L. Hall

Significance: Issues regarding trial publicity emerge from two opposing principles: the right of the accused to a fair trial and the constitutional imperative that court proceedings be public. The two concerns conflict when trial publicity threatens to bias the outcome of a trial.

Traditionally, tacit professional limitations were imposed on attorneys, restricting the information they could reveal to the news media. By the late twentieth century the potential for instantaneous, in-depth trial coverage by electronic media made trial publicity a broader social issue involving the whole judicial system, the public's right to know, and the professional conduct of journalists. The result is freer movement of information to the public and less accountability for any one party or institution.

The principle of publicity was key to the development of modern mass democracies in Europe and America. It was through the publicizing of the private affairs of kings and other ruling authorities that a public sphere of discourse developed. Consequently, most modern constitutions call for conducting the affairs of state in public. The Sixth Amendment to the U.S. Constitution states that "the accused shall enjoy the right to a speedy and public trial." This ensures that justice will be carried out under the watchful eye of other private citizens.

In the eighteenth and nineteenth centuries the right to a public trial meant that private citizens and print journalists could attend court proceedings. In the twentieth century access was sometimes extended to radio and television broadcasters as well. However, the U.S. Supreme Court has been reluctant to grant to broadcast journalists the access given to citizens and print journalists. The Supreme Court takes the position that broadcast technology adversely affects court proceedings.

In some cases the individual's right to privacy takes precedence over the public's right to know. In certain states an attorney can move to close the courtroom. If the attorney shows good cause the judge may remove spectators from the courtroom for part or all of the proceedings. This is most often done in cases involving juveniles, adoptions, or rape. Judges may also clear the courtroom if witnesses must provide embarrassing evidence, usually in cases involving sexual assault.

Typically, trial publicity is limited to coverage of a crime, the police investigation, and regular reports on courtroom testimony. In the majority of trials, publicity is not a problem. If a judge believes that trial publicity may bias the proceedings, a gag order can be issued restricting what parties in the trial may say to journalists. A judge may also sequester a jury by cutting off their access to news broadcasts and newspapers and by restricting them to their hotel rooms and court facilities. However, it is rare for gag orders to be enforced or for a jury to be sequestered.

If excessive local publicity presents a problem, a judge may also call for a change of venue by moving the trial to an area in which the pool of potential jurors is less exposed to news coverage of the case in question.

Thomas J. Roach

Further Reading

Chermak, Steven M. *Victims in the News: Crime and the American News Media*. Boulder, Colo.: Westview Press, 1995.

Chiasson, Lloyd, ed. *The Press on Trial: Crimes and Trials as Media Events*. Westport, Conn.: Greenwood Press, 1997.

Clehane, Dianem, and Nancy Grace. *Objection! How High-Priced Defense Attorneys, Celebrity Defendants, and a 24/7 Media Have Hijacked Our Criminal Justice System*. New York: Hyperion, 2005.

Surette, Ray. *Media, Crime, and Criminal Justice*. 2d ed. Pacific Grove, Calif.: Brooks/Cole, 1998.

See also Attorney ethics; Celebrity criminal defendants; Celebrity trial attorneys; Change of venue; Constitution, U.S.; Gag orders; Inquests; Jury sequestration; Jury system; News source protection; Print media; Radio broadcasting; Simpson trials; Television news; *Voir dire.*

Trial transcripts

Definition: Official records of trial proceedings

Criminal justice issues: Appeals; trial procedures

Significance: Trial transcripts are used chiefly by appellate courts in evaluating whether errors have occurred in the trial courts in which the records were created.

A trial consists in the main of statements made by lawyers and the judge and of the questions asked of witnesses and the answers given by them. A court reporter normally records these matters as they are spoken and produces a formal trial transcript. With the benefit of special training and equipment, court reporters can produce a verbatim record of the words spoken in a proceeding.

Sometimes the transcript of the trial is used during the trial itself. For example, a lawyer cross-examining a witness might wish to confront the witness with statements made during direct examination. In these cases, the lawyer requests that the court reporter produce a transcript of the witness's testimony so that the lawyer can present it to the witness and question the witness about it.

More commonly, however, the trial transcript is a key portion of the material considered by an appellate court when a case is appealed. On appeal, the appellate court does not conduct a trial again and hear the testimony of witnesses and the arguments of lawyers. Instead, the appellate court reviews what happened in the trial court to determine whether legal errors were made. The appellate court reviews the record of the trial, which includes the trial transcript, the evidence offered by the parties, and any official court documents filed with the trial court. Of these items, the trial transcript is normally the most important source for the appellate court to determine what happened during the trial.

Although the court reporter does not charge the parties in the case for transcribing the proceedings, the reporter does charge for making a formal transcript. This charge can be quite substantial, especially in cases that last for extended periods of time. The party wishing to appeal a case must normally shoulder the cost of having a transcript prepared, because the appellate court generally does not consider an appeal without a record (including the transcript) of the trial.

In at least some cases the U.S. Supreme Court has found that due process of law requires that indigent persons not be denied access to courts simply because they lack the financial resources to pay for a trial transcript. In *Griffin v. Illinois* (1956), for example, the Supreme Court determined that a state must furnish a free trial transcript for indigent criminal defendants if the transcript is necessary for appellate review. Similarly, in *M.L.B. v. S.L.J.* (1996) the Court ruled as unconstitutional a state law that prevented a parent from appealing the termination of parental rights to a child unless the parent paid for a record of the termination proceedings. In *M.L.B.* these costs amounted to $2,352.36.

Timothy L. Hall

Further Reading

Bergman, Paul. *Transcript Exercises for Learning Evidence*. St. Paul, Minn.: West Publishing, 1992.

Coffin, Frank M. *On Appeal: Courts, Lawyering, and Judging*. New York: W. W. Norton, 1994.

Del Carmen, Rolando V. *Criminal Procedure: Law and Practice*. 6th ed. Belmont, Calif.: Thomson/Wadsworth, 2004.

Emanuel, S. L. *Criminal Procedure*. Aspen, Colo.: Aspen Publishing, 2003.

See also Clerks of the court; Court reporters; Evidence, rules of; Inquests; Testimony; Trials; Witnesses.

Trials

Definition: Formal processes of adjudication, from arraignment through verdicts

Criminal justice issues: Courts; defendants; judges; trial procedures

Significance: Judicial trials represent a high point in criminal justice processing and symbolize justice. When they are conducted fairly, they reinforce public confidence in the criminal justice system, raise public awareness that crime does not pay, and demonstrate the principle that under constitutional government, the innocent are vindicated.

Judicial trials take two forms: bench trials and jury trials. Bench trials are nonjury trials in which judges act as the sole arbiters. Jury trials are judicial processes in which groups of selected impartial average citizens are sworn to reach verdicts by considering relevant facts to find the truth. The history of jury trials is deeply rooted in English history, going back at least as far as King John's signing in 1215 of the Magna Carta, which granted the right to trial by jury of peers to English noblemen.

In the United States, jury trials are a right guaranteed by the U.S. Constitution, which provided that trials of all crimes were to be by juries selected in the states in which the crimes were al-

legedly committed. That right was further affirmed in 1791 by the ratification of the Bill of Rights, whose Sixth Amendment, which gives accused persons the right to speedy and public trials by impartial juries in all criminal prosecutions.

Fundamental to court trials is the fact that the United States practices an adversarial system of justice, which is based on the premise that every dispute has two sides to it. Trials offer the opposing sides—prosecution and defense—the opportunity to present their evidence and arguments before judges or impartial juries.

Typical court trial processes consist of a series of major steps, beginning with opening statements and ending with the verdict. The underlying purpose of all trials is to find the truth—guilty verdicts when charges against defendants are proven, and acquittals when the charges are not proven beyond a reasonable doubt. Where not guilty verdicts are rendered, the accused are immediately discharged. When guilty verdicts are rendered, sentencing and appeals may follow.

Types of Trials

The two basic types of court trials in the United States are criminal and civil. Criminal trials are proceedings designed to enforce or protect public rights. Penalties in criminal trials range from simple fines to death, depending on the charges and the circumstances in which the crimes are committed.

Civil trials, on the other hand, are proceedings designed to permit individuals, organizations, and institutions to seek monetary redress, to protect private rights, and prevent private wrongs. Penalties in civil trials are almost always monetary awards.

Stages in Judicial Trials

The first step in any jury court trial is jury selection. It begins with the summoning of eligible citizens—whose names are taken from the master jury lists—who are then questioned in a process known as *voir dire* to determine their eligibility to serve as jurors. The master jury list is usually compiled from voter registration lists, driver's license lists, or city telephone directories. By employing unlimited challenges for cause and limited peremptory challenges, counsel for the prosecution and the defense whittle down the numbers of potential jurors to the required size, which is usually twelve jurors and several alternates.

The second step is presentation of brief opening statements by prosecutors and defense attorneys that outline what each side intends to prove in evidence. The primary purpose of opening statements is to acquaint judges and jurors with the essentials of the cases and to prepare them for the arguments that are to come. These statements are often limited to the scope of what the prosecutors and defense attorneys intend to cover in evidence. The prosecution usually presents its opening statement first.

Prosecution Strategies and Procedures

The next step in court trial is the fuller presentation of the plaintiff or prosecution's case. In ju-

The longest phase of almost every criminal trial is the prosecution's presentation of its case, as the prosecution bears the burden of proof. The prosecution presents every scrap of evidence that it can collect to prove its case beyond a shadow of a doubt. *(Brand-X Pictures)*

dicial trials, the plaintiff or prosecution is typically the first to present its case to the judge or jury. It is an opportunity to call and lead witnesses in evidence, as well as to present other evidence that will bolster the case. Prosecution witnesses present their evidence through direct examination as led by the prosecutors. They may include victims, eyewitnesses, police officers, and expert witnesses such as forensic scientists and medical specialists.

Four basic types of evidence may be presented at trial: real evidence, testimonial evidence, direct evidence, and circumstantial evidence. Real evidence includes physical objects of almost any kind, such as weapons, documents, and other tangibles, that are related to the case. Testimonial evidence consists of statements of any sort by competent witnesses. Direct evidence consists of eyewitness testimony by third parties who have observed incidents relating to the cases. Circumstantial evidence is indirect evidence, that is, indirect proofs of material facts relating to cases without direct observation of the action.

After prosecutors directly examine witnesses, the defense attorneys are given the opportunity to cross-examine the same witnesses. In cross-examinations, the defense attorneys ask questions to clarify the defendants' roles in the cases. The defense also uses cross-examination to point out inconsistencies in witnesses' testimony that damage their cases and, if possible, raise doubts in the minds of the juries about the credibility of the witnesses and their testimony.

In like manner, the defense may also challenge the reliability and relatedness of other types of evidence presented by the prosecution. However, the judges ultimately rule on the admissibility or nonadmissibility of contested evidence. Prosecutors may reexamine their own witnesses after defense cross-examinations are

Hollywood Goes to Court

Film depictions of trials are often unrealistic, but it is unusual for films to stray as far from legal reality as *Suspect* (1987) and . . . *And Justice for All* (1979). In director Peter Yates's *Suspect*, singer Cher stars as a public defender assigned to represent a homeless deaf man (Liam Neeson) accused of murder. During the ensuing trial, one of the jurors (Dennis Quaid) secretly offers advice to the public defender, then helps her actively investigate the case and develops a romantic relationship with her. Although suspenseful, *Suspect* receives low marks for accuracy in the depiction of a criminal case. Contact between lawyers and jurors is specifically prohibited, and it is inconceivable that a defense counsel would pursue a relationship with a juror in the midst of a trial. The film also makes other kinds of errors. For example, the prosecutor at trial, with little evidence to prove the guilt of the homeless defendant, offers evidence of the defendant's previous criminal behavior. Similar evidence is commonly spotlighted in movie trials but is not generally admissible in real-life trials. In the main, rules of evidence prevent prosecutors from trying to show that because defen-

dants have done something wrong in the past, they have probably done something wrong more recently.

In director Norman Jewison's . . . *And Justice for All* Al Pacino plays a lawyer who is representing a judge (John Forsythe) accused of rape. After the lawyer discovers that his client is actually guilty, he announces this fact during his opening statements at his client's trial. This action, completely unbelievable, would certainly lead to the lawyer's disbarment. In fact, almost nothing about the film's treatment of legal issues is realistic. For example, the judge-defendant elects to be tried by another judge, not by a jury. In real life, no criminal defense lawyer would allow his client to be tried by a judge—especially one known as a law-and-order judge, as is the film's judge. The film also misrepresents plea bargains, which are agreements between prosecutors and defense attorneys, not between defense attorneys and judges, as the film seems to suggest. Finally, lawyers are not allowed to have private conversations with judges about pending cases; such *ex parte* communications are strictly forbidden.

Timothy L. Hall

completed to provide answers to new information and points raised during cross-examination.

Defense Tactics and Procedures

Immediately following the presentation of the prosecution's case, the defense may request the court to dismiss the case on grounds of failure of the prosecution to prove its case. If the motion is sustained, the judge will direct the jury to acquit the defendant and then dismiss the case. If motion is denied, then the defense presents its own case.

Defense attorneys present their cases in the same manner as the prosecution by calling their own witnesses. The defense usually involves direct examination of defense witnesses and presentation of other types of evidence. As the defense finishes examining witnesses, the prosecution can cross-examine them. The prosecution tries to establish inconsistencies in the defense witnesses' testimony, just as the defense has earlier tried to discredit the prosecution witnesses.

It should be noted that because defendants are

deemed innocent until proven guilty, the defense may elect not to present any witnesses or evidence at all. The prosecution carries the burden of proof—the legal standard requiring it to prove the accused guilty beyond any reasonable doubt.

Rebuttal and Surrebuttal

At the conclusion of the defense case, the prosecution may present rebuttal witnesses or evidence. Rebuttal evidence is evidence that tends to refute the opponents' evidence or undermine their alibis. It may also take the form of discrediting the credibility of defense witnesses based on misrepresentations of facts or proof of incentives to lie, especially for witnesses who have criminal conviction records of their own.

Sometimes rebuttals may involve bringing in new evidence that was not introduced during the prosecutors' case. The defense may choose to exercise a surrebuttal by examining rebuttal witnesses, and may in turn introduce other evidence or witnesses. Surrebuttal is evidence directed toward countering rebuttal evidence, or strengthening the defense evidence. Rebuttal/surrebuttal exchanges may continue indefinitely, until both parties exhaust all witnesses and new evidence. When that happens, the defense may again submit a motion for directed verdict. If the motion is denied, both the prosecution and defense present their closing arguments.

From Closing Arguments to Jury Deliberation

Closing arguments are summary statements delivered by the prosecution and the defense following the presentation of all evidence. Defense attorneys usually present their arguments first, followed by the prosecutors, who wrap up the cases. The goal of each closing statement is to attack the credibility of the opponent's evidence and witnesses. Closing statements must be based on facts, supported by evidence, and aimed at convincing judges or juries as to why they must rule in favor of their arguments. Factual summaries may be either short or prolonged.

After the closing arguments, the judges inform jurors of the general legal principles and standards they are to observe as they deliberate to reach their verdicts. Judges typically remind jurors that the accused are be deemed innocent until they are proven guilty and that convictions must be based on proof beyond a reasonable doubt. The judges also advise jurors on any special aspects of the crimes in question that may be relevant to their deliberations.

Because jurors are mostly average citizens, the instructions they receive are designed to educate them on the legal rules, principles, and standards applicable to the particular cases, as well as general principles. The instructions are also designed to clear away any misconceptions that may constitute grounds for appeal. Sometimes, judges invite the prosecutors and defense attorneys to participate in drawing up their jury instructions.

After jurors hear the judges' instructions, they retire into seclusion to discuss the cases and reach verdicts. Deliberation processes may involve exhaustive discussions and analyses of all evidence presented at trial. When in doubt about specific points, the jurors may call for clarification from the judges on aspects of their instructions or for portions of the case transcripts.

During their deliberations, jurors are cut off from all outside influences until they reach their verdicts. Deliberations may last only a few hours or drag on for several days. When jurors cannot reach verdicts in one day, they are instructed by the judges not to discuss the cases with anyone until they return the next day to continue their deliberations. In highly politicized or celebrated cases, jurors may be sequestered in jury or hotel rooms and not allowed to leave until after they reach verdicts. Sequestration is the keeping together of juries and separating them from the general public

In the American system of justice, criminal trials are adversarial proceedings in which judges play roles similar of those of referees in sporting events, overseeing the interplay between opposing attorneys to make sure that they follow correct procedures and to ensure that each side has a fair chance to make its case. *(Brand-X Pictures)* throughout trials or deliberation processes to protect them from outside influences that may affect their decisions unfairly.

Verdicts

Verdicts represent the jurors' final decisions after detailed analyses of all evidence presented in cases. Typical jury verdicts are either guilty or not guilty. Jury decisions must be unanimous in all criminal cases, and guilty verdicts must meet the standard of proof beyond all reasonable doubt, that is, a clear and convincing belief that any reasonable person would accept that the defendant is guilty as charged.

When jurors fail to reach agreement after deliberating, the trials are said to end in hung juries. In some jurisdictions, a hung jury constitutes grounds for a judge to declare a mistrial and dismiss the jury. Mistrials mean the termination of trials before verdicts are reached due to intervening circumstances that make it impossible to secure fair trials or for the trials to continue. When hung juries or mistrials are declared, charges are dismissed and the defendants are released. However, prosecutors reserve the right to file for new trials of the defendants on the same charges without breaching the defendants' constitutional right against double jeopardy.

When juries inform the judges that they have reached verdicts, they are invited back into the courtrooms to announce their verdicts. Trial verdicts of not guilty bring cases to an end, and the defendants are freed of all pending bonds. On the other hand, when jury forepersons announce guilty verdicts, the jurors are usually polled individually to voice their decisions in open court. After guilty verdicts are finalized, judges order presentencing investigations and set dates for sentencing the convicted defendants.

Postverdict Motions and Sentencing

After guilty verdicts are announced, defense attorneys can file two types of postconviction motions in the hope of giving their clients second opportunities at freedom. The first type of motion is a motion in arrest of judgment. This type of motion asks the court to set aside and reverse the jury verdict on grounds that errors were made by the jury in the trial that require the case to be dismissed and the defendant acquitted. The second

type is a motion for a new trial. This unusual request is based on assertions that serious errors have been made at trial by either the trial judge or the prosecutor. Sometimes the motions are based on newly discovered evidence that justifies setting aside a guilty verdict and granting a new trial. However, such motions are rarely granted by presiding judges.

Sentences are penalties imposed by courts on persons found guilty of criminal wrongdoing. It is the responsibility of the presiding judges to impose criminal sentences. Penalties are often tied to recommendations made by probation officers in presentence investigation (PSI) reports. Types of judicial penalty include monetary fines, probation, imprisonment, restitution, intermediate sanctions, commitment to hospitals or other treatment agencies, and death. Judicial sanctions may combine two or three of these punishments.

Appeals

Appeals mark the end of the road in court trial processes. Losing sides in trials may file for judicial reviews from appellate courts when the trial court judges refuse their post-trial motions for relief from the verdicts. Possible reasons for appeals include refusals of trial judges to admit relevant or exculpatory evidence during trial, inclusion of irrelevant or damaging evidence at trial, and improper jury instruction—especially when the losing attorneys' objections to such measures are ignored by the trial judges.

The first major step in the appeals process involves the filing of formal notice of appeal document in the appellate court. The next phase is to apply for a transcript proceeding from the trial court. On fixed dates, both the prosecution and the defense present their cases to the appeals courts under a regulated schedule. Appellate court decisions may include upholding the rulings of the lower court or reversing the trial court decisions and discharging the cases. Appellate courts may also reverse and remand cases for fresh trials.

Emmanuel C. Onyeozili

Further Reading

Baum, Lawrence. *American Courts: Process and Policy*. 5th ed. Boston: Houghton Mifflin, 2001. Standard textbook covering all aspects of U.S.

courts, from their organization and structure to the procedures they employ.

Bodenhamer, David J. *Fair Trial: Rights of the Accused in American History*. New York: Oxford University Press, 1997. Succinct history of changing constitutional rulings that have steadily ensured greater fairness in criminal procedures.

Carp, Robert A., and Ronald Stidham. *Judicial Process in America*. 5th ed. Washington, D.C.: CQ Press, 2001. Congressional Quarterly, 1996. General survey of trial procedures in the larger context of criminal justice processes.

Epstein, Lee, and Thomas G. Walker. *Constitutional Law for a Changing America: Rights, Liberties, and Justice*. 5th ed. Washington, D.C.: CQ Press, 2004. Up-to-date study of constitutional law with considerable attention to the role of the Supreme Court.

Mauet, Thomas A. *Trial Techniques*. 6th ed. New York: Aspen Publishers, 2002. Textbook explaining trial procedures and the tactics and strategies that prosecution and defense attorneys can employ.

Neubauer, David W. *America's Courts and the Criminal Justice System*. 8th ed. Belmont, Calif.: Wadsworth/Thomson Learning, 2005. Comprehensive analysis of the dynamics of criminal justice in action as seen in the relationship of judge, prosecutor, and defense attorney.

Siegel, Larry J. *Criminology*. 8th ed. Belmont, Calif.: Wadsworth/Thomson Learning, 2004. Gives a thorough overview of the discipline of criminology and the entire criminal justice process, legal concepts, and justice perspectives, featuring high-profile cases, events, and relevant materials in a comprehensive, balanced, and objective fashion.

Wellman, Francis L. *The Art of Cross-Examination*. 4th ed. New York: Macmillan, 1936. Reprint. New York: Simon and Schuster, 1998. Reprint of a classic work on the crucial trial attorney skill of cross-examination.

See also Acquittal; Bifurcated trials; Burden of proof; Court types; Criminal prosecution; Discovery; Dismissals; District attorneys; Evidence, rules of; Hung juries; Judges; Judicial system, U.S.; Jurisdiction of courts; Jury duty; Mistrials; Reasonable doubt; Speedy trial right; Verdicts; Witnesses.

Unabomber

Identification: Theodore J. Kaczynski, the perpetrator of a bombing campaign between 1978 and 1995

Born: May 22, 1942; Evergreen Park, Illinois

Criminal justice issues: Terrorism; violent crime

Significance: The Unabomber, as Theodore Kaczynski made himself known to the police, conducted a bombing campaign for more than seventeen years before he was arrested and convicted. In the process, he baffled the police and received extensive coverage by the news media.

On May 25, 1978, a parcel exploded at Northwestern University in Chicago, injuring one person. This marked the beginning of a lengthy bombing campaign by Theodore Kaczynski, a brilliant Harvard-trained mathematician, who sought the overthrow of modern industrial society, toward which he had become embittered.

The Unabomber soon began a selective campaign of well-organized attacks with increasingly advanced bombs. In November, 1979, one exploded in the cargo hold of a passenger plane, forcing the plane's emergency landing. This attack sparked the launch of a major police investigation into the crimes that in 1980 they codenamed "Unabom" because of an attack on a United Airlines executive and university-based targets. Although the profile of the criminal developed by police proved accurate, clues to Kaczynski's identity proved scarce because of his careful pattern of allowing time between attacks, building his own bombs, and traveling to avoid exposure.

These initial attacks wounded and permanently maimed some individuals. In December, 1985, a bomb killed a Sacramento computer dealer. The fatality prompted the police to publicize that a serial bomber was responsible for a series of attacks. The first major break in the case occurred in 1987, when in Salt Lake City a woman spotted the Unabomber planting a bomb. A composite drawing based on her description of a man wearing sunglasses and a hooded tracksuit appeared in the media.

"Unabomber" Theodore Kaczynski being escorted from a federal courthouse in Montana by federal agents in April, 1996. *(AP/Wide World Photos)*

After a six-year hiatus, in 1993, the Unabomber renewed his attacks and contacted the media to publicize the motivations for his crimes. In September, 1995, the key moment in the case occurred, when *The Washington Post* and *The New York Times* published the Unabomber's thirty-five-thousand-word manifesto, titled "Industrial Society and Its Future," in response to the author's pledge to end the attacks. Among those reading the document was David Kaczynski, who recognized similarities in the ideas and writing style of his brother. In February, 1996, David Kaczynski passed his suspicions on to the Federal Bureau of Investigation, which arrested Theodore Kaczynski at an isolated Montana cabin two months later.

With a trial scheduled for early 1998, Theodore Kaczynski found himself in dispute with his lawyers, who sought to use a defense of mental illness. Their client, however, wished to defend his attacks on political grounds. In the end, Kaczynski bypassed his lawyers' strategy by striking a plea bargain that involved pleading guilty to thirteen counts of bombing and murder. He received several sentences of life imprisonment.

Steve Hewitt

Further Reading

Chase, Alton. *Harvard and the Unabomber: The Education of an American Terrorist.* New York: W. W. Norton, 2003.

Graysmith, Robert. *Unabomber: Desire to Kill.* New York: Regnery, 1997.

Unabomber. *The Unabomber Manifesto: Industrial Society and Its Future.* New York: Jolly Roger Press, 1995.

See also Bombs and explosives; Crime; Defendant self-representation; Defense attorneys; Federal Bureau of Investigation; Insanity defense; Juvenile delinquency; Plea bargaining; Print media; Psychological profiling; Ten-most-wanted lists; Terrorism.

Uniform Crime Reports

Identification: National crime statistics compiled from government law-enforcement records

Date: Begun in 1929

Criminal justice issues: Crime statistics; criminology; law-enforcement organization

Significance: The Uniform Crime Reports (UCR) provide information on fluctuations in crime levels in the United States. Criminologists and criminal justice professionals use the statistics for varied research and planning purposes.

Uniform Crime Report Definitions

The definitions listed below are provided to reporting agencies by the Federal Bureau of Investigation's UCR program. On the surface, these definitions may appear to be clear-cut and straightforward; however, they lend themselves to a wide variety of interpretations by the police personnel who classify crimes. The UCR program provides a *Uniform Crime Reporting Handbook*, from which the following definitions were obtained.

Murder and nonnegligent manslaughter: Willful (nonnegligent) killing of one human being by another.

Forcible rape: Carnal knowledge of a female forcibly and against her will.

Robbery: Taking or attempting to take anything of value from the care, custody, or control of a person or persons by force or threat of force or violence or by putting the victims in fear.

Aggravated assault: Unlawful attack by one person upon another for the purpose of inflicting severe or aggravated bodily injury. This type of assault is usually accompanied by the use of a weapon or by means likely to produce death or great bodily harm.

Burglary: Unlawful entry into a structure to commit a felony or a theft.

Larceny theft: Unlawful taking, carrying, leading, or riding away of property from the possession or constructive possession of another.

Motor vehicle theft: Theft or attempted theft of a motor vehicle.

Timothy M. Bray

The Uniform Crime Reporting Program was developed during the late 1920's by the International Association of Chiefs of Police. Since 1930, it has been under the management of the Federal Bureau of Investigation (FBI). The primary objective of UCR is to generate a valid set of crime statistics for use in law-enforcement administration, operation, and management. Over the years UCR has also become one of the country's leading social indicators. More than 17,000 federal, state, and local law-enforcement agencies nationwide participate in the program.

UCR crime data are reported in two formats: Summary UCR and National Incident-Based Reporting System (NIBRS). Summary UCR is an agency-level count of eight criminal offenses (murder, rape, robbery, aggravated assault, burglary, theft, motor vehicle theft, and arson) and an accounting of criminal arrests for a variety of offenses. These crime counts are aggregated to state, regional, and national totals and summarized each year in the FBI's annual report *Crime in the United States*.

NIBRS was developed in the mid-1980's to collect detailed information about each criminal incident reported to the police. It is anticipated that NIBRS reporting will one day replace Summary UCR. In addition to these two sub-programs, UCR also collects detailed information on criminal homicides, hate crimes, and law-enforcement officers who are killed or assaulted in the line of duty.

James J. Nolan III

Further Reading

Akiyama, Yoshio, and James J. Nolan. "Methods for Understanding and Analyzing NIBRS Data." *Journal of Quantitative Criminology* 15, no. 2 (1999): 225-238.

Barnett, Cynthia. *The Measurement of White-Collar Crime Using Uniform Crime Reporting (UCR) Data*. Washington, D.C.: U.S. Department of Justice, FBI, CJIS Division, 2002.

Federal Bureau of Investigation. *Crime in the United States, 2002*. Washington, D.C.: U.S. Government Printing Office, 2003.

Gove, Walter R., Michael Hughes, and Michael Geerken. "Are Uniform Crime Reports a Valid Indicator of Index Crimes? An Affirmative Answer with Minor Qualifications." *Criminology* 23 (1985): 451-501.

Uniform Crime Reports on the Web

UCR publications can be found on the FBI Web site at www.fbi.gov/publications.htm. Additional UCR crime data can be found on the National Archive of Criminal Justice Data's Web site at www.icpsr.umich.edu/NACJD/index.html.

See also Arson; Bureau of Justice Statistics; Carjacking; Crime; Crime Index; Criminal history record information; Law enforcement; National Crime Information Center; National Crime Victimization Survey; President's Commission on Law Enforcement and Administration of Justice; Rape and sex offenses; Vandalism; Wickersham Commission.

Uniform Juvenile Court Act

The Law: Federal model law outlining significant changes recommended for state juvenile courts

Date: Enacted in 1968

Criminal justice issues: Constitutional protections; courts; juvenile justice

Significance: The Uniform Juvenile Court Act served as a model that the individual states could follow to make their own juvenile justice systems more uniform in their purposes, scopes, and procedures.

After years of criticism regarding the lack of procedural safeguards afforded juveniles in state courts, the Uniform Juvenile Court Act was drafted by the National Conference of Commissioners on Uniform State Laws. With the express goal of developing a model juvenile justice system that could be used as a blueprint for state juvenile courts, the law addressed the issues of decreasing the stigmatization of delinquent youth and helping to maintain family units. The act also addressed the need to preserve recently recognized constitutional rights of youth. These rights included the right to legal counsel, articulated in the U.S. Supreme Court's *In re Gault* ruling in 1967, and the right to due process, articulated in *Kent v. United States* in 1966.

Additionally, the model law outlined how state courts might accomplish these goals. Philosophically, the model system aimed to blend the original juvenile courts' goal of treating children as capable of reform and rehabilitation while still holding them accountable for their misdeeds. In short, it outlined the need for judicial intervention when necessary for the care of dependent children and for the treatment and rehabilitation of juvenile delinquents, while ensuring fair and constitutional procedures.

Rachel Bandy

Further Reading

Champion, Dean John. *The Juvenile Justice System: Delinquency, Processing, and the Law.* 4th ed. Upper Saddle River, N.J.: Prentice-Hall, 2003.

Cox, Steven M., John J. Conrad, and Jennifer M. Allen. *Juvenile Justice.* 5th ed. New York: McGraw-Hill, 2002.

Hess, Karen M., and Robert W. Drowns. *Juvenile Justice.* 4th ed. Belmont, Calif.: Wadsworth/Thomson Learning, 2004.

See also Counsel, right to; *Gault, In re*; Juvenile courts; Juvenile delinquency; Juvenile Justice and Delinquency Prevention Act; Juvenile Justice and Delinquency Prevention, Office of; Juvenile justice system; Juvenile waivers to adult courts; *Parens patriae*.

United States Code

The Law: The official collection of federal statutes in force, which are edited to eliminate duplication and arranged under appropriate headings

Date: First compiled in 1926

Criminal justice issues: Federal law; law codes

Significance: The U.S. Code provides easy access to federal legislation which has been "codified"—that is, assembled and presented in a uniform format.

Prior to 1926, when Congress authorized preparation of the U.S. Code, federal laws were added as they appeared to the Revised Statutes of 1875. This agglomeration of legislation was difficult to use, because laws were often redundant and their relevance often unclear. The first U.S. Code rearranged the laws in force in 1926 under fifty titles and published them in four volumes; subsequently these were updated annually with a cumulative supplement. Every six years, the federal government publishes a new edition of the code following the same format, and the number of volumes continues to grow. Another official collection of federal legislation, the United States Code Annotated (USCA), is similarly structured. It contains, in addition to the texts of federal laws, notes on state and federal judicial decisions applying individual laws, together with cross-references to other sections of the code, historical annotations, and library references.

The laws enacted by Congress are also collected in a chronological arrangement; issued annually, this arrangement is known as the United States Statutes at Large. The U.S. Statutes at Large are indexed but are not arranged by subject matter. Congress numbers the volumes of the Statutes at Large, which also contain amendments to the Constitution and presidential proclamations.

Lisa Paddock

Further Reading

Dubber, Markus Dirk. *Criminal Law: Model Penal Code.* New York: Foundation Press, 2002.

Federal Criminal Code and Rules. St. Paul, Minn.: West Group Publishing, 2003.

See also Annotated codes; Coast Guard, U.S.; Common law; Constitution, U.S.; Counterfeiting; Criminal law; Environmental crimes; Motor vehicle theft; United States Statutes at Large.

United States Parole Commission

Identification: Agency within the U.S. Department of Justice

Date: Created as the United States Board of Parole in 1930; renamed United States Parole Commission in 1976

Criminal justice issues: Federal law; pardons and parole; punishment

Significance: The United States Parole Commission grants, alters, and revokes paroles to federal criminals and supervises parolees.

In May, 1976, the Parole Commission and Reorganization Act renamed the United States Board of Parole, in existence since 1930, the United States Parole Commission (USPC). The major responsibility of the USPC was to make parole decisions for eligible federal offenders. In 1984, the Sentencing Reform Act ended parole eligibility for individuals who committed federal offenses after November 1, 1987. Since then, the USPC has made parole decisions only for offenders who committed offenses prior to November 1, 1987.

In 1997, the authority of the USPC was extended to include the District of Columbia federal prisoners, a responsibility previously delegated to the District of Columbia Board of Parole. The USPC also has jurisdiction for conducting hearings and setting release dates for U.S. citizens who are sent home to the United States to serve sentences imposed by foreign countries. The commission also has authority to grant or deny parole to military prisoners who are serving sentences in facilities of the U.S. Bureau of Prisons. In all of its decisions, the USPC applies the least restrictive sanctions that ensure justice and public safety.

On three different occasions between 1992 and 2002, federal legislation was passed that would have abolished the USPC. On each occasion, however, it was determined that no other federal agency was ready to assume the duties of the USPC, so it was maintained. In 2002, realizing that the parole functions regulated by the USPC were still necessary, the U.S. Congress extended the lifetime of the agency through at least November 1, 2005.

Alvin K. Benson

Further Reading

United States Parole Commission. *History of the Federal Parole System.* Washington, D.C.: U.S. Department of Justice, 2003.

_____. *An Overview of the United States Parole Commission.* Washington, D.C.: U.S. Department of Justice, 1997.

See also Criminal justice in U.S. history; Criminal justice system; Criminals; Law enforcement; Marshals Service, U.S.; Military justice; Pardons; Parole; Prison and jail systems; Sentencing; United States Sentencing Commission.

United States Sentencing Commission

Identification: Independent federal judicial agency responsible for developing federal sentencing guidelines and acting as a research resource for the executive and legislative branches of the federal government

Date: Established in 1984

Criminal justice issues: Federal law; judges; sentencing

Significance: The commission is responsible for determining federal sentencing guidelines, thereby removing discretion from federal judges.

The United States Sentencing Commission was established by the Sentencing Reform Act of 1984 as an independent federal agency located within the judicial branch of the government. The commission is tasked with setting the lower and upper bounds of permissible punishments for federal offenses.

The commission's duties also include collecting and analyzing federal sentencing data and determining its effect on the federal criminal justice system. The commission uses this data to recommend federal sentencing changes to Congress.

It also reviews various crime and sentencing research and refines the federal guidelines based on the findings of this research. The commission also monitors the outcomes and cases from the Court of Appeals and congressional action. In addition, the commission trains thousands of criminal justice professionals in the proper use of the federal sentencing guidelines and publishes numerous reports every year (all of which are posted on its Web site).

The makeup of the commission is mandated by federal statute. Seven voting members are appointed by the president and confirmed by the Senate for six-year terms. Also included are two nonvoting members. One additional voting member is appointed by the commission's chairperson. No more than three of the commissioners may be federal judges, and no more than four may belong to the same political party. In addition, the U.S. attorney general and the chairperson of the U.S. Parole Commission are ex officio members of the commission.

The commission was established in an effort to combat disparity in federal sentencing. Prior to the Sentencing Reform Act of 1984, federal judges were not required to use the same sentencing standards. Judges could impose sentences ranging from probation to the statutory maximum for any given offense. The Sentencing Reform Act was passed in an attempt to achieve greater fairness and certainty of punishment in the federal courts.

Since its inception, the sentencing commission has been a point of contention between the federal judiciary and the legislative branch of government. In April, 2003, the Protect Act was passed, requiring the commission to issue new limits to federal judges' discretion in sentencing above or below the sentencing guidelines. The federal judiciary voted in the fall of 2003 to support legislation counter to the Protect Act in an effort to restore more judicial discretion. This places the commission in the middle of a political battle between the federal judiciary and some members of Congress.

The Protect Act and the more recent sentencing guideline changes open federal judges to more scrutiny in their sentencing practices, both by the public and by the appellate courts. Under the new rules, judges who depart from the sentencing guidelines face the possibility of their sentencing records being made public.

The Justice Department and Republican members of Congress tend to support the new rules, stating that they are needed in order to keep sentencing in the federal courts uniform and to keep maverick judges in line. The protests from the judiciary are not just from a few disgruntled liberal judges. Chief Justice William Rehnquist has also protested the changes, stating that they go too far in eliminating judicial discretion and flexibility. Statistics from the sentencing commission show that federal judges depart from the guidelines about 18 percent of the time, usually at the request of prosecutors, as a reward for cooperative defendants.

Jennifer R. Albright

Further Reading

Stith, Kate, and Jose A. Cabranes. *Fear of Judging: Sentencing Guidelines in the Federal Courts*. Chicago: University of Chicago Press, 1998.

United States Congress Committee on the Judiciary Subcommittee on Criminal Justice Oversight. *Oversight of the United States Sentencing Commission: Are the Guidelines Being Followed? Hearing Before the Subcommittee on Criminal Justice Oversight of the Committee on the Judiciary, United States Senate, One Hundred Sixth Congress, Second Session, October 13, 2000*. Washington, D.C.: U.S. Government Printing Office, 2001.

Von Hirsh, Andrew, Michael Tonry, and Kay Knapp. *Sentencing Commission and Its Guidelines*. Boston: Northeastern University Press, 1987.

See also Comprehensive Crime Control Act; Discretion; Just deserts; Mandatory sentencing; Sentencing; Sentencing guidelines, U.S.; United States Parole Commission.

United States Statutes at Large

Identification: Legal publication
Date: First published in 1845
Criminal justice issues: Federal law; law codes
Significance: Also called Statutes at Large, the United States Statutes at Large is a chronological compilation of federal law that serves as an important reference tool for legal research.

Published by the Office of the Federal Register at the National Archives in Washington, D.C., the United States Statutes at Large is a compilation of the entire body of federal law, encompassing every law that Congress has ever enacted, all treaties and international agreements signed prior to 1948, treaties with Native Americans and foreign nations, and presidential proclamations. Statutes at Large includes the text of both public laws, which apply to the general public, and private laws, which are specific to individual persons, corporations, or localities.

The Statutes at Large also includes the full text of the Declaration of Independence, the Articles of Confederation, the U.S. Constitution and its amendments, and laws repealed or rendered obsolete. It was first published by the Boston book publisher Little, Brown in 1845 pursuant to a joint resolution of the U.S. Congress. In 1874 responsibility for publication was transferred to the U.S. Government Printing Office in Washington, D.C., which began publishing annual volumes in 1937.

Potential difficulties researchers face in using Statutes at Large include the lack of a cumulative index and the time frame under which it is published. Laws enacted during a particular congressional session are typically not published until approximately one year after the end of the session, by which time they have usually been made available as supplements to commercial publications such as United States Code Annotated (USCA). Nevertheless, Statutes at Large remains the definitive and comprehensive source for research into federal law.

Michael H. Burchett

Further Reading

Bourdeau, John, and Sonja Larsen. *Legal Research for Beginners*. Hauppauge, N.Y.: Barron's Educational Series, 1997.

Conklin, Curt E. *An Historical and Bibliographic Introduction to the United States Statutes at Large*. Washington, D.C.: Government Publications Press, 1992.

See also Annotated codes; Bill of particulars; Constitution, U.S.; Counterfeiting; Model Penal Code; Statutes; United States Code.

Vagrancy laws

Definition: Vagrancy, or the condition of being without "visible means of support," is not a crime per se, but ordinances and statutes have often made it a punishable public offense

Criminal justice issues: Deviancy; victimless crime

Significance: Dealing with the homeless vagrant has become a major urban problem that cannot be solved through the strict enforcement of outmoded vagrancy laws that are no longer practical or constitutionally appropriate.

Under English common law, a "vagrant" was construed as any able-bodied and destitute individual who refused work and attempted to live by begging. Before the Industrial Revolution most rural workers were agrarian laborers, and vagrants who roamed the land in search of better wages violated statutes against internal migration.

Economic factors forced changes in such laws. The enclosure movement ended much tenant farming, thereby ending the need to tie workers to the land. Next, the Industrial Revolution encouraged unemployed workers to seek factory jobs in mushrooming urban centers. The older vagrant and poor laws had restricted those who were unable to work to their home parishes and sent itinerant "loafers" and "idlers" to workhouses or forced them to return to their home communities. Under the new conditions, with worker migration inevitable, vagrancy laws shifted their focus to community worries about potential criminal behavior and the financial burden of caring for indigent drifters.

Eventually vagrancy came to be viewed as a form of disorderly conduct, and that association is reflected even in the earliest vagrancy laws in the United States. Under the Articles of Confederation, "paupers" and "vagabonds" were denied the right of free movement from one state to another, and both colonial and ensuing state vagrancy statutes had similar restrictions on the movement of indigent individuals. Under most vagrancy laws, indolent drifters could be jailed or required to move outside the legal jurisdiction of the enforcing agency.

In bad economic times, vagrancy laws could be stringently enforced. For example, during the Great Depression, some states used such laws to justify burning "Hoovervilles" (makeshift settlements of homeless people) and erecting blockades to prevent migrants from entering to look for work. Police have at times put the laws to other questionable uses—for example, in the service of controlling labor unrest or upholding community standards based on racial or class discrimination.

Beginning in the 1960's, in part as a result of the Civil Rights movement, vagrancy laws increasingly came under judicial review. In 1972, the U.S. Supreme Court, in *Papachristou v. City of Jacksonville*, struck down a Florida vagrancy law because of its vagueness and condemnation of innocent behavior. Because the Florida law was very similar in scope and wording to laws in other states, the Court's finding forced the revision of many state laws. Most were refashioned to comply with the Model Penal Code, which makes no mention of idleness, the original basis of vagrancy statutes in common law. Civil rights advocates have argued that the code itself contains constitutionally suspect provisions against loitering and prowling. Given the growing concerns over the nation's high crime rate, however, it remains to be seen whether the civil rights of "potential criminals" will gain much additional protection.

John W. Fiero

Further Reading

Feldman, Leonard C. *Citizens Without Shelter: Homelessness, Democracy, and Political Exclusion*. Ithaca, N.Y.: Cornell University Press, 2004.

Levinson, David, ed. *Encyclopedia of Homeless-*

ness. Thousand Oaks, Calif.: Sage Publications, 2004.

Smith, Christopher E. *Courts and the Poor*. Chicago: Nelson-Hall, 1991.

See also Breach of the peace; Commercialized vice; Disorderly conduct; Indecent exposure; Model Penal Code.

Vandalism

Definition: Willful or malicious destruction, injury, disfigurement, or defacement of public or private property

Criminal justice issues: Juvenile justice; morality and public order; vandalism

Significance: Although vandalism arrests have declined since the early 1990's, vandalism remains an ongoing problem that adversely affects cities, schools, businesses, and residential communities across the United States, and it accounts for a large portion of juvenile arrests.

The word "vandalism" derives from the name of a Germanic people called the Vandals, who were known for their frequent and spirited raids into the Roman Empire during the fifth century C.E. In modern times, the term "vandal" has come to be applied to individuals who willfully damage and deface public and private structures and vehicles. During the twentieth century, vandalism became a widespread problem throughout the United States and in other industrialized nations. It includes such acts as ravaging schoolrooms and offices, smashing windows and mailboxes, and painting graffiti on buildings, vehicles, and public places.

One of the most common and most visible expressions of vandalism in the United States is graffiti—words and pictures painted on walls, signs, buildings, buses, and other vehicles and public places. Usually applied with aerosol spray-paint products and other permanent markers, graffiti is closely associated with youth gangs, which use it in many cities to mark distinctive symbols and words on their "turf"—the areas they claim as their own territories. Such graffiti advertises the gangs' presence and serves to warn members of rival gangs to stay away. Ironically, the same graffiti sometimes also assists police to identify and track gang activity within their jurisdictions.

In many urban neighborhoods, graffiti is also recognized as street art that symbolizes more than simple vandalism. Its creators view their paintings as forms of artistic self-expression and symbols of neighborhood and cultural pride. However, although graffiti art may have nothing to do with gang activity, it is nevertheless regarded as a form of vandalism, and property owners must deal with the reconstruction and cleanup of the art left by these individuals. Communities try to reduce graffiti by banning the sale of spray-paint products to minors.

Prevalence

The news media tend to convey the impression that vandalism is a crime that is always on the increase. However, Federal Bureau of Investigation (FBI) crime statistics have shown that arrests for vandalism were actually declining in the early twenty-first century. In fact, vandalism has gone through several historical cycles in the past. Between 1980 and 1982, arrests for vandalism declined, and then gradually increased each year until 1994. They then began another period of decline until 1997. Overall, during the ten-year period between 1993 and 2002, total arrests for vandalism of persons under the age of eighteen in the United States decreased by 33.3 percent. However, the FBI's Uniform Crime Reports also showed that vandalism in some suburban and rural areas increased by slightly more than 3 percent.

According to the National Crime Victimization Survey, which is conducted by the Census Bureau for the U.S. Department of Justice, vandalism of private residences has also shown a steady decrease. In 1994, 9 percent of the families in the United States experienced incidents of vandalism. After that year, the rate went down steadily until it reached 5 percent in 2002.

Although vandalism has declined, it remains a major problem, and one that is estimated to cost cities, schools, homeowners, and business owners more than $15 billion a year. In the year 2000, about 6.1 million households experienced inci-

Burned-out Hummer in a West Covina, California, automobile dealership that lost several dozen Hummers and sport utility vehicles (SUVs) to vandalism in August, 2003. During the first years of the twenty-first century a new form of vandalism emerged that was closely allied to ecoterrorism: the destruction and disfiguring of expensive oversized vehicles by radical environmentalists opposed to what they regard as wasteful consumption. *(AP/Wide World Photos)*

dents of vandalism that cost approximately $1.7 billion in repairs and cleanup. According to the National Crime Victimization Survey, 44 percent of the damage occurred to motor vehicles, while 13 percent of the damage was done to mailboxes, 13 percent to structures, and 9 percent to yards and garden areas. The most common types of damage were broken windows, graffiti, driving over properties, and leaving burn marks on houses and yards.

Schools are also common targets for vandals. In studies conducted by the U.S. Department of Education in 1999-2000, approximately 51 percent of the schools in the United States—a total of more than 42,000 different schools—reported at least one incident of vandalism, for a total of more than 200,000 separate incidents. Most of the damage reported included broken windows, graffiti, and defacement of school property.

Businesses have also been targets of vandals for many years. According to the Small Business Administration, they spend more than $1 billion every year to repair damage caused by vandals. Vandalism costs are then reflected in higher prices charged by businesses, which are passed on to the consumer, and can even appear in the form of higher taxes by cities and schools that must repair and replace the damage.

Male offenders account for about 83 percent of all vandalism arrests in the United States, and white offenders account for about 76 percent of arrests, while African Americans account for only about 22 percent. Although people of all ages are arrested for vandalism, most acts of vandalism are committed by youthful offenders. In 2002, the FBI's Uniform Crime Reports listed a total of 75,955 arrests for vandalism cases for those under the age of eighteen.

After the turn of the twenty-first century, vandalism still ranked as one of the most serious offenses of all property crimes that are reported to law-enforcement officials. Police officers spend enormous amounts of time investigating vandalism complaints from a wide variety of victims. Among the frequent complaints they hear are those concerning graffiti, which appears on walls, freeways, buildings, and other noticeable public properties. It is difficult to apprehend perpetrators because they tend to leave few clues and can disappear rapidly.

Adults who are arrested for vandalism are usually charged with misdemeanor offenses, which are punishable by one year or less in jail or prison. However, most vandals are under the age of eighteen. Juveniles arrested for vandalism usually make contact with juvenile probation officials, who conduct presentence investigations to understand the individual cases and offenders. The officials typically interview family members, school officials, and other people with connections with the offenders to learn as much as they can about the offenders. After cases are referred to juvenile courts, decisions are made whether to handle them formally or informally.

When cases are handled informally, the juveniles may be sent to diversion programs or similar first-offender programs. The goal of the courts is to keep youths out of the juvenile justice system. Approximately 49 percent of vandalism cases are handled informally, and about one-half of those cases are dismissed after the offenders meet all of the requirements set forth by judges. Most cases require offenders to participate in community service, pay fines, or furnish restitution.

In approximately 54 percent of the vandalism cases that are handled formally, youthful offenders are adjudicated as juvenile delinquents. In these cases, formal probation is generally ordered for the majority of the offenders, and restitution may be required, along with fines and community service.

Jerry W. Hollingsworth

Further Reading

Clement, Mary J. *Juvenile Justice System: Law and Process*. 2d ed. Woburn, Mass.: Butterworth-Heinemann, 2001. Textbook that discusses vandalism in the broader context of juvenile justice in the United States.

Leet, D., G. Rush, and A. Smith. *Gangs, Graffiti, and Violence: A Realistic Guide to the Scope and Nature of Gangs in America*. 2d ed. Incline Village, Nev.: Copperhouse, 2000. Text well suited to students that discusses gang problems in jargon-free language.

MacDonald, Nancy. *The Graffiti Subculture: Youth, Masculinity and Identity in London and New York*. Basingstoke, England: Palgrave, 2001. Comparative study of how male youths in the largest cities in the United States and Great Britain incorporate graffiti into their culture.

Phillips, Susan A. *Wallbangin': Graffiti and Gangs in L.A.* Chicago: University of Chicago Press, 1999. Profusely illustrated study of African American and Latino gangs in Los Angeles by an anthropologist who pays particular attention to the role of graffiti.

Taylor, Ralph. *Breaking Away from Broken Windows: Baltimore Neighborhoods and the Nationwide Fight Against Crime, Grime, Fear and Decline*. Boulder, Colo.: Westview Press, 2001. Case study of juvenile delinquents in Baltimore, Maryland, who are examined in the broader context of national crime problems.

See also Bureau of Justice Statistics; Burglary; Graffiti; Juvenile courts; Juvenile delinquency; Misdemeanors; National Crime Victimization Survey; Probation, juvenile; Restitution; School violence; Uniform Crime Reports; Youth gangs.

Vehicle checkpoints

Definition: Stoppages of motorists by police for such purposes as apprehending criminals, preventing criminal behavior, and obtaining information

Criminal justice issues: Crime prevention; investigation; search and seizure; traffic law

Significance: Vehicle checkpoints have been proven to be effective tools in law enforcement, but their use has raised constitutional challenges that have won court decisions that limit their use.

One of the most publicly visible and useful tools in law enforcement is the use of vehicle checkpoints, in which police officers stop traffic passing through certain locations in order to question drivers and passengers and to perform quick visual inspections of vehicles. The specific purposes of individual checkpoints vary. Some are set up to apprehend criminal fugitives in emergencies, and others are set up on holidays to check for drunk drivers and to discourage drunken driving by their mere presence. Vehicle checkpoints take at least five different forms:

✓ general crime control checkpoints
✓ border patrol checkpoints
✓ driver's license checkpoints
✓ sobriety checkpoints
✓ informational checkpoints.

Despite their frequent usefulness in deterring crime and apprehending criminals, the use of vehicle checkpoints has raised legal challenges because of their perceived infringement on civil liberties. For example, general crime control checkpoints, including those set up to search for illegal drugs, have been ruled constitutionally unreasonable in several landmark decisions of the U.S. Supreme Court. On the other hand, the Supreme Court has upheld them as legal, under certain circumstances, in a number of cases. For any type of vehicle checkpoint to be considered reasonable and constitutional, there is a fine balancing act between the public interest the stop serves and the right of individuals to be free from governmental interference.

The Fourth Amendment of the U.S. Constitution gives citizens the right to be secure in their persons, houses, papers, and effects against unreasonable searches and seizures. The individuals in some Supreme Court cases claimed that their Fourth Amendment rights were violated when they were stopped at vehicle checkpoints. Although the amendment has been interpreted to permit informational vehicle checkpoints, the crimes about which information is sought must be serious. Under court rulings, such checkpoints must be narrowly tailored to the investigative purpose. Moreover, all checkpoint stops must be brief and systematic. Arbitrary stops are unconstitutional.

Informational Checkpoints

Informational checkpoints are used by police to ask motorists if they have information about recent crimes and other matters. They can be useful tools, especially when they succeed in finding witnesses to crimes who might otherwise not come forward. In 2003, the Supreme Court heard the case of *Illinois v. Lidster*, which challenged the constitutionality of vehicle checkpoints for informational purposes. A bicyclist had been struck and killed by a vehicle at approximately the same time of day as the checkpoint was being conducted. Police were stopping individual vehicles for only about ten to fifteen seconds each, in order to hand drivers flyers to ascertain if they had been witnesses to the fatal hit-and-run. The officers did not ask motorists for their names or any other information. The police roadblock was set up purely for informational purposes.

When a motorist named Robert Lidster approached the vehicle checkpoint, a police detective smelled alcohol on his breath and noticed that Lidster's speech was slurred. He asked Lidster for his driver's license and insurance card and directed him to a side street, where another officer performed a sobriety test. After Lidster failed the test, he was arrested and charged with driving under the influence of alcohol. Later, Lidster argued that the checkpoint was unconstitutional because he was seized without suspicion. Lidster said that his Fourth Amendment rights were being violated, and he motioned to suppress the evidence of his offense.

In the trial that followed, Lidster was found guilty of driving under the influence of alcohol, despite his argument that he successfully completed all of the roadside sobriety tests. Afterward, he appealed his conviction, arguing that the hindrance to drivers that the checkpoint created outweighed its possible usefulness in obtaining information. An Illinois appellate court agreed and reversed the trial court's decision, but the case later reached the U.S. Supreme Court, which upheld the trial court's original ruling.

Other Checkpoint Cases

Another U.S. ruling bearing on vehicle checkpoints, *Brown v. Texas* (1979), originated in a Texas case in which police officers stopped two men in a neighborhood with a high incidence of

U.S. Border Patrol agent using a drug-sniffing dog at a vehicle checkpoint along Vermont's border with Canada in late 2004. After the terrorist attacks of September 11, 2001, the U.S. Border Patrol tripled the number of agents along the Canadian border. *(AP/Wide World Photos)*

drug traffic merely because they looked suspicious. One man refused to identify himself and was arrested. The Supreme Court ruled that this violated the man's Fourth Amendment rights. The Court's decision ruled that a Texas statute requiring individuals to identify themselves to police violated the Fourth Amendment because it could be applied when officers lacked any reasonable suspicion to believe that suspects were engaged in criminal conduct.

The Supreme Court's ruling in *Indianapolis v. Edmond* (2000) involved a vehicle checkpoint system that had been established by the city of Indianapolis in 1998 to intercept unlawful drugs. Secondary purposes of the system were to keep impaired drivers off the road and to verify motorists' license and registration information. Police stopped selected vehicles at a checkpoint and spent less than five minutes per vehicle

searching for signs of driver impairment, conducting open-view examinations of the vehicles, and leading a drug-sniffing dog around the vehicles.

Later, two motorists, James Edmond and Joell Palmer, filed a class-action suit in a federal district court, claiming that the vehicle stop violated their rights under the Fourth Amendment and Indiana's own constitution. When their case reached the U.S. Supreme Court, the Court ruled that a checkpoint program was unconstitutional if its only purpose was to uncover "ordinary criminal wrongdoing."

Heidi V. Schumacher

Further Reading

Hall, John Wesley. *Search and Seizure*. 3d ed. Charlottesville, Va.: LEXIS Law Publishing, 2000. Textbook focusing on issues surrounding search and seizure, including vehicle checkpoints.

LaFave, W. R. *Search and Seizure: A Treatise on the Fourth Amendment*. 3d ed. St. Paul, Minn.: West Publishing, 1995. Comprehensive overview of search and seizure with special attention to the constitutional issues that the subject raises.

McWhirter, Darien A. *Search, Seizure, and Privacy*. Phoenix, Ariz.: Oryx Press, 1994. Book written to make subjects such as search and seizure, the exclusionary rule, and privacy rights interesting for high school and undergraduate college students.

Miller, Marc L., and Ronald F. Wright. *Criminal Procedures: The Police: Cases, Statutes, and Executive Materials*. New York: Aspen Law & Business Publishers, 1998. Discussion of both police-citizen interactions and appeals processes in the U.S. justice system.

Wetterer, Charles M. *The Fourth Amendment: Search and Seizure*. Springfield, N.J.: Enslow, 1998. Discussion of various aspects of search and seizure law and how the courts have interpreted the Fourth Amendment.

See also Automobile searches; Border patrols; Consent searches; Drunk driving; Fourth Amendment; Plain view doctrine; Probable cause; Search and seizure; Sobriety testing; Speeding detection.

Verdicts

Definition: Formal decisions or findings made by juries or judges upon matters of fact submitted to them for deliberation and determination

Criminal justice issues: Trial procedures; verdicts

Significance: Verdicts in criminal justice cases can differ from those in civil cases, as defendants who are issued verdicts of acquittal cannot be tried again.

In legal cases the court interprets the applicable law associated with a given case and explains the law to the jury. Based on the presented evidence the jury must determine the facts in the case and make a proper application of the law relating to those facts to arrive at a verdict. In general, the jury's verdict must be unanimous, but many states have modified the condition of unanimity, particularly in civil cases, so that verdicts can be rendered by designated majorities of the juries.

Verdicts may be either general or specific. A general verdict is that in which the jury pronounces "guilty" or "not guilty" and thus decides whether the plaintiff or the defendant wins the case. A general verdict is the verdict most often rendered in criminal cases. Moreover, in criminal cases the verdict must generally be unanimous and must be returned by the jury to the judge in open court. This verdict is based on every material fact submitted for the consideration of the jury. The court may also submit to the jury appropriate forms for a general verdict and, in some cases, a list of written questions concerning one or more of the relevant issues to the case that must be answered in the process of determining the verdict.

When the jury is asked by the court to answer specific questions of fact but leaves any decisions based on the law to the court, it is called a special verdict. The court often requires that the jury return a special verdict in the form of a special written finding upon each issue of fact, and the court determines if the defendant is guilty or not based on those answers. Civil cases may be decided by either a general or a special verdict.

When the verdict is presented in court, the defendant and all the jury members must be present. In most jurisdictions, both the plaintiffs and the defendants have the right to have the jury polled. When they are polled, the jury members are asked if the stated verdict is the one that they favored. A verdict will not stand if the required number of jurors does not answer this question in the affirmative.

When the evidence conclusively dictates a clear verdict in favor of one of the litigants, the judge has the authority in many states to direct the jury to render a verdict in favor of either the plaintiff or the defendant. If it is evident to the court that a verdict is against the weight of the evidence, the court may order a new trial. However, in criminal cases, a verdict of acquittal is conclusive upon the prosecution (the state) so that the defendant will not be subjected to double jeopardy. However, in the event that the jury cannot reach a verdict, the defendant may be tried again.

Alvin K. Benson

Further Reading

Kavlen, Harry, and Hans Zeisel. *The American Jury*. Boston: Little, Brown, 1966.

Litan, Robert E., ed. *Verdict: Assessing the Civil Jury System*. Washington, D.C.: Brookings Institution, 1993.

See also Acquittal; Convictions; Defendants; Dismissals; Double jeopardy; Hung juries; Jury system; Mistrials; Punitive damages; Reasonable doubt; Reversible error; Testimony; Trials.

Vicarious liability

Definition: Legal concept that someone in a supervisory role, such as an employer or parent, may be held liable for harm done by their subordinates or employees

Criminal justice issues: Law codes; legal terms and principles

Significance: Under the concept of vicarious liability, supervisors may be held responsible for injuries or damage caused by the negligent acts or omissions of their subordinates, whether or not those acts or omissions are specifically authorized by the employers.

Vicarious liability is based on the doctrine of *respondeat superior*, wherein a supervisor can be held liable for harm done by subordinates while acting within the scope of their agency or employment. The intent behind the concept is that the proper party must be held responsible when harm is done, even if that party is not directly involved.

There are many situations in which a party may be charged with vicarious liability. Contractors may face vicarious liability if their subcontractors perform a job incorrectly or are found guilty of contract violations. Parents may face vicarious liability when the actions of their children cause harm or damage. Employers may be liable vicariously for sexual harassment or dis-

crimination by an employee, even if that employee acts against the employer's policies. Vicarious liability suits have expanded; for example, manufacturers of mobile phones whose use contributes to car crashes have been being charged with vicarious liability.

In *Faragher v. City of Boca Raton* and *Burlington Industries v. Ellerth*, the U.S. Supreme Court decided that an employer is responsible for sexual harassment or other unlawful actions of its employees, unless the employer had taken steps to prevent workplace harassment and employees failed to take advantage of preventive opportunities provided by the employer.

Linda Volonino

Further Reading

Buckley, William, Cathy Okrent, and Cathy J. Okrent. *Torts and Personal Injury Law*. 3d ed. Albany, N.Y.: Delmar, 2003.

Hall, Daniel E. *Criminal Law and Procedure*. 4th ed. Albany, N.Y.: Delmar, 2003.

See also Circumstantial evidence; Conspiracy; Criminal law; Criminal liability; Environmental crimes; High-speed chases; *Mens rea*; Police civil liability; Sexual harassment; Strict liability offenses.

Victim and Witness Protection Act

The Law: Federal law providing guidelines for treatment of victims and witnesses in federal trials

Date: Enacted on October 12, 1982

Criminal justice issues: Crime prevention; victims; witnesses

Significance: The multiple changes enacted by the Victim and Witness Protection Act of 1982 affected the experiences of victims within the criminal justice system in a multitude of ways.

The Victim and Witness Protection Act of 1982 (VWPA) was established to address the important role crime victims and witnesses play in a federal trial and to guide criminal justice professionals in their treatment of victims and witnesses. The VWPA called for fair treatment of victims and witnesses throughout the court process and also was formulated as a model for state and local legislation.

Specifically, the VWPA called for protection of crime victims and witnesses from intimidation or retaliation by defendants, consideration of victims in regard to privacy when at trial, restitution, victim impact statements to be included in presentence reports, return of property listed as evidence, and safety when assigning bail to defendants. It also included a provision offering employer intervention services for crime victims and witnesses. To aid criminal justice professionals working with victims and witnesses, the VWPA provided for training and education for federal law-enforcement officers and government attorneys. Additionally, the VWPA prohibited federal felons from profiting from their crimes through literary or other profit-based avenues.

Subsequent amendments to the act include allowing for an oral or written statement at the hearing and assigning U.S. attorneys as federal prosecutors with the responsibility of informing victims of parole hearings.

Elizabeth Quinn DeValve

Further Reading

Karmen, Andrew. *Crime Victims: An Introduction to Victimology*. 5th ed. Belmont, Calif.: Wadsworth, 2004.

Office for Victims of Crime. *New Directions from the Field: Victims' Rights and Services for the Twenty-first Century*. Washington, D.C.: U.S. Department of Justice, 1998.

See also National Crime Victimization Survey; Organized Crime Control Act; Trials; Victimology; Victims of Crime Act.

Victim assistance programs

Definition: Advocacy and support services, often funded or administered by government, that guide victims of crime through the legal system and help them cope with emotional distress

Criminal justice issues: Domestic violence; medical and health issues; victims; women's issues

Significance: Victim assistance programs address a common criticism of the criminal justice system: that by focusing on justice for defendants and society at large, it overlooks the emotional, legal, and physical needs of crime victims.

The first victim assistance programs in the United States were created during the early 1970's. They were located in large urban areas and focused primarily on sexual assault of women. These programs offered limited support services to women for whom the criminal justice system might seem intimidating and insensitive. Since that time, victim assistance programs have expanded in number and scope. By the mid-1990's programs were in place throughout the country, addressing victims not only of sexual assault but also of child abuse, spousal battery, and other violent crimes.

Victim assistance programs typically offer services in three general areas: counseling and support, legal assistance, and public awareness and legislative reform. Counseling and support is perhaps the most common function, helping victims to cope with posttraumatic stress disorder, rape trauma syndrome, and other conditions caused by an assault. Individual and group counseling, crisis intervention, medical referrals, and relocation services are some of the resources typically available. Programs also offer legal assistance for crime victims who are testifying, seeking restraining orders, or otherwise facing the criminal justice system. Services include orientation to the justice system and courtroom assistance. Finally, victim assistance services act as advocates for crime victims generally, raising public awareness of certain crimes and how to prevent them, and advocating legislative reforms.

The federal government has promoted victim assistance programs through legislation and funding. The federal Law Enforcement Assistance Administration funded the creation of model victim assistance programs in 1974. The federal Victim and Witness Protection Act of 1982 established "fair treatment standards" for victims and witnesses of crimes. Two years later, the Victims of Crime Act (VOCA) established a fund which provides grants to states to compensate crime victims, and for state and local programs that provide direct assistance to crime victims and their families. In 1994 the Violent Crime Control and Law Enforcement Act augmented the VOCA fund and authorized funding of more than $1 billion for fighting violence against women.

National nongovernment organizations also have been established for promoting victims' rights and victim assistance. Two advocacy groups, the National Organization for Victim Assistance (NOVA) and the Victims' Assistance Legal Organization (VALOR), were created in 1975 and 1981, respectively. In 1985, the National Victim Center was established to help promote the rights and needs of crime victims by working with thousands of local criminal justice and victim service organizations around the country.

Further Reading

Karmen, Andrew. *Crime Victims: An Introduction to Victimology.* 5th ed. Belmont, Calif.: Wadsworth, 2004.

Office for Victims of Crime. *New Directions from the Field: Victims' Rights and Services for the Twenty-first Century.* Washington, D.C.: U.S. Department of Justice, 1998.

See also Criminal justice system; Domestic violence; National Organization for Victim Assistance; Rape and sex offenses; Restorative justice; Victimology; Victims of Crime Act.

Victim-offender mediation

Definition: Facilitated meetings between offenders and victims of their crimes with the intent to discuss the effects and triggers of the harm and to provide options of developing an agreement to repair the harm

Criminal justice issues: Probation and pretrial release; restorative justice

Significance: Part of the "new wave" of community justice decision-making practices known as restorative justice, victim-offender mediation emphasizes restoration and rehabilitation as opposed to traditional retributive justice system practices which highlight retribution and punishment.

Victim-offender mediation gained popularity in the United States during the 1990's, rising with the tide of the restorative justice movement, which sought alternatives to the conflict resolution practices of the (still dominant) retributive justice system. Sharing elements with other restorative practices, such as family group conferencing and circle sentencing, it appeals to community partnerships for crime control and crime prevention and represents a significant shift from the state governance of crime matters.

In 2004, victim-offender mediation programs were widespread across the United States and the world. In the United States they are most often conducted by nonprofit organizations, which receive referrals from courts and probation or parole officers. Mediators are trained volunteers or paid staff members who function as facilitators so that victim and offender may exchange their experiences of the harm, and if they are agreed, help them reach a final contract, which usually involves restitution (monetary or other) and apologies for the victim, and possibly some form of assistance to the offender aimed at circumventing future offenses. This may or may not be court-enforceable.

Victim-offender mediation is used in place of formal adjudication or in addition to it, or as a condition of parole or probation. It is used with lower level, moderately serious, and serious offenses, including capital murder cases. With careful preparation of both parties, mediation

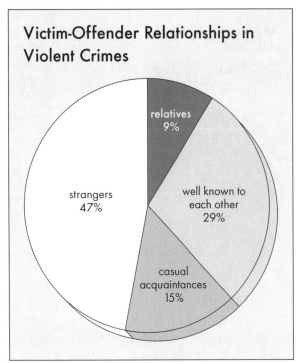

Victim-Offender Relationships in Violent Crimes

relatives
9%

strangers
47%

well known to
each other
29%

casual
acquaintances
15%

Source: U.S. Bureau of Justice Statistics, *Criminal Victimization*. Percentages reflect data for all violent crimes reported in the United States in 2002.

can register great success, as illustrated by the high rates of satisfaction reported by victims and offenders, their perceptions of fairness with both the process and the outcome, and their reports that they would choose mediation over court proceedings in the future. In addition, victims who participate in mediation are far more likely to feel that the justice system has treated them fairly and have been found to enjoy reduced fear and anxiety, while there is significant evidence that mediation is positively related to lower recidivism rates among offenders. These results indicate that wider public policy consideration should be given to increasing the availability of victim-offender mediation services, perhaps as a basic right for all victims and offenders.

Victim-offender mediation addresses aspects of social and criminal justice that are not built into the criminal justice system: It considers public safety beyond simple imprisonment, it makes victims central to decision making, and it makes offenders accountable while simultaneously allowing them to make amends and learn about the

impact of their crime, thus increasing a sense of responsibility rather than inadequacy and rejection.

Michael J. Coyle

Further Reading

Miethe, Terance D., and Robert F. Meier. *Crime and Its Social Context: Toward an Integrated Theory of Offenders, Victims, and Situations*. Albany: State University of New York Press, 1994.

Umbreit, Mark S. *The Handbook of Victim Offender Mediation: An Essential Guide to Practice and Research*. San Francisco: Jossey-Bass, 2001.

See also Civilian review boards; Community-based corrections; Rehabilitation; Restitution; Restorative justice.

Victimless crimes

Definition: Legally prohibited activities or exchanges among willing parties that do not directly harm anyone except, possibly, the parties willingly involved; typical examples include gambling, prostitution, and drug use

Criminal justice issues: Criminology; morality and public order; victimless crime

Significance: The concept of victimless crimes—also called consensual crimes or public order offenses—is frequently applied to debates about decriminalization and the advisability of attempting to legislate morality.

Although the concept of victimless crime was suggested in the work of criminologists in the 1950's, it first found explicit statement in a 1965 study by Edwin Schur that was published under the title *Crimes Without Victims*. Schur identified and discussed three types of behavior as examples of victimless crimes: abortion, drug addiction, and homosexuality. As he stated, "In each case the offending behavior involves a willing and private exchange of strongly demanded yet officially proscribed goods and services: this element of consent precludes the existence of a victim—in the usual sense."

Other scholars who have made use of the concept of victimless crimes include criminologist Jerome Skolnick, who applied it to offenses such as gambling, marijuana use, and prostitution, and jurist Herbert Packer, who cited fornication and narcotic use as crimes without victims. A number of other offenses, including drinking in public, vagrancy, and selling or viewing pornography, have also been called victimless crimes.

At issue is the debate over whether the law should forbid activities for which it is difficult or impossible to determine precisely who is being harmed and how. It has been argued that the law should not forbid activities as long as they harm no one except, perhaps, the people willingly involved in them. Some legal scholars argue that the United States has become an "overcriminalized" society. On the other hand, others point out that some supposedly "victimless" crimes indeed generate harm (for example, drug addiction leads to theft and robbery as addicts try to support their habit). There is also a widespread belief that certain activities should be prohibited because they are harmful to society at large—this is essentially a moral and philosophical position and is therefore difficult to evaluate empirically.

The concept of victimless crime has been used in efforts to reform criminal law by reducing the kinds of conduct subject to criminal penalties. Some argue that criminal offenses which lack victims in the traditional sense are good candidates for decriminalization. Decriminalization frequently entails reducing punishments from possible jail time to a fine; public drunkenness and the possession of small amounts of marijuana are offenses that have been decriminalized in some states.

Schur points out that victimless crimes often involve conduct about which there is a lack of public consensus that the conduct is seriously wrong. Moreover, the fact that many such offenses cause no measurable harm (except for possible harm to the participating individuals) gives rise to serious difficulties with enforceability. If there is no clear harm to another, there is no complainant (a crime victim who requests that an alleged criminal be prosecuted). Law-enforcement officials therefore have difficulty detecting such crimes and gathering evidence to establish the guilty parties. Thus, efforts to control more serious crimes may suffer because of the time-consuming distractions of investigating victimless crimes. Two further undesirable effects are often cited. One is that criminalizing such conduct often gives rise to illicit traffic in the goods and services legally proscribed. The conduct is not actually discouraged, and law enforcement faces the additional problem of dealing with a thriving black market. The second unwelcome consequence is that otherwise law-abiding persons are stigmatized as criminals and are thus degraded.

Despite its initial attractiveness and apparent utility, the appeal of the notion of victimless crimes has declined; by the early 1990's, criminologists were more likely to talk of consensual crimes or public-order offenses. An early manifestation of difficulty with the concept of victimless crime was that different authors provided different lists of such crimes, suggesting that the concept lacked clarity and focus. An underlying difficulty is the fact that defining "victim" or "victimization" is a complex and controversial undertaking. Being physically injured or being de-

Examples of Victimless Crimes

No list of victimless crimes will find full acceptance by everyone. The activities listed here are merely those most commonly cited as meeting the definition of the concept.

✓ Alcoholism
✓ Breaking age-based curfews
✓ Bungee jumping
✓ Drinking in public
✓ Drug use
✓ Fornication
✓ Gambling
✓ Loitering
✓ Not wearing motorcycle helmets
✓ Not wearing seat belts
✓ Pandering
✓ Polygamy
✓ Prostitution
✓ Public nudity
✓ Selling or viewing pornography
✓ Suicide and assisted suicide
✓ Vagrancy

prived of a valued possession are clear-cut cases of victimization. It is also arguable, however, that damaging another person's reputation or esteem or causing mental distress or anguish through one's actions or insults should be considered as victimizing that person. Feminist critiques of pornography and prostitution, for example, condemn such practices as degrading and demeaning to the women involved and, in effect, to all women. Even if meaningful consent were present, they contend, there would still be real victims of these practices.

Mario F. Morelli

Further Reading

Fernandez, Justin. *Victimless Crimes: Crime, Justice, and Punishment*. Philadelphia: Chelsea House Publishers, 2002. Brief discussion of victimless crime issues written for young adult readers.

Hardaway, Robert M. *No Price Too High: Victimless Crimes and the Ninth Amendment*. New York: Praeger, 2003. Argument built on rights implied in the Ninth Amendment that the criminalization of victimless crimes violates citizens' constitutional rights.

Meier, Robert F., and Gilbert Geis. *Victimless Crime? Prostitution, Drugs, Homosexuality, and Abortion*. Los Angeles: Roxbury Publishing, 1997. Examination of the three basic categories of victimless crimes defined by Schur in 1965, with the additional category of prostitution.

O'Donnell, Tim. *American Holocaust: The Price of Victimless Crime Laws*. Lincoln, Nebr.: Writer's Showcase Press, 2000. Case against victimless crime laws arguing that such laws have a devastating effect and are based on the narrow moral views of the majority in power and represent a form of religious persecution.

Schur, Edwin M., and Hugo Adam Bedau. *Victimless Crimes: Two Sides of a Controversy*. Englewood Cliffs, N.J.: Prentice-Hall, 1974. Although this book may now appear somewhat dated, it presents clear and concise arguments on both sides of the victimless crime debate that are still relevant.

See also Antismoking laws; Breach of the peace; Commercialized vice; Drug legalization debate; Drugs and law enforcement; Mann Act; Pornography and obscenity; Prohibition; Public-order offenses; Suicide and euthanasia.

Victimology

Definition: Scientific study of victims of crime
Criminal justice issues: Crime prevention; criminology; hate crime; victims
Significance: Studying the victims of crime is an essential part of any study of criminal justice.

The discipline known as victimology emerged at a time when some of the traditional research found within the field of criminology was shifting from studies of those who commit crimes to those who are adversely affected by crimes committed against them. "Victimology" was quickly acknowledged as a branch of criminology and later became an independent discipline dedicated to studying the reasons why certain individuals and members of certain groups become victims of crime.

Victimology is now a rapidly growing academic field with interests that incorporate sociology, criminology, psychology, criminal justice, legal studies, and rehabilitative sciences. Victimology differs from these other fields in developing theories about how different lifestyles can affect the chances that individuals or members of groups have of becoming victims of crime. The goal of victimology studies is to promote long-term solutions to stop victimization from occurring.

Victimologists study the effectiveness that the criminal justice system has upon the public, specifically those individuals who have had crimes committed against them. The earliest victimologists studied the effects of violent crime on victims of rape and murder. Current victimologists tend to study children, women, the elderly, immigrants, indigenous peoples, and frequently persecuted people whose sexual orientations are nonheterosexual: gay men, lesbian women, bisexuals, and those who are transgendered. Studies of hate crimes and the impact that these

What Makes a Person a Victim?

A central difficulty in defining "victims" of crimes lies in drawing nonarbitrary lines between indirect victims and others. For example, if a person's home is burgled, and the next-door neighbor then purchases a home security system to avoid being similarly burgled, should that neighbor be considered an indirect victim? Or, suppose that a person driving into a convenience store parking lot sees an armed robbery taking place within the store and then suffers a serious injury in a collision while rushing to exit the lot to seek police help. Is that person a victim of the armed robbery crime?

crimes have upon members of persecuted communities are excellent examples of research done by victimologists.

Victimologists research not only the impact of physical harm and personal loss experienced by victims, but also the handling of such victims by the criminal justice system itself. Often, the actual roles of law-enforcement officials, especially police officers, lawyers, judges, and probation officers, are studied and compared to their ideal roles. Broadly speaking, victimologists explore interactions between victims and offenders, victims and the criminal justice system, and victims and society.

Finally, victimologists study public reactions to victims of crime, as portrayed by the mass media. Victimologists research legal issues raised by the public along with new advocacy groups that emerge in response to crimes and victimization. Such advocacy groups include Mothers Against Drunk Driving (MADD), one of the largest organizations devoted to victims of crime. Other manifestations of the fruits of public campaigns undertaken by advocacy groups are laws that are named after highly publicized victims of crime. One of the best-known examples is New Jersey's Megan's Law, which requires convicted sex offenders to register with local police departments after they are released from prison.

Emily I. Troshynski

Further Reading

Beloof, D. *Victims in Criminal Procedure*. Raleigh, N.C.: Carolina Academic Press, 1999.

Bergen, R., ed. *Issues in Intimate Violence*. Thousand Oaks, Calif.: Sage Publications, 1998.

Johnstone, Gerry. *Restorative Justice: Ideas, Values, Debates*. Portland, Oreg.: Willan, 2002.

Karmen, Andrew. *Crime Victims: An Introduction to Victimology*. 5th ed. Belmont, Calif.: Wadsworth, 2004.

See also Battered child and battered wife syndromes; Date rape; Domestic violence; Just deserts; National Crime Victimization Survey; Rape and sex offenses; Restitution; Stalking; Victim and Witness Protection Act; Victim assistance programs; Victims of Crime Act.

Victims of Crime Act

The Law: Federal legislation that established funding for compensating and assisting victims of crime
Date: Signed into law on October 12, 1984
Criminal justice issues: Restorative justice; victims; women's issues
Significance: The Victims of Crime Act demonstrated the federal government's commitment to assisting crime victims and encouraged the funding of victim-assistance programs throughout the United States.

Victims have existed as long as there have been crimes, and the methods and efforts of restoring the victims and their losses have been variously addressed. One of the earliest known documents that described government intervention and restoring victims was the code of the eighteenth century B.C.E. Babylonian ruler Hammurabi. In the eighteenth century, Italian criminologist Cesare Beccaria began addressing criminals' rights.

During the 1960's, various movements raised the issues of inequities in the rights of various communities in the United States. One of these communities was made up victims of crime, and the issue of their rights began gaining national attention. The developing victims' movement adopted many of the methods of the Civil Rights and women's movements and raised public awareness of victim status and treatment in the criminal justice system. As a result, some local efforts were attempted in providing assistance for crime victims, most notably in California.

During the early 1980's, President Ronald Reagan ordered the establishment of a Presidential Task Force on Victims of Crime. That initiative led to recommendations for legislative assistance and protection of crime victims and resulted in the passage of the federal Victims of Crime Act (VOCA) in 1984. The law established federal funding for the states to provide compensation and assistance to crime victims. In addition, the law established the Office for Victims of Crime (OVC) as an agency of the Department of Justice. That agency was given responsibility for administering the federal funds made possible through VOCA. In addition, the OVC was to provide advocacy and assistance for victims.

The Victims of Crime Act was a major step in changing the rights for victims of crime. By 1992, all U.S. states had established offices for victims' compensations and assistance.

Richard L. McWhorter

Further Reading

Doerner, William G. *Victimology*. Cincinnati: Anderson Publishing, 2002.

Estrich, Susan. *With Justice for Some: Victims' Rights in Criminal Trials*. Reading, Mass.: Addison-Wesley, 1995.

Karmen, Andrew. *Crime Victims: An Introduction to Victimology*. 5th ed. Belmont, Calif.: Wadsworth, 2004.

See also National Organization for Victim Assistance; Victim and Witness Protection Act; Victim assistance programs; Victimology.

Vigilantism

Definition: Illegal assumption of law-enforcement responsibilities by organized groups of private citizens

Criminal justice issues: Morality and public order; punishment

Significance: Vigilantism still exists in parts of the world where law enforcement is weak or corrupt, but no nation has ever developed a vigilante tradition as strong as that of the United States.

During the eighteenth and nineteenth centuries, a tradition of vigilantism developed on America's Western frontier because of the slowness with which authorized law enforcement caught up with new settlements. This situation contrasted with that of Canada, where the forerunners of the Royal Canadian Mounted Police arrived in frontier towns to provide order almost as quickly as the towns arose. One reason for this difference was that law enforcement was regarded as almost exclusively a local responsibility in the United States, and new settlements often lacked the resources to pay for their own policing. Where local law enforcement did exist on the frontier, it generally lacked the resources to pursue criminals beyond its own jurisdiction.

During the eighteenth and nineteenth centuries, approximately five hundred vigilante movements arose to dispense local justice in the United States and its frontier territories. During the nineteenth century alone, American vigilantes executed at least 700 suspected criminals and subjected many thousands of others to whippings and other corporal punishments and expulsions from communities.

Vigilantism has not been unknown in other nations, especially those that developed their own frontiers, such as nineteenth century New Zealand. In nineteenth century Russia, peasants formed vigilante committees to combat horse thieves. Even Great Britain had vigilante movements, and these gave rise to such terms as "Cowper law," "Jeddart justice," and "Lydford law."

The Nature of Vigilantism

Vigilante groups, or "committees," as they often called themselves, were usually not disorganized mobs. They tended to have organized hierarchical structures, with the most powerful and wealthiest men in communities serving as their leaders. Most members of vigilante groups were from the middle class. A typical vigilance committee included several hundred men. Vigilantes considered themselves to be upholding law and order. They thus differed from organizations such as the Ku Klux Klan in not wearing masks or disguises. Vigilantes occasionally even held formal trials before punishing the criminal suspects they captured, and sometimes their trials even produced acquittals.

Vigilantism is, by definition, a group activity. In the modern United States, the term "vigilante" is sometimes applied to lone citizens who take the law into their own hands to seek personal revenge on criminals or conduct private crusades against crime, but the term is not properly applied to individual action.

The Early Frontier

Some of the earliest documented American vigilantes appeared during the 1760's in the back country of South Carolina in response to the predations of gangs that kidnapped girls to live as their wives in outlaw communities and robbed, raped, and tortured their victims. As the back country had neither courts nor sheriffs, middle- and upper-class citizens formed a vigilante committee called the Regulators. Within two years, the Regulators destroyed the outlaw gangs and drove their survivors out of the area. However, the Regulators did not stop there. They abused their newfound power by whipping other people merely for such crimes as idleness. To oppose the Regulators, a new vigilante group called the Moderators was formed. The Moderators fought the Regulators until 1769, when South Carolina's colonial government finally provided local courts and sheriffs.

During the Revolutionary War of the late eighteenth century, Virginia vigilantes were led by Colonel Edward Lynch. Because rural Virginia then had no courts, Lynch set up his own courts to try people who were suspected of aiding the British. When his unofficial courts convicted suspected traitors, lynch mobs formed to whip the offenders and drive them out of town.

Vigilantism in the West

Soon after the Revolutionary War ended in 1783, a variant of vigilantism arose in the development of the anti-horse thief movement, which arose in the East and spread throughout the country rapidly. In many states anti-horse thief associations became official adjuncts of profes-

President Andrew Jackson. *(Library of Congress)*

sional law-enforcement bodies and helped to combat the serious crime of horse stealing. As late as the early twentieth century, branches of the movement claimed hundreds of thousands of members, but the movement died out as automobiles displaced horses in transportation.

Meanwhile, the election of Andrew Jackson to the presidency in 1828 represented an important change in American political values. Common citizens became more confident in their ability to administer the government and less deferential toward elites. The years of Jackson's two terms in office saw a great increase in vigilantism, and President Jackson himself even applauded vigilantism at one point. During his presidency, many towns along the Mississippi and other major navigable rivers suffered from the vices associated with gambling rings, which also promoted robbery and murder. In Vicksburg, Mississippi, for example, vigilantes drove out gamblers and killed some of them. An antigambling crusade inspired other vigilante movements up and down the Mississippi and its tributaries.

More typical, however, were vigilante groups

that arose in response to specific local problems and disbanded as soon as the local problems were resolved. For example, during the early 1840's, outlaw gangs controlled several northern Illinois counties, whose legal governments were too weak to oppose them. In response, a bank president and a wealthy settler organized middle-class farmers into a committee called the Illinois Regulators. They used whippings and executions to break the power of the outlaw gangs.

One of the most famous vigilante groups of the nineteenth century was the San Francisco Committee of Vigilance that formed in 1851 in response to the growing violence caused by the huge influx of drifters attracted to the city by California's gold rush. The city's criminal justice system was unable to cope with the violence, and criminal gangs—such as the Sydney Ducks from Australia—so terrorized the city that law-abiding citizens became afraid to testify against them. Eventually, the city's vigilantes arrested ninety-one people; they executed four of them, whipped one, sent fourteen back to Australia, and drove fourteen others out of California. Of the remaining fifty-eight whom they arrested, fifteen were handed over to government authorities, and the rest were released.

Although the 1851 San Francisco vigilantes were generally praised at the time, modern historians have taken a more critical view of their activities. They point out that one of the effects of the city's vigilantism was to wrest control of San Francisco politics away from Irish Catholics and deliver it to the middle- and upper-class Protestants who formed the nucleus of the vigilantes.

In 1856, San Francisco saw the formation of the largest American vigilance committee ever created in a single area. During the six months before the vigilantes assembled, about one hundred murders occurred in the city. During the three months that the new vigilante committee was active, only two murders two place, and four people were executed by the committee.

During the early 1860's, Bannack, Montana, faced a unique crime problem because the town's own sheriff was the head of a local criminal gang. In response to that situation, citizens of Bannack and nearby Virginia City formed vigilance committees that met openly, chose officers by election, arrested suspects, and conducted trials. Dur-

ing the winter of 1863-1864, these committees hanged thirty criminals, including Bannack's sheriff.

Vigilantes as Heroes

One of the Montana vigilante leaders, Wilbur Fiske Sanders, later founded Montana's state bar association and was one of the first two men that Montana elected to the U.S. Senate when it became a state in 1889. Other vigilante leaders elected to high office included Wyoming governors Fennimore Chatterton and John Osborne, Missouri senator Francis Cockrell, New Mexico governor and congressman George Curry, Illinois governor Augustus French, Louisiana governor and senator Alexander Mouton, and California governor and senator Leland Stanford, Sr., who also founded Stanford University. Another former vigilante, Idaho governor and senator William John McConnell, published an autobiography, titled *Frontier Law: A Story of Vigilante Days* (1924), that was acclaimed as a model of good citizenship for American youth.

David B. Kopel

Further Reading

Abrahams, Ray. *Vigilant Citizens: Vigilantism and the State*. Cambridge, England: Polity Press, 1998. Exploration of vigilantism in a variety of modern contexts in various nations.

Brown, Richard Maxwell. *Strain of Violence: Historical Studies of American Violence and Vigilantism*. New York: Oxford University Press, 1977. Essays on vigilantism by the leading scholar of American vigilantism.

Dimsdale, Thomas J. *The Vigilantes of Montana: Being a Correct and Impartial Narrative of the Chase, Trial, Capture, and Execution of Henry Plummer's Notorious Road Agent Band*. Norman: University of Oklahoma Press, 1953. Firsthand account by one of the Bannack, Montana, vigilantes. First published in 1866 and reprinted in many later editions.

Moses, Norton H. *Lynching and Vigilantism in the United States: An Annotated Bibliography*. Westport, Conn.: Greenwood Press, 1997. Comprehensive bibliography of American vigilantism.

Neely, Richard. *Take Back Your Neighborhood: A Case for Modern-Day "Vigilantism."* New

York: Penguin, 1990. Appeal by the chief justice of West Virginia's supreme court of appeals to create neighborhood citizen patrols.

Stewart, George R. *The Committee of Vigilance: Revolution in San Francisco, 1851.* Boston: Houghton Mifflin, 1964. Fascinating history of one of the most famous vigilante episodes.

See also Bounty hunters; Citizen's arrests; Criminal justice in U.S. history; Ku Klux Klan; Lynching; Outlaws of the Old West; *Posse comitatus*; Sheriffs; Slave patrols.

Violent Crime Control and Law Enforcement Act

The Law: Comprehensive federal crime-fighting law

Date: Enacted on September 13, 1994

Criminal justice issues: Crime prevention; federal law; violent crime

Significance: The most comprehensive federal anticrime bill enacted in U.S. history, this act expanded federal and state criminal justice and law-enforcement powers, weapon prohibitions, and crime-prevention efforts.

The Violent Crime Control and Law Enforcement Act was an achievement of the 103d Congress and President Bill Clinton's administration. The bipartisan bill was enacted when the nation was expressing an ever-diminishing tolerance for criminal activity. Some polls reported that as many as 70 percent of all Americans believed that combating crime required emergency action, and 54 percent regarded crime as a more serious problem than the national economy, the environment, or health care.

Responding to the national concern, President Clinton outlined five components of crime legislation that he wanted Congress to approve, in August, 1993. Legislative action began in October. The House Judiciary Committee chairman faced battles in getting a crime bill out of committee. However, within months of the president's announcement, several sensational events captured congressional attention. A young girl was murdered by a repeat violent offender, a gunman killed several people on a commuter train, the state of Washington passed a three-strikes law, and Virginia elected a governor who promised "truth-in-sentencing" laws. These events almost forced Congress to take action. The bill that Congress eventually passed authorized $30.2 billion in spending over six years for law enforcement and crime prevention, including funding for seventeen grant programs.

The law banned the manufacture of numerous assault weapons, expanded the federal death penalty, allowed prosecution of some juvenile offenders as adults, and required all states to register sex offenders and double penalties for repeat sex offenders. The law also prohibited the sale of firearms to domestic abusers, strengthened firearm licensing laws, provided stiffer penalties for gang activity, expanded categories of fraud, and stiffened expectations on border control and deportation laws. Finally, it enacted three-strikes laws with mandatory life imprisonment for felony offenders with three or more convictions for serious violent offenses and drug-trafficking offenses.

The new grant programs created by the law included implementation of the Brady Bill for states to upgrade criminal-history records; Byrne Grants for state law-enforcement purposes; competitive community policing programs to put 100,000 additional police officers in neighborhoods, and a prison-expansion program for states to implement truth-in-sentencing laws that would require violent offenders to serve at least 85 percent of their prison sentences. Crime-prevention grant initiatives included delinquent and at-risk youth programs, drug-treatment and court programs, credit to community development corporations, and efforts in reducing and preventing crimes against women.

Carrie A. Pettus

Further Reading

Marion, Nancy E. *A History of Federal Crime Control Initiatives, 1960-1993.* Westport, Conn.: Praeger, 1994.

Reams, Bernard D., Jr., comp. *The Omnibus Anti-Crime Act: A Legislative History of the Violent Crime Control and Law Enforcement Act of 1994.* Buffalo, N.Y.: W. S. Hein, 1997.

Violent Crime Control and Law Enforcement Act of 1994: Briefing Book. Washington, D.C.: U.S. Department of Justice, 1994.

See also Criminal justice in U.S. history; Domestic violence; Drug courts; Firearms; Juvenile waivers to adult courts; Police; Sentencing; Three-strikes laws; Violent Criminal Apprehension Program.

Violent Criminal Apprehension Program

Identification: National database of information on serial murders and other violent homicides

Date: Launched online in 1985

Criminal justice issues: Crime prevention; crime statistics; investigation

Significance: The Violent Criminal Apprehension Program, or ViCAP, allows wide access to patterns of murderous violence and characteristics of missing persons so that personnel working in various law-enforcement jurisdictions can share information.

ViCAP is a national online database that was launched in 1985. It serves as a clearinghouse of information for use by law-enforcement officers at the municipal, state, and local levels when investigating serial murders, missing persons, and unidentified remains. Los Angeles detective Pierce Brooks originally envisioned the ViCAP system in the 1950's, but the technology needed to put the idea into practice would not be available for three decades.

With approximately sixteen thousand separate law-enforcement agencies nationwide, officers and investigators from different locales needed a way to compare and share information with agencies in other jurisdictions. This is particularly true in investigating roaming serial murderers and sexual killers who strike over wide geographic regions. ViCAP was developed so that officers could have access to information on crimes that occurred in other jurisdictions, allowing them to discern patterns of violence that could be useful for their own investigations.

Some serial killers are highly mobile and move from one jurisdiction to another to commit murders and evade detection. ViCAP provides the opportunity for officers from different locales to identify suspects or otherwise advance their own investigations. Among the information maintained by ViCAP is the case status (open or closed), age and ethnicity of the offender and the victims, what caused the crime, any known relationships between the offender and victims, and weapon types.

Criteria for submission of cases to ViCAP vary by the crime. Homicide cases can be solved or unsolved and should appear to be random, motiveless, sexual, or serial. Missing persons cases must involve strong suspicion of a violent end. Unidentified bodies of those who appear to be homicide victims are also ViCAP reportable. The primary goal of ViCAP is to allow law-enforcement agencies to exchange information that could uncover investigative leads in victimology; modi operandi; suspect characteristics; behaviors before, during, and after the crime; and other details that could contribute to the emergence of a pattern and the identification of a common perpetrator.

The original version of ViCAP was cumbersome and underused, particularly by urban agencies. ViCAP was redesigned in 1996 to be more streamlined and user-friendly. ViCAP can now store and display images, so that crime scene photographs can be accessed and viewed. Other upgrades planned for the future included the introduction of graphic information system (GIS) data so that locations of events could be mapped and displayed. The program's mission to foster cooperation and communication among agencies in order to identify, apprehend, and prosecute violent offenders will remain an integral part of the criminal justice system.

David R. Champion

Further Reading

Osterbug, James W., and Richard H. Ward. *Criminal Investigation.* 3d ed. Cincinnati: Anderson, 2000.

Ressler, Robert K., Ann W. Burgess, and John E. Douglas. *Sexual Homicide: Patterns and Motives.* Lexington, Mass.: Lexington Books, 1988.

Witzig, Eric W. "The New ViCAP: More User-Friendly and Used by More Agencies." *FBI Law Enforcement Bulletin* (June, 2003).

See also Computer information systems; Criminal justice in U.S. history; Geographic information systems; Murders, mass and serial; National Commission on the Causes and Prevention of Violence; Police; Violent Crime Control and Law Enforcement Act.

Virginia v. Black

The Case: U.S. Supreme Court ruling on cross burning

Criminal justice issues: Civil rights and liberties; hate crime

Date: Decided on April 7, 2003

Significance: In this case, the Supreme ruled that state laws criminalizing cross burning that is done with the intent to intimidate do not violate the First Amendment.

After the Civil War, cross burning was used as a form of intimidation by southern white supremacists. A Virginia statute prohibited cross burning in public places or on private property when it was done for the purpose of intimidation. In 1998, Barry Black, a Ku Klux Klan (KKK) member who supervised a cross burning in an open field, was convicted by a Virginia jury whose members were instructed that burning a cross was sufficient evidence of an intent to intimidate. In another incident, Richard Elliott and Jonathan O'Mara attempted to burn a cross on a neighbor's lawn. O'Mara pleaded guilty, and Elliott was convicted by a jury that was instructed to find that the defendant intended to intimidate his neighbors when he burned the cross. The Virginia Court of Appeals upheld the convictions in both cases, but the Virginia Supreme Court found the state's anti-cross-burning law unconstitutional. Virginia appealed to the U.S. Supreme Court, which granted certiorari.

Justice Sandra Day O'Connor delivered the opinion for the Court on the question of the constitutionality of a state statute prohibiting cross burning. Writing for a six-member majority, she held that a state could single out cross burning done with the intent to intimidate, even if the state did not criminalize all other intimidating messages. As the Court had held in *R.A.V. v. City of St. Paul* (1992), its leading hate speech case, a state could prohibit the worst illustrations of the very reason that an entire category of speech is unprotected. Cross burning, she concluded, was a particularly virulent form of intimidation practiced by the KKK–the kind of true threat that the First Amendment permits states to ban.

When the court turned to the question of the constitutionality of the Virginia statute, seven justices agreed that the Virginia statute was unconstitutional, but there was no majority opinion. Justice O'Connor in a plurality opinion, joined by Chief Justice William Rehnquist and Justices John Paul Stevens and Stephen Breyer, found that the Virginia statute violated the First Amendment, because it permitted the jury to ignore the fact that a cross may be constitutionally burned at Klan rallies as a symbol of solidarity and to infer from the cross burning itself that the defendant had the intent to intimidate.

In a separate opinion, Justices David Souter, joined by Justices Anthony Kennedy and Ruth Bader Ginsberg, found that the Virginia statute was an unconstitutional content-based distinction, because it had selected a symbol with a particular content from the field of all proscribable intimidating or threatening expressions and made its use criminal.

As the Supreme Court's first opportunity in a decade to revisit *R.A.V. v. City of St. Paul*, *Virginia v. Black* confirmed that cross burning with the intent to intimidate is not protected by the First Amendment. As a result, states may punish cross burning done with the intent to intimidate as long as their criminal laws clearly require prosecutors to prove that the cross burning is intended as a threat.

William Crawford Green

Further Reading

Gerstenfeld, Phyllis B. *Hate Crimes: Causes, Controls, and Controversies*. Thousand Oaks, Calif.: Sage Publications, 2004.

Levin, Jack. *The Violence of Hate: Confronting Racism, Anti-Semitism, and Other Forms of Bigotry*. Boston: Allyn & Bacon, 2002.

Perry, Barbara. *In the Name of Hate: Understanding Hate Crimes*. New York: Routledge, 2001.

Streissguth, Thomas. *Hate Crimes*. New York: Facts on File, 2003.

See also Hate crime; Ku Klux Klan; *R.A.V. v. City of St. Paul*; Supreme Court, U.S.

Voir dire

Definition: Preliminary process in selection of persons to serve on juries

Criminal justice issues: Juries; legal terms and principles; trial procedures

Significance: The process of empaneling jurors can be one of the most important and most difficult tasks of the trial process.

A French legal phrase, *voir dire* means "to speak the truth." It is the process by which prospective jurors are questioned to determine whether they hold any biases or prejudices that might interfere with their role as objective jurors. The circumstances of cases or high-profile status of persons involved in cases make it difficult at times for jury selection to remain bias-free. *Voir dire* allows defense attorneys and prosecutors to eliminate jurors whom they believed are biased or who may be unlikely to accept their sides' versions of events. This is done using two types of challenges—challenges for cause and peremptory challenges.

Challenges for cause can be made by either set of attorneys and are unlimited in number. However, judges make the final decisions about excusing specific prospective jurors. Challenges for cause are rarely made and are rarely granted.

Peremptory challenges are made by either side and are limited in number. However, judges are not involved in these decisions to exclude jurors. Peremptory challenges are strategically used and require no explanation to the judges. In the past, such challenges were used systematically to remove jurors on the basis of their race or gender—a practice that is now legally prohibited.

As with other aspects of the trial process, *voir dire* exists to protect the integrity of the system.

It is meant to allow citizens to participate in the trial process while allowing that process to be as unbiased and impartial as possible.

Jenifer A. Lee

Further Reading

Abadinsky, H. *Law and Justice: An Introduction to the American Legal System*. Upper Saddle River, N.J.: Prentice-Hall, 2003.

Rabe, Gary A., and Dean John Champion. *Criminal Courts: Structure, Process, and Issues*. Upper Saddle River, N.J.: Prentice-Hall, 2002.

See also Death qualification; Defendants; Defense attorneys; District attorneys; Judges; Jury duty; Jury system; Mistrials; Print media; Trial publicity; Trials.

Voting fraud

Definition: Use of illegal tactics and practices to influence political elections in U.S. history

Criminal justice issues: Fraud; government misconduct, organized crime; political issues

Significance: Although the U.S. political system was founded on principles of equal rights and democratic rule, voting fraud has influenced the outcomes of political elections through the nation's history and has thereby threatened the legitimacy of the nation's democratic institutions.

Although the alleged improprieties of the 2000 presidential election came as a shock to many Americans, voting fraud has a long and rich history in the United States. In large part, voting fraud stems from the primary rule in politics: Get elected. Whether political candidates have been motivated by their thirst for power or their desire to serve their fellow citizens, the American political landscape has often reflected the importance of getting elected at any cost. This attitude has led to innumerable creative attempts to gain office, many of which fall outside the bounds of legality.

Political Machines

Early American politics, particularly in urban centers, was dominated by what came to be known as political machines—informal organizations, commonly aligned with political parties, that were designed to control the governments of local jurisdictions. Because of the elitist nature of early American politics and the high levels of poverty in American cities, most citizens had little knowledge of the inner workings of the political system. Meanwhile, the "machines" worked to deliver votes to particular candidates and parties by both legal and illegal means. From the early nineteenth century until the late twentieth century, such machines exercised a powerful influence on the American political sphere.

The best known and most infamous political machine was New York City's Tammany Hall. After the American Revolution, that organization took its name from the Delaware Indian chief Tamanend, who was said to have signed a peace treaty with William Penn. Tammany Hall was simply one part of a larger organization of Tammany societies that were located throughout the United States. Its motto was "freedom our rock," and its members fought primarily for the rights of poor citizens and immigrants. Although the political goals of the Tammany societies were noble, the societies were also pioneers of voting fraud.

The ways in which Tammany Hall bosses ensured allegiance were similar to those of organized crime groups. In exchange for political loyalty, the organizations helped members secure jobs, and they provided food, clothing, shelter, and even legal representation for both immigrants and poor Americans. In addition, the organizations helped immigrants to become citizens— always in exchange for voter loyalty. When those inducements were not sufficient to win support, Tammany Hall simply offered voters money. By the 1830's, the practice of buying votes was firmly established within America's cities. The going rate at the time was five dollars per vote—an amount roughly equivalent to one hundred dollars in the early twenty-first century—but it could go as high as twenty dollars or more. Although the practice of vote buying was no secret to anyone, it was difficult to detect.

Although Tammany Hall was the best known

political machine to buy political loyalty, it was by no means the only group to do so. Throughout much of American history, all sides of the political spectrum actively participated in what was viewed as the most efficient manner to secure the votes of apathetic citizens. The dimensions of voting fraud can be seen in the results of a New York City election in 1868. An audit of that election found that of the 156,000 total votes cast, 25,000 were fraudulent—a figure large enough to decide most elections.

Another creative and illegal means of winning elections was the practice of repeat voting. The phrase "Vote early and vote often" is now merely a jest; however, it was a serious admonition during the days of machine politics. Individual machine loyalists often managed to find ways to vote several times in a single election. One technique was simply to bribe poll watchers to turn their backs while casting extra ballots. A more devious technique was to vote under the names of people who had recently died, before those names were removed from voting registers. Because few people carried personal identification on them during the nineteenth and early twentieth centuries, one merely had to present oneself at a polling place under the name of a recently deceased person. Around the turn of the twentieth century, Philadelphia's Gas Ring Machine not only had many dead people voting for its candidates, it also counted the names of horses, cats, and dogs among its voters.

If buying off voters and polling place workers was not sufficient to secure victory, political machines might attempt to buy off the election officials. Once a machine purchased or won the loyalty of the people who actually counted votes, it did not matter who actually voted for whom; victory was assured. When carried out properly, this practice was the most efficient means to secure political office.

Modern Voter Fraud

Modern voters are far more politically savvy and sophisticated than their nineteenth century and early twentieth century predecessors; however, that fact has not immunized modern voters from political fraud. As late as the 1950's, political machines continued to exert influence over the election processes. For example, when

Lyndon B. Johnson was running for the U.S. Senate in Texas in 1948, the Democratic Party's local machine is said to have secured votes through bribes, intimidation, and even ballot burning. When it appeared that Johnson had lost the election by only 112 votes, another 201 votes for him were suddenly found that gave the Senate seat to him.

The presidential election of 1960 has also long been believed to have been tainted by fraud. According to charges that have never been substantiated, associates of Joseph Kennedy, the wealthy father of presidential candidate John F. Kennedy, went through West Virginia doling out cash to local sheriffs in return for voter loyalty. It has also been charged that Kennedy received considerable support from dead voters in Chicago.

While electoral reforms and improved voting technology offer the promise that voting fraud is in the past, allegations of fraud have continued. The U.S. presidential election of 2000 and the congressional elections of 2002 were rife with accusations of voter intimidation and unconstitutional election practices.

Theodore Shields

Further Reading

Dionne, E. J., Jr., and William Kristol, eds. *Bush v. Gore: The Court Cases and Commentary*. Washington, D.C.: Brookings Institution, 2001. Analysis of the 2000 presidential election, which was decided by the U.S. Supreme Court after the results of voting in Florida became hopelessly confused amid charges and countercharges of voting fraud.

Grossman, Mark. *Political Corruption in America: An Encyclopedia of Scandals, Power, and Greed*. Santa Barbara, Calif.: ABC-Clio, 2003. Encyclopedic reference work on people, laws, scandals, and basic concepts associated with political corruption, including voting fraud, in the United States.

McCaffrey, Peter. *When Bosses Ruled Philadelphia*. University Park: Penn State University Press, 1993. Study of machine politics during the nineteenth and early twentieth centuries in the city in which the U.S. Constitution was drafted.

Rakove, Jack N., ed. *The Unfinished Election of 2000: Leading Scholars Examine America's Strangest Election*. New York: Basic Books, 2001. Engaging essays by seven scholars and legal experts on the controversial presidential election of 2000.

Scher, Richard K., Jon L. Mills, and John J. Hotaling. *Voting Rights and Democracy*. Chicago: Nelson-Hall, 1997. Survey of the changes in voting rights in the United States through the late twentieth century, when American politics was transformed by federal voting rights legislation.

See also Conspiracy; Fraud; Organized crime; Political corruption.

Walnut Street Jail

Identification: Historic U.S. penal institution
Date: Opened in 1773
Place: Philadelphia, Pennsylvania
Criminal justice issues: Prisons; rehabilitation
Significance: The Walnut Street Jail promoted the rehabilitation of criminals and was the forerunner of the modern prison system in the United States.

Designed by architect and builder Robert Smith, the Walnut Street Jail was constructed in Philadelphia in 1773. At the time, deplorable conditions existed in U.S. penal institutions. It was commonplace for men, women, and children to be incarcerated in a common locked area, where aggression and sexual exploitation frequently occurred. Encouraged by the Philadelphia Society for Alleviating the Miseries of Public Prisons, administrators of the Walnut Street Jail eventually used that jail as a model for improving the imprisonment system.

Starting during the late 1780's, instead of using the Walnut Street Jail strictly as a place for punishment of prisoners, it was redesigned to reform inmates and help prevent them from committing crimes after they were released. Men, women, and children were separated from one another in clean, solitary cells. Prisoners received basic education and religious instruction and were encouraged to treat one another humanely. Highlights of the new approach included the use of solitary confinement, special times for prisoner meditation and reflection, and training of inmates for future employment. The discipline system employed at the Walnut Street Jail became known as the Pennsylvania System.

Because of overcrowding, the Walnut Street Jail was remodeled and converted into the Walnut Street Prison in 1790, the first state prison in Pennsylvania and the birthplace of the modern U.S. prison system. Several new ideas were implemented to help rehabilitate criminals, particularly an increased focus on a variety of prison industries which included making nails, sawing rocks, weaving, and making shoes. The more hardened criminals were sentenced to hard labor during the day and at nighttime.

Alvin K. Benson

Further Reading

Blomberg, Thomas G. *American Penology: A History of Control*. New York: Aldine de Gruyter, 2000.

Peterson, Charles E. *Robert Smith: Architect, Builder, Patriot, 1722-1777*. Philadelphia: Athenaeum, 2000.

See also Criminal justice in U.S. history; Prison and jail systems; Prison health care; Prison industries; Prison overcrowding; Prison violence.

War crimes

Definition: Crimes against humanity that go beyond the acts normally considered permissible in international armed conflicts
Criminal justice issues: International law; military justice; victims
Significance: Since the mid-nineteenth century, the world has moved steadily to impose greater international control over the conduct of war and to call to account individual persons and states that violate human rights.

Wars are, by their nature, international conflicts, and the behaviors that constitute war crimes are largely defined by international humanitarian laws. These laws are made up of humanitarian principles and international treaties aimed at minimizing the suffering of combatants and noncombatants during international or noninternational armed conflicts. They are designed to protect persons and property that are affected by conflicts and to limit the rights of belligerent states to use whatever weapons and methods to forward their interests that they choose.

Taken collectively, these international rules limit the means and extent of permissible violence in armed conflicts. In the modern world, all actors involved in military conflicts are bound by international law. Accordingly, when actors violate these rules, their actions may be deemed war crimes and may be subject to penalties imposed by either domestic or international courts.

International Conventions

In response to the immense human suffering and devastation caused by wars throughout history, international laws of war have been developed to define and regulate acceptable behaviors during wartime. The first attempt to regulate acts during war was made at the Diplomatic Con-

ference of Geneva in 1864. It resulted in the first treaty to establish international humanitarian law, also known as the rules of war: The Geneva Convention for the Amelioration of the Condition of the Wounded in Armies in the Field.

Later conferences extended the laws of war to other categories, including principles for war at sea (Hague Convention of 1899) and for treatment of prisoners including their status (Geneva Conventions of 1907), the Hague Rules of Aerial Warfare of 1923, the Geneva Convention of 1929, and the International Military Tribunals of German War Criminals, which laid down the Nuremberg Principles of 1945. After Nazi war criminals were tried at Nuremberg at the end of World War II, the United Nations took the first step to combine previously established rules of war into four separate conventions. It also added provi-

German defendants at the Nuremberg Trials. The boxes beside the defendants give their surnames and sentences. Adolf Hitler's confidante Hermann Goering (center foreground) was sentenced to hang but managed to commit suicide before his sentence could be carried out. In contrast, Hitler's architect, Albert Speer (center rear) served his twenty-year sentence and afterward published a best-selling book, *Inside the Third Reich* (1970). *(AP/Wide World Photos)*

sions for the protection of civilians during armed combat in the Geneva Conventions of 1949.

The first of the four 1949 Geneva Conventions provided for the care of the wounded and sick combatants to eliminate torture, murder, and biological experiments. The second convention covered wounded, captured and sick combatants at sea. The third convention covered the humane treatment of prisoners of war, requiring that they be provided with adequate housing, food, clothing, and medical care and not be subjected to torture, medical experiments, acts of violence, or insults and public curiosity. The fourth convention was written to protect civilians. It requires all parties in military conflicts to distinguish between civilians and combatants and direct their operations only against military targets. Under that convention, civilians must be permitted to conduct their lives as normally as possible during wartime and to be protected against murder, pillage, torture, reprisals, indiscriminate harm, indiscriminate destruction of property, and being taken hostage. Combatants must also respect the honor, family rights, and religious freedoms of civilians. Military forces occupying captured territories are required to ensure the safe passage of food and medical supplies and establish safety zones for the wounded, sick, elderly, children, expectant mothers, and mothers of young children. Protocols added to the 1949 conventions added more protections guaranteed to civilians in international conflicts and extended protections to civilians in noninternational conflicts, such as civil wars.

In 1998, international humanitarian law was against expanded by the Rome Statute of the International Criminal Court (ICC). The International Criminal Court utilizes customary law, human rights law, and the Geneva Conventions to define what constitutes war crimes. However, there is no single unified convention or text for the laws of war.

The rules of war constitute a significant body of law aimed at constraining excessive violence and harm during conflicts. The essential body of law that defines war crimes has been expanded throughout history at specific historical contingencies. The rules of war also include two other components for regulating armed conflict behaviors that are crimes against peace and crimes against humanity. Although these crimes include war crimes, they encompass broader principles.

Legal Actions for War Crimes

Individual offenders who violate the rules of war may be criminally charged for "grave breaches" of the Geneva Conventions and their protocols and for other violations of the laws and customs of war. Nation-states can also be charged with war crimes and brought to justice. Charges leveled against one state by another are heard through the International Court of Justice at The Hague or through the establishment of a special international military tribunal. Examples of international tribunals include the Nuremberg Trials after World War II, the International Military Tribunals that followed the genocide in Rwanda, and the Former Yugoslavia International Military Tribunals.

There are several ways in which perpetrators of war crimes can be punished. Individuals accused of such crimes can be tried and punished by the states in which they are citizens. In the United States, offenders can be prosecuted for war crimes under the federal War Crimes Act of 1996. The U.S. Congress enacted this legislation to permit the United States to exercise its sovereignty by prosecuting its own citizens for breaches of international law. In 1997, the Expanded War Crimes Act amended and redefined the circumstances that were necessary for state prosecution and recognition of international law. Trials for war crimes can be conducted in both civilian and military courts.

International Monitoring Organizations

The primary oversight agency of war crimes is the International Red Cross, a nongovernmental humanitarian organization based in Geneva, Switzerland, that is considered the official guardian of international humanitarian law. When the Red Cross detects abuses, it notifies the offending states or organizations. If its notifications fail to bring relief, it publicly announces its grievances. The Red Cross is not empowered to take action itself but acts merely as a guardian.

Other nongovernmental organizations that monitor armed conflicts include Amnesty International and Human Rights Watch. Governmental organizations that may track war crimes include the United Nations Commission for Human Rights and the Coalition for a Criminal Court. These organizations oversee a larger body of international law that includes international human rights and international humanitarian law.

International human rights are principles articulated to help guide the behavior of states toward their own citizenry. Simply stated, human rights are stated expectations of inherent rights all persons should receive as human beings. Nonetheless, these nongovernmental organizations often document and publicly disclose war crime offenses as a component of human rights violations to bring this information to the general public as well as officials of nation-states.

Dawn Rothe

Further Reading

Bahmueller, Charles F., ed. *Human Rights Violations*. 3 vols. Pasadena, Calif.: Salem Press, 2003. Collection of more than one hundred articles on major incidents of human rights abuses during the twentieth century, including many articles on war crimes.

Bass, Gary. *Stay the Hand of Vengeance: The Politics of War Crimes Tribunals*. Princeton, N.J.: Princeton University Press, 2002. Critical study of international tribunals that pays special attention to the tribunals set up to try abuses of human rights in the former Yugoslavia and Rwanda.

Bassiouni, M. Cherif. *International Criminal Law*. 2d ed. Vol. 1. Ardsley, N.Y.: Transnational Publishers, 1999. Descriptive legal account of international criminal law with detailed commentaries.

Bassiouni, M. Cherif, and Veda Nanda. *A Treatise on International Criminal Law*. Vol. 1: *Crimes and Punishment*. Springfield, Ill.: Charles C Thomas, 1973. Descriptive account of international crimes and venues for punishment such as international military tribunals.

Cassesse, Antonio. "On the Current Trend Towards Criminal Prosecution and Punishment of Breaches of International Humanitarian Law." *European Journal of International Law* 9, no. 1 (1998): 2-19. Description of the current forms utilized for prosecution and penalization of war crimes, crimes against humanity, and crimes of peace.

Gutman, Roy, and David Rieff, eds. *Crimes of War: What the Public Should Know*. New York: W. W. Norton, 1999. Guide to war crimes for nonspecialist readers.

Neier, Aryeh. *War Crimes: Brutality, Genocide, Terror, and the Struggle for Justice*. New York: Times Books, 1998. Survey of human rights abuses throughout the world, with special attention to recent history.

Politi, Mauro, and Giuseppe Nesi, eds. *The Rome Statute of the International Criminal Court: A Challenge to Impunity*. Burlington, Vt.: Ashgate, 2001. Comprehensive description of the Rome Statute and relevant issues of international crimes.

Sadat, Lela. *The International Criminal Court and the Transformation of International Law: Justice for the New Millennium*. Ardsley, N.Y.: Transnational Publishers, 2002. Legal descriptive of the Rome Statute and its impact on international law.

See also Courts-martial; International law; International tribunals; Military justice; Treason; World Court.

Warren Commission

Identification: A government commission charged with investigating the circumstances of President John F. Kennedy's assassination

Date: Created November 29, 1963; issued final report September 24, 1964

Criminal justice issues: Government misconduct; investigation

Significance: The Warren Commission is widely regarded as having carried out its investigation poorly, thus leaving the door open for numerous theories as to who might have been involved in the assassination and why.

President John F. Kennedy was assassinated in Dallas, Texas, on November 22, 1963, while riding in a motorcade. Lee Harvey Oswald was

Warren Commission members, from left to right: Congressman Gerald R. Ford, Congressman Hale Boggs, Senator Richard Russell, Chief Justice Earl Warren, Senator John Sherman Cooper, New York banker John J. McCloy, former Central Intelligence Agency director Allen W. Dulles, and J. Lee Rankin, who served as the commission's general counsel. *(AP/Wide World Photos)*

charged with the assassination, but before he could be brought to trial he was in turn assassinated by Jack Ruby. A week after Kennedy's assassination, President Lyndon Johnson established a fact-finding commission to investigate the tragedy. He appointed Chief Justice Earl Warren to head the commission. Other members included Allen Dulles, Gerald Ford, and Arlen Specter. The commission was to determine whether Oswald had been a lone assassin or whether there were others involved.

The Warren Commission released its twenty-six-volume report in September, 1964. The commission concluded that Kennedy had been killed by a single assassin: Oswald had acted alone, and no domestic or foreign conspiracy was involved. Doubts about this conclusion surfaced immediately, and they have increased as the years have gone by. Substantial problems and oversights in

the commission's investigation show that the commission was at best inept and at worst trying to bend the evidence to prove that there was only one man involved. Based on the testimony of 552 people and on physical and photographic evidence, the Warren Report held that there was "no credible evidence" of a conspiracy. Oswald, it said, had shot Kennedy from the Texas Book Depository with a rifle he owned; Oswald's rifle ballistically matched a bullet found on a stretcher. Among the problems with this theory, however, are unanswered questions about the seemingly improbable angles and pattern of bullet wounds and the fact that a number of witnesses reported hearing a gunshot from a grassy knoll to the front and right of Kennedy.

The primary legacy of the Warren Commission has been to encourage distrust of "truth" as it is presented by government; subsequent events, including the Vietnam War and the Watergate hearings, added to this distrust. Shortly after the Warren Report, New Orleans district attorney Jim Garrison embarked on a personal crusade to uncover a conspiracy, but although he generated interest and publicity, he did not marshal convincing evidence of a plot. A congressional committee created in 1976 concluded that Kennedy was "probably" assassinated as the result of a conspiracy.

During the early 1990's, after the 1991 film *JFK* brought the issue to national prominence again, President Bill Clinton appointed a panel to release numerous documents relating to the assassination that Johnson had classified as secret. A number of facts came to light, but again, no concrete evidence of conspiracy emerged. Thousands of articles and books have tried to unravel the mystery. A number of theories have been proposed as to who might have been involved. One idea is that the CIA and/or Cuban leader Fidel Castro conspired with the Soviet Union to kill Kennedy; another is that organized crime planned the assassination.

Sterling Harwood

Further Reading

McKnight, Gerald. *Breach of Trust: How the Warren Commission Failed the Nation and Why.* Lawrence: University Press of Kansas, 2005.

Remington, Rodger A. *The Warren Report: Evidence v. Conclusions.* Philadelphia: Xlibris Corporation, 2003.

Warren Commission. *Investigation of the Assassination of President John F. Kennedy.* 26 vols. Washington, D.C.: Government Printing Office, 1964. Full report of the Warren Commission; also issued in a one-volume condensation.

See also National Commission on the Causes and Prevention of Violence; President, U.S.; Watergate scandal.

Watergate scandal

The Event: Scandal arising from a break-in at the Democratic national headquarters in Washington, D.C.'s Watergate Hotel and a subsequent cover-up by the Nixon administration that led to the resignation of President Richard M. Nixon

Date: June 17, 1972-August 9, 1974

Place: Washington, D.C.

Criminal justice issues: Government misconduct; political issues; robbery, theft, and burglary

Significance: Caused by the obstruction of justice committed by President Richard M. Nixon and several of his most influential assistants, the Watergate scandal created a constitutional crisis. Nixon denied personal involvement in the Watergate cover-up for more than two years, but after proof of his guilt was eventually revealed, he became the first U.S. president to resign from office.

During the spring of 1972, opinion polls indicated that President Richard Nixon would easily win reelection against the expected Democratic nominee, Senator George McGovern from South Dakota. Several members of the Committee to Reelect the President, however, did not want to take any chances. Wanting to learn of the strategy the Democrats planned to use in their campaign against Nixon, they decided to break into the national headquarters of the Democratic Party in Washington's Watergate Hotel. A custodian in the Watergate Hotel noticed a door ajar in the Democratic Party offices and notified the District of Columbia police, who arrested the would-be burglars. They were charged with breaking and entering.

Although three of the criminals, E. Howard Hunt, James McCord, and G. Gordon Liddy, worked for the Committee to Reelect the President, no one could prove at that time that any member of the Nixon administration had been involved in planning the break-in or in paying money to the seven defendants to remain quiet. More than two years later it was proved that on June 23, 1972, President Nixon himself had ordered the Central Intelligence Agency to interfere with the Federal Bureau of Investigation's probe of the break-in. Moreover, Nixon's main assistants, John Ehrlichman and Bob Haldeman, approved the secret payment of large sums of money to the seven defendants. Nixon clearly hoped that the defendants would not reveal the participation of their superiors in the break-in. Throughout the remaining months before the November, 1972, election, the cover-up was successful. President Nixon and his staff stated repeatedly that no one other than the seven defendants had been involved in the crime. Nixon won a landslide victory against Senator McGovern.

Judge Sirica's Role

During their trial in January, 1973, the defendants affirmed that they had acted alone, thereby committing perjury. The cover-up began to unravel in March, 1973, however, when the time came for federal district court judge John Sirica to sentence the five defendants who had pleaded guilty and the two whom the jurors had found guilty. Judge Sirica suspected that he had been lied to during the trial, and he was determined to do something to discover the truth. He offered the seven felons a choice: If they chose to cooperate with prosecutors and the recently formed Senate Select Committee on Presidential Campaign Activities, chaired by Senator Sam Ervin, Jr., from North Carolina, they would not serve much time in jail, but if they continued to be uncooperative, he would sentence each of them to forty-five years in federal prison, the maximum sentence permitted for their crime.

Judge Sirica's tactic astounded President Nixon's assistants in the White House, but it also produced the desired effect by persuading James McCord, one of the convicted felons, that it was in his self-interest to cooperate with Sirica. McCord wrote a letter to Sirica explaining that he and his partners had been paid to perjure themselves during the trial. McCord admitted that others had been involved in the cover-up. Nixon decided to continue to deny his personal involvement in the cover-up and to blame others in his administration for the scandal, which was threatening to endanger his presidency. He revealed a complete lack of loyalty to those who had served him faithfully for several years; he also abused his authority by the false claim of executive privilege to con-

ceal his own participation in the Watergate scandal. His contempt for the rule of law and his abuse of the great power of the White House caused some Americans to lose respect for the office of the presidency. Although Nixon strove mightily to remain in power, eventually even most members of his own party abandoned him. He was forced to resign in disgrace in August, 1974. Many unexpected events had occurred between Judge Sirica's decision in March, 1973, and Nixon's resignation in August, 1974.

The Special Prosecutor and the Senate Hearings

On April 30, 1973, Nixon accepted the resignations of Ehrlichman, Haldeman, his personal counsel John Dean, and Attorney General Richard Kleindienst, all of whom had participated in the cover-up. He appointed a well-respected Republican, Elliot Richardson, as his new attorney general and granted Richardson the authority to appoint an independent special prosecutor. Nixon badly misjudged the character of both Richardson and Archibald Cox, the new special prosecutor. He thought that he could somehow control them. Richardson was a Republican, and Cox was a Democrat (Cox was teaching law at Harvard University). Despite their political differences, neither Richardson nor Cox would compromise their ethical beliefs. Neither had political ambitions, and both were very honest lawyers. Soon after his appointment as special prosecutor, Cox made it clear that he would seek the truth, no matter where the search led him. Richardson strove to reestablish the integrity of the Department of Justice, which had been used for political purposes by Richard Kleindienst and his predecessor, John Mitchell.

After Senator Ervin's Select Committee began its hearings in May, 1973, it became clear that many morally questionable decisions had been made by influential people in the Nixon White House and that specific laws had most probably been violated by many members of his administration. It remained unclear whether President Nixon himself had been involved in the cover-up. Senator Howard Baker of Tennessee, the ranking Republican member of the committee, asked many witnesses what the president knew and when the president had learned of certain facts.

These hearings, which were televised live, persuaded the American public that the four Democratic and three Republican senators on the select committee were objectively seeking truth. Although many people believed that President Nixon must have known of the Watergate cover-up, there was no proof that he had committed the high crimes and misdemeanors that would justify removing him from office.

The White House Tapes

An unexpected revelation, one that would eventually produce the necessary proof of President Nixon's personal involvement in the criminal obstruction of justice, was made before the Ervin Committee on July 16, 1973, when Alexander Butterfield, who had previously served as an assistant in the White House, stated under oath that from 1971 until his departure from the White House on March 14, 1973, all conversations in the Oval Office had been secretly recorded and that these tapes had been kept by order of the president. Senators Ervin and Baker and Special Prosecutor Cox immediately understood that these tapes could provide incontrovertible proof of the president's innocence or guilt. In response to subpoenas from the Senate Committee and Archibald Cox, President Nixon invoked "executive privilege" and refused to turn over the relevant tapes.

The American public understood that President Nixon's actions had provoked a constitutional crisis. Would the United States remain a country governed by law, or would the president be free to disregard laws that displeased him? After Nixon's refusal to comply with the subpoena from Archibald Cox, the special prosecutor asked Judge Sirica to enforce this subpoena. Sirica did so, and the Federal Appeals Court of the District of Columbia upheld the validity of the subpoena in October, 1973. Unless the U.S. Supreme Court voted to overrule the decision of the appeals court, Nixon would have to turn over the relevant tapes or be held in contempt of court, which would most certainly cause his impeachment by the House of Representatives and removal from office by the Senate.

In a desperate attempt to put an end to the work of the special prosecutor, Nixon ordered Attorney General Richardson on Saturday, October 20, 1973, to fire Cox and to abolish the office of the special prosecutor. Both Attorney General Richardson and Assistant Attorney General William Ruckelshaus refused to implement this unethical order, and they were both fired by President Nixon. Robert Bork, then the U.S. solicitor general and third in command in the Department of Justice, complied with Nixon's wishes and fired Cox. This abuse of presidential power came to be known as the "Saturday night massacre." On November 1, 1973, President Nixon had to appoint yet another attorney general, Senator William Saxbe of Ohio. Leon Jaworski was appointed as

President Richard M. Nixon bidding farewell before boarding the helicopter that took him from the White House on August 9, 1974, the day his resignation took effect. *(AP/Wide World Photos)*

the new special prosecutor. President Nixon's attempt to destroy the independence of the American judicial system had failed, and he was even forced to agree that he would not attempt to fire special prosecutor Jaworski without the approval of Republican and Democratic leaders from the House and the Senate.

Nixon's Resignation

Although Richard Nixon would not resign for several months, it was clear that the end was near. President Nixon's special counsel, James St. Clair, asked the U.S. Supreme Court to reverse the decision of the Federal Appeals Court of the District of Columbia, but in a unanimous decision written by Chief Justice Warren E. Burger (*United States v. Nixon*), the U.S. Supreme Court affirmed on July 24, 1974, the decision of the lower court and ordered President Nixon to turn over the subpoenaed tapes to the special prosecutor. Nixon's guilt soon became obvious to almost everyone: In a conversation recorded on June 23, 1972, he had ordered the CIA to interfere with the FBI's investigation of the break-in. This action clearly constituted criminal obstruction of justice. By a vote of 27 to 11, the House Judiciary Committee under the chairmanship of Congressman Peter Rodino from New Jersey voted on July 27, 1974, to impeach President Nixon. All twenty-one Democrats on the committee as well as six of the seventeen Republicans voted for impeachment. When it was explained to President Nixon by such Republican leaders as Senators Hugh Scott of Pennsylvania and Barry Goldwater of Arizona that almost no Republicans would support him in either the House of Representatives or the Senate, Nixon finally decided to resign in order to avoid the public humiliation of being impeached by the House of Representatives and then removed from office by the Senate.

Vice President Gerald Ford was sworn in as president on August 9, 1974. On September 8, 1974, President Ford granted Richard Nixon a full pardon for all crimes that he had committed during his presidency. Many of Nixon's top assistants, including Ehrlichman, Haldeman, and Mitchell, were later convicted of their crimes and sentenced to prison. The Watergate scandal cast a long shadow over the presidency and to some extent—especially combined with the deep divisions caused by the Vietnam War—the government as a whole for many years. In particular, both politicians and the public were suspicious of presidential power, and special prosecutors were appointed on a number of occasions to investigate possible wrongdoing. Among the activities investigated by special prosecutors were the Iran-Contra scandal that tainted the Reagan and Bush administrations and the Whitewater allegations against Bill Clinton and members of his administration.

Edmund J. Campion

Further Reading

Bernstein, Carl, and Bob Woodward. *All the President's Men*. 2d ed. New York: Simon & Schuster, 1994. Updated edition of the best-selling 1974 journalistic exposé of the Watergate scandal by the reporters whose work helped to bring down the Nixon administration.

Doyle, James. *Not Above the Law: The Battles of Watergate Prosecutors Cox and Jaworski*. New York: William Morrow, 1977. Detailed study of the work of the special prosecutors both before and after Nixon's resignation.

Ervin, Sam, Jr. *The Whole Truth: The Watergate Conspiracy*. New York: Random House, 1980. Inside view of the Watergate scandal by the chairman of the Senate Select Committee on Presidential Campaign Activities,

Mankiewicz, Frank. *U.S. v. Richard M. Nixon: The Final Crisis*. New York: New York Times Books, 1975. Penetrating examination of Nixon's unsuccessful attempts to manipulate public opinion during the Watergate crisis.

White, Theodore H. *Breach of Faith: The Fall of Richard Nixon*. New York: Atheneum Press, 1975. Clear history of the Watergate scandal by a distinguished journalist who spent decades covering presidential politics.

Woodward, Bob. *Shadow: Five Presidents and the Legacy of Watergate*. New York: Simon & Schuster, 2000. Study of the impact of Watergate on Nixon's first five successors in the White House by the coauthor of the classic *All the President's Men*. Woodward examines the effects of post-Watergate ethics laws, Congress's altered views of the executive branch, and media treatment of the presidents.

See also Attorney general of the United States; Corporate scandals; Pardons; Political corruption; President, U.S.; Subpoena power; Warren Commission.

Weather Underground

Identification: Primarily student political organization that advocated revolution and guerrilla warfare
Date: Established in 1968
Criminal justice issues: Political issues; terrorism; violent crime
Significance: One of the most notorious radical organizations of its era, the Weather Underground advocated the violent overthrow of the U.S. government and called for war in the streets. By assassinating government officials and bombing governmental institutions, the organization became the target subject of intense and effective law-enforcement investigation and prosecution.

The turbulent 1960's saw the rise of many revolutionary groups in the United States. One of the best known of these was Students for a Democratic Society (SDS), which advocated revolution in the streets to stop the war in Vietnam. In 1968, SDS sponsored a demonstration against the war at Columbia University, where more than seven hundred students were arrested. Afterward, it became philosophically fractured, and a small but militant faction separated to form the Weathermen. This new group took its name from a Bob Dylan song lyric, "You Don't Need a Weatherman to Know Which Way the Wind Blows." During the early 1970's, the organization changed its name to Weather Underground.

Members of the Weather Underground believed that the only way to bring about change was through violence. They advocated guerrilla warfare, bombings, firebombings, and assassinations. The organization identified with other militant groups of the time, such as the Black Panther Party, and were philosophically aligned with North Vietnamese leader Ho Chi Minh. Meanwhile, the group continued its bombings and other guerrilla activities, steadily escalating its violent behavior. On March 6, 1970, several members of the group accidentally detonated a bomb in the basement of a brownstone home in Lower Manhattan. The blast killed three members and injured two others, who fled before police arrived.

The Weather Underground dissolved after North Vietnam won the Vietnam War and U.S. troops withdrew completely from Vietnam, thereby removing the organization's primary focus. Three decades later, several Weather Underground members remained in prison. Others, who have been released, continued to advocate resistance against the government, but not as militantly as they had during the 1970's.

Lawrence C. Trostle

Further Reading

Ayers, Bill. *Fugitive Days: A Memoir*. New York: Penguin Books, 2003.

Jacobs, Ron. *The Way the Wind Blew: A History of the Weather Underground*. New York: Verso, 1997.

Jones, Thai. *A Radical Line: From the Labor Movement to the Weather Underground, One Family's Century of Conscience*. New York: Free Press, 2004.

Varon, Jeremy. *Bringing the War Home: The Weather Underground, the Red Army Faction, and Revolutionary Violence in the Sixties and Seventies*. Berkeley: University of California Press, 2004.

See also Chicago Seven trial; Terrorism.

Weeks v. United States

The Case: U.S. Supreme Court ruling on use of evidence in criminal trials
Date: Decided on February 24, 1914
Criminal justice issues: Evidence and forensics; privacy; search and seizure
Significance: In order to enforce the privacy values of the Fourth Amendment, the Supreme Court ordered that illegally obtained evidence must be excluded from criminal trials in federal courts; this order is commonly called the "exclusionary rule."

After Fremont Weeks was arrested for illegally sending lottery tickets through the U.S. mail service, a federal marshal accompanied by a police officer, without a search warrant, broke into Weeks's private home and seized incriminating evidence. Although the defendant argued that the search and seizure contradicted the requirements of the Fourth Amendment, the resulting evidence was used to convict him in a federal district court. Weeks appealed his case to the Supreme Court.

Until the *Weeks* decision, American courts had followed the common-law practice of allowing federal prosecutors to use evidence unlawfully seized by law-enforcement officers. Many constitutional scholars had argued that the traditional practice encouraged governmental violations of liberties guaranteed in the Constitution, and they insisted that it was inconsistent with the Fourth Amendment's purpose of treating people's houses as their castles. Based on this point of view, the Supreme Court in *Boyd v. United States* (1886) criticized and implicitly rejected the common-law practice, but the Court stopped short of explicitly ruling the inadmissibility of evidence obtained illegally. The *Boyd* pronouncements on privacy values, without any means of enforcement, appeared to have no impact on the behavior of those who enforced the laws.

In *Weeks* an impatient Court unanimously required federal courts thereafter to apply the exclusionary rule in all criminal prosecutions. In the official opinion, Justice William Day declared that without the exclusionary rule, the Fourth Amendment was of "no value" and "might as well be stricken from the Constitution." The noble goal of punishing the guilty must not be used as an excuse to sacrifice the "fundamental rights" established by the Constitution. Day's opinion did not clearly articulate whether the application of the exclusionary rule was an individual right guaranteed by the Constitution or whether it was simply a judicial device developed to prevent unreasonable searches and seizures. Although these two views would continue to be debated by the Court, most justices have accepted Day's conclusion that the exclusionary rule is the only practical means of requiring government to conform to constitutional rules.

The immediate impact of the *Weeks* decision

was limited, because it did not apply to state courts, where most criminal prosecutions took place. When the Court ruled that the Fourth Amendment was binding on the states in *Wolf v. Colorado* (1949), the Court did not require states to follow the exclusionary rule, and until *Elkins v. United States* (1960), the so-called silver platter doctrine permitted federal prosecutors to make use of evidence illegally seized by agents of the states. Finally, in *Mapp v. Ohio* (1961), the Supreme Court required the application of the exclusionary rule in state courts. The exclusionary rule has always been controversial, for it sometimes makes it more difficult to prosecute criminals. Critics argue that there are alternative means of protecting the rights of the Fourth Amendment, but defenders reply that the alternatives do not provide effective protection.

Thomas Tandy Lewis

Further Reading

Barnett, Randy. "Resolving the Dilemma of the Exclusionary Rule: An Application of Restitutive Principles of Justice." *Emory Law Journal* 32 (1983).

Lynch, Timothy. "In Defense of the Exclusionary Rule." *Harvard Journal of Law and Public Policy* 23 (2000).

McWhirter, Darien A. *Search, Seizure, and Privacy.* Phoenix, Ariz.: Oryx Press, 1994.

Osborne, Evan. "Is the Exclusionary Rule Worthwhile?" *Contemporary Economic Policy* 17 (1999).

See also *Brown v. Mississippi*; *Chimel v. California*; Exclusionary rule; Fourth Amendment; Incorporation doctrine; *Mapp v. Ohio*; Search and seizure; Search warrants; Supreme Court, U.S.

White-collar crime

Definition: Crimes committed by corporations, government agencies, and corporate and government officials against criminal and regulatory laws

Criminal justice issues: Business and financial crime; government misconduct; white-collar crime

Significance: White-collar crime challenges popular assumptions about crime. By itself, it probably does more economic, physical, and social harm to the United States than all serious conventional crimes combined. Nevertheless, it is also the least controlled form of crime. Its existence demonstrates that the rich, as well as poor, commit crime; that crime can be committed by collectivities, as well as individuals; and that the powerful can influence the making of laws and the administration of justice to insulate themselves from culpability for their own offenses.

Ever since sociologist Edwin Sutherland introduced the term in his presidential address to the American Sociological Society in 1939, "white-collar crime" has been a controversial subject. More than sixty-five years later, many basic questions about white-collar crime remained unresolved. Among them are such questions as whether white-collar crime constitutes "real" crime, whether it produces physical as well as financial harm, whether its offenders should be treated as criminals, and what types of offenses should be included in the definition. These unresolved questions combined with the inherent complexity of many white-collar offenses, their relative invisibility, the wide dispersal of their victims, the difficulties of enforcement, and their historical neglect by academic criminology, have brought numerous attempts at redefinition.

Sutherland himself originally defined white-collar crime as offenses committed by persons of respectability and high social status in the course of their legitimate occupations. He was referring primarily to business crime at a time when American businesses were weakly regulated. As a result, what Sutherland called "socially injurious harms," were seen by some of his contemporary critics, such as sociologist Paul Tappan, as merely the consequences of normal business practices. In their view, what Sutherland called "white-collar crimes" were not criminal acts. Tappan himself argued that crimes can be committed only when acts violate criminal laws; to be criminals, offenders must be convicted by criminal courts of violating statutory laws. Thanks to the powerful influence that large businesses had over lawmakers and the public during that era, the kinds of practices to which Sutherland was alluding were not crimes, but Sutherland argued that they should be redefined as crimes. He also argued that repeat violators of regulatory statutes should be seen as corporate recidivists.

Elements of White-Collar Crime

Individuals, organizations, or government agencies committing white-collar crimes use the power, skills, and opportunities afforded by their otherwise legitimate occupations, professions, businesses, and public offices, to deceive their victims. Many white-collar crimes involve violations of trust to gain money, materials, or services by deceptive means. Other crimes are perpetrated to obtain political or social advantages. In the process victims may also suffer material, psychological, or physical harm, including death, as well as violations of their human rights.

While definitions of white-collar crime may differ, the concept rests on three essential criteria that are central to any definition of the term:

✓ Offenders must occupy legitimate occupational positions in society that constitute their primary activities. This criterion thus excludes officers in criminal enterprises, such as organized crime leaders, and makes it possible to avoid confusing activities of organizations such as the Mafia with those of corporations such as Enron.

✓ The crimes that white-collar offenders commit must involve the use of the power afforded to them through their legitimate positions, and they must use that power for the purpose of increasing the economic, political, or social standing of themselves, their organizations, or both. Moreover, that use must result in harm to one or more victims.

✓ Finally, both individuals and large groups of individuals can be either offenders or victims of white-collar crime. Thus white-collar crime focuses on systemic problems; on "bad barrels" (organizations and processes) as well as "bad apples" (individuals).

A controversial definitional issue is whether the concept of white-collar crime should apply exclusively to crimes committed by the powerful, or whether it should apply to crimes committed by any employees—regardless of their positions—in the course of their legitimate occupations. To address questions such as this, alternative terms have been proposed; however, the term "white-collar crime" has proven to have resiliency.

White-collar crime is generally seen as taking any of three basic forms: economic, physical, or political. Examples of white-collar crime that has produced economic harm include:

✓ antitrust price-fixing, as was formerly practiced by Standard Oil, General Electric, and Archer Daniels Midland
✓ consumer fraud, such as that which brought about savings and loan institution collapses during the 1980's and the 2001 Enron scandal
✓ charging for unnecessary services, as Sears formerly did in its auto repair stores
✓ charging or billing for unnecessary medical procedures—a common practice in Medicare and Medicaid fraud
✓ willfully deceptive advertising, such as Juicy Fruit's advertising a "100 percent" apple juice product that contained no apple juice
✓ corporate tax evasion
✓ illegal stock manipulations and insider trading, such as that made famous during the 1980's by Ivan Boesky and Michael Milken and in 2001 by Martha Stewart

The range of white-collar crimes that produce physical harm may be narrower than the range of white-collar economic crimes, but this category's potential for causing harm to human beings may be much greater. Examples of such crimes include:

✓ environmental pollution, such as that caused by the disastrous oil spill of the tanker *Exxon Valdez* off the coast of Alaska in 1989; a disaster that had even worse consequences was a lethal gas leak at the Union Carbide plant in Bhopal, India, in 1984 that killed more people than the September 11, 2001, terrorist attacks on the United States

✓ violations of worker health and safety standards, such as the failure to provide proper emergency exits for employees that resulted in the deaths of 146 workers in New York City's Triangle Shirtwaist Company factory fire in 1911 and 25 workers in North Carolina's Imperial Chicken plant in 1991
✓ unsafe production methods, such as the manufacture of asbestos by Johns-Manville
✓ food and drug violations, such as Jack-in-the-Box's selling of hamburgers with *Escherichia coli* (*E. coli*)
✓ manufacture of faulty or dangerous products, such as Ford Motor Company's Pinto model with gas tanks that were prone to explode

White-collar crimes that produce political harm may be the most difficult to identify and quantify. The most obvious example is the acceptance of bribes and kickbacks by politicians such as were taken by members of Congress in the Abscam scandal of the late 1970's and by a federal cabinet officer in the Teapot Dome scandal of the 1920's.

Corporate and Occupational Crime

In their 1994 study of criminal behavior, sociologists Marshall Clinard and Richard Quinney distinguished between "corporate" and "occupational" crime. They applied the former term to offenses committed by corporate officers, primarily on behalf of their corporations, and by corporations as a whole through their collective decisions, policies, and practices. They applied the term "occupational crime" to offenses committed by individuals, primarily for their own interests, in the course of their occupations.

Corporate crime has also been called business crime, organizational crime, elite deviance, crimes of privilege, and corporate deviance. Some scholars have referred to it as "crimes of the powerful" or "suite crime." In this context, the term "power" is meant to refer to the offenders' positions in society's occupational or class hierarchies, rather than to the use of power in actual offenses, such as the use of physical force, weapons, or threats.

The term "elite deviance" includes crimes perpetrated by governments—which are also called "state crime." Such crimes include bribery and corruption, police entrapment, systemic police corruption, invasion of privacy, improper medical experiments, human rights violations against citizens, and political repression of other nations.

In contrast, the term occupational crime is applied to offenses by officials, professionals, or employees—whether committed by individuals or by groups—against employers, employers' businesses, customers and clients, and the government. The utility of this term is limited by the fact that it lumps together individual crimes (motivated by personal gain) committed by persons in powerful occupational positions, such as lawyers, accountants, and executives, with crimes by lower-level workers. For this reason, some scholars differentiate between crimes of the occupationally powerful and those of the occupationally powerless and call offenses of the latter "blue-collar crimes."

The Impact of White-Collar Crime

Given the diversity and complexity of white-collar crime and its varied and dispersed victims, estimates of its economic costs vary enormously. An additional problem is the absence of systematically gathered data on corporate offenses and their costs—a shortcoming for which both governments and criminologists have received much criticism. An often-quoted figure for the cost of white-collar crime is $174-231 billion per year. However, that is merely an estimate made by a U.S. Senate judicial subcommittee during the 1970's.

Some experts put the annual dollar costs of white-collar crime at between five and twenty-five times the total cost of conventional crime. Consumer fraud is estimated to account for more than one-half of this cost. The 1980's savings and loan crisis alone is conservatively estimated to have cost about $500 billion, and about 70 to 80 percent of that cost is believed attributable to white-collar crime. The bankruptcy of the Enron energy corporation in 2001 resulted from the false and inflated financial statements its directors issued; that bankruptcy cost Enron's shareholders $60 billion and 4,200 employees lost their jobs.

During 1975-1976, Clinard and Peter C. Yeager

conducted a study of civil and criminal actions filed with twenty-five federal agencies against 477 of the largest manufacturing corporations and 105 of the largest wholesale and retail services in the United States. They found that 60 percent of the companies had at least one legal action against them, with an average of 4.2 violations. Multiple violators that averaged 23.5 violations each accounted for 13 percent of those charged (8 percent of all the corporations studied), and 38 companies committed 52 percent of all violations. Another study found that between 1975 and 1985, two-thirds of Fortune 500 companies had convictions on charges ranging from price fixing to hazardous waste dumping.

Contrary to popular belief, public opinion research has found that the majority of Americans regard certain white-collar crimes as more serious offenses than some conventional crimes and favor harsh punishments, including imprisonment, for white-collar offenders. A national household study conducted by the National White Collar Crime Center in 1999 found that increasingly members of the public were becoming more concerned about all forms of white-collar crime, particularly those involving both monetary losses and erosion of public trust. The same study also found that one in three U.S. households had been victimized by white-collar crimes in the previous year, but less than one in ten had reported the crimes to authorities. Respondents to the survey viewed white-collar crimes that caused physical harm—such as allowing tainted meat to be sold—as more serious than such street crimes as robbery that caused serious injury. Similarly, respondents regarded contractor fraud and embezzlement as more serious than street thefts that caused equal monetary losses. Respondents also regarded politicians who accepted bribes as substantially worse than the people who offered them the bribes. Likewise, respondents regarded medical professionals who filed false insurance claims as worse than patients who did the same.

The Criminal Justice Information Services of the Department of Justice found that between 1997 and 1999, selected white-collar crimes in the United States claimed 5.8 million victims—a figure that included individuals, businesses, financial institutions, government and religious organizations, and society as a whole. The study also reported that offenders were predominantly white, male, and in their late twenties to early thirties.

Overall, it took more than fifty years, from the time that Sutherland articulated the concept of "white-collar crime" for the public, politicians, criminologists, and corporations to acknowledge that the problem is both "real" and serious and to press for effective measures to control it.

Investigation

Detecting white-collar crime is inherently difficult. Its victims are often unaware of their own victimization, and independent audits of businesses and government agencies can be unreliable, even when they are not compromised. Many of the most egregious white-collar offenses have been detected as a result of the actions of individual "whistleblowers"—employees who detect wrongdoing and publicize their observations, as happened at Enron in 2001.

Lawrence Fox speaking at the annual meeting of the American Bar Association (ABA) in San Francisco in August, 2003; Fox protested a narrowly approved change in the ABA's ethics rules that permitted attorneys to blow the whistle on clients who they discover are keeping false books or looting their companies' treasuries. The ABA's policy board voted the change in its ethics rules in response to growing concern over white-collar crime; however, some attorneys objected to the change because it might compromise attorneys' ethical obligations to their clients. (AP/Wide World Photos)

Formal control of white-collar crime involves investigation, prosecution, and punishment. Because of the complexity of the crimes, investigation is unusually costly and time-consuming. Government investigators concerned with white-collar crime include a variety of federal regulatory agencies and the Federal Bureau of Investigation (FBI). The U.S. Department of Justice and state attorneys general prosecute these offenses.

Before the 1970's, the United States tried to deal with corporate and organizational wrongdoing through laws designed to control individual persons. That approach changed as new regulatory agencies were established and formal penalties were increased. However, the most relevant laws were still regulatory, rather than criminal, and they contained numerous loopholes that were the products of corporate lobbying when the

laws were being written. Moreover, enforcement agencies have been typically understaffed and have been particularly short of inspectors. In addition, corporations practice a politics of resistance and use preemptive public relations campaigns to confuse issues after revelations of wrongdoing emerge. They also take full advantage of extensive and expert legal advice and plead *nolo contendere* (no contest) to avoid civil liability in about three-quarters of the antitrust cases that lead to convictions.

Prosecution

It is difficult to establish the total numbers of arrests and convictions for white-collar crimes because government data are available only for selected offenses, such as fraud, counterfeiting, forgery, and embezzlement, as well as certain corporate crimes such as antitrust violations and government crimes such as corruption of public office. Furthermore, the disparate number of regulatory agencies makes it difficult to arrive at a cumulative assessment.

According to the U.S. Bureau of Justice Statistics, in 2001 there were 323,308 arrests in the United States for fraud. Of the people arrested, 68 percent were white, 31 percent were black, and 97 percent were over the age of eighteen years. Interestingly, 55 percent of fraud arrestees were male and 45 percent female. This is the highest proportion of female arrests for any kind of property offense except the white-collar crime of embezzlement, whose arrestees were 50 percent female. In 2002, 1,136 government officials were indicted for abuse of public office; 1,011 were convicted—a rate seven times higher than that of 1973.

In the 1980's, local prosecutors began prosecuting, at an increasing rate, economic crime, oc-

cupational safety and health violations, and illegal toxic dumping. However, they were limited by a lack of resources, the complex and technical nature of the offenses, the difficulty of establishing intent, and the reluctance of victims of the crimes to cooperate. By the mid-1990's, changes in the federal government had reversed the trend toward stronger enforcement and had weakened legislation by placing limits on penalties—many of which were already viewed as too inadequate to be effective. By 2001, after a rash of major corporate scandals, prosecutions and penalties again increased. However, some critics contended that this development was merely a symbolic and temporary increase.

In 2001, U.S. attorneys prosecuted 7,988 defendants charged with a variety of white-collar crimes, including various forms of fraud, antitrust violations, and bank embezzlement. This figure was a 40 percent increase over the 5,721

Former Enron chief executive officer Kenneth Lay reading a prepared statement to the U.S. Senate subcommittee investigating the Enron scandal in February, 2002. Lay announced that he would exercise his Fifth Amendment right not to answer questions that might incriminate him. (AP/Wide World Photos)

defendants prosecuted in 1992. The conviction rate for 2001 was 82 percent.

By contrast, Department of Justice data show that antitrust cases filed by the federal government in U.S. district courts dropped from 90 cases in 2000 to 44 in 2001. The government also filed 44 antitrust cases in both 2002 and 2003. These were the lowest figures since 1975. Meanwhile, of the 238 cases in 2001 in which U.S. district courts imposed fines and restitution on parties convicted of antitrust violations, bribery, fraud, embezzlement, money laundering, environmental pollution, and food, drugs, and agricultural violations, the average restitution order was $4 million and the average fine was $2.1 million.

In 2000, state courts convicted 82,700 defendants of fraud, forgery, and embezzlement. Ninety-eight percent of those convicted pleaded guilty; 59 percent were male and 41 percent female; 58 percent were white and 40 percent were black; and 97 percent were over twenty years of age, and the average age was thirty-three. Forty-six percent of those convicted received probation and 54 percent received prison or jail time, with average maximum sentences of 34 months; 27 percent of those convicted received additional penalties in the form of fines, 26 percent restitution, 8 percent treatment, and 6 percent community service.

Of the 5,262 persons serving federal sentences for fraud, embezzlement, and other white-collar offenses in 2000, the time actually served was 16 months; 13 months for tax fraud, but 19 months for regulatory offenses. Interestingly, while those released from federal prisons in 1994 had a reconviction rate of 19 percent and those released in 1986-1997 a rate of 13 percent, those released from state prisons for fraud had a reconviction rate of 42 percent.

Limits to Enforcement

Even at its best, enforcement of laws against white-collar crime has been lax and has had little follow-through. Sixty percent of convicted corporations do not pay their fines. This is reflected in public opinion surveys that reveal little confidence in big businesses. A national household survey on white-collar crime conducted in 1999 by the National White Collar Crime Center found

that 74 percent of the respondents believed that common robbers had a greater chance of being apprehended than fraudsters. Moreover, 84 percent of the respondents believed robbers would be punished more severely, although 69 percent believed that fraudsters should be punished equally or more severely. Likewise, 65 percent believed that the resources devoted to combating white-collar crime should be at least equal to, if not greater than, the resources devoted to combating street crime.

With regard to reforms, many call for increased funding for enforcement agencies, such as the Securities and Exchange Commission (SEC) and the Department of Justice's Corporate Crime Division and increasing the number of inspectors, random inspections, interagency cooperation, and independent research. More support is called for whistleblowing and some encourage employees to take video recorders into corporate board rooms. Others advocate changing American corporate structures—including the implementation of corporate chartering, licensing, and strict liability rules for executives—and making boards of directors directly accountable for a corporation's actions, granting shareholders the right to nominate and elect boards of directors, and requiring shareholder approval of major business decisions. Some favor banning federal contracts for serious or repeat corporate offenders. Sentencing suggestions include: use of negative publicity and public shaming, corporate divestiture, community and public service, and funding for research on prevention of white-collar crime.

One serious attempt to control corporate crime was the passage of the Sarbanes-Oxley Act by the U.S. Congress in 2002. It provides for overseeing accounting and auditing of publicly traded companies, and limits the ability of accounting firms to serve as both auditors and consultants for the same firms, while increasing the size of fines and the terms of incarceration. However, critics point out that this law was considerably weakened by corporate influence over Congress. Until political influence is curtailed—by controlling lobbyists, political action committees, and campaign financing—little sustainable reform is likely to occur.

Stuart Henry

Further Reading

Barnett, Cynthia. *The Measurement of White-Collar Crime Using Uniform Crime Reporting (UCR) Data*. Washington, D.C.: U.S. Department of Justice, FBI, CJIS Division, 2002. Federal government survey of statistics on white-collar crime.

Benson, Michael L., and Francis T. Cullen. *Combating Corporate Crime: Local Prosecutors at Work*. Boston: Northeastern University Press, 1998. Penetrating study of the role of local prosecutors in controlling corporate crime.

Clinard, Marshall B., Richard Quinney, and John Wildeman. *Criminal Behavior Systems: A Typology*. 3d ed. Cincinnati, Ohio: Anderson Publishing, 1994. Classic work on criminals that classifies offenders by the types of crimes they commit and provides some insights into people involved in organized crime.

Coleman, James William. *The Criminal Elite: Understanding White-Collar Crime*. 5th ed. New York: Worth Publishers, 2002. Discusses illegal acts committed by middle- and upper-class persons in conjunction with their ordinary occupational pursuits.

Ermann, M. David, and Richard J. Lundman, eds. *Corporate and Governmental Deviance*. 6th ed. New York: Oxford University Press, 2002. Excellent anthology on various dimensions of white-collar crime that has been a standard college text since the early 1980's.

Friedrichs, David O. *Trusted Criminals: White Collar Crime in Contemporary Society*. 2d ed. Belmont, Calif.: Wadsworth, 2003. Comprehensive textbook on white-collar crime by one of the leading authorities in the field.

Levi, Michael, and Andrew Pithouse. *Victims of White Collar Crime: The Social and Media Construction of Business Fraud*. New York: Oxford University Press, 2005. Study of the international dimensions of white-collar crime, with special attention to Great Britain, Australia, and developing nations, as well as the United States.

Podgor, Ellen S., and Jerold Israel. *White Collar Crime in a Nutshell*. 3d ed. St. Paul, Minn.: West, 2004. Broad study of white-collar crime that covers specific offenses in detail and also discusses punishments.

Reiman, Jeffrey H. *The Rich Get Richer and the Poor Get Prison: Ideology, Class, and Criminal Justice*. 7th ed. Boston: Pearson/Allyn and Bacon, 2004. Now a standard text, this book presents a powerful indictment of the criminal justice system's failure to address white-collar crime with the seriousness that it demands.

Rosoff, Stephen M., Henry N. Pontell, and Robert H. Tillman. *Profit Without Honor: White-Collar Crime and the Looting of America*. 3d ed. Upper Saddle River, N.J.: Prentice-Hall, 2004. Comprehensive study of white-collar crimes that includes extensive case studies.

Sutherland, Edwin. *White Collar Crime: The Uncut Version*. New Haven, Conn.: Yale University Press, 1985. Corrected reprint of the classic study of corporate crime first published in 1949. This edition presents Sutherland's text as he originally wrote it—complete, with the names of corporate offenders discussed in case studies.

See also Antitrust law; Computer crime; Consumer fraud; Corporate scandals; Embezzlement; Fraud; Identity theft; Insider trading; Mail fraud; Money laundering; Political corruption; Regulatory crime; Tax evasion; Teapot Dome scandal.

Whren v. United States

The Case: U.S. Supreme Court ruling on Fourth Amendment protections

Date: Decided on June 10, 1996

Criminal justice issues: Police powers; search and seizure

Significance: This Supreme Court decision upheld the authority of police officers to stop automobiles whenever there is probable cause of minor traffic violations, even if circumstances suggest that the officers are motivated by considerations of race or physical appearance of the motorists.

In what is considered a "high-drug area" of Washington, D.C., plainclothes officers in an unmarked vehicle noticed a truck occupied by two young African Americans who were waiting at a stop sign for about twenty seconds. The truck then turned without signaling and left the intersection at an excessive speed. When the officers stopped the truck—presumably to warn the driver about a possible traffic violation—they observed plastic bags that appeared to contain cocaine. The officers arrested the two men, who were later convicted of violating federal drug laws.

At trial, defense attorneys argued unsuccessfully that the evidence should be suppressed. Because plainclothes officers almost never enforce minor traffic violations, the attorneys asserted that the officers' justification for stopping the truck was pretextual. Indeed, the circumstances of the case strongly suggested that the officers were motivated by vague suspicions that were influenced by the location and race of the defendants. To prevent abuses such as racial profiling, the defense attorneys proposed an alternative test for automobile stops.

After reviewing the case, the Supreme Court unanimously upheld the original convictions and rejected the alternative test proposed by the defense. In the opinion for the Court, Justice Antonin Scalia wrote, "the decision to stop an automobile is reasonable where the police have probable cause to believe that a traffic violation has occurred." He argued that the Court's precedents had never held that the existence of probable cause depends on the subjective motivation of police officers. Although acknowledging that the Fourth Amendment prohibits selective law enforcement based on considerations such as race, Scalia could see "no reasonable alternative to the traditional common-law rule that probable cause justified a search and seizure."

Many civil libertarians criticized the *Whren* decision as inconsistent with the spirit of the Fourth and Fourteenth Amendments. The broad scope of the ruling allows the police almost unfettered discretion for deciding to stop select vehicles for minor traffic violations that would usually be ignored. After making stops, the police may then seize suspicious objects in plain view, check drivers for the smell of alcohol, frisk occupants for weapons based on reasonable suspicion, and request permission to search the entire vehicle.

Critics argue that the *Whren* holding provides a rationale for selectively investigating individuals based on an intuitive hunch rather than

probable cause. Such discretion is especially controversial because of evidence that officers sometimes engage in racial profiling, because of either unconscious bias or supervisors' instructions. Some African Americans complain that the decision has increased the practice of stopping drivers for "the crime of driving while black."

Thomas Tandy Lewis

Further Reading

O'Brien, David M. *Constitutional Law and Politics.* 6th ed. New York: W. W. Norton, 2005.

Whitebread, Charles, and Christopher Slobogin. *Criminal Procedures: An Analysis of Cases and Concepts.* 4th ed. New York: Foundation Press, 2000.

See also Automobile searches; Consent searches; Exclusionary rule; Fourth Amendment; Plain view doctrine; Racial profiling; Search and seizure; Supreme Court, U.S.

Wickersham Commission

Identification: Commission appointed by President Herbert Hoover to examine the enforcement of laws throughout the United States

Date: Created in 1929; issued final report in June, 1931

Criminal justice issues: Government misconduct; law-enforcement organization; professional standards

Significance: The first federal study of the administration of justice, the Wickersham Commission placed crime on the national public policy agenda.

Formally known as the National Commission on Law Observance and Enforcement, the government commission chaired by George Wickersham from 1929 to 1931 was created to conduct an objective, scientific study of the administration of justice because of public concern and distrust of the justice system that arose during the Prohibition era. The commission examined the police, courts, and corrections, and published its findings in a series of thirteen official reports.

The commission's findings of widespread official corruption and lawlessness, including a special condemnation directed at police for the use of the "third degree" or torture in interrogations, ignited intense public discussions and led to a series of Supreme Court decisions protecting the rights of those in custody. Identification of other critical problems—such as inadequate recruitment standards and inadequate training in law enforcement, inept and corrupt management, and invasive political influence—spawned the movement for professionalization of police.

The Wickersham Commission advocated a systems approach to criminal justice; endorsed probation, parole, and rehabilitation programs for offenders; and endorsed the development of a national system for collecting statistical data on crime. The commission's *Report on the Causes of Crime* held the seeds for sociological approaches to the study of crime and juvenile delinquency. Its analysis of the effects of inadequate enforcement of Prohibition and its encouragement of organized crime became the foundation for modern discourses on drug policies.

The commission's work is one of the most important events in the history of the American criminal justice system. The long-term effects of its recommendations continue to shape public policy and criminal justice procedures in the twenty-first century.

Susan Coleman

Further Reading

Calder, James D. *The Origins and Development of Federal Crime Control Policy.* Westport, Conn.: Praeger, 1993.

Friedman, L. M. *Crime and Punishment in American History.* New York: Basic Books, 1993.

Walker, Samuel. *Popular Justice: A History of American Criminal Justice.* 2d ed. New York: Oxford University Press, 1997.

See also Criminal justice in U.S. history; Organized crime; Peace Officers Standards and Training; Police brutality; Police corruption; Political corruption; Prohibition; Uniform Crime Reports.

Wilson v. Arkansas

The Case: U.S. Supreme Court ruling on Fourth Amendment protections

Date: Decided on May 22, 1995

Criminal justice issues: Constitutional protections; privacy; search and seizure

Significance: This Supreme Court decision held that police officers, when conducting searches, are normally expected to knock and announce their presence before entering private homes, except when special circumstances justify exceptions to this common-law requirement.

In 1992, Sharlene Wilson sold illegal drugs to undercover agents working for the Arkansas state police. Based on this information, police officers obtained warrants to arrest Wilson and search her home. When they arrived, the main door to the house was open and the screen door was unlocked. After entering the house without knocking, the officers notified her of the warrants. They placed her under arrest, and their search uncovered substantial amounts of illicit narcotics.

At Wilson's trial, her defense attorneys entered a motion to have the evidence collected in her home suppressed. They asserted that the search had been unconstitutional because the police had ignored the common-law obligation of knocking and announcing their presence and authority before entering a private home. The motion was denied, and Wilson was found guilty. After Arkansas's highest court upheld the conviction, the U.S. Supreme Court agreed to review the case.

A unanimous Supreme Court held that the knock-and-announce principle is a significant part of an inquiry into whether a search-and-seizure passes the reasonableness standards of the Fourth Amendment. In writing the official opinion in the case, Justice Clarence Thomas referred to a long-standing endorsement of the knock-and-announce principle in the common law, combined with a wealth of founding-era commentaries, statutes, and cases supporting the principle. Based on this history, Thomas concluded that an unannounced entry into a home is unreasonable in most circumstances.

However, the Court's opinion also acknowledged that the common-law principle has never been applied as an inflexible rule that requires announcement before entry in all situations. Law enforcement may be faced with exigent circumstances, including a credible threat of physical harm to the police or reasons to believe that physical evidence would probably be destroyed if advance notice were given. The Court therefore remanded the case back to the state courts and directed the judges to consider whether the police had a reasonable justification for neglecting to knock and announce their presence before entering Wilson's home. If the police were unable to articulate a strong rationale, the conviction of Wilson would be rendered invalid, and in the event of another trial, prosecutors would not be able to introduce the seized narcotics as evidence. The *Wilson* ruling sent a firm message to law-enforcement officers not to ignore the principle of knock-and-announce.

Thomas Tandy Lewis

Further Reading

Franklin, Paula. *The Fourth Amendment.* New York: Silver Burdett Press, 2001.

LaFave, Wayne R. *Search and Seizure: A Treatise on the Fourth Amendment.* 3d ed. St. Paul, Minn.: West Publishing, 1996.

O'Brien, David M. *Constitutional Law and Politics.* 6th ed. New York: W. W. Norton, 2005.

Wetterer, Charles M. *The Fourth Amendment: Search and Seizure.* Springfield, N.J.: Enslow, 1998.

See also Arrest warrants; Fourth Amendment; No-knock warrants; Search and seizure; Search warrants; Supreme Court, U.S.

Wiretaps

Definition: Electronic surveillance method of eavesdropping by a third party to monitor or record communications of individuals or groups under investigation

Criminal justice issues: Investigation; privacy; technology

The Patriot Act

Title III of the Patriot Act of 2001 permits law-enforcement officers to enter buildings covertly for the purpose of installing the listening devices needed for electronic surveillance. However, covert entry is authorized only when Title III warrants are issued. To obtain warrants, law-enforcement officers must show:

✓ Probable cause that specific offenses are about to occur, have occurred, or are occurring.

✓ That evidence is likely to be obtained by the intercept or wiretap.

✓ That all other investigative techniques either have failed or will fail to provide the necessary evidence, or that they are too dangerous to employ.

✓ That the locations of the proposed wiretaps are sites of criminal activity.

✓ That telephones are being used to conduct criminal activity at those sites.

Significance: Wiretaps can be effective law-enforcement tools for gathering information that helps identify criminal activity and often lead to successful prosecutions; however, they are controversial because they have often been used illegally and pose the threat of increasing government intrusions on privacy.

Federal law-enforcement agencies, such as the Federal Bureau of Investigation and the Drug Enforcement Administration, and more than thirty-two states allow electronic interception of conversations. Intercepted conversations may include oral, wired, or cellular transmissions. During the early years of the twenty-first century, the number of court-ordered interceptions ranged from slightly more than six hundred to as many as one thousand per year. All such intercepted conversations are legally required to be reported to the administrative office of the U.S. Courts, which makes an annual report to the Congress. A device called a pen register, which records the telephone numbers called and requires judicial approval, is often used to provide probable cause for the wiretap.

By the 1960's, technology had been developed that was being used frequently by both law-enforcement officers and private detectives to monitor telephone conversations of individuals who had a reasonable expectation of privacy. In response to complaints about such activity, Congress passed Title III of the Omnibus Crime Control and Safe Streets Act of 1968. That law established guidelines and standards for both federal and state law enforcement and still governs actions of court-ordered wiretaps.

In 2001, Congress passed the Patriot Act, which expanded powers granted to law-enforcement agencies by the Foreign Intelligence Surveillance Act of 1978 to gather foreign intelligence information. Title III of the new law allowed wiretaps to be used to investigate possible terrorism within the United States. These powers included roving wiretaps, which allow electronic surveillance to continue even after suspects change their telephones, venues, or Internet accounts. Title III also prohibits all private wiretaps.

Enforcement

The President's Commission on Law Enforcement and Administration of Justice, the President's Commission on Organized Crime in 1983, the Pennsylvania Crime Commission, and the McClellan Committee of the late 1950's all concluded that traditional law-enforcement methods were not effective against complex criminal organizations such as the Mafia, South American drug cartels, triads, outlaw motorcycle gangs, and—in the twenty-first century—terrorists. Wiretaps have been successful, when combined with traditional law-enforcement methods, against such crime bosses as John Gotti (the head of the Mafia's Gambino family) and Pablo Escobar (the head of Colombia's Medellin drug cartel).

Leaders of criminal organizations have traditionally been skilled at insulating themselves against arrest and prosecution, typically by having others in their organizations carry out their criminal acts. The leaders usually engage in conversations with their subordinates only when

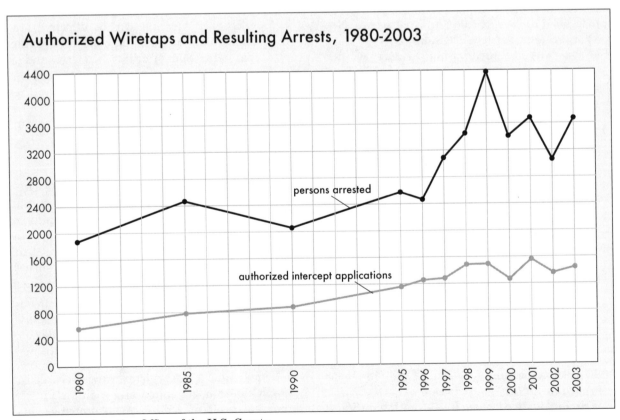

Source: Administrative Office of the U.S. Courts.

giving them orders or discussing criminal activities. Telephones are frequently used as communication devices and thus are excellent sources of evidence that can be intercepted by wiretaps.

Wiretaps can be very expensive, owing to the legal requirements requiring the presence of two monitors, in addition to the officers who actually conduct the surveillance of the suspects. The monitors are necessary for the corroboration and identification of callers. Electronic monitoring also often entails overtime wages, expensive equipment and training, and the costs of transcribing recordings. Monitors also take notes that are part of the record and are used to verify what is said on the communication devices. Monitors must be alert to noticing when conversations are not criminal so that they can stop recordings when conversations have no evidentiary value.

Wiretapping is a complex operation requiring analytical, legal, and technological expertise. Moreover, because many conversations are conducted in codes, analysts experienced in decoding may be required. Intelligence analysts synthesize information to develop probable cause to obtain judicial approval of a wiretap order/warrant. Targets of wiretaps must be notified that their conversations have been intercepted within ninety days after termination of the judicial orders. Most orders permit wiretaps for thirty days and require judicial reviews for extensions.

Wiretaps often collect valuable evidence that is used against major violators, but they sometimes produce little or no useful evidence. They can be potent tools in the arsenal of criminal investigation, but tools that require considerable thought and planning before they are implemented.

Stephen L. Mallory

Further Reading

Adams, James A., and Daniel D. Blinka. *Electronic Surveillance: Commentaries and Statutes*. Notre Dame, Ind.: National Institute for Trial Advocacy, 2003. Practical survey of legislation relating to surveillance since September 11, 2001, including issues relating to wiretapping.

Brzezinski, Matthew. *Fortress America: On the Frontline of Homeland Security—An Inside Look at the Coming Surveillance State*. New York: Bantam Books, 2004. Critical examination of the new Department of Homeland Security and the post-September 11 sacrificing of civil liberties in the name of national security.

Diffie, Whitfield, and Susan Landau. *Privacy on the Line: The Politics of Wiretapping and Encryption*. Cambridge, Mass.: MIT Press, 1999. Examination of the growing need for more secure methods of electronic communication.

Keefe, Patrick Radden. *Chatter: Dispatches from the Secret World of Global Eavesdropping*. New York: Random House, 2005. Critical examination of the failings and potential for abuse in the global electronic surveillance network used by the United States to protect national security.

Schulhofer, Stephen J. *The Enemy Within: Intelligence Gathering, Law Enforcement, and Civil Liberties in the Wake of September 11*. New York: Century Foundation Books, 2002. Examination of the wide-ranging new surveillance and law-enforcement powers acquired by the federal government that have eroded civil liberties.

See also Comprehensive Crime Control Act; Electronic surveillance; Espionage; Fourth Amendment; Gangsters of the Prohibition era; Omnibus Crime Control and Safe Streets Act of 1968; Organized crime; Organized Crime Control Act; Patriot Act; Privacy rights; Surveillance cameras.

Wisconsin v. Mitchell

The Case: U.S. Supreme Court ruling on hate crime and free expression

Date: Decided on June 11, 1993

Criminal justice issues: Constitutional protections; hate crime

Significance: This hate crime case was the first of its type to be heard by the U.S. Supreme Court; this landmark decision has opened the way for more extensive hate crime legislation, and it signals that such legislation will be upheld as constitutional by the Court in most cases.

Following a showing of the 1988 film *Mississippi Burning*, several African American men and boys congregated in a Wisconsin apartment complex to talk about the film. After discussing a scene from the film in which a young African American boy is beaten by a white man, Todd Mitchell asked those who joined him outside if they were ready to go after a white man. Meanwhile, walking on the opposite side of the street and saying nothing, fourteen-year-old Gregory Riddick approached the complex. Mitchell selected three individuals from the group to go after Riddick. The victim was beaten, and his tennis shoes were stolen.

In a Kenosha, Wisconsin, trial court, Mitchell was convicted as a party to the crime of aggravated battery. By Wisconsin law, this crime carries a maximum prison sentence of two years. Mitchell's sentence was extended to four years, however, under a state statute commonly known as the hate crimes statute. This statute provides for sentence extensions if it can be determined that the victims have been selected because of their race, religion, color, disability, sexual orientation, national origin, or ancestry.

Mitchell appealed his conviction and the extended sentence. His conviction was upheld by the court of appeals, but the Supreme Court of Wisconsin reversed the decision of the appellate court. The top Wisconsin court held that the hate crimes statute violated the defendant's First Amendment protection for freedom of speech because it was unconstitutionally overbroad and punished only what the state legislature found to be offensive. Moreover, the state supreme court believed that this statute would have a "chilling effect" on a citizen's freedom of speech; that is, a citizen would fear reprisal for actions which might follow the utterance of prejudiced or biased speech.

The U.S. Supreme Court reversed the state court's decision. Chief Justice William Rehnquist wrote the opinion in this unanimous decision. The Court held that Mitchell's First Amendment rights to free speech had not been violated. The Court pointed out that the statute was aimed not at speech but at conduct, which is not protected by the First Amendment. The Court also addressed the "chilling effect" of the statute, finding that such would not be the case and that the state supreme court's hypothesis was far too speculative to be entertained. This decision indicates that the Supreme Court appears ready to uphold

legislation designed to enhance punishment for criminal acts based on bigotry and bias without making bigoted or biased speech itself a crime.

Donna Addkison Simmons

Further Reading

Bell, Jeannine. *Policing Hatred: Law Enforcement, Civil Rights, and Hate Crime.* New York: New York University Press, 2002.

Gerstenfeld, Phyllis B. *Hate Crimes: Causes, Controls, and Controversies.* Thousand Oaks, Calif.: Sage Publications, 2004.

Levin, Jack. *The Violence of Hate: Confronting Racism, Anti-Semitism, and Other Forms of Bigotry.* Boston: Allyn & Bacon, 2002.

Perry, Barbara. *In the Name of Hate: Understanding Hate Crimes.* New York: Routledge, 2001.

Streissguth, Thomas. *Hate Crimes.* New York: Facts on File, 2003.

See also Hate crime; *R.A.V. v. City of St. Paul*; Supreme Court, U.S.

Witherspoon v. Illinois

The Case: U.S. Supreme Court ruling on juries in capital punishment cases

Date: Decided on June 3, 1968

Criminal justice issues: Capital punishment; juries

Significance: In this groundbreaking decision, the Supreme Court decided that prospective jurors with reservations about the death penalty could not be excluded from service in criminal proceedings.

The Sixth Amendment to the U.S. Constitution guarantees accused citizens the right to trial by an impartial jury of peers. This deceptively simple guarantee has come under fire in cases too numerous to mention. During the 1960's, many noteworthy cases advanced to the Supreme Court regarding the composition and unanimity of the jury in criminal cases. In 1968, the *Witherspoon* case compounded the jury-selection question with the issue of capital punishment.

Using an Illinois statute, the prosecution at

William Witherspoon's murder trial in Cook County, Illinois, eliminated almost half of the potential jurors by challenging those who had reservations about their ability to impose a death sentence. This exclusion occurred without any determination of the level of reservation; that is, the potential jurors were excluded for any degree of uncertainty about imposition of a death sentence. The defendant, Witherspoon, appealed his case on the grounds that such a broad exclusion of jurors prevented him from being tried by an impartial jury as guaranteed in the Sixth Amendment. Witherspoon claimed that a jury absent of those opposed or at least uncertain about capital punishment would under no circumstances be impartial or representative of the community.

The Supreme Court agreed in a majority opinion written by Justice Potter Stewart. Witherspoon's death sentence was voided by the Court; however, his conviction was not overturned. The Court agreed with the defendant that a jury devoid of objectors to capital punishment was sure to be "woefully short" of the impartiality guaranteed by the Sixth Amendment and extended to the states under the Fourteenth Amendment. In the majority opinion, the Court stated that those prospective jurors who expressed a total disinclination toward ever imposing the death penalty could be excluded; however, persons who merely had reservations in the matter could not be excluded for their reservations alone.

The Court went on to state that juries must attempt to mirror the feelings of the community. In any given community there will be a certain number of people who are unsure of their feelings about capital punishment. This point of view should not be avoided in jury selection, the Court ruled, as inclusion of such undecided jurors will ensure neutrality on the sentencing issue and will allow the jury more adequately to reflect the conscience of the community.

While ruling that a jury totally committed to the imposition of the death penalty cannot be selected deliberately, as this would deprive a defendant of life without due process, the Court did not issue a constitutional rule that would have required the reversal of every jury selected under the Illinois statute. The Court did not state that a jury composed of persons in favor of capital punishment would be predisposed to convict, only

that such a jury would be predisposed in the sentencing element of a trial.

The *Witherspoon* decision was an early test of the Supreme Court's position on capital punishment as well as on jury composition and selection. The Court indicated its willingness to uphold criminal convictions while examining the sentencing procedures being used in the states. At no point in its opinion did the Court express disfavor for the death penalty; rather, the opinion targeted only the constitutional implications of the jury-selection process. In other words, the *Witherspoon* decision indicated that within constitutional bounds, communities would be left to choose whether or not to impose the death penalty.

Donna Addkison Simmons

Further Reading

Bohm, Robert M. *Deathquest: An Introduction to the Theory and Practice of Capital Punishment in the United States*. Cincinnati: Anderson Publishing, 2003.

Carter, Linda E., and Ellen Krietzberg. *Understanding Capital Punishment Law*. Newark, N.J.: LexisNexis, 2004.

Latzer, Barry, ed. *Death Penalty Cases: Leading Supreme Court Cases on Capital Punishment*. 2d ed. Burlington, Mass.: Butterworth Heinemann, 2002.

Sarat, Austin. *When the State Kills: Capital Punishment and the American Condition*. Princeton, N.J.: Princeton University Press, 2001.

See also Capital punishment; Criminal law; Criminal procedure; Death qualification; Jury system; Supreme Court, U.S.

Witness protection programs

Definition: Government programs designed to ensure the safety of key witnesses during and after court proceedings

Criminal justice issues: Crime prevention; trial procedures; witnesses

Significance: Witness protection programs provide security for witnesses whose testimony is critical in important court proceedings.

Witness Protection in Canada

Canada passed its own Witness Protection Program Act in 1996. A wealth of information on this law and its application can be found on the Canadian Department of Justice Web site, at laws.justice.gc.ca/en/W-11.2.

Some U.S. states have developed state-managed witness protection programs. The most frequently used program is the federal Witness Protection Program. Since the program's inception, under Title V of the Racketeer Influenced and Corrupt Organizations (RICO) Act of 1970, as a tool to combat organized crime, more than five thousand witnesses have been part of the Witness Protection Program. Beyond providing for the safety of witnesses, the program also provides for the health, relocation, psychological welfare, and social adjustment of witnesses. Federal protection through the Witness Protection Program has been extended to provide protection for any witnesses and their families who are recommended to the attorney general by a state U.S. attorney's office. After the program was evaluated by the Witness Security Review Committee in 1977, the Witness Security Reform Act, part of the Comprehensive Crime Control Act of 1984, was adopted to correct a number of deficiencies that existed in the original 1970 act.

A victim's compensation fund was established through an adjustment made to the Witness Protection Program by the Reform Act. This fund compensates persons or beneficiaries for death or physical injury that may occur during relocation. However, injuries that occur to witnesses cannot be used as a cause of action against the United States. Also, for those witnesses who are sentenced to and remain in prison, placement in one of the five protected witness units in special areas of federal penitentiaries is necessary. Located throughout the country, these units are operated by the federal Bureau of Prisons.

Guidelines and Procedures

Before accepting witnesses in the Witness Protection Program, the attorney general considers the danger in which a community will be placed if a witness is relocated there. The safety of the town or region must be considered, because many of the witnesses in the program are criminals who, in exchange for revealing information, are provided with protection and a reduction in fines or prison time. However, the significance of witnesses' testimony may outweigh the danger in which the witnesses place the community. Witnesses and those close to them must have their criminal histories reviewed and pass a psychological examination.

The attorney general, with aid from the U.S. marshals, assists witnesses accepted into the program in a variety of ways. Witnesses may be provided with new identities, including new names and social security cards. Those involved in the program may then use the new information to obtain other pieces of identification, such as driver's licenses. Consequently, witnesses' birth identities cease to exist in the public domain, and the records of witnesses' birth identities are turned over to the marshals service.

Once the decision to relocate a witness is made, local law-enforcement officials are notified that there is a protected witness in their territory. A relocation inspector is provided to witnesses to help them adjust to their new locations and identities. The inspector advises the witnesses about improved living strategies, such as answering people's questions about the past. The witnesses are also provided with housing. For some, this may be a temporary safe house; for others, it may be a new permanent location. The transportation of previously owned household furniture and personal property to the witnesses' new locations may also be provided. However, the type of personal property relocated with the witnesses is regulated, because certain personal items could connect the witnesses to their previous identities.

The witnesses are provided with a stipend to meet basic living expenses. The amount and duration of the stipend are regulated by the attorney general. Once witnesses are able to support themselves, monetary aid ceases. They are also assisted with obtaining employment. Although employment aid from the government entails paying for job training, government aid does not include providing false job résumés or references. Beyond these specific guidelines, witnesses generally are assisted in other ways that are necessary to achieve independence. The decision to reveal or not to reveal witnesses' identities or locations is made by the attorney general after weighing the danger to the witnesses, to the public, to the success of the program, and to the forthcoming trial. However, the attorney general must reveal any requested information if ordered to do so by the court.

Witness Agreement

Once approved for the program, witnesses must sign a memorandum of understanding with the attorney general. The memorandum of understanding includes the agreement to testify and to provide information related to the proceedings to appropriate law-enforcement officials. To provide for the safety of the community, protected witnesses must agree not to commit any crimes and to take necessary steps to avoid detection. The witnesses must comply with legal obligations and civil judgments and must cooperate with reasonable requests of government employees who are involved in the protection process. Witnesses are allowed to designate persons to serve as their agents, who make sworn statements regarding the witnesses' legal obligations, such as child custody and any outstanding debts. Witnesses are also advised to resolve the issue of child custody before entering the program, ensuring that their children's best interests are considered in making a decision. Protected witnesses must inform witness protection officials of probation and parole responsibilities, of other activities, and of their current addresses.

Memorandums of understanding are entered into with all participants in the protection program who are over eighteen years of age. Before completing the evaluation that determines whether witnesses qualify for the program, the attorney general may decide to provide protection to witnesses immediately. Immediate protection is necessary in situations in which the lack of immediate protection would harm the investigation. The attorney general also has the power to terminate the protection of the witnesses if the memorandum of understanding is breached or the witnesses provide false information. The decision to terminate protection is not open to judicial review.

Kim Kochanek

Further Reading

Earley, Pete, and Gerald Shur. *WITSEC: Inside the Federal Witness Protection Program*. New York: Bantam Books, 2002. Inside view of the federal Witness Protection Program, based on Shur's twenty-five-year career as an attorney in the Department of Justice.

Fyfe, Nicholas R. *Protecting Intimidated Witnesses*. Aldershot Burlington, Vt.: Ashgate, 2001. Detailed study of a witness protection program in Great Britain, with emphasis on Scotland.

Hill, Henry, with Gus Russo. *Gangsters and Goodfellas: The Mob, Witness Protection, and Life on the Run*. New York: M. Evans, 2004. Firsthand account of a former criminal living under the Witness Protection Program by the man whose criminal life was dramatized in the film *Goodfellas* (1990).

Sabbag, Robert. "The Invisible Family." *New York Times Magazine* (February 11, 1996). Offers a personal understanding of the witness protection program and general information.

See also Immunity from prosecution; Marshals Service, U.S.; Organized crime; Testimony; Witnesses.

Witnesses

Definition: Persons whose testimony under oath or affirmation is received as evidence in courts of law or in depositions

Criminal justice issues: Evidence and forensics; trial procedures; witnesses

Significance: Under the common law, witnesses should speak only what they know firsthand and testify only as to facts. That is, they cannot offer opinions, make inferences, or draw conclusions.

The rule requiring firsthand personal knowledge has been preserved by the Federal Rules of Evidence (FRE). Because the meaning of the key terms "fact" and "opinion" is often unclear, the FRE have also liberalized the admissibility of lay opinions. Lay opinions are now allowed whenever they would be helpful, provided that they are rationally based on the witness's perceptions. The latter requirement simply means that the witness must have firsthand (personal) knowledge of the matter at issue. Thus, witnesses are allowed to say that a person was (or appeared to be) angry, kidding, dying, strong, sober, or drunk. Speed may be estimated, even sometimes in such terms as fast or slow. Other examples include "It was a sturdy fence" and "The apple was rotten."

The requirement of firsthand knowledge should not be confused with the hearsay rule. If a witness states "Jack shot Mary" but knows this only from others, the witness violates the firsthand personal knowledge rule. If the same witness in the same circumstances testifies that "Joe told me Jack shot Mary," the firsthand rule is not violated, but the hearsay rule may be violated. Hearsay rules govern the admissibility of a declarant's out-of-court statements. Accordingly, hearsay may be recounted in court pursuant to an exception or exemption; in such instances, the lack of firsthand knowledge would affect the weight rather than the admissibility of the witness's testimony.

Incompetency or Disqualification of Witnesses

Competent witnesses are those who testify to what they have seen, heard, or otherwise observed. Trial courts recognize two kinds of witness incompetencies that result in automatic disqualification: lack of personal knowledge and failure to take the oath or affirmation regarding telling the truth.

In the past, witnesses have been ruled incompetent because they have personal interests in cases, past criminal convictions, drug or alcohol intoxication or addiction, marital relationships with involved parties, or mental incapacity. Moreover, persons who are too young may be disqualified as witnesses. Such matters are mainly deemed factors to consider for whatever they are worth in the realms of relevance and credibility.

Persons who are to be offered as witnesses are often subjected to a special series of questions (of-

---

Attorneys as Witnesses

Inherit the Wind, a 1960 film directed by Stanley Kramer, is a fictional re-creation of the famous Scopes "monkey" trial of 1925, when a high school biology teacher was charged with violating a Tennessee state law prohibiting the teaching of evolution in classrooms. The film's climactic moment occurs when the counsel for defense (Spencer Tracy), a lawyer modeled on Clarence Darrow, cross-examines the prosecutor (Fredric March), who is modeled on the historical William Jennings Bryan. Such an occurrence is highly unusual in trials, but the film scene is based on an actual courtroom confrontation between Darrow and Bryan. Lawyers are not generally permitted to serve as both advocates and necessary witnesses in cases, except in matters of what would considered noncontroversial issues—such as the fees they are entitled to be paid for their work in cases.

Timothy L. Hall

---

ten outside the presence of the jury) to ascertain foundational facts. This series of questions is to determine whether prospective witnesses understand the duty to tell the truth, can distinguish fact from fantasy, and have the ability to communicate meaningfully with the jury. Children over six years old are rarely found to be incompetent. Although state laws may differ, the FRE generally treat children, at least in principle, no differently from other witnesses. These rules allow for the exclusion of child witnesses only for compelling reasons, which must be something other than mere age.

Witness Preparation and Sequestration

There are almost no formal limits on bona fide efforts to prepare a prospective witness for taking the witness stand. Thus, in preparing to testify, a witness may review documents, recordings, notes, and other pieces of documentation. The witness may also be rehearsed by attorneys but not prompted to tell an untruth.

In most jurisdictions there is a process called "sequestration," whereby witnesses may be prevented from listening to other testimony in the case. Questions have arisen as to whether this bars trial witnesses from reading transcripts, attending depositions, listening to oral reports of what transpired at hearings, or watching televised portions of trials. The Oklahoma bombing trials of the late 1990's raised the question as to whether families of the deceased victims were permitted to view the trial if they planned to give victim-impact statements at the death-penalty sentencing phase. The trial judge, upheld by the court of appeals, concluded that they could not. The U.S. Congress then legislated, specifically with retroactive effect, that such witnesses in such cases could view the trials.

Additionally, the FRE exempts from sequestration witnesses who are parties, the designated representatives of organizations that are parties, or essential persons, such as experts needed at counsel's table to assist the attorneys. This rule also requires the judge to enter a sequestration order upon an attorney's request or upon the judge's own motion. The judge's order serves to clarify the scope of witness sequestration in a particular case.

Procedure for Examining Witnesses

The basic pattern of trials after jury selection and the opening statements of counsel is that plaintiffs present their cases through witnesses, documents, and other evidence. Then the defendants present their cases, which may consist of both denying facts asserted in the plaintiffs' cases and establishing affirmative defenses.

A witness presented at either phase will normally be examined directly by the attorney presenting the witness, by the attorney from the opposing side during cross-examination, by the proponent to redirect examination and repair the damage caused during cross-examination, and finally by the opposing attorney in a second cross-examination to repair the damage of the proponent. In the absence of an exercise of the judge's discretion, repair is the only acceptable purpose of the last two sequences. Furthermore, repair may be severely limited or disallowed completely by the judge when the contribution of additional examination would be minimal. Further redirects and recrosses are always possible if necessary.

The order of presentation of witnesses in both civil and criminal trials is basically the same. The most significant difference is that the U.S. Constitution's Fifth Amendment privilege against self-incrimination prohibits the prosecution from calling criminal defendants to the stand as witnesses. In civil trials the plaintiff's lawyers often call defendants before other witnesses.

On direct examination attorneys usually must ask for and get yes-no or short answers. However, many jurisdictions give the judge discretion to permit extended narratives to the extent that they help develop the witness's testimony. Leading questions, those that suggest the answer, are generally improper on direct examination, with exceptions for forgetful, older, young, hostile, or adverse witnesses. In the case of forgetful, older, or young witnesses, leading questions serve a valid function in refreshing their memory or directing their attention. When lawyers call hostile or adverse witnesses to the stand, the danger that the witness will consciously or unconsciously acquiesce to the examiner's version of the truth is minimal, and leading questions are thus allowed. When witnesses are hostile to the examiner, the need for forcing them to answer the lawyer's questions is greater than the danger that leading questions present.

In common-law jurisdictions there are restrictions not only on leading questions but also on those deemed argumentative, misleading, compound, or otherwise multifaceted. The FRE treat these matters by reposing power in the judge to supervise witness examinations. Specifically, the FRE exhort the judge to take reasonable measures to promote effectiveness and efficiency in ascertaining the truth and to protect witnesses from harassment or undue embarrassment.

There are two views as to the permissible scope of cross-examinations. The restrictive rule confines the cross-examiner to matters within the scope of direct examination. The wide-open rule allows any material issue in the case to be explored. The federal rules adopt the restrictive rule but allow the judge to make exceptions. Convenience of witnesses and trial efficiency often dictate that the judge exercise discretion regarding the proper scope of a witness's cross-examination.

Witnesses' Character and Credibility

By introducing personal testimony about a witness's character, it is possible to judge whether the witness has testified accurately, lied, or made a mistake; whether a person did or did not commit rape; whether a person was or was not careful; or whether a person turned a corner in an automobile in a particular way. However, such character-type propensity evidence is sometimes prejudicial, misleading, too time-consuming, or unfair. Accordingly, there is a general ban on the use of character-type propensity evidence unless it fits special rules for special exceptions. The exceptions are many.

It must be shown that reputation or character witnesses are familiar with the reputation of the person about whom they are testifying. Thus, in the case of reputation testimony, courts normally require that the witness and the subject have lived or done business in reasonable proximity to each other for a substantial period in the fairly recent past. Also, the reputation reported must be the subject's reputation in the relevant community and relatively current.

A prerequisite for the admissibility of personal opinions about another's propensities is that the person providing personal opinions had some substantial recent contact or relationship with the other person that would furnish a reasonable basis for a current opinion. Weaknesses in these foundational elements affect the weight rather than the admissibility of character-type propensity evidence. Rules of impeachment govern the efforts to test the opposing witnesses' credibility.

Witnesses in *The Caine Mutiny* Court-Martial

One of the most famous trials in American fiction occurs in Herman Wouk's 1951 novel *The Caine Mutiny*, a story made even more famous by the 1954 film adaptation starring Humphrey Bogart. The novel's trial is a court-martial proceeding against Lieutenant Steve Maryk, the executive officer of the USS *Caine*, a Navy minesweeper, and it realistically portrays both the inconsistencies in testimony of witnesses to the same events and the difficulty of punishing perjurers.

Early in *The Caine Mutiny*, Maryk is harassed by fellow lieutenant Thomas Keefer's constant complaints about the irrational behavior of their captain, Lieutenant Commander Philip Francis Queeg. Finally, when the ship's safety is threatened in a typhoon, Maryk concludes that Captain Queeg is mentally unbalanced and relieves him of command—a momentous action for any naval officer to undertake. Afterward, Maryk is court-martialed for "conduct to the prejudice of good order and discipline." However, his attorney, Lieutenant Barney Greenwald, wins his acquittal. Although Keefer has been the lead instigator of Queeg's removal from command, at trial he betrays Maryk by denying that Queeg is unbalanced. However, under intense cross-examination by Greenwald, Queeg himself begins acting erratically on the witness stand, becoming the defense's most persuasive witness.

The trial in *The Caine Mutiny* is realistic in that events that seem to be of clear import at one time are found by the time of trial to be subject to differing interpretations. For a time, at least, before he is rattled by Greenwald's cross-examination, Queeg is able to present himself in a different light from that in which his ship's crew has seen him while at sea. Also realistic is Keefer's willingness to perjure himself and his ability to get away with this conduct. Although witnesses appear in court under oath, it is ordinarily difficult to marshal evidence sufficient to convict a lying witness of perjury.

Lieutenant Maryk's defense attorney (José Ferrer) questions Captain Queeg (Humphrey Bogart), as Maryk (Van Johnson) nervously looks on from the rear. *(AP/Wide World Photos)*

Timothy L. Hall

Everyone's Duty to Testify

Two kinds of witnesses may appear at a trial or deposition: ordinary lay witnesses or expert witnesses. A properly subpoenaed witness who fails to show up at the time and date specified is subject to arrest. Except for the reimbursement of costs of coming to court, ordinary witnesses may not be paid to testify. Because of the truth-seeking function of the court, parties and other witnesses can be compelled to give testimony, even if it is damaging to themselves or others. Accordingly, a person normally cannot prevent another person from disclosing confidences, secrets, or other matters. However, privileges are a narrow exception to these general rules. The privileges for confidential communications in the attorney-client, physician-patient, psychotherapist-patient, and husband-wife contexts are examples of such exceptions. Privileges operate to exclude relevant evidence in the name of some other social objective. Most true privileges are designed to promote certain kinds of relationships and particularly to promote confidential communications within these socially desirable relationships.

W. Dene Eddings Andrews

Further Reading

Bergman, Paul. *Transcript Exercises for Learning Evidence.* St. Paul, Minn.: West Publishing, 1992. Practical workbook containing various questions, answers, and judicial rulings from a variety of civil and criminal cases. This book is helpful for understanding the legal propriety of common objections.

_____. *Trial Advocacy in a Nutshell.* 3d ed. St. Paul, Minn.: West Publishing, 1995. This book and the book Bergman coauthored with Berman-Barnett, listed below, are easy-to-read, helpful, and inexpensive paperbacks. They review the fundamentals of direct examinations and cross-examinations and offer numerous examples.

Bergman, Paul, and Sara J. Berman-Barnett. *Represent Yourself in Court: How to Prepare and Try a Winning Case.* 2d ed. Berkeley, Calif.: Nolo Press, 1998.

Graham, Kenneth. *Casenotes Law Outlines: Evidence.* Santa Monica, Calif.: Casenotes, 1996. Offers discussions of the evidence rules on which common objections are based.

Loftus, Elizabeth F. *Eyewitness Testimony.* 2d ed. Cambridge, Mass.: Harvard University Press, 1996. Discussion by a psychologist of research on conditions influencing the reliability of eyewitness testimony.

Rothstein, Paul F., Myrna Raeder, and David Crump. *Evidence: State and Federal Rules in a Nutshell.* 3d ed. St. Paul, Minn.: West Publishing, 1997.

Technical Working Group for Eyewitness Evidence. *Eyewitness Evidence: A Guide for Law Enforcement.* Washington, D.C.: U.S. Department of Justice, Office of Justice Programs, National Institute of Justice, 1999. Practical guide for law-enforcement professionals in evaluating testimonies of witnesses.

See also Cross-examination; Depositions; Diplomatic immunity; Discovery; Expert witnesses; Objections; Perjury; Privileged communications; Subpoena power; Testimony; Trial transcripts; Trials; Witness protection programs.

Women in law enforcement and corrections

Definition: Women who work as police officers, corrections and probation officers, and security guards, and in other related fields

Criminal justice issues: Civil rights and liberties; professional standards; women's issues

Significance: Women first entered law enforcement and corrections work in the United States during the early nineteenth century, but significant numbers of women were not given the full responsibilities and opportunities available to men until after the passage of federal civil rights legislation in the late twentieth century. The numbers of women in law enforcement and corrections then grew dramatically, only to level off as women in those professions encountered workplace discrimination and harassment.

The roles and scope of women in law enforcement and corrections have changed significantly since the beginning of the twentieth century. Women began working in policing during the mid-nineteenth century, but their duties confined them primarily to clerical work and to working with other women and children. Since the U.S. Congress passed the Civil Rights Act of 1964 and the Equal Employment Opportunity Act of 1972, women have entered police patrol work and have become police officers with job functions similar to their male counterparts.

In the early nineteenth century, the reformatory movement in corrections opened new avenues of employment for women as matrons in prisons because they were viewed as having the abilities necessary to redirecting female offenders to the types of lives they were expected to live after their release. As in policing and other law-enforcement positions, however, women now enter and work in the same kinds of corrections jobs, with the same security, benefits, and salaries, as their male counterparts. Finally, with the rise in the use of security officers in the private sector, increasing numbers of women are finding employment as security personnel in restaurants, shopping malls, and other locations.

Policing

In 1845, the New York City Police Department became the first department officially to employ women. However, the women it hired served as matrons and were essentially social workers who assisted the women and children with whom the department dealt. Their hiring met opposition from male police officers and citizens, but by 1885, other cities were also beginning to utilize women officers as matrons.

In 1893, the mayor of Chicago officially appointed Marie Owens, the widow of a Chicago police officer, as the first woman "patrolman" with powers of arrest. Seventeen years later, Los Angeles made Alice Stebbins Wells the first woman to be classified as a "policewoman." Wells, who had previously worked as a social worker, was initially appointed for prevention and protection principles related to youth. Although she was later given powers of arrest, her duties were limited to enforcing laws in places such as dance halls, movie theaters, amusement parks and arcades, and other places of recreation frequented by women and children. It would be many years before limitations placed on women in policing

would be eased through U.S. Supreme Court decisions and legislation.

The 1970's was the decade that set in motion the modern era for women in policing. In *Reed v. Reed* (1971), the Supreme Court ruled that police departments that discriminated on the basis of sex were in violation of the equal protection clause of the Fourteenth Amendment. The Equal Rights Amendment and its subsequent Equal Employment Opportunity Act of 1972 provided for the advancement of women in policing and other law-enforcement positions. In 1972, two women successfully completed Federal Bureau of Investigation (FBI) training, New York City's police began hiring and training women for patrol duty, and Pennsylvania's state police began giving women increased duties.

After the 1970's, the numbers of sworn female police officers increased dramatically, from a handful across the United States, to more than 50,000 in 2004. However, despite these advances, the total number of women in law enforcement remains small, and their progress has been slow. Although women constituted 47 percent of the nation's workforce in 2004, they held only about 12-14 percent of sworn law-enforcement positions in the country. Moreover, the progress that women were making toward the end of the twentieth century actually regressed slightly. According to the Feminist Majority Foundation's National Center for Women and Policing's annual survey, women are not promoted as often as men, and they hold only about 7.5 percent of top command decision-making positions and only 9.6 percent of supervisory positions.

A final indication of the lack of progress being made by women in law enforcement is the fact that in 2004 only thirty of the one hundred largest municipal police agencies in the United States had women in top command positions. Federal and state agencies employ even fewer women overall, with even fewer promoted to upper echelons in their agencies. The barrier popularly known as the "glass ceiling" is especially evident in law enforcement.

Barriers to Women in Policing

Possible explanations for the low numbers of women found in law-enforcement positions, especially those of higher rank, may be rooted in the continuing problems of disparate practices concerning societal gender bias, work assignments, and sexual harassment. Once on the job, women in law enforcement often face discrimination, harassment, and intimidation from their male colleagues, especially as they move up the ranks.

Despite more than a century of evidence showing that women are as capable of police work as men, widespread bias in recruitment policies, selection practices, hiring, and promotions keep their numbers disproportionately low. Although discriminatory size requirements were discarded during the early 1970's, modern entrance tests continue to bar qualified women from entering policing. Many mandatory physical agility tests have a significant negative effect on the representation of sworn female officers, as most departmental entry exams overemphasize physical strength, thereby disqualifying many suitable female applicants.

Another obstacle is the stereotype of policing as a male job because of its association with crime and danger. The prevailing attitudes of policing styles have focused on use of force with emphasis on paramilitary environments. In these conditions, male officers perceive their female counterparts as weak and unimposing, unable to carry out the duties required by their positions. Thus, the primary obstacle that women must overcome is the attitudes of male officers. However, despite negative male ideas about women police officers, time and experience have shown that male and female officers are equally effective in their activities—as measured by productivity on patrol, commitment to law-enforcement organizations, and performance evaluations.

Women employed in policing often encounter hostile workplaces, facing sexual harassment on the job. Despite legislation and departmental policies prohibiting sexual harassment in the workplace, women in law enforcement face such problems in many agencies across America. Found mainly in smaller departments, the "good old boy" system exemplifies stereotypical attitudes and often allows such misconduct. One of the major reasons cited for the high turnover rate

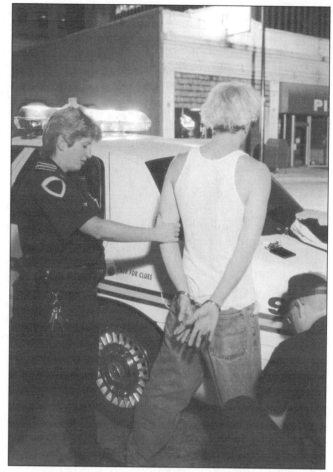

Since the passage of the federal Civil Rights Act of 1964 and the Equal Employment Opportunity Act of 1972, increasing numbers of women have taken on the full range of police duties that had previously been restricted to male officers. *(Brand-X Pictures)*

found among female officers is sexual harassment.

Notwithstanding the barriers that female officers confront, they bring to policing a style that relies more on communication skills than physical force. The citizenry they serve sees them as more respectful, and by using tactics and techniques that defuse potentially violent situations, female officers often successfully resolve situations that might otherwise lead to serious injury or death. Finally, because of their emphasis on communication, female officers are also able to respond more effectively to cases of domestic violence, which represent almost one-half of all violent crime calls to police agencies.

Corrections Work

The advancement of women into policing jobs was actually established by female correctional matrons. Between 1822 and 1832, the first women were hired as jail matrons and prison guards, thus paving the way for female police officers by legitimizing women working within the criminal justice field.

The background and history of women working in corrections is similar to that of women in policing. Impacted by women's reform groups, such as the Women's Christian Temperance Union and the American Female Moral Reform Society, female jail and prison matrons were essentially social workers who were interested in the morality of women arrested and detained for prostitution and other forms of commercial vice, as well as wayward juveniles. Matrons were intended to serve as role models who could influence female inmates and young women in the "ways of being a lady." Their work often required them to lead classes on such domestic skills as cooking, cleaning, and sewing.

From the beginning, as with policing, women in corrections were relegated to lower positions of authority. Female correctional officers did not hold the same pay grades as men in similar positions, and the facilities in which they served were often below the standard of those used by men. The pay of correctional matrons was similar to that of domestic servants. Like domestic servants, they worked long shifts with few days off. Moreover, they often lived and worked alongside the inmates they were charged to supervise.

As the reformatory movement in corrections rose and fell in the early twentieth century, women worked as correctional officers for the same pragmatic reasons as did men. No longer focused on the ideals of reform, women went into corrections for job security and steady paychecks. No longer were female corrections officers concerned with reforming their charges. Instead, they became custodial employees whose main duties revolved around prevention of violence within, and escape from, jail and prison facilities.

Corrections has historically been the most sex-segregated and male-dominated component of the criminal justice system. However, since the late twentieth century, and because of the same laws and decrees that affected police, correc-

tional staffs have become more gender integrated. Now, female officers are allowed to work in prisons for both women and men. This advancement is not without problems, however. As with policing, male colleagues often do not take female officers seriously. Consequently, female officers feel a constant need to prove their abilities and often confront sexual harassment by inmates and male officers alike.

Work in corrections also presents problems of cultural differences. Corrections officers often work mostly in rural environments where most lockup facilities are located, and they supervise inmates from urban areas with whom they share little in common. Correctional work is particularly difficult for working mothers, as the shifts are long and often rotating, and involuntary overtime work is common. Correctional officers cannot easily leave their jobs for personal emergencies, especially as most correctional facilities operate shorthanded or with minimal staff supervision.

Many women work in the subfield of corrections known as "intermediate sanctions," which is better suited to their schedules. This field includes the supervision of all persons in the correctional pipeline who instead of being incarcerated in jails or prisons are housed in halfway houses, boot camps, and the like. The most common jobs for women in this field are as probation officers who monitor the conduct and behavior of criminal offenders (both juvenile and adult) serving probation terms in lieu of incarceration. Some jurisdictions combine probation with parole, requiring officers to monitor the reintegration of criminal offenders into communities during their conditional release from prison.

As in policing, many correctional experts have observed that female corrections officers have better listening and communication skills than men. They can have a calming effect on prisoners, are less confrontational, and are better than men at exercising control without using force.

Security Work

A variety of private police services, including the private detective and security businesses, have arisen to compete with traditional law enforcement. Moreover, the U.S. Department of Labor reports that this twelve-billion-dollar-a-year industry, which employs more than ten million men and women in such protective services as store detectives, undercover investigators, and security guards, is rapidly growing to meet increasing demand. This is also an area of law enforcement in which women are more welcome than in the traditional areas of policing and corrections, as women have a greater ability than men to "blend in with the crowd" with which they work.

Conclusion

Most modern agencies attempt to recruit women, and all positions are at least theoretically open to them. The adage that "everything old is new again" now applies, as law-enforcement recruiters are returning to the traditional sources of female officers from the nineteenth century, attempting to attract social workers and other caregivers from whom the first police matrons were drawn in the early nineteenth century.

However, the numbers of women in policing or corrections in general, or in supervisory roles, has not increased significantly, as these occupations remain traditionally male in nature with women having to continually prove themselves in their everyday work experiences. For women in law enforcement, the "glass ceiling" remains firmly in place, and until women are fully integrated into the profession, incidents of sexual harassment and obstacles in employment, promotions, and other advancements will likely remain in place.

Pati K. Hendrickson

Further Reading

Gall, Gina. *Armed and Dangerous: Memoirs of a Chicago Policewoman*. New York: Tom Doherty Associates, 2001. Memoirs of a female police officer with sixteen years of experience in Chicago.

Gold, Marion E. *Top Cops: Profiles of Women in Command*. Chicago: Brittany Publications, 1999. Follows the career of one of the few women to break through the "glass ceiling."

Heidensohn, Frances. *Women in Control? The Role of Women in Law Enforcement*. New York: Oxford University Press, 1992. Comparative study of women in law enforcement in Great Britain and the United States.

Martin, Susan E., and Nancy C. Jurik. *Doing Justice, Doing Gender: Women in Law and Criminal Justice Occupations*. Thousand Oaks, Calif.: Sage Publications, 1996. Examination of the historical and current roles of women employed in the criminal justice system.

Muraskin, Roslyn. *It's a Crime: Women and Justice*. 2d ed. Upper Saddle River, N.J.: Prentice Hall, 2000. Comprehensive text on women in criminal justice that includes topical readings on subjects related to the involvement of women in crime and treatment of women offenders by the criminal justice system.

Scarborough, Kathryn E., and Pamela A. Collins. *Women in Public and Private Law Enforcement*. Woburn, Mass.: Butterworth-Heinemann, 2002. Detailed analysis and description of the struggles women have faced and the challenges they have overcome in law enforcement.

See also Criminal justice system; Law enforcement; Parole officers; Police; Police academies; Prison and jail systems; Prison guards; Private police and guards.

Work camps

Definition: Alternative form of incarceration that requires less security than regular prisons and offers inmates practical work experience

Criminal justice issues: Prisons; punishment; rehabilitation

Significance: Work camps are an alternative form of incarceration designed to meet objectives of inmates, correctional management, and society. The rehabilitative needs of inmates are served by giving them opportunities to repay their debts to society and to develop vocational and personal skills. Management needs are met as camps reduce overcrowding in secure facilities, provide placements for minimum-custody inmates, and result in costs savings associated with the use of inmate labor. Society benefits as inmates, after being punished for their crimes through involuntary work, are often returned to society with a work ethic that enhances their chances of succeeding.

The emergence of modern prison work camps can be traced to the 1970's, when prison populations began to increase dramatically. Since that time, work camps have been established throughout the United States. Typical work camps house from 40 to 250 minimum-custody inmates in barracks resembling dormitories. Most inmates in the camps have been convicted of nonviolent crimes, such as drug trafficking, white-collar crimes, and lesser property offenses. Convicted murderers are occasionally admitted to work camps, but only after they have served major portions of their sentences and have demonstrated exemplary behavior in prison.

The architectural designs of most prison camps are open and are often similar to academic campuses. The camps often have perimeter fences, but their purpose is generally to provide security for the inmates themselves. When the camps are part of larger, more secure prisons, they are usually placed outside the prisons' security fences or walls. Camp living quarters are generally arranged around central buildings that contain cafeterias, recreation centers, classrooms, medical units, post offices, churches, commissaries, and administrative offices.

Specialized Camps

Some work camps are designed to serve the special needs of specific vocations, such as forestry maintenance, farming, and road maintenance. Forestry camps are usually located in national and state forests, where inmates assist in reforestation work, fighting forest fires, clearing underbrush, and building firebreaks. Their work is usually supervised by forestry personnel, with security and discipline matters attended to by prison personnel.

Work camps in which inmates engage in farm-related tasks are usually located in rural farming communities. The specific types of farming in which they engage are usually determined by the regions and acreage available to them. For example, vegetable cultivation requires mild and wet climates, while wheat cultivation is best suited for arid climates. Pork and poultry production re-

quires warmer climates, while beef and sheep production is best in cooler locations.

Work camps that focus on road maintenance are also suitable for rural communities, whose roads often need repair. Mild climates are best, so inmates can work outside throughout the year. When work camps are part of larger, more secure institutions, their inmates typically engage in such maintenance work as painting, carpentry, plumbing, groundskeeping, and electrical work. Camp inmates also perform service-related jobs by helping to meet the needs of higher-custody inmates, such as food preparation and service, laundry, and janitorial tasks.

Camps as Alternative Incarceration

Local, state, and federal correctional systems use work camps as an alternative form of placement for inmates. For example, the Leon County Sheriff's Department in Tallahassee, Florida, has a work camp that functions as part of the Leon County Jail. The work crews consist of inmates from the county jail who clean litter and remove undergrowth from roads. Participants in this shock-probation program are sentenced to the work camp by the court as a condition of their probation.

The Work Ethic Camp in Nebraska is an example of a state-level program. Its inmates are provided structured programming that includes work programs, vocational training, behavior management and modification, money management, substance abuse awareness, counseling, and opportunities to continue their academic educations. Inmates selected for the camp are nonviolent prison-bound offenders who are provided this plea-agreement alternative to regular incarceration to help relieve overcrowding and reduce recidivism. The mission of the program is the rehabilitation of program participants.

An example of a federal work camp can be found in Pleasanton in Northern California. Its inmates, who have been convicted of federal offenses, work for twelve to fourteen cents an hour and are housed in remodeled military barracks.

Some work camps are designed for special populations, such as geriatric inmates. One such camp is Florida's River Junction Work Camp in Chattahoochee for minimum- and medium-custody inmates who are elderly. Eighty percent of camp inmates are over the age of fifty years. They work in state mental hospitals and for the city of Chattahoochee.

The success of work camps, like that of other correctional programs, is generally measured by assessing the recidivism rates of program graduates. The recidivism rates of inmates who have completed work-camp programs tend to be better than those of inmates incarcerated in traditional prison settings. In an evaluation of Florida work camps, for example, researchers found that 86 percent of 720 offenders released from work camps had not returned to state prisons, and 51 percent had not returned to prison or any form of supervision. As is true of traditional prison inmates, recidivism rates of work-camp inmates are inversely related to the inmates' ages. As the ages of prisoners at the time of their release increase, the less likely they are to return to incarceration.

Elizabeth H. McConnell

Further Reading

Allen, Harry E., Clifford E. Simonsen, and Edward J. Latessa. *Corrections in American: An Introduction*. 10th ed. Upper Saddle River, N.J.: Pearson Education, 2004. Introductory discussion of the history of corrections in the United States, with some attention to alternatives to traditional forms of incarceration, such as work camps.

Gido, R. L., and T. Alleman. *Turnstile Justice: Issues in American Corrections*. 2d ed. Upper Saddle River, N.J.: Pearson/Prentice-Hall, 2002. Critical readings on issues facing corrections, including alternatives to incarceration.

Haas, Kenneth C., and Geoffrey P. Alpert. *The Dilemmas of Corrections*. 4th ed. Prospect Heights, Ill.: Waveland Press, 1999. Readings on rehabilitation, community-based corrections, and critical problems and issues faced by corrections institutions.

Mays, L. G., and T. L. Winfree. *Contemporary Corrections*. 2d ed. Belmont, Calif.: Wadsworth, 2002. Textbook that focuses on issues relating to the role that corrections plays in society. Includes a variety of discussions ranging from the history of corrections to new advances in community corrections.

Murphy, Jeffrie, comp. *Punishment and Rehabilitation*. 3d ed. Belmont, Calif.: Wadsworth, 1995. Collection of essays on rehabilitative and other justifications for punishment.

Wiersma, B., and K. Siedschlaw. "Nebraska's Work Ethic Camp: The First Year." *Corrections Compendium* 28 (2004): 1-7. Brief study of Nebraska's experimental work camp, whose program includes vocational training, behavior management and modification, and other forms of counseling and training.

See also Boot camps; Bureau of Prisons; Chain gangs; Community-based corrections; Elderly prisoners; Forestry camps; Halfway houses; Prison industries; Prison overcrowding; Probation, adult; Recidivism; Rehabilitation; Work-release programs.

Work-release programs

Definition: Alternative to traditional incarceration that places accused and convicted offenders into the community to work at jobs paying standard wages

Criminal justice issues: Probation and parole; punishment; rehabilitation; sentencing

Significance: Work release is an alternative to incarceration that is expected to be used more widely in the future because of its proven benefits.

Work-release programs serve a variety of needs. They may be used as a form of pretrial release, as sentencing options, or as privileges awarded to incarcerated inmates with exemplary records. Accused offenders who are authorized for the programs during their pretrial release are allowed to maintain their existing jobs but must spend their nights or weekends, or both, in work-release facilities or jails. The same conditions also apply to convicted offenders who are sentenced to work release instead of prison. In addition, work release may be given as a privilege to inmates of prisons, jails, and halfway houses. In all cases, inmates in the programs are allowed to leave the facilities in which they are housed to work in the community.

Work release has been used in the United States since 1913, when Wisconsin became the first state to allow convicted misdemeanants to continue working at their jobs while serving short jail sentences. In 1957, North Carolina became the first state to permit convicted felons to leave prison during the day to work in the community. The Federal Prisoner Rehabilitation Act, passed by the U.S. Congress in 1965, allowed work release for prisoners of federal institutions.

Regardless of whether work release is given at the state or federal level, the working conditions of accused and convicted offenders are similar to those experienced by civilians. Job requirements are identical, and work supervision is by civilians. Moreover, like any free citizens, participants in work-release programs are usually responsible for their own transportation to and from work.

Those on work release are paid as civilians and typically receive their salaries directly from their employers. However, they usually have to turn their paychecks over to corrections officials, who extract portions of the money to reimburse the facilities for room and board. Some of the income may also be deducted to cover costs of transportation and other incidental expenses. Further deductions may also be made to pay for restitution or victim compensation. After the deductions are made, the balance of the money is deposited into the inmates' savings accounts.

Released inmates benefit from having supervised savings accounts. Some also benefit by avoiding the risk of losing their current jobs. Those who have not worked for some time may benefit from learning new job skills and raising their self-esteem. In addition, participants in work-release programs are less adversely affected by confinement than other inmates because they can enjoy more normal societal interactions that facilitate their reintegration into the community, and their recidivism is usually reduced. Work release may also be used as an inmate-management tool. Because participation in work release is highly desired but not guaranteed, corrections administrators may use it to reward good behavior of inmates.

Pauline K. Brennan

Further Reading

McCarthy, Belinda Rodgers, Bernard J. McCarthy, and Matthew C. Leone. *Community-Based Corrections.* 4th ed. Belmont, Calif.: Wadsworth Publishing, 2001.

Turner, Susan, and Joan Petersilia. *Work Release: Recidivism and Corrections Cost in Washington State.* Washington, D.C.: National Institute of Justice, 1996.

Wees, Greg. "Work and Educational Release, 1996." *Corrections Compendium* (May, 1997): 8-23.

See also Arraignment; Community-based corrections; Halfway houses; Parole; Prison overcrowding; Recidivism; Rehabilitation; Sentencing; Work camps.

World Court

Identification: International Court of Justice
Date: Held first session in April, 1946
Place: The Hague, the Netherlands
Criminal justice issue: International Law
Significance: Legal systems have historically been established solely within sovereign nations. The International Court of Justice—or World Court, as it is better known—handles cases among nations and international disputes that are beyond the scope of any one nation's justice system.

Although the International Court of Justice (ICJ) was created as part of the United Nations after World War II, it was neither the first attempt to establish a mechanism to arbitrate disputes among countries nor the first World Court. However, it is the first court to become truly global in membership and recognition. The weakness of the court is that it cannot coerce participation by its sovereign member countries, nor can it enforce judgments. Even with these weaknesses, however, the court is seen by most to play a positive role within the international community.

Forerunners to the World Court include the Permanent Court of Arbitration, which was established in 1899 to assist in cases of international arbitration and other related matters. The

Chamber of the World Court within The Hague's Peace Palace. *(AP/Wide World Photos)*

first international body with independently appointed justices who heard cases brought before it was the Permanent Court of International Justice (PCIJ). Operating from 1922 to 1946, this court was created in conjunction with the League of Nations but was not formally part of the League.

Post-World War II plans for the United Nations included the International Court of Justice. The new World Court was understood to be a successor to the PCIJ with broader powers. In contrast to its predecessor body, the new World Court was created as an integral part of the United Nations. In 2005, it recognized the right of 191 sovereign nations to bring cases before it.

The court comprises fifteen justices who serve nine-year terms. One-third of them are elected every three years, and no two justices may be from the same country. The justices are elected by the U.N. General Assembly and Security Council, which vote separately on nominations. The function of the court is to settle disputes between independent countries (contentious cases) and to give opinions on international matters, as requested by agencies within the United Nations (advisory opinions).

The court hears contentious cases between two nations only when the governments of both nations agree to accept the court's jurisdiction over their dispute. From its inception through mid-2004, the court delivered seventy-nine contentious-case rulings and twenty-five advisory opinions. The court's activities were not spread evenly over those years, as its activities reflected changing global political moods. For example, between July, 1962, and August, 1971—at the height of Cold War tensions—only one new case was brought before the court and only one advisory opinion was sought. Between 1990 and 2004—after the Cold War ended—more than forty-five contentious cases (many interrelated) were brought before the court; however, the court did not rule in all these cases.

As the world's nations were becoming more comfortable with the idea of international tribunals, a new international court came into existence in 1998: the International Criminal Court. Completely independent of the World Court, this new court deals exclusively with matters of international crimes.

Donald A. Watt

Further Reading
Broomhall, Bruce. *International Justice and the Criminal Court: Between Sovereignty and the Rule of Law*. New York: Oxford University Press, 2003.
Cassese, Antonio. *International Criminal Law*. New York: Oxford University Press, 2003.
Kolba, Boris. *International Courts*. Milwaukee: World Almanac Library, 2004.
Meyer, Howard N. *The World Court in Action: Judging Among the Nations*. Lanham, Md.: Rowman & Littlefield, 2002.

See also Canadian justice system; Diplomatic immunity; International law; International tribunals; Jurisdiction of courts; War crimes.

Y

Youth authorities

Definition: Inclusive term for the various state agencies and officials involved in juvenile justice

Criminal justice issues: Crime prevention; juvenile justice; rehabilitation

Significance: Within the criminal justice system, state youth authorities are delegated the responsibility of dealing with juvenile offenders in matters ranging from probation and parole to incarceration, education, and many other areas.

State youth authorities (SYA) are a relatively new development within the criminal justice system, as many were not created until after the 1940's. Originally, their primary responsibility was management and operation of state reformatories, as well as provision of job training and education to their juvenile charges.

After courts commit them to the care of SYAs, youths are provided services ranging from receiving educational assistance and psychological treatment for interpersonal problems to job training for specific occupations. Most youths handled by SYAs are referred by juvenile and criminal courts; however youths committed by criminal courts are transferred to the state corrections departments on their eighteenth birthday, if their sentences are not already completed.

Goals

An important difference between adult and juvenile offenders is that adults are placed in correctional facilities for the primary purpose of being punished, with rehabilitation a distant secondary goal, while the first goal for juvenile offenders is rehabilitation. The youth authorities believe that if young offenders are caught early enough, major life changes are possible for them. Hence, rehabilitation and education are primary focuses for youth authorities.

In addition to managing and administering youth correction facilities, youth authorities are also in charge of state parole and probation services for juveniles and are responsible for the care and upkeep of youth offenders remanded in their custody. Their other functions include providing improvements and any construction needed for the day-to-day running of correctional facilities.

Youth authorities are also often involved at state and local levels in efforts to prevent crime and delinquency. Youth authority officials visit schools and provide delinquency prevention advice to teachers and students, and they often address community service organizations and religious groups. In many states, youth authorities provide shelters for children aged six through seventeen, with services provided for runaways, homeless minors, and abused and neglected children. The primary goal for most of these shelters is survival—meeting the immediate needs of the children and their families for food, clothes, and safe places to sleep.

Within major urban areas such as New York City, Los Angeles, and Chicago, youth authorities work with other state agencies to combat gang violence. One strategy in this effort has been the construction of youth centers, where juveniles can receive help in job training, health, fitness, citizenship skills, pregnancy prevention, and counseling.

The philosophy behind youth centers is the belief that children need structured environments. Busy youths are expected to be less likely to experiment with drugs and alcohol, less likely to become pregnant, and less likely to get into trouble with the law. These benefits, in turn, increase youths' chances of finishing high school. Youth centers provide structured activities during nonschool hours, offering juveniles opportunities to become involved in positive activities. Other youth center services include mentoring and training in music, arts and crafts, and the culinary arts, as well as other potentially enjoyable activities.

Shortcomings

While youth authorities strive to maintain decent living conditions for the youths in their custody, problems often arise. For example, increases in the number of juvenile arrests during the early years of the twenty-first century have made overcrowding an issue. Old facilities are forced to house more youths than they are designed to accommodate. In some places, as many as three to four juveniles share rooms designed for only one person.

Another major issue has been punitive living conditions. In one center, male youths were routinely locked in bare cells for as many as eighteen hours per day. They were not allowed to keep anything of a personal nature beyond the clothes on their backs and Bibles. In addition, personal hygiene products and common items like toothpaste and soap were forbidden.

Other problems have included the use of abusive discipline without due process. Many facilities operate without offering any positive incentives for good behavior, instead relying on negative disciplinary procedures. Guards, whose own educations are often only marginally better than those of their wards, routinely administer inappropriate punishments, ranging from verbal threats to physical force. Sexual harassment and assault are also areas needing attention. Moreover, many institutions lack sufficient numbers of trained women guards for their female wards. As a result, there have been sexual assaults against girls by male staff members.

Although youth authorities assert that hiring qualified teachers for their wards is a priority, many institutions have too few educators to provide adequate schooling. This is an especially serious problem, as the wards of youth authorities have a much higher than average rate of learning disabilities.

The federal Individuals with Disabilities Education Improvement Act of 2004 provides for youths with learning disabilities in correctional facilities with special education and related services. However, providing appropriate services for these students is a challenge. Issues having an impact on the provision of appropriate special education include the transience of the student population, conflicting goals for security and rehabilitation, shortages of adequately pre-pared personnel, and limited interagency coordination.

Cary Stacy Smith

Further Reading

Hubner, John, and Jill Wolfson. *Ain't No Place Anybody Would Want to Be: Conditions of Confinement for Youth*. Washington, D.C.: Coalition for Juvenile Justice, 1999. Exposé of the harsh conditions provided by youth authorities to their wards by two California journalists.

Jonson-Reid, M. "Child Welfare Services and Delinquency: The Need to Know More." *Child Welfare* 83, no. 2 (2004): 157-174. Sociological study of the relationship between juvenile delinquency and the services provided by youth authorities.

Shoemaker, D. J. *Theories of Delinquency: An Examination of Explanations of Delinquent Behavior*. 4th ed. New York: Oxford University Press, 2000. Survey of theoretical approaches to explaining delinquent behavior. Clearly written evaluations of the various individualistic and sociological theories.

Siegel, L. J., Brandon C. Welsh, and Joseph J. Senna. *Juvenile Delinquency: Theory, Practice, and Law*. 8th ed. Belmont, Calif.: Wadsworth/ Thomson, 2002. Comprehensive examination of juvenile justice along with policies, theories, landmark court decisions, and contemporary issues.

Tanenhaus, David S. *Juvenile Justice in the Making*. New York: Oxford University Press, 2004. Examination of three thousand juvenile case files from Chicago during the early twentieth century that are used to address fundamental questions about how juvenile offenders should be treated under the law.

Whitehead, J. T., and S. P. Lab. *Juvenile Justice: An Introduction*. 4th ed. Cincinnati: Anderson Publishing, 2003. Introductory textbook examining the history of juvenile justice in the United States, from its nineteenth century roots to the early twenty-first century.

See also Juvenile courts; Juvenile delinquency; Juvenile Justice and Delinquency Prevention, Office of; Juvenile Justice and Delinquency Prevention Act; Juvenile justice system; Probation, juvenile.

Youth gangs

Definition: Self-defined group of adolescents whose value systems and activities encourage deviant behavior

Criminal justice issues: Juvenile justice; vandalism; violent crime

Significance: Although juvenile crime has tended to decline since the mid-1990's, crimes associated with youth gangs have continued to increase as gangs have proliferated across the United States and as gang members have engaged in more serious forms of crime.

Youth gangs have received considerable attention in criminal justice since the beginning of the twentieth century but no universally accepted definition of what constitutes a gang has yet emerged. The consensus among scholars and people in criminal justice is that a gang is a group with at least three members who engage in delinquent behavior. Gangs are more than merely groups of delinquent peers; they are unique in that the values of their members support the deviant behavior of both the individual members and the gang as a whole. Many researchers also agree that an important element of youth gangs is their adoption of distinctive identifying names. Moreover, gang members also tend to identify themselves by wearing distinctive clothing and tattoos and by marking neighborhoods with distinctive graffiti—all of which reinforces group cohesiveness.

History and Theory

The first documented youth gangs emerged in the Five Points District of New York City at the beginning of the twentieth century. Members of these early gangs were predominantly white and included many newly arrived immigrants from Europe. These early gangs were forerunners to organized crime groups—a fact that makes them different from their modern gang counterparts. Early attempts to explain the criminal behavior of youth gangs focused on social disorganization. However, during the 1920's, researchers took on the challenge of specifically explaining the gang phenomena.

It was not until the mid-twentieth century that Los Angeles and Chicago saw the emergence of what would become modern youth gangs. These later gangs were similar to the earlier gangs in that their membership was made up of mostly new immigrants. These new gangs also included groups whose members were moving around throughout the United States. Most of their members were African Americans and Hispanics. The modern gangs developed in response to conditions of poverty, discrimination, and other social problems in developing urban areas in big cities. Research on gangs during the mid-twentieth century leaned toward "strain theory"—an emerging explanation of general criminal behavior that focused on lack of legitimate opportunities in society and the resulting need for value adaptation.

A major difference between these modern gangs and the earlier gangs is that instead of dissolving or seeing their members move into organized crime, the modern gangs have tended to become more deeply entrenched in street crime. Part of the reason for this development has been the inability of gang members to gain access to legitimate employment opportunities.

The continuity of gangs has been reinforced by the continued involvement of members into their adulthood, and twenty-first century gangs have their roots in the mid-twentieth century gang movement. The perpetuation of gangs has encouraged a resurgence of scholarly interest in gang theory. A notable development in theory has been the application of general criminological theory to explain why individuals join gangs. Money, gang members in the family, friendship, respect, protection, and self-esteem are among the reasons that have been noted for joining gangs.

The late twentieth century saw increased levels of gang violence and a proliferation of gangs across the United States. Cities that had never had youth gangs before the 1980's suddenly had to deal with gangs. Much of this change has been attributed to deindustrialization and a consequent need to rely more on criminal activities, especially drug sales. Large gangs expanded across the United States, and entirely new gangs emerged in many cities.

One of the most visible changes in modern gangs has been their trend toward multiracial membership. Also, many gangs are taking in female members. The age structures of gangs are also changing. Gangs are taking in more younger members than ever before, and increasing numbers of members are remaining active in their gangs into their young adulthood. There also seem to be growing connections between street gangs and prison gangs that were not evident in earlier years.

Structure and Behaviors

The evolution of gangs over time has brought with it variety in the structure of the groups and the criminal behaviors of its members. The structures of gangs appear to be related to the gangs' behaviors. For example, gangs lacking cohesion are generally less organized than others are and are more likely to engage in random deviant behavior. More cohesive groups have tighter struc-

tures and engage in more organized criminal activities. The longer gangs are in existence, the more cohesive they become. Gangs whose members stay in longer are also more likely to develop greater cohesion and stronger organization. However, most gangs are not formally organized, and most members are transitional and do not stay in gangs for life.

Emergent gangs with low levels of cohesion tend to have weak leadership. Their members tend to engage in random and diverse deviant behaviors that are individually based and do not benefit the gangs as a whole. Many members of such gangs engage only in minor forms of delinquency. Members of gangs of this type are the most likely to quit before they reach adulthood, and the gangs themselves are prone to disband. Many gangs in the United States can be classified as emergent.

Members of Los Angeles's Diamond Street gang sit by a wall with distinctive graffiti marking their territory. *(AP/Wide World Photos)*

When emergent gangs continue to evolve, they become more cohesive. They often have initiation rituals that test members' loyalty and strength. Eventually, formal rules develop, and members who violate the rules may face consequences. Meanwhile, more leadership structures develop, and the deviant behaviors of individual members may monetarily benefit a gang as a whole.

Most gangs never become solidified and tightly organized, but a few "supergangs," such as the Latin Kings, have reached advanced levels of organization. Gangs of this nature have intricate leadership structures with multiple tiers and elaborate rules for members to follow. Highly organized groups often have branches dispersed throughout the United States, and their criminal activities are well structured. Such gangs tend to operate as organizations and often benefit from the criminal activities of their individual members. Their members generally avoid outward displays of their gang affiliation to avoid attracting the attention of police.

Criminal Activities

Criminal activity of gangs range from minor delinquent behaviors, such as shoplifting and drinking, to such serious crimes as robbery and homicide. Most gang members engage in deviant behavior before joining their gangs, but their deviant behaviors increase after they join. Reasons for this tend to revolve around the common value systems and group mentalities of the gangs.

Among the most common criminal activities of gangs are graffiti marking, drug trafficking, and seemingly random violence, such as homicides and drive-by shootings. A traditional gang behavior, graffiti marking serves multiple purposes, including creating artistic displays (tagging), marking territory, honoring fallen members, and communicating with rival gangs. However, increasing violence in gang-ridden urban areas has overshadowed this relatively minor deviant behavior. Gang violence takes the form of intergang wars and drive-by shootings. The result has been staggering death rates among young urban male members of minority groups.

Much of modern youth gang violence is due partly to increased availability of guns and personal transportation, which has expanded rivalry areas. It has also been suggested that this violence is a function of increased drug sales, which rely heavily on tough enforcement of street-level rules.

Prevention and Intervention

As law enforcement and scholars have tackled problems of youth gangs and street crime, strategies for preventing gang violence have proliferated. Some of these strategies are implemented at the individual level to keep youths from joining gangs and to encourage those already in gangs to renounce their gang lifestyles. Prevention and intervention are important because of both the short and long-term consequences of gang membership.

The effect of gang membership stays with many members long after they leave their gangs. Gang-prevention programs strive to raise awareness of the effects of gangs and give youths the skills necessary to resist membership. Those at higher risk for membership may require more intensive efforts, including family counseling and mentoring programs. For youths who are already gang involved, outreach and street-worker programs provide job skills training and guidance to help with the transition to legitimate adulthood activities.

Gang membership affects not only individual members but also entire communities, which suffer from gang activities. Several prevention and intervention efforts aim to strengthen communities and reduce criminal behavior in high-crime areas. Community organization efforts encourage community efforts to combat the effects of social disorganization. Working together ultimately strengthens communities and helps to protect them against escalating crime. An example of this type of approach is neighborhood watch programs. Other avenues for organization utilize key community stakeholders, such as religious leaders and business owners.

The criminal justice system also plays a role in the reduction of gangs and gang activity. While community-oriented policing is an important endeavor in community relations, law enforcement also plays a role in suppressing the criminal gang activities. The toughest police approaches to gangs may include zero-tolerance enforcement and specialized gang units.

In some instances, tough police policies have backfired and strengthened gangs. The U.S. Supreme Court seems to recognize the potentially negative effects of hard-core gang enforcement in its 1999 ruling in *Chicago v. Morales*, which limited police discretion in handling suspected gang members. At the same time, programs such as Boston's Ceasefire Program, which combines suppression with other intervention efforts, have shown favorable results.

Efforts to control youth gang activity have also been strengthened as a result of administrative and legislative changes that include civil injunctions, enhanced sentencing, and gang-specific prosecutions. However, enhanced sentencing and more efficient detection and prosecution of gang activity have also led to problems within correctional institutions. Increases in gang activity on the streets have been accompanied by the increased presence of gangs in correctional facilities, which have been accompanied by growing connections between street and prison gangs.

Kimberly Tobin

Further Reading

Esbensen, Finn-Aage, Larry K. Gaines, and Stephen G. Tibbetts. *American Youth Gangs at the Millennium*. Long Grove, Ill.: Waveland Press, 2004. Substantial collection of new and reprinted articles on all aspects of youth gangs in the United States.

Miller, Jody, Cheryl Maxson, and Malcolm Klein, eds. *The Modern Gang Reader*. 2d ed. Los Angeles: Roxbury Publishing, 2000. Collection of essays on youth gangs.

Rodríguez, Luis J., et al. *East Side Stories: Gang Life in East LA*. New York: Powerhouse Books, 2000. Collection of essays about gangs in Los Angeles's predominantly Hispanic East Los Angeles community. Profusely illustrated with photographs.

Shakur, Sanyika. *Monster: The Autobiography of an L.A. Gang Member*. New York: Grove Press, 2004. Poignant memoir of a former gang member who was notorious for an exceptionally violent career that began when he was only eleven years old. After being sent to prison, he renounced his past and became an advocate of black nationalism.

Sheldon, Randall G., Sharon K. Tracy, and William B. Brown. *Youth Gangs in American Society*. Belmont, Calif.: Wadsworth, 2003. Diverse collection of articles on a wide variety of aspects of youth gangs, with special attention to gangs in Los Angeles, Milwaukee, and Chicago.

Valdez, Al. *Gangs: A Guide to Understanding Street Gangs*. 3d ed. San Clemente, Calif.: Law Tech Publishing, 2000. Well-written and fascinating survey of gangs in the United States by a veteran of a police special gang unit with vast experience working with gang members.

See also Drive-by shootings; Graffiti; Juvenile delinquency; Juvenile justice system; Neighborhood watch programs; Organized crime; School violence; Vandalism; Violent Crime Control and Law Enforcement Act.

Appendices

Appendices

Bibliography of Basic Works on Criminal Justice

General

Barkan, Steven. *Criminology: A Social Understanding*. 3d ed. Upper Saddle River, N.J.: Prentice Hall, 2005. This edition provides readers with a sociological perspective on crime. The central theme of this book focuses on social inequality as a correlate of crime, and interactive scenarios at the close of each chapter will actively engage readers on integral issues concerning society's treatment of criminals. Topics unique to this edition include the following: death penalty, terrorism, stalking, identity theft, computer crime, and white collar crime.

Champion, Dean. *The American Dictionary of Criminal Justice*. 3d ed. Los Angeles, Calif.: Roxbury, 2005. Comprehensive guide to any terms, events, and significant course cases in the field of criminal justice.

Fagan, James A. *Criminal Justice: 2005 Update*. New York: Allyn & Bacon, 2005. The main focus of this update to the introductory text is to address the effect of the Patriot Act of 2001 and the establishment of Homeland Security on the criminal justice system.

Fuller, John Randolph. *Criminal Justice: Mainstream and Crosscurrents*. Upper Saddle River, N.J.: Pearson/Prentice-Hall, 2006. Provides a showcase of how financial constraints and errors on the part of policymakers and enforcers affect the goals of the criminal justice system. "Crosscurrents" sections at the close of each chapter provide readers with true-life examples of the administration of justice throughout the United States.

Jacoby, Joseph, ed. *Classics of Criminology*. 3d ed. Long Grove, Ill.: Waveland Press, 2004. Collection of sixty-five of the most influential writings from the past 240 years that attempt to explain crime. Presented chronologically in three sections: classic descriptions of crime, theories of causation of crime, and social responses to crime.

Palacios, William P., Paul F. Cromwell, and Roger G. Dunham, eds. *Crime and Justice in America: Present Realities and Future Prospects*. 2d ed. New York: Prentice Hall, 2002. Provides a diverse range of thirty original articles that focus on the critical issues challenging the criminal justice system.

Potter, Gary W., and Victor E. Kappeler, eds. *Constructing Crime: Perspectives on Making News and Social Problems*. Long Grove, Ill.: Waveland Press, 1998. Collection of fifteen original essays addressing the truths behind media portrayals of criminality in American society. The second part of the book focuses on the potential impact of the media on policymakers, law enforcement, and researchers and on the media's ability to depict crime accurately.

Schmalleger, Frank. *Criminal Justice Today: An Introductory Text for the Twenty-first Century*. 8th ed. Upper Saddle River, N.J.: Pearson/Prentice-Hall, 2005. Introduction to the criminal justice system with a special section on the U.S. war on terrorism since the September 11, 2001, attacks. Also offers Internet research exercises.

Siegel, Larry J. *Criminology*. 9th ed. Belmont, Calif.: Thomson/Wadsworth, 2005. In addition to offering an introduction into all facets of the criminal justice system, this edition examines such modern crime issues as terrorism and cybercrime.

Siegel, Larry J., and Joseph J. Senna. *Introduction to Criminal Justice*. 10th ed. Belmont, Calif.: Thomson/Wadsworth, 2004. This newly revised edition presents the latest statistical data to date, updated research on such current criminal justice issues as terrorism and identity theft. Particular attention is given to recent technological advances in criminal justice.

Territo, Leonard, James B. Halsted, and Max L. Bromley. *Crime and Justice in America: A Human Perspective*. 6th ed. New York: Prentice Hall, 2004. This edition of a now standard text merges theoretical concepts with practical applications relating to all aspects of criminal justice. Other new additions include sections in each chapter describing careers in the field, Web site references, and a comprehensive listing of media resources.

Corrections

Champion, Dean John. *Corrections in the United States: A Contemporary Perspective*. 4th ed. Upper Saddle River, N.J.: Prentice Hall, 2005. Historical overview of the American correctional system, extensive jail and prison coverage, a discussion of juvenile corrections, and a discussion of officer recruitment and training.

Clear, T. R., and G. F. Cole. *American Corrections*. 6th ed. Belmont, Calif.: Thomson/Wadsworth, 2003. Comprehensive analysis of modern corrections in the United States.

Cromwell, Paul, ed. *In Their Own Words: Criminals on Crime*. 3d ed. Los Angeles, Calif.: Roxbury, 2003. Collection of articles offering the perspectives of offenders on motivations, perceptions, decision-making strategies, and rationalizations for committing of crime.

Flanagan, T. J., J. W. Marquart, and K. G. Adams, eds. *Incarcerating Criminals: Prisons and Jails in Social and Organizational Context*. New York: Oxford University Press, 1998. Provides historical perspectives on the origins and development of correctional institutions and showcases current issues of overcrowding, substance abuse treatment, and health care.

Gray, Tara, ed. *Exploring Corrections: A Book of Readings*. Boston: Allyn & Bacon, 2002. Collection of contrasting viewpoints on the correctional system and the need for alternatives to incarceration.

Irwin, John. *The Warehouse Prison: Disposal of the New Dangerous Class*. Los Angeles, Calif.: Roxbury, 2005. Thorough examination of the implementation of new technology and prison regimes from 1980 to 2000.

Latessa, Edward J., A. Holsinger, J. W. Marquart, and J. R. Sorenson, eds. *Correctional Contexts: Contemporary and Classical Readings*. 2d ed. Los Angeles, Calif.: Roxbury, 2001. Collection of readings tracing the history of corrections in the United States.

Mays, G. Larry, and L. Thomas Winfree, Jr. *Essentials of Corrections*. 3d ed. Belmont, Calif.: Thomson/Wadsworth, 2005. Contributions to the timeless debate about what constitutes appropriate punishments for crimes, with attention to the widespread dissatisfaction with the American corrections system.

Paluch, James A., Jr., T. J. Bernard, and R. Johnson. *A Life for a Life: Life Imprisonment (America's Other Death Penalty)*. Los Angeles, Calif.: Roxbury, 2003. Firsthand account of the realities and culture of prison life by a convict serving a life sentence.

Russ, J. I., and S. C. Richards. *Convict Criminology*. Belmont, Calif.: Thomson/Wadsworth, 2003. Mixture of autobiographical accounts with research that presents convict perspectives on prison life and the problem of reentrance into the community.

Criminal Law

Boyce, R. N., and R. M. Perkins. *Criminal Law and Procedure: Cases and Materials*. 7th ed. Westbury, N.Y.: Foundation Press, 1989. Case studies concerning common law, modern codification, and the model penal code.

Hemmens, C., J. L. Worrall, and A. Thompson. *Criminal Justice Case Briefs: Significant Cases in Criminal Procedure*. Los Angeles, Calif.: Roxbury, 2004. Critical review of the most important legal cases relating to criminal justice.

Merlone, A. P., and A. Karnes. *The American Legal System: Foundations, Processes, and Norms*. Los Angeles, Calif.: Roxbury, 2003. Thorough introduction to the relationship between private and public law that aids in understanding the legal system.

Nemeth, C. P. *Law and Evidence: A Primer for Criminal Justice, Criminology, Law, and Legal Studies*. Upper Saddle River, N.J.: Prentice Hall, 2001. Review of the various forms of evidence, with advice on how best to utilize it.

Neubauer, D. W. *America's Courts and the Criminal Justice System*. 3d ed. Belmont, Calif.: Brooks/Cole, 1988. Textbook designed to bridge the gap between the history and ideology as to what should be done in court and the actual practice of court procedures.

Schubert, Frank A. *Criminal Law: The Basics*. Los Angeles, Calif.: Roxbury, 2004. Provides readers with the fundamentals of substantive criminal law.

Domestic Violence

Berry, Dawn Bradley. *Domestic Violence Sourcebook*. 3d ed. New York: McGraw-Hill, 2001. Comprehensive overview of the historical, psychological, social, and legal developments surrounding domestic violence. Also includes chapters that describe prevention and treatment strategies for victims of domestic violence and a detailed resource guide.

Buzawa, Eve, and Carl Buzawa. *Domestic Violence: The Criminal Justice Response.* 3d ed. Thousand Oaks, Calif.: Sage Publications, 2002. Examination of domestic violence from the victims' perspective.

Geffner, R. A., and A. Rosenbaum. *Current Interventions, Research, and Implications for Policies and Standards.* Binghamton, N.Y.: Haworth Press, 2002. Detailed examination of treatment strategies and intervention techniques for male batterers arrested for domestic violence.

Gelles, R. J., and D. R. Loseke, eds. *Current Controversies on Family Violence.* Thousand Oaks, Calif.: Sage Publications, 1993. Side-by-side comparison of opposing viewpoints on the conceptualization, definition, measurement, causes, and social intervention of domestic violence.

Kubany, E. S., M. A. McCaig, and J. R. Laconsay. *Healing the Trauma of Domestic Violence: A Workbook for Women.* Oakland, Calif.: New Harbinger Publications, 2004. Examination of posttraumatic stress disorder suffered by women as a consequence of becoming victims of domestic violence.

Lee, M. W., J. Sebold, and A. Uken. *Solution Focused Treatment of Domestic Violence Offenders: Accountability for Change.* New York: Oxford University Press, 2003. Study of new approaches to increasing accountability among domestic violence offenders by offering positive solutions to prevent incidences of domestic violence.

Mignon, S. I., C. J. Larson, and W. M. Holmes. *Family Abuse: Consequences, Theories, and Responses.* Boston: Allyn & Bacon, 2001. The authors integrate a theoretical framework and research findings to examine relationships between familial abuse and deviant behavior.

Mills, Linda G. *Insult to Injury: Rethinking Our Responses to Intimate Abuse.* Princeton, N.J.: Princeton University Press, 2003. Critique of the failure to consider racial, ethnic, and religious issues in domestic violence theories.

Roberts, Albert, ed. *Handbook of Domestic Violence Intervention Strategies: Policies, Programs, and Legal Remedies.* New York: Oxford University Press, 2002. Book designed to provide professionals with the tools necessary to address the specific needs of women and children falling victim to domestic violence.

Homicide and Capital Punishment

Bohm, Robert. *Deathquest: An Introduction to the Theory and Practice of Capital Punishment in the United States.* 2d ed. Cincinnati, Ohio: Anderson, 2003. Exhaustive review of the history of the controversy surrounding the implementation of the death penalty in the United States.

Del Carmen, Rolando V., et al. *The Death Penalty: Constitutional Issues, Commentaries, and Case Briefs.* Cincinnati, Ohio: Anderson, 2005. Survey of the history and foundation of the death penalty followed by the constitutional issues associated with its successful implementation.

Geberth, Vernon J. *Sex-Related Homicide and Death Investigation: Practical and Clinical Perspectives.* Boca Raton, Fla.: CRC Press, 2003. With a thirty-eight-year background in homicide investigation, the author provides a multitude of techniques for use in the investigation of certain types of sex-related homicides including sexual asphyxia, interpersonal violence, rape, lust murder, serial murder, and child abduction.

Hickey, Eric. *Serial Murderers and Their Victims.* 4th ed. Belmont, Calif.: Thomson/Wadsworth, 2005. Detailed examination of the biological, cultural, psychological, and religious factors influencing more than four hundred serial murderers throughout the world. The book features updated statistical information and profiles of some of the most famous serial killers.

Mandery, Evan J. *Capital Punishment: A Balanced Examination.* Sudbury, Mass.: Jones and Bartlett, 2005. Comprehensive review of the constitutional implications of the implementation of capital punishment in America.

Shipley, S. L., and B. A. Arrigo. *The Female Homicide Offender: Serial Murder and the Case of Aileen Wuornos.* Upper Saddle River, N.J.: Prentice Hall, 2005. Thorough examination of female criminality with special attention to the case of Aileen Wuornos.

Juvenile Justice

Cox, S. M., J. J. Conrad, and J. M. Allen. *Juvenile Justice: A Guide to Theory and Practice*. 5th ed. New York: McGraw-Hill, 2003. Innovative approach to exploring the juvenile justice system through the assessment of those involved in the system, changes in the law, and the development of a theoretical framework to explain the origins of delinquency.

Decker, Scott. *Policing Gangs and Youth Violence*. Belmont, Calif.: Thomson/Wadsworth, 2003. Proposes a community-oriented policing approach in promoting community-wide involvement in the prevention of gang violence and juvenile delinquency.

Grennan, S., M. T. Britz, J. Rush, and T. Barker. *Gangs: An International Approach*. Upper Saddle River, N.J.: Prentice Hall, 2000. History of the origin of gangs with discussion of their structures and organizations, followed by chapters on specific ethnically-based gangs.

Lundman, R. J. *Prevention and Control of Juvenile Delinquency*. 3d ed. New York: Oxford University Press, 2001. Analysis of intensive supervision programs, patterns of delinquency, incapacitation, and deterrence. Includes recommendations for instillment of community-based treatment programs for the vast majority of chronic offenders.

Miller, Jody, Cheryl L. Maxson, and Malcolm W. Klein, eds. *The Modern Gang Reader*. 2d ed. Los Angeles, Calif.: Roxbury, 2001. Anthology of original articles addressing salient contemporary issues relating to gang activity.

Sanborn, J. B., and A. Salerno. *The Juvenile Justice System: Law and Process*. Los Angeles, Calif.: Roxbury, 2005. Comprehensive overview of the history of juvenile justice in the United States, jurisdiction of the courts, prevalence and incidence of delinquent behavior, trial and sentencing phases, community and institutional corrections, and recommendations for the future.

Siegel, L. J., B. C. Walsh, and J. J. Senna. *Juvenile Delinquency: Theory, Practice and Law*. 9th ed. Belmont, Calif.: Thomson Learning, 2005. Overview of all facets of the juvenile justice system, including theories; social, community, and environmental influences; and the organization of the system itself.

Law Enforcement

Caldero, M. A., and J. P. Crank. *Police Ethics: The Corruption of Noble Cause*. 2d ed. Cincinnati, Ohio: Anderson, 2004. Study of the day-to-day ethical challenges confronting police officers and factors contributing to police corruption.

Hess, John. *Interviewing and Interrogation for Law Enforcement*. Cincinnati, Ohio: Anderson, 1997. A former FBI instructor explains interrogation techniques that have been used successfully in preventing crime.

Klotter, John C. *Legal Guide for Police: Constitutional Issues*. 6th ed. Cincinnati, Ohio: Anderson, 2001. Textbook that provides law-enforcement officers with a convenient guide to laws and procedures associated with arrest, search and seizure, detention authority, interrogation, and pretrial identification.

Lersch, Kim Michelle. *Policing and Misconduct*. Upper Saddle River, N.J.: Prentice Hall, 2002. Examination of the various aspects of the historical development of appropriate police conduct and ethical behavior.

Ortmeier, P. J. *Introduction to Law Enforcement and Criminal Justice*. 2d ed. Upper Saddle River, N.J.: Prentice Hall, 2005. Comprehensive overview of the historical development of law-enforcement and criminal justice philosophies.

Thurman, Q. C., and J. D. Jamieson. *Police Problem Solving*. Cincinnati, Ohio: Anderson, 2004. Provides useful problem-solving techniques for police working in domestic security and dealing with troubled youth, auto theft, prostitution, gangs, and crime in public housing.

Wadman, R. C., and W. T. Allison. *To Protect and Serve: A History of Police in America*. Upper Saddle River, N.J.: Prentice Hall, 2004. Detailed examination of the historical development, theory, and practice of police organizations.

Miscellaneous

Mann, C. R., and M. S. Zatz, eds. *Images of Color, Images of Crime: Readings*. Los Angeles, Calif.:

Roxbury, 1998. Comprehensive guide to the exploration of the dynamics of race, crime, and the criminal justice system. Each of the twenty-two original essays stresses links between images of color and crime based on gender, class, and heritage.

Saferstein, Richard. *Criminalistics: An Introduction to Forensic Science*. 8th ed. Upper Saddle River, N.J.: Prentice Hall, 2004. Examines the latest technological advances employed in the use of trace evidence to link offenders to crime scenes that in turn lead to eventual apprehension and prosecution.

Salter, Ann. *Predators: Pedophiles, Rapists, and Other Sex Offenders—Who They Are, How They Operate, and How We Can Protect Ourselves and Our Children*. New York: Basic Books, 2003. The authors use case histories to investigate varying types of predators and offer strategies to be employed in minimizing risks of victimization.

Taylor, R. W., T. J. Caeti, K. Loper, E. J. Fritsch, and J. Liederbach. *Digital Crime and Digital Terrorism*. Upper Saddle River, N.J.: Prentice Hall, 2006. The authors use case studies to illustrate the historical development, incidence, and prevalence of digital crime as well as the types of legislation being put in place to prevent this rapidly growing criminal enterprise.

Terry, Karen J. *Sexual Offenses and Offenders: Theory, Practice, and Policy*. Belmont, Calif.: Thomson Learning/Wadsworth, 2005. Discussion of the history of sexual offenses, definitions, incidence, and prevalence, with information on offender typologies. The book examines such issues as Megan's law and legislation designed to combat sexual offenses.

Weston, Paul B., and Charles A. Lushbaugh. *Criminal Investigation: Basic Perspectives*. 10th ed. Upper Saddle River, N.J.: Prentice Hall, 2006. With a combined fifty years of law-enforcement experience, the authors present a comprehensive review of the basic concepts concerning all aspects of criminal investigation.

Theories

Agnew, Robert. *Why Do Criminals Offend? A General Theory of Crime and Delinquency*. Los Angeles, Calif.: Roxbury, 2004. The author integrates past and current research to develop a general theory of crime that incorporates theories of social learning, social control, self-control, strain, labeling, and social support.

Akers, R. L., and C. S. Sellers. *Criminological Theories: Introduction, Evaluation and Application*. 4th ed. Los Angeles, Calif.: Roxbury, 2004. Exhaustive review of the leading theories influencing the field of criminology, with empirical evaluations of each theory.

Cullen, Francis T., and R. Agnew, eds. *Criminological Theory: Past to Present Essential Readings*. 2d ed. Los Angeles, Calif.: Roxbury, 2003. Anthology of readings that trace the development of criminological theory from past to present.

Curran, D. J., and C. M. Renzetti. *Theories of Crime*. 2d ed. Boston: Allyn & Bacon, 2001. Summaries of the major theoretical perspectives in criminology followed by empirical tests of the theories.

DeKeseredy, W. S., D. Ellis, and S. Alvi. *Deviance and Crime: Theory, Research, and Policy*. 3d ed. Cincinnati, Ohio: Anderson, 2005. Comprehensive examination of the discordance among the academic community, policymakers, and the population at large concerning the construction of social policies aimed at preventing social deviance.

Gottfredson, Michael R., and T. Hirschi. *A General Theory of Crime*. Palo Alto, Calif.: Stanford University Press, 1990. Controversial book that dismisses classical sociological theories and focuses on control theory and successful socialization as being predictors of subsequent criminality.

Hunter, Ronald D., and Mark L. Dantzker. *Crime and Criminality: Causes and Consequences*. Upper Saddle River, N.J.: Prentice Hall, 2001. Analysis of the core criminological theories that attempts to bridge gaps among different social science explanations of crime.

Lilly, R., F. Cullen, and R. Ball. *Criminological Theory: Context and Consequences*. 2d ed. Thousand Oaks, Calif.: Sage Publications, 1995. History of criminological theory and the interconnections among social context, theory, and policymaking. This edition offers a new chapter on feminist perspectives.

Paternoster, Raymond, and Ronet Bachman, eds.

Explaining Criminals and Crime: Essays in Contemporary Criminological Theory. Los Angeles, Calif.: Roxbury, 2001. Collection of articles on the historical development, basic tenets, and controversies surrounding the contemporary criminological theories, including biological, strain, social and self-control, social reaction, social learning, social disorganization, radical and feminist, rational choice, routine activities, and integrated theory.

Renzetti, C. M., D. J. Curran, and P. J. Carr, eds. *Theories of Crime: A Reader*. Boston: Allyn & Bacon, 2003. Collection of writings by leading criminologists on contemporary sociological, biological, and psychological theories of crime.

Thornberry, Terence P. *Developmental Theories of Crime and Delinquency*. Somerset, N.J.: Transaction, 2004. The author describes the evolution of criminal behavior that typically begins in adolescence and carries forward throughout the life course.

Vold, G. B., T. J. Bernard, and J. B. Snipes. *Theoretical Criminology*. 5th ed. New York: Oxford University Press, 2002. Overview of a wide range of theories addressing crime, including classical theory, positivism, biological and psychological theories, mainstream sociological theory, and theoretical integration.

Williams, Frank P., and Marilyn D. McShane, eds. *Criminology Theory: Selected Classic Readings*. 2d ed. Cincinnati, Ohio: Anderson, 1998. Anthology of readings explaining the foundations of classical and modern criminological theory.

Terrorism

Benjamin, Daniel, and Steven Simon. *The Age of Sacred Terror: Radical Islam's War Against America*. New York: Random House, 2003. Nearly a year before the September 11, 2001, attacks on the United States, the director and senior director of the National Security Council began writing this book in an attempt to warn the public about a newly emerging breed of terrorists determined to kill large numbers of Americans.

Dyson, William E. *Terrorism: An Investigator's Handbook*. 2d ed. Cincinnati, Ohio: Anderson, 2005. Comprehensive guide to the appropriate investigatory procedures to initiate and specific actions to be taken in response to terrorist attacks.

Frum, David, and Richard Perle. *An End to Evil: How to Win the War on Terror*. New York: Random House, 2003. A former presidential speechwriter and a secretary of defense wrote this book to present their views on foreign policy in an effort to win the war on terror.

Posner, Gerald. *Why America Slept: The Failure to Prevent 9/11*. New York: Random House, 2003. Attempt to uncover the truth behind the failed U.S. intelligence investigations during the time leading up to the September 11, 2001, attacks.

White, Jonathon. *Terrorism and Homeland Security*. 7th ed. Belmont, Calif.: Thomson/Wadsworth, 2005. The author has combined two previously written books to provide a comprehensive guide to the latest information on terrorism in the West, Middle East, Europe, and Latin America.

Criminal Behavior and Typologies

Bartol, C. R., and A. M. Bartol. *Criminal Behavior: A Psychological Approach*. 7th ed. New York: Prentice Hall, 2005. Examination of behavioral, emotional, and cognitive aspects of criminals in an effort to uncover the causes, classification, and intervention of criminals and crime.

Cassel, E., and D. A. Bernstein. *Criminal Behavior*. New York: Allyn & Bacon, 2000. Detailed exploration of the origins of criminal behavior and its development over the life courses of offenders; also includes a typology of all violent and property crimes from the perspectives of both offenders and victims.

Clinard, M. B., R. Quinney, and J. Wildeman. *Criminal Behavioral Systems: A Typology*. 3d ed. Cincinnati, Ohio: Anderson, 1994. Typologies of perpetrators of violent, personal, property, public order, conventional, political, occupational, corporate, organized, and professional crimes.

Dabney, Dean A., ed. *Crime Types: A Text/Reader*. Belmont, Calif.: Thomson/Wadsworth, 2004. Compilation of original essays exploring typologies of homicide and assault, violent sex crimes, robbery, burglary, common property crimes, public order crimes, and organizational crime.

Miethe, T. D., and R. McCorkle. *Crime Profiles: The Anatomy of Dangerous Persons, Places, and Situations*. Los Angeles, Calif.: Roxbury, 1998. Summary of the seven major forms of crime: homicide and aggravated assault, sexual assault, robbery, burglary, motor vehicle theft, occupational and organizational crime, and public order crimes.

Violence

Barnett, O., C. L. Miller-Perrin, and R. Perrin. *Family Violence Across the Lifespan: An Introduction*. 2d ed. Thousand Oaks, Calif.: Sage Publications, 2005. Provides readers with a better understanding of the methodology, etiology, prevalence, treatment, and prevention of family violence. The chapters chronologically address the following areas as they relate to violence over the life course: child physical, sexual, and emotional abuse; courtship violence; date rape; spousal abuse; battered women; batterers; and elder abuse.

Gilbert, P. R., and K. K. Eby. *Violence and Gender: An Interdisciplinary Reader*. Upper Saddle River, N.J.: Prentice Hall, 2004. Multidisciplinary approach to understanding violent behavior in order to develop strategies for its reduction.

Holmes, Stephen T., and Ronald M. Holmes, eds. *Violence: A Contemporary Reader*. New York: Prentice Hall, 2004. Collection of readings on violence in diverse settings, including inner cities, families, schools, and workplaces.

Lopata, H. Z., and J. A. Levy. *Social Problems Across the Life Course*. Lanham, Md.: Rowman and Littlefield, 2003. Study of how society develops social problems through personal hardships confronted by individuals at varying stages in life.

Meadows, Robert J. *Understanding Violence and Victimization*. 3d ed. New York: Prentice Hall, 2003. Provides a multitude of varying perspectives on causes surrounding victimization, the dynamics of victim-offender relationships, and legal and behavior responses to victims.

Toch, Hans. *Violent Men: An Inquiry into the Psychology of Violence*. Washington, D.C.: American Psychological Association, 1992. Portrayal of the motivational factors, attitudes, assumptions, and perceptions among chronic violent offenders and others with established propensities toward violence.

Zahn, M. A., H. H. Brownstein, and S. L. Jackson, eds. *Violence: From Theory to Research*. Cincinnati, Ohio: Anderson, 2004. Anthology of original works applying various criminological theories.

Careers in Criminal Justice

Most of these books are similar in approach, offering descriptions of criminal justice jobs, the qualifications necessary to obtain them, and practical advice on applying for the jobs. Persons considering careers in criminal justice would do well to make sure they get hold of the latest editions of any of these books they wish to consult.

Ackerman, Thomas. *Guide to Careers in Federal Law Enforcement: Profiles of 225 High-Powered Positions and Surefire Tactics for Getting Hired*. East Lansing, Mich.: Hamilton Burrows Press, 2001.

Hutton, D. B., and A. Mydlarz. *Guide to Homeland Security Careers*. Hauppage, N.Y.: Barron's Educational Series, 2003.

Justice Research Association. *Your Criminal Justice Career: A Guidebook*. 2d ed. Upper Saddle River, N.J.: Prentice Hall, 2003.

Peat, Barbara. *From College to Career: A Guide for Criminal Justice Majors*. Boston: Allyn & Bacon, 2004.

Stephens, W. Richard. *Careers in Criminal Justice*. 2d ed. Boston: Allyn & Bacon, 2003.

Stinchcomb, James. *Opportunities in Law Enforcement and Criminal Justice Careers*. 2d ed. New York: McGraw-Hill, 2002.

Taylor, Dorothy. *Jumpstarting Your Career: An Internship Guide for Criminal Justice*. 2d ed. Upper Saddle River, N.J.: Prentice Hall, 2004.

Lisa Landis Murphy

Glossary

abuse of discretion. Standard that an appellate court uses to reverse actions or decisions of a lower court that are clearly wrong.

accessory. Person who secondarily assists in the commission of a crime.

accomplice liability. Liability for assisting someone else commit a crime.

accused/accused person. Person formally charged with having committed a crime; a defendant.

ACLU. American Civil Liberties Union, an organization devoted to protecting individual rights.

acquittal. Judgment of a criminal court based on the verdict of a jury or, in cases without a jury, on the court's decision, that a criminal defendant is not guilty of the crimes charged against that defendant.

actus reus. Act that violates the law; a guilty act.

adjudication. Arrival by a court at a decision.

adversary system. System—such as prevails in the United States—in which the opposing parties in a case, rather than the judge, have the primary responsibility for presenting evidence necessary to decide the case.

advocate-witness rule. Rule of legal ethics that generally prohibits an attorney from acting both as an advocate and a witness in the same case.

affidavit. Written statement made under oath.

aggravation/aggravating circumstances. Circumstances relating to the commission of a crime that cause it to be treated more seriously than average instances of the same crime.

alias. Alternative name under which a person is known.

American Bar Association. Most prominent national association of lawyers in the United States.

amicus curiae **brief.** Brief filed with a court by persons or organizations who are interested in the issues raised by a case even though they are not official parties to the case.

amnesty. Pardon granted to a person guilty of having committed political crimes.

annotated codes. Statutes organized by topic and accompanied by brief descriptions of cases referring to the statutes.

antitrust law. Legislation that provides for civil and criminal penalties against businesses that act or conspire unreasonably to limit competition in the marketplace.

appeal. Request to a higher court to review the decision of a lower court.

appearance. Act of coming into a court and submitting to that court's authority.

appellant. Person who is appealing the decision of a lower court to a higher court.

appellate jurisdiction. Authority of a higher court to hear a case appealed from a lower court.

appellee. Person who receives a favorable decision in a lower court that is being appealed by another person, an appellant, to a higher court.

arraignment. Point in criminal proceeding when the accused of a crime is brought before a court to be informed of the charges against the person and to enter a plea as to those charges.

arrest. Act of taking a person into custody for the purpose of charging that person with having committed a crime.

arrest warrant. Document issued by a judicial officer directing a law-enforcement officer to arrest a person accused of committing a crime.

arson. Unlawful destruction of property by fire or explosion.

assault. Attempt to inflict bodily harm on another, even if such harm is not inflicted. When combined with actual physical harm, it becomes assault and battery.

asset forfeiture. Government seizure of personal property derived from, or connected to, criminal activity.

assignment of error. Points made by party appealing a case that specify the mistakes allegedly made by a lower court.

attempt. Effort to commit a crime that may be punished even if the crime is not carried out.

attorney. Person who, with appropriate education and training, is admitted to practice law in a particular jurisdiction and thus authorized to advise and represent other persons in legal proceedings.

authenticate. To demonstrate that an item is genuine.

autopsy. Medical examination of a dead body undertaken to determine the cause and other circumstances of a death.

aver. To allege or assert.

background check. Search undertaken to verify the identity of, and information about, an individual.

bail. Money or other property given to obtain the release from custody of a criminal defendant and to guarantee that the defendant will thereafter appear in court.

bail bond. Agreement made by one party to procure the release of a criminal defendant that specifies that the party will pay a specified amount if the defendant thereafter fails to appear in court.

bail-enforcement agent/bail agent. See **Bounty hunter**

bailiff. Person assigned to keep order in a courtroom and superintend arrangements for the jury.

ballistics. Analysis of firearms, ammunition, and explosive devices.

bar exams. Comprehensive tests of legal knowledge given to persons desiring to become lawyers as a condition to earning the right to practice law.

battered child and battered wife syndromes. Reactions to violence perpetrated by parents, guardians, or spouses that lead victims to adopt coping mechanisms that may lock them into cycles of violence.

battery. Harmful touching of another.

bench warrant. Order issued by a court directing that a law-enforcement officer bring the person named in the warrant before the court, usually because that person has failed to obey a previous order of the court to appear.

beyond a reasonable doubt. Degree of proof required to convict a person accused of having committed a crime.

bifurcated trial. Legal proceeding in which two or more separate hearings, or trials, are held on different issues of the same case.

bigamy. Crime of marrying a person while a previous marriage to another person is still in effect; usually characterized by deceit.

bill of attainder. Unconstitutional action by a legislature that singles out particular persons for punishment without a trial.

bill of particulars. Detailed document itemizing charges against a defendant.

Bill of Rights, U.S. First ten amendments to the United States Constitution, which safeguard various individual liberties, including rights for persons suspected, or accused, of having committed crimes.

billable hours. Hours spent working on a client's matter, for which a lawyer bills an agreed upon hourly rate.

blackmail. Attempt to extort money by the threat of inflicting violence upon or exposing some wrongdoing of another; closely related to extortion.

Black's Law Dictionary. Foremost American dictionary of legal terms.

blended sentences. Types of sentences in which judges simultaneously impose both juvenile and adult sanctions on juvenile offenders.

blue laws. State and local regulations banning certain activities, particularly on Sundays.

booking. Official entry of a record of detention after the arrest of a person identifying the person arrested.

boot camps. Alternative form of incarceration using rigid discipline modeled on military training camps.

border patrols. Units of a federal agency that oversee the coastal and land boundaries of the United States.

bounty hunter/bail-enforcement agent/bail agent. Person who tracks bail skippers, defendants who flee after bail-bond companies post their bail.

breach of the peace. Disturbance of public order.

bribery. Attempt to influence some public person in the discharge of a public duty by offering something of value to the person.

brief. Concise statement of the facts and arguments in a case, or a written document presenting an argument to a court about some matter.

burden of proof. Duty of prosecution to prove a particular issue in a case; in criminal cases, for example, the duty of the prosecutor to prove beyond a reasonable doubt that an individual has committed a crime.

burglary. Entrance into a building for the purpose of committing a felony such as theft.

campus police. Law-enforcement departments based on college and university campuses.

capital crime. Crime punishable by death.

capital punishment. Punishment by death.

carjacking. Theft of a vehicle that is committed while the vehicle owner is inside or near the vehicle.

case law. Law derived from the decisions of courts.

cease-and-desist order. Order from court or agency prohibiting certain persons or entities from continuing certain conduct.

certiorari, writ of. Application to the United States Supreme Court, or a state appellate court, seeking review of a lower court decision.

chain gang. Group of prisoners who are chained together while performing manual labor outside a prison or work camp.

chain of custody. Account of the possession of the evidence from its discovery and initial possession until it is offered as evidence in court.

change of venue. Relocation of a trial from one jurisdiction to another.

chambers. Private office of a judge.

charge. Claim that an individual has committed a specific criminal offense.

check kiting. Unlawful use of two or more checking accounts to write worthless checks.

circumstantial evidence. Evidence from which a primary issue may be inferred.

citation. Order issued by a court or law-enforcement officer requiring a person to appear in court.

cite. To order someone to appear in court; to refer to legal authority in support of one's argument.

citizen's arrest. Taking of a person into physical custody by a witness to a crime other than a law-enforcement officer, for the purpose of delivering the person into the physical custody of law-enforcement officials.

civil disobedience. Deliberate act of law breaking undertaken to dramatize or protest a law or governmental policy that the offender regards as immoral.

civilian review board. Official group of citizens who examine the merits of complaints against members of the local police department.

clear and present danger test. Principle holding that political speech is protected unless it creates a "clear and present danger" to the nation.

clearance rate. Ratio of crimes reported as to the number of crimes solved.

clemency. Act of an executive official reducing a criminal sentence as a matter of leniency.

clerk of the court. Court official who maintains the court's official records and files.

closing argument. Summary of the arguments in a case made by the prosecution and the defense at the conclusion of a trial.

COINTELPRO. Secret federal government counterintelligence programs designed to neutralize radical political organizations in the United States during the late 1950's and the 1960's.

cold case. Unsolved criminal case, usually involving a homicide, on which active police work has ceased.

color of law. Action that has the appearance of authority and legality but is actually unauthorized and illegal.

commercialized vice. Business enterprises catering to various human desires that lead to statutory crimes; examples include prostitution, gambling, and pornography.

common law. Body of law, going back into early English history, that arises from judicial decisions, rather than from written statutes, that reflect customs, tradition, and precedent.

community-based corrections. Use of sentencing options that permit a convicted offender to remain in a community under conditional supervision rather than serve a sentence in prison.

community-oriented policing. Philosophy of law enforcement that encompasses aspects of social service as police officers work with members of the communities.

community service. Sentencing arrangement that requires criminal offenders to spend time performing public service supervised by a community agency.

competency, legal. Capacity to understand and to act rationally.

compulsory process. Right of a person charged with a crime to summon witnesses to court on his behalf.

computer crime. Illegal intrusions into computers and the use of computers for the perpetration of other crimes.

computer forensics. Search of computers, networks, and communication devices for existing or deleted electronic-evidence.

computer information system. System designed to bring together people, computers, and departmental rules and procedures to gather, store, retrieve, analyze, and apply information to meet an organizations' goals.

concurrent jurisdiction. Authority of two or more courts to hear the same case.

concurrent sentence. Sentence imposed after conviction of a crime that is to be served at the same time as a sentence for another crime.

concurring opinion. Judicial opinion that agrees with the result in the case reached by other judges but states different reasons for this result.

confession. Admission of guilt.

conjugal rights. Rights of married couples including companionship and sex.

consecutive sentence. Sentence served in sequence after a sentence for another crime, thus increasing the maximum time an offender is incarcerated.

consent decree. Court decree based upon the agreement of the parties to a case.

consent search. Search by law enforcement that is based on permission, usually given by the party who is the object of the search.

conspiracy. Agreement among two or more parties to commit a criminal act.

Constitution, U.S. Law: Foundation document representing the supreme law of the United States of America, as applied to the body of law dealing with offenses against the state, which may be penalized by fine or imprisonment.

consumer fraud. Intentional deception of consumers with untruthful or misleading information about goods, services, and other aspects of business.

contempt of court. Conduct that disobeys a court order, disrupts court proceedings, or undermines the dignity of a court.

contingency fees. Fee (not generally permitted in criminal cases) payable to a lawyer only if the lawyer achieves some successful result.

continuance. Delay of court proceedings until some future date.

contributing to delinquency of minors. Acts or omissions perpetrated by adults that encourage juveniles to engage in behaviors that may lead to delinquency.

controlled substance. Drug proscribed by law, such as marijuana, cocaine, and heroin.

conviction. Final determination that a criminal defendant is guilty made as a result of a trial or a plea bargain.

coroner. Public official who investigates the circumstances of violent or suspicious deaths; may or may not also be a medical examiner.

corporal punishment. Physical punishment.

corpus delicti. Meaning literally, "the body of crime," and referring to facts that demonstrate a crime has occurred.

corroborate. To support or confirm.

counsel, right to. Entitlement provided for criminal defendants by the U.S. Constitution to receive representation by an attorney during a criminal proceeding.

counterfeiting. Copying something and illegally passing the copy off as an original.

court-martial. Military tribunal convened to try members of the armed forces accused of violating the Uniform Code of Military Justice.

court reporter. Person who creates a verbatim record of proceedings in court.

crime. Any violation of a criminal law that commands or bans acts whose commission or omission are subject to penalties.

Crime Index. Part of the Federal Bureau of Investigation's annual Uniform Crime Reports that is the most complete compilation of national reported crime statistics for the eight most serious types of crime, as determined by the FBI.

crime lab. Facility—mostly government-run—designed to analyze physical evidence of crimes.

crime of passion. Crime committed under the influence of strong emotion.

crime scene investigation. Meticulous preservation of physical evidence at specific locations by use of photographs, sketches, and collection and preservation.

Glossary

criminal. Perpetrator of criminal offenses.

criminal history record information. Record, or a system of records, that includes the identification of a person and describes that person's arrests and subsequent court dispositions. Also known as a rap sheet.

criminal intent. Wrongful or guilty purpose.

criminal justice system. Interrelationships among all law-enforcement bodies, the courts, corrections, and juvenile justice throughout the United States.

criminal law. Body of law that defines criminal offenses and sets out appropriate punishments for convicted offenders.

criminal liability. Accountability under criminal law.

criminal negligence. Act that fails to exercise the appropriate care needed to avoid foreseeable harmful consequences.

criminal procedure. Stages and points at which particular decisions are made in the criminal justice process that are mandated by statutes and constitutional judicial decisions.

criminal record. Official documents that list an individual person's past convictions for misdemeanors and felonies and that sometimes include arrests that do not result in convictions.

criminology. Interdisciplinary field that relies heavily on scientific methods to study crime phenomena, including patterns and rates of crime and victimization, etiology of crime, social responses to crime, and crime control.

cross-examination. Questioning of a witness called by an opponent in a court proceeding.

cruel and unusual punishment. Punishment that is disproportionately severe in relation to a crime or otherwise excessive.

cryptology. Science of enciphering and deciphering codes, ciphers, and cryptograms.

culpable. Worthy of criminal sanction.

cultural defense. Legal defense designed to diminish or eliminate criminal responsibility by establishing that the cultural traditions of the defendants have led them reasonably to believe in the propriety of their otherwise criminal acts.

cybercrime. Crimes that involve use of the Internet and computers.

date rape. Rape committed by a person with whom the victim is voluntarily engaging in a social outing.

de minimus. Legal matter that is considered trivial or unimportant.

deadly force. Killing of people by police officers through the use of choke holds, firearms, or other methods of physical control.

death certificate. Official document recording the fact of an individual's death.

death qualification. Procedure used in selecting jury members to try death-penalty cases.

death-row attorney. Lawyer who specializes in representing criminal defendants sentenced to death in appeals of their convictions.

declaratory judgment. Court order declaring the rights or obligations of parties without awarding monetary relief or specifically ordering any party to act or not act in particular ways.

decriminalization. Process of lessening or removing penalties for violations of specified laws.

default. Failure to perform some legal duty.

defendant. Person accused of having committed a crime in a criminal case.

defendant self-representation. Situations in which criminal defendants reject professional legal counsel and represent themselves.

defense attorneys. Attorneys who are engaged to represent criminal defendants and are usually paid by the clients.

defenses to crime. Justifications and excuses offered by criminal defenses in attempts to win cases or have charges dropped or reduced.

deportation. Removal of a person from a country.

deposition. Questioning of a witness under oath outside of court that is transcribed by a court reporter or otherwise recorded.

deterrence. Effect of discouraging individuals from future involvement in criminal conduct that is produced—or believed to be produced—by harsh punishments of convicted offenders.

dictum. Language in a court opinion that is not necessary to the decision.

dilatory tactics. Attempts to delay the progress of a legal proceeding.

diminished capacity. Defense tactic used to reduce the culpability of a criminal defendant.

diplomatic immunity. Legal immunity that exempts foreign diplomats and their families from the laws of the host countries in which they work.

direct examination. Questioning of a witness by the party who called the witness.

discovery, pretrial. Procedures for allowing parties to a court case to exchange and discover relevant information prior to the trial.

discretion. Flexibility allowed to the police and the courts to make decisions such as whether to arrest and prosecute individuals.

discrimination. Treating persons or matters differently when no reasonable grounds exist for doing so.

dismiss, motion to. Motion made by defense in a criminal case arguing that grounds exist to discontinue charges against a defendant without a trial, or—in some cases after a trial has begun—without submitting the case to a jury for a verdict.

dismissal. Formal termination of a legal proceeding.

disorderly conduct. Illegal conduct that disturbs the public peace.

dissenting opinion. In cases, such as appeal cases, decided by more than one judge, an opinion written by one or more judges who believe a case should have been decided with a different result than that adopted by a majority of the court.

district attorney. Prosecuting attorney who represents the government within a particular judicial district.

diversion. Decision that may be made at several stages of the juvenile justice process to avoid formal court processing.

DNA testing. Comparison of DNA (deoxyribonucleic acid) samples from body tissues and fluids to identify people.

docket. Brief record of the proceedings in a case.

document analysis. Forensic techniques used to ascertain the authenticity of documents.

domestic violence. Emotional, sexual, or other physical abuse committed by a spouse, intimate partner, or other relatives living in the same household.

double jeopardy. To expose a criminal defendant a second time to prosecution for an offense for which the defendant has already been acquitted or that has already been finally dismissed.

drive-by shooting. Use of firearms to shoot at people from a moving vehicle passing through a neighborhood; typically associated with gang violence.

drug court. Less formal alternative to regular criminal courts in which drug-related offenses are adjudicated.

"drug czar." Nickname for the federal government official in charge of the Office of National Drug Control Policy.

drunk driving/DUI. Operating or controlling a motor vehicle while under the influence of intoxicants; also known as "driving under the influence" (DUI).

due process of law. Constitutional requirement that individuals be accorded legal procedures consistent with the orderly operation of law and with fundamental rights.

DUI. See **Drunk driving**

duress. Condition under which a person is forced to act against his or her will.

effective counsel. Legal representation of clients by fully qualified attorneys who are committed to providing their clients with the best possible defenses.

electronic surveillance. Investigative techniques used to monitor telephone conversations, electronic mail, pagers, wireless phones, computers, and other electronic devices.

embezzlement. Unlawful appropriation of money or property held in trust by one person for another.

en banc. Decision of a case by all the judges who serve on a court.

enjoin. To command that something be done or not done.

entrapment. Unlawful or improper inducement of one to commit a crime.

environmental crimes. Violations of environmental laws, such as the dumping and discharging of pollutants into the atmosphere and water and the illegal production, handling, use, and disposal of toxic substances and hazardous wastes.

equal protection of the law. Constitutional requirement that persons similarly situated be accorded the same treatment under law.

espionage. Attempting to secure secret information from a country or a company, using illegal or covert means.

ethics. Sets of moral principles and values that differentiate between good and bad behavior.

euthanasia. Intentional taking of the life of another or allowing, through intentional neglect, another life to end.

evidence, rules of. Rules governing the admissibility of all forms of evidence at trial.

ex parte. Communication, typically with a judge, by only one side of a case without the other side's knowledge or participation.

***ex post facto* laws.** Laws enacted "after the fact" of actions or occurrences that retrospectively alter the legal consequences of those original actions or occurrences.

exclusionary rule. Rule of constitutional criminal procedure that prevents the use of evidence in a criminal trial that was obtained illegally.

execution. Carrying out of death penalty.

execution of judgment. Process of carrying into effect the orders, judgments, or decrees of courts.

expert witness. Person who offers testimony in a legal proceeding based on a specialized knowledge of a subject.

extortion. Use of illegal threats by one party to obtain money or property from another; closely related to blackmail.

extradition. Surrender by one country to another of a person accused or convicted of a crime in the other country.

eyewitness testimony. Account given by a person who has directly observed a crime or an action related to a crime.

false conviction. Occasion in which an innocent person is convicted of a crime that the person did not commit.

felony. Serious crime, as distinguished from a misdemeanor, normally punishable by death or a prison sentence rather than a jail sentence.

fiduciary. Person with special obligation to act on another's behalf.

fine. Monetary payment required of a defendant that provides compensation to either the government or the victim of the defendant's crime.

firearm. Small weapon that uses gunpowder to fire lethal projectiles.

first-degree murder. Willful, premeditated murder.

forensic accounting. Integration of accounting, auditing, and investigative skills to assist in legal investigations of possible fraud and other white-collar crimes.

forensic anthropology. Analysis and identification of human skeletal remains that sometimes uses archaeological methods to recover buried remains.

forensic entomology. Use of insects and their by-products as evidence in legal investigation, prosecution, and defense.

forensic odontology. Examination of teeth to identify human remains, or to match bite marks to the teeth of an individual.

forensic palynology. Use of pollen and spore data to help solve crimes.

forensic psychology. Application of psychology to legal issues.

forensics. Application of science to the legal arena, particularly criminal investigations.

forestry camp. Minimum-security facility in which low-risk adult and juvenile offenders work with local, state, and federal forestry departments to maintain public forests.

forgery. Illegal creation of a document or alteration of an existing document to accomplish a fraudulent purpose.

fraud. Intentional misrepresentation or distortion of facts.

fugitive. Person who flees from justice to avoid being tried or serving a sentence.

gag order. Court order that prevents parties, attorneys, or others from discussing matters pertaining to a case.

gambling. Playing of games and placing of bets to win money or other prizes; may be legal or illegal, depending on the jurisdiction and the form that the gambling takes.

gangster. Member of a professional crime organization; the term is most closely associated with criminals during the Prohibition era of the 1920's and early 1930's, when organized crime profited from the illegal sale of alcohol.

geographic information system. System that is used to plot and analyze geographic locations of such data as crimes.

good time. Reduction of prison sentences based on good behavior or participation in some kind of program by inmates.

graffiti. Unauthorized drawing, writing, or painting on a surface in a public space.

grand jury. Citizens appointed to hear evidence relating to crimes and to determine whether criminal indictments should be brought against particular individuals.

habeas corpus, **writ of.** Application to a court to consider whether a person held in custody is being held lawfully.

halfway house. Supervised-living facility, usually in an urban area, that provides an alternative to incarceration that is midway between incarceration and release.

harmless error. Legal mistake made during the course of a defendants' progress through the justice system that is not considered to be damaging.

hate crime. Crime perpetrated against a person because of the person's race, ethnicity, religion, sexual orientation, or other group characteristic.

hate crime statutes. Laws that impose penalties or increase penalties for crimes motivated by racial prejudice or other specified forms of hatred.

hearing. Legal proceeding other than a trial in which evidence is taken or legal arguments presented.

hearsay. Out-of-court statement offered to prove the truth of some matter at issue in a legal proceeding.

high-speed chase. Vehicular pursuit by law-enforcement officers of a suspected or known criminal or traffic law violator.

highway patrol. State government law-enforcement agency whose primary responsibilities are traffic management and traffic law enforcement.

hit-and-run accident. Vehicular accident in which the responsible driver leaves the scene prior to the arrival of police.

homicide. Killing of another person.

house arrest. Intermediate form of sanction that allows offenders to remain in their homes under specific restrictions.

hung jury. Jury that cannot agree to the extent specified by law—whether unanimously or otherwise—on a verdict.

identity theft. Crime of wrongfully obtaining and using the personal data of others for one's own profit.

ignorance of the law. Criminal defense based on defendants' claims to have been ignorant of the laws they have broken.

illegal alien. Colloquial term for a foreign-born person who enters the United States without legal authorization or one who enters legally but violates the terms of admission or fails to acquire permanent residence status.

immunity from prosecution. Legally binding promise not to prosecute a potential defendant, typically offered in exchange for testimony.

impanel. To select and install the members of a jury.

impeach. To discredit the testimony of a witness or the behavior of judges or other public officials.

in forma pauperis. Latin phrase, meaning "as a poor pauper," that is applied to legal matters involving poor persons.

inalienable. Incapable of being transferred or surrendered, such as inalienable rights.

incapacitation. Aim or rationale of punishment that seeks to control crime by rendering a criminal unable, or less able, to commit crimes, such as incarceration of the offender.

inchoate crime. Crime that is intended to lead to another crime, such as the crime of solicitation to commit murder.

incompetent to stand trial. Condition, often the result of a mental illness, under which a criminal defendant is unable to understand the charges and proceeding against him or to assist in the preparation of his own defense.

incorporation doctrine. Process through which the U.S. Supreme Court has extended U.S. Bill of Rights protections to the states.

incorrigible. Not capable of being reformed.

incriminate. To provide evidence that would implicate someone, including one's self, of having committed a crime.

indecent exposure. Unlawful and intentional exposure in public places of one's normally covered body parts.

indeterminate sentencing. System of awarding prison sentences whose terms are defined by minimum and maximum lengths.

indictment. Formal accusation made by a grand jury that a particular individual has committed a crime.

indigent. Poor.

information. Formal accusation by a public official such as a judge that an individual has committed a crime, used in many states as an alternative to a grand jury indictment.

injunction. Order by a court for someone to do or not do something.

inquest. Official investigation of whether a crime has occurred, especially in connection with a death.

insanity. In criminal law, the state of being either temporarily or permanently unaware of one's actions, or unable to determine whether one's actions are right or wrong.

insanity defense. Defense tactic used to reduce the culpability of a criminal defendant.

insider trading. Purchase or sale of securities by persons who have access to information that is not available to those with whom they deal or to traders generally.

insurance fraud. Willful misrepresentations or fabrications by claimants or providers of facts concerning accidents, injuries, or thefts for the purpose of monetary gain.

interlocutory. Temporary or provisional action, such as a court order pending a final determination of some matter or an appeal pending the conclusion of a trial.

internal affairs. Units within police departments that investigate charges of police misconduct.

international law. Body of international norms and practices established by national governments to deter and to punish criminal acts of international consequence.

international tribunal. Court established by countries at the regional or global level to try war criminals.

Interpol. International Criminal Police Organization, the largest international police organization in the world.

involuntary manslaughter. Unintentional killing that is not murder but for which criminal liability is imposed.

jaywalking. Crossing of public streets at illegal locations.

J.D. Doctor of jurisprudence; a postgraduate degree normally necessary to practice law in the United States.

Jim Crow laws. Discriminatory laws of the past that were designed to disfranchise and segregate African Americans in the South.

judge. Appointed or elected public official who is charged with authoritatively and impartially resolving disputes presented in a court of law.

judicial review. Power of courts to review the constitutionality of actions taken by other branches of government.

jurisdiction. Authority of a court to hear and decide a particular case.

jurisprudence. Philosophy of law.

jury duty. Obligation of citizens to respond to summonses to serve the legal system by hearing evidence and rendering decisions in trials.

jury nullification. Power of juries to render verdicts that alter the law or the facts in cases.

jury sequestration. Confinement of a jury during a trial or jury deliberations to prevent jury members from being improperly influenced by contact with others.

just deserts. Concept that punishments for crimes should match the severity of the crimes themselves.

justice. Administration of rewards and punishments according to rules and principles that society considers fair and equitable.

justifiable homicide. Killing of another person, as in self-defense, that is permitted by law.

juvenile court. Court specializing in cases involving juvenile offenders.

juvenile delinquent/juvenile offender. Minor who has committed a crime.

juvenile waiver to adult courts. Formal process of moving a case from a juvenile court to an adult court.

kidnapping. Unlawful detention of a person by force against the person's will.

larceny. Illegal taking of another's personal property with the intent to steal it.

latent evidence. Evidence that is left behind by fingers or other body parts on surfaces that they come into contact with; such evidence is typically biological material.

law enforcement. Component of the criminal justice system that is responsible for such functions as crime prevention and fighting, order maintenance, conflict management, and other services.

leading question. Question asked during the examination of a witness that suggests the answer desired; generally permitted during cross-examination of a witness but not during the direct examination of a witness.

lesser-included offense. Crime necessarily proven by proof that a more serious crime has been committed.

Lindbergh law. Congressional legislation making kidnapping for ransom and carrying victims across state lines a federal crime.

loitering. Standing idle or wandering about aimlessly without a lawful purpose.

LSAT. Law School Admission Test; a standardized test used to measure the qualifications of potential law students.

lynching. Extralegal means of social control in which individuals—typically members of mobs—take the law into their own hands to inflict physical punishment or even death upon persons seen as violating local customs and mores.

magistrate. Judicial official with authority to decide preliminary matters or minor cases.

mail fraud. Use of government postal services to conduct fraudulent schemes.

mala in se. Action that is considered wrong in itself.

mala prohibita. Action, such as driving on the wrong side of the road, that is considered wrong only because the law defines it as such.

malfeasance. Wrongful or illegal conduct.

malice. Intent to commit a wrongful act.

malice aforethought. Predetermined intent to commit a wrongful act.

malicious mischief. Spiteful destruction of personal property.

mandamus, **writ of.** Court order requiring a lower court or government agency to carry out its lawfully mandated duties.

mandatory sentencing. Laws requiring judges to impose predetermined penalties for certain specified crimes or third felony convictions.

manslaughter. Negligent or otherwise unlawful killing of a person without malice aforethought.

martial law. Use of armed forces or National Guard units to help maintain public order during emergencies.

medical examiner. Official responsible for investigating the circumstances of suspicious or violent deaths.

mens rea. Criminal intent.

mental illness. Illness, disease, or condition that substantially impairs sufferers' thought processes, perceptions of reality, and sense of judgment, while grossly impairing their behavior and emotional well-being.

military justice. System of justice designed to maintain order and discipline within the armed forces.

minor. Person who has not reached age of adulthood defined by law.

Miranda rights. Requirement that individuals be advised of certain constitutional protections at the time of their arrest.

miscarriage of justice. Legal act, verdict, or punishment that is clearly unfair or unjust.

misdemeanor. Minor crime punishable by a fine or imprisonment for a relatively brief period, generally less than one year in most jurisdictions, and generally in a local jail as opposed to a prison.

misprision of felony. Concealment of or failure to report a felony under circumstances where the law requires one to report the felony.

missing persons. Persons who are abducted or who inexplicably leave home or remain away from home for an extended period.

mistrial. Premature termination of a trial because of some misconduct or other unusual occurrence.

mitigating circumstances. Circumstances relating to violations of law that may cause decreases in the sentences.

M'Naghten rule. Legal test for insanity in criminal cases, that asks whether a defendant knew the nature of his actions and whether those actions were right or wrong.

Model Penal Code. Code of criminal provisions developed by the American Law Institute and intended to standardize criminal law among the various states.

modus operandi. Method by which a crime is carried out.

money laundering. Methods of concealing the source of illegally obtained money.

moral turpitude. Act characterized by dishonesty or depravity.

motion. Request for a court to take some action.

motive. Reason a person commits a crime.

multiple jurisdiction offense. Criminal offense that is subject to prosecution in more than one jurisdiction.

murder. Unlawful killing of another person with malice aforethought.

murder, mass. Killing of multiple victims in a short period of time.

murder, serial. Killing of multiple victims over a period of time, often using the same methods.

natural law. Legal principles derived from general moral intuitions.

naturalization. Process by which a person not born a citizen is granted citizenship in a country.

negligence. Failure to act with due care.

night court. Court holding its sessions during evening hours.

no-knock warrant. Written order allowing police to enter a structure without first announcing their presence.

nolle prosequi. Announcement made into a court record that a plaintiff or prosecutor will not proceed forward with a lawsuit or indictment.

nolo contendere **plea.** Plea according to which a criminal defendant neither denies nor admits guilt.

nonlethal weapon. Weapon designed to control living persons and animals when used properly, without killing or causing serious bodily injury.

nonviolent resistance. Active use of nonviolent strategies to resist laws and policies regarded as unjust and to promote social and political change.

objection. Challenge to testimony or other evidence offered in court, or to other action taken in court.

obscenity. Patently offensive sexual material lacking serious literary, artistic, political, or scientific value.

obstruction of justice. Crime of interfering with the administration of justice such as by improperly influencing a witness or destroying evidence.

offender. Perpetrator of a crime.

offer of proof. Means of preserving a record of evidence not admitted in a trial, so that an appellate court can determine whether the evidence was improperly excluded from the trial record.

opinion. Written statement of a judge or court summarizing the facts of a case, the issues raised in the case, and the reasons for the court's decision.

ordinance. Law adopted by a local political body such as a city council.

organized crime. Syndicated enterprises characterized by pyramidal structures, specialization of functions, and unity of command that engage in ongoing criminal activities.

original jurisdiction. Authority of a court—such as a trial court—to make the initial determination of a particular issue, in contrast with appellate jurisdiction.

overrule. For a court to deny an objection in a case or to overturn the legal authority of a prior case.

oyez. Meaning literally "Hear Ye," a phrase used to call a judicial proceeding to order.

pandering. Encouraging another person to engage in prostitution.

paralegal. Nonlawyer with legal skills who works under the supervision of an attorney.

pardon. Exempting, by the U.S. president or the governor of a state, of one accused of a crime from punishment.

parens patriae. Legal doctrine granting authority to the government to take responsibility for the welfare of children.

parole. Release of a prisoner, generally subject to conditions, prior to the time a sentence has been completed.

parole officer. Government employee charged

with supervising parolees, convicted criminals who have been released, or exempted, from incarceration.

parole violation. Violation of one or more of the conditions of parole, for which parole may be revoked and a person who has been released on parole returned to incarceration.

pedophilia. Adult sexual disorder that makes children sex objects.

penal code. Collection of laws defining criminal conduct.

peremptory challenge. Objection to the seating of a particular person on a jury that need not be supported by specific reasons.

perjury. Deliberate false statement made under oath.

personal recognizance. Pretrial release of criminal defendant without bail, on the basis of defendant's reasonably relied upon promise to appear for trial.

pickpocketing. Form of larceny that involves the sudden or stealthy stealing of property directly from persons, usually in public places.

plain error rule. Rule allowing an appellate court to reverse a trial court decision on some issue even if the person appealing did not complain about the issue at trial, as is normally required.

plain view doctrine. Rule allowing law-enforcement personnel to seize items in plain view even if they do not have a proper search warrant.

plea. Response of a criminal defendant to the charge or charges contained in an indictment.

plea bargain. Agreement between a prosecutor and a criminal defendant disposing of a criminal matter.

police. Officers of municipal law-enforcement agencies whose primary mission is to protect their communities from crime and other threats.

police academy. Training school for new police recruits.

police brutality. Abuses of authority that amount to serious and divisive human rights violations involving the excessive use of force that may occur in the apprehension or retention of civilians.

police chief. Top officer in an urban police department.

police civil liability. Police officers' obligations to refrain from acts within the course of duty that may cause undue harm to another.

police corruption. Unethical, dishonest, and other criminal conduct or deviant behaviors by police officers that involve abuses of their authority.

police detective. Police officer who specializes in criminal investigations.

police dog. Dog used by law-enforcement professionals to help find missing persons and criminal suspects and to sniff out controlled substances.

police lineup. Investigative tool used by police to identify possible suspects of a crime by lining them up, side by side, as victims and eyewitnesses attempt to pick out perpetrators.

police powers. Authority conferred on law-enforcement officers to enforce the law.

political corruption. Misuse of public office for personal gain.

polling a jury. Asking each member of a jury whether he or she agrees with the verdict that the jury has announced.

polygamy. Condition of having more than one spouse at the same time; differs from bigamy in not being undertaken deceitfully.

polygraph. Device used to test whether a person is telling the truth.

pornography. Depiction of erotic behavior that is intended to arouse sexual excitement.

positive law. Law created or enacted by an appropriate lawmaking authority, such as a legislature or a court, in contrast with natural law.

posse comitatus. Group of people pressed into service to help civilian officials enforce the law.

post mortem. Official examination of a body after death has occurred.

precedent. Decision of a court that is used to resolve a subsequent legal case.

preemption. Doctrine of constitutional law, based on the Supremacy Clause, that stipulates that federal laws on a subject (including the U.S. Constitution) are superior to and override inconsistent state and local laws.

preliminary hearing. In criminal proceedings that do not involve a grand jury indictment, a court hearing to determine whether there is probable cause to believe that an accused person has committed a crime.

preponderance of the evidence. Standard for deciding whether a person who brings a civil lawsuit will prevail, which requires evidence sufficient to suggest that it is more likely than not that an asserted claim is true. Contrasted with the more demanding standard used for deciding whether a government has proved that an individual has committed a crime, which requires proof beyond a reasonable doubt.

presentence investigation. Report drafted by a probation officer or court officials that details significant information that may be used in sentencing a defendant.

presumption of innocence. Requirement that government affirmatively prove that an individual has committed a crime.

preventive detention. Confinement of a criminal defendant before final conviction and sentencing.

price fixing. Agreement between competitors establishing prices, generally prohibited by state or federal antitrust laws.

prima facie case. Presentation of evidence sufficient to prevail in a case absent some response from an opponent.

prisons and jails. Government facilities that hold individuals suspected of, or convicted of, committing crimes.

private detectives. Nongovernment investigators who hire out to attorneys, companies, and private citizens.

private police and guards. Nongovernment security personnel who provide protective services that supplement law-enforcement protection.

privileged communication. Communication between two individuals, such as an attorney and a client or a physician and a patient, whose confidentiality the law protects, made in circumstances in which the individuals intend for the communication to remain secret. This communication cannot be admitted into evidence in a judicial proceeding without the permission of the parties to the communication.

pro bono legal work. Legal services provided by an attorney without charge.

pro se representation. Representation of one's self in a legal proceeding, in contrast with being represented by an attorney.

probable cause. In criminal proceedings that do not involve a grand jury indictment, information sufficient for a judge to conclude that it is likely enough that an accused person has committed a crime to justify proceeding with a trial; in the case of search warrants, information sufficient for a judge to conclude that evidence relating to a crime may be found at a particular location.

probation. Sentencing procedure through which offenders convicted of crimes are released by courts and remain out of prison, so long as they adhere to conditions set by the judges.

Prohibition. Historical period during which a federal constitutional amendment banned the production, sale, and distribution of alcoholic beverages throughout the United States, thereby enabling organized crime to make large profits through the sale of contraband alcohol.

proof, burden of. See **burden of proof**

prosecutor. Lawyer, such as a district attorney or a United States attorney, who represents the government in cases against persons accused of having committed crimes.

prostitution. Criminal act of engaging in the sale of sexual services.

proximate cause. Action that results in an event, particularly an injury or damage, due to negligence or intentionally wrongful behavior.

psychological profiling. Method of identifying probable offender characteristics, including behavioral, personality, and physical attributes, based on crime scene evidence.

psychopathy/sociopathy. Psychological disorder marked by a constellation of personality traits, including dishonesty, guiltlessness, and callousness.

public defender. Attorney appointed by government to defend a person accused of crime when that person cannot afford to hire a lawyer.

public nuisance. Unlawful interference with a community's use of public property.

public-order offense. Act that interferes with the operations of society and its ability to maintain order.

public prosecutor. Attorney serving as the public official responsible for overseeing the prosecution of criminal cases by setting charges, conducting plea negotiations, and presenting evidence in court on behalf of the government.

punishment. Intentional infliction of harm by government on individuals for offenses against law.

punitive damages. Money awarded in civil tort actions to punish intentional wrongdoers and to deter them and others from engaging in similar such behavior in the future.

race riot. Short-lived but violent conflict—usually in an urban area—that pits members of different racial groups against each other.

racial profiling. Police practice of using race or ethnicity as a primary reason for stopping, questioning, searching, or arresting potential suspects.

rape. Criminal act of engaging in sexual intercourse with an individual against his or her will.

reasonable doubt. Absence of moral certainty of a defendant's guilt.

reasonable doubt, proof beyond a. Standard of proof required in criminal cases according to which the government must offer proof such as to preclude the reasonable possibility of innocence.

reasonable force. Amount of physical force that police officers may use while making arrests.

reasonable suspicion. Amount of certainty that illegal actions are taking place that law-enforcement officers must have to stop suspects in public—the standard amounts to something greater than mere hunches but less than probable cause.

receiving stolen property. Crime of accepting possession of property when it is known to be stolen.

recess. Temporary adjournment of legal proceedings in a case.

recidivism. Possessing the characteristic of having repeatedly engaged in criminal conduct.

reckless endangerment. Willful engaging in conduct that shows a conscious disregard for the safety and welfare of others.

recuse. For a judge to withdraw from consideration of a matter because of some prejudice or conflict of interest.

regulatory crime. Business practices that are banned under regulatory law instead of criminal or civil law.

rehabilitation. Punishment designed to reform offenders so they can lead productive lives free from crime.

release. Liberation from incarceration.

remand. Order by a higher court returning a proceeding to a lower court for further action consistent with the higher court's decision in the case.

reprieve. Postponement of the execution of a criminal sentence.

resisting arrest. Crime arising out of the preventing of law-enforcement officers from detaining or arresting suspects.

restitution. Legal remedy requiring someone to restore property or money to the person from whom it was originally taken or obtained.

restorative justice. Philosophy of justice that focuses on repairing harm caused by offenses.

restraining order. Court order in the form of an injunction, usually temporary, that forbids a specified party or parties from doing specified acts.

retainer. Fee for legal services paid in advance.

reversible error. Significant error committed by a trial court sufficient to justify an appellate court to overrule the result obtained at trial.

right to bear arms. Right of citizens to own and carry guns.

robbery. Taking of one's property within one's presence by force or the threat of force.

scienter. Knowledge.

search and seizure. Law-enforcement practice of searching people and places in order to seize evidence or suspects.

search warrant. Judicial order allowing law-enforcement personnel to enter and search a particular location.

seditious libel. Criminal act of undermining government by publishing criticism of it or of public officials.

self-defense. Protection of one's person or property from attack by another.

self-incrimination. Testimony by an individual that tends to suggest that the individual has committed a crime.

self-incrimination, privilege against. Privilege found in the Fifth Amendment to the U.S. Constitution that protects persons from being compelled to be witnesses again.

sentencing. Pronouncing of punishment on a person convicted of having committed a crime.

sex discrimination. Unequal treatment of similarly situated individuals based on their sex.

sex offender registries. Law-enforcement databases that contain the names, crimes, and current addresses of convicted sex offenders released from custody.

sexual battery. Act of having sexual intercourse with one who is unable to consent to the intercourse because, for example, he or she is intoxicated or unconscious.

sexual harassment. Unwelcome gender-based treatment of individuals in workplaces and other arenas.

sheriff. Chief law-enforcement administrator of a county; usually an elected official.

shoplifting. Stealing goods from a retail establishment.

side bar. Discussions between a judge and attorneys in a case that cannot be heard by the jury or spectators.

skyjacking. Hijacking of aircraft in flight by armed persons or groups, usually for the purpose of perpetrating other crimes.

slave patrol. Summoned body of citizens charged with enforcing laws restricting the activities and movement of slaves in the antebellum South.

sobriety testing. Methods of determining whether drivers are operating vehicles while under the influence of alcohol or drugs.

solicitation to commit a crime. Enticing or inducing someone to commit a crime.

solicitor general of the United States. Lawyer appointed by the U.S. president to represent the United States in cases argued before the Supreme Court.

solitary confinement. Confinement of prisoners in isolation from other prison and jail inmates.

sovereign immunity. Doctrine that prevents suits against the government for damages un-less the government has previously authorized such suits.

spam. Unsolicited and usually unwanted electronic mail.

special weapons and tactics teams (SWAT). Specialized police units designed to resolve dangerous crises.

speedy trial requirement. Right provided to criminal defendants by the Constitution's Sixth Amendment to be tried without excessive delay.

stakeout. Tactical deployment of law-enforcement officers to a specific location for the purpose of surreptitiously observing criminal suspects.

stalking. Willful, malicious, or repeated following of another person.

standards of proof. Rules determining how much and what sort of evidence is enough to win cases in courts of law.

stare decisis. Principle that courts should generally follow the decisions of previous cases in the interest of consistency of legal stability.

state police. Law-enforcement organizations that operate directly under the authority of state governments, rather than under municipalities.

status offense. Offense such as truancy, incorrigibility, or running away from home that is considered a crime when is it committed by a juvenile.

statute. Law enacted by the legislative branch of government, whether at the federal or state level.

statutes of limitations. Laws that disallow prosecution of crimes after specified periods of time elapse.

statutory rape. Crime of having sexual intercourse with an underage female.

sting operation. Undercover police operation in which police officers pose as criminals in order to trap law violators.

stop and frisk. Power of police to stop and search suspects or their property when there is reason to believe that the suspects have committed crimes or may be carrying concealed weapons.

strict liability offenses. Offenses for which people are responsible, whether they mean them to occur or not.

subornation of perjury. Crime of inducing another to commit perjury.

subpoena. Order for a witness to appear in court to testify.

suicide. Voluntary taking of one's own life.

summons. Judicial instrument used to initiate a legal proceeding or to command the appearance of persons before courts or other bodies.

supermax prison. Modern innovation in American corrections that separate the most dangerous inmates from general prison populations and keep them in what amounts to long-term solitary confinement.

surveillance cameras. Video cameras mounted on elevated locations in public areas such as highways, parking lots, and spaces within or between buildings for the purpose of spotting and recording criminals in action and collecting video evidence for possible prosecution.

suspect. Person under investigation for possible criminal activity who has not yet been charged.

suspended sentence. Postponement of the execution of a sentence handed down by a court.

sustain. For a court to agree with an objection made by a lawyer or for a higher court to uphold the ruling of a lower court.

SWAT team. See **special weapons and tactics teams**

tax evasion. Deliberate failure to pay legally due taxes—particularly income taxes—or to submit required returns and other documents.

telephone fraud. All uses of telephones to defraud or cheat victims.

ten-most-wanted lists. Federal Bureau of Investigation program that publicizes the names and images of the most dangerous and sought-after criminal fugitives.

terrorism. Coercive use, or threat, of violence to terrorize a community or society to achieve political, economic, or social goals.

testimony. Statement made in a legal proceeding by a witness under oath.

theft. Taking of a person's property without that person's consent.

three-strikes law. Statute that requires repeat criminal offenders to be punished with long prison terms, regardless of the severity of any of the three offenses.

toxicology. Science concerned with the effects of harmful and toxic substances on living organisms.

trace evidence. Forms of physical evidence at crime scenes that are usually not visible to the naked eye.

traffic court. Special court that deals only with infractions of traffic laws that are considered less serious than misdemeanors and felonies.

traffic fine. Monetary penalty imposed for a traffic violation.

traffic law. Branch of law comprising rules for the orderly and safe flow of pedestrian and vehicular traffic.

transcript. Official record of a legal proceeding.

treason. Crime consisting of rebellious action toward one's government.

trespass. Crime of interfering with the property rights of another.

trial. Formal process of adjudication, from arraignment through verdicts.

trial transcript. Official record of a trial proceeding.

Uniform Crime Reports. National crime statistics compiled from government law-enforcement records.

vacate. In criminal justice proceedings, to set aside or rescind a court order or decision.

vandalism. Crime of willfully destroying property.

vehicle checkpoint. Stoppages of motorists by police for such purposes as apprehending criminals, preventing criminal behavior, and obtaining information.

venire. List of those who have been summoned for jury duty.

venue. Jurisdiction in which a legal action, such as a trial, arises.

verdict. Formal decision, or finding, made by a jury or a judge upon matters of fact submitted to them for deliberation and determination.

vicarious liability. Legal concept that someone in a supervisory role, such as an employer or parent, may be held liable for harm done by their subordinates.

victim assistance program. Advocacy and support services, often funded or administered by government, that guide victims of crime through the legal system.

victim-offender mediation. Facilitated meetings between offenders and victims of their crimes with the intent to discuss the effects and triggers of the harm.

victimless crime. Legally prohibited activities or exchanges among willing parties that do not harm anyone except, possibly, the parties willingly.

vigilantism. Illegal assumption of law-enforcement responsibilities by organized groups of private citizens.

voir dire. Examination of potential jurors to determine whether they should be seated on a jury or the preliminary examination of a witness to determine whether the witness is competent to testify.

voting fraud. Use of illegal tactics and practices to influence political elections.

war crimes. Crimes against humanity that go beyond the acts normally considered permissible in international armed conflicts.

warrant. Order permitting an official to take some action, such as an order permitting law-enforcement personnel to arrest someone or to search certain property.

white-collar crime. Nonviolent crimes committed by professional workers.

wiretap. Surreptitious monitoring of telephone conversations by law-enforcement officials.

witness. Person who offers testimony in a legal proceeding.

witness protection program. Government program designed to ensure the safety of key witnesses during and after court proceedings.

work camp. Alternative form of incarceration that requires less security than regular prisons and offers inmates practical work experience.

work-release program. Alternative to traditional incarceration that places accused and convicted offenders into the community to work at jobs paying standard wages.

youth authorities. Inclusive term for the various state agencies and officials involved in juvenile justice.

Timothy L. Hall and the Editors

Crime Rates and Definitions

Accurate measurement of crime is of vital importance for public and private agencies in determining priorities and policies regarding crime and for the evaluation of existing programs. The two main sources of crime data in the United States are the Uniform Crime Reports (UCR) of the Federal Bureau of Investigation (FBI) and the National Crime Victimization Surveys (NCVS) of the U.S. Census Bureau.

The FBI's Uniform Crime Reporting (UCR) program, which began in 1929, collects, publishes, and archives crime data voluntarily provided by nearly 17,000 law-enforcement agencies across the United States. The data collected represent well over 90 percent of the U.S. population. The UCR program classifies offenses into two groups. Part I crime counts are based on crimes reported to the police, and Part II crime counts are based on arrests made. This distinction exists because many Part II crimes are not reported. In counting crimes, the FBI uses a hierarchical rule: In multiple-offense situations—those in which several offenses are committed at the same time and place—only the highest-ranking offense is scored, after classifying all Part I offenses. All other crimes are ignored, regardless of the numbers of offenders and victims.

Each year since 1973, the U.S. Census Bureau (under the U.S. Department of Commerce) on behalf of the Bureau of Justice Statistics (under the U.S. Department of Justice) has collected data on the frequency, characteristics, and consequences of six types of crime victimizations. These data are collected from a nationally representative sample of roughly 49,000 households in the United States that contain more than 100,000 persons twelve years of age and older. The survey collects information not only on crimes and their circumstances but also on such characteristics of victims as age, sex, race, ethnicity, income, and marital status. Victims are also asked whether they have reported the crime incidents to police and, in cases of personal violent crimes, they are asked about their relationships to the offenders and characteristics of the offenders.

The UCR calculates crime rates by dividing the numbers of crimes by the population of an area—for example, city, region, and country—and then multiplying by 100,000, yielding rates per 100,000 persons. The NCVS reports two types of rates: crimes against persons and crimes against households. Person crime rates are equal to the numbers of person crimes divided by the numbers of people and then multiplied by 1,000; the resulting figures are rates per 1,000 people. Household crime rates are calculated by dividing the numbers of household crimes by the numbers of households and multiplying those results by 1,000 to determine the rates per 1,000 households.

Uniform Crime Reports: Crime Definitions and Rates per 100,000 Population

Part I Offenses (those reported to police)

1993	2002	Offense	Definition
9.5	5.6	Criminal homicide	Murder and non-negligent manslaughter: the willful (non-negligent) killing of one human being by another.
41.1	33.0	Forcible rape	Carnal knowledge of a female forcibly and against her will. Rapes by force and assaults or attempts to rape, regardless of the age of the victim, are included. Statutory offenses (no force used—victim under age of consent) are excluded.
256.0	145.9	Robbery	Taking or attempting to take anything of value from the care, custody, or control of persons by force or threat of force or violence and/or by putting the victims in fear.

1993	2002	Offense	Definition
440.5	310.1	Aggravated assault	Unlawful attack by one person upon another for the purpose of inflicting severe or aggravated bodily injury. This type of assault usually is accompanied by the use of a weapon or by means likely to produce death or great bodily harm. Simple assaults are excluded.
1,099.7	746.2	Burglary (breaking or entering)	Unlawful entry of a structure to commit a felony or a theft. Attempted forcible entry is included.
3,033.9	2,445.8	Larceny/theft	Unlawful taking, carrying, leading, or riding away of property from the possession or constructive possession of another. Examples are thefts of bicycles or automobile accessories, shoplifting, pocket-picking, or the stealing of any property or article which is not taken by force and violence or by fraud. Attempted larcenies are included. Motor vehicle theft, embezzlement, confidence games, forgery, worthless checks, and similar offenses, are excluded.
606.3	432.1	Motor vehicle theft	Theft or attempted theft of a motor vehicle—any self-propelled vehicle that runs on solid surfaces and not on rails. Motorboats, construction equipment, airplanes, and farming equipment are specifically excluded from this category.
n/a	n/a	Arson	Willful or malicious burning or attempt to burn—with or without intent to defraud—a dwelling house, public building, motor vehicle or aircraft, personal property of another, and so forth. Although arson is included in Part I offenses, insufficient data are available to calculate rates.

Part II Offenses (arrests made; rates prior to 1995 are not available)

1995	2002	Offense	Definition
496.5	449.3	Other assaults (simple)	Assaults and attempted assaults in which no weapons are used and which do not result in serious or aggravated injury to the victim.
46.8	40.5	Forgery and counterfeiting	Making, altering, uttering, or possessing—with intent to defraud—anything false in the semblance of that which is true. Attempts are included.
162.9	113.6	Fraud	Fraudulent conversion and obtaining money or property by false pretenses. Confidence games and bad checks, except forgeries and counterfeiting, are included.
5.9	6.9	Embezzlement	Misappropriation or misapplication of money or property entrusted to one's care, custody, or control.
65.1	44.5	Stolen property offenses	Buying, receiving, and possessing stolen property, including attempts.
118.5	96.8	Vandalism	Willful or malicious destruction, injury, disfigurement, or defacement of any public or private property, real or personal, without consent of the owner or persons having custody or control. Attempts are included.
95.3	57.7	Weapons offenses	All violations of regulations or statutes controlling the carrying, using, possessing, furnishing, and manufacturing of deadly weapons or silencers. Attempts are included.

1995	2002	Offense	Definition
41.4	28.6	Prostitution and commercialized vice	Sex offenses of a commercialized nature, such as prostitution, keeping a bawdy house, procuring or transporting women for immoral purposes. Attempts are included.
36.8	33.1	Other sex offenses	Statutory rape and offenses against chastity, common decency, morals, and the like. Attempts are included. Forcible rape, prostitution, and commercialized vice are excluded.
582.5	537.7	Drug abuse violations	State and/or local offenses relating to the unlawful possession, sale, use, growing, and manufacturing of narcotic drugs. Specified drug categories: opium or cocaine and their derivatives (morphine, heroin, codeine); marijuana; synthetic narcotics—manufactured narcotics that can cause true addiction (Demerol, methadone); and dangerous non-narcotic drugs (barbiturates, Benzedrine).
8.0	3.7	Gambling	Promoting, permitting, or engaging in illegal gambling.
53.4	47.6	Offenses against the family and children	Nonsupport, neglect, desertion, or abuse of family and children. Attempts are included.
526.0	497.4	Driving under the influence	Driving or operating any vehicle or common carrier while drunk or under the influence of liquor or narcotics.
221.6	226.1	Liquor laws	State and/or local liquor law violations, except drunkenness and driving under the influence. Federal violations are excluded.
268.4	201.7	Drunkenness	Offenses relating to drunkenness or intoxication. Driving under the influence is excluded.
285.9	235.4	Disorderly conduct	Breach of the peace.
10.4	9.6	Vagrancy	Begging, loitering, and so forth. Includes prosecutions under the charge of suspicious person.
1,486.3	1.270.6	Other offenses	All violations of state and local laws not listed above and traffic offenses.
4.6	3.7	Suspicion	No specific offense; suspect released without formal charges being placed.
58.5	50.3	Curfew and loitering laws	Offenses relating to violations by persons under the age of eighteen of local curfew or loitering ordinances where such laws exist.
96.6	44.0	Runaways	Limited to juveniles (under the age of eighteen) taken into protective custody under provisions of local statutes.

National Crime Victimization Survey: Crime Definitions and Rates per 1,000 Population

1993	2002	Offense	Definition
42.9	19.8	Assault	Unlawful physical attack or threat of attack. Assaults may be classified as aggravated or simple. Rape, attempted rape, and sexual assaults are excluded from this category, as well as robbery and attempted robbery. The severity of assaults ranges from minor threats to incidents that are nearly fatal.
12.1	4.3	Aggravated assault	Attack or attempted attack with a weapon, regardless of whether or not an injury occurs and attack without a weapon when a serious injury results.

1993	2002	Offense	Definition
3.4	1.4	Aggravated assault with injury	Attack without a weapon when serious injury results or an attack with a weapon involving any injury. Serious injuries include broken bones, lost teeth, internal injuries, loss of consciousness, and any unspecified injury requiring two or more days of hospitalization.
8.7	2.9	Threatening with weapon	Threat or attempted attack by an offender armed with a gun, knife, or other object used as a weapon, not resulting in victim injury.
30.8	15.5	Simple assault	Attack without a weapon resulting either in no injury, minor injury (for example, bruises, black eyes, cuts, scratches, or swelling) or in undetermined injury requiring fewer than two days of hospitalization. Also includes attempted assault without a weapon.
6.4	3.9	Simple assault with minor injury	Attack without a weapon resulting in such injuries as bruises, black eyes, cuts or in an undetermined injury requiring fewer than two days of hospitalization.
24.4	11.6	Simple assault without injury	Attempted assault without a weapon not resulting in injury.
1.5	0.7	Rape/attempted rape	Forced sexual intercourse including psychological coercion as well as physical force. Forced sexual intercourse means vaginal, anal, or oral penetration by the offenders. This category also includes incidents in which penetration is from a foreign object, such as a bottle.
0.8	0.4	Completed rape	
0.7	0.3	Attempted rape	Includes verbal threats of rape.
6.1	2.2	Robbery	Completed or attempted theft, directly from a person, of property or cash by force or threat of force, with or without a weapon, and with or without injury.
3.9	1.7	Completed/property taken	Successful taking of property from a person by force or threat of force, with or without a weapon, and with or without injury.
1.3	0.7	Completed with injury	Successful taking of property from a person, accompanied by an attack, either with or without a weapon, resulting in injury.
2.6	0.9	Completed without injury	Successful taking of property from a person by force or the threat of force, either with or without a weapon, but not resulting in injury.
2.3	0.5	Attempted to take property	Attempt to take property from a person by force or threat of force without success, with or without a weapon, and with or without injury.
1.8	0.4	Attempted without injury	Attempt to take property from a person by force or the threat of force without success, either with or without a weapon, but not resulting in injury.
0.5	0.2	Attempted with injury	Attempt to take property from a person without success, accompanied by an attack, either with or without a weapon, resulting in injury.
0.8	0.3	Sexual assault	Wide range of victimizations, separate from rape or attempted rape. These crimes include attacks or attempted attacks generally involving unwanted sexual contact between victim and offender. Sexual assaults may or may not involve force and may include such acts as grabbing and fondling. Sexual assault also includes verbal threats.

1993	2002	Offense	Definition
59.9	27.7	Burglary (also household burglary)	Unlawful or forcible entry or attempted entry of a residence. This crime usually, but not always, involves theft. The illegal entry may be by force, such as breaking a window or slashing a screen, or may be without force by entering through an unlocked door or an open window. As long as the person entering has no legal right to be present in the structure, a burglary occurs. Furthermore, the structure need not be the house itself for a burglary to take place; illegal entry of a garage, shed, or any other structure on the premises also constitutes household burglary. If breaking and entering occurs in a hotel or vacation residence, it is still classified as a burglary for the household whose member or members are staying there at the time the entry occurs.
48.3	23.7	Completed burglary	Form of burglary in which a person who has no legal right to be present in the structure successfully gains entry to a residence by use of force or without force.
18.6	9.2	Forcible entry	Form of completed burglary in which force is used to gain entry to a residence. Some examples include breaking a window or slashing a screen.
29.7	14.3	Unlawful entry without force	Form of completed burglary committed by someone having no legal right to be on the premises, even though no force is used.
11.6	4.2	Attempted forcible entry	Form of burglary in which force is used in an attempt to gain entry.
19.6	9.0	Motor vehicle theft	Stealing or unauthorized taking of a motor vehicle, including attempted thefts.
12.9	7.1	Completed motor vehicle theft	Successful taking of a vehicle by an unauthorized person.
6.7	1.9	Attempted motor vehicle theft	Unsuccessful attempt by an unauthorized person to take a vehicle.
2.4	0.7	Purse snatching/ Pocket picking	Theft or attempted theft of property or cash directly from the victim by stealth, without force or threat of force.
0.4	0.2	Completed purse snatching	Successful snatching of a purse.
0.2	0.0	Attempted purse snatching	Unsuccessful snatching of a purse.
1.8	0.4	Pocket picking	
242.6	122.3	Theft	Completed or attempted theft of property or cash without personal contact. Incidents involving theft of property from within the sample household would classify as theft if the offender has a legal right to be in the house (such as a maid, delivery person, or guest). If the offender has no legal right to be in the house, the incident would classify as a burglary.
230.4	118.2	Completed theft	Successful taking, without permission, property or cash without personal contact between the victim and offender.
12.3	4.1	Attempted theft	Unsuccessful attempt to take property or cash without personal contact.

Composite Rates

Both the UCR and the NCVS construct composite rates that are used to track changes and trends in amounts of crime more often than are individual rates. The UCR constructs a violent crime rate, which incorporates murder, forcible rape, robbery, and aggravated assault, and a property crime rate that incorporates burglary, larceny-theft, and motor vehicle theft. Similarly, the NCVS constructs a violent crime rate that incorporates rape, robbery, aggravated assault, and simple assault and a property crime rate that incorporates burglary, theft, and motor vehicle theft.

The UCR also creates the Crime Index, which is the sum of selected offenses used to indicate changes in the overall rate of crime reported to law enforcement. Offenses included in the Crime Index total include the violent crimes of murder and non-negligent manslaughter, forcible rape, robbery, and aggravated assault, and the property crimes of burglary, larceny-theft, and motor vehicle theft.

The table below shows these rates for 1983, 1993, and 2002. The UCR rates are per 100,000 population, while the NCVS property crime rates are per 1,000 people and the NCVS violent crime rates are per 1,000 households.

UCR and NCVS Composite Rates

	UCR (per 100,000 population)		NCVS (per 1,000 population)		
Year	property crime	violent crime	property crime	violent crime	Crime Index
1983	4641.1	538.1	428.4	46.5	5179.2
1993	4740.0	747.1	318.9	49.1	5487.1
2002	3624.1	494.6	159.0	22.8	4118.8

Comparing UCR and NCVS Rates

Both UCR and NCVS rates show that crimes of both types were lower in 2002 than in 1983 or 1993. However, the table also shows that the UCR and NCVS do not always agree on the direction and degree of change in property or violent crime over time. For example, the UCR indicates property crime increased slightly from 1983 to 1993, while the NCVS shows a substantial decrease. A 2001 study by Michael R. Rand and Callie M. Rennison found that between 1972 and 2000, year-to-year violent crime rate changes

from the NCVS and UCR moved in a different direction, either up or down, about 40 percent of the time, and property crime rates moved in a different direction about 25 percent of the time. As both UCR and NCVS rates are considered valid indicators, one wonders how they can vary so frequently and by so much.

The NCVS was created to complement the UCR. Each has its advantages, and each has its flaws. The UCR measures only crimes reported to law-enforcement agencies, and research indicates that fewer than 40 percent of crimes are reported in a given year. By interviewing victims, the NCVS measures both reported and unreported crimes. However, the NCVS excludes homicide, arson, commercial crimes, and crimes against children under the age of twelve, all of which are included in UCR rates. Furthermore, being based on a sample of American households, the NCVS is subject to sampling error, meaning a different sample might yield different results.

The UCR data are, in most cases, based on actual counts of offenses reported by law-enforcement jurisdictions. However, officers in law-enforcement agencies responsible for compiling data for the UCR can and do make errors. Similarly, another source of error in the NCVS is that victims may not accurately recall how many times they were crime victims in the six-month reference period, either forgetting some victimizations or including some that occurred prior to the reference periods.

The basic counting units of the NCVS are individual victimizations. Victimizations are reported by victims, and thus each person victimized is counted as a victimization. The basic counting unit for the UCR is the offense. An offense can have one or more victims. If two people are robbed in a single incident, the UCR would count this as one offense, while the NCVS would count it as two victimizations.

Neither crime measure is necessarily better than the other. Together they give a better idea as to crime volume and trends than either alone could. The UCR is likely to be a better measure for more serious offenses, since these are more likely to be reported to the police. This is especially the case for murder as it cannot be included in the NCVS, and virtually all murders come to the attention of the police. The NCVS is likely to be the better measure for less serious offenses, which often go unreported.

Jerome L. Neapolitan

Crime Trends

Policymakers such as legislators, mayors, and police chiefs need up-to-date, accurate information to make their decisions. In recognition of that need, the Federal Bureau of Investigation (FBI) created the Uniform Crime Reporting (UCR) program to collect information from the states about the numbers of crimes reported to the police. The eight basic crime categories tracked most regularly since the late twentieth century are known as Part I, or Index offenses. They include murder and non-negligent manslaughter, forcible rape, robbery, aggravated assault, burglary, larceny theft, motor vehicle theft, and arson. Because of special rules surrounding the reporting of arson, arson rates are generally not reported along with other Part I crimes. To control for variations over

time in the numbers of crimes due to changes in the population, this information is often reported in the form of rates: numbers of offenses per 100,000 population.

Recognizing that not all crimes are reported to the police, the U.S. Department of Justice began the National Crime Victimization Survey (NCVS) in 1973. This survey, conducted annually through telephone calls to a random sample of 42,000 households, asks all persons age twelve and older in each household about their victimization experiences. Generally, the NCVS expresses victimization rates as numbers of victimizations per 1,000 population—also of persons aged twelve and older.

Figure 1 shows the forty-four-year trend in

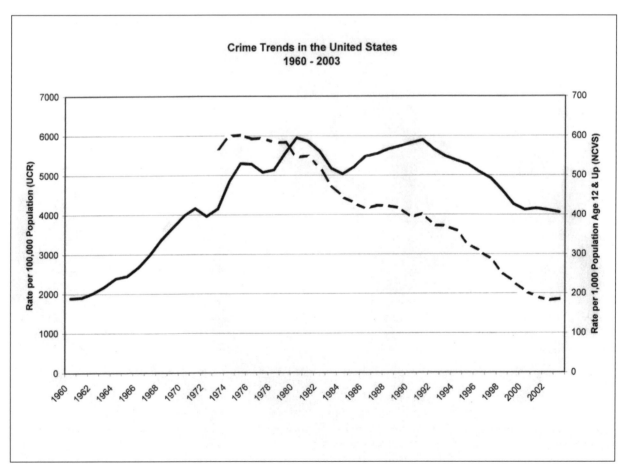

Figure 1: Crime trends, 1960-2003. UCR rate is solid line; NCVS rate is broken line.

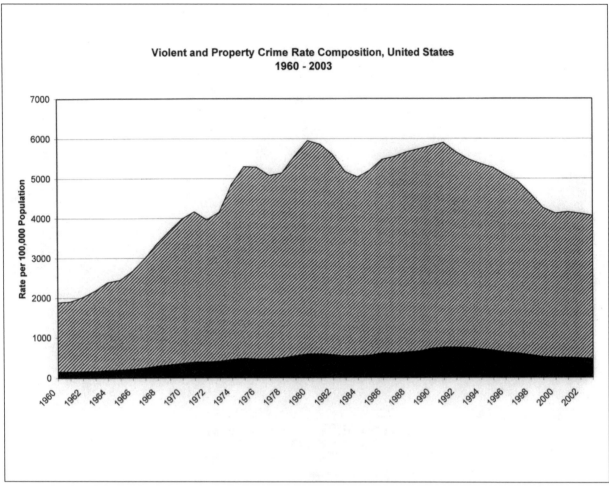

Figure 2: UCR crime rates, 1960-2003 (violent crimes are black; property crimes are gray).

UCR offenses known to police, and the thirty-one-year trend in NCVS victimization estimates. As UCR data in figure 1 show, crime rates in the United States rose steadily throughout the 1960's and 1970's and peaked in 1980, when 5,950 offenses per 100,000 population were reported. The victimization data, depicted by the dashed line and interpreted on the second axis, show a slightly earlier peak, with 602 victimizations reported per 1,000 population aged twelve and older.

After a brief decline through the early 1980's, the crime rate again approached its 1980 peak in 1991. Between then and 2003, the overall crime rate dropped by slightly more than 30 percent, approaching lows not seen since the early 1970's. The trends in victimizations reported in the sur-

vey data largely match those recorded in the official report data.

The Composition of the Crime Rates

As already mentioned, the UCR's Part I index crimes comprise eight main categories, seven of which are reported regularly. These seven categories are not equally represented in the crime rates that are reported. One major distinction used by police is that of separating violent crime from property crime. In the UCR data, violent crimes include murder and non-negligent manslaughter, forcible rape, robbery, and aggravated assault. Property crimes include burglary, larceny theft, and motor vehicle theft. As figure 2 shows, the vast majority of offenses reported to police between 1960 and 2003 were property crimes.

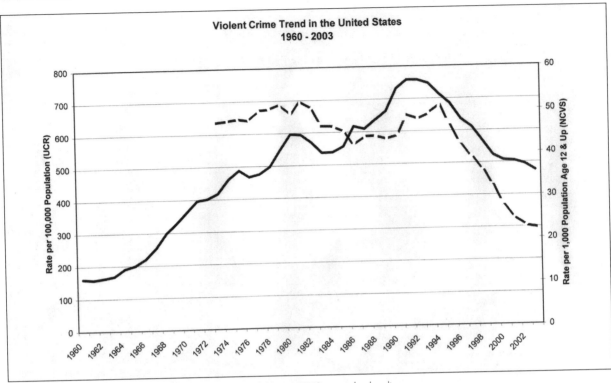

Figure 3: Violent crime rates, 1960-2003. UCR rate is solid line; NCVS rate is broken line.

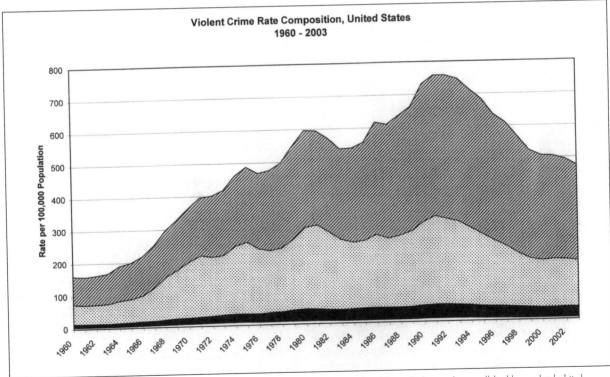

Figure 4: UCR violent crime rates, 1960-2003. Top to bottom: assault (dark gray), robbery (light gray), rape (black), murder (white).

Figures 3 and 4 depict trend and composition information for violent crime between 1960 and 2003. As figure 3 shows, reported incidents of violent crime in the United States steadily rose to 596.6 incidents per 100,000 population in 1980. Then, after a brief decline, they again rose to reach a high of 758.1 in 1991. As the dashed line shows, the National Criminal Victimization Survey data closely track the official report trend, though they did not reflect as steep a post-1980 increase.

Further examining the violent crime composition reveals that not all violent crimes equally contribute to the rate. As figure 4 shows, the bulk of violent crimes reported to police are assaults and robberies; murders and rapes generally account for less than 8 percent of the UCR violent crime rate.

Similar patterns can be observed in the property crime data displayed in figures 5 and 6. As figure 5 shows, reported incidents of property crime in the United States followed the same trend seen in the violent crime rates of figures 3 and 4, steadily rising to a peak rate of 5,353.3 incidents per 100,000 population in 1980. After a brief decline, they rose to a new high of 5,139.7 in 1991. As with violent crime, the dashed line shows the National Criminal Victimization Survey data closely tracking the official report trend. Again, the victimization data show a peak victimization rate of 553.6 per 1,000 population (age twelve and older) in 1975, five years before the UCR peak in 1980.

Further examining property crime composition reveals that, while not all property crimes contribute equally to the rate, the distribution is

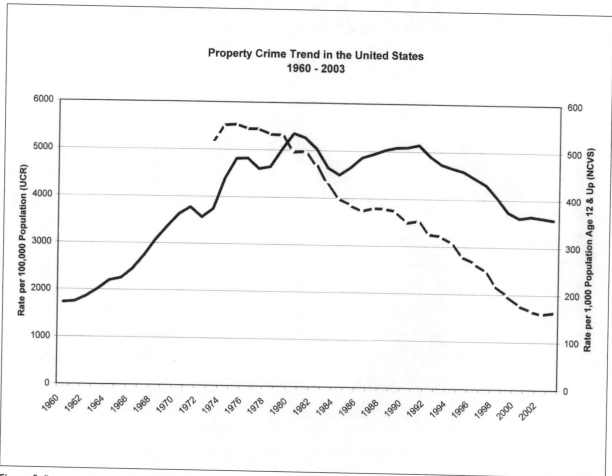

Figure 5: Property crime trends, 1960-2003. UCR rate is solid line; NCVS rate is broken line.

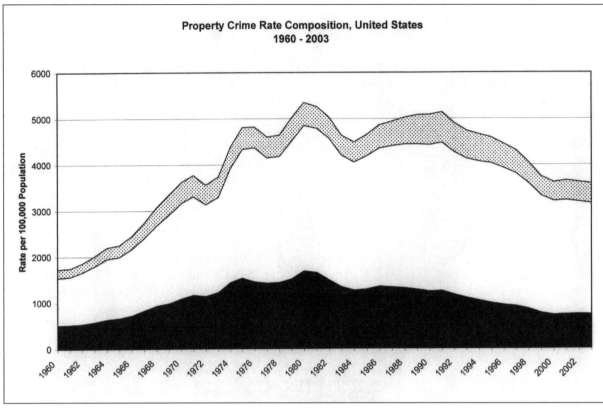

Figure 6: UCR property crime rates, 1960-2003. From top to bottom: motor vehicle theft (gray), larceny theft white), burglary (black).

not nearly as uneven as that seen in violent crime. As figure 6 shows, the major contributor to the nation's property crime rate is larceny theft, averaging almost 62 percent of total property crime rates. The motor vehicle theft rate makes the smallest contribution, but as the UCR reporting manual indicates, the motor vehicle theft category is a special category of the general crime of larceny theft.

Timothy M. Bray

Supreme Court Rulings on Criminal Justice

Cases marked with asterisks (*) are subjects of essays within the main text.

Year	Case	Relevance to criminal justice
1884	*Hurtado v. California* *	Held that due process under the Fourteenth Amendment does not require indictments by grand juries in state murder prosecutions.
1900	*Maxwell v. Dow*	Held that trial by jury in state courts is not a necessary requisite of due process of law.
1908	*Twining v. New Jersey*	Held that protection against self-incrimination is not required in state trials under the Fourteenth Amendment due process clause.
1914	*Weeks v. United States* *	Established the exclusionary rule whereby illegally obtained evidence may not be used in federal prosecutions.
1927	*Tumey v. Ohio*	Ruled that due process is denied when suspects are tried before judges who have direct, personal, substantial, and pecuniary interests in deciding against them.
1928	*Olmstead v. United States* *	Held that the Fourth Amendment does not preclude use of wiretapping by federal agents.
1932	*Powell v. Alabama* *	In this first Scottsboro case, ruled that the due process clause of the Fourteenth Amendment requires that defendants in state capital cases are entitled to counsel.
1935	*Norris v. Alabama*	In this second Scottsboro case, held that systematic exclusion of African Americans from service on grand and trial juries denies black defendants equal protection guaranteed by the Fourteenth Amendment.
1936	*Brown v. Mississippi* *	Held that due process under the Fourteenth Amendment prohibits the use of confessions coerced by physical torture.
1937	*Palko v. Connecticut* *	Held that due process under the Fourteenth Amendment may incorporate Bill of Rights protections that are "the very essence of a scheme of ordered liberty"; double jeopardy is not one of those provisions.
1938	*Johnson v. Zerbst*	Ruled that the Sixth Amendment requires appointment of counsel for all felony defendants in federal courts.
1940	*Chambers v. Florida*	Held that the Fourteenth Amendment's due process clause prohibits admissibility of confessions coerced by psychological or nonphysical means.
1942	*Betts v. Brady*	Held that the appointment of counsel for indigents in state felony cases depends upon the special circumstances of the cases.
1942	*Skinner v. Oklahoma ex rel. Williamson*	Held that equal protection is violated by state laws requiring sterilization of habitual criminals.

Year	Case	Relevance to criminal justice
1943	*McNabb v. United States*	Voided a conviction, not on grounds of unconstitutional self-incrimination, but because prisoners had not been taken before the nearest judicial officer without unnecessary delay for hearing, commitment, or release on bail, as required by statute.
1947	*Adamson v. California*	Self-incrimination clause of the Fifth Amendment does not apply to the states; dissent in this case articulated total incorporation doctrine.
1947	*Louisiana ex rel. Francis v. Resweber*	Held that the Eighth Amendment ban against cruel and unusual punishment does apply to states; however, defendant in this case had to face the electric chair a second time, even though it malfunctioned during the first attempt to execute him.
1948	*In re Oliver*	Incorporated the Sixth Amendment right to a public trial to apply to the states.
1948	*Cole v. Arkansas*	Incorporated the Sixth Amendment notice clause to apply to the states.
1949	*Wolf v. Colorado*	Incorporated the Fourth Amendment search and seizure protections to apply to the states but did not incorporate exclusionary rule.
1957	*Mallory v. United States*	Broadened the 1943 *McNabb* rule to invalidate even a voluntary confession made before arraignment.
1961	*Mapp v. Ohio**	Applied the exclusionary rule to the states.
1962	*Robinson v. California**	Incorporated Eighth Amendment protections against cruel and unusual punishment to apply to the states while finding that narcotics addiction is not in itself a crime.
1963	*Gideon v. Wainwright**	Required counsel for indigent defendants in all state felony cases.
1964	*Escobedo v. Illinois**	For first time, recognized suspects' right to counsel during police interrogations in states.
1964	*Malloy v. Hogan*	Incorporated Fifth Amendment protection against self-incrimination to apply to the states.
1964	*Massiah v. United States**	Held that incriminating statements elicited by federal agents during the absence of the defendant's attorney deprived the defendant of his right to counsel under the Sixth Amendment; the statements collected could not be used as evidence in trial.
1965	*Pointer v. Texas*	Incorporated the confrontation clause of the Sixth Amendment to apply to the states.
1966	*Parker v. Gladden*	Incorporated Sixth Amendment right to an impartial jury to apply to the states.
1966	*Miranda v. Arizona**	Announced Miranda rule requiring specific procedures for police to follow during interrogations and declared that any statements elicited in violation of these procedures would be inadmissible.
1967	*In re Gault**	Held that minors are entitled to certain procedural rights including adequate notice, right to counsel, privilege against self-incrimination, and the rights of confrontation and sworn testimony.

Year	Case	Relevance to criminal justice
1967	*Katz v. United States**	Held that because the Fourth Amendment protects people, not places, electronic surveillance is an unreasonable intrusion into privacy.
1967	*Klopfer v. North Carolina*	Incorporated Sixth Amendment right to a speedy trial to apply to the states.
1967	*United States v. Wade*	Allowed accused suspects to be compelled to participate in police lineups and to utter the words attributed to offenders in crimes.
1967	*Washington v. Texas*	Incorporated Sixth Amendment compulsory process clause to apply to the states.
1968	*Chimel v. California**	Held that arresting suspects does not empower police officers to conduct widespread searches of the arrestees' homes without search warrants.
1968	*Duncan v. Louisiana*	Incorporated Sixth Amendment jury trial protections to apply to the states.
1968	*Harris v. United States**	Established plain view exception to search warrant requirements.
1968	*Witherspoon v. Illinois**	Held that excluding jurors opposed to capital punishment results in an unrepresentative jury on the issue of guilt or substantially increases the risk of conviction.
1969	*Benton v. Maryland*	Incorporated Fifth Amendment protection against double jeopardy to apply to the states.
1970	*Brady v. United States**	Approved most forms of plea bargaining, in which defendants agree to plead guilty in return for reduced charges or sentences.
1970	*Illinois v. Allen*	Allowed disruptive defendants to be removed from courtrooms without violating their constitutional right to be present and to confront witnesses against them.
1970	*Williams v. Florida*	Held that the right of trial by jury does not require state to provide defendants with twelve-person juries in noncapital cases.
1971	*Bivens v. Six Unknown Named Agents**	Held that plaintiffs can—under certain conditions—seek damages when federal officials violate their Fourth Amendment protection against unreasonable searches.
1971	*Santobello v. New York**	Held that when defendants rely on prosecutors' plea bargain promises, due process requires that the promises be kept or that the defendants be given some form of relief, such as withdrawal of their guilty pleas.
1971	*Schilb v. Kuebel*	Incorporated Eighth Amendment protection against excessive bail to apply to the states.
1972	*Apodaca v. Oregon*	States may allow nonunanimous jury verdicts in noncapital cases.
1972	*Argersinger v. Hamlin**	Requires counsel for indigent defendants in all state misdemeanor cases in which imprisonment in jail is the penalty for conviction.

Year	Case	Relevance to criminal justice
1972	*Barker v. Wingo**	Developed a "balancing test" in applying Sixth Amendment speedy trial protections, thus requiring such cases to be approached on an ad hoc basis.
1972	*Furman v. Georgia**	Invalidated the death penalty as then administered as a violation of the cruel and unusual punishment clause of the Eighth Amendment applied to the states by the Fourteenth Amendment.
1973	*Roe v. Wade*	Decriminalized abortions under certain conditions.
1975	*Faretta v. California**	Held that defendants have a constitutional right to proceed *pro se*, that is, to represent themselves in criminal trials.
1976	*Gregg v. Georgia**	Reversed the 1972 *Furman* decision, finding that the death penalty is a constitutionally permissible punishment for carefully defined categories of murder; required carefully controlled discretion of sentencing authority, with bifurcated trial procedures.
1977	*Coker v. Georgia**	Held that death sentences for the crime of rape are grossly disproportionate and excessive punishment and are therefore forbidden by the Eighth Amendment as cruel and unusual punishment.
1978	*Ballew v. Georgia*	Held that juries for state criminal trials must have at least six members.
1979	*Burch v. Louisiana*	Held that when juries have only six members in state criminal trials for nonpetty offenses, nonunanimous verdicts violate the Sixth and Fourteenth Amendments.
1980	*Rummel v. Estelle**	Ruled that Texas's mandatory life sentence for a three-time recidivist felon did not constitute cruel and unusual punishment under the Eighth and Fourteenth Amendments.
1983	*Illinois v. Gates**	Adopted the "totality of the circumstances" approach for determining whether an informant's tip establishes probable cause for issuance of a warrant.
1983	*Solem v. Helm**	Held that the Eighth Amendment's cruel and unusual punishments clause prohibits sentences that are disproportionate to the crimes and that a state's sentence of life imprisonment without the possibility of parole for recidivist criminals violates that clause.
1984	*United States v. Leon**	Created the good faith exception to the exclusionary rule, holding that evidence gained by officers acting in good faith is admissible even when their search warrants prove to be invalid.
1984	*Massachusetts v. Sheppard**	Held that police officers are not required to disbelieve judges who advise them that the warrants they possess authorize them to conduct the searches they request.
1984	*Nix v. Williams*	Held that evidence obtained in violation of the *Miranda* decision need not be suppressed if the same evidence would have been inevitably discovered by lawful means.

Year	Case	Relevance to criminal justice
1984	*Schall v. Martin**	Upheld a state preventive detention statute authorizing pretrial detention of juveniles as a legitimate protection of society from the hazards of pretrial crime.
1985	*New Jersey v. T.L.O.**	Permits school officials to search students who are under their authority without warrants.
1985	*Tennessee v. Garner**	Held that a state law authorizing police officers to use deadly force against apparently unarmed and nondangerous fleeing suspects violates Fourth Amendment protections; such force may not be used unless necessary to prevent the escape and officers have probable cause to believe that suspects pose a significant threat of death or serious physical injury to them or others.
1986	*Batson v. Kentucky**	Held that states excluding persons from jury service on account of race are in violation of the equal protection clause of the Fourteenth Amendment.
1986	*Bowers v. Hardwick**	Upheld Georgia's antisodomy law, finding no fundamental right for homosexual offenders.
1986	*Ford v. Wainwright**	Held that the Eighth Amendment prohibits state from inflicting the death penalty upon prisoners who are mentally ill.
1986	*Terry v. Ohio**	Authorized the "stop and frisk" exception to warrant requirements.
1987	*Illinois v. Krull**	Held that the Fourth Amendment exclusionary rule does not apply to evidence obtained by a police officer who acted in objectively reasonable reliance upon a state statute authorizing a warrantless administrative search of an automobile wrecking yard that was subsequently found to violate the Fourth Amendment.
1987	*McCleskey v. Kemp**	Rejected claims based on statistical studies that Georgia's capital punishment process discriminated on the basis of the race of the murder victim, in violation of the Eighth and Fourteenth amendments.
1987	*United States v. Salerno*	Upheld the Bail Reform Act of 1984, which authorized judges to deny bail to defendants to ensure the safety of other persons and the community.
1987	*Tison v. Arizona**	Created a flexible Eighth Amendment standard for applying the death penalty to felony-murder accomplices who demonstrate reckless disregard for human life even though they do not directly participate in killing victims.
1987	*Turner v. Safley*	Announced a four-pronged test to determine whether prison regulations impinging on inmates' constitutional rights are reasonable, concluding that regulations are valid if they are reasonably related to legitimate penological interests.
1988	*Coy v. Iowa*	Struck down a state law permitting children who claim they are victims of sexual abuse to testify in court from behind screens.

Year	Case	Relevance to criminal justice
1989	Stanford v. Kentucky*	Sustained the constitutionality of imposing the death penalty on individuals for crimes committed at the age of sixteen or seventeen.
1989	Texas v. Johnson*	Struck down a state flag-desecration law because it is not viewpoint-neutral.
1990	Maryland v. Buie*	Held that the Fourth Amendment permits properly limited protective sweeps in conjunction with in-home arrests when the searching officers possess reasonable beliefs, based on specific and articulable facts, that the areas to be swept harbor persons posing dangers to those on the arrest scenes.
1990	Maryland v. Craig*	Held that the Sixth Amendment's confrontation clause does not guarantee criminal defendants an absolute right to face-to-face meeting with the witnesses against them at trial.
1990	Minnick v. Mississippi*	Held that when suspects request counsel, their interrogation must cease, and officials may not reinitiate interrogations without counsel present—whether or not the accused consult with their attorneys; the requirement that counsel be "made available" to the accused refers not to the opportunity to consult with attorneys outside the interrogation room, but to the right to have the attorney present during custodial interrogation.
1991	Arizona v. Fulminante*	Held that tainted testimony erroneously admitted as evidence at trial need not overturn convictions if sufficient independent evidence supporting guilty verdicts also is introduced.
1991	Harmelin v. Michigan*	Held that the Eighth Amendment does not prohibit imposing mandatory life sentences without possibility of parole for possessing more than 650 grains of cocaine.
1991	Payne v. Tennessee*	Upheld use of victim impact evidence and emotional impact of crimes on victims' families by juries in capital sentencing procedures.
1992	United States v. Alvarez-Machain*	Held that the forcible abduction of a defendant in Mexico did not prohibit his trial in a U.S. court for violations of U.S. criminal laws; defendant may not be prosecuted in violation of the terms of an extradition treaty; however, when a treaty has not been invoked, a court may properly exercise jurisdiction even though the defendant's presence is procured by means of a forcible abduction.
1992	Jacobson v. United States	Employed federal approach to entrapment defense requiring proof that accused was disposed to commit a criminal act prior to first being approached by government agents.
1992	R.A.V. v. City of St. Paul*	On the basis of the First Amendment, invalidated a municipal ordinance outlawing fighting words (hate speech) because it involved viewpoint-based distinctions among different topics.
1993	Wisconsin v. Mitchell*	Upheld a state-enhanced penalty for aggravated battery hate crimes that are unprotected by the First Amendment.

Year	Case	Relevance to criminal justice
1995	*United States v. Lopez**	Held that the Gun-Free School Zones Act of 1990 exceeded Congress's commerce clause authority because possessing guns in local schools is not an economic activity that might have a substantial effect on interstate commerce; characterized the law as a criminal statute that has nothing to do with "commerce" or any sort of economic enterprise.
1995	*Wilson v. Arkansas**	Held that the common-law knock-and-announce principle forms a part of the Fourth Amendment reasonableness inquiry when police enter a suspect's residence.
1996	*Whren v. United States**	Found that the temporary detention of motorists upon probable cause to believe that they have violated the traffic laws does not violate the Fourth Amendment's prohibition against unreasonable seizures, even if reasonable officers would not stop the motorists absent some additional law-enforcement objective.
1997	*Hudson v. United States*	Held that the double jeopardy clause permits government to fine persons for fraud and other regulatory law violations and later use the criminal process to prosecute the same persons for the same offenses.
1998	*United States v. Balsys*	Held that resident aliens may not invoke the self-incrimination clause to withhold information from the U.S. government out of fear that disclosure might lead to prosecution by a foreign nation.
1998	*California v. Greenwood**	Held that the Fourth Amendment does not prohibit warrantless search and seizure of garbage left in plastic bags for collection on street curbs.
1998	*Knowles v. Iowa**	Held that a police officer's search of an automobile with neither the driver's consent nor probable cause, after the driver was issued a citation for speeding, violates the Fourth Amendment.
2000	*Dickerson v. United States*	Ruled that the *Miranda* case is so embedded in routine police practice that the warnings have become part of American national culture.
2000	*Illinois v. Wardlow**	Held that police officers stopping suspects and conducting protective pat-down searches for weapons on public streets in areas known for heavy narcotics trafficking do not violate the Fourth Amendment.
2001	*Atwater v. City of Lago Vista**	Held that the Fourth Amendment does not forbid warrantless arrests for minor criminal offenses, such as misdemeanor seatbelt violations punishable only by fines.
2001	*Illinois v. McArthur**	Ruled it permissible under the Fourth Amendment for police officers who have probable cause to believe that suspects have hidden marijuana in their homes to prevent the suspects from reentering their homes for up to two hours while they obtain search warrants.

Year	Case	Relevance to criminal justice
2001	*Kyllo v. United States**	Held that using thermal imaging devices, which are not in general public use, to explore details of private homes that would be unknowable without physical intrusion constitutes a Fourth Amendment "search" and is presumptively unreasonable without a warrant.
2002	*Atkins v. Virginia*	Held that executing murderers with mental disabilities violates the Eighth Amendment.
2002	*United States v. Drayton*	Ruled that during random searches for drugs or weapons on buses, police are not required to inform passengers that they may refuse to be searched.
2002	*Ring v. Arizona*	Held that the Eighth Amendment requires that only juries—not judges—can award the death penalty.
2003	*Ewing v. California*	Held that the Eighth Amendment does not prohibit sentencing repeat felons to prison terms of twenty-five years under a "three-strikes" law, as the sentence of the appellant in the case was not grossly disproportionate.
2003	*Lawrence v. Texas*	Struck down state antisodomy law as violation of liberty guarantees of due process.
2003	*Virginia v. Black**	Upheld a state law prohibiting cross burning when it is undertaken with the intent to intimidate.
2004	*Blakely v. Washington*	Held that the Sixth Amendment's guarantee of trial by jury prevents judges from making factual findings that increase defendants' sentences beyond the usual ranges for the crimes under state sentencing guidelines; juries must find such facts beyond a reasonable doubt.
2004	*Crawford v. Washington*	Reaffirmed that the Sixth Amendment's guarantee that defendants have the right to face their accusers has few exceptions and that prosecutors cannot introduce statements from absent witnesses (for example, on tape), unless defendants have opportunities to cross-examine such witnesses at earlier hearings or in previous trials.
2004	*Hamdi v. Rumsfeld*	Held that U.S. citizens captured on foreign battlefields in the war on terrorism have a due process right to a "meaningful opportunity" to contest the factual basis for their detention.
2004	*Hiibel v. Sixth Judicial District Court of Nevada*	Held that police are entitled to obtain the names of persons they suspect are involved in crimes, even in the absence of the probable cause normally necessary to make arrests.
2004	*Missouri v. Seibert*	Ruled that police cannot withhold Miranda warnings during initial phases of questioning in order to induce inadmissible confessions that the suspects might be persuaded to repeat after receiving their Miranda warnings; in such cases, the second confessions are not admissible either.

Theodore M. Vestal

U.S. Supreme Court Justices

Alphabetical listing of all justices who served on the Supreme Court. Their dates of tenure on the Court are given in the second column. Asterisks (*) indicate tenures of chief justices. Crosses (†) after names indicate justices who died in office.

Justice	Tenure	Party, state of origin	Notable stances
Henry Baldwin†	1830-1844	Democrat from Pennsylvania	Proponent of states' rights.
Philip P. Barbour†	1836-1841	Democrat from Virginia	Defended slavery and sovereignty of the states.
Hugo L. Black	1937-1971	Democrat from Alabama	Liberal on criminal due process and civil rights. Advocated "total incorporation," or applying all provisions of the first eight amendments of the U.S. Constitution to the states; wrote a defense of the Japanese relocation in *Korematsu v. United States* (1944); emphasized freedom of expression, rejected doctrine of substantive due process, and opposed most restrictions on speech and press.
Harry A. Blackmun	1970-1994	Republican from Minnesota	Became increasingly liberal on criminal procedures, civil rights, and affirmative action; eventually decided that capital punishment is unconstitutional; voided laws prohibiting abortions in *Roe v. Wade* (1973).
John Blair, Jr.	1789-1796	Federalist from Virginia	Was a delegate to the Constitutional Convention in 1787 but left no clear mark on the nation's jurisprudence.
Samuel Blatchford†	1882-1893	Republican from New York	Wrote one of earliest opinions defending privilege against self-incrimination in *Counselman v. Hitchcock* (1892); defender of emerging substantive due process doctrine.
Joseph P. Bradley†	1870-1892	Republican from New Jersey	Wrote first expansive interpretation of the Fourth and Fifth Amendments in *Boyd v. United States* (1886); conservative on civil rights; defended law prohibiting women from practicing law in *Bradwell v. Illinois* (1873).
Louis D. Brandeis	1916-1941	Democrat from Massachusetts	Coauthored an influential article on privacy rights in 1890; also wrote that wiretapping fell under the Fourth Amendment in a dissent in *Olmstead v. United States* (1928); argued that the liberty of the Fourteenth Amendment went beyond property rights to protect personal freedoms of the Bill of Rights; a strong defender of free speech.
William Brennan, Jr.	1950-1990	Democrat from New Jersey	Was a prominent liberal voice in the Warren and Burger courts who consistently defended broad constitutional rights for defendants, privacy rights, freedom of expression, and affirmative programs; argued that capital punishment is unconstitutional in *Furman v. Georgia* (1972).
David J. Brewer	1890-1910	Republican from Kansas	Was a conservative who supported substantive due process and racial segregation; defended the imprisonment of Eugene Debs for violating a federal injunction; asserted that the United States "is a Christian nation."

Justice	Tenure	Party, state of origin	Notable stances
Stephen G. Breyer	1994-	Democrat from Massachusetts	Is a consistent supporter of the Court's liberal wing on issues of criminal procedures, generic privacy, abortion rights, affirmative action, and federalism.
Henry B. Brown	1891-1906	Republican from Michigan	Took a narrow view of defendants' rights; authored the "separate but equal" doctrine in *Plessy v. Ferguson* (1896); defended property rights and substantive due process.
James F. Brynes	1941-1942	Democrat from South Carolina	Was a judicial conservative who wrote sixteen majority opinions during his single year on the Court; had little sympathy for convicted felons; strengthened the constitutional right to travel in *Edwards v. California* (1941).
Warren E. Burger	1969-1986*	Republican from Minnesota	Was a moderate conservative who criticized but failed to reverse the Warren-era expansion of due process rights for criminal defendants; presented a three-pronged test for obscenity in *Miller v. California* (1973); held that "gag orders" in criminal trials were the last resort in *Nebraska Press Association v. Stuart* (1976).
Harold H. Burton	1945-1958	Republican from Ohio	Was a moderate known for his careful research and well-crafted opinions; upheld state prosecutions of noncapital felonies without appointed counsel in *Bute v. Illinois* (1948); usually voted to uphold anticommunist policies of the Truman administration. Outspoken opponent of racial segregation.
Pierce Butler	1923-1939	Democrat from Minnesota	Regarded as one of the conservative "Four Horsemen" who opposed Franklin D. Roosevelt's New Deal reforms; rejected right to counsel in his dissent to *Powell v. Alabama* (1932) but condemned the use of wiretaps in *Olmstead v. United States* (1928); defended liberty of contract and some prior restraint of the press.
John A. Campbell	1853-1861	Democrat from Alabama	Defended states' rights and concurred in *Scott v. Sandford* (1857); took a narrow view of federal admiralty jurisdiction; resigned after the Civil War began and served in the Confederate government as assistant secretary of war.
Benjamin N. Cardozo	1932-1938	Democrat from New York	Was a liberal advocate of sociological jurisprudence and insisted on fundamental fairness of trials; argued for the incorporation of fundamental rights of first eight amendments to states in *Palko v. Connecticut* (1937); restricted freedom of contract doctrine; defended New Deal programs.
John Catron†	1837-1865	Democrat from Tennessee	Defended states' right and slavery but strongly opposed the secession of the southern states; during the Civil War, upheld suspension of *habeas corpus* and confiscation laws.

Justice	Tenure	Party, state of origin	Notable stances
Salmon P. Chase†	1864-1873*	Republican from Ohio	Before the Civil War was an abolitionist and Abraham Lincoln's treasury secretary; took a broad view of war powers of the president in his dissent to *Ex parte Milligan* (1866); upheld the right of women to practice law in *Bradwell v. Illinois* (1873); disagreed with the majority's narrow interpretation of the Fourteenth Amendment in the *Slaughterhouse* cases (1873).
Samuel Chase†	1796-1811	Federalist from Maryland	A signer of the Declaration of Independence, was the only eighteenth century justice on the Court to reject federal common law of crimes; defended doctrine of judicial review and a natural law interpretation of the Constitution in *Calder v. Bull* (1798).
Tom C. Clark	1949-1967	Democrat from Texas	Was a moderate who applied the exclusionary rule to states in *Mapp v. Ohio* (1961); dissented in *Miranda v. Arizona* (1966); broadened concept of conscientious objector in *United States v. Seeger* (1965); overturned a criminal conviction because of prejudicial publicity in *Sheppard v. Maxwell* (1966).
John H. Clarke	1916-1922	Democrat from Ohio	Upheld restrictions on speech with a bad tendency test in *Abrams v. United States* (1919); defended broad congressional powers to regulate business.
Nathan Clifford†	1858-1881	Democrat from Maine	Supported President Abraham Lincoln's wartime suspension of constitutional rights but opposed radial Reconstruction; took an expansive view of judicial review.
Benjamin R. Curtis	1851-1857	Whig from Massachusetts	Wrote the Court's first extended analysis of the due process clause in the *Murray's Lessee v. Hoboken Land Improvement Co.* case (1856); enunciated the "selective exclusiveness" doctrine of congressional power to regulate commerce; resigned after the rancor from his strong dissent in *Scott v. Sandford* (1857); was a critic of Lincoln's suspension of *habeas corpus*.
William Cushing†	1790-1810	Federalist from Massachusetts	Defended the Sedition Act and the doctrine of judicial review.
Peter V. Daniel†	1842-1860	Democrat from Virginia	Supported states' rights and concurred in *Scott v. Sandford* (1857); opposed military trials of citizens during Civil War.
David Davis	1862-1877	Republican from Illinois	Was a friend of Abraham Lincoln; wrote *Ex parte Milligan* (1866), which disallowed military trials when civil courts were available.
William R. Day	1903-1922	Republican from Ohio	Established the exclusionary rule in federal Fourth Amendment cases in *Weeks v. United States* (1914); defended the idea of national police power based on the commerce clause of the Constitution; upheld the Mann Act in *Hoke v. United States* (1913).

Justice	Tenure	Party, state of origin	Notable stances
William O. Douglas	1939-1975	Democrat from Connecticut	Defended expansive views of individual liberties, including application of first eight amendments to the states; reluctantly supported Japanese relocation in *Korematsu v. United States* (1944); opposed governmental restrictions on obscenity and favored a constitutional right of privacy; wrote thirty books.
Gabriel Duvall	1811-1835	Republican from Maryland	Had strong antislavery views and usually agreed with John Marshall; wrote that the right to freedom was more important than the right to property.
Oliver Ellsworth	1796-1800	Federalist from Connecticut	Defended powers of federal courts; expanded federal admiralty jurisdiction over navigable rivers and the Great Lakes.
Stephen J. Field	1863-1897	Democrat from California	Was a zealous advocate of inalienable rights, especially property rights based on substantive due process; opposed loyalty oath requirements for elected offices.
Abe Fortas	1965-1969	Democrat from Tennessee	Successfully argued the *pro bono* case *Gideon v. Wainwright* (1963), which established the right of indigents to counsel in felony cases; interpreted the due process clause of the Constitution as a broad guarantee of fairness in procedures and substance; expanded due process protections for juvenile offenders in *In re Gault* (1967).
Felix Frankfurter	1939-1962	Independent from Massachusetts	Advocated judicial self-restraint, with justices carefully balancing complex constitutional principles; denied that all the Bill of Rights applied to the states in concurring opinion in *Adamson v. California* (1947); made a subjective interpretation of due process as fairness in *Rochin v. California* (1952); held that the states were not required to follow the exclusionary rule in *Wolf v. Colorado* (1949); was a strong proponent of desegregation.
Melvin W. Fuller	1888-1910	Democrat from Illinois	Was a strong defender of private property; wrote that the Tenth Amendment prohibited federal police powers in his dissent to *Champion v. Ames* (1903); accepted racial segregation and wrote that the Fourteenth Amendment produced "no revolutionary change."
Ruth Bader Ginsburg	1993-	Democrat from New York	Is a consistent supporter of rights for criminal defendants, affirmative action, and an expansive role for the federal government; has held especially strong views on reproductive rights and equality for women, as in *United States v. Virginia* (1996).
Arthur J. Goldberg	1962-1965	Democrat from Illinois	Emphasized equality and the rights of criminal defendants; recognized the right of defendants to remain silent in absence of counsel in *Escobedo v. Illinois* (1964); ruled that foreign travel was protected by the Fifth Amendment in *Aptheker v. Secretary of State* (1964).

Justice	Tenure	Party, state of origin	Notable stances
Horace Gray†	1882-1902	Republican from Massachusetts	Supported an expansive view of congressional powers and attempted to limit applications of substantive due process; upheld the U.S. citizenship of Asians born in the United States.
Robert C. Grier	1846-1870	Democrat from Pennsylvania	Sanctioned both federal and state prosecution of persons who aided runaway slaves in *Moore v. Illinois* (1852); defended dual sovereignty and states' rights; wrote defense of wartime blockade in *Prize Cases* (1863).
John Marshall Harlan	1877-1911	Republican from Kentucky	Wrote more dissenting opinions that later became law than any other justice; argued for incorporation of all the first eight amendments into the Fourteenth Amendment in his dissent to *Hurtado v. California* (1884); opposed racial segregation and was a critic of the freedom of contract doctrine.
John Marshall Harlan	1955-1971	Republican from New York	Interpreted the due process clause as a body of evolving principles rather than a shorthand formula for the first eight amendments; opposed the *Miranda* restrictions on police interrogations; interpreted the Fourth Amendment as requiring a "reasonable expectation of privacy" in *Katz v. United States* (1967); interpreted the Smith Act so that prosecution of subversive activities was difficult; defended states' rights and marital privacy.
Oliver W. Holmes, Jr.	1902-1932	Republican from Massachusetts	Often considered the most influential justice of the twentieth century; formulated a libertarian "clear and present danger" test for regulating speech in his dissent to *Abrams v. United States* (1919); did not believe that wiretaps were forbidden by the Fourth Amendment; urged judicial restraint when applying the substantive due process doctrine.
Charles E. Hughes	1910-1916; 1930-1941*	Republican from New York	Was a moderately progressive justice who strongly defended free expression rights; insisted on fair procedures in criminal trials, as in *Powell v. Alabama* (1932); limited application of substantive due process.
Ward Hunt	1873-1882	Republican from New York	Usually voted to uphold legislation protecting rights of African Americans.
James Iredell†	1790-1799	Federalist from North Carolina	Dismissed the natural law approach to judicial review and argued that the Court should overturn statutes only when they contradicted the written Constitution; supported the Sedition Acts.
Howell E. Jackson†	1893-1895	Democrat from Tennessee	Supported an expansive role for the national government and dissented when the Court voided the income tax.
Robert H. Jackson†	1941-1954	Democrat from New York	Balanced expressive freedom with the need for public order; supported vigorous enforcement of the Smith Act in *Dennis v. United States* (1951) and other cases; advocated caution when overturning racial segregation; opposed extension of exclusionary rule to the states; argued for judicial self-restraint in his book *The Struggle for Judicial Supremacy* (1941); also served as a prosecutor at the Nuremberg Trials after World War II.

Justice	Tenure	Party, state of origin	Notable stances
John Jay	1789-1795*	Federalist from New York	Was a committed nationalist who, as the first chief justice, made substantial contributions to the development of a strong Supreme Court.
Thomas Johnson	1792-1793	Federalist from Maryland	Wrote only one opinion during his brief tenure on the Court.
William Johnson†	1804-1834	Republican from South Carolina	Held that federal judges had no power to create or enforce common-law crimes in *United States v. Hudson and Goodwin* (1912); was a slave owner who was vilified by fellow southerners for his broad reading of congressional powers; denounced the denial of due process to the slave rebel Denmark Vessey.
Anthony M. Kennedy	1988-	Republican from California	Has been a moderate conservative who has often been a swing vote on issues of individual liberty, due process, and abortion; approved mandatory drug tests when they were justified for public safety in *Skinner v. Railway Labor Executives Association* (1989); wrote several decisions defending gay rights.
Joseph Lamar†	1911-1916	Democrat from Georgia	Held conservative views but had little impact on the Court.
Lucius Q.C. Lamar†	1888-1893	Democrat from Mississippi	Endorsed broad legislative discretion but insisted on making distinctions between commerce and manufacturing.
Henry B. Livingston†	1807-1823	Republican from New York	Endorsed state prosecutions of seditious libel while on the New York State Supreme Court; took a broad interpretation of the Constitution's full faith and credit clause.
Horace H. Lurton†	1910-1914	Democrat from Tennessee	Was a former confederate officer who supported states' rights but accepted the concept of national police power.
Joseph McKenna	1898-1925	Republican from California	Defended an expansive view of federal police power legislation in cases such as *Hoke v. United States* (1913) and *Adair v. United States* (1908, dissent).
John McKinley†	1838-1852	Democrat from Kentucky	Was firmly committed to state sovereignty.
John McLean†	1830-1861	Democrat from Ohio	Was an opponent of slavery who dissented in *Scott v. Sandford* (1857) but agreed that Congress had constitutional authority to pass the fugitive slave law in *Jones v. Van Zandt* (1847); was a moderate on states' rights.
James C. McReynolds	1914-1941	Democrat from Tennessee	Was one of the "Four Horsemen" with conservative views on individual liberties, defendants' rights, and economic regulations; saw no constitutional necessity for the appointment of counsel in capital cases in his dissent to *Powell v. Alabama* (1932); supported prosecution for displaying a red flag in *Stromberg v. California* (1931) but took a liberal view of the Fourth Amendment in *Carroll v. United States* (1925).

Justice	Tenure	Party, state of origin	Notable stances
John Marshall†	1801-1835*	Federalist from Virginia	Considered the "great chief justice" who established the dominant role of the Court in constitutional interpretation; defended a broad interpretation of congressional powers and took a narrow view of states' rights; ruled that the Bill of Rights did not apply to the states in *Barron v. Baltimore* (1833).
Thurgood Marshall	1967-1991	Democrat from New York	Was a liberal African American justice who consistently defended expansive rights of criminal defendants, individual liberties, affirmative action programs, and the right to privacy; argued that the death penalty was always unconstitutional in his dissent to *Gregg v. Georgia* (1976).
Stanley Matthews†	1881-1889	Republican from Ohio	Held that a grand jury indictment was not essential under the due process clause of the Fourteenth Amendment in *Hurtado v. California* (1884); supported antipolygamy laws; voted to strike down the Ku Klux Klan laws in *Harris v. United States* (1883).
Samuel F. Miller†	1862-1890	Republican from Iowa	Narrowly interpreted the Fourteenth Amendment so that none of the first eight amendments applied to the states in the *Slaughterhouse* cases (1873).
Sherman Minton	1949-1956	Democrat from Indiana	Advocated judicial restraint; tended to uphold convictions and accepted warrantless searches as reasonable in *United States v. Rabinowitz* (1950); accepted restrictions on free speech and association in the interest of national security.
William H. Moody	1906-1910	Republican from Massachusetts	Took an expansive view of congressional power over interstate commerce; was a Progressive but refused to apply the privilege against self-incrimination to the states in *Twining v. New Jersey* (1908).
Alfred Moore	1800-1804	Federalist from North Carolina	Wrote only one opinion, which defended congressional action in time of war.
Frank Murphy†	1940-1949	Democrat from Michigan	Was a liberal who asserted that the Fourteenth Amendment made all of the first eight amendments, plus other fundamental rights, binding on the states; argued that the Fourth Amendment exclusionary rule should apply to the states in *Wolf v. Colorado* (1949); denounced "legalization of racism" in his dissent to *Korematsu v. United States* (1944).
Samuel Nelson	1845-1872	Democrat from New York	Emphasized states' rights and defended rights of slaveholders; extended federal admiralty jurisdiction to inland rivers and lakes.
Sandra Day O'Connor	1981-	Republican from Arizona	Is a moderate conservative whose subtle distinctions have often swung Court decisions; allowed police to conduct noncoercive requests to search private belongings in *Florida v. Bostick* (1991); upheld right to abortion but approved regulations not "unduly burdensome"; has upheld many affirmative action programs judged by the "strict scrutiny" test.

Justice	Tenure	Party, state of origin	Notable stances
William Patterson†	1793-1806	Federalist from New Jersey	Was one of the Framers of the Constitution who supported supremacy of the federal government over the states and espoused the judicial review doctrine.
Rufus W. Peckham†	1896-1909	Democrat from New York	Was a laissez-faire constitutionalist who authored many substantive due process cases; denied that the first eight amendments were binding on the states.
Mahlon Pitney	1912-1922	Republican from New York	Took a narrow view of defendants' rights in cases such as *Frank v. Mangum* (1915); was a strong defender of liberty of contract doctrine; rejected freedom of speech claims against the Espionage Act of 1917.
Lewis F. Powell, Jr.	1972-1987	Democrat from Virginia	Was a moderate "balancer" who often provided swing votes on the Court; limited federal *habeas corpus* reviews of alleged Fourth Amendment violations in *Stone v. Powell* (1976); established a balancing test for determining speedy trial requirement in *Barker v. Wingo* (1972); prohibited disproportionately severe penalties in noncapital cases in *Solem v. Helm* (1983); was the author of the "open fields" exception to Fourth Amendment.
Stanley F. Reed	1938-1957	Democrat from Kentucky	Was moderately conservative on issues of civil liberties and rights; wrote that the privilege against self-incrimination did not apply to the states in *Adamson v. California* (1947).
William H. Rehnquist	1972-1986; 1986- *	Republican from Arizona	Is a consistently conservative justice who has defended capital punishment and opposed most Warren-era expansions of defendants' rights; formulated the public safety exception to the *Miranda* rule in *Quarles v. New York* (1984); rejected the right to abortion and has emphasized states' rights.
Owen J. Roberts	1930-1945	Republican from Pennsylvania	Was a justice whose decisions often appeared to lack consistency; denied that states must provide counsel for indigent defendants in *Betts v. Brady* (1942); opposed internment of Japanese Americans during World War II; expanded the right of political dissent in *Herndon v. Lowry* (1937).
Wiley B. Rutledge, Jr.†	1943-1949	Democrat from Iowa	Was a staunch liberal who held that all of the first eight amendments plus other rights were binding on the states; defended the preferred position of First Amendment freedoms; endorsed Japanese American resettlement during World War II.
Edward T. Sanford	1923-1930	Republican from Tennessee	Was a moderate who wrote that the freedom of speech guarantee of the First Amendment was binding on the states in the landmark *Gitlow v. New York* (1925) case.
Antonin Scalia	1986-	Republican from Ohio	Is a conservative who has advocated emphasis on the text in *A Matter of Interpretation* (1997); has usually rejected claims of defendants' rights; has denied that the Constitution guarantees a generic right of privacy; has consistently opposed affirmative action; has usually defended freedom of expression, as in flag burning and hate speech cases.

Justice	Tenure	Party, state of origin	Notable stances
George Shiras, Jr.	1892-1903	Republican from Pennsylvania	Supported liberal views of due process rights in criminal prosecutions, as in *Brown v. Walker* (1896); endorsed the substantive due process doctrine.
David H. Souter	1990-	Republican from New Hampshire	Called a "closet liberal"; usually upheld expansive views of defendants' rights and defended substantive due process in right of privacy cases.
John Paul Stevens	1975-	Republican from Illinois	Is considered the most liberal justice of the early twenty-first century; has consistently voted in favor of defendants' rights, privacy rights, and affirmative action; held that police usually need warrants to enter private homes to make arrests in *Payton v. New York* (1980); overturned an anti-indecency statute for the Internet in *Reno v. American Civil Liberties Union* (1997).
Potter Stewart	1958-1981	Republican from Ohio	Was a moderate who often broke tie votes on the Court; liberalized Fourth Amendment protections for persons in *Katz v. United States* (1967); expanded Eighth Amendment rights in *Robinson v. California* (1962); upheld capital punishment with due process in *Gregg v. Georgia* (1976); consistently voted in favor of strengthening free speech; endorsed the right to abortion in 1973.
Harlan Fiske Stone†	1925-1941; 1941-1946*	Republican from New York	Was a moderate liberal who wrote the seminal "footnote four" in *United States v. Caroline Products Co.* (1938), suggesting heightened scrutiny for restrictions of fundamental rights; asserted "preferred position" of First Amendment; wrote many liberal dissents later accepted by the Court's majority.
Joseph Story†	1811-1845	Republican from Massachusetts	Aggressively asserted federal jurisdiction over the states in *Martin v. Hunter's Lessee* (1816); tried to harmonize natural justice and positive law in cases such as *Le Jeune Eugenie* (1822); wrote the influential *Commentaries on the Constitution* (1833).
William Strong	1870-1880	Republican from Pennsylvania	Defended the right of African Americans to serve on juries in *Strauder v. West Virginia* (1880); supported laws mandating Christian practices.
George Sutherland	1922-1938	Republican from Utah	Spokesman for substantive due process and property rights; favored selective application of the first eight amendments to the states; wrote opinions expanding rights of counsel in *Powell v. Alabama* (1932); held liberal views on free expression.
Noah H. Swaine	1862-1881	Republican from Ohio	Defended legislative and executive restrictions on rights during the Civil War; his dissent in the *Slaughterhouse* cases (1873) broadly interpreted individual rights under the Fourteenth Amendment.

Justice	Tenure	Party, state of origin	Notable stances
William H. Taft	1921-1930*	Republican from Ohio	Was usually conservative; held narrow interpretations of Fourth Amendment, as in approval of wiretaps without warrant in *Olmstead v. United States* (1928); articulated "automobile exception" in *Carroll v. United States* (1925); restricted congressional powers under the Tenth Amendment.
Roger Brooke Taney†	1836-1864*	Democrat from Maryland	Defended fugitive slave laws and was an apologist for slaveholders' rights in *Scott v. Sandford* (1857); condemned President Abraham Lincoln's "arbitrary arrests" in *Ex parte Merryman* (1861); provided more support for states' rights and less protection for private property than the Marshall court.
Clarence Thomas	1991-	Republican from Georgia	Is a conservative who has predictably voted to restrict defendants' rights, affirmative action, and the rights of privacy and abortion; has had expansive views of the takings clause of the Constitution and states' rights under the Tenth Amendment.
Smith Thompson†	1824-1843	Republican from New York	Defended states' authority over commerce unless directly conflicting with federal law; recognized sovereignty of Native American nations.
Thomas Todd†	1807-1826	Republican from Kentucky	Consistently supported decisions of Chief Justice John Marshall.
Robert Trimble†	1826-1828	Republican from Kentucky	Usually agreed with Chief Justice John Marshall's views on federalism.
Willis Van Devanter	1910-1937	Republican from Wyoming	Was one of the conservative "Four Horsemen" who consistently voted to support states' rights and economic rights; usually supported government repression of political dissent; endorsed bad tendency test for limits on speech.
Fred M. Vinson†	1946-1953*	Democrat from Kentucky	Was a moderate conservative who defended restrictions on free speech for national security, as in *Dennis v. United States* (1951). Expansive views of legislative powers under the commerce clause.
Morrison R. Waite†	1874-1888*	Republican from Ohio	Held that a criminalization of polygamy did not violate the First Amendment in *Reynolds v. United States* (1879); restricted the authority of Congress to protect civil rights in *United States v. Cruikshank* (1876); rejected substantive due process as a barrier to government regulations of business.
Earl Warren	1953-1969*	Republican from California	As chief justice, presided over an unprecedented expansion of individual liberties and civil rights; demanded due process principles in congressional investigations in *Watkins v. United States* (1957); held that police must inform detained suspects of their constitutional rights in *Miranda v. Arizona* (1966); struck down antimiscegenation laws in *Loving v. Virginia* (1967); interpreted the Eighth Amendment in terms of "evolving standards of decency" in *Trop v. Dulles* (1958).

Justice	Tenure	Party, state of origin	Notable stances
Bushrod Washington†	1799-1829	Federalist from Pennsylvania	Favorite nephew of George Washington who liberally defined the privileges and immunities of national citizenship in *Corfield v. Coryell* (1823); enforced the Sedition Act of 1798 while riding circuit.
James M. Wayne†	1835-1867	Democrat from Georgia	Was a slaveholder who concurred in *Scott v. Sandford* (1857) but endorsed special legislative and executive powers during the Civil War.
Byron R. White	1962-1993	Democrat from Colorado	Was usually liberal on civil rights but conservative on criminal procedures; opposed the requirement of Miranda warnings and asserted "good faith" exception to exclusionary rule in *United States v. Leon* (1984); endorsed many restrictions on obscenity, defended prosecution of flag desecration; dissented in *Roe v. Wade* (1973) and upheld prosecution of homosexual practices in *Bowers v. Hardwick* (1986).
Edward D. White†	1894-1910; 1910-1921*	Democrat from Louisiana	Erratic on substantive due process held that the Fifth Amendment did not apply to Native American courts in *Talton v. Mayes* (1896); endorsed military conscription in the *Selective Draft Law Cases* (1918).
Charles E. Whittaker	1957-1962	Republican from Missouri	Was a nonideological conservative who often provided the swing vote in 5-4 decisions; supported antisubversive laws and opposed application of exclusionary rule to the states; insisted on rights of aliens to due process.
James Wilson†	1789-1798	Federalist from Pennsylvania	Was one of the Framers of the U.S. Constitution in 1787; combined the ideas of popular sovereignty and a strong national government in *Lectures on Law* (1790-91); asserted doctrine of judicial review in *Hayburn's Case* (1792).
Levi Woodbury†	1845-1851	Democrat from New Hampshire	Held that the Fugitive Slave Act of 1793 did not violate the due process clause of the Fifth Amendment in *Jones v. Van Zandt* (1847).
William B. Woods†	1880-1887	Republican from Georgia	Narrowly interpreted the Fourteenth Amendment and held that the first eight amendments were not binding on the states, as in *Presser v. Illinois* (1886); wrote the majority opinion in *Harris v. United States* (1883), which invalidated federal Ku Klux Klan laws.

Thomas Tandy Lewis

Famous American Trials

Date	Trial	Charge or Issue	Result or Significance
1634	Roger Williams	Religious dissent	Williams was found guilty of blasphemy and exiled from Massachusetts Bay Colony; he subsequently founded Rhode Island.
1636	Anne Marbury Hutchinson	Religious dissent	Hutchinson was convicted of sedition and contempt and exiled; she founded Portsmith, Rhode Island.
1690	Rebecca Nurse and others	Witchcraft	During the Salem witchcraft trials, Rebecca Nurse and five others (all old men and women) were convicted of witchcraft and hanged.
1735	John Peter Zenger	Seditious libel	Zenger published a newspaper opposed to the New York colonial government. He was arrested and imprisoned. Defended by Alexander Hamilton, Zenger proved that his statements were true and was acquitted. His trial set the pattern for freedom of the press in America.
1770	William McCauley and others	Manslaughter	McCauley and six other British soldiers were tried for killing five men in a riot on Boston Commons in March, 1770 (the "Boston massacre"). Future president John Adams defended them. Four were acquitted and two were convicted. The latter were branded and released.
1804	Samuel Chase	Impeachment	Associate Justice Chase was impeached by Jeffersonian Democrats for his opposition during sedition trials, but the Senate refused to convict him.
1807	Aaron Burr	Treason	Burr planned to create a personal empire in the Mississippi Valley. President Thomas Jefferson charged him with treason. The judge, Chief Justice John Marshall, narrowly defined the charge, and Burr was quickly acquitted. Popular sentiment was so much against Burr, however, that he was forced into European exile for a number of years.
1859	John Brown	Treason and murder	Brown's trial on charges stemming from his abolitionist raid on the federal arsenal at Harpers Ferry lasted four days. Supporters' plans to free him failed. The jury convicted him in forty-five minutes, and he was hanged two months later.
1862	Rda-in-yan-ka, Big Eagle, and others	Murder	After a Sioux uprising in 1862 in Minnesota in which more than four hundred white settlers were killed, a mass trial was held. Three hundred and six Indians were sentenced to death and eighteen to prison. President Abraham Lincoln commuted all but thirty-nine of the death sentences. Rda-in-yan-ka was hanged and Big Eagle was imprisoned.
1865	Mary Surratt	Conspiracy to murder and treason	Linked to the assassination of President Abraham Lincoln because the conspirators stayed at her boardinghouse, Surratt was found guilty and hanged although there was no direct evidence against her.
1866	Samuel A. Mudd	Conspiracy to murder	A physician, Mudd treated John Wilkes Booth after he killed Lincoln. Although he claimed he did not know of the assassination, he was sentenced to life imprisonment.

Date	Trial	Charge or Issue	Result or Significance
1868	Andrew Johnson	Impeachment for high crimes and misdemeanors	A southern pro-Union Democrat, Johnson became president after Lincoln's assassination. The Republican Congress passed a law limiting his ability to control his cabinet. When he refused to abide, an impeachment trial in the Senate began. Johnson was acquitted when seven Republicans refused to join the others in a guilty verdict: The charge failed by one vote to reach the required two-thirds majority.
1873	Susan B. Anthony	Illegal voting	After voting in Rochester, New York, in a federal election, Anthony was arrested for illegal voting because she was a woman. When she was later tried, the judge would not let her testify and instructed the jury to find her guilty. She was convicted and fined one hundred dollars and court costs, but she refused to pay. She petitioned Congress to remit her unjust fine, but Congress ignored her petition.
1875	John Doyle Lee	Murder	A Mormon and Indian agent, Lee was involved in a dispute with a band of California-bound settlers. He encouraged a group of Paiute Indians to kill them and participated in the massacre at Mountain Meadows, Utah. After two trials he was executed.
1881	Charles J. Guiteau	Murder	The assassin of President James Garfield, Guiteau was convicted and executed.
1886	August Spies and others	Accessory to murder	Spies and seven others were tried for abetting the murder of policemen killed by a bomb during a labor demonstration in Chicago (the Haymarket Riot). Although their connection to the crime could not be proved, they were charged because they were labor leaders and outspoken anarchists. They were convicted—seven sentenced to hang and one, Oscar Neebe, to life imprisonment. One committed suicide. Two death sentences were commuted. Four of the men were hanged, including Spies. The remaining three were pardoned by Illinois governor John Peter Altgel in 1893.
1893	Lizzie Borden	Murder	When Borden was thirty-two years old, her father and stepmother were brutally killed by blows from an axe in their Massachusetts home in 1892. The circumstantial evidence against Borden was strong, but she was acquitted of murder in a jury trial. Nevertheless, her name was ever afterward associated with her parents' murder.
1901	Leon Czolgosz	Murder	Czolgosz was the anarchist assassin of President William McKinley. He was rapidly tried and convicted in Buffalo, New York, where the assassination took place. He was executed by electrocution.
1906	William Dudley ("Big Bill") Haywood	Murder	Haywood was accused with others of murdering Frank Steunenberg, the governor of Idaho. They were defended by Clarence Darrow and acquitted.
1907	Harry Thaw	Murder	A wealthy socialite married to the dancer Evelyn Nesbit, Thaw shot and killed Nesbit's lover, prominent architect Stanford White. He was acquitted on grounds of insanity.

Date	Trial	Charge or Issue	Result or Significance
1911	J. J. and J. B. McNamara	Murder	The McNamara brothers bombed the *Los Angeles Times* building during a labor dispute, killing twenty-one persons. Their attorney, Clarence Darrow, pleaded guilty to save their lives. They were sentenced to long prison terms.
1914	Joe Hill (Joe Emmanuel Hagglund)	Murder	A Swedish-born labor organizer and composer, Hill was falsely charged with murder. He was convicted on doubtful evidence and executed despite widespread appeals for reconsideration, including one from President Woodrow Wilson.
1917	Margaret Sanger	Creating a public nuisance	A nurse and advocate of artificial birth control, then illegal in most states, Sanger was arrested and convicted of creating a public nuisance. She was sentenced to thirty days in jail.
1917	Emma Goldman	Hindering conscription	An anarchist and pacifist, Goldman opposed American entry into World War I. She was tried for impeding conscription, denaturalized, and returned to her native Russia in 1919.
1918	Eugene V. Debs	Sedition	A labor leader and pioneer American socialist, Debs was tried and convicted of violating the Espionage Act. Sentenced to ten years, he was pardoned by President Warren G. Harding in 1921.
1921-1922	Roscoe "Fatty" Arbuckle	Manslaughter	A comedic film star, Arbuckle was arrested after the death of a young actress at a Hollywood party. After three trials he was acquitted, but his film career was ruined because of the scandal.
1924	Nicola Sacco and Bartolomeo Vanzetti	Murder and robbery	Sacco and Vanzetti were Italian-born anarchists who were tried and convicted of armed robbery and murder in 1924. Although the evidence against them was flimsy and some evidence pointed toward other possible culprits, the authorities refused appeals and new trials. Sacco and Vanzetti were convicted largely because of their anarchist political beliefs. The case provoked worldwide condemnation and mass demonstrations. Sacco and Vanzetti were executed in 1927. Fifty years later, Massachusetts governor Michael Dukakis issued a proclamation formally exonerating them of any guilt or stigma.
1924	Nathan Leopold and Richard Loeb	Murder	This celebrated case involved the brutal homosexual rape and murder of young Bobby Franks by two wealthy young men, Leopold and Loeb. Clarence Darrow successfully argued against the murderers' execution in a bench trial, and they were given life imprisonment. Loeb was killed in prison in 1936; Leopold was paroled in 1968 and died three years later.
1925	John T. Scopes	Teaching evolution	In what was dubbed the "monkey trial," Scopes, a high school teacher, deliberately broke Tennessee's law against teaching Darwinian evolution. The trial gained national publicity because it pitted William Jennings Bryan as prosecutor against Clarence Darrow for the defense. Scopes was convicted and given a nominal fine. The U.S. Supreme Court overturned Scopes's conviction, but the statute remained.
1926	Albert Fall	Accepting bribes	The secretary of the interior under President Warren G. Harding, Fall was at the center of the Teapot Dome scandal, giving out generous leases on public land. He was convicted and served one year in prison.

Date	Trial	Charge or Issue	Result or Significance
1927	Harry Daugherty	Conspiracy to defraud the government	President Harding's attorney general, Daugherty was also involved in the Teapot Dome scandal. His two trials ended in hung juries.
1931	Haywood Patterson and others	Rape	Patterson and eight other African Americans were falsely charged with rape in Scottsboro, Alabama. All-white juries quickly convicted them in three trials, and all nine were sentenced to execution. The "Scottsboro" case drew national attention and involved complex political and racial issues. The U.S. Supreme Court overturned the convictions because the defendants were denied due process and the right to counsel.
1931	Al Capone	Income tax evasion	A notorious gangster involved in the illegal manufacture and sale of alcohol and other rackets, Capone had long evaded arrest. Federal authorities finally charged him with violating the tax laws. He was convicted and sentenced to eleven years in prison and fined $80,000.
1936	Bruno Hauptmann	Kidnapping and murder	Hauptmann was charged in the sensational Lindbergh kidnapping case. He was accused of kidnapping and murdering the son of famous aviator Charles Lindbergh. Although the evidence was circumstantial, he was convicted and executed. The media reporting of the event was extremely controversial.
1941	Louis (Lepke) Buchalter	Murder	The leader of Murder Incorporated, Buchalter's organized crime assassination ring in 1930's New York, was convicted in one of a series of trials against racketeers that brought District Attorney Thomas E. Dewey to prominence. Buchalter was executed.
1948	Caryl Chessman	Kidnapping	Chessman forced his victim from one car to another and raped her. In a trial in which he defended himself, he was convicted on the technical charge of kidnapping, rather than rape, and was sentenced to death. His execution was postponed for twelve years, during which time he wrote a number of successful books. The controversial nature of the charge, the length of the delay, and his personal publicity made his case a *cause célèbre*.
1949	Julius and Ethel Rosenberg	Espionage	The Rosenbergs were convicted of passing atomic secrets to the Soviet Union in a controversial trial. Despite many appeals for their sentences to be commuted to life imprisonment, they were executed.
1950	Alger Hiss	Perjury	Hiss was tried and convicted in a second trial after a first one ended in a hung jury. He was charged with lying about his communist connections. The trials were public sensations, contributing to the hysteria of the McCarthy period.
1951	Elizabeth Gurley Flynn	Smith Act (membership in the Communist Party)	A prominent radical labor leader and Communist Party member, Flynn was convicted under the Smith Act of 1940.
1954	Sam Sheppard	Murder	Sheppard was convicted of murdering his wife and sentenced to life imprisonment. The U.S. Supreme Court in 1965 overturned the conviction because the publicity associated with the case had denied him a fair trial.

Date	Trial	Charge or Issue	Result or Significance
1964	Jack Ruby	Murder	The killer of President John F. Kennedy's alleged assassin, Lee Harvey Oswald, Ruby was defended by attorney Melvin Belli. He was convicted and sentenced to death, but the conviction was reversed in 1966 on appeal, and he died while awaiting a new trial.
1967	Jimmy Hoffa	Jury tampering and mishandling union funds	The leader of the mob-ridden Teamsters Union, Hoffa was an object of the U.S. Department of Justice's war on union corruption. He was convicted in 1967 after several trials and then pardoned in 1971.
1968	James Earl Ray	Murder	Ray was convicted of murdering civil rights leader Martin Luther King, Jr., and sentenced to life imprisonment.
1969	Angela Davis	Accessory to murder	Charged because her guns were used in a prison escape attempt, Davis was acquitted in a case that brought international publicity. Her membership in the Communist Party was thought to be part of the reason behind the charge.
1969-1970	Rennie Davis and others	Conspiracy and intent to incite riot	The "Chicago eight" (later seven), were arrested for disrupting the 1968 Democratic convention. Conspiracy charges were dismissed, but five were convicted of intent to incite riot; they were sentenced to five years and fined. Prominent attorney William Kunstler defended them. The convictions were reversed in 1972.
1971	Charles Manson and others	Murder	The leader of a counterculture commune known as the "Manson family," Charles Manson was charged with the murder of actor Sharon Tate and more than six others. Although the murders were carried out by his followers, and he was not present at any of them, he was seen as primarily responsible. Manson was sentenced to death, but later the sentence was commuted when California overturned its death penalty. The trial attracted international attention.
1971	William J. Calley	Murder	A U.S. Army lieutenant, Calley commanded a platoon that massacred women and children in the South Vietnamese village of My Lai during the war. The publicity about the event forced a court-martial of Calley. He was convicted and sentenced to twenty years, but he served little time before being pardoned.
1971	Daniel Ellsberg	Theft, espionage, and conspiracy	Ellsberg leaked the Pentagon Papers, secret documents that contained information on U.S. violations of international law in the Vietnam War. He was indicted, but the charges were dismissed because of improper government actions in preparing their case.
1973	Spiro Agnew	Accepting bribes	Charged with accepting bribes and other wrongdoing while he had held public offices—including the governorship—in Maryland, Vice President Agnew pleaded no contest and was sentenced to three years' probation and a $10,000 fine. He resigned as vice president.
1973	John Dean	Perjury	A key figure in the Watergate scandal, Dean pleaded guilty of perjury in the cover-up and was sentenced to prison.
1974	G. Gordon Liddy	Burglary, conspiracy, and wiretapping	One of the principal "plumbers" in the Watergate affair, Liddy was convicted of burglarizing and bugging the Democratic headquarters and was sentenced to seven to twenty years.

Date	Trial	Charge or Issue	Result or Significance
1974-1975	John Mitchell, H. R. Haldeman, John Ehrlichman, and others	Conspiracy	Seven high-ranking members of the Nixon administration, White House staff, and Republican National Committee were indicted for illegal conspiracy relating to the 1972 election. Five, including Mitchell, Haldeman, and Ehrlichman, were convicted and given sentences ranging from two and one-half to eight years.
1974	E. Howard Hunt and others	Burglary, conspiracy, and wiretapping	Along with G. Gordon Liddy, Hunt directed the Watergate burglary. He and his four codefendants actually carried out the burglary. Hunt pleaded guilty and was sentenced to thirty months to eight years.
1975	Patricia Hearst	Armed robbery	Kidnapped by the radical terrorist Symbionese Liberation Army, Hearst, the daughter of a newspaper magnate, joined the group and participated in its bank robberies. Her criminal career, capture, and trial were a media sensation. She claimed to have been "brainwashed" but was convicted and sentenced to seven years, commuted by President Jimmy Carter after two and one-half years.
1976	Gary Gilmore	Murder	Gilmore was convicted of two murders and sentenced to death. His case became controversial when he requested (and received) execution rather than following up the appeals process, and his 1977 execution was the first in the United States since the U.S. Supreme Court had ordered executions halted in 1972.
1982	Claus von Bulow	Attempted murder	A financial consultant married to a New England socialite, von Bulow was convicted of trying to kill her by administering an insulin overdose. He was sentenced to thirty years. The conviction was overturned in 1985 when von Bulow was represented by attorney Alan Dershowitz.
1984	Raymond James Donovan	Falsifying documents, business records	President Ronald Reagan's secretary of labor, Donovan was hounded through his tenure of office by charges of corruption linked to organized crime. He was indicted, tried, and acquitted.
1984, 1986	John DeLorean	Drug trafficking, racketeering, and fraud	In two trials, automobile entrepreneur DeLorean was acquitted on all counts.
1986	Jim Bakker	Conspiracy and fraud	A television evangelist, Bakker lost his ministry because of a sex scandal and then was convicted of diverting donations from his ministry to his personal use and other frauds. He was sentenced to forty-five years in prison. His conviction was upheld in appeal, but his sentence was reduced to eighteen years and he was released even sooner.
1989	Oliver North	Conspiracy to defraud and obstruction of Congress	A staff member on the National Security Council, North was a key figure in the Iran-Contra scandal (the Reagan administration's illegal trading of arms for hostages). He was convicted of covering up the affair and sentenced to a three-year suspended sentence, probation, a fine, and community service.

Date	Trial	Charge or Issue	Result or Significance
1990	John Poindexter	Conspiracy, perjury, and obstruction of Congress	As secretary of the Navy, Poindexter lied during the congressional investigation of the Iran-Contra scandal. He was convicted on all counts and sentenced to six months. The conviction was reversed on appeal.
1990	Marion Barry	Drug possession	The mayor of Washington, D.C., Barry was convicted of cocaine possession and sentenced to six months. After serving his term he was again elected mayor.
1992	Jeffrey Dahmer	Murder	A serial killer, Dahmer enticed his victims to his apartment, murdered them, and saved parts of their bodies. He also engaged in cannibalism. The gory nature of his crimes made his trial a sensation. He was ruled sane, convicted of murder, and sentenced to sixteen life terms. He was killed in prison in 1994.
1992	Mike Tyson	Rape	The heavyweight boxing champion was accused and convicted of raping a participant in a beauty contest in which he was a judge.
1992	William Kennedy Smith	Rape	A member of the prominent Kennedy family, Smith was accused of rape by a woman he invited to the family's compound in Florida. He was acquitted after a televised trial.
1992, 1993	Stacey Koon, Laurence Powell, and others	Police misconduct, violation of civil rights	Four Los Angeles police officers were charged with using excessive force in arresting African American motorist Rodney King for a traffic violation. The beating of King was videotaped by a witness. The police officers were acquitted by a suburban jury, causing five days of rioting in Los Angeles. In a second trial in federal court, Koon and Powell were convicted of civil rights violations and sentenced to two-and-a-half years.
1993	Lorena Bobbitt	Malicious wounding	Bobbitt cut off her husband's penis in retaliation for spousal abuse. (Doctors were able to restore the organ surgically.) She was acquitted and became a feminist icon for standing up to male abuse.
1993-1994, 1995-1996	Erik and Lyle Menendez	Murder	In a much-publicized case, the Menendez brothers, who were accused of murdering their wealthy parents, pleaded innocent on the basis that they had been abused as children. Their first trial was declared a mistrial. In their second trial, they were both convicted of first-degree murder and sentenced to life in prison without the possibility of parole.
1994	Byron de la Beckwith	Murder	Beckwith assassinated prominent civil rights activist Medgar Evers in 1963. Although he was known to have committed the crime, racial prejudice in Mississippi—where the murder occurred—resulted in two hung juries. A new trial took place in 1994. He was convicted and sentenced to life imprisonment.
1995	Susan Smith	Murder	After murdering her two young sons, Smith claimed that they were kidnapped. She was convicted and sentenced to life imprisonment.
1995	O. J. Simpson	Murder	In a sensational, nationally televised trial lasting almost a year, celebrity and former football star Simpson was charged with murdering his former wife and her friend. A jury took less than a day to acquit him in a decision that had racial overtones and divided the nation.

Date	Trial	Charge or Issue	Result or Significance
1996	Timothy McVeigh	Bombing	Two days after the bomb blast that killed 168 people in a federal office building in Oklahoma City, Oklahoma, McVeigh and his friend Terry Nichols were arrested. A federal grand jury later indicted them for first-degree murder, conspiracy to use a weapon of mass destruction, and destruction by explosives. McVeigh was later tried by himself, found guilty on all counts, and executed.
1999	Jack Kevorkian	Murder	A medical doctor and outspoken practitioner of assisted suicide, Kevorkian repeatedly challenged state laws by assisting with more than one hundred suicides until he was convicted of second-degree murder in Michigan and sentenced to ten to twenty-five years in prison.
1999	Bill Clinton	Impeachment	In late 1998, the House Judiciary Committee approved four articles of impeachment against President Clinton: perjury before a grand jury, obstruction of justice, perjury in a civil deposition, and abuse of power. After the full House approved two of the articles, the impeachment trial opened in the Senate in January. The trial ended with the Senate voting 45 to 55 for conviction on the perjury count and 50 to 50 on the obstruction of justice count. As conviction requires a two-thirds vote, the president was acquitted.
2002	Andrea Yates	Murder	Suffering from severe mental disorders, Yates drowned all five of her young children in a bathtub. A Texas jury rejected her insanity defense and convicted her of murder but sentenced her to life in prison. In 2005, her conviction was overturned because of faulty expert testimony in her trial, but she remained in prison under psychiatric care.
2002	Winona Ryder	Shoplifting	The shoplifting charges against Ryder were comparatively minor, but her fame as an actor attracted great public interest in her case, particularly because of the apparent senselessness of the crime of shoplifting by a wealthy person. Convicted on two counts of felony theft, she was sentenced to paying restitution and community service, but her felony convictions were later reduced to misdemeanor convictions.
2004	Martha Stewart	Conspiracy, making false statements, obstruction of justice, and securities fraud	Stewart was investigated for insider trading but was tried for only a variety of technical offenses. Because of her fame as a television and publishing personality, her trial was closely watched by the media. In early 2004, she and her stockbroker were convicted on all charges, and she was sentenced to five months in a federal prison.
2004	Scott Peterson	Murder	Four months after Peterson's pregnant wife, Laci, disappeared, Peterson was charged with both her murder and the murder of her unborn child. Peterson's subsequent trial attracted wide interest because of public curiosity about how such an attractive and apparently loving couple's marriage could end in murder and because of legal questions about whether the killing of a fetus could constitute murder.

Date	Trial	Charge or Issue	Result or Significance
2004-2005	Jayson Williams	Manslaughter	A wealthy former basketball star, Williams shot to death his chauffeur in what was apparently a drunken accident in 2002. The charge against Williams was manslaughter, but the issue was whether the homicide was aggravated manslaughter or merely negligent manslaughter. In Williams's first trial, a jury acquitted him of aggravated manslaughter, but afterward, a judge ordered that he be retried for reckless manslaughter.
2005	Robert Blake	Murder	Blake was tried for murdering his wife and for attempting to solicit murder. The circumstantial evidence against him was strong, but the prosecution failed to prove its case beyond a reasonable doubt, and he was acquitted by a jury.
2005	Michael Jackson	Child molestation	A decade after a scandal in which the famous pop singer was alleged to have paid millions of dollars to silence a child who had charged him with sexual molestation, Jackson was brought to trial in another molestation case that turned into a true media circus. After a trial that heard the testimony of more than 130 witnesses over the course of fourteen weeks, a jury deliberated for seven days and then ruled Jackson not guilty on all counts.

Frederick B. Chary
Updated by the Editors

Television Programs

This is a listing of representative television programs of the past and present with criminal justice themes: police procedurals, crime dramas, courtroom programs, and others. For additional information on these and other television programs, consult the articles on television in the main text and check the listings in the general index.

American Justice (A&E, 1992-   , Bill Kurtis, executive producer) Criminal justice programming. Tackles tough, real-life contemporary issues—from the death penalty, to drug sentencing, false confessions, and racial inequities—through cases that challenge and change the law. Told by key players from police to the victims to the perpetrators, the program offers a rare inside view that enables viewers to understand the complex legal principles at stake. Presents insightful perspectives on the most controversial aspects of criminal law in the United States. Critically acclaimed episodes include: "Why O. J. Simpson Won"; "Justice Denied: The Hurricane Carter Story"; "Erin Brockovitch"; "Von Bulow: A Wealth of Evidence"; and "We, the Jury," a special look at the system of trial by jury, the cornerstone of American justice.

America's Dumbest Criminals (Syndicated, 1996-   , Steve Angus, director). Light entertainment. This series combines actual surveillance camera footage collected from law-enforcement agencies with narration, dramatic reenactments, and comedy music to demonstrate the ineptness of most perpetrators of crime. Examples include thieves trying to make fast getaways, only to find they have locked their keys in their getaway cars; burglars having to call 911 after becoming trapped inside the buildings they are robbing; defendants who raise their hands to identify themselves in court when prosecutors ask victims to identify the wrongdoers.

America's Most Wanted (Fox, 1988-   , John Walsh, host; renamed *America's Most Wanted: America Fights Back* in 1996). Mixture of real-life facts and entertainment. Comprising vignettes in which actors reenact actual crimes, the series targets and starts a relentless pursuit of dangerous fugitives. Features interviews with victims, their families and friends, and the police, as well as film and photographs of suspects. Viewers are urged to telephone police or the program with information about the crimes and suspects covered in the programs. New episodes update earlier broadcasts with film clips of captured fugitives and follow-up reports on fugitives who are still at large. The program has reportedly assisted in the capture of more than eight hundred criminals, including fifteen from the Federal Bureau of Investigation's ten-most-wanted lists. The show is also an active voice for victims' rights.

Charlie's Angels (ABC, 1976-1981, Aaron Spelling and Leonard Goldberg, producers). Fantasy-detective drama about three gorgeous former policewomen. The original "angels," Sabrina Duncan (Kate Jackson), Jill Munroe (Farrah Fawcett-Majors), and Kelly Garrett (Jaclyn Smith), worked with their trusty male counterpart, John Bosley (David Doyle), for a private detective agency. Their boss, Charlie—who was known to them only by his voice—gave them their assignments via a speaker phone. A perfectly turned-out and accessorized force to be reckoned with, the angels traveled each week to new and exotic locales, where—despite their stunning good looks—they always fit into everyday situations with everyday people. No crime was ever too perplexing and no murder scene was ever too mundane for the technologically talented, martial arts-trained trio. Dubbed the original "jiggle TV" detective program, the show was built on guns, hairstyles, and makeup. An instant pop-culture phenomenon, *Charlie's Angels* remained popular even as new angels rotated through the cast because it was mostly about women fighting crime in a man's world. This show also inspired the popular and more serious 1980's drama *Cagney & Lacey*, and with reincarnated angels spawned a motion picture series in 2000.

CHiPs (NBC, 1977-1983, Rick Rosner, creator).

Police procedural drama about California Highway Patrol officers working in Los Angeles. The main characters were officers Jon Baker (Larry Willcox) and Frank "Ponch" Poncherello (Erik Estrada), two motorcycle officers always on the street, saving lives and driving home the violent consequences of criminal activity.

Cold Case Files (A&E, 1998-   , Bill Kurtis, executive producer). Reality police program that examines the most fascinating cases on crime books, showing how law-enforcement authorities use a combination of timing, persistence, and high-tech forensics to solve criminal cases that have long gone cold. Kurtis is one of the few producer/performers in criminal justice television shows with a law degree.

Columbo (ABC, 1968-2002, Richard Levinson and William Link, creators). Drama about an eccentric Los Angeles police detective. Many fictional criminals made the mistake of underestimating Lieutenant Columbo (Peter Falk), a homicide investigator with a crumpled trench coat and beat-up car who appeared to be an incompetent bumbler. Columbo was so polite to suspects and talked so much about his wife (who never appeared) that he lulled even the shrewdest murderers into a false sense of security. The dramatic structure of the programs was unusual in that audiences saw the crimes committed at the beginning of each episode. Suspense was built around Columbo's painstaking and methodical efforts to get the killers to reveal the mistakes in their seemingly perfect crimes.

COPS (Fox, 1988-   , John Langley, creator and executive producer). Reality police program in which television cameras accompany real police to film stories as they unfold. Each week, a camera crew follows the activities and daily beats of officers of a different city's police department. Actual footage shows police in action in incidents such as routine traffic stops that evolve into charging the subjects with drug-related offenses; domestic violence; high-speed chases; stakeouts and raids. Audiences see and hear much of what police see and hear as events happen. This approach has been touted as the "real thing"; however, programs are edited to concentrate on the most visually

interesting sequences. Uninteresting video is deleted and clips from stock footage are added. Moreover, *Time* magazine reported that every episode is reviewed by the police who are involved before it is aired, "to make sure no investigations are compromised." Sometimes called the original reality show, this half-hour series features police officers performing their daily duty "to serve and protect" the public.

Courtroom Television Network (Court TV, 1991-   , Steven Brill, founder). Basic cable network that provides a window on the U.S. system of justice through distinctive programming concerning law and justice. The show has broadcast gavel-to-gavel coverage, or portions, of more than 740 civil and criminal trials and other proceedings, including parole hearings, death-penalty hearings, and proceedings in municipal and night courts around the United States. Differentiating its coverage from sound bites and "spin" frequently a part of out-of-court media coverage of judicial proceedings, Court TV claims its video camera constitutes a "thirteenth juror" that helps to ensure fair trials by making them public. Court TV has covered a wide variety of criminal trials that have raised important social, economic, political, and cultural questions; among the most notable have been the trials of accused murderer O. J. Simpson; accused rapist William Kennedy Smith; Louise Woodward, the British nanny accused of murder; convicted murderers Erik and Lyle Menendez; four New York City police officers accused of shooting Amadou Diallo; the Los Angeles police officers accused of brutalizing Rodney King; Lorena Bobbitt, the penis amputator; and Joseph Hazelwood, the former captain of the *Exxon Valdez*, who was accused of illegally spilling oil in pristine Alaskan waters. The network's schedule has included documentaries hosted by Al Roker, Martin Sheen, Andrea Thompson, Cynthia McFadden, and others; series such as *Forensic Files*; *The System*; *Catherine Crier Live*; *Dominick Dunne's Power*; *Privilege and Justice*; *I, Detective*; and *Body of Evidence: From the Case Files of Dayle Hinman*; and specials, including some original films; plus popular off-network series, such as *NYPD Blue*, *Profiler*, and *COPS*. Court Television's Web site has aired more than 150 trials involving such notables as television talk show host Jenny Jones and assisted-suicide advocate Jack Kevorkian.

Crime & Punishment (NBC, 2002-   , Dick Wolf, creator and executive producer). Documentary. Sometimes described as a real-life *Law & Order*, this series is an unscripted documentary about real-life court cases in San Diego, California. Typical episodes follow prosecuting attorneys as they interview witnesses, gather evidence, and present their cases at trial. Filmed in high-definition video, the series combines cinema verité footage with three-camera courtroom coverage, giving it the look and feel of a fictional drama series. In contrast to other shows, this show contains no interviews, no narration, and no reenactments; everything is real as it unfolds on the screen. *Crime & Punishment* also provides toll-free telephone numbers of services that offer assistance to viewers in dangerous situations that are similar to those explored on the show. Organizations such as ChildHelp USA, the National Domestic Violence Hotline, and the National Sexual Assault Hotline have reported 100 percent increases in calls following broadcasts on which they are mentioned.

CSI, also known as *CSI: Crime Scene Investigation* (CBS 2000-   , Anthony E. Zuiker, creator/executive producer). Crime drama series in which a team of forensic investigators from the Las Vegas police use forensic evidence at crime scenes to solve cases. Lead scientist Gil Grissom (William Petersen) utilizes a fully functional crime lab with real equipment provided by vendors who are pleased to get their wares on network television. The program provides shock with the intellectual appeal of a science class. Viewers travel inside the human body to see such things as the damage bullets inflict as they pass through ribs and lungs and how blood spatters in particular patterns in slow motion. *CSI* has also inspired several CBS spin-off series: *CSI: Miami* (2002-   ) and *CSI: New York* (2004-   ).

The Defenders (CBS, 1961-1965, Herbert Brodkin, producer). Legal drama that is arguably the most socially conscious lawyer-centered series yet produced. The program focused on topical issues with a penchant for controversial social commentary that resonated with New Frontier liberalism. Episodes followed the cases of a father-and-son team of New York defense attorneys: Lawrence Preston (E. G. Marshall), the veteran litigator, and his inexperienced and idealistic son Kenneth (Robert Reed). While exploring the machinery of the law, the vagaries of legal processes, and the system's capacity for justice, *The Defenders* established the model for other social-issue programs that followed during the early 1960's, marking a trend toward dramatic shows centering on nonviolent, professional heroes.

Dragnet (NBC, 1952-1959; 1967-1970; Jack Webb, producer/director). Police procedural drama. This archetypal television police series left an indelible mark on American culture. It was the first successful television crime drama to be shot on film and one of the few prime-time series of any type to return to production after its initial run. Applauded for its realism, *Dragnet* made use of actual police cases, voice-over narration that provided information about the workings of the police department, and a generally low-key, documentary style. Episodes began with a prologue promising that "the story you are about to see is true; the names have been changed to protect the innocent," then faded to a vista of Los Angeles. Filming the series permitted the use of stock shots of Los Angeles Police Department operations and location shooting in Los Angeles. This was a contrast to the stage-bound "live" detective shows of the period. *Dragnet* emphasized authentic police jargon, the technical aspects of law enforcement, and the often tedious drudgery of such work. Protagonist Joe Friday (Webb) was a serious Los Angeles police sergeant (later promoted to lieutenant but was again a sergeant in the show's second incarnation). Rather than engaging in fights and gun battles, Friday and his partner, originally Officer Frank Smith (Ben Alexander) and later Officer Bill Gannon (Harry Morgan), spent much screen time making phone calls, questioning witnesses, and following up on leads. Scenes of the detectives simply waiting and engaging in mundane small talk were common. Programs always concluded with epilogues detailing the criminals' fates, accompanied by footage of the characters shifting about uncomfortably before the camera. *Dragnet* created the benchmark by which subsequent police procedurals would be judged.

Hard Copy (Syndicated, 1989-1999, Burt Kearns, producer). Tabloid television program. When *Hard Copy* first aired in 1989, it was a new kind of program combining the formats of investigative news shows and daytime talk shows to present news in a sensational, gossipy form. This "infotainment" program focused on celebrities and scandals and sometimes involved criminal justice issues. In the case of William Kennedy Smith, accused of rape, a representative of *Hard Copy* purportedly offered a prospective juror gifts for her story.

Hill Street Blues (NBC, 1981-1987, Steven Bochco, producer). Police procedural and melodrama that revolutionized television cop shows by combing elements from sitcoms, soap operas, and cinema verité-style documentaries, all tied together with haunting theme music composed by Mike Post. Dubbed the original "ensemble drama," the show explored the lives and work of the staff of an inner-city police precinct. Each episode charted a "day in the life" on the Hill, beginning with a roll call that concluded with the desk sergeant's memorable line, "Let's be careful out there." Technically, the show's realistic texture of sound and visuals was set with its hand-held camera, quick cuts, furious pace, complexity, and congestion that mirrored the city's life. Actors spoke lines as they moved toward and away from microphones and often purposefully overlapped dialogue. Recurring characters included Captain Frank Furillo (Daniel Travanti), attorney Joyce Davenport (Veronica Hamel), Sergeant Phil Esterhaus (Michael Conrad), Officer Bobby Hill (Michael Warren), and Officer Andy Renko (Charles Haid).

Homicide: Life on the Street (NBC, 1993-1999, Barry Levinson, executive producer). Detective drama. Perhaps the most reality-based of police dramas, the series was shot entirely with hand-held cameras on location in the Fells Point community of Baltimore, Maryland. A police homicide investigation unit closed cases, but actual crimes were seldom shown. Recurring characters included Detective Beau Felton (Daniel Baldwin), Detective Stan Bolander (Ned Beatty), and Detective John Munch (Richard Belzer).

Ironside (NBC, 1967-1993, Joel Rogosin, executive producer). Detective drama about a brilliant former chief of detectives named Robert T. Ironside (Raymond Burr), who was confined to a wheelchair after being disabled by an assassination attempt and became a crime consultant to the San Francisco Police Department. Detective Sergeant Ed Brown (Don Galloway), policewoman Eve Whitfield Barbara Anderson), and ex-convict Mark Sanger (Don Mitchell) joined with Ironside to crack perplexing criminal cases. The show was a testament to successful careers in law enforcement by the physically challenged.

Judge Greg Mathis (Syndicated, 1999-   , Bo Banks, executive producer). Reality courtroom sessions. As a teenager growing up in the housing projects of Detroit, Greg Mathis dropped out of school, was in and out of jail, and yet overcame these adversities to be elected a superior court judge for Michigan's Thirty-sixth District (the youngest judge in the state's history). In presiding over his television court, Mathis brings a unique perspective to his dealings with people. He is compassionate yet street smart and not about to tolerate disregard for the law. He runs his courtroom with a no-nonsense style, often using his own life as an example to those who appear before him.

Judge Hatchett (Syndicated, 2000-   , Michael Rourke, executive producer). Reality courtroom sessions in which Judge Glenda Hatchett presides over a diverse mix of family court, juvenile court, and unusual small-claims cases. What distinguishes this series from other "Judge shows" is its trademark "intervention segments"—creative sentences handed out by the judge to help litigants understand the implications of their actions and to learn how to handle future problems (a technique earlier developed in Hatchett's Georgia courtroom). For example, Hatchett has sent drug users on visits to prisons in which felons who committed drug-related offenses live. These reality-check experiences are shot on locations throughout the country and offer guidance that can be blunt, confrontational, enriching, and motivational. After some cases, Hatchett takes the litigants into her chambers to have discussions with them. She gives the impression that she really does care about the litigants and urges viewers to become mentors to at-risk youths in their own communities.

Judge Joe Brown (Syndicated, 1997-   , Peter Brennan, executive producer). Reality courtroom sessions with Judge Brown, a lawyer who served for a decade as a judge of the Shelby County Criminal Courts in Memphis, Tennessee. While still on the bench, Brown also launched a television career in Los Angeles. Having grown up in one of the toughest neighborhoods in South Central Los Angeles, Brown has a special interest in following up on cases and helping teenagers stay out of trouble. Using his show as a springboard, Brown encourages youngsters to be productive members of society instead of potential prison inmates.

Judge Judy (Syndicated, 1995-   , Timothy Regler, producer). Reality courtroom sessions with Judge Judy Sheindlin, a former judge from New York who tackles real-life small-claims cases with her no-nonsense attitude. By her side is Bailiff Petri Hawkins-Byrd, who keeps order in the court. After cases are closed, defendants and plaintiffs briefly confront each other outside the courtroom.

Kojak (CBS, 1973-1978, Matthew Rapf and Abby Mann, creators/executive producers). Police drama revolving around Theo Kojak (Telly Savalas), an outspoken and streetwise New York City police detective who was not above stretching the law when doing so helped him crack cases. Kojak operated on instinct and decency and solved complex criminal schemes followed around by a cast of mostly inept officers incapable of intelligent action except at the direction of their wise leader. A bald police detective with an appetite for lollipops, Kojak battled crime with little sympathy for the constitutional rights of criminal suspects. With a fiery righteous attitude about bringing criminals to justice, he held the crime-control, as opposed to due process, point of view about his difficult work. The series was marked by an unrealistic overemphasis on shootouts between cops and bad guys. Considerable location filming of the series was done in New York. In 2005, the USA Network launched a new version of *Kojak*, with Ving Rhames in the title role.

L.A. Law (NBC, 1986-1994, Steven Bochco, creator and executive producer) Ensemble drama set in a large Los Angeles law firm, McKenzie, Brackman, Chaney & Kuzak, and delving into both the personal lives and professional activities of the partners, associates, and staff. Stories centered on courtrooms and the law offices and treated controversial, headline-making cases. Protagonist attorneys and clients were economically well off, but their personal problems rivaled those of the most wretched characters of the cop shows. Recurring characters included Victor Sifuentes (Jimmy Smits), Benny Stulwicz (Larry Drake), and Leland McKenzie (Richard Dysart).

Law & Order (NBC, 1990-   , Dick Wolf, creator/executive producer). A drama filmed on location in New York City, this realistic program looks at crime and justice from a dual perspective. During the first half-hour of each episode, police detectives Lennie Briscoe (Jerry Orbach) and Edward Green (Jesse L. Martin) investigate crimes and apprehend suspects under the supervision of their precinct lieutenant, Anita van Buren (S. Epatha Merkerson). During the second half-hour, the focus shifts to the criminal courts. Assistant district attorneys Jack McCoy (Sam Waterston) and Serena Southerlyn (Elisabeth Rohm) work within the justice system to prosecute the accused. Cases are multifaceted, the investigations challenging, prosecutions complicated, and decisions about legal procedures and plea-bargaining vexing. Lives often hang in the balance in the complex process of determining guilt and innocence. Plots highlight legal, ethical, and personal problems that plague contemporary society. The show has inspired such NBC spin-offs as *Law & Order: Special Victims Unit* (1999-   ), *Law & Order: Criminal Intent* (2001-   ), and *Law & Order: Trial by Jury* (2005-   ).

Monk (USA Network, 2002-   , Anthony Santa Croce and David Breckman, producers). Detective comedy/drama. Adrian Monk (Tony Shalhoub), a brilliant detective who suffers from obsessive-compulsive disorder, has been suspended from his position as a legendary homicide detective on the San Francisco police force. Due partly to the tragic unsolved murder of his wife, Monk has developed an abnormal fear of germs, heights, crowds, and almost everything else—all of which provides an unusual challenge to solving crimes. The plots are sometimes far-fetched, and Monk is not a believable character, but the show makes realistic points about the importance of subtle evidence. Most episodes rest on Monk's ability to see clues that other detectives miss. Taken collectively, the cases that Monk builds may be exaggerated, but the individual clues that he finds are mostly realistic.

Moonlighting (ABC, 1985-1989, Glenn Gordon Caron, creator). Detective comedy/drama. Fashion model Maddie Hayes (Cybill Shepherd) was about to sell one of her few assets, the Blue Moon Detective Agency—until the brash employee David Addison (Bruce Willis) talked her out of it, saving his job and launching a new career for her. What followed was an often witty series, with Maddie and David sniping at each other like the stars of an old screwball comedy. Sexual chemistry was the leitmotif of solving mysteries.

Murder, She Wrote (CBS, 1984-1996, Richard Levinson, William Link, and Peter S. Fischer, creators). Drama/mystery in which famed mystery writer and amateur sleuth Jessica Fletcher (Angela Lansbury) of the fictional seaside village of Cabot Cove, Maine, had a gift for solving crimes. Fletcher remains close to old friends in the village, including Dr. Seth Haslett (William Windom) and bumbling Sheriff Amos Tupper (Tom Bosley), who sometimes helped her discover who committed murder. Each episode began with a murder, followed by Fletcher's investigation that uncovered various means, motives, and opportunities and eliminated suspects. She noticed—and the camera lingered on—details that seemed inconsequential but later proved central to the solutions. Minutes before each program ended, Fletcher suddenly realized the last piece of the puzzle and announced that she

knew who the killer was. She then confronted the killer privately or in a group with authorities observing off camera. The killer almost always confessed, and Jessica presented the person to the police. *Murder, She Wrote* was the only significant dramatic series on American television to feature an older woman in the sole leading role. The world, as the profession of the mystery writer demonstrates, is not a safe place. The wisdom and acute mental capacity of this older woman are weapons in an ongoing struggle for order.

The Naked City (ABC, 1958-1961, Stirling Silliphant, writer). Crime drama filmed on location in New York City. *The Naked City* broke new ground in the medium and changed the face of television cop shows forever. Senior detective Lieutenant Dan Muldoon (John McIntire) and the neophyte detective Jim Halloran (James Franciscus) starred in stories centered less on the crimes than on the people involved. Showing compassion as well as requisite toughness, the detectives were not above becoming emotionally involved in their cases. Every episode, featuring gritty, semi-documentary cinematography, was intended to be a look into the lives of real human beings. Unlike other shows of the era that were made on Hollywood back lots, *The Naked City* was filmed entirely in the streets and buildings of New York City. In 1960, a new hour-long version premiered on ABC with its title abbreviated to *Naked City*. As police stories, the shows had their share of violence and grimness, but they also included humor, absurdity, and occasional romance.

Nero Wolfe (A&E, 2001-2002, Timothy Hutton and Michael Jaffe, executive producers) In what the *Los Angeles Times* called a "witty, beguiling, colorful, pulse-pounding hoot of a weekly series," genius detective Nero Wolfe (Maury Chaykin) and his arch, wisecracking right-hand man, Archie Goodwin (Timothy Hutton), solved seemingly impossible crimes. Wolfe was the larger-than-life hero of seventy-three novels and novellas written by Rex Stout between 1934 and his death in 1975. In this critically acclaimed short-lived series, Chaykin masterly portrayed Wolfe as a petulant, blustery gourmand and misogynist who preferred to tend his orchids in his Manhattan home rather than visit the scenes of the crimes. He usually nailed the bad guys in focus groups in his own opulent study. Goodwin and Wolfe engaged in an endless game of wry and sly one-upmanship in a repertory theater cast of splendid character actors.

NYPD Blue (ABC, 1993-2005, Steven Bocho and David Milch, creators/executive producers). Police drama. Set against the gritty backdrop of New York City, this series portrayed realistic characters devoting themselves to the pursuit of justice in the city's Fifteenth Precinct while attempting to integrate their personal lives. The cases often dealt with the worst elements the city has to offer. Detective Andy Sipowicz (Dennis Franz) provided continuity while running through a series of partners and driving other cast members off the force, except for the anxious and sensitive Detective Greg Medavoy (Gordon Clapp) who somehow stayed put. In some southern states local ABC affiliates refused to carry the show because of the potential images created by the introductory warning to each episode: "This police drama contains adult language and scenes with partial nudity. Viewer discretion is advised."

Perry Mason (CBS, 1957-1966, Erle Stanley Gardner, creator). Legal drama/mystery. Los Angeles lawyer Perry Mason (Raymond Burr), assisted by his secretary Della Street (Barbara Hale) and private detective Paul Drake (William Hopper), worked to clear their innocent clients of murder charges brought by the formidable district attorney Hamilton Burger (William Talman). As evidence mounted against his clients, Mason pulled off legal maneuvers that proved them innocent and identified the true culprits, who, remarkably, were always in the courtroom. The memorable endings featured Mason's efforts to free his clients, Drake's frequently bringing in surprise witnesses in the closing courtroom scenes, and dramatic courtroom confessions. The show was not realistic but made memorable use of the legal profession and trials as forums for detective work. *Perry Mason* was the longest-running lawyer show in American television history.

Peter Gunn (NBC 1958-1960; ABC, 1960-1961;

Blake Edwards, creator) Peter Gunn (Craig Stevens) was a private detective in the *film noir* tradition of the 1930's. What set him apart from the detectives of the past were his elegantly furnished office and his fashionable clothing and hip manner. Gunn usually operated out of Mother's Jazz Club in Los Angeles, where he rubbed shoulders with the "in" people of the time and admired his girlfriend Edie Hart (Lola Albright), a jazz singer. Police lieutenant Jacoby (Herschel Bernardi) often assisted Gunn in solving mysteries. This was the first detective show in which the music was an integral part of the action; viewers could usually tell what was happening by the type of music accompanying the action. Henry Mancini's scores for *Peter Gunn* won a Grammy at the first Grammy award presentation. Peter Gunn was the model for all the sophisticated, hip television detectives who came after him.

The Practice (ABC, 1997-   , David E. Kelley, producer) Lawyer drama in which a firm of Boston attorneys brings passion to their pursuit of justice. Legal maneuvering is the firm's modus operandi, making even the most questionable arguments convincing. The attorneys confront serious ethical and moral issues of conscience while pursuing justice in provocative, issue-related stories. Recurring characters include Bobby Donnell (Dylan McDermott), a passionate lawyer; Jimmy Berluti (Michael Badalucco), a hard-working good guy with a winning record; and Jamie Stringer (Jessica Capshaw), a young associate fresh out of law school.

Quincy, M.E. (NBC, 1976-1983, Glen Larson and Lou Shaw, creators). Dramatic series about a medical examiner, Dr. R. Quincy (Jack Klugman) of the Los Angeles County Coroner's office. Medical examiners rarely serve as investigators, but Quincy (whose first name is never revealed) thrives on being the catalyst behind investigations. In addition to determining causes and times of death, Quincy often pushes police and homicide detectives to solve cases no matter the cost—financial or personal. The show combined the twin perennial favorites of medical and police dramas and was praised for its sensitive handling of controversial subject matter. Quincy may have had more influence than any other assistant medical examiner in the history of modern crime-fighting, and pains were taken to make the show's science as accurate as possible.

Rescue 911 (CBS, 1989-1996, Jean O'Neill and Arnold Shapiro, executive producers). Reality show. Hosted by William Shatner, the show consisted of re-enactments of actual emergency situations and documentaries of hospitals, police, and firefighters.

Remington Steele (ABC, 1982-1987, Michael Gleason and Robert Butler, creators). Detective drama. Laura Holt (Stephanie Zimbalist) got no respect as a private investigator, so she changed the name of her agency and made up a fictitious boss with the name "Remington Steele." Business then flowed in, but a dashing, handsome, and mysterious thief assumed the Remington Steele identity (Pierce Brosnan). Eventually, the interloper came to be an investigator and becomes a great crime-solving partner for Holt. Fed by the sexual tension between Steele and Holt, the series worked on the old combination of mystery and romance.

The Rockford Files (NBC, 1974-1980, Roy Huggins and Stephen J. Cannell, creators). Detective drama about a pardoned ex-convict-turned-private investigator with a weakness for Oreo cookies, Jim Rockford (James Garner), rarely carried a gun and when he did, he seldom fired it. Rockford hated trouble, would not hesitate to quit in the middle of a case if things got too rough, and had no qualms about saying why. He did have real talent, however, for solving cases that the Los Angeles Police Department had either closed or considered unsolvable. This made Rockford most unpopular with the police with whom he had to work. Audiences loved him, however, in this well-written and memorable character-laden series that was energized by a lively musical theme by composers Mike Post and Pete Carpenter.

The Shield (FX, 2002-   , Shawn Ryan, creator/executive producer). Police drama. The road to justice is twisted in this dark cop drama that plays out in a tough morally ambiguous world in which the line between good and evil is crossed everyday. This story of an inner-city Los Angeles police precinct, some of whose cops are not above breaking the rules or working against their associates to keep the streets safe and their self-interests intact, has earned a reputation as one of the most violent shows on television. Captain Monica Rawling (Glenn Close) commands the Barn (the station) and empowers Detective Vic Mackey (Michael Chiklis) to implement her controversial antigang policies.

The Sopranos (HBO, 1999-2006, David Chase, creator/executive producer). Drama centered on mob boss Tony Soprano (James Gandolfini), who tries desperately to balance the needs of his dysfunctional suburban family with the needs of his mob "family." His double life causes him severe depression and panic attacks, which send him to seek the help of psychiatrist Dr. Jennifer Melfi (Lorraine Bracco). Soprano's struggle to reconcile the mundane and the monstrous in his life strains his marriage to Carmela (Edie Falco) and creates problems in his waste-management business. The series reveals the media gangster at the center of a highly emotional mode of storytelling in which the pleasures of action and violence exist to speak not only about macho aggressiveness, but also about vulnerabilities that even tough guys encounter and about troubling cultural conditions. The characters are richly drawn in episodes written and performed with remarkable subtlety. The dialogue is sharp and sly, and some of the best scenes come when the criminal world brushes up against "decent" society. With the criminal family pursued by agents of the U.S. Justice Department, Tony's Uncle Junior (Dominic Chianese) and nephew Christopher Moltisanti (Michael Imperioli) fuel Machiavellian plot turns. In this most successful HBO series, viewers frequently empathize with career criminals, often at the expense of empathy with law-abiding citizens.

The Streets of San Francisco (ABC, 1972-1977, Edward Hume, developer). Police drama. Filmed entirely on location in San Francisco, this series followed the adventures of veteran detective Mike Stone (Karl Malden) and Steve Keller (Michael Douglas), a rookie detective who is a college-educated misfit in a workingman's police department. The two partners thwart Bay Area criminals in shows featuring car chases with soaring autos on San Francisco's hills, crazy haircuts, big sideburns, and wide ties indicative of the 1970's.

Texas Justice (Syndicated, 2001-   , Arthur Bergel, director). Pseudo-reality courtroom sessions. A Houston attorney portrays Judge Larry Joe Doherty to hear small-claims cases and deliver folksy verdicts in small-claims interpersonal conflicts. Unlike other judge shows, *Texas Justice* takes place in a courtroom of dubious certification. In the show's credits, Doherty is identified as "Larry Joe Doherty, Esquire." Clearly, he is a lawyer, not a judge. The show's participants are never formally sworn in or addressed as "litigants," and they do not officially agree to "have their disputes settled" in "the court."

Third Watch (NBC, 1999-   , John Wells and Edward Allen Bernero, creators). Ensemble police drama set in New York City, where the police of the Fifty-fifth Precinct put in a full day's work in each shift. The series depicts the brave and dedicated police, paramedics, and firefighters on the "third watch"—the shift from 3:00-11:00 P.M.—as they strive to keep the streets safe.

24 (Fox, 2001-   , Joel Surnow and Robert Cochran, producers). Counter-terrorist Unit (CTU) drama. The story of this unique drama is told in real time; the episodes of an entire season take place within the span of one twenty-four-hour day. Agent Jack Bauer (Kiefer Sutherland) is in and out of work with an elite team of CTU agents who, despite all the unbelievable odds against them, uncover an assassination plot targeting a presidential nominee, stop a massive nuclear weapon from destroying Los Angeles, thwart a drug cartel threatening to release a deadly virus, and rescue a kidnapped secretary of defense. Bauer races the clock to triumph over evil, while dealing with moles and bureaucrats inside the agency and with his egregious personal problems. Neither the bad guys nor the CTU play by polite rules. Technological wonders give the government an edge. The action is gripping, if unbelievable.

Unsolved Mysteries (NBC, 1988-1997; CBS 1998-1999; Lifetime, 2001-2002; John Cosgrove, director/producer). Documentary/mystery series that was one of the most popular reality programs during the late 1980's and the inspiration for numerous network and syndicated imitators. Robert Stack (of untouchable Eliot Ness fame) was the longest-serving host of the series that investigated baffling crimes, reunited missing persons, sought the heirs to unclaimed fortunes, and looked into persistent legends. Stories were reenacted as minidramas, usually three or four in an hour. An 800 telephone number was provided for viewers to call in clues. The show claimed to have been responsible for the capture of about 40 percent of all fugitives profiled on the series, the solving of nearly 300 cases, and 93 reunions.

The Untouchables (ABC, 1959-1963, Quinn Martin, producer). Crime drama that evoked a realistic mood because it was about Eliot Ness (Robert Stack), a real G-man, and his elite team of incorruptible treasury agents—dubbed the "Untouchables" by newspaper reporters—who battled organized crime in 1930's Chicago. The enormously popular programs maintained an earthy grittiness with stark sets and dark, studio back lot exterior sequences. The series narrator was real-life celebrity media columnist Walter Winchell. While the fictional Ness and his agents were somewhat lifeless characters, the back-stories and motivations established for the series' criminals were well defined and acted by a splendid roster of talented actors. The programs were criticized for what at the time was deemed excessive and senseless violence and for stereotyping ethnic characters as criminals. The Italian American community protested the series' use of Italian names for criminal characters. The family of organized crime boss Al Capone brought an unsuccessful million-dollar libel suit against the series creators, Desilu Productions. *The Untouchables* inspired two revivals: a 1980's movie and a 1990's syndicated television series.

Theodore M. Vestal

Time Line

Year	Event
1692	Salem witchcraft trials result in the execution of twenty people in Massachusetts.
1773	Walnut Street Jail opens in Philadelphia.
1776	Continental Congress approves the Declaration of Independence, which formally begins the American Revolution.
1783	Treaty of Paris formally ends the American Revolution.
1787	U.S. Constitution is framed in Philadelphia in 1787 and becomes effective in 1789.
1789	The first U.S. Congress passes the First Judiciary Act to provide for an attorney general, the Supreme Court, and the establishment of the U.S. Marshals; Federal Crimes Act, the first law to define federal crimes.
1790	U.S. Supreme Court holds its first session.
1791	Ratification of the Bill of Rights adds major new rights protections to the U.S. Constitution.
1792	Congress passes the Uniform Militia Law, which authorizes creation of the National Guard.
1803	U.S. Supreme Court's *Marbury v. Madison* decision establishes the Court's power of judicial review over congressional legislation.
1804	Associate Justice Samuel Chase is impeached but is acquitted by the Senate.
1807	Former vice president Aaron Burr is tried and acquitted for treason on charges of attempting to lead a secessionist movement.
1820's	New York State opens Auburn and Sing Sing prisons.
1824	Society for the Reformation of Juvenile Delinquents is founded.
1830	First U.S. race riots occur against abolitionists and African Americans.
1831	Downtown Bank of New York City is the first in the United States to be robbed.
1843	M'Naghten rule establishes the use of the insanity defense in a criminal court.
1845	Macon B. Allen is the first African American lawyer admitted to the bar, in Worcester, Massachusetts.
1845	Federal government begins publishing the United States Statutes at Large.
1851	First of several San Francisco vigilante groups forms to combat lawlessness brought on by the California gold rush.
1859	John Brown is convicted of treason after leading an abolitionist raid on the federal arsenal at Harpers Ferry, Virginia; he is hanged in December.
1861-1865	Civil War; President Abraham Lincoln declares martial law and suspends the writ of *habeas corpus* in Washington, D.C., and Confederate territories occupied by Union troops during the war.
1862	Internal Revenue Service is established.
1865	Mary Surratt is the first woman to be executed in the United States after being convicted of participating in the conspiracy to assassinate President Abraham Lincoln.
1865	U.S. Secret Service is established to combat counterfeiting of currency.

Year	Event
1866	Ku Klux Klan is organized.
1868	Andrew Johnson is the first president to be impeached by the House of Representatives but is acquitted by the Senate.
1868	Ratification of the Fourteenth Amendment establishes, among other things, the principle of equality before the law, strengthens constitutional protections of due process, and creates a basis for incorporating the protections of the Bill of Rights to the states.
1870	Ratification of the Fifteenth Amendment guarantees voting rights to African American men, prompting southern states to manipulate their voting laws to exclude black voters.
1870	Organizations founded: U.S. Justice Department; American Correctional Association; National Prison Association.
1873	Congress passes the Comstock law, which amends postal regulations prohibiting the use of the mails to send sexually suggestive material, including birth-control information.
1878	American Bar Association is established.
1879	President Rutherford B. Hayes signs a bill allowing female attorneys to argue cases before the Supreme Court.
1881	Charles J. Guiteau shoots President James Garfield, who dies two and one-half months later; Guiteau is convicted of murder and hanged the following year.
1884	In *Hurtado v. California*, the Supreme Court finds, for the first time, that the due process clause of the Fourteenth Amendment might apply some provisions of the Bill of Rights to the states.
1889	New York law legalizes the use of the electric chair for execution; William Kemmler becomes the first person to be executed by electric chair, despite a legal appeal to have electrocution ruled cruel and unusual punishment.
1890	Congress passes the Sherman Antitrust Act to prohibit restraints on trade.
1891	Federal Immigration and Naturalization Service is established.
1893	Lizzie Borden is tried for the axe-murder of her father and stepmother and is acquitted.
1893	International Association of Chiefs of Police is established.
1894	Yale University hires two New Haven, Connecticut, police officers, who become the forerunners of the first campus police in the United States.
1896	In *Plessy v. Ferguson*, the Supreme Court upholds a Louisiana segregation law and articulates the principle of "equal but separate," which governs legal tests of segregation over the next six decades
1896	The first documented American serial killer, "Dr. H. H. Holmes," is hanged.
1899	Illinois establishes the first juvenile court in the United States.
1901	Anarchist Leon Czolgosz assassinates President William McKinley; after a rapid trial, is executed by electrocution.
1907	National Council on Crime and Delinquency is established.
1907	New York City's police are the first in the United States to use police dogs.
1908	The forerunner of the Federal Bureau of Investigation, the Bureau of Investigation is established under the U.S. Department of Justice.
1909	Congress passes the Opium Exclusion Act, which bans the importation of opium and opium compounds, except those used expressly for medicinal purposes

Year	Event
1910	Congress passes the Mann Act to prohibit the interstate transportation of women for immoral purposes.
1912	National Automobile Theft Bureau is founded.
1914	Congress passes the Clayton Antitrust Act, which strengthens the Sherman Antitrust Act by regulating practices such as price discrimination, and the Harrison Narcotic Drug Act, the first federal antidrug act.
1914	In *Weeks v. United States*, the Supreme Court establishes the exclusionary rule to prohibit the use of illegally obtained evidence in federal criminal trials.
1914	Federal Trade Commission (FTC) is established to protect consumers.
1915	The forerunner of the federal Drug Enforcement Administration is established as a branch of the Bureau of Internal Revenue.
1915	Police Activities League program begins in New York City.
1917	Congress passes the Espionage Act, which imposes twenty-year prison terms for offenders; anarchist Emma Goldman is convicted under the Espionage Act and is later deported to Russia.
1917	Major race riot erupts in East St. Louis, Illinois.
1918	Congress passes the Sedition Act, which outlaws spoken and printed attacks on the U.S. government, constitution, and flag.
1918	Socialist labor leader Eugene V. Debs is convicted of violating the Espionage Act and is sentenced to prison; President Warren G. Harding pardons him two years later.
1919	Most of Boston's police go on strike for ten days, and a crime wave sweeps the city.
1919	Race riots erupt in twenty cities, including Charleston, South Carolina; Washington, D.C.; Knoxville, Tennessee; and Chicago.
1919	Ratification of the Eighteenth Amendment to the Constitution and passage of the Volstead Act outlaw the manufacture, sale, and transportation of intoxicating liquors, beginning in January, 1920.
1919	The forerunner of the modern Bureau of Alcohol, Tobacco, Firearms and Explosives, the federal Alcohol Prohibition Unit, is established.
1920's	Scandal unfolds as high-ranking officials in President Warren G. Harding's administration are found to have profited from the illegal awarding of oil leases to federal lands at Teapot Dome, Wyoming and Elk Hills, California.
1920	Nineteenth Amendment to the Constitution gives women the right to vote in federal elections.
1920	In the so-called Palmer raids, federal law-enforcement agents sweep through dozens of American cities to arrest alien residents suspected of being radicals.
1920	League of Nations establishes the International Court of Justice, later known as the World Court.
1920	American Civil Liberties Union is established to protect constitutional rights.
1921-1922	Film star Roscoe "Fatty" Arbuckle is acquitted on manslaughter charges in the death of a young woman at a Hollywood party.
1923	Interpol, the International Criminal Police Organization, is created.
1924	U.S. Border patrol is established.

Year	Event
1924	Italian-born anarchists Nicola Sacco and Bartolomeo Vanzetti are convicted of armed robbery and murder in Massachusetts; despite worldwide protests, they are executed in 1927.
1924	Nathan Leopold and Richard Loeb are convicted of the rape and murder of young Bobby Franks in Chicago and are sentenced to life imprisonment.
1925	In *Carroll v. United States*, the Supreme Court finds that search warrants are not necessary when police officers have probable cause to search vehicles for contraband or evidence of crimes.
1925	Tennessee schoolteacher John T. Scopes is convicted of violating a state law against teaching evolution in what becomes known as the "Scopes monkey trial"; live radio broadcasts from the trial inaugurate radio coverage of crime.
1926	Federal government compiles the first United States Code.
1928	In *Olmstead v. United States*, the Supreme Court finds that wiretaps placed outside suspects' homes do not violate Fourth Amendment rights to privacy because the interiors of the homes are not trespassed upon.
1929	Gangsters under Al Capone's command gun down seven men from a rival Chicago gang in the St. Valentine's Day massacre.
1929	International Association of Chiefs of Police begins issuing the Uniform Crime Reports.
1929	National Commission for Law Observance and Enforcement is established.
1929	President Herbert Hoover appoints the Wickersham Commission to review law enforcement throughout the United States; the commission issues its final report in 1931.
1930	U.S. Department of Justice creates the United States Board of Parole (later renamed the United States Parole Commission).
1930	Federal Bureau of Prisons is established.
1931	Gangster leader Al Capone is convicted of federal income tax evasion and is sent to prison.
1931-1937	Nine young African American men falsely accused of rape in Scottsboro, Alabama, are convicted by all-white juries and subjected to years of incarceration.
1931	International Association of Auto Theft Investigators is founded.
1932	In *Powell v. Alabama*, the Supreme Court rules that the concept of due process requires states to provide effective counsel in capital cases when indigent defendants are unable to represent themselves.
1932	Federal Bureau of Investigation's Scientific Crime Detection laboratory opens in Washington, D.C.
1932	In response to the kidnapping and murder of aviator Charles Lindbergh's infant son, Congress passes the Lindbergh law, making kidnapping a federal offense when kidnappers cross state boundaries; Congress also passes the Fugitive Felon Act, designed to prevent interstate travel to avoid prosecution.
1933	Ratification of the Twenty-first Amendment to the Constitution repeals Prohibition.
1933	Federal Securities and Exchange Commission is established.
1934	Alcatraz receives its first federal prisoners, who are regarded as America's "most dangerous."
1934	Congress passes the Anti-racketeering Act, making it unlawful to engage in acts interfering with interstate commerce; the National Stolen Property Act, which prohibits trafficking of stolen property; and the National Firearms Act, which imposes a tax on the transfer of machine guns, short barreled rifles, and shotguns.

Year	Event
1935	Bureau of Investigation is renamed the Federal Bureau of Investigation (FBI).
1936	In *Brown v. Mississippi*, the Supreme Court finds that coerced confessions violate the due process clause of the Fourteenth Amendment.
1936	Bruno Hauptmann is convicted of kidnapping the Lindbergh baby and is executed.
1937	In *Palko v. Connecticut*, the Supreme Court establishes an influential test for determining which fundamental rights contained within the Bill of Rights are incorporated into the Fourteenth Amendment's due process clause.
1937	Congress passes the Marijuana Tax Act, which levies fines on possession of untaxed marijuana.
1937	National Council of Juvenile and Family Court Judges is founded.
1938	Congress passes the National Firearms Act to regulate interstate commerce in firearms.
1939	Congress passes the Hatch Act to combat political corruption among government employees.
1940	Congress passes the Alien Registration Act—also known as the Smith Act—making it illegal to advocate overthrowing the government, and the Selective Service Act, which allows African Americans to serve in the military.
1941	After the surprise Japanese attack on Pearl Harbor, the governor of Hawaii declares martial law, with President Franklin D. Roosevelt's endorsement.
1945	Federal Rules of Criminal Procedure establish all rules governing criminal proceedings.
1945-1946	Associate Justice Robert H. Jackson serves as chief U.S. prosecutor in the Nuremberg War Trials after World War II.
1946	Association of Trial Lawyers of America is established.
1946	World Court holds its first session at The Hague, the Netherlands.
1947	Congress passes the Hobbs Act to enhance federal antiracketeering legislation and the National Security Act, which establishes the Central Intelligence Agency.
1949	International Association of Arson Investigators is founded.
1950	FBI publishes its first ten-most-wanted list.
1950	One of the most sensational robberies in U.S. history takes nearly three million dollars in cash and securities from Boston's Brinks Bank.
1950	Alger Hiss is convicted of perjury for lying to Congress about his communist connections.
1950	National District Attorneys Association is established.
1952	Institute for Judicial Administration is founded.
1953	Julius and Ethel Rosenberg, who have been convicted of espionage, become the first Americans executed for that crime during peacetime.
1954	Congress passes the Espionage and Sabotage Act to make engaging in these acts during times of peace a capital offense; the Communist Control Act, which outlaws the Communist Party in the United States; and the Immunity Act, which requires witnesses to appear in national security cases.
1954	U.S. Court of Appeals decision establishes the Durham rule, which provides an insanity test to prove an accused person has a mental disorder at the time of committing a crime.
1954	Ohio physician Sam Sheppard is convicted of murdering his wife and sentenced to life imprisonment—a decision that the U.S. Supreme Court overturns in 1965.

Year	Event
1956-1971	Federal government's secret counterintelligence programs (COINTELPRO) are conducted to neutralize radical political organizations in the United States.
1957	Organized Crime and Racketeering Section (OCR) is created.
1958	Congress passes the Federal Aviation Act, which makes it a crime to board or attempt to board aircraft with concealed weapons.
1958	International Association of Campus Law Enforcement Administrators is founded.
1959	First Peace Officers Standards and Training (POST) programs begin.
1960	Convicted rapist Caryl Chessman is executed in California after spending twelve years on death row and becoming a national symbol in the fight against capital punishment through his writings.
1960	International Narcotic Enforcement Officers Association is founded.
1961	President John F. Kennedy appoints Thurgood Marshal a judge in the U.S. Circuit Court of Appeals.
1961	In *Mapp v. Ohio*, the Supreme Court rules that illegally obtained evidence must be excluded from criminal trials in state courts, a rule that previously had been applied to federal trials in 1914.
1961	Manhattan Bail Project is undertaken to identify what kinds of defendants are the best risks for pretrial release.
1961	Center for the Study of Crime, Delinquency, and Corrections is founded.
1962	In *Robinson v. California*, the Supreme Court finds that narcotics addiction by itself is not a crime and incorporates the Eighth Amendment's protection against cruel and unusual punishment to the states.
1962	American Law Institute publishes the Model Penal Code.
1963	Civil rights leader Medgar Evers is assassinated in Mississippi; Byron de la Beckwith is tried for Evers's murder in 1964 but is released after two hung juries; in 1994 Beckwith is tried again and convicted.
1963	President John F. Kennedy is assassinated in Dallas, Texas; Lee Harvey Oswald is arrested for the crime but is himself assassinated by Jack Ruby before he can be tried. President Lyndon B. Johnson appoints the Warren Commission to investigate the assassination.
1963	Federal prison on Alcatraz Island closes after sending all its inmates to other federal facilities.
1963	In *Gideon v. Wainwright*, the Supreme Court finds that all indigent offenders are entitled to have court appointed counsel represent them in felony cases.
1963	Organizations founded: Academy of Criminal Justice Sciences; Center for Criminology Library; International Association for Police Professors.
1964	Rioting erupts in New York City's Harlem district.
1964	In *Escobedo v. Illinois*, the Supreme Court finds that law-enforcement questioning has shifted from investigatory to accusatory; the suspect has a right to counsel and can refrain from speaking until counsel is present.
1964	In *Massiah v. United States*, the Supreme Court finds that a taped conversation between an indicted suspect and his friend constituted an interrogation and violation of rights because the friend was acting on the instructions of government, and the suspect was without counsel during the interrogation.
1964	Organizations founded: International Brotherhood of Police Officers; International Halfway House Association.

Year	Event
1965	Six-day riot ravages Los Angeles's Watts district.
1965	Malcolm X is assassinated.
1965	President Lyndon B. Johnson establishes the President's Commission on Law Enforcement and Administration of Justice to study sequences of events in the criminal justice system.
1965	Organizations founded: Institute for Law and Criminal Procedure; Office of Law Enforcement Assistance.
1966	In *Miranda v. Arizona*, the Supreme Court makes a landmark ruling by requiring police officers to inform suspects of their right not to incriminate themselves, thereby limiting police interrogations and inaugurating a revolutionary change in arrest procedures.
1966	Organizations founded: Americans for Effective Law Enforcement; American Federation of Police; Vera Institute of Justice; National Polygraph Association; Black Panther Party.
1967	Teamsters Union president Jimmy Hoffa is convicted on federal corruption charges; he is pardoned in 1971.
1967	New rioting erupts in Newark, New Jersey; Tampa, Florida; Cincinnati, Ohio; Atlanta, Georgia; and Detroit, Michigan.
1967	In *In re Gault*, the Supreme Court establishes the right of juvenile defendants to counsel, the right of cross-examination of witnesses, sufficient notice of charges when punishments are involved, and protection against self-incrimination.
1967	In *Katz v. United States*, the Supreme Court establishes the principle that electronic surveillance constitutes a search subject to the Fourth Amendment's warrant and probable cause provisions.
1967	Congress passes the Freedom of Information Act, which allows private citizens to obtain confidential government files.
1967	Organizations founded: Center for Administration of Criminal Justice; National Crime Information Center; Federal Judicial Center.
1968	Civil rights leader Martin Luther King, Jr., is assassinated in Memphis, Tennessee; James Earl Ray is convicted of his murder and is sentenced to life in prison.
1968	In *Bruton v. United States*, the Supreme Court finds that defendants have the right to cross-examine their accusers, even if they are accomplices.
1968	In *Chimel v. California*, the Supreme Court rules that in searches incidental to arrests, arrest warrants entitle police only to search the persons and areas within their immediate vicinity, unless proper search warrants are issued.
1968	In *Harris v. United States*, the Supreme Court finds that anything in plain view in an automobile is subject to seizure and admissible in a court of law.
1968	In *Witherspoon v. Illinois*, the Supreme Court finds that prospective jurors cannot be excluded as part of the *voir dire* process for voicing objections to the death penalty as long as they can make fair and impartial decisions.
1968	Congress passes the Uniform Juvenile Court Act, a precursor to the Juvenile Justice and Delinquency Prevention Act of 1974, and the Omnibus Crime Control and Safe Streets Act, which is designed to reform the criminal justice system.
1968	President Lyndon B. Johnson appoints the National Commission on the Causes and Prevention of Violence to investigate the causes, consequences, and prevention of violence in American society.

Year	Event
1968	Organizations founded: Law Enforcement Assistance Administration; National Juvenile Detention Association; National Institute of Justice; Afro-American Police League.
1969	Center for Criminal Justice is established at Harvard University.
1969-1970	"Chicago Seven" are tried for conspiracy, inciting to riot, and other offenses relating to protest demonstrations at the 1968 Democratic Party National Convention.
1970	Congress passes the Comprehensive Drug Abuse Prevention and Control Act, which creates a single system of control for both narcotic and psychotropic drugs for the first time; the Organized Crime Control Act, which establishes the Witness Protection Plan; and the Racketeer Influenced and Corrupt Organizations Act, which authorizes asset forfeiture in the war on organized crime.
1970	New York City creates the Knapp Commission, which issues its report in 1972.
1970	In *Brady v. United States*, the Supreme Court acknowledges the validity of plea bargaining by asserting that it offers a "mutuality of advantage" for both defendant and the state.
1970	Organizations founded: Environmental Protection Agency; Insurance Crime Prevention Institute.
1971	Forty-two inmates and guards die in the Attica prison riot in New York State.
1971	Charles Manson and his followers are convicted of the murder of actor Sharon Tate and others; Manson is sentenced to death, but his sentence is later commuted when California overturns its death penalty.
1971	U.S. Army lieutenant William J. Calley is convicted in a court-martial for his role in commanding an Army platoon that massacred women and children in the Vietnamese village of My Lai in 1968; Calley's life sentence is reduced to twenty years, but he ultimately serves only three and one-half years.
1971	In *Bivens v. Unknown Named Agents of Federal Bureau of Narcotics*, the Supreme Court finds that in certain federal actions, plaintiffs have the right to claim civil damages when federal officials violate the Fourth Amendment protection against unreasonable search and seizure.
1971	In *Santobello v. New York*, the Supreme Court confirms the binding nature of plea-bargaining agreements made by prosecutors and defendants in criminal proceedings.
1971	Organizations founded: National Crime Information Center (branch of the Federal Bureau of Investigation); National Computerized Criminal History System; Institute for Court Management; National Center for State Courts; National Disabled Law Officers Association.
1972	In *Furman v. Georgia*, the Supreme Court finds that administration of the death penalty constitutes a form of cruel and unusual punishment because of its random and unpredictable application.
1972	In *Argersinger v. Hamlin*, the Supreme Court finds that indigent defendants have a right to counsel if they are charged with offenses punishable by incarceration.
1972	In *Barker v. Wingo*, the Supreme Court finds that defendants must request speedy trials to ensure compliance with the speedy trial provision of the Sixth Amendment.
1972	Division of Alcohol, Tobacco, and Firearms separates from the Internal Revenue Service and is renamed the Bureau of Alcohol, Tobacco, and Firearms.
1972	Organizations founded: Citizens United for Rehabilitation of Errants; National Association of Blacks in Criminal Justice.

Year	Event
1972-1974	A break-in at the Democratic national headquarters in Washington, D.C.'s Watergate Hotel by Republican Party operatives and the subsequent cover-up by the Nixon administration leads to the criminal prosecution of top administration officials and the resignation of President Richard M. Nixon.
1973	Vice President Spiro Agnew pleads no contest to charges of corruption while he was an elected official in Maryland; he is sentenced to three years' probation, a fine, and restitution, and he resigns the vice presidency.
1973	In *Roe v. Wade*, the Supreme Court decriminalizes abortion by ruling that a woman's right to abortion falls within the right of privacy implied by the Fourteenth Amendment.
1973	Organizations founded: Drug Enforcement Administration; Institute for Law and Social Research; International Association of Bomb-Technicians and Investigators; National Crime Survey (later becomes known as the National Crime Victimization Survey); Academy for Professional Law Enforcement.
1974	Newspaper heiress Patricia Hearst is kidnapped by the Symbionese Liberation Army, which later involves her in its robberies; Hearst is eventually caught and convicted of bank robbery.
1974	Congress passes the Juvenile Justice and Delinquency Prevention Act, which creates the Office of Juvenile Justice and Delinquency Prevention and promotes the development of community treatment programs for youthful offenders; Congress also passes the Speedy Trial Act (amended in 1979 and 1984) to ensure that defendants are brought to trial within seventy days of the time that formal charges are brought against them.
1974	Organizations founded: National Clearinghouse on Child Abuse and Neglect Information; Commission on Accreditation for Corrections; Criminal Justice Statistics Association; National Military Intelligence Association; Office of Juvenile Justice and Delinquency Prevention (OJJDP).
1975	Teamsters Union president Jimmy Hoffa disappears near Detroit, Michigan; his disappearance remains unexplained thirty years later.
1975	In *Faretta v. California*, the Supreme Court finds that defendants have a right to self-representation in criminal proceedings.
1975	Organizations founded: National Association of Legal Assistants; Task Force on Juvenile Justice and Delinquency Prevention; National Organization for Victim Assistance (NOVA).
1976	In *Gregg v. Georgia*, the Supreme Court rules that the death penalty itself is not a cruel and unusual punishment, but that procedural safeguards are required to prevent its use in an arbitrary and unpredictable manner.
1976	Organizations founded: American Law Enforcement Officers Association; Integrated Criminal Apprehension Program; National Center for the Prevention and Control of Rape.
1976	Crime Stoppers is founded to gain community involvement by offering monetary rewards for information leading to the capture and conviction of criminals.
1976	United States Board of Parole is renamed the United States Parole Commission.
1977	Convicted murderer Gary Gilmore is the first person executed in the United States since the Supreme Court's 1972 ban on capital punishment.
1977	Congress passes the Foreign Corrupt Practices Act, which establishes antibribery provisions from foreign entities, and the Juvenile Justice Reform Act, which imposes mandatory sentencing on juveniles based on age, previous criminal activity, and the nature of their crimes.
1977	In *Coker v. Georgia*, the Supreme Court rules that the death penalty is an inappropriate punishment in rape cases when the victims' lives are not taken.

Year	Event
1978	Ted Kaczynski—who publicly calls himself the "Unabomber"—begins his terrorist bombing campaign.
1978	Serial killer David Berkowitz, better known as "Son of Sam," is sentenced to twenty-five years to life for each of the six murders he has committed.
1978	Organizations founded: International Union of Police Administration; National Coalition of Jail Reform; National Forensic Center.
1979	Organizations founded: Commission on Accreditation for Law Enforcement Agencies (CALEA); Office of Justice Assistance, Research, and Statistics.
1980	Seventeen people are killed during three days of racially charged rioting in Miami, Florida, after the criminal justice system fails to convict police officers for the death of a black businessman.
1980	Inmates in the New Mexico state penitentiary seize control of the prison for thirty-six hours, killing thirty-three inmates and taking twelve guards hostage before surrendering to authorities.
1980	In *Rummel v. Estelle*, the Supreme Court rules that application of Texas's mandatory life-imprisonment statute on a habitual small-time offender does not constitute cruel and unusual punishment.
1980	National Crime Prevention Council creates McGruff the Crime Dog.
1980	Organizations founded: Aid to Incarcerated Mothers; Mothers Against Drunk Driving.
1981	President Ronald Reagan is wounded in a failed assassination attempt by John Hinkley, Jr.
1981	Sandra Day O'Connor becomes the first woman justice on the U.S. Supreme Court.
1981	Organizations founded: International Association of Law Enforcement Intelligence Analysts; National Center for Community Anti-Crime.
1982	Congress passes the Victim and Witness Protection Act, which protects victims and witnesses in criminal proceedings.
1982	Law Enforcement Assistance Administration is abolished.
1983	In *Illinois v. Gates*, the Supreme Court finds that when the totality of circumstances suggests that a crime has been committed and suspects are identified, police are not in violation of the Fourth Amendment by obtaining search warrants.
1983	In *Solem v. Helm*, the Supreme Court finds that the Eighth Amendment's prohibition on cruel and unusual punishments limits states' power to impose life sentences for multiple convictions on nonviolent felony charges.
1983	First DARE program is founded to help deter schoolchildren from taking up drug use.
1983	Criminal Justice National Council on Crime and Delinquency is founded.
1984	Congress passes the Comprehensive Crime Control Act, revising bail and forfeiture procedures; the National Narcotics Act, which establishes a government board to coordinate law-enforcement efforts in the federal war on drugs; the Victims of Crime Act, which improves services to crime victims; the Sentencing Reform Act, which creates the United States Sentencing Commission; the Bail Reform Act, which establishes procedures for the release or detention of suspects under arrest; the Trademark Counterfeiting Act to combat trafficking in counterfeit goods; the Insanity Defense Reform Act, which shifts the burden of proof for insanity pleas from the prosecution to the defense; and the Missing Child Act, which establishes a hotline for information reporting and coordination of public and private programs in the location of missing children.

Year	Event
1984	In *United States v. Leon*, the Supreme Court establishes a good faith exception to the exclusionary rule, ruling that evidence may be admissible in court if officers act in good faith, believing the search warrants they use are valid.
1984	In *Massachusetts v. Sheppard*, the Supreme Court finds that police officers acted in good faith by executing a revised and re-written search warrant because the judge advised that the warrant was valid.
1984	In *Schall v. Martin*, the Supreme Court finds that detention of a juvenile based on false information given by him to law enforcement does not violate due process.
1984	Organizations founded: National Bureau of Document Examiners; Office of Justice Programs (OJP); Community Patrol Officer Program.
1985	The city of Philadelphia's attempt to evict illegal squatters belonging to an organization called MOVE culminates in a bombing that kills eleven people and destroys sixty-one homes.
1985	In *New Jersey v. T.L.O.*, the Supreme Court finds that school officials only need reasonable suspicion to search students and their possessions on school property.
1985	In *Tennessee v. Garner*, the Supreme Court nullifies the fleeing felon rule for using deadly force, finding that deadly force may only be applied to fleeing suspects if they pose threats to the lives of law-enforcement officers or others.
1985	The Violent Criminal Apprehension Program (ViCap) is launched on the Internet.
1986	In *Terry v. Ohio*, the Supreme Court establishes acceptable "pat and frisk" procedures for police searches of suspects.
1986	In *Ford v. Wainwright*, the Supreme Court holds that the criminally insane cannot be executed and that Florida's procedures for determining competence are inadequate.
1986	In *Bowers v. Hardwick*, the Supreme Court upholds a Georgia sodomy law criminalizing homosexual relations—a decision that the Court will overturn in *Lawrence v. Texas* in 2003.
1986	In *Batson v. Kentucky*, the Supreme Court rules that peremptory challenges used to exclude prospective jurors must not be racially discriminatory.
1986	Organizations founded: International Law Enforcement Instructors Agency; American Crime Prevention Institute.
1987	In *McCleskey v. Kemp*, the Supreme Court finds that Georgia's death penalty is not arbitrary, capricious, or discriminatory.
1987	In *Tison v. Arizona*, the Supreme Court finds that accomplices who do not actually murder others but assist in murders can receive the death penalty.
1987	In *Illinois v. Krull*, the Supreme Court establishes the "good-faith exception," which allows evidence gathered from warrantless searches to be admitted at trial when investigators act in good faith.
1987	U.S. Sentencing Guidelines are created to guide discretionary power of judges.
1987	International Association for Asian Crime Investigators is founded.
1988	In *California v. Greenwood*, the Supreme Court determines that warrantless searches of garbage are permissible because the right to privacy is relinquished when things are placed in public areas.
1989	Serial killer Ted Bundy is executed.

Year	Event
1989	In *Stanford v. Kentucky*, the Supreme Court finds that the Eighth Amendment's prohibition against cruel and unusual punishment does not forbid executions of offenders who are juveniles at the time they commit their capital crimes.
1989	In *Texas v. Johnson*, the Supreme Court upholds symbolic forms of expression, including flag burning in political demonstrations.
1990	Washington, D.C., mayor Marion Barry is convicted of cocaine possession and sentenced to six months in prison; after his release, he is reelected mayor.
1990	In *Maryland v. Buie*, the Supreme Court rules that contraband goods or evidence of crimes seen in plain view during an arrest is a reasonable seizure under the Fourth Amendment.
1990	In *Minnick v. Mississippi*, the Supreme Court rules that a reinitiated interrogation of a murder suspect who was advised of his Miranda rights and received counsel still violated the suspect's Fifth Amendment rights because it was conducted without counsel being present.
1990	In *Maryland v. Craig*, the Supreme Court finds that the Sixth Amendment right to cross-examine accusers is not violated when children testify via closed circuit television.
1991	Los Angeles police officers stop motorist Rodney King and savagely beat him. The incident is recorded on videotape, prompting criticisms of the police department that lead to the establishment of the Christopher Commission to investigate and report on the police misconduct.
1991	In *Arizona v. Fulminante*, the Supreme Court rules that coerced confessions wrongly admitted as evidence cannot be subjected to "harmless error" analysis and may not be grounds for automatic invalidation of criminal convictions.
1991	In *Payne v. Tennessee*, the Supreme Court finds that victim impact statements are not in violation of an offender's Eighth Amendment rights at sentencing hearings.
1991	In *Harmelin v. Michigan*, the Supreme Court upholds a Michigan drug possession law carrying a mandatory term of life imprisonment, rejecting the plaintiff's argument that the sentence is "cruel and unusual punishment," in violation of the Eighth Amendment.
1992	Serial killer Jeffrey Dahmer is sentenced to life in prison in Milwaukee, Wisconsin.
1992	Federal agents raid the communal home of Randy Weaver—who is wanted for illegal gun sales—at Ruby Ridge, Idaho; in the ensuing shootout, Weaver's wife and son are killed.
1992	Rioting erupts in Los Angeles after the four police officers responsible for beating Rodney King are acquitted in a criminal trial.
1992	California executes Robert Alton Harris for a 1978 double murder, marking the first time in twenty-five years the state has put a man to death.
1992	Kathleen Hawk Sawyer becomes the first woman director of the federal Bureau of Prisons.
1992	In *United States v. Alvarez-Machain*, the Supreme Court finds that the abduction of criminal offenders from other countries is legal for the purpose of returning them to the United States for trial.
1992	In *R.A.V. v. City of St. Paul*, the Supreme Court holds that a local ordinance criminalizing cross-burning for the purpose of racial harassment is unconstitutional, even though such acts motivated by hate are reprehensible.
1992	National Insurance Crime Bureau is founded.
1992	Operation El Dorado is formed by U.S. Customs and the Department of Treasury as one of the nation's most successful money-laundering task forces.

Year	Event
1993	Terrorist bombing damages one of the World Trade Center towers in New York City, killing six people and injuring more than one thousand.
1993	Agents of the federal law-enforcement agencies, National Guard troops, and local law-enforcement officers destroy the compound of the Branch Davidian cult outside Waco, Texas, raising questions about the use of excessive force.
1993	Congress passes the Brady Handgun Violence Prevention Act, which imposes five-day mandatory waiting periods for handgun purchasers.
1993	In *Wisconsin v. Mitchell*, the Supreme Court upholds the constitutionality of state laws increasing punishments of offenders who target their victims on the basis of race.
1993-1996	Brothers Erik and Lyle Menendez are tried for the murder of their parents; their first trial ends in a mistrial; they are convicted in their second trial.
1994	The U.S. prison population reaches more than one million inmates for the first time in history.
1994	Congress passes the Violent Crime Control and Law Enforcement Act to provide funding for law enforcement and crime prevention initiatives, such as the establishment of a three-strikes provision for violent offenders.
1994	New Jersey passes Megan's Law, which requires convicted sex offenders to register with local law-enforcement agencies so that they may inform the public.
1994	Office of Community Oriented Policing is founded.
1995	Terrorist bomb blast destroys the Murrah Federal Building in Oklahoma City, Oklahoma, killing 168 people; Timothy McVeigh is quickly arrested and is later convicted and executed.
1995	Former football star O. J. Simpson is acquitted of the murder of his former wife and another man in Los Angeles; Simpson later loses a wrongful death suit brought against him in civil court by the murder victims' families.
1995	In *Wilson v. Arkansas*, the Supreme Court holds that police officers, when conducting searches, are normally expected to knock and announce their presence before entering private homes, except in special circumstances.
1995	In *United States v. Lopez*, the Supreme Court finds that possession of a firearm in a school zone does not violate the interstate commerce clause since it is not considered an economic activity.
1996	Congress passes the Anti-Terrorism and Effective Death Penalty Act, which imposes limits on *habeas corpus* claims filed by inmates on death row and reduces lengths of appeals in capital cases.
1996	In *Whren v. United States*, the Supreme Court upholds the authority of police officers to stop automobiles whenever there is probable cause of minor traffic violations, even if circumstances suggest that the officers are motivated by considerations of race or physical appearance of the motorists.
1998	Ramzi Ahmed Yousef is sentenced to life imprisonment for his role in the 1993 World Trade Center bombing.
1998	International tribunal makes the Rwandan Jean-Paul Akayesu the first person in world history to be convicted of genocide.
1998	In *Knowles v. Iowa*, the Supreme Court limits the authority of police to search cars while conducting routine traffic stops.
1999	President Bill Clinton is acquitted by the Senate after the House of Representatives impeaches him on charges of perjury and obstruction of justice.

Year	Event
1999	Two teenage boys enter Littleton, Colorado's Columbine High School with an assortment of firearms and homemade bombs and kill thirteen people, including themselves.
1999	Physician Jack Kevorkian is convicted of second-degree murder in Michigan and is sentenced to ten to twenty-five years in prison after assisting more than one hundred people to commit suicide.
1999	Organizations founded: Academy of Experimental Criminology; National Center for Analysis of Violent Crime (under FBI).
2000	In *Illinois v. Wardlow*, the Supreme Court expands the powers of police to stop and frisk suspects by holding that taking flight in high-crime areas gives police enough evidence to undertake such actions.
2001	On September 11, Middle Eastern terrorists hijack four U.S. airliners; they fly two of the planes into New York City's World Trade Center towers, which later collapse; one plane is flown into Washington, D.C.'s Pentagon Building; and the fourth plane crashes into a western Pennsylvania field—apparently because of an effort by passengers to retake the plane.
2001	In response to the hijackings, the United Nations adopts a resolution to establish measures to combat terrorism, and the U.S. Congress passes the Patriot Act to increase the authority of federal officials to track and intercept communications relating to international and domestic terrorists.
2001	In *Atwater v. City of Lago Vista* the Supreme Court rules that warrantless arrests for misdemeanor traffic violations do not violate the Fourth Amendment right to be free from unreasonable search and seizure.
2001	In *Illinois v. McArthur*, the Supreme Court permits police officers with probable cause to believe that criminal evidence is located within private homes to use reasonable means to prevent destruction of that evidence while they await search warrants.
2001	In *Kyllo v. United States*, the Supreme Court rules that government use of technology not commonly employed by the public to sense images, sounds, or smells coming from homes is a form of search and thus requires a warrant.
2002	Congress passes the Homeland Security Act, which calls for the reorganization of government law-enforcement and investigative agencies under the new U.S. Department of Homeland Security, which is established in 2003.
2003	In *Virginia v. Black*, the Supreme Court finds that a ban on burning of a cross violates the First Amendment right to freedom of expression, except when such acts are undertaken for the purpose of intimidation.
2003	In *Lawrence v. Texas*, the Supreme Court overturns its 1986 *Bowers v. Hardwick* ruling on homosexuality.
2004	Media mogul Martha Stewart is convicted on federal charges of perjury, conspiracy, obstruction of justice, and securities fraud stemming from an investigation of possible insider trading; she is sentenced to five months in a federal prison.
2004	Congress passes the Justice for All Act to enhance protections of victim rights in federal crimes, increase resources to combat crimes with DNA technology, and reduce the risk of conviction and execution of innocent persons.
2005	Pop singer Michael Jackson is tried and acquitted on child molestation charges in Southern California.

Lisa Landis Murphy and the Editors

Criminal Justice Sites on the World Wide Web

Site	*Web address*
Consumer Protection Sites	
Anti-Phishing working group	antiphishing.org
Better Business Bureau	www.bbb.org
Coalition Against Insurance Fraud	www.insurancefraud.org
Consumer World	www.consumerworld.org
Federal Government Consumer Information	www.consumer.gov
Federal Trade Commission: For the Consumer	www.ftc.gov/ftc/consumer.htm
Federal Trade Commission: ID Theft Home	www.consumer.gov/idtheft
National Fraud Information Center	www.fraud.org
National Institute for Consumer Education	www.emich.edu/public/coe/nice/index2.html
Office for Victims of Crime	www.ojp.usdoj.gov/ovc
Taxpayers Against Fraud	www.taf.org
U.S. Postal Service Consumer Tips	www.usps.gov/websites/depart/inspect/consmenu.htm
Corrections	
Bed Search	www.bedsearch.org
Bureau of Justice Corrections Statistics	www.ojp.usdoj.gov/bjs/correct.htm
Correctional Law Materials	www.law.cornell.edu/topics/corrections.html
Correctional Services Canada	www.csc-scc.gc.ca
Corrections Telecommunication and Technology	www.lib.jjay.cuny.edu/ctt
Death Penalty Laws	www.law.cornell.edu/topics/death_penalty.html
Federal Bureau of Prisons	www.bop.gov
Jail Net: The Global Corrections Source	www.jail.net
Juvenile Information Network	www.juvenilenet.org
National Commission on Correctional Healthcare	www.ncchc.org
National Institute of Corrections Information Center	www.nicic.org
Prison Issues Desk	www.prisonactivist.org
U.S. Parole Commission	www.usdoj.gov/uspc/parole.html
Courts and Adjudication	
Administrative Office of the Courts	www.uscourts.gov
Center for Court Innovation	www.courtinnovation.org
Court Directory	www.courts.net
Court Technology Vendors List	www.ncsc.dni.us/ncsc/vendor/vindex.htm
Federal Judicial Center	www.fjc.gov
National Center for State Courts (NCSC)	www.ncsconline.org
National Center on Institutions and Alternatives	www.sentencing.org
National Clearinghouse for Judicial Educational Information	jeritt.msu.edu
National Council of Juvenile and Family Court Judges	www.ncjfcj.org
NCSC Technology Information Service	www.ncsc.dni.us/NCSC/TIS/TIS99/Tiscover.htm
Pretrial Services Resource Center	www.pretrial.org
Sentencing Project	www.sentencingproject.org
State Justice Institute	www.statejustice.org

Site	*Web address*
U.S. Courts: The Federal Judiciary	www.uscourts.gov
U.S. Sentencing Commission	www.ussc.gov

Criminal Justice Information and Resources

Application for Consumer Sentinel	www.ftc.gov/sentinel/reg_forma.html
California Law and Resources	www.leginfo.ca.gov
Criminal Justice Links	www.criminology.fsu.edu/cjlinks
FBI Law Enforcement Bulletin	www.fbi.gov/publications/leb/leb.htm
Forensics Science Resources	www.tncrimlaw.com/forensic
Government Information Sharing Project	govinfo.kerr.orst.edu
Investigators Guide to Sources of Information	www.gao.gov/special.pubs/soi.htm
Justice Institute of British Columbia	www.jibc.bc.ca
National White Collar Crime Center-training and resources	www.nw3c.org
Police Executive Research Forum	www.policeforum.org
Police Resource List	police.sas.ab.ca/prl/index.html
Royal Canadian Mounted Police	www.rcmp-grc.gc.ca
Web of Justice: Criminal Justice Technology Links	www.co.pinellas.fl.us/bcc/juscoord/etech.htm

Federal Departments and Law-Enforcement Agencies

Bureau of Alcohol, Tobacco, Firearms and Explosives	www.atf.treas.gov
Code of Federal Regulations	www.gpoaccess.gov/cfr/index.html
Department of State International Information Programs	usinfo.state.gov
Drug Enforcement Administration	www.usdoj.gov/dea
Environmental Protection Agency	www.epa.gov
Federal Bureau of Investigation	www.fbi.gov
Federal Citizen Information Center	fic.info.gov
Federal Communications Commission	www.fcc.gov
Federal Register of the National Archives and Records Administration	www.gpoaccess.gov/fr/index.html
Immigration and Naturalization Service	www.bcis.gov/graphics/index.htm
Law Databases	www.internets.com/slegal.htm
Library of Congress	www.loc.gov
National Security Agency	www.nsa.gov
Office of National Drug Control Policy	www.whitehousedrugpolicy.gov
Office of Science and Technology	www.ojp.usdoj.gov/nij/about_sci.htm
Thomas U.S. Congress on the Net	thomas.loc.gov
U.S. Court of Appeals Federal Circuit	www.law.emory.edu/fedcircuit
U.S. Customs Service	www.customs.ustreas.gov
U.S. Department of Justice	www.usdoj.gov
U.S. Department of Treasury	www.ustreas.gov
U.S. General Accounting Office	www.gao.gov
U.S. General Services Administration	www.gsa.gov
U.S. Marshals Service	www.usdoj.gov/marshals
U.S. Parole Commission	www.usdoj.gov/uspc/parole.htm
U.S. Postal Service	www.usps.gov
U.S. Secret Service	www.treas.gov/usss
U.S. Sentencing Commission	www.ussc.gov
U.S. Supreme Court Cases	www.findlaw.com/casecode/supreme.html
White House	www.whitehouse.gov

Site	*Web address*
Forensic Science	
Crime Scene Investigation	www.crime-scene-investigator.net/index.html
Federal Laboratory Consortium	www.fedlabs.org
Forensic Science Communications	www.fbi.gov/hq/lab/fsc/current/index.htm
Forensic Toxicology Links	home.lightspeed.net/~abarbour/links.htm
National Center for Forensic Science	ncfs.ucf.edu/home.html
National Cybercrime Training Partnership	www.cybercrime.org
National Fish and Wildlife Forensics Laboratory	www.lab.fws.gov
National Forensic Science Technology Center	www.nfstc.org
GIS/Mapping Sources	
Crime Mapping News	www.policefoundation.org/docs/library.html
GeoPlace.com	www.geoplace.com
GIS Portal	www.gisportal.com
Spatial News Crime Mapping Resources	www.spatialnews.com/features/crimemaps/crimeresources.html
Information Clearinghouses	
Central Banking Resource Center	patriot.net/~bernkopf/
Federal Reserve National Information Center	www.ffiec.gov/nic
FedWorld Information Network	www.fedworld.gov
Financial Crimes Enforcement Network	www.fincen.gov/.
FirstGov: U.S. Government Information Source	firstgov.gov
IACP Law Enforcement Information Management	www.iacptechnology.org
Integrated Justice Information Systems	www.ijis.org
National Center for Missing and Exploited Children	www.missingkids.com
National Check Fraud Center	www.ckfraud.org
National Clearinghouse on Child Abuse and Neglect	nccanch.acf.hhs.gov
National Technical Information Service	www.ntis.gov
Partnerships Against Violence Network	www.pavnet.org
Privacy Rights Clearinghouse	www.ucan.org/prc/prc4ucan.htm
Securities Class Action Clearinghouse	securities.stanford.edu
Transactional Access Records Clearinghouse	www.trac.syr.edu/aboutTRACgeneral.html
United Nations Crime and Justice Information Network	www.uncjin.org
U.S. Government Printing Office GPO Access	www.gpoaccess.gov/index.html
Intelligence/CounterIntelligence	
Center for the Study of Intelligence	www.odci.gov/csi
Central Intelligence Agency	www.cia.gov
Criminal Intelligence Services of Canada	www.cisc.gc.ca
Factbook on Intelligence	www.odci.gov/cia/publications/facttell
Interagency International Fugitive Lookout	www.usdoj.gov/criminal/oiafug/fugitives.htm
Interpol	www.interpol.com/Default.asp
Terrorism Research Center	www.terrorism.com
U.S. Intelligence Community	www.columbia.edu/cu/lweb/indiv/dsc/intell.html

Site	*Web address*
Investigative Resources	
Computer Crime Related Links	www.crime-research.org/eng/links.html
Computer Incident Advisory Capability	ciac.llnl.gov/ciac
Economic Research Service (USDA)	www.ers.usda.gov
InterNet Bankruptcy Library	bankrupt.com
Internet Directory of Expert Witnesses	www.expertwitness.com
Internet Scam Busters	www.scambusters.org
Internet Tracing tools	www.samspade.org
Investigative Links and Resources	techcrime.com
Investigative Resources International	www.factfind.com
Investigator's Toolbox	pimall.com/nais/in.menu.html
National Insurance Crime Bureau	www.nicb.com
Research It	www.itools.com/research-it/research-it.html
The Seeker: Locating Missing Individuals	www.the-seeker.com
Sex Offender.Com	www.sexoffender.com
Stolen Computers Registry	www.stolencomputers.org
Virtual Librarian	www.virtuallibrarian.com/index2.html
World's Most Wanted	www.mostwanted.org
Juvenile Justice	
Boot Camps	www.boot-camps-info.com
Center for Prevention of School Violence	www.ncdjjdp.org/cpsv
Center on Juvenile and Criminal Justice	www.cjcj.org
Children Now	www.childrennow.org
Children's Defense Fund	www.childrensdefense.org
Children's Legal Protection Center	www.childprotect.org
Corners Report-Resources on Gang Intervention	www.gangwar.com
Gang Resources Library	www.virtuallibrarian.com/gangs
Gangs in Los Angeles and Ventura Counties	www.csun.edu/~hcchs006/table.html
Gangs in Los Angeles County	www.streetgangs.com
Gangs or Us	www.gangsorus.com
Juvenile Boot Camps	www.juvenile-boot-camps.com/?source = overture
Mothers Against Gang Wars	home.inreach.com/gangbang/magw.htm
National Center for Missing and Exploited Children	www.ncmec.org
National Center for Youth Law	www.youthlaw.org
National Center on Education, Disability and Juvenile Justice	www.edjj.org
National Council on Crime and Delinquency	www.nccd-crc.org
National Major Gang Task Force	www.nmgtf.org
National Youth Court Center	www.youthcourt.net
National Youth Gang Center	www.iir.com/nygc
Office of Juvenile Justice and Delinquency Prevention	www.ojjdp.ncjrs.org
Online Resource to Gangs and Graffiti	www.enhancementcourses.edu/gangs/gang_resources.htm
Youth Activism Project	www.youthactivism.com
Law Enforcement	
Community Policing Consortium	www.communitypolicing.org
Join Together	www.jointogether.org/home
Law Enforcement Links Directory	www.leolinks.com
Life on the Beat	www.lifeonthebeat.com

Site	Web address
National Center for Community Policing	www.cj.msu.edu/~people/cp
Office of Community Oriented Policing Services	www.cops.usdoj.gov
Officer.com: The Source for Law Enforcement	www.officer.com
Police Discussion List	www.police-l.org
Police Foundation	www.policefoundation.org
Police World.Net	www.policeworld.net/forums/index.php

Professional Associations

Academy of Criminal Justice Sciences	www.acjs.org
AFSCME Corrections United	www.afscme.org/acu/index.html
American Academy of Forensic Sciences	www.aafs.org
American Arbitration Association	www.adr.org/index2.1.jsp
American Bar Association	www.abanet.org/crimjust/links.html
American Civil Liberties Union	www.aclu.org
American College of Forensic Examiners	www.cfenet.com/splash
American Judges Association	aja.ncsc.dni.us
American Probation and Parole Association	www.appa-net.org
American Psychological Association	www.apa.org
American Society for Industrial Security (ASIS)	www.asisonline.org
American Society of Crime Laboratory Directors	www.ascld.org
American Society of Criminology	asc41.com
American Society of Questioned Document Examiners	www.asqde.org
Association of Pretrial Professionals	www.appf.org
California Financial Crimes Investigators Association	www.cfcia.info
Evidence Photographers International Council	www.epic-photo.org
Federal Bar Association	www.fedbar.org
High Tech Crime Investigation Association	www.htcia.org
International Association for Identification	www.theiai.org
International Association of Chiefs of Police	www.theiacp.org
International Association of Computer Investigative Specialists	www.cops.org
International Association of Crime Analysts	www.iaca.net
International Association of Financial Crimes Investigators	www.iafci.org
International Association of Forensic Nurses	www.forensicnurse.org
International Association of Law Enforcement Intelligence Analysts	www.inteltec.com/ialeia.htm
International Association of Law Enforcement Planners	www.ialep.org
International City/County Management Association	www.icma.org
International CPTED Association	www.cpted.net
International Society of Crime Prevention Practitioners	www.iscpp.net
Justice Research and Statistics Association	www.jrsainfo.org
Midwestern Criminal Justice Association	www.geocities.com/midwestcja/home.html
National Alliance of Gang Investigators Association	www.nagia.org

Site	Web address
National Association of Attorneys General	www.naag.org
National Association of Counsel for Children	naccchildlaw.org
National Association of Document Examiners	www.expertpages.com/org/nade.htm
National Association of Drug Court Professionals	www.nadcp.org
National Association of Pretrial Services	www.napsa.org
National Association of State Judicial Educators	nasje.unm.edu
National District Attorneys Association	www.ndaa.org
National Futures Association	www.nfa.futures.org
National Sheriffs Association	www.sheriffs.org
Society of Forensic Toxicologists	www.soft-tox.org

Statistics

Criminal Statistics Tutorial and Links	www.crime.org/do/Home
Economic Statistics Briefing Room	www.whitehouse.gov/fsbr/esbr.html
Federal Bureau of Prisons Quick Facts	www.bop.gov/fact0598.html
Federal Justice Statistics Resource Center	fjsrc.urban.org/index.cfm
Fedstats: One Stop Shopping For Federal Statistics	www.fedstats.gov
Geospatial and Statistical Data Center	fisher.lib.virginia.edu
Grass Roots	www.crime.org
Justice Research and Statistics Association, Incident-Based Reporting Resource Center	www.jrsa.org/ibrrc
National Archive of Criminal Justice Data	www.icpsr.umich.edu/NACJD/archive.html
National Criminal Justice Reference Service	www.ncjrs.org
National Institute on Drug Abuse	www.nida.nih.gov/Infofax/Infofaxindex.html
NCJRS Statistics Publications	virlib.ncjrs.org/Statistics.asp
Population Reference Bureau	www.prb.org
RAND Institutes Criminal Justice System	www.rand.org/psj
SEARCH National Consortium for Justice Information and Statistics	www.search.org
Sourcebook of Criminal Justice Statistics	www.albany.edu/sourcebook
U.S. Bureau of Justice Statistics	www.ojp.usdoj.gov/bjs
U.S. Bureau of Justice Statistics Courts and Sentencing Statistics	www.ojp.usdoj.gov/bjs/stssent.htm
U.S. Bureau of Labor Statistics	stats.bls.gov
U.S. Bureau of Transportation Statistics	www.bts.gov
U.S. Census Bureau	www.census.gov
U.S. Department of Commerce, Stat-USA	www.stat-usa.gov
U.S. Office of Highway Safety	safety.fhwa.dot.gov/

Topics by Subject Category

List of Categories

APPEALS

LEGAL TERMS AND PRINCIPLES

Index to Court Cases

Index to Laws and Acts

Indexes

Personages Index

Subject Index